MUNDARI GRAMMAR AND EXERCISES

MUNDARI GRAMMAR
AND
EXERCISES

THE REVD. J HOFFMANN, S.J.

GYAN PUBLISHING HOUSE
NEW DELHI - 110002

MUNDARI GRAMMAR AND EXERCISES

ISBN : 81-212-0763-0

Published in 2001 in India by
Gyan Publishing House
5, Ansari Road, New Delhi—110002

Phones : 3261060, 3282060, Fax : 3285914
E-Mail : gyanbook@del2.vsnl.net.in
Visit Our Web Site At http:\\www.gyanbooks.com

Leser type setting c' : Apex Computer
Printed at : Mehra Offset Printers

CONTENTS

PART 1

APPENDIX

PART II

PART 1

PART I

AN INTRODUCTION

SHOWING THE STRUCTURAL OUTLINES OF MUNDARI AND POINTING OUT THE MORE STRIKING DIFFERENCES BETWEEN KHOLARIAN AND ARYAN LANGUAGES

MUNDARI, Santhali, and Ho are the chief among the surviving Kholarian dialects. They do not differ much from each other. The Koroas, Asurs, and Birhors, as well as some other numerically insignificant tribes, also speak Kholarian dialects.

Mundari is chiefly spoken in southern and western parts of the Ranchi district and in the north of Singhbhum.

The terms *Munda* and *Mundari* are used by foreigners only to designate the Kholarians of the Ranchi district and their language.

The Mundas call themselves *Hoṛoko* : *the Men*, and their language, *Hoṛo Kaji*: *the Man-language*, or simply *Hoṛo*. *Mundari* is a Hindi and English Adjective which is never used by the Mundas themselves. With them the word *Munda* means a landed proprietor or a rich man. Again, every Munda village is divided into two *khunts* or classes—the Munda *khunt* and the Pahaṇṛ *khunt*. The head of the Munda *khunt* is the civil chief of the village, whereas the head of the Pahanr khunt is the religious chief or sacrificer. Hence in Mundari the word *Munda* is used (1) to distinguish landed proprietors from mere tenants or raiyats; (2) to denote the village chief ; (3) to distinguish the members of the Munda *khuṇt* from those of the Pahaṇṛ *khunt*.

The vocabulary and especially the structure of Kholarian dialects show that these languages are by no means as closely related to the Dravidian languages as they have, by some writers, been supposed to be, nor do they seem to stand closer, genealogically speaking, to any of the other non-Aryan languages of India. Until comparative philology has accomplished for that vast number of non-Aryan and non-Semitic languages what it has done for the Aryan and Semitic families, it will hardly be possible to ascertain the exact *genealogical position* of Kholarian speech.

From the purely *morphological* or *structural point of view*, the case is of course quite different, for the grammar of any language shows at once to what class or group it belongs.

Morphologically languages are divisible into three great groups—the *Isolating*, the *Agglutinative*, and the *Organic* or *Flexiona language*.

In an Isolating language (Chinese) every root constitutes a complete word with a meaning of its own, and undergoes no phonetic change when in contact with other roots: hence complex ideas, such, *v. gr.,* as are signifed by the various forms of our declensions and conjugations, are here expressed by the mere juxtaposition of perfectly independent roots. Consequently a different arrangement or grouping of the same unaltered and unalterable elements will yield phrases and propositions of totally different meanings.

Organic languages.—(1) In these the *current words* are no longer *bare original roots*. Even such monosyllables as the Latin word *lex* or the English *law* are compounds of at lèast two original roots.

(2) In these compounds there is no such thing as mere juxtaposition of independent roots, but there is a real *subordination* of one or more *secondary* roots to one *primary* root. The primary root denotes a certain general idea, and the secondary roots are grouped around it according to fixed laws and subordinated to it for the purpose of variously specifying or modifying that general idea. Hence these secondary roots are also called *the formative elements*.

Thus in *lex, legislator, eligo, praelego, -s, islator, e, -o, pra-o* are so many *formative elements* which determine the *de facto* meaning of one and the same primary root *lec*. They are in a real subordination to the primary root, for we cannot change their position in any of the above words without destroying it as a Latin word: *lec-s* is a Latin word, whereas *s-lec* means nothing any more.

(3) The roots thus concurring to form words react on each other according to fixed phonetic laws, so that both *the primary* as well as *the secondary* roots become liable to changes in their original form. These changes are visible not only through the different languages of the same family, but also in the various forms of a given compound in the same language. *Cfr., lex, loi, law, lego, lire, lisant, lu.* In all of these the original primary root is *lec.*

(4) In the secondary roots especially the changes caused by the phonetic laws are so great that the original form of these roots is generally quite mutilated. They dwindle down to mere terminations, inflexions or vowel and consonantal changes, which have no longer any meaning at all if detached from the word they concurred to form *Cfr.*, the Case-endings of Nouns and the Personal pronominal desinences of Verbs, and in fact nearly all the formative elements of Organic words. It even happens that some secondary roots disappear entirely from a compound, although the particular function for which they were originally affixed to a primary root still continues to live. Thus *lego* still means *I* read, yet there is no trace of a personal pronominal desinence left in *lego*. The phonetic laws presiding over the formation of Organic words, and therefore over the whole development or growth of Organic languages, constantly tend to weaken strong forms and to grind down formative elements. The effect of this tendency is generally called *phonetic decay*. Hence we say that the phonetic interdependence of the component elements must

always leave full play to the phonetic decay of primary as well as secondary roots through the various branches of the same family. Organic words may therefore in a certain sense be called real *combinations* of originally distinct complete roots into a new *totum*, even as distinct atoms combine to form molecules. Though these roots be really in the combination or compound word as far as *their functions* are concerned, yet their *original forms* can no longer be ascertained without the aid of philological analysis.

The *Agglutinative languages* stand midway between the Isolating and the Organic groups.

(1) In these, as in the Isolating languages, bare roots may be complete words.

(2) But when it becomes necessary to use two or several roots together for the purpose of expressing a complex idea, then these languages adopt a process differing from that used by either the Organic or the Isolating language: the roots concurring to form a word are neither completely *independent* of each other nor yet so *interdependent* as to phonetically react on each other *to any great extent*. In other words, there is neither *mere co-ordination* of completely independent roots nor is there such a degree of mutual dependence as to produce a *reciprocal reaction* with its consequent blending as it were of various elements into one organic whole. But there is, in these compound words, an *attraction* exercised by the *primary* on the *secondary roots*. The latter stand to the primary root in the relation of *prefixes* or *suffixes* or *infixes*. These secondary roots, to accommodate themselves to the primary, will submit to some vowel or consonant changes, or even to partial mutilation. But they seem to do so only reluctantly, and as if trying to preserve their original form as far as possible. The primary root, however, sacrifices nothing to the secondary roots. It always preserves its original form intact. The following may serve to illustrate this:—*dal* is a bare root meaning to strike ; *dal*-me ! do strike ! *dal*-tanae : he strikes ; *dal*-kedae : he struck ; *dal*-oáe: he will be struck ; *dal*-entanae : he strikes himself ; *dal*-kení : the one who struck. In these languages, therefore, phonetic decay is restricted to the secondary roots. They left the Isolating stage the moment they began that incipient subordination of secondary to primary roots, which has just been described. They begin to enter the Organic stage the moment they allow the secondary roots to react phonetically on the primary root. There is little if any doubt that the Organic languages have passed through the Agglutinative stage. By far the greater number of the world's languages are still in this stage. Their one common feature is the preservation of the form of primary roots. In many other respects they differ widely from each other. Thus, in some the secondary roots are for the most part *prefixes*, whilst in others they are *suffixes* ; in some the secondary roots undergo comparatively strong changes, whilst in others they hardly suffer any change; in some the so-called law .of the *harmony of vowels* reigns supreme, whereas in others we hardly find any traces of it; in some the order of words in the proposition is the reverse of what it is in others; in some,

again, Parts of Speech are recognisable as such by some permanent prefix, suffix or infix, whereas in others the context in which a bare root occurs, will alone show what function the word actually performs in a given proposition. In a word, some Agglutinative languages approach more closely to the Organic stage, whilst others are still far removed from it.

The Kholarian dialects, through now spoken only by a few numerically insignificant tribes, are in several respects a very interesting and remarkable specimen of the Agglutinative group.

Before entering on the details of Mundari Grammar, I think it advisable to first describe the great outlines of the language. This will show that neither the method nor the whole of the terminology of Organic grammars can be applied successfully to Mundari, or, for the matter of that, to any Agglutinative language.

If the Kholarians had, before the Aryan invasion, attained any civilisation worth the name, traces of that civilisation would no doubt be met with in their language. However, both the number and kind of Mundari words, as well as the manner in which those words are handled, seem to show that neither civilisation nor intellectual activity have so far exercised any marked influence on the language.

NUMBER AND KIND OF MUNDARI WORDS

Ever since the Mundas retreated before the Aryan invaders into the forests of the Chota Nagpur plateau, they have lived in the most rigorous seclusion. A deep aversion for their former conquerors constantly repelled all that civilisation and thought which have existed for centuries around them among the Hindu and Mussulman populations. Though they live in the land which is reputed the birth-place of the art of writing, their language as well as that of other Kholarians remained unwritten and altogether unknown beyond the limits of the small woody mountainous tracts they occupied. It was only towards the second half of the last century that Mundari and Sonthali were written by Missionaries,—the one in Hindi and the other in Bengali characters. Even at the present day the Mundas generally disdain every trade or art. That they were once keen hunters may be inferred from the obligatory yearly hunts in which every boy and grown-up man of the village must join if he wants his name to be remembered by the Singbonga (Sungod), as well as from the *eṛa sendera* (the women's hunts),which is proclaimed after stated cycles of years. In this *eṛa sendera* the women don the men's clothes, and carrying the men's arms raid the neighbouring villages. Any goats, sheep, pigs or fowls they meet outside the houses on that occasion are their legitimate prey, if they succeed in cutting them down. The Mundas still prefer the forest to the cultivated country. To carry on a cultivation of the most rudimentary kind in clearances made by themselves, and lead an idle, improvident life cheered by nightly dances to the sound of the *dumang* (a deep-toned drum), and by as much intoxicating rice-beer as they can procure, seems to be their highest ideal of life. Hence names of trades, products, and implements belonging to a somewhat advanced culture are not to be met with in the purely Mundari vocabulary. Their list of words denoting concrete objects is therefore exhausted by that part of the *fauna* and *flora* which interests the hunter and tiller, and by names of places, objects, and implements of practical value and in a life of the simplest kind. Even the rudimentary plough now in common use has got a Hindi name.

The number of words exclusively denoting forms of activity, such as our Verbs and certain of our Abstract Nouns, is by no means as large as we might expect it to be. For (1) all such forms of activity as belong exclusively to a higher culture have no means in Mundari, for the simple reason that they are unknown. (2) Purely intellectual forms of activity have received but scanty attention, and even that little throws a peculiar light on the pleasure they would seem to take in the exercise of our noblest faculties. *Urú* denotes sadness and gloom. It means also to be sad, to be gloomy. At the same time it is the only word they have to denote *thought* or to say that *they are thinking*. (3) Every Mundari word may, without undergoing any change of its original form, be used with the function of a Verb. Thus *ora* means *house*. It also means *to make a house, to settle down in a certain place or village. Urí* means *bullock*. It may also be used to denote *the acquisition of cattle*. *Aiar* means *ahead*. Hence it also means *to advance*. Thus, then, while we have, besides our Nouns, Adjectives, etc., a distinct set of words to denote forms of activity, viz.,Verbs, the Munda simply uses the existing roots denoting persons, animals, objects or relations, with a transitive or intransitive function, and thereby considerably reduces the size of his vocabulary.

Their religious system is neither very clear nor homogeneous. It is made up of three distinct cults : the worship of *Sing-bonga, ancestor worship*, and the cult of certain minor deities, called simply *bongako*. These seem to be local deities worshipped by former aborigines, who were partly destroyed, partly crowded out by the Mundas.

I.—The Worship of Sing-bonga.—Sing is one of the current words for *day*; *singi* means *the sun*. It would appear from certain expressions that formerly the word *bonga* was used to denote *the moon* and perhaps also *the sun*. Now the Hindi word *chand*, Mundarized into *chandú*, is used to signify the *moon*. The word *bonga* is now entirely restricted to denote all those spirits who are believed to have power or influence over the destinies of man. As such it may be added to the name of any deity. If used alone, it always signifies only the minor or local deities.

The word *Sing-bonga* therefore literally means the *Sun-god*, or the spirit of light. Whereas the minor deities are considered as spiteful and as the immediate causes of all kinds of sickness and misfortune, the *Sing-bonga* is conceived as essentially kind and good. He is entitled to a *daily* cult or *adoration*, which consists in a respectful greeting every morning at sunrise. I have heard the complaint that in these days of legal strife and coolie-trade the Mundas have become very remiss in this practice. The *soka* or soothsayer advises occasionally to sacrifice a fowl or a goat to *Sing-bonga*. Those fowls or goats must be *white*. That the *Sing-bonga* is conceived as *personal* and as *distinct* from the orb of the sun appears from the following points of belief still common among the Mundas: (1) He has made the sun as well as everything else; (2) He is invisible; (3) Though believed to be chiefly residing in the sun, he is everywhere— "*in the four corners of the world and in the four worlds* ;" (4) He directs everything; (5) He is the *Maranguterni*, i.e., the utterly great or the supreme one ; (6) All the other *bongas* are not only inferior to him, but they have been made *bongas* by him; (7) In great misfortunes the first instinctive complaint is generally addressed to him: *Hela singa-bonga ! Chikanamentem enkajáiña* ? Hela Singbonga ! Why dost thou treat me thus ? (8) In solemn asseverations he is called on as a witness by the words : *Haní leljáiña* ! or *Hani ituanae* ! Yonder One sees me ! or Yonder One knows ! (9) When the cause of some sickness is enquired into by the *soka* or *denonran* (soothsayer), the *Sing-bonga* is first called upon as *the All-knowing* to reveal the name of the particular *bonga* who requires propitiation.

II.—Ancestor-worship.—This is still deeply rooted in the Kholarian mind. It seems to be a cult they brought with them when they retreated into Chota Nagpur and the adjacent hilly tracts, and one which they probably had already when they entered India. The fact that the present system of private and public sacrifices to the local deities or *bongas* has pushed ancestor-worship somewhat to the background and reduced it almost entirely to a domestic cult has caused the notices so far written about these tribes to underestimate or overlook altogether this distinctly Kholarian cult.

The Mundas say that formerly they burnt their dead, but that now they have adopted the practice of burying from their Christian fellow- Mundas. The first disposal of dead bodies is, as it were, only provisional and outside the religious observance; for they have a special burial feast once a year, which is called *Jang-tõpa*, — Burial of bones. After burning a body the remaining bones were gathered into a small earthen vessel and kept in the *ading*. The *ading* is a side-room in the hut or house, in which the spirits of the deceased are believed to reside. It is also used as a store-room. On the *Jang-tõpa* feast bones are with some ceremonies placed under the horizontal stone-slabs, which are invariably met with in or near every Munda village. If the deceased were first buried, then either some bones are dug out or some earth is taken from the recent grave and placed similarly under the slabs at the *Jang-tõpa* feast. On that day all the villagers, though they may not have any remains to dispose of that year, turn out and anoint the burial slabs with oil in honour of their ancestors. Those stone slabs are called *sasan-diri*. Members of the village family who may have settled in other villages as mere tenants bury their dead provisionally in their actual place of residence. But on the *Jang-tõpa* day they carry the remains to their ancestral village to be there placed under the common *sasandiris*. It is only when emigrants have acquired land enough to found a separate hamlet or village that they will place slabs in their new home and observe the yearly burial day there. In honour of prominent men, and, as I have been told, in memory of some people who have been carried off by tigers, upright stone slabs of sometimes considerable height are erected in or near the village. These are called *bid'-diri*.

The *sasan-diris* are not only religious monuments : they serve, also as proofs of membership in the village family, and therefore as a sort of title-deed to partnership in the village property. Hence the saying: *Sasandiriko Mundakoá pata*,—The burial slabs are the Mundas' title-deeds. None but a real or formally-adopted member of the village family would ever be allowed to place a *sasan-diri* in the village Remains of children who have died before the age of reason are buried under some tree near the village and left there. Women dying in child-birth are buried as far away as possible from the village, near some stream. They are believed to turn into ghosts, called *churin*, who always want to come back and haunt the house. To prevent them from doing so, long thorns are driven into the soles of their feet just before the burial. All other members of the village family, whether men, women or children, receive the customary burial honours, are accounted among *the Ancestors*, *Haramko*, and have a share in the Ancestor-worship.

Some two or three days after the death of any person entitled to Ancestor-worship, the rite of recalling the deceased's soul or spirt to the house is performed. This rite is called *Umbul-ăder,—The taking or bringing in of the shade.* The ceremonies are briefly as follows:-

In the evening two persons remaining in the house of the deceased place some food in a leaf-cup, strew the floor with ashes, and then close the house-door. Meanwhile the villagers go to the place where the deceased was burnt or lies buried. There one man addresses the *shade* or spirit of deceased as follows: "Here we have come to call thee back to the house ; thou hast now been long enough in the chill and the cold!" A silent procession is then formed towards the house. During the progress two ploughshares are at short intervals struck against each other. Arrived at the house, the speaker, on behalf of the *shade*, asks that the door be opened to him. A short dialogue ensues, during which the two persons inside express misgivings regarding the intentions and character of him who seeks admission. When the *shade* has satisfied them the door is opened. Then the floor and the leaf-cup are examined. The slightest trace of real or imaginary disturbance in the ashes on the floor or the food in the leaf-cup is considered as a proof that the *shade* has taken his abode permanently in the *ading* with the *ancestors*. If no traces at all can be found, the whole process is gone through a second and sometimes even a third time. If after that no real or imaginary traces are found, they resign themselves, saying that the *shade* must be dissatisfied with something or another, and has probably taken up his abode in some tree or stone.

These *shades* are often called *Oṛá-bongako, house spirits*. None of the other *bongas* (local deities) ever enter a Munda's house.

Like the *Singbonga,* the *Oṛá-bongako*, or *shades* of the ancestors, are entitled to a *daily cult*. Before every meal the Mundas drop a few grains of rice on the ground as an offering to the *Oṛá-bongako*. Similarly, a few drops of rice-beer must be allotted to the *shades* before the living put the cup to their own lips.

Besides this there is every year a special feast in honour of the ancestors, viz., the *Bá-parob* or *Flower feast*. It is preceded by a vigil, which is a strict fast-day. On the feast itself the head of the family offers a sacrifice of fish, pulse, and fine rice to the *shades* in the *ading*. He alone partakes of the dainty meal; then sticking a sâl-tree blossom over his ear he turns to the family and says: *Mar nádo báanpe* ! *Now then adorn yourselves with flowers*! Immediately everybody sticks sâl-tree blossoms in his hair; garlands of the same flowers are hung about the house, and the feast commences with banqueting and winds up with a dance, which lasts the whole night through.

The *Oṛá-bongako* are also believed to cause in others (chiefly) that particular sickness of which they themselves died. The sacrifices of propitiation consist of cooked rice, pulse, fish, flowers, a black fowl, or red goat, and sometimes a bullock. This last item shows that the *shades* of the Mundas have not allowed themselves to be *Hinduizsed* out of their taste for cow-flesh. All the local deities, except the *Baranda Buru Bonga*, a Mahali deity, do not accept offerings of cow-flesh.

Munda girls always marry out of their village in another *kili*. Now it happens sometimes that one of her own *Orábongako* follows her on the road to her new home, and staying somewhere on that road causes the newly-married person to get frequently sick until she with her husband returns some evening along that road and there at some spot both offer a sacrifice, asking that particular shade to return home and leave the girl unmolested. Such *shades* are called *Horatenkoá bonga*,—Spirits of those who wander, i.e., leave home.

III. The Local Deities

(1) *The Nage eṛako, the wives of the Nages or Azurs*,—The myth relating to the origin of these *bongas* is 'given in an appendix. It is strongly tinged with Hindu notions. The *caste* of the birds, the term *bejait* for *outcast*, the exclusion of cows and bullocks from the list of sacrificial animals, the *incarnation* of Singbonga, the introduction of a *wife* of Singbonga, and the division of the village family into a civil and sacerdotal class, viz., Munda-Khuṇt and Pahaṇṛ-Khunt, are so many distinct Hindu features. Hinduism has, nevertheless, been unable to destroy or even deeply modify the original Kholarian religion, and it has had practically no influence on their social system: that *female Singbonga* of the legend has never

succeeded in getting any official recognition. Not only has she no trace of a cult, but she has not even got a name. She exists only in that one passage of the Azur legend. The division of the village into a civil and sacerdotal *Khunt*, though accepted, is in no respect either as deep or as thoroughgoing as it is in the Brahmanic system; for it creates neither social nor religious privileges. There is absolutely no trace of caste-distinctions or social exclusiveness between Mundas and Pahanrs. The marriage law rests still exclusively on the original custom of not marrying within one's own *kili* ; nor are there any *sacred* lands allotted to the Pahanrs on the ground of their sacerdotal character. Whatever lands they hold are theirs simply by the ordinary Munda law of inheritance. Again, the man who is now Pahaṇṛ may, on account of circumstances, become Munda and *vice versâ.* Sometimes one and the same person is both Munda and Pahanr. It is only in villages from which the Mundas have been crowded out by Uraons or Hinduized aborigines that the superstition of the new owners tries to retain a Pahaṇṛ of the Munda race, because they believe them more able to propitiate the local deities. In such villages a special grant of lands, going by various names, is made to the Pahaṇṛ. In purely Mundari villages the patriarchal system is still in full force, viz., the head of each family is the high priest or sacrificer for all the needs of the .family. The work of the Pahaṇṛ as such is limited to a few public sacrifices on behalf of the whole village at fixed periods or festivals.

Though the *bongas* are stated by the legend to have been the women-folk of the exterminated Azurs, they are not now considered as female deities : they are simple *bongas* or *spirits*. Finally, the word *Doisa Nagar* stamps the legend as comparatively recent.

These local deities are not entitled to a *daily* worship like the Singbonga and the *Shades of the Ancestors*. Their cult consists of eight public sacrifice offered by the Pahaṇṛ for the success of the ploughing, sowing, weeding, reaping and threshing operations, for a successful hunt in the month of *Phagun* (February - March), and to celebrate a particularly unclean festival called *Mage-parob* (January-February).

Besides these public sacrifices, the head of a family afflicted with sickness offers an occasional propitiatory sacrifice to some particular *bonga*, who is either suspected by himself or pointed out by the *soka* as the cause of the sickness.

(2) *The Baranda Buru bonga.*—This is a deity of the Mahali tribe. He has no feast. Recourse is had to him only in cases of child-birth. Unlike the preceding class of *bongas*, he accepts sacrifices of bullocks.

(3) *The Pangruabonga.*—Though supposed to reside in a pond caused by a waterfall near the Pangrua village, some 12-miles south of Khunti, he has no cult among the Mundas except in the three villages closest to his residence. But the Larka Khols of Kholan worship him.

(4) *The Aun Disum bonga* or *Disum bonga.*—He has no feast and no worship among the Mundas, but is considered a spirit who stuck to the country even after the above-mentioned local deities had occupied it.

The Karam-Kahani, or the story of *Karma and Dharma*, though given sometimes as a Mundari legend, is unknown to those Mundas who live still secluded from other races ; so are the rites and sacrifices based on that story. The *Karam* is the principal religious feast of what appear to be Hinduised aborigines and of the Uraons. No Mundas, except those who live scattered among other tribes, observe the *Karam* feast.

The word *ondoka* signifies a minister of human sacrifices. These *ondokas* are supposed to be chiefly emissaries of wealthy Hindu zamindars. It is said, however, that certain Mundas, Uraons and others do not shrink from occasional human sacrifices. The belief in the existence of sacrificers of this kind is so universal and so deeply rooted that almost every year, especially at sowing time, rumours of real or attempted human sacrifices run through the country and spread such torror in out-of-the way places that people keep a close watch over their children, and that even grown-up men dare not venture alone on a journey through lonely spots.

The word *nájom* denotes a wizard or more frequently a witch who can in various ways excite some *bonga* against this or that family or individual. The *najom* is said to eat the life or soul of his victim. The *soka* is applied to for the purpose of discovering *nájoms*. Formerly they used to suspend wizards and witches to a branch of a high tree and roast them to death slowly by means of a fire kindled under the tree. Hardly a village can be found where there is not a house suspected or convicted of witchcraft by the *soka*. The social position of these poor people becomes exceedingly difficult. They are *chilan*, i.e., precluded from eating or drinking with the other villagers sometimes for years and years; and when first pointed out by the *soka* they are invariably fined to furnish the animals for expiatory sacrifices, and generally they have to undergo a certain amount of bodily ill-treatment. They are sometimes altogether expelled from the village, and even now-a-days they do not always escape with their lives.

The numberless superstitions and their theories about dreams need not be mentioned here, as they do not give rise to special words. Boulders of limestone are believed to be the bones of fiendish proud giants, called *raksha*. The word is evidently not a Mundari one.

The little the Mundas have of popular stories is singularly devoid of bright imagination and ideality, and therefore, linguistically so to say, valueless. The Hindi word *kahani* is the only existing equivalent for *story*. Distinctively Kholarian accounts of the origin of man and of the great flood are exceedingly meagre and do not enrich the vocabulary of the language.

Dalton gives the following as a Kholarian version :—

"The first man and women were placed in a delightful valley and lived there in great simplicity. It was only when their creator descended and taught them the art of making *ili* (intoxicating rice-beer) that they began to get offspring."

Instead of the deluge they speak of a rain of fire which long ago destroyed everything living except a brother and sister, who were both blind. These two getting drunk one day on rice-beer got offspring and became the parents of the present human race.

This unsavory detail of drunkenness met with in both these accounts throws an unfavourable light on the *reputed* simplicity of the race. That *simplicity* as well as the *reputed truthfulness* of the Khols are two myths, which only show how rash it is for mere tourists or even temporary residents to rush into print with interesting ethnographical notes about races whose languages they do not understand and of whose customs and real inner life they could not possibly have acquired any but the most superficial knowledge.

Words which, like our Adjectives, denote qualities concretely, are not very numerous.

(1) For the purely moral qualities there are hardly any words: such Adjectives as *constant, generous, faithful, courageous, discreet, pious, abstemious, modest*, etc., have no equivalents in Mundari. It would, however, be wrong to conclude from this that the Mundas have no ethical perceptions, for they have words to denote the corresponding moral deformities or vices. They will say that a man is *miserly, deceitful, crafty, spiteful, jealous, dishonest, lazy*, and the like. All these deficiencies have struck them as morally wrong : they are all *et'kan*, i.e., *bad.* But they have so far not given any serious attention to the study and classification of the various kinds of virtues. These must be satisfied with the general term *bugin*, i.e., *good. Bugi* means primarily *to be in good health* as well as to *cure*. I have heard the terms *sotô* and *pokto* used as qualificatives of praise. *Sotõ horo* means a man on whose word one can rely to a great extent. *Pokto hoṛo* is a morally ambiguous praise: it means a man of resource to carry out any work, whether it be a piece of consummate rascality or of moral merit. These seem to be the Mundarized Hindi words *sut* and *puckcka.*

(2) All intellectual accomplishments are summed up in the single word *sẹraṇan. Sẹraṇ* means primarily to come to the age of reason. It is also used to denote *wisdom*, *cleverness*.

(3) What seems more surprising still is the fact that they have only three *generic* terms for colours. The pure blue sky of Chota Nagpur, the light green rice-fields, the forests with their numberless hues as well as everything else that is not white or red are all simply called *hende*, i.e., *black*. From light grey to the purest white everything is *pundi, white*. Whatever colour does not fall under these two denominations is *aṛá*, i.e., *red.* And yet the Mundas are by no means colour-blind, nor are they indifferent to colours. They delight in them, A profusion of bright colours is especially relished. They denote it by a jingle, "*chiribiri-chiribiri*".

If they are urged to specify some kind of red, they will tell you that it is *red like saffron* or *red like this* or *that flower*. To specify some kind of their wide range of blackness, they will say that something is *black like the rice-fields*, or *like the leaves of this or that tree*, or *like the sky*, or *like the night*. Though they are probably the darkest race in India, they distinguish between the *esel* or *fair*, and the *hende* or *black* individuals of their kinsfolk. For the newcomer from Europe it takes some time before he perceives the difference. They have also a certain number of words entirely restricted to denoting the colours of domestic animals and fowls. The coat of the man-eating Bengal tiger has vividly struck their imagination. Hence they denote his colour by a jingle, *bangad'-bungud' bangad'-bungud'*. The leopard, owing to his greater daring-in cattle-stealing, is as much an object of terror as the tiger. His coat is honoured too with a special jingle, " *bangra-bungru bangra-bungru*."

As against their three generic terms for colour, they have at least six or seven to denote qualities affecting the sense of taste.

The Munda's arithmetical notions are, of course, very simple. He has as many Cardinal numbers as he has fingers on both hands, or toes on both feet, viz., *ten* distinct forms. And as though he had summed up fingers and toes into one grand total, he has adopted a special word for twenty, viz., *hisi*. Generally he will place the word *mid'* or *mod'* before *hisi* and say *mod' hisi*, one twenty, just as we say *one hundred, one thousand*. Eleven becomes *gelmid'*, i.e., ten-one ; thirty is *mod' hisi gelea*, one-twenty-ten ; forty is *bar hisi* or two twenties. Thus he runs up to five and sometimes to six twenties. A special word for *a hundred* or anything beyond it does not exit in Mundari. That number appears to have exceeded their imagination as much as it exceeds the modest sums changing hands in their commerical transactions.

Of *Ordinal* Numbers they have but two, *viz*., *sida*, the first, and *etá*, the other.

Distributive Numerals they form by reduplicating the first syllable of the Cardinal numbers. V.gr., baria, two; *babaria*, two by two.

Proportional Numerals are formed by means of a suffix literally meaning *towards*. V.gr., *bar-sá* : twice.

The English rule is gradually bringing home to the Munda the necessity of counting further than five or six twenties. But instead of perfecting his own system, he finds it more convenient to adopt the Hindi one. Now-a-days the Mundari Numerals are hardly used except in out-of-the-way places, where the Hindu money-lender and zamindar have not yet found it profitable enough to establish themselves.

The whole geometrical terminology is limited to the word *gota* : *to be round, to round off*. But this word means also and primarily *whole, entire*. Even Hindi equivalents for such terms as *triangular, square*, etc., have not yet found their way into the Mundari vocabulary.

A race whose aims and ambitions do not rise beyond the most rudimentary civilisation is not likely to indulge much in those abstract forms of thought which divide being into substance and accidents or compare and classify qualities. As for those still higher and subtler abstractions which are indulged in chiefly for the intense satisfaction they afford to an active mind, they are sure to find no favour with a race for whom thought is synonymous with gloom and recollection or remembrance with sorrow. Hence we need not look for abstract words of a higher kind in Mundari. A kind of abstract nouns of a low type is formed by the insertion of *n* after the first vowel of certain words. That vowel is repeated after the *n*. Thus *argu* means *to lower, to let down*; *anargu* means *a slope*; *bolo*: *to enter*; *bonolo*: *entrance*.

On the other hand, there exist sets of totally *distinct* roots for objects of the same class as well as for states or for forms of activity of the same kind, where we would expect one *generic* term to be specified according to need by various qualitatives. Thus, *v.gr.*, five different words denote the various sitting postures to which the Mundas are accustomed. There are as many as ten different words to designate baskets of different sizes and varying but slightly in form. But this very profusion points to the same fact as the above-mentioned scarcity of words of another kind, viz., the comparative absence of those higher forms of thought which tend to generalize and classify. With regard, then, to words indicative of civilisation and intellectual activity, Mundari may deservedly be called a poor language.

The manner in which the Munda handles his scanty materials appears to point equally to an inability to grapple successfully with the higher forms of abstract thought. So far, however, as it goes, it is certainly a remarkable product of the spontaneous working of human reason. It differs so totally from anything we are accustomed to in Organic languages that a somewhat lengthy exposition seems necessary to place it in its proper light. This exposition comprises three distinct considerations, viz., (i) *the nature of Mundari words as such*. Here we consider the words simply as signifying units, leaving aside the connotation of all those interrelations which arise solely from the exigencies of the proposition, (ii) *The manner in which words are treated when they do enter as parts into a proposition*, or the manner in which the Kholarian mind conceives the relations existing between the different parts of the proposition. (iii) *The structure or form of the Mundari proposition*.

FUNCTIONS OR SIGNIFYING POWER OF MUNDARI WORDS

(1) With regard to their signifying power, roots have been divided into two categories: *Predicative roots* and *Demonstrative roots*.

Predicative roots are those which primarily denote living beings, inanimate objects, qualities, stages, or actions.

Demonstrative roots are those whose primary office it is either (1) to point out distinctions between living beings or inanimate objects (*v.gr.*, Pronouns), or (2) to signify relations of space and time as well as other relations (*v.gr.*, Prepositions or Postpositions). This division applies, of course, to Mundari roots as well as to those of any other language.

In Organic languages words, as already stated, are no longer bare roots. Organic words are divided into *Parts of Speech*, *viz.*, Nouns, Verbs, Adjectives, Pronouns, Numerals, Adverbs, Conjunctions, and Interjections. Each Part of Speech has its own separate function. Thus *Concrete Nouns* denote either living beings or inanimate objects. *Abstract Nouns* denote qualities, states or actions considered abstractly. *Adjectives* denote qualities concretely only, i.e., as inherent in some subject, whereas *Verbs* denote states or actions concretely, i.e., transitively or intransitively, viz., as referred to some subject or agent in a given proposition; and so on for the other Parts of Speech. These Parts of Speech remain permanently restricted each to its own particular function. The Noun cannot perform the function of a Verb; the Adjective always remains an Adjective; the Adverb remains an Adverb.

Furthermore, these various Parts of Speech are even in the living Organic languages frequently distinguished from each other by their outward form. The extent to which the *functions* of Organic words are thus recognizable from the *word-form* depends on the greater or lesser extent to which the laws of phonetic decay have been at work : in a given language; for the outward sign of the function now performed by a Part of Speech was originally some permanent prefix, suffix or infix with a fōrm and a meaning of its own. Hence, in the more ancient languages we meet with a greater number of these characteristic desinences, whereas English has hardly any of them left.

Now, what is the purport of these Parts of Speech? How far and how closely do they follow thought itelf, i.e., how far and in what sense do they signify *concepts*? In a word, *what is their real and full power as signifying agents*? Though the answer to this question be implied in the above description, it may be useful to give it more explicitly here, in order to bring out fully the contrast between the signifying power of Organic Parts of Speech and that of Mundari words. If that contrast is well understood, it will be seen that precisely that which we are accustomed to consider as the better part of the value and power of our own words, is by no means essential to *words as such*, and is actually wanting in *Mundari words*.

Bare roots denote living beings, objects, qualities, actions, states, and relations. *Parts of Speech* have the very same *denotative power*. They too denote living beings, objects, etc. But they are not restricted to this *modicum* : they superadd something to it. They *connote* at the same time the *varying* manner in which the mind, *may* and *does conceive* at different times the living beings, objects, qualities, states, actions, and relations thus *denoted*. They are therefore not, like bare roots, *merely* spoken or written signs of things, actions, etc., but they are also signs of *various forms of abstract thought*. Let us, by way of illustrating this, consider the words *to divide, division, divisible, divisibility*. These are all easily recognized as resulting from the combination of the same primary root with various secondary ones. All four of them denote *one and the same action*. But they do not at all denote that action in *one and the same manner*. The intellect may conceive an action—

(1) *As a physical reality*, viz., as an actual modification of some agent. The concept thus obtained represents the action as referred to a real subject or agent. Now, *the Verb "to divide"* denotes the action precisely as conceived by the mind in that particular manner which has just been described. The Organic Verb therefore does not merely denote action in a loose, vague manner, *independently* of the various ways in which the mind may conceive them. But it directly *denotes* the actions, and at the same time it *connotes* one and *only one* of the ways in which they may be conceived by the mind. It is therefore something more than the spoken or written sign of an action: it is also the sign of *one particular, well-defined degree of abstract thought*.

(2) The intellect may conceive the same action *independently* of its relation to an agent. It may tear it away from all real relations, and thus transform it into a purely ideal entity—one which, as now conceived, can have no existence out of the thinking mind; for an action without an agent is a physical impossibility. Now the *Abstract Noun "division"* is precisely the spoken or written sign of the concept thus formed. It *directly denotes* the same action which is denoted by the Verb *to divide*. But it *connotes* a degree of thought or abstraction *distinct* from and *higher* than the one connoted by the Verb.

(3) The intellect may compare the *concept* represented by the Noun "*division*" with the *concept* of some concrete object in order to see whether that object be susceptible or not of the action in question. If it find the object susceptible of that action, it may conceive that object *precisely*, and *only* as susceptible of the action, leaving out of consideration all its other qualities. *The Adjective "divisible"* becomes the written or spoken sign of the concept thus obtained. It implies therefore a degree of abstraction *distinct* from and *higher* still than the one connoted by the *Noun "division."* Here the action is conceived as an actual modification or quality of an object.

(4) Finally, instead of conceiving the action in the way just described, the mind may consider it as apart from every *object* as well as from every *agent*. It thus transforms it into a purely ideal entity for the purpose of considering it *in itself*, and comparing its *essential characteristics* with those of other similarly obtained *concepts*. Thus it may oppose *divisibility* to *simplicity* or *the ideal geometrical point*, etc. This is, again, a much higher degree of abstraction than the one connoted by the *Adjective "divisible"*. The *Abstract Noun "divisibility"* is the spoken or written sign for *this particular concept* or *degree of abstraction*.

Now, in the outward form of the above four words, there is absolutely nothing more which could intelligibly and explicitly signify the widely different meanings conveyed by those words. The change of *d* into *s*, the endings *ion, ible, ibility* have no longer a trace of signifying power if taken by themselves. They are the meaningless remnants of former complete secondary roots added to the primary for the purpose of obtaining an adequate expression of the *four concepts* just described. Though we be no longer conscious of *the manner* in which these meanings were originally obtained, the Aryan mind instinctively grasps those meanings. *The functions* of the elements composing the words remain in our *explicit* consciousness, though *the elements themselves* have to a great extent dropped out of *that explicit consciousness. The Parts of Speech* therefore are a kind of crystals which offer to the mind *ready-made spoken or written signs* for every kind and degree of abstract thought the mind is capable of. It is not difficult to see how the formation and existence of such words enriches and strengthens a language. It endows it with an almost indefinite power to express in a comparatively simple manner the highest abstractions of the mind, and gives it a pliability which can follow thought into its most intricate varieties and its finest shades. Deprive words of this character and immediately the expression of even simple forms of thought becomes heavy and obscure. The words by themselves alone no longer convey the full meaning of the speaker's mind: hence the context of the proposition and the circumstances under which it is uttered must, as far as they can, make up for the deficiency in the words' signifying power. Often this will not suffice. Circumlocution must be used where otherwise a single word would do. It may even perhaps be said that no amount of circumlocution can bring home certain abstractions to a race so long as that race has not gone through the hard intellectual effort of making its own language a fit vehicle for those abstractions. Thus, *v. gr.*, the single term *divisibility* is by itself alone equivalent to some such propositions as the following : *We conceive quantity as susceptible of being decomposed either really or ideally into an indefinite number of parts.* The Adjective *divisible* is equivalent to the sentence—'*This* or *that* "*quantum*" *(real or ideal) is susceptible of being decomposed into so or so many equal parts*. Hence in the proposition—*twelve is divisible by four*, the Adjective equals the following circumlocution: the number *twelve can be decomposed into four parts, each of which contains the same number of units*. Our Parts of Speech save us the trouble of composing each time such explicit verbal expressions for these abstractions. In this way they powerfully assist the habit of abstract thought, and confer on the mind an ever-increasing facility to move with both greater ease and rapidity in the higher regions of intellectuality. The evolution of roots into Parts of Speech is therefore an intellectual acquisition of immense value. That mental energy and activity have a great, deal to do with that evolution need hardly be stated.

In Mundari this evolution can scarcely be said to have seriously begun. Here we look in vain for four perfect equivalents of the words *to divide, division, divisible*, and *divisibility*. The word *hating* means indeed *to divide*, but it is not, like the English Verb, restricted to this function, and consequently does not, by itself alone, *connote the manner* in which the mind conceives the action; for the very same word denotes also a *part*. Again, the same word signifies *the act of division*. In this signification it has a substantive function. But it has not the *abstract connotative power* of the English Noun *division*. It is a functional equivalent to the English Infinitive in such phrases as *to divide this is easy*. The insertion of *n* after the first vowel yields a real *Abstract Noun*, viz., *hanating, the division, the partition*. But, as a matter of fact, the Mundas use this Noun to denote both *the action* and its *result*. Thus *hanating* means also *a part*. Primarily, however, it signifies *the action itself*, and it does signify it with a certain emphasis. This particular formation is in reality a decided step towards a higher evolution, and if the Mundas were given a little more to abstract thought, forms of this kind would undoubtedly soon be used exclusively as perfect equivalents of our Abstract Nouns. The Adjective *divisible* can only be rendered by the phrase *hating darioa*: *it can be divided*, or by the circumlocution, *hatingó-lekageá* : *it is like being divided* (*hatingó* is the Passive of *hating*, and therefore means *to be divided*, whereas *lekagea* means *it is like*). For the Noun *divisibility* the Munda has not only no single word, but he would be sadly at a loss if he had to render the term in any intelligible way at all. Anything like a concise translation of the arithmetical chapter on division is, up to date, an impossibility in Mundari. Instead, then, of Parts of Speech with well-defined functions and a precise but rich denotative and connotative power, we meet in Mundari with words of great functional elasticity, and therefore of a vague signifying power— words which, whilst *denoting* living beings, actions, qualities, and relations, do generally not by themselves *connote* the *manner* in which the mind conceives the things signified. That *connotation* is generally left to the context of the proposition or the circumstances under which it is uttered; for (1) every Mundari root, whether predicative or demonstrative, may perform at least two functions, viz., (a) its own primary function; (b) the function of a Transitive or an Intransitive Verb; (2) A number of words are susceptible of quite a variety of functions. By way of illustration let us take the word *oró*. It is the ordinary equivalent of the English Conjunction *and*. It may therefore be called a *Conjunction*. However, it is just as much a *Quantitative Adjective* meaning *more*, v. gr., *ọró hoṛoko* : *more men*. But instead of being thus used adjectively in connection with a Noun, it may stand by itself alone, and thus perform the function of an *Indefinite Quantitative Pronoun*, v. gr., *Ọró omaingme*: give me *more of it*. The same unchanged form may be used as *an Adverb* and thus mean: *again, once more*. Finally, it may assume the functions of either a *Transitive* or *an Intransitive Verb*. Thus used *ọró* may mean—(1) *To do more, to say more, to ask for more, to give more*. (Here it is the Adjective *oró* which is used as a Verb.) (2) *To do something again, to ask for something again, to say something again.* (Here it is the Adverb *oró* which is used as a Verb.) This Verb *oró* may in its turn be used as a *Noun.*

Thus the same unchanged form is at the same time *a Conjunction, an Adjective, a Pronoun, an Adverb, a Verb,* and *a Noun,* or, to speak more precisely, it may become a Conjunction, an Adjective, etc., etc. but by itself alone it *is none of them.* It is simply a vague elastic word, capable of signifying, in a vague manner, several distinct concepts, *i.e., of assuming a variety of functions.* It does assume this or that function only when it enters actually as part and parcel into a proposition. The function it performs in such a proposition is generally gathered either from the context, or from the position it occupies or from some Suffix assumed temporarily for a particular purpose. I say *assumed temporarily,* because the original form *oró,* through all its possible functions, is not only incapable of any internal changes, but it repudiates every *permanent Suffix.* In this respect therefore Mundari differs not only from Organic languages, but also from those Agglutinative languages which have evolved Parts of Speech and distinguish Substantives, Verbs, etc., by characteristic and permanent suffixes, prefixes, or by reduplication.

The following series of propositions shows the word *oró* in its various functions:-

(1) *Conjunction.*—	Horoko *oṛó* Dikuko menákoa,—	Here are Mundas *and* Hindus.
(2) *Adjective.*—	*Oṛó* Dikuko hijútanako,—	*More* Hindus are coming.
(3) *Pronoun.*—	*Oṛó* mená,—	There is *more of it.*
Pronoun.—	*Oṛó-ko* hijútanako,—	*More of them* are coming.
(4) *Adverb.*—	*Oṛó-ko* hijútana,—	They are coming *again.*
(5) *Verb.*—	*Oṛó*-a-ko,—	They *will do* or *say it again.*
	Oṛó-a-ko.—	They *will ask* or *give* or *say more.*
(6) *Noun.*—	*Oṛó* ena rabala,—	*To do it again* is easy, or *to ask for more* is easy.

N.B.— The *ko* suffixed to the Pronoun in (3) stands as Plural suffix, whereas the same suffix in (4) stands as Pronominal subject to the Predicate *hijútana.*

(II) What has just been said of the vagueness and functional elasticity of *simple words* devoid as yet of any specifying prefixes, infixes or suffixes applies equally to Mundari *compound words.** This term is not here restricted to those words which we generally call compound words such as *corn-flour dark-blue, interfere,* but it includes all those varying forms of simple words which arise directly out of the exigencies of the proposition such as case-forms of Nouns, tense-forms of Verbs etc. *v.gr.,* *father's, came, wrote*. For all these are in Mundari easily recognised as compounds, in which the primary roots stand out clear and distinct from the secondary roots or the so-called *formative elements*. It is precisely in this class of compounds that the functional difference between Organic and Mundari words shows itself most strikingly.

In Organic languages the case-endings of a Noun or Pronoun, the desinences or auxiliaries indicating Voice, Mood, and Tense of a Verb, the personal pronominal desinences of Verbs, and the ending indicating degrees of comparison in Adjectives or Adverbs do add something to the signification of Nouns, Pronouns, Verbs, and Adjectives, but they do not change the nature of their signifying power. The Noun still remains a Noun, the Adjective remains Adjective, and the Verb still performs the function of a Verb. This kind of desinences or formulative elements simply point out the particular relation in which the words specified by them stand to some other words of the same proposition. In the proposition *Thy brother's horse runs faster than mine*, the word brother's is the spoken sign of the same kind of being and of the same concept of which the word *brother* is a sign. But the desinence's exhibits that being as standing in the relation of owner to a being denoted by the word *horse*. *Runs* denotes the same concrete action which is denoted by *run*, but the *s* refers the action to a particular subject, viz., *horse*. *Faster* signifies the same generic modification of an action which is denoted by *fast*. But the ending *er* exhibits it as exceeding in intensity the speed of the second horse spoken of in the same sentence. We cannot *conjugate* Organic Nouns, Adjectives or Conjunctions, nor can we *decline* the Tense-forms of Organic Verbs, nor can we add *desinences* indicative of *degrees of comparison* to any Part of Speech except Adjectives and Adverbs. And the reason of this lies precisely in the fact that this kind of *secondary elements* is exclusively destined to point out the *intra-propositional relations* of words which are already perfect as Parts of Speech.

A consequence of this is another fact which we must attend to when we compare the *functional character* of these Organic forms with their Mundari equivalents. It is this. The Organic forms under consideration, if taken by themselves alone, do not satisfy the mind, because their special formative elements raise questions which can only be answered by the context of a proposition. Thus, the form *would come* makes us ask instinctively: who ? and under what circumstances or conditions would he or they come? In this sense therefore we

---

* In considering the functional elasticity of Mundari compounds, we abstract entirely from the manner in which they are obtained. That indeed is a consideration quite apart. Here we simply take them as we find them ready-made, and contrast their functional character with that of their Organic equivalents.

may say that these forms have no existence independently of a proposition. Nevertheless, if we do detach them from their context, they still *are always capable of suggesting to the mind a complete and well-defined concept*. Thus, *v. gr.*, the forms *brother's* and *would come* at once call up in the mind the very same concepts which are signified by the Nominative *brother* and the Infinitive *to come*; although the case-ending'*s* and the auxiliary *would* cause the mind to ask for a context in order to bring out fully the meaning suggested by these formative elements.

Mundari can produce compounds denoting the very same relations which are denoted by Organic *Cases* or *Tenses*. It has even a greater number of Tense-suffixes than any Organic language can show. The compounds thus obtained resemble their Organic equivalents in this that they can have no existence independently of a proposition, but they differ from them in this that *very often* they cannot even incipiently suggest to the mind any definite concept at all if torn away from every context. In order to know what such a compound may mean, it is necessary that we should know (1) what function its primary root performs in a given proposition; (2) what functions its secondary root or roots perform in the same proposition. But frequently all this can only be gathered from the circumstances under which that proposition is uttered. Hence (3) it is often necessary that we should know those circumstances. When therefore the Munda has formed a compound by infixing or suffixing to *the primary root* such *secondary ones* as denote Case, Voice, Mood or Tense, he does not yet obtain a *Part of Speech* or a sign exclusively representing one sharply-defined concept. All he obtains is a *compound word* which, within the logical limits of the new specifications caused by these secondary roots, is as little restricted to one single function as any *simple* predicative or demonstrative root. Such a compound may, without undergoing a further change of form, assume all those functions which are still in any way compatible with the limitations or specifications denoted by its secondary roots. Hence we meet with material *Case-forms* assuming the functions of an Organic Verb, and with *Tense-forms* taking the Case-suffixes of Nouns; *v. gr., reá* is one of the five Mundari Genitive suffixes; *ọrá* means *house*. The compound *ọrá-reá* therefore means *of the house*. But it may just as well be an Intransitive form, and thus mean *it is in the house* or *they* (viz., inanimate objects) *are in the house*. Unless, therefore, we know the circumstances under which this compound is uttered, it is impossible to know what function it actually performs. Nor can the word by itself alone call up any definite concept in the mind, precisely because under one set of circumstances it may directly denote an object, viz., *house*, whereas under different circumstances it may denote *a state*, viz., the state of some thing being then and there in a house.

As a further illustration of the functional elasticity of Mundari compounds, take the various meanings of *ọró-ko* in the following propositions :—

(1) Nereko kamikeda *ọróko* senójana,—They worked here *and then they*

went away.

(2) Hijúdoko hijúlena mendo *oṛóko* senójana,—They really did côme, but *they* went away *again.*

(3) Hanre ka beseá enreo *oṛóko* senójanako,—It is not good over there; nevertheless—*more of them* have gone (thither).

(4) *Oṛóko* sajaikom—Punish those who will do it again.

In (1) and (2) the suffix *ko* is the Personal Pronoun standing as Subject to the Predicates senójana. It is therefore impossible to ascertain the function of the compound *oṛóko* from this suffix. Can it be ascertained from the primary root *oṛó* ? No, for there is nothing in the form of either proposition which allows us to conclude anything with certainty regarding the function of *oṛó*'. It may be the Conjunction *and* or the Adverb *again* in either of the two propositions. Hence the circumstances must decide whether here the primary root performs the function of a Conjunction or that of an Adverb.

In (3) and (4) *ko* performs the function of a Plural suffix. In (3) it is the Plural suffix to *oṛó* used as an Indefinite Pronoun. This can be made out from the existence of a distinct Pronominal subject *ko* suffixed to *senójana.* In (4) *ko* acts as Plural suffix to the Future Tense used as a Participial Noun of Agency. That here *oróko* is a Noun of Agency will at once be felt instinctively by the Munda. But that little sentence, *Oṛóko sajaikom*, would puzzle many a foreigner, though he may have spoken *his own Mundari* perhaps already for years.

Tense-forms are best suited to illustrate the functional elasticity of Mundari compounds in a striking manner.

The Mundari equivalent of an Organic Transitive Verb has *four Voices*, *five Moods*, and *twenty-one Tenses*. Each Tense has *three Numbers*—-Singular, Dual, and Plural, with altogether *eleven Personal forms* and *one Impersonal form.* All this array of Voices, Moods, and Tenses can be tabulated into a scheme of great regularity, apparently resembling a scheme of Organic Conjugations very much indeed. It is then not astonishing that beginners should look on these as exclusively equivalent to Organic Verb-forms, and therefore as restricted to the functions of Transitive Predicates. But that is a fatal mistake; for Mundari has not only *no Conjugation* in our sense of the word, but it has not even any *Verbs* at all, as we shall see by and bye. The twenty-one Mundari Tense forms may indeed *be Transitive Predicates*, but they are just as well *Adjectives, Adverbs* or *Concrete* or *Abstract Nouns*. Frequently they are equivalent to *whole Relative Clauses* or *to Circumstantial Clauses of Place, Time* or *Manner*.

The root or word *om* denotes *the act of giving* substantively as well as transitively. It means therefore also *to give.* The Tense-suffix of the Simple Past in the Active Voice is *ked.* Hence *omked* is the Simple Past Tense. I call it *bare Tense-form* because it contains only the primary root *plus* that element which connotes time. In this respect, then, it is equivalent to the Latin *ded* or the Greek *ëδwk* (*ëδw*) and the English *gave*.

This bare Tense-form may, like its Latin and Greek equivalents, stand as Predicate, i.e., it may be referred to a Subject. This act of reference is in Latin and Greek effected by the mere fact of the Personal desinences being added to the bare Tense-form or theme. Ded-*i* or epsiton means *I* gave. In Mundari the reference of the Transitive or Intransitive Predicate to a Subject is made by means of the Copula *á* or *a*; *ing* means *I*. Hence *omked-a-ing* = *dedi*, *ëδwka*, or, *I gave*. Here is the complete scheme of the Simple Past Tense:—

Predicate. Copula. Subject.	*Pred. Subj.*	*Subject.*	*Predicate.*
Omked — a — ing	= *ëδwk—a*,	I	gave.
Omked — a — m	= *ëδwk—a*,	thou	gavest.
Omked — a — e	= *ëδwk—ε*,	he *or* she	gave.
Omked — a —		it	gave.
Omked — a — lang,		thou and I	gave.
Omked — a — ling,		he *or* she and I	gave.
Omked — a — ben,		you two	gave.
Omked — a — king,		these *or* those two	gave.
Omked — a — bu	= *ëδo—-μεν*,	you and we	gave.
Omked — a — le		they and we	gave.
Omked — a — pe	= *ëδo—τε*,	you	gave.
Omked — a — ko	= *ëδo—kaν*,	they	gave.

Neither the Copula *á* nor the Personal Pronouns figuring as Subjects in the above Mundari scheme are mere desinences in the sense in which the corresponding Greek Personal Subjects are desinences exclusively belonging to a Transitive Predicate.

For (1) the Mundari Subjects are the current Personal Pronouns of the language, whereas the Greek Subjects are so no longer.

(2) The Greek Subjects must be *suffixed* to the bare Tense-form or theme, whereas the Mundari Subjects are not restricted to that position. In fact, whenever a word precedes the Predicate, those Subjects are detached from the Predicate and suffixed to that word, so as to form the last syllable of it, so far as pronunciation is concerned. Thus in the propositions : I, thou, he, etc., gave yesterday, we get in Mundari the following : Hola.-*ing* omkeda, hola-*m* omkeda, hola-*e* omkeda, etc.

As for the *a* in conjunction with a *bare Tense-form,* it is not restricted to the function of a Copula or link-word between a Predicate and a Subject. It can act equally as formative element of a Noun. Thus the form *omkedá* by itself alone means *that which some one has given.* This derivative from an Active Tense has no single-worded equivalent in any Organic language. The closest literal translation—"the somebody having given thing"—sounds barbarous. Yet it is the manner in which this particular signification is conceived by the Munda mind.

In comparing Organic with Mundari Tense-forms, we must attend to the following points:—

(1) *Bare* Organic Tense-forms, such as *ded*, *ëδωκ*, are incomplete and meaningless if separated from the Personal desinences; *ded* and *ëδωκα* mean nothing : they are not *words*; whereas *dedi* and *ëδωκα*, are words and mean *I gave.*

(2) The *mechanism* of Organic languages (if I may so call the particular lines along which the Aryan languages have developed) precludes them from using their bare Tense-forms either adjectively or substantively. If they want to use a Tense-form either substantively or adjectively, they must have recourse to Infinitive or Participial desinences. These special desinences *may* affect the theme or primary element *in its form*. Thus *ëδωκ*, and *ëδωκ*, are the Participle and Infinitive of *ëδωκα*, *I gave,*

(3) That same mechanism tends to limit the power of even this process more and more. Thus Latin has already fewer Infinitives and Participles than Greek, and modern languages have fewer than Latin.

In Mundari the case is very different:-

(1) The bare Tense-form *omked* is a complete word by itself alone. It has not only one, but several meanings. That is why we must see it in a context in order to know which of its possible functions it actually performs.

(2) This complete word may, without the aid of any special suffix, be used either substantively or adjectively. *Omked* is equivalent to *ëδωκ*, *dedisse*, *to have given*, as well as to *δovs*, *having given.*

(3) Every one of the 21 Mundari *bare Tense-forms* may thus be used either substantively or adjectively.

In other words, though Mundari has no special Infinitive or Participial *forms*, it has, *functionally*, as many Infinitives and Participles as it has Tenses in any of its four voices. Of course most of the Tense-forms thus used substantively or adjectively cannot be translated into English, except by Relative Clauses.

When used as Participial Adjectives, they are placed immediately before the Noun they qualify, and they never take any suffixes indicative of either Gender, Number or Case. V.gr., *omked horo, the man who give*; *omked horoking, the two men who gave*; *omked horoko, the men who gave.*

The dissimilarity between the two processes of treating Tense-forms does not end here. The Organic Infinitive, though it has a substantive function, will not allow itself to be treated in every respect like other Nouns. It refuses the ordinary Case-suffixes, nor can it be governed by Prepositions. *ëδνκα*, cannot be declined, nor could we say in Latin: *Gratias refero tibi*, pro-dedisse *librum*, I thank thee *for to have given* the book.

The Mundari Tense-form, on the contrary, behaves in every respect both like an ordinary Adjective and like an ordinary Noun. In its substantive function it may take all the suffixes any other word, such as v. gr., *orá*, house, may take. Besides suffixes denoting relations of space, it may take suffixes of time distinct from the Tense-suffixes. In fact, every suffix denoting any function which is at all compatible with the general concept of an action may be added to a bare Mundari Tense-form. A few examples will show this more clearly:—

1st.—We have seen that in its adjective function the Tense-form precedes the Noun. But a Noun can always be replaced by a Personal Pronoun. Hence instead of *Tense* followed, by *Noun*, we may have *Tense* followed by *Pronoun*. But since the ordinary Mundari Personal Pronouns are always *suffixes*, this combination of Tense *plus* Pronoun yields one single word.

Omked *horo,*—	The *man* who gave.	Omked*í*,—	*The one* who gave.
Omked *horoking*,—	The *two men* who gave.	Omked*'king*,—	*The two* who gave.
Omked *horoko,*—	The *men* who gave.	Omked*'ko*,—	*Those* who gave.

2nd—A Mundari Adjective is turned into an Adverb of Manner by means of the suffixes *leka, lekage,lekate, lekatege*, v.gr., *bugilekate*; literally, good-like, *i.e.*, properly, in the right way. These same suffixes may be used to transform any Tense-form into an Adverb of Manner. But Adverbs of this class can never be translated by a single word into English. *Atkarjáiña* means *I feel* and *I am under the impression*. Hence *Omked'-leka at'karjaiña* means *I feel like having given*, i.e., *I am under the impression that I did give*.

3rd.—*á* means *it*. Hence, *omked-á* means *that which someone gave*.

4th.—*Rá* is a Genitive suffix to Nouns. Hence *omked'- rá* rasika,—The Joy one experiences for having given (*literally*, the joy *of* having given).

5th.—*Te* denotes cause. Hence *omked'-te*-ko sukujana,—They are happy *because* they gave (*literally*, they rejoice *on account of* having giving).

6th.—*Re* means *in*, and I also used to denote condition. Hence *omked'-re-ko* sukujana honage ; *literally*, in the having given they would have rejoiced, *i.e.*, they would be happy now if they had given.

7th.—*Táre* means *there* and *there where*. Hence *omked'-táre-ko* lelkia,—They saw him *at the very place where he gave*.

8th.—*Imtage* means "at the very moment." Hence *omked-imtage* lelkíako,—They saw him *at the very moment when he gave*.

Tense -forms used subtantively never become perfect functional equivalents of our Abstract Nouns, which cannote that the action is there and then conceived as abstracted from all real relations; for they still signify the action *as refered to an agent* and *as having a real terminus* or *object*. This is clearly proved by the following fact:-

The Munda inserts Direct and Indirect Pronominal Objects into his Transitive Predicates. In the Definite Present and the Definite Imperfect, these Objects must stand between the primary root and the Tense-suffix. Example—*Dal* means *to strike*; the Definite Present suffix is *tan*; the Definite Imperfect suffix is *tan* + *taiken*; *ko* means *they* and *them*.

Hence, he is striking them now, { Root. Dir. obj. T.suff. Cop. Subj
Dal - *ko* - tan - a - e.

In the Imperfect Tenses the Subject generally stands between *tan* and *taiken*.

Hence, he was striking them then, { Root. Dir. obj. Tense. Subj. Tense. Copula.
Dal - *ko* - tan - e - taeken - a.

This is of course pronounced like one word—dalkotanetaikena.

In all the other Tenses Direct and Indirect Objects stand between the Tense-suffix and the Copula. Hence—

Simple Past.—He struck them: Dalked'-*ko*-a-e.
Anterior Past.—He struck them first: Dalled'-*ko*-a-e.

Whenever the Direct or Indirect Object to a Transitive Predicate is a living being, Pronominal Objects *must be* inserted into the Predicate according to the above rules. When no Pronominal Object is inserted, it is understood *ipso facto* that the Direct Object is an inanimate being.

Now, whenever a Transitive Predicate is detached from its Copula and Subject in order to be used adjectively or substantively, it is detached together with its Pronominal Objects—

Dal-ko-tan horo,—Tho man who strikes *them* now.

Dal-ko-tan-í,—The one who strikes *them* now; *Dal-ko-tan-king,*—The two who strike *them* now; *Dal-ko-tan-ko,*— Those who strike *them* now.

Dallked'-ko-ní—The one who struck *them*; *Dalled'-ko-king,*—The two who struck them first.

Datted'-ko-reá sajai,—The punishment incurred for having struck *them* first (*literally*, the punishment of the act of striking *them* first).

Dalled'-ko-táre-king lelkía,—Both saw him there where he struck *them* first.

The suffix of the Possessive Genitives is *á*. Hence *Dallea'-ko-niá orá* means "The house of the one who struck *them* first."

To denote presence in a certain place or near a person or object, it suffices to suffix *re*, *in* or *táre*, *near* to the word denoting the place or person or object, add the Subject to these suffixes, and then add the Copula *a*. This transforms the word into an Intransitive Predicate.

Noun. Suff. Subj. Cop.

Hence, Dalled'-ko-niá—*orá - re - ko - á*,—They are in the house of the one who struck *them* first.

Dalled'-ko-ní-táre-ko-á,—They are near the one who struck *them* first. Here, then, we have an example of a Tense-form being used substantively, and then being retransformed into an Intransitive Predicate denoting presence near a person, but still retaining its original Transitive function. The compound *orárekoá* exhibits the Locative Case of a simple Noun, transformed into a similar Intransitive Predicate.

As a further illustration of the utter functional instability of both simple and compound Mundari words, I shall add the following examples :—*Martobe* is an Interjection meaning *all right! let us begin ! Martobe-pe-a* means: *now, then, say martobe, i.e.*, begin the work like fellows who say *martobe* ! (Here the Interjection is used as an Imperative with the *Familiar* Interjection *a* suffixed.)

Boys having learned to begin a race after counting in Hindi up to three-*ek, do, tin*! by way of signal, will transform thee Numerals into a so-called Verb in order to says—Let us begin after counting one, two, three—*ekdotin-e-a-bu. Bu* is the Subjects, *a* the Copula, the *e* is euphonic. *Literally*, this means *we shall ekdotin it*, i.e., we shall start after the singal *ek,do, tin*!

Sim means a fowl. *Simked'-ko-a-le*—literally, *we fowled them*. This generally means *we have acquired* (*them*) *the fowls*. But it may also mean *we have killed fowls to eat them*, i.e. (to-day), we have fowl for our dinner.

Mahara means a cowherd; *akad* is the Suffix of the Perfect Tense. Hence, *Maharaakad'koale*,—*We have cowherded them*, i.e., *our cattle*; *we have entrusted our cattle to a cowherd*. But it may also mean *We have engaged them* (these men) *as cowherds*. Of course this Tense-form may go again through the modification indicated above. Thus, *Maharaakad'koni*,—The one who has his cattle grazed by a cowherd.

It may be said that this method of treating words is very handy and expeditious. No doubt it is so in a certain way. But it would have to be abandoned were the Mundas to take to literature; for the ' above examples suffice to show how absolutely necessary it is for the listener to know the circumstances under which such compounds are uttered. As clear and self-sufficient *signifying agents*, these compounds are practically useless. They are too narrow, too material, too dependent on trivial circumstances to be of use in literature; they can only do real service in a very familiar conversation about narrow domestic or village matters, where all the circumstances are supposed to be known to the listener.

Still proceeding on this fundamental principle of his language, the Munda retransforms *whole propositions* into *compound words*, and uses them as Predicates in other propositions. Take the following proposition: *Hoka-a-lang*, Thou and I shall stop *or* cease. Here *hoka* is Predicate, *a* is Copula, *lang* is Subject. The addition of a new Pronominal Subject and Copula transforms this proposition into a mere compound Predicate, thus—

Dir. object. Subj. Predicate. Copula.
Neado - le hõkaalang - á.

Literally, this we *hokaalang* it, *i.e.*, this we express by saying (*hokaalang*) thou and I shall stop. *Nájom*, a sorcerer. *Nájomkoako*, they treat them as sorcerers:-

Dir. object. Subj. Predicate. Copula.
Neado - le - nájomkoako - á.

This (process) we express by saying "they treat them as sorcerers."

Sarti means *true*; *sarti-á* means *it is true*. Hence, *sartiákedako* means "they believed it"—*literally*, they *it is trued it*, i.e., they said to themselves *it is true*.

It is easy to see how deeply the functional elasticity of Mundari roots and compounds affects the grammar of the language. Not only does it give to its etymological part a character widely different from the etymology of an Organic language, but it does away altogether with a great part of Organic syntax; for by substituting compound words for every kind of Organic Subordinate Clauses, it eliminates with one stroke the complicated laws which regulated the Moods and the so-called sequence of Tenses in the Subordinate Clauses.

THE MUNDARI PROPOSITION OR SENTENCE

Isolated words, whether simple or compound, bare roots or organic forms, are the spoken signs of concepts. But the mind is not satisfied with isolated concepts: it cannot rest until it has wrought at least two such concepts into an *intellectual totum*, which might be called a *mental picture*. When, for instance, we join the concepts denoted by the words *horse* and *run* we obtain such a mind-picture. This is translated into language by the proposition : *the horse runs*. These are of course quite distinct from mere sense-perceptions and the picturings of the imagination.

We may at times seem to be working on a single idea or concept, but in that case we are in reality decomposing a complex idea into its elements for the purpose of selecting some two or three of these elements to rearrange them into a mental picture which will exhibit one particular aspect of the idea we were working on. This process we go through each time we formulate some definition. *V. gr.*, the concept denoted by the term *man* includes in an implicit or embryonic manner all the essential characteristics of man. But it is impossible for the mind to represent to itself at any one instant explicitly and clearly all that is contained implicitly in this complex concept. It can only picture man to *itself* under one particular aspect at a given moment. It may at one moment represent him as a moral being, at another as an intelligent being, at another, again, as a being composed of both matter and mind. Thus it obtains successively the different mind-pictures which are signified by the propositions: *man is a responsible being*; *man is an intelligent being; man is a rational animal.* If a speaker only uttered the isolated word *man*, a listener, though understanding the term, would still be at a loss to know what he was driving at. But by uttering one of the above sentences he calls up in the listener's mind a definite mind-picture. The listener then knows that the same picture exists at that moment in the speaker's mind He understands him. The act of thus uniting two or more concepts into a mind-picture is, in logical terminology, called a *judgment*. Since the mind can think only by judgments, we may call the judgment the working unit of the intellect. Hence concepts are related to the judgment as constitutive elements are related to the whole or *totum*.

Considered as a mental act, the judgment is in reality a perfectly simple act, for it consists essentially in the perception of either agreement or disagreement between two concepts.

Hence, *an affirmative judgment* is that act of the mind by which we refer one concept to another as either necessarily or contingently belonging to it.

A *negative judgment* is that act of the mind by which we separate one concept from another as disagreeing with it.

When we examine two concepts thus concurring into a judgment, we find that one of them always acts as a kind of substratum, or rather as an element requiring a closer specification or determination—an element about which the mind may be said to ask a question. This concept is called the *Subject.* The second concept contains the particular specification which is required by the Subject. It answers the question which the mind puts concerning the Subject. This concept is called *the Predicate*, i.e., that which is then and there predicated of the Subject. The Predicate being the determining element may be considered as the more important factor. Thus every judgment consists necessarily of *two* primary or essential elements—*a Subject* and *a Predicate*. The mind may introduce other elements into the judgment, but these do not affect the *constitutive duality* of the judgment; for they are all merely explicitation's or extensions or explanations of either the Subject or the Predicate. For instance, Predicates denoting actions generally imply a *terminus*. Thus the idea of seeing implies an object which is seen. This terminus is called the *Direct Object*. Many words denoting actions imply a double terminus, *v. gr*, the idea of giving implies not only an object which is given, but also a being to whom the object is given. Such a second terminus is called the *Indirect Object*. Both Direct and *Indirect Objects* are therefore only natural complements or explicitations of the Predicate. They are part of the Predicate, but do not form a new constitutive element of the judgment. The same is true of any additions or explanations which may be added either to the Subject or to the Predicate.

From what has just been said we see that in a judgment concepts are not merely juxtaposed at random. Such a juxtaposition would as little yield a judgment as the random juxtaposition of colours would produce a picture. Even as the painter blends different colours into a material picture, so does the mind, in its judgments, blend various concepts into an intellectual picture. That blending is done by aptly correlating and subordinating them to each other. But this presupposes in the mind an innate power of grasping purely intellectual relations and of instinctively and rapidly classifying the different concepts of a judgment under the various categories of apprehended relations.

It is in this act that the superiority of intellect or reason over mere sense manifests itself so strikingly; and since all languages are a more or less perfect physical imitation of this purely intellectual act, it has been said with truth that language constitutes an insuperable barrier between man and the mere animal world.

The spoken sign of a *judgment* is *the proposition* or *sentence*, just as *words* are the spoken signs of *concepts*. Since the proposition is the physical counterpart of the mental judgment, it is evident that it cannot merely juxtapose at random the words denoting the various concepts which constitute a judgment. It must in some way or another connote at the same time all the relations in which the concepts stand one to another. These relations are a set of purely mental abstractions quite distinct from the abstractions described above ? as implied in the Organic Parts of Speech. They arise directly out of the exigencies of the judgment as such. Some of them are purely logical and necessary relations, such as, *v. gr.,* those which exist between the Subject and the Predicate; others are external and contingent, such as, for instance, the various relations of space, time or manner.

The means which language has at its disposal are necessarily limited, and may be summed up under three heads—

(1) A particular and fixed order of words in the Preposition.
(2) Reduplication of the first or last syllable of certain words.
(3) The use of special words used to directly denote relations of space and time. These are the simple or compound Demonstratives, such as Pronouns, Prepositions or Postpositions of space and time, etc.

The three methods are used simultaneously in all languages; but not to the same extent nor yet in the same manner. Some use the order of words more extensively for the purpose of connoting the grammatical relations, whereas others have recourse more freely to the use of Demonstratives. Again, it happens that two different languages using the order of words to connote one and the same relation do not arrange the correlated words in the same order.

The methods used by the Kholarian dialects differ in most respects widely from those used by the Aryan languages. As a consequence of this divergence the Mundari proposition bears an aspect very different from its Aryan equivalent. It is regulated by laws which find no application in the Aryan proposition. A comparison between the Aryan and Kholarian methods on a few essential points will bear out this statement.

1.—Methods of connoting the relation between the Subject and the Predicate.

This relation is a logical or necessary one; for whatever we predicate in a proposition may roughly be defined as either a state or an action. But a state necessarily implies some subject, and every action implies an agent. Hence the Subject and the Predicate are each the natural complement of the other, and *as thus implying each other*, they constitute the very essence of the judgment. They are blended into a new mental unit.

The words denoting the two concepts thus blended being physical elements cannot, of course, perfectly imitate this mental process. Nevertheless, since language is the natural outward imitation of thought, we may expect it to instinctively tend towards welding the terms denoting Subject and Predicate into one compound word or at least to juxtapose them immediately. As a matter of fact, however, though juxtaposition be used extensively, it has, so to say, been judged insufficient by a certain number of languages. Organic languages have recourse to it only when the Predicate denotes an action conceived as a reality, *i.e.*, when it is *a Verb*. In that case the Subject is suffixed to the Predicate in the shape of a Personal Pronoun. Predicate and Subject reacting on each other have produced those peculiar compounds which we meet chiefly in the more ancient organic conjugations, where the Pronominal Subject has become a mere desinence and the root of the Predicate itself has sacrificed something of its original form to the welding of Subject and Predicate into a single word. That the position of the Pronoun immediately after the Predicate is really intended to connote the relation between Subject and Predicate is clearly shown by the fact that these Pronominal desinences must remain even in those propositions where the Subject is expressed by a separate Noun or a current Pronoun, *v. gr.*, Rex da-*t*,—The king give-s.

The Organic languages went a step further still. To Nouns standing as Subject they also affixed a demonstrative root for the purpose of connoting the relation between such Nouns and the Predicate. Thus they obtained eventually a special *Subject form* of Nouns, viz., the *Nominative Case*, which, like the Verb, consists of the bare Noun + a firmative element or desinence. These Nominative desinences are extended to Pronouns and Adjectives. Hence when the subject of a proposition is a Noun or a Pronoun, and the Predicate is a Verb, then the relation between Subject and Predicate is connoted twice, viz., *first*, by the Pronominal desinence of the Predicate; *secondly*, by the Nominative desinence of the Noun or Pronoun. Thus Duc-*s* (dux) veni-*t*.

Whenever the Predicate of a proposition is either a Noun or an Adjective, Organic languages use a link-word or Copula to connect tho Predicate with the Subject, *v. gr.* this man *is* a European. They *are* honest.

Not this Copula behaves like an ordinary Verb Predicate, inasmuch as it takes Pronominal desinences agreeing with the Subject in Number and Person.

Hence here the relation of Subject to Predicate is *directly* or *primarily* denoted first by the Copula, second by the Nominative desinence of the Copula as well as by the Nominative desinence of the Noun or Adjective standing as Predicate, *v. gr.* Rec-*s* nost-*er es-t* duc-*s* bon-*us*. Whereas the Copula *est* connects the Predicate *dux bonus* with the Subject *rex noster,* the several Nominative desinences of the Nouns and Ajectives perform the function of exhibiting the concepts denoted as perfectly co-ordinated in one and the same logical relation.

Thus, then, the method used by Aryan languages to connote the relation between Subject and Predicate does, as a matter of fact, divide Organic propositions into two classes, so far as their outward form is concerned:—

(1) Propositions without a formal link-word.

(2) Propositions with a formal link-word.

The phonetic decay of the personal pronominal desinences has in modern Aryan languages largely increased the number of propositions belonging to the second class. The word used as Copula is generally the so-called Substantive Verb *to be*, and this is treated as an ordinary Verb. Some of its forms are taken from a root meaning *to become*. This copula directly and primarily denotes either *existence* (real or ideal) or *a rising into* existence. Hence the function it performs as link-word is a secondary one superadded to its primary meaning for the particular purpose of referring Predicates to their Subjects.

The Mundari method of connoting the relation between Subject and Predicate differs very radically from the Aryan method—more radically even than it appears at first sight. Mere juxtaposition of the Subject and Predicate is not used. The short questions and replies in which *Substantive Predicates* are occasionally placed immediately after the Subject in affirmative, or before it, in interrogative propositions are in reality merely elliptic propositions. Thus *Munda okoe ?*—Who (is) village-chief ? *Ní Munda,*—This one (is) village-chief.

(1) Every Mundari Predicate is connected with its Subject by means of a Copula.

(2) The word denoting existence, viz., *mená*, is not used as Copula.

(3) There are in Mundari *two distinct Copulas*, viz., *tan* and *á* or *a*. *Tan* is used as link-word only when the Predicate is a Noun or Pronoun, whereas *a* is used when the Predicate is either an Adjective or a Verb.

(4) Mundari propositions too are therefore divided into two classes, but division rests on a different principle from the one on which the Aryan classification is based.

(5) Nouns, Pronouns, and Adjectives take no suffix indicative of the relation here under discussion. There is therefore in Mundari *no Subject* or *Nominative-Case suffix* of Nouns, Pronouns, and Adjectives.

(6) Neither *tan* nor *á* (*a*) ever undergo any change or mutilation of form.

(7) Nevertheless, *tan* and *a* are not the sole exponents of the relation between

Subject and Predicate, for *tan* must alway take the current Personal Pronoun as *immediate Subjective suffix* even in propositions where the concept standing as Subject is expresed by neither a Noun or another Pronoun. Hence it is the Copula *tan* plus *the Pronominal suffix* which connotes the relation.

Subj.	Cop.	Pred.	Pred.	Cop.	Subj.
I	am	a Munda.	Hoṛo	*tan-*	*ing.*
Thou	art	a Munda.	Hoṛo	*tan-*	*me.*
He	is	a Munda.	Hoṛo	*tan-*	*í.*

Subj.	Cop.	Pred.	Subj.	Pred.	Cop.	Subj. Suff
This servant	is	a Munda,	Ne dasi	Hoṛo	*tan-*	*í.*
These two servants	are	Mundas.	Ne dasiking	Hoṛoking	*tan-*	*king.*
These servants	are	Mundas.	Ne dasiko	Hoṛoko	*tan-*	*ko.*

Similarly, a Subjective Pronominal Suffix must be used together with the Copula *á* (*a*) to connote the relation between Adjective and Transitive or Intransitive Predicates and their Subject. But in this case the construction differs slightly ; whereas the Copula *tan* is not a suffix or syllable of the Predicate, the Copula *á* (*a*) is always immediately suffixed to Adjective or Transitive and Intransitive Predicates. The Subjective Pronominal suffix is added to the Copula only when no other word precedes the Predicate. Whenever another word precedes the Predicate, the Pronominal suffix is added to that word, and thus forms its last syllable. Adjectives standing as Predicates generally take the enclytic *ge, v. gr.*, *bugin*, well (in good health), *buginge*—

	Predic. Cop. Subj.		Predic. Cop. Subj.
I am well,—	Buginge-*a* -*ing.*	Thou and I are well,—	Buginge-*a-lang.*
Thou art well,—	Buginge-*a* -*m.*	He and I are well,—	Buginge-*a-ling.*
He is well,—	Buginge-*a* -*e.*	You two are well,—	Buginge-*a-ben.*

Senken is the Simple Past Tense of *sen*, to go. Hence it means *went*—

Subj.	Predic	Predic.Cop Subj.	Subj. Pred.	Predic. Cop. Subj.
I	went,—	Senken -*a* -*ing.*	Thou and I went,—	Senken- *a* - *lang.*
Thou	wentst,—	Senken -*a* -*m.*	He and I went,—	Senken- *a* - *ling.*
He	went,—	Senken -*a* -*e.*	You two went,—	Senken- *a* - *ben.*

	Subj.	*Pred.*	*Subj.*	*Pred. Cop.*
	I	went yesterday,—	Hola *-ing*	senken *-a.*
	Thou	wentst yesterday,—	Hola *-m*	senken *-a.*
	He	went yesterday,—	Hola *-e*	Senken *-a.*

Subject.	*Pred.*	*Subj.*	*Pr. Subj.*	*Prod. Cop.*
The servant	went yesterday,—	Dasi	hola- *e*	senken *-a.*
The two servants	went yesterday,—	Dasiking	hola- *king*	senken *-a.*
The servants	went yesterday,—	Dasiko	hola- *ko*	senken *-a.*

In the Imperfect Tenses the Tense-sign consists of two distinct suffixes, viz., the suffix of a particular Past or Present Tense, *plus* the generic Imperfect suffix *taiken*. Thus, for instance, *sentan* is the Definite Present of *sen*. Hence *sentan taeken* is the Definite Imperfect, meaning *was going along at that moment*. In these Tenses the Pronominal Subject generally stands between the particular Tense-sign and the Imperfect sign *taeken*—

Subj.	*Predicate.*	*Predicate.* *Subj.*	*Cop.*
I	was going along,—	Sentan *-ing-*	taeken *-a.*
Thou	wast going along,—	Sentan *-em-*	taeken *-a.*
He	was going along,—	Sentan *-e-*	taeken *-a.*

From these examples we see that the Pronominal Subjects, though not restricted to one fixed position with regard to the Predicate, must, nevertheless, be in *immediate contact* either with the Copula or with the Predicate. No word can ever intervene between these Pronominal Subjects and the Predicate or between them and the Copula. This particular kind of contact is no doubt intended to assist in its way towards the connotation of the relation between Subject and Predicate.

The division of Organic propositions into two classes, viz., one class without a link-word, and the other with a link-word, is not based directly on the logical nature of the Predicate-concept, but on the etymological form of the word which denotes that concept. This is clear from the fact that whenever an Organic language uses an Adjective, *i.e.*, a Participial form as Predicate in certain Tenses that Predicate must be connected with its Subject by means of a Copula. In the sentence *Rex proficiscitur* there is no Copula, whereas in *Rex profectus est* we meet with a Copula, although the idea denoted by *profectus* is specifically the same as that which is denoted by *proficiscitur*.

It is hardly to our purpose to point out here the logical reason underlying the use of the participial forms. This much, however, may be said that a great amount of abstract thought is embodied in these as well as in all other Organic word - forms. The Aryan has the advantage of being able to use the abstractions thus stereotyped in his words without having necessarily an *explicit consciousness* of either the abstractions themselves or of the manner in which the forms embodying them were obtained. Hence in the formation of his propositions he may allow himself to be guided by his rich word-forms to a much greater extent than a race whose words do not embody the same amount of thought. Such races must, in the framing of their propositions base themselves more directly on the *nature* of the *judgment itself* in order thus to throw into the form of the proposition those essential abstractions which they have, as it were, neglected to express in their word-forms.

In Mundari the division of propositions into two classes is directly based on *the logicul nature* of the Predicate-concept. The form of the word denoting that concept has nothing to do with it. This is shown by the following facts:—

(1) The very same word-form is at one time referred to its Subject by means of the Copula *tan*, at another of the Copula *á* (*a*) according to the nature of the concept it denotes. Thus, horo *tan-í* means he *is* a Munda; horo-*a*-*e* means he *speaks* Mundari.

(2) A certain number of words denoting occupations, offices, etc., are primarily Nouns in Mundari just as they are in Organic languages; v. gr., *Munda*, village-chief ; *pahanr*, sacrificer; *manki*, district-chief; *dasi*, servant. Such Nouns may stand as Subjects or Direct and Indirect Objects in a proposition, but they cannot as such perform the function of Predicates. To use them as Predicates, the Munda attaches to them an intransitive function, adds the Perfect Tense-suffix, and then connects them with the Subject by means of the Copula *a*. Thus—

S. C. *Predicate.*	*Predicate. C. S.*		
He is the village-chief,—	*Munda-akan-a-* e;	*literally*,	He is village-chiefed.
He is the district-chief,—	*Manki-akan -a-* e;	,,	He is district-chiefed.
He is a servant,—	*Dasi-akan -a-* e;	,,	He is a-serving.
He is a king,—	*Raja-akan -a-* e;	,,	He is kinged.

Hence the statement that Substantive Predicates are referred to their Subject by means of the Copula *tan* does not mean that *every Mundari Noun* can stand as a Substantive Predicate and take the Copula *tan*. It only means that no Predicate except a Substantive can take the Copula *tan*. It is *the logical nature* of the concept denoted by a Noun which decides whether that Noun can stand as Substantive Predicate, or whether it must assume an intransitive function before it can be used as Predicate at all.

From the Organic point of view, the whole Mundari method of signifying the relation between Subject and Predicate may perhaps at first sight appear rather arbitrary. However, in language there is really nothing either arbitrary or merely conventional. A short examination of the nature of Predicates in general will, I think, show that the Munda's method is perfectly logical, and that what may appear to us anomalous is in reality of a transparent regularity.

The mind throws all its concepts into two great categories: substances and accidents. A *substance* is conceived as a something which has either a real or possible *separate existence* of its own, *v,gr.*, a man, a tree, the sun. If we analyse the concept of a substance, we find it to contain as it were a bundle of characteristics, each of which is conceived as an essentially necessary constitutive element of that particular substance, so that we cannot remove even one of them without destroying that concept as such, *v, gr*, the concept *plant* necessarily implies *matter* and *life*; the concept *animal* similarly implies *matter*, *life*, and *sense*; and the concept *man* implies *reason* and *will* in addition to *matter*, *life*, and *sense*. Logicians divide these concepts into the so-called natural genera, species and individualities. *Natural genera* are concepts embracing classes of beings conceived as having certain essential characteristics in common, *v. gr.*, plant, animal. *Natural species* as subdivisions of genera are conceived as sets of beings having in common certain essential characteristics not included in the concept of the genera under which they fall, *v. gr.*, *dog* (under the genus animal). *Individualities* are conceived as possessing, besides the characteristics of a so-called *species infima*, certain characteristics by which they are distinguishable from all the other individuals of that species, *v. gr.*, *this* dog, *that man*.

Accidents are conceived as mere modifications of substances, *i.e.*, as something which cannot have a separate existence of its own, but requires a substance as substratum, a so-called *subject of inherence*. Thus, for instance, we conceive colour as belonging to something and able to exist only in that something. Again, we primarily conceive walking, writing, thinking as the acts or modifications of some agent, some substance. Furthermore, we conceive these modifications as not being part of those essential characteristics which make up our concepts of substances. Though a man has and must have some colour, we do not conceive any particular colour as in any way affecting or modifying humanity as such. This is true even of forms of activity, *the capacity for which* constitutes an *essential characteristic* of a substance. Thus the *capacity* of thinking is conceived as essential in man. But the *actual exercise of it* at any given moment is conceived as merely contingent. Hence the name *accident*, which implies that all the ideas of this category are conceived as contingent, as mere modes of being which whether actually present or not cannot change the intrinsic nature of a substance.

In Organic languages ideas conceived as substances are denoted by *Nouns*, also called *Substantive*. However, not all Nouns denote substances. Thus, for instance, Abstract Nouns, such as *whiteness, virtue,* etc., directly denote accidents and connote a particular manner of conceiving them, as shown above. Again, many Concrete Nouns, such as, *v. gr., king, servant,* etc., although denoting individuals, are, nevertheless, primarily intended to designate particular accidents as inherent in those individuals. They directly denote offices, occupations, trades, etc., as inherent in certain classes of individuals. The king and the servant would still remain substantially the same individuals even though, their respective social positions were suddenly reversed.

Ideas conceived as accidents are denoted (1) by Adjectives, (2) by Verbs (3) by Abstract Nouns, and (4) by certain Concrete Common Nouns, as just stated.

Now the office of the Predicate consists entirely and solely in specifying the Subject, *i.e,* in stating *how* the mind conceives the Subject in a given judgment. Hence in judgments where the Predicate denotes a substance, the mind considers or pictures the Subject in its essentially permanent aspect. In judgments where the Predicate signifies an accident, the mind pictures the Subject in one of its contingent or varying aspects. In doing this the mind implicitly knows that particular feature it thus pictures is not an intrinsic constitutent of Subject's nature or essence.

From a purely logical point of view, therefore, judgement do really fall into classes, viz., *essential* and *accidental* judgments.

Essential judgements are those in which the Predicate denotes a *substance.*

Accidental judgements are those in which the Predicate denotes an *accident.*

The Kholarians would seem to have transferred this logical division instinctively into their language. For in their propositions they recognize the division (1) *materially* by the adoption of two distinct link-words, one of which, viz., *tan,* is strictly reserved to connect with the Subject only such Predicates as denotes substances, whereas the other, viz., *á* (*a*), is used only to connect with the Subject such Predicates as denote accidents. (2) They furthermore recognize the division *formally* by the very meaning of these two link-words.

To judge from the generic functions it performs in the compounds where it occurs, the root *ta* denotes fixity in space and permanence in time in the widest sense. If narrowed down by the Demonstrative *ne* (this), it becomes *tan.* This used intransitively means *to remain, to endure, to last, to be necessarily so or so, to be essentially.* Hence the proposition Horo *taní* would literally mean—He *necessarily* is a man. (The form *taen* is the current word for *to remain,* and as such is an ordinary Intransitive Predicate.)

A' is the current Impersonal Pronoun meaning *it, something.* It therefore denotes "being" or "somethingness" in the widest sense, *i.e.,* that vaguest of all concepts which is equally applicable to substances and accidents. Now, if this be used in transitively, it must mean either *to be something* or *to become something.* That the Copula *á* (*a*) is in reality nothing but the Impersonal Pronoun used intransitively will be shown in the Chapter on Mundari equivalents of Organic Verbs. By the fact that *tan* exclusively connotes *substance* in the Predicates which it refers to their Subject, it is sufficiently understood that the kind of *being* connoted by *á* (*a*) in the Predicates it connects with their Subject is a merely accidental mode of being. Hence the proposition *Ne sadom hendege-a-e* literally means: This horse a black-something-he. And if-we translate *a* by *is*, we get—This horse black-is-he. *Hijútan* means coming now. Hence *Hijutan-a-ko* literally means : A coming-now-something-they. If we translate *a* by the Organic form *are*, we get: Coming-now-are-they. The word *raja* used transitively means *to make some one king*. *Rajaó* is the Passive Voice, and means to become a king. The Perfect Tense of the Passive Voice is denoted by *akan*. Hence *rajaakan* is a Participial form, literally meaning *rex factus* (who has) become king, i.e., is king now. Hence, he *is* the king must be rendered into Mundari by *Rajaakan-a-e*; literally, a having-become-king-*being*-he, or having become king *is* he.

The mind frequently forms judgments which are logically quite distinct from those which have just have been described ; for it often represents things under an aspect which do neither exhibit their substance nor yet any of their inherent accidental modications. We may, for instance, represent to ourselves a man as *present* in a particular place. Thus we say : the servant is in the garden. Now presence here or there does not affect the substance of the subject nor does it add anything to the accidental modications which are *inherent* in it. In such judgments the mind simply represents to itself the outward spatial relation of the subject to other real beings. Again, *real existence* as such does not form part of our concept of substances. When, for instance, we think of a future generation of men, we conceive their subtances exactly in the same way as we conceive our own. Their coming into existence some day changes nothing in those essential features which make up our concept of a man: nor can we call their existence, when realized, a mere accidental modifcation of those men. Their existence or coming into actual being is conceived by us as their entering into actual relations with the existing universe. In English this idea of real existence as well as that of presence in, or absence from, a particular place is generally denoted by the same word which serves as Copula to connect Substantive and Adjective Predicates with their Subjects, viz., by the Substantive Verb *to be*. There *is* a God means—God *exists*. He *is* in the house means he is *present* in the house or he *now exists* in the house. He *is not* in the house means he *is absent* from the house. In these propositions therefore the word *to be* does not perform the office of link-word, but it is by itself alone the real Predicate.

The Munda never uses either of his two link-words to denote existence. This alone goes some way to show that he attaches to both *tan* and *á* (*a*) a meaning which cannot well bear the concept implied in the English word *existence*. It is therefore in its way an argument in favour of the meaning which has been attributed to *tan* and *á* in the preceding pages.

Existence and *non-existence* are, in Mundari, denoted by two quite distinct words : *Mená* means *to exist* and *banó* means *not to exist*. At the same time these two words are generally used to denote presence and absence respectively—*Mená, to be present*, and *banó, to be absent*. These two words when used intransitively do not, like other Intransitive Predicates, take the Copula *a* before the Personal Pronominal Suffix but after it—

Mená-*iñ*-a,—	I exist or I am present.	Bangá-*iñ*-a,—	I do not exist or I am absent.
Mená-*me*-a,—	thou exists, thou art present.	Bang-*me*-a,—	thou doest not exist, etc.
Mená,-*i*-a,—	he or she exists, etc.	Bangá-*i*-a,—	he or she does not exist.
Mená,—	it or they exist, etc.	Banó-a,—	it does not exist, etc.
Mená-*lang*-a,—	thou and I exist, etc., etc.	Bang-*lang*-a,—	thou and I do not exist, etc.

There is in Mundari no Transitive equivalent of the English Verbs *to possess, to have, to own.* This idea is expressed by *mená* and its contradictory by *banó.* The construction used to predicate possession is similar to the Latin construction in which the Verbs *case* is used to denote possession, viz., the being possessed stands as Subject, whereas the name of the owner stands as Indirect Object, *v.gr.*, I have a horse,—*Equus est mihi; Aiñ-á* (to me) *sadom* (a horse) *mená-i-a* (exists), or *Sadom* (a horse) *menáia-taing* (exists to me).

Instead of expressing the idea of presence by means of *mená* the Mundas very frequently have recourse to a different construction.

The name of the place in which something or some one is present stands first with the Suffix *re, in.* To this is added the required Personal or Impersonal Pronoun, and then the link-word *á*—

They are here,—*Nere-ko-á.*	They are there,—*Enre-ko-á.*
They are in the house,—*Oráre-ko-á.*	They are on the mountain,—*Burure-ko-á.*

What has so far been said about the manner in which the Kholarian mind denotes the relation between Subject and Predicate may be summed up as follows :—

Propositions are divided into two great categories—

(I) Propositions in which the predication falls directly and solely on the Subject considered in itself alone.

(II) Propositions in which the predication falls directly on the relations in which the Subject stands to other beings.

The first category of propositions is subdivided into two classes—

(1) *Essential propositions*, or those in which the Predicate denotes a *substance.* In these the predication falls on the essential and intrinsically

necessary features of the Subject.

(2) *Accidental propositions,* or those in which the Predicate denotes *accidents.* In these the predication falls on such contingent modifications as may be inherent in the Subject.

In the Essential propositions the Predicate is connected with the Subject by means of the Copula *tan.* In the Accidental propositions the Predicate is connected with the Subject by means of the Copula *á* (*a*).

These two link-words are not restricted to the bare function of simply connecting the Subject and the Predicate, but they do by their very meaning point out the logical nature of the Predicate. In other words, they point out both *the fact* of the agreement and *the nature* of that agreement; for *tan* denotes a logically necessary agreement between the Subject and the Predicate, whereas *á* (*a*) implies a merely contingent agreement.

The propositions of the second category predicate, besides existence or non-existence, the space relations of presence or nearness and absence and the relation of ownership in which the Subject may stand to other beings. These relations are denoted by *mená* and *banó* together with the Copula *á* (*a*). But the position of the Personal Pronominal Affixes is, in these Predicates, never the same as in the Accidental propositions of the first category—

I.—Category

	Pred.	*Cop.*	*Subj.*	*Subj.* / *Cop.* / *Pred.*
Ess. Prop.	Horo ... -	*tan* ...	- í	He ... is ... a Munda.
Acc. Prop.	Marangge ... -	*á* ...	-e	He ... is ... great.
	Rajaakan ... -	*a* ...	-e	He ... is ... a king.
	Hijúlen ... -	*a* ...	-e	He ... ... came.

II.—Category

	Subj.	*Pred.*	*Pronom.*	*S. Cop.*	*Pred.* *Subj.* *Subj.* *Pred.*
1. *Existence*	Pormesor ...	mená ...	-i ...	-a	There is... a God *or* God ...exists.
2. *Presence*	Soma ...	nere mená	-i ...	-a	... ... Soma ... is here.
	Soma ...	ner ...	-i ...	-a	

Subj. Pred. Pronoun. S. Cop. Possess. Aff. Possessor.

3. *Possession*	Sadom mená ... -i ... -a ... -ta ... -ing	
	Possessor. Possess Aff. Subj. Pred. Pronom. S. Cop.	*Subj. Pred. Dir. Obj.*
ñ	Aifi... -á... sadom mená ... -i ... -a	I .... have ... a horse.

This table shows at a glance how difficult it is for a beginner to translate the English Verb *to be* always correctly into Mundari. Yet it is most important that in this matter mistakes be avoided because the use of the wrong Copula or the use of *mená* instead of the required Copula will frequently change the meaning of the proposition, *v.gr.*— Hoṛo *mená*-ia. means—There *is* a Munda *here*, or the Munda *is present*. Hoṛo *tan-í* means—He *is* a Munda. Hoṛo-a-e means—He *can speak* Mundari.

The correct translation of the Verb *to be* is increased still more by a rule which I did not state above. It is this—

Concrete Nouns denoting states, offices, and occupations may in certain cases stand as Predicates, and are then connected with the Subject by means of the Copula *tan*. This happens whenever the speaker intends directly to point out, not the *state, office* or *occupation* denoted by the Noun, but the *individuality* of the person who happens to be in that state or office. Thus the question : *What is* that man? is answered by Raja*akanae*, Munda*akanae*, dasi*akanae*, etc. He *is* a king, he *is a* village-chief, he *is a* servant, etc. But the question *Who is* that man? is answered by Raja *taní*, Munda *taní*, dasi *taní*, etc. He *is the* king, he *is the* village-chief, he *is the* servant, etc. The reason of this difference in construction is clearly based on the principles exposed above concerning the logical nature of Predicates. In the first set of answers the Predicate directly points out mere accidental modifications of the Subject in answer to a question concerning the state, office, etc., of the Subject. These answers are therefore *accidental propositions*. In the second set of answers, on the contrary, the Predicate points out primarily and directly the individuality of the Subject. In them the words *raja*, *munda*, *dasi* are like Proper Nouns. The sentences are equivalent to—That man is the one who is king; that man is the person who is village-chief. The qualifications denoted by the Nouns are here used only for the purpose of clearly pointing out *the individual*. Hence these sentences are *Essential propositions*. In English the Definite and Indefinite Articles will often point out the nature of such Predicates, and thus serve as a guide to the correct use of the Copula, *v.gr.*, in—He is *the* king, the Article shows that here the personality of the king is primarily pointed out; whereas in—He is *a* king, the Article shows that the dignity or office is primarily insisted on.

2.—Methods of connoting the relation between Transitive or Intransitive Predicates and their Direct or Indirect Objects

Transitive and Intransitive Predicates always denote actions in their concrete circumstances, *i.e., real* actions. Even as we cannot conceive a real act of *seeing* without referring it to some subject who does see, so can we not conceive that act without thinking of some object or another which is seen. Similarly, the real act of *giving* implies not only an object which is given, but also a being to whom that object is given. Thus real actions have always one or two *termini*. These are the so-called *Direct* and *Indirect Objects*.

The relation between Transitive or Intransitive Predicates and their Objects bears therefore the same character of a *logical necessity* as the relation between Subject and Predicate.

Organic languages denote this relation by means of special Case desinences in Nouns and Pronouns denoting the Direct and Indirect Objects. In the Predicate itself there is nothing indicative of the relation.

Direct Objects are marked as such by the Accusative Case desinences, *v.gr.*, Rex mittit ministr-*um*. Rex mittit ministr-*os*.

Indirect Objects are marked by the Dative Case desinences or by special Demonstrative words (Prepositions and a Case desinence), *v.gr.*, Bex dat pecuniam ministr-*o*. Rex accepit nuntium *a* ministr-*o*.

Modern Organic languages in which the Case desinences have partly or almost wholly succumbed to the action of phonetic decay have chiefly recourse to current Demonstrative words for the purpose of signifying this relation. Besides the use of Case desinences or of current Demonstrative words, juxtaposition is used; for there is a marked tendency to place the Objects immediately after or immediately before the Predicate. However, no very great stress is laid on this factor as an exponent of the relation.

In Mundari, on the contrary, *the position* of the Objects is *the sole exponent* of the relation; for no kind of affix is ever added to any Noun or Pronoun for the purpose of signifying it.

On this point Mundari differs not only radically from Organic, but also from most Agglutinative languages. It is not satisfied with mere immediate juxtaposition, but it *inserts* Pronominal Direct and Indirect Objects *into* the very body of the Predicate-word. Even as *the mental* Object is conceived as a necessary complement of the concept denoting the action, and thus coalesces with that concept into one complete *mental* Predicate, so does the *spoken* Object in Mundari coalesce with the term denoting the action into one single *Predicate-word.*

The Pronominal Objects are inserted according to the following rules: —

(1) In the Definite Present and the Definite Imperfect they stand between the root and the Tense-suffix.

(2) In all the other Tenses they stand between the complete Tense-form and the copula.

The inserted Pronouns are always the unmodified bare root-forms—

Predicate.

Root. Dr. ob. Tense-suff,. Cop. Subj.

D. Pr.	Lel - *ko* - tan	- a - ing,—I am seeing them now.
D. Imp.	Lel - *ko* - tantaeken	- a - ing,—I was seeing them then.

Predicate.

Root. Tense-suff. Dir. Ob. Cop.Subj

Ind. Pr.	Lel - jad' -	*ko* -	a - ing,—I see them.	
S.Past.	Lel - ked' -	*ko* -	a - ing,—I saw them.	

As already stated, in all Imperfect Tenses the Pronominal *Subjects* are by preference inserted between the original Tense-suffix and the generio Imperfect suffix *taeken*. Thus—

I saw them then ... { Lel-ko-tan taeken-a-*ing*. or Lel-ko-tan-*ing*-taeken-a. }

I had seen them ... { Lelked'-ko-taeken-a-*ing* or Lelked'-ko--*ing*-taeken-a. }

In this kind of Mundari proposition therefore all the purely logical relations, viz., those between Subject and Predicate as well as those between the Predicate and its Objects, are welded together into one polysyllabic word, and this word constitutes the whole proposition as such. Any additional words which may be met with are mere explanations of either the Pronominal Subject, or the Predicate, or the Pronominal Direct and Indirect Objects.

As a physical imitation of the mental judgment, this is no doubt driven as close as possible. In itself, however, it is not a perfection; for it renders language heavy and sometimes obscure. Thus, for instance, whenever the Pronominal Subject and Direct Object are in the same Number and Person, the Mundari proposition is ambiguous, though either of the two be explained by an additional Noun. Raja-*e* lelked-*i*-a may mean "the King saw him" as well as "he saw the King". This construction is another proof that the Kholarian mind has so far been *de facto* unable to grapple successfully with the mind's higher abstractions and the connex problem of translating these into clear and easy language. It exhibits him in a way as unable to clearly formula the abstract concept of action on the one hand and the abstract concept of the Objects or *termini* of action on the other. He cannot pronounce the word *to see* without *at the same instant* naming in a way the object seen. That this is so is shown by the fact that the Pronominal Objects must be inserted even if the Object is named by some separate Noun or Pronoun in the proposition, *v. gr*, I saw the *servants*,—*Dasiko*-ing leiked'-*ko*-a. In this respect, then, the Kholarian resembles the Red Indians of America, whose languages are similarly tied down to slavish imitation of concrete realities.

The following facts seem to indicate that the kholarians themselves feel this method of expressing the relation between Predicate and Objects as inconveniently heavy:—

(1) If the principle on which the insertion of Direct and Indirect Objects undoubtedly rests were carried out to its entire extent, then a number of Predicates would have to insert *two* Objects, *viz*., a *Direct* and an *Indirect* one at the same time. *I give these horses to them* would therefore stand thus : Ne sadomko-ing om-*ko-ako*-tana. But it was evidently felt that this would bo overloading a word and throwing the Tense-suffix too far from the root it specifies. Hence two Objects are never inserted into one and the same Predicate. The speaker in such cases is free to insert either the Direct or the Indirect Object. One of the two must occupy a separate position outside the body of the Predicate. Hence either Ne *sadomko*-ing om-*ako*-tanaing (here the Indirect Object is inserted) or Ne sadomko *akotá*-ing om-*ko*-tanaing (here the Direct Object is inserted and the Indirect Object stands before the Predicate in the shape of an emphatic Personal Pronoun *ako* with the suffix *tá*, *to*).

(2) The logically correct practice of distinguishing Indirect Objects by the prefix *a, to*, from Direct Objects is found to interfere too much with euphony in most Tenses. Hence in the Simple Past, instead of leaving this prefix immediately before the Pronominal Object, they throw it before the Tense-suffix. Thus in the sentence *I gave it to them*, we get om-*a*-ked-*ko*-aing instead of omked-*ako*-aing. This transposition is made no doubt because *omkedako* is by itself alone a complete proposition, where *ko* is Subject and *a* Copula and it means *they gave it*. Since this compound would call up that judgment in the mind before the addition of the intended Copula *a* and the Subject *ing* would be pronounced in *omkedakoaing*, they had recourse to the transposition of the prefix *a* in order to avoid that inconvenience. But the form om-*a*-ked'-*ko*-aing is *never* used in its entirety. From the fact that *a* belongs to the Pronominal Object there arises an instinctive hurrying over the Tense-suffix *ked*, and this brings about the elision of the two first letters, *k* and *e*. Hence the current form om-*a*-d' *ko*-aing instead of omaked' koaing.

In the insertion of the 1st and 3rd Persons Singular, viz., *ing* and *i* the Mundas of some districts go a step further in the way of alleviating the overloaded Predicate. By rapidly passing over the letter *d'* and compensating for it by the peculiar jerk represented by the graphic sign (') they obtain the forms omá*iñ*ae and omá*i*ae, instead of *omadiñae* and *omadiae*,—He gave it *to me* and he gave it *to him*. This process is in its way as strongly Organic as anything we meet with in the treatment of the formative or demonstrative elements by the Aryan languages; for here the whole Tense-suffix is sacrificed to the principle which requires the insertion of the Pronominal Object into the Predicate. Most Mundas, however, find this process too much for their Agglutinative instincts, and they stick to the forms oma*d*iña and oma*d*ia.

The other Tenses in which the Pronominal Objects stand after the Tense-suffix do not lend themselves to the above transposition and its consequent elisions. The Perfect Tense-form om-*akad* cannot afford an additional *a* before *akad* : Oma-akad'*ko* aing would be more heavy even than om-akad-*ako*-aing.

In the Indefinite Present *omjad* and the Anterior Past *omled* the transposition would present no more difficult than in the Simple Past *omked*. But then the result would be that these three tenses become identical in form; for the elision of *ja* and *le* in om-*a*-jad' *ko*-aing and om-*a*-led'-*ko*-aing would lead to om-*a-d'-ko*-aing, which is accepted as the Simple Past form.

Now what does the Munda do in these cases ? Rather than throw his troublesome Indirect Object entirely outside the Predicate, he sacrifices the Prefix *a*, *to*, completely and leaves to the listener the trouble of discovering from context or circumstances whether the Simple Personal Pronouns inserted into these Tenses are then and there *Direct* or *Indirect* Objects. Hence—

Omjad'-*ko*-aing may mean—I gave *them* (to some one), or I gave it *to them*,

Omled'-*ko*-ainrig may mean—I first given *them* (to some one), or I first gaven it *to them*.

Omaked'-*ko*-aing may mean—I have given *them* (to some one), or I have gaven it *to them*.

The other relations which may arise between the various terms of a proposition are relations of space, time and manner. They are denoted by Postpositions, so-called Adverbs and Numerals. They need not be considered here in detail because the manner in which they are signified does not affect the essential outlines of the proposition.

If now we want to apply the Organic grammatical terminology to the Kholarian mode of signifying the relations arising directly out of the nature of a judgment, we shall be led to a couple of statements which must at first sight shoek our accepted grammatical notions—

I.—*Mundari Nouns, Pronouns and Adjectives have no Nominative, no Accusative, and no Dative Case*. For whatever meaning we may attach to the term *Nominative*, we must admit that it does not apply to Mundari Nouns or Pronouns. If by *Nominative* we mean only that material *word-form* which has arisen out of the combination of the Original Nominative Affix with the Noun's root or theme, as, *v.gr.*, rex, murus, in contradistinction to the theme, and the other Case-forms, such as *regis, regem*, the term cannot be applied to Mundari Nouns and Pronouns because such forms as Root *plus* Nominative Affix or Theme *plus* Nominative Affix do not exist. However, that is hardly the real meaning of our term; for we do not say that all the Nouns and Pronouns of a dictionary stand in the *Nominative Case,* although they there appear in the same form which they have when standing as Subject of a proposition. What we really mean to designate by the term *Nominative Case* is *the function* which that particular *word-form* performs. This function consists in pointing out the Noun or Pronoun as the real Subject of a given proposition, and it is therefore part of the Organic method of denoting the relation between Subject and Predicate. But there is no suffix in Mundari whose function it is to point out any Noun or Pronoun as Subject of the proposition. Nouns and independent Pronouns do not assist by anything in their *form* to denote the relation between Subject and Predicate. The real grammatical Subject in the Mundari proposition is the Personal or Impersonal Pronominal suffix, which stands either at the end of the Predicate or immediately before it. Additional Nouns or Pronouns are, strictly speaking, only specifications of the Pronominal or real Subject. In *dasi hijúlenae* the word "*hijúlenae*" is the grammatically complete proposition; *dasi* explains the Pronominal suffix *e*, as though we said *he*, namely, the servant, *came*.

The same remark applies to the terms *Accusative* and *Datire*; for the whole denotation of the relation between Predicate and Direct or Indirect Objects is exclusively performed by the inserted Pronominal Objects.

In certain cases where the Indirect Objects are thrown out of the Predicate, they are pointed out as such by Postpositions denoting clearly a relation of space. Hence if a *Case* at all, it is a *Locative of motion*.

Add to this the very peculiar manner in which the Organic *Genitive Case* is split up into five different forms, four out of which are pure *Locatives* and only one a genuine *Possessive Case. V. gr.*—

The house *of the servant*,—Dasi-*á orá*. The beasts *of the* forest,—Bir-*ren* jontuko.

The cattle *of the* servant,—Dasi-*táren* uríko. The trees *of the* forest,—Bir-*reá* daru.

If ring *of* gold,—Samrom-*rá* mudam.

If, then, we want to force the terms *Declension* and *Case* on Mundari Nouns and Pronouns, we should say that the whole Mundari Declension consists of a *Possessive Case*, an *Instrumental Case*, and a certain number of *Locatives of rest or motion*.

To say that the *Nominative*, *Dative* and *Accusative* are identical in form is meaningless. If the term *Case* be insisted on, the bare root-form of Nouns might be called the *Indeterminate Case*, inasmuch as that form does not perform any function as regards the denotation of relations. This form may in a certain very restricted sense be called an *Equivalent* of Organic *Nominatives*, *Datives* and *Accusatives*.

II.—If we take the term *Case* as denoting, not a particular word-form, but the grammatical function of signifying the relation between Predicate and Direct and Indirect Objects, then we may say that in Mundari *Transitive* and *Intrasitive Predicates* have, besides Voice, Mood and Tense also an *Accusative* and a *Dative Case.* Furthermore, since the relation between Subject and Predicate is exclusively denoted by the Pronominal Subject, we might say that they have also a *Nominative Case*.

III.—The term *Verb* denotes a class of words exclusively denoting states or actions as referred to a subject or agent. We associate with it at the same time that peculiar Organic process which is called *Conjugation*. But Mundari has no particular class of words restricted to that function nor has it a conjugation in our sense of the term.

Mundari equivalents of our Verbs fall under the head of Accidental Predicates as regards their nature, and the mode of connecting them with their Subject is the same as that by which simple Adjectives are connected with the Subject. Hence the term *Verb* can in no sense be applied to them. Those equivalents represent *a mere grammatical function*. They are *Predicates*. To distinguish them from ordinary *Adjective*-Predicates the qualification *Transitive* or *Intransitive* is added to them. Hence the term *Transitive* and *Intransitive Predicates* is in these pages substituted for the word *Verb*.

So much for the more striking differences existing between the internal relations of the Mundari and those of the Organic proposition. If now we consider the proposition as a whole, we find that in that respect too Mundari differs strongly from the Aryan methods.

Besides the *Simple Proposition*, we have in Organic languages Compound Propositions or Sentences. In these there is one *Principal Proposition* with its own Subject and Predicate and one or more *Subordinate Propositions* with their own Subjects and Predicates. *V. gr*., the man (*Subj*,) who (*Subj.*) gave (*Pred.*) you this letter is an Uraon (*Pred.*). Though this sentence signifies but one single judgment or mind-picture, it contains two Subjects and two Predicates. We understand that the whole of the above Relative Clause is but an explanation of the real or *Principal Subject* of the judgment.

But the Munda never tolerates more than one Subject and one Predicate in even the most complex proposition. Subordinate clauses with special Subjects and Predicates can never occur in a Mundari Proposition. It is here that he brings into play his numerous Tense-forms. By using them either with a Substantive, an Adjective or an Adverbial function he obtains compounds which, with or without additional suffixes, render any of our subordinate clauses.

It is exceeding difficult for a foreigner to translate compound Organic sentences fluently and correctly into Mundari: when he has acquired a certain facility in this matter, he may not yet flatter himself with the idea that he will understand all those perplexing compounds as fast as they drop from the Munda's lips. Often and often he will have to acknowledge to himself that he does not know what his interlocutor is driving at, though every word of the sentence sounds familiar to him. Nothing but a prolonged intercourse with Mundas can help him over this difficulty. To get into a correct rendering from English into Mundari the following is the safest and the shortest method, though apparently rather long. *First*, translate your subordinate clause into a complete Mundari proposition; *then* cut off the Copula and the Pronominal subject; *finally*, place the remnant thus obtained in its proper place of the Mundari principal proposition. *Ex.*, "The man *who brought this letter* is an Uraon." Since there are no Relative Pronouns in Mundari, all English Relatives must be replaced by corresponding Personal Pronouns. Hence *Who brought this letter* becomes *he brought this letter*,—Ne chiti-e (*Sub.*) auked-a (*Pred.*). Throw out *e* and *a* and you obtain *Ne chili auked,* these three words being a qualificative of the Subject; *The man, horo,* precede that word. Hence—

Hence—

Subject.	*Pred.*	*Cop.*	*Pr. Subj.*
Ne-chiti auked horo	Uraon	tan	-í

The man *who gave this letter to you* is a Hindu. He gave this letter to you—Ne chiti omad'me-a-e. Cut off the Cop. *a* and the Subj. *e* :

Subject.	*Pred.*	*Cop.*	*Pr. Subj.*
Ne chiti omad'me horo	Diku	tan	-í

I saw the men *who beat him.* They beat him,—*dalkí-a-ko* (here *í*is the Pronominal Dir. Object). Cut off the Copula *a* and the Pron. Subj *ko*. Hence—

Direct Object.	*Predicate.*	*Cop.*	*Subj.*
Dalkí horoko	leiked'ko -	a -	ing

or Dalkí horoko-ing lelked'koa. *Literally,* the him having beaten men I saw them.

An additional difficulty arises in other kinds of subordinate clauses where the Tense-form, severed from its Copula and Pronominal Subject, requires other modifying suffixes. This of course pre-supposes a knowledge of the functions performed by the various Postpositions. In those propositions we meet turns which defy every attempt at anything like an approximatively literal translation into English.

A last peculiarity of the Mundari proposition is the absence of the so-called *Oratio obliqua* or *Indirect Speech.* The words of a third person are always left in the *direct form.* This necessitates the *co-ordination* of two complete propositions into one sentence. It is the only instance of a Mundari sentence containing *two Subjects, two Predicates*, and *two Copulas*.

The sentence *He said he would come to-morrow* must, in Mundari, be turned as follows : *I* will *go* to-morrow, saying he said,—Gapa-ing sen-a mente (saying) kajilá-e.

He affirms that he never saw you, becomes, *I* never saw *him*, saying he affirms.

This construction is very simple in itself. It eliminates the last trace of the troublesome *sequence of Tenses* from the syntax. But it requires some attention on the part of the foreigner to make the requisite transposition of words when he translates from English into Mundari. A slight mistake in this matter would make him say what he never intended to.

It will readily be perceived that the method to be followed in a Mundari grammar must differ widely from that which is usally followed in the elementary grammars of Organic languages. A rigorous adhesion to the divisions and classifications of those grammars would create difficulties where there are none, and give the appearance of anomalies to forms and constructions which are but the logical consequences of the principles on which the language is based.

As regards *the terminology* used in Organic grammars, very little of it applies to Mundari if taken in its current meaning. It is to be hoped that the rapidly increasing study of non-Aryan languages may soon create a rational terminology which will be applicable to Isolating and Agglutinative as well as to Organic languages. This ought not to present great difficulties if the terms to be partly selected and partly created be based exclusively on *the functions* performed by the various Predicative and Formative or Demonstrative elements and on *the ideal relations* existing between the constituents of a judgment; for *functions* and *relations* being purely mental and abstracting from the material word-form, are fundamentally the same in all languages:

Some of our terms, such as *Noun* and *Pronoun*, can hardly be objected to from that point of view; whereas others would undoubtedly have to be modified. Thus *Adjectives* are not always mere qualifying additions to Nouns, because they may stand as Predicates of a proposition. The term *Verb* is unfortunate even in Organic languages, since it really indicates neither a grammatical function nor the outward form of the particular class of words it designates. The mere fact of their occurring more frequently as Predicates does not entitle those words being called the *word par excellence*. Functionally it belongs to the same class of Predicates to which ordinary Qualificatives (Adjectives) belong. Adverb is a very inadequate term even in those languages which use the term Verb. For it there is applied not only to words which *modify* Verbs, but also to words which modify Adjectives, *v. gr., sightly* bitter. *Preposition* and *Postposition* again do neither touch the function nor the form of the class of Demonstratives they designate. They merely point out their relative position with regard to other words.

A common terminology serving to give an accurate analytic description of *the proposition* in all languages may appear to offer more serious difficulties owing to the very divergent methods used by different groups of languages for the purpose of expanding, explaining or modifying either the Subject or the Predicate. If, however; the fact that the most complex and complicated sentences of any language have always only *one main Subject* and *one main Predicate* and that everything else in the sentence is for a particular purpose grouped around these two essential constituents—if, I say, this fact were made the exclusive basis of the common terminology, the difficulty would be found more apparent than real. But until a universal terminology be really adopted, the creation of new terms for a comparatively insignificant language, such as Mundari is, would probably cause more confusion than the use of the Organic terms with such modifications in their current meanings as the character of Mundari necessarily implies. Thus, *v. gr.*, the terms *Noun*, *Adjective*, *Adverb*, etc., must be understood to denote, not word-forms, but simply *grammatical functions*. *Clause* never denotes a subordinate proposition with a Subject and Predicate of its own, but merely a compound word with or without additional words which stand as mere Qualificatives or Modificators or Expansions of either Subject or Predicate.

That in Mundari Etymology and Syntax coincide, so to say, completely is evident enough. Hence a division of the grammar into Etymology and Syntax is out of the question. The method best adapted to the character of language appears to be the following:—

The whole subject is divided into four parts—

- *The First Part* treats of the so-called Demonstratives. Beginning with the simplest Demonstratives, it gives their signification and shows how the simple forms concur to form Compound Demonstratives. It contains eight chapters, viz., (1) Definite, Indefinite, and Interrogative Demonstratives used adjectively, (2) Personal Pronouns, (3) Definite Indefinite, and Interrogative Pronouns, (4) Postpositions, (5) Numerals, (6) Words used adverbially, (7) Conjunctions, (8) Interjections.
- *The Second Part* shows how Simple and Compound Demonstratives concur with Nouns and Pronouns to form compounds equivalent to Organic declensional or Case-forms. The formation of Possessive Adjectives and Possessive Pronouns as well as of certain Nouns falls in naturally with the subject-matter of this part. To this is added a word on the degrees of comparison in Adjectives.
- *The Third Part* treats of the manner in which Demonstratives concur with Predicative roots to form equivalents of Organic conjugational forms. It considers these compounds as Transitive or Intransitive Predicates, and therefore comprises chapters on Mood, Voice and Tenses. It considers them next as performing various other functions with or without additional Demonstrative suffixes.
- *The Fourth Part* explains how the Tense-forms are used as subordinate clauses in propositions.

A few necessary remarks on the Mundari vowels and consonants, and on grammatical Gender, Number, and the distinction between living beings and inanimate objects precede the first chapter of the First Part.

MUNDARI VOWELS AND CONSONANTS

The vowels *a*, *e*, *i*, *o*, *u* are pronounced as in Latin or German.

Any two vowels may stand side by side: *ae*, *ai*, *ao*, *au*, *ea*, *ei*, *eo*, *eu*, etc. When thus occurring together each vowel retains its original sound. Fusions of two vowels into a new sound, such as occur, *v. gr.*, in the English word *broad*, do not exist, nor are two vowels together used to form a long one. Each vowel is either long, short, or neutral, *i.e.*, so short that it is difficult to distinguish between an *â* and an *ĕ*.

All the vowels may be na salized. In that case I use the mark *n* after the vowels, *v, gr.*, *anri*, a fig-tree; *chenre*, a bird. They occur only before *d* and *r*.

The semi-vowels *y* and *w* are rare. *y* is used only instead of *e* when this occurs between two vowels, *v. gr.*, *loyong* for *loeong,* a rice-field. *w* takes the place of *o* between two vowels, *v. gr.*, *hewa* for *heoa*, accustom.

The consonants *f*, *x* and *z* do not exist.

g is always pronounced like the *g* in *good*, never like the *g* in *George.*

j is a purer sound than the English *j*. It may be said to stand between the German and the English *j;* but it has nothing of the French *j.* The same remark applies to *ch*.

d and t are pure dentals as in German, hence different from the English sounds.

r is always pronounced distinctly as in German, never like the affected French guttural.

s is a sharp palatal rather than a dental consonant.

n (1) in the beginning of a word is pronounced like the English *n* in *never*.

(2) In connection with a dental it becomes a pure dental.

(3) When it precedes the consonants *g* or *k* it is pronounced like the *n* in the English *ring* and the German *Enkel*.

In this conjunction of *n* and *g*, the *g* is pronounced like in the English *ring* when it is the last letter of the word ; but when it is followed by another letter, the *g* is pronounced somewhat harder like in the English *linger, v, gr.,* *dungui,* short. With regard, however, to this combination of *ng* and *nk*, attention must be paid to the following rules :—

(1) When the vowel following *g* is the first part of a distinct Suffix, *v. gr.*, the Perfect Tense Suffix *akan*, then the *g* is pronounced like the *g* in the word *English* or the German word *Engel*, *v. gr.*, *dinga-kana*,—full of water.

(2) When the *n* preceding the consonants *g* or *k* belongs to the Demonstrative Prefix *en* that, then the *n* must be pronounced as a distinct dental, *v. gr., enkate=en-kate*, that way or thus; *inku=en-ko* ; *literally*, that they, *i.e.*, those.

In this we see the instinctive tendency of an Agglutinative language trying to preserve the primary root against even the slightest encroachments on the part of secondary roots.

I do not think it necessary to adopt a diacritic mark for the purpose of distinguishing between the cases where the *n* and *g* or *k* sounds are preserved quite pure, and those where they are, so to say, melting into each other, because a slight knowledge of the language will naturally lead a foreigner to observe the above rules.

Besides the *n* described above, there exists in Mundari the so-called *n mouillé*'s. This I write *ñ*. It is used when the Pronoun *aing* or *ing* of the first Person Singular is followed by the Suffix *á*, *v. gr.*, the Possessive *aiñá*, to me or of me, my; *kaiñá*,—I won't.

To the above consonants must be added the cerebrals *ḍ*, *ṭ* and *ṛ*, which is readily interchanged with ḍ. We might add ṇ, which is used to transform ordinary vowels into nasals before ḍ and ṛ.

h occurs both in the beginning as well as in the body of words, *v. gr.*, *hoṛo*, man; *mahara*, cowherd.

Moreover, all consonants may take the aspirate; hence *dh* and and *ḍh, th* and *ṭh*, etc.

It is a curious fact that the Mundas of the Mankipati districts, who are generally not acquainted with Hindi or Sadhani, frequently drop the aspirate in adopted Hindi words.

It is difficult for most Europeans to get into a correct pronunciation of the aspirate consonants, and especially of the cerebrals ḍ, ṭ, ṛ, and ṇ. But it is, I believe, quite impossible for any foreigner to acquire a perfectly correct pronunciation of the peculiarly checked vowels which occur so frequently in Kholarian languages. All the vowels may be thus checked. This peculiar sounding of the vowels may be described as follows: The pronunciation of a vowel, commenced in the ordinary way, is suddenly checked by a rapid partial contraction of the muscles used in its formation, and then, by a relaxation of those muscles the breath or sound is allowed to flow out without receiving any further modulation.

This process gives to the vowel the sound of two vowels, of which the first is very distinct, smart, and short; whereas the second sounds somewhat like a slight short echo of the first. I represent these sounds by a wedge-shaped apostrophe above the letter, in order to distinguish it from the ordinary apostrophe: *á é í ó ú. á*, a bow, sounds somewhat like *a-â*, *dé*, to climb *de-*

ê. The consonants *b* and *d* preceded by vowels are frequently treated in the same manner. For *d* this is the case not only at the end of words, but also each time that this letter is followed by a *k* or a *t* in the middle of a word, *v. gr.*, *ub*', hair ; *med*', eye; *had*', to cut. *Ked* is the Simple Past Tense Suffix. The *d* of this becomes *d'* in *v. gr.* lelke*d*' koaing,—I saw them; lelke*d'*te,—having seen it. The consonant *d'* thus checked sounds somewhat as though it were followed by a slight m; *ub'* = ub-m. The consonant *d'* sounds as if it were followed by a slight *n*, med' = med-n. In reality, however, there is neither an *m* nor an *n* attached to these consonants. These *m*-and-*n*-like echoes arise naturally from the flow of the breath after the check whilst the lips and tongue are still in that position in which they were when the formation of the consonants *b* and *d* was commenced.

The consonant *t* in *et'kan*, bad, seems to undergo the same check. The checking of *d* in the Tense-suffixes before *k* and *t* seems to be used for the purpose of preserving this final letter of a tense-form which would otherwise naturally become *t* before and in contact with *k* and *t*.

These checks disappear and reappear in certain connections in a manner which seems to be almost, arbitrary. Again, some Mundas will use them where others do not use them. As I have so far not been able to fully ascertain the laws which regulate them, it would hardly be of use to put down here such observations as I have been able to make.

In dissyllabic words the accent is generally on the first syllable even when the last syllable is checked, *v, gr.*, *lija*, a cloth; *rebed*', squeeze. There are few exceptions to this rule. They must be learned by practice. I have so far not ascertained the reason of the accentuation of the last syllable in those words. In general it may be said that accentuation is by far not as pronounced as in German or English. Barring some very short vowels, the accentuated has hardly more stress than the non-accentuated syllable.

The law of harmony of vowels which plays such a prominent part in Ural-Altaic languages has comparatively little influence in Mundari. Vowels of Tense-suffixes, for instance, never change for the purpose of harmonizing with the root-vowel, *do-akad, de-akad, ti-akad, nu-akad*.

However, some vowel-changes are evidently traceable to this law. *V. gr.*, the Plural kuṛi*ku* used as well as kuṛi*ko*. Again, *i*ni-instead of *e*n-í etc.

There is neither a *Definite* nor an *Indefinite Article* in Mundari. The context in which a Noun occurs must decide whether that Noun, when rendered into English, should be preceded by the Definite or by the Indefinite Article. Thus-

horo may mean, *the* man or *a* man.

horoko may mean, *the* men or men.

REMARK.—The Numeral *mid*' or *miad*', *one*, is often used, especially in narrations, where, in English, the *Idenfinite Article a, an* or the phrase *a certain* would stand.

GENDER

Mundari does not recognise *Grammatical Genders*. Hence—

(1) Nouns do not take any suffixes indicative of Gender.

(2) One and the same pronominal form denotes both male and female beings. Thus, *Aé* means *he* as well as *she*; *ko* means they, *i.e.*, the French *ils* or *elles*; *ní* means this one, *i.e.*, both *celui-ci* as well as *celle-ci.*

(3) One and the same adjective form is used to qualify Nouns denoting male or female or neuter beings. Thus, *bugin* apu, a good father*; bugin* enga, a good mother; *bugin* orá, a good house.

The only Mundari Nouns connoting sex are the patronymics, *i.e.*, words denoting family relations. The following is, so far as I could ascertain, a complete list of those words:—

apu, father, vocative, *aba !; enga*, mother, vocative, *eang*! (aiang).

koṛa, man, husband ; *kuṛi*, woman, wife.

herel, husband; *eṛa*, wife; *bau*, senior brother; *misi*, senior sister.

aṛa, son-in-law, also junior brother-in-law ; *kimin,* daughter-in-law, also junior sister-in-low.

hatom, senior paternal aunt, *i.e.*, father's senior sister, or wife of father's senior brother.

gari, junior aunt, *i.e.*, father's junior sister or wife of father's junior brother.

hili, senior sister-in-law.

guiram is used by *men* only when speaking of or to the brothers of their sister-in-law.

nataia is used by *women* only when speaking of or to the wife of their brother-in-law. In other words, women who are married to brothers call each other *nataia.*

saḍigi is used by men when speaking of or to the husband of a sister-in-law. Two men having married sisters call each other *saḍigi*,

boko denotes both a junior brother and a junior sister.

honjar denotes both a *senior* brother-in-law and a senior sister-in-law.

tenja denotes both a *junior* brother-in-law and a junior sister-in-law. It is used by *men* speaking of or to their wife's junior brothers or sisters.

irul denotes both a *junior* brother-in-law and a junior sister in-law. It is used by *women* speaking of or to their husband's junior brothers or sisters.

hon denotes a child as well as the young one of any animal irrespective of sex.

sumdi denotes both the parents and the uncles and aunts of a son-in-law or a daughter-in-law,

To distinguish between the male and female beings denoted by the words just enumerated, the words *koṛa,* man, and *kuṛi*, woman, are added, respectively—

boko-koṛa, junior brother.	*boko-kuṛi*, junior sister.
tenja-koṛa, junior brother-in-law.	*tenja-kuṛi*, junior sister-in-law.
irul-koṛa, junior brother-in-law.	*irul-kuṛi*, junior sister-in-law.
hon-koṛa, son.	*hon-kuṛi*, daughter.
sumdi-koṛa, father or uncle of one's daughter or son -in-law.	*sumdi-kuṛi*, mother or aunt of one's son or daughter-in-law.

N.B.—The word *honjar* prefixes the words *bau* and *misi; bau-honjar*, senior brother-in-law ; *misi honjar*, senior sister-in-law.

The words *koṛa* and *kuṛi* are more generally placed before the word *hon* : thus, *koṛa-hon* oftener than *hon-koṛa,* son; *kuṛi-hon* oftener than *hon-kuṛi*, daughter.

To complete their catalogue of patronymics the Mundas have borrowed the following terms from the Hindus. In these words the masculine gender is connoted by the ending *a* or *u,* the feminine by *i*—

aja, paternal or maternal grandfather.	*aji*, paternal or maternal grandmother, also senior sister.
dada, senior brother. (This is the vacative of address to the Mundari word *bau*.	*dai*, senior sister. (Vocative of address to the Mundari word *misi.*)
baṛa, senior parternal uncle.	*baṛi,* senior paternal aunt.
kaka, junior paternal uncle.	*kaki*, junior paternal aunt.
mamu, senior or junior maternal uncle.	*mami*, senior or junior maternal aunt.
kuku, one's aunt's husband.	*kukui*, paternal uncle's wife.

aji-hanar, senior sister-in-law, *i.e.* one's wife's senior sister.

N.B.—This last is a combination of Hindi and Mundari, and corresponds to the term *bau-honjar*.

There exist a few terms destined chiefly to connote the age of domestic animals or the work they are used for. Of these, some do at the same time connote sex—

haṛa, a bullock used for ploughing.	*gundi*, a cow used for ploughing.
nauṇkì, a female buffalo.	*paṭia*, a female goat not yet bearing.
gaia, a capon.	*kaluti,* a grown chicken not yet laying.

urí denotes both cattle in general and bullocks in particular.

The words *andia*, bull*; bacha*, a young bull; *gai*, cow*; bhains*, buffalo cow; *bakra*, he-goat; *khassi,* gelded goat; *boda*, he-goat, are borrowed from Hindi.

If required to distinguish between the sex of animals, the words *saṇdi* male, or *enga*, female, are placed before the Nouns denoting animals. Thus—

Sim, fowl; *saṇdi-sim*, cock; *enga-sim*, hen.

Sadom, horse; *saṇḍi-sadom*, stallion ; *enga-sadom*, mare.

DISTINCTION BETWEEN LIVING BEINGS AND INANIMATE OBJECTS

The distinction between living beings and inanimate objects is constantly attended to, and from a grammatical point of view is most important; for it regulates the Grammatical Numbers and thus plays a conspicuous part in the formation of those compounds which are the equivalents of Organic Declensions and Conjugations.

All heavenly bodies as well as the causes of natural phenomena, such as rain, thunder, lightning, hail, are considered as living beings: hence the Munda says: *He* rains, etc. On the other hand, plants are treated as inanimate objects.

GRAMMATICAL NUMBERS

1st. Nouns denoting living beings have three Numbers—*the Singular, the Dual*, and *the Plural*.

2nd. Personal Pronouns, *i.e.*, those which stand for Nouns denoting living beings, have *distinct forms* for the Singular, the Dual, and the Plural.

3rd. Other Pronouns standing for Nouns denoting living beings form their *Dual* and *Plural* like the Nouns they stand for.

4th. Nouns denoting inanimate objects have, generally speaking, no *Dual* and *Plural.*

5th. Pronouns standing for Nouns denoting inanimate objects have no *Dual* and *Plural* forms.

6th. Adjectives never take the *Dual* or *Plural* suffixes whether they qualify Nouns denoting living beings or inanimate objects.

Formation of Numbers

The Singular of Nouns is always the bare root, *i.e.*, no suffix is ever added to any Noun for the purpose of pointing out the Singular Number.

king is the Dual form of the Personal Pronoun of the third person and means *both, the two*.

ko is the Plural form of the same Pronoun and means *they*.

The Dual of Nouns is formed by suffixing *king* to the Singular.

V. gr. *horo, man ; horoking*, two men*; literally*, man-the two.
ipil, star ; *ipilking*, two stars „ star-the two.

The Plural is formed by suffixing *ko* to the Singular : *horoko*, men; literally, man-they *; ipilko*, stars; *literally,* star-they.

Nouns denoting inanimate objects never take the Dual and Plural Suffixes in ordinary conversation or narration. Thus *daru* may mean one or more trees. The context must decide what number is actually meant.

There are only two cases in which those Suffixes are added to Nouns denoting inanimate objects, *viz.*—

1st.—When it is required to strongly *emphasise* the duality or plurality of objects.

2nd.—In enumerations of inanimate objects. Here every Noun of the series takes the Plural Suffix *ko*, even those which in English have no Plural. Thus—

What didst thou buy ?—Chikanam kiringla' ? Salt, tobacco, rice,—bulung-*ko*, tamaku-*ko,* chauli-*ko*.

Head, chest, stomach, in short the whole body, is paining me,—Bó-*ko*, kuram-*ko*, laí-*ko,* gota hormo-*ko* hasujáiña.

The Plural form is even used when any single part of the body is spoken of as ailing. Thus—Kuram-*ko* hasujáiña,—My chest pains me.

Remark.—When a Munda speaks of his wife to a third person, he always uses the Plural form of the word : *kuri* wife. This dispenses with the use of the Possessive Adjective, thus— Who is sick ? Okoe hasujáiña, ? My wife,—kuri-*ko*.

Married women always use the Exclusive Dual form of the Personal Pronoun when speaking of themselves. V. gr., *Ka-ling* sena instead of Ka-*ing* sena,—*I* will not go. Again, any one speaking to a married woman is supposed to use the Dual form of the Personal Pronoun. *V. gr.,* Sena-*ben* chi ka-*ben* sena ? instead of Sena-*m* chi ka-*m* sena?— Wilt *thou* go ?

It would be considered both rude and indecent were any one to address a married woman with the Singular form of the second person. Husbands may use the Singular form, but even they generally observe the above rule.

The Dual form of the Pronoun is also very frequently used when speaking- of married women in the third person. V. gr., Ka-*king* sena instead of Ka-*e* sena,—She will not go. Hence also ni*king* instead of *ni*, this (woman), celle-ci; in*king* instead of *ini*, that (woman), celle-lá.

This peculiarity is the more striking, because the Mundas not only have none of the ceremonial or polite forms which abound in some other Agglutinative languages, but they never even use any honorific Plural or Dual of address. *Am*, *thou* is used to address superiors as well as equals and inferiors. The reason of this peculiar use of the Dual lies in the manner in which the Munda conceives the family, viz., as a moral unity. Hence the wife always includes her husband in the Pronoun of the first person. *Aling* in fact means literally *he* and *I.* That this is the real reason will be shown fully lower down where the Possessive Suffixes are explained.

Very frequently unmarried girls use the Dual forms of themselves in the same manner. But this is not general, and evidently arises only from a desire of aping their seniors.

DEMONSTRATIVES AND INTERROGATIVES USED AS ADJECTIVES

I.—Definite Demonstratives

The following, when used adjectively, occupy an independent position in the proposition, *i.e.*, they are neither suffixes nor prefixes.

They stand before the word they qualify and never take any suffix indicative of Number.

ne, this; *en*, that; *han*, yonder, that . .yonder; *nimin*, this much of, this number of; *niminang*, just this much; *imim*, that much, so much; *iminang*, just that much, just so many.

The forms *nimin* and *imin* qualify Nouns denoting living beings, whereas *niminang* and *iminang* qualify Nouns denoting inanimate objects.

Ne horo, this man; *ne* sadomking, these two horses; *en* honko, those children; *han* daru, yonder tree ; *niminung* bulung, this much of salt ; *imin* simko, just so many fowls.

Remark—The stronger forms *hen* for *en*, *niminung* for *niminang* and *iminung* for *iminang* occur very often.

The forms *nendŭr* or *nendŭro, handŭr* and *handŭro* occur chiefly in the dialect of the Larkas.

Note :

1. *Ne*, *en* (*hen*) and *han* appear to be but different modulations of one and the same root; the changes in the position and strength of the vowels serving to mark the relative distance of the object pointed out. The aspirate *ha*, placed before the consonant *n*, indicates a very great distance. To point out an object that is less distant, *ha* ia softened down into *he* or more frequently into e. To point out something that is quite close to the speaker, this *e* is still further weakened by being thrown behind the consonant *n*. Thus, then, the consonant is the unvarying element of the simple Definite Demonstrative root. This *n* occurs in many compounds both as infix and suffix as a specifying or limiting agent. The power of expressing proximity or distance by mere vowel changes is not limited to Mundari. Max Müller in "Turanian Languages" says it is shared by several Agglutinative languages, *cfr*. Canarese: *ivanu*, this one; *avanu*, that one.
2. *Nimin* and *imin* are compounds of *ne min* and *en min* ; literally, *this much*, *this many*, and *that much* or *that many*. In *nemin* the stronger vowel *i* influences the weaker *e* so as to harmonize it with the vowel *i*. In *en min* the same influence is exerted over the *e* by *i*, and then the *n* being thrown out for euphony's sake the form *imin* is obtained.

   Hence *min* may be considered as a Definite Demonstrative of quantity, whether continuous or discreet.

3. The forms *nendur* and *handur* may perhaps be a combination of the Mundari *ne* and the Hindi *idhar*; literally, this here, and of the Mundari *han* and the Hindi *udhar* ; literally, that or yonder there. When Mundas borrow from the Hindi, they generally replace aspirate letters by the corresponding simple ones. They not unfrequently add a vowel in harmony with the root-vowel of the adopted, word.
4. *Ne* occurs as Definite Demonstrative with but slight modifications in a number of Agglutinative languages.

II.—Indefinite Demonstratives

N.B.—The abbreviations (1. b.) and (i. o.) stand for the words *living beings* and *inanimate objects* respectively.

The Adjectives marked below by the abbreviation (1. b.) are used to qualify Nouns denoting living beings ; those marked by the abbreviation (i. o.) qualify Nouns denoting inanimate objects.

The following, placed before Nouns, perform the function of Indefinite Demonstrative Adjectives, and as such never take any suffix indicative of Number:—

Oko, some; *ja* (1, b.), any at all; *jan* (i. o.), any at all; *jeta* (1. b.), some; *jetan* (i. o.), some, any; *mid'* (*miad', mod' moiad'*), some, one *tara*, several; *tara tara* or *tatara* and *taramara*, many; *isu*, much, many; *purá*, much, many; *isu purá,* very much, very many; *huṛing* or *huduṛing*, little, few; *hupuṛing*, very little, very few; *oṛó, oḍó or onḍó*, more; *jad'ka,* more ; *huṛingleka,* a little, a few; *nimpirang* or *nimpirung*, this little, as little as this; *jaiminang* or *jaiminung* any amount of, any number of.

Ja hoṛo, any man at all; *jan* kami, any work whatever; *oko* honko, some children ; *Purá* diri, many stones.

Remark.—The enclytic *ge* is always suffixed to the above Demonstratives in short replies to questions, where the Noun specified by the Interrogatives in the question is understood, but not expressed in the answer.

Chimin hoṛoko senako ? How many men will go ? *Purádge*, many; Oṛó chauling omamea ? Shall I give you more rice ? *Oṛóge*, yes, more.

III.—Interrogative Demonstratives

The following placed before Nouns perform the function of Interrogative Adjectives, and, as such, remain always unchanged :—

Oko ? What? *Chikan* ? What kind or what sort of ? *Chilekan* ? Of what quality? *Literally*, what like? *Chimin* ? (1. b.) How many? *Chiminang* ? (i. o.) How many? How much?

Oko ? is an Indefinite Adjective ; all the others are Definite.

Remark.—*Chimin* is chiefly used to qualify Nouns denoting living beings; *Chiminang* chiefly qualifies Nouns denoting inanimate objects. This distinction, however, is not always rigorously observed.

The other Interrogatives are used indiscriminately both with Nouns denoting living being and with those denoting inanimate objects.

Note 1.—*Chi* is an interrogative particle used both as suffix and as prefix. When suffixed to the last word of a proposition, it transforms that proposition into an interrogative one *v. gr,*, Hoṛoko hijútanako means,—The men are coming; Hoṛoko hijútanakochi ? means,—Are the men coming ?

As prefix it is used only to form Interrogative Compounds.

2. *Kan* is the equivalent of *tan*, which, as stated in the Introduction, is used as Copula when the Predicate of a proposition is a Noun or Pronoun. It is therefore best rendered by the English *is* or *it is*, in its copulative meaning.

Leka means like, similar.

Hence *Chikan* ? is a compound of the interrogative particle *chi* and the Copula *kan*, and means literally *what is it* ? This Adjective then enquires after the *kind* or *class* to which something belongs.

Chilekan ? is a compound of three words, viz., the Particle *chi,* the word *leka* and the Demonstrative *en*, that, the vowel of the latter being dropped. Hence it literally means,—What like that ? Therefore it enquires after the *qualitfy* of something.

Chimin, a compound of the interrogative *chi* and the quantitative *min* literally means: how many ? how much ?

Chiminang is possibly a compound of *chi*, *min*, and *ena*, the Neuter Demonstrative Pronoun, *that*. If so, it literally means how much that, *i.e.*, how much of that. This might account for the form being chiefly used with Nouns denoting inanimate objects—

Oko hoṛo ? What man ? *Hani'*, Yonder one.

Chikan hoṛoko ? What kind or class or race of men ? *Mundako*, Mundas.

Chilekan hoṛo? What sort of man? *Salangi esel hoṛo*,—A tall, fair man.

Chimin sadomko? How many horses? *Chiminang* daru? How many trees ?

Chiminang chauli? How much rice?

II.—PERSONAL PRONOUNS

1.-Simple Personal Pronouns

The Personal Pronoun of the first person has two distinct forms both for the Dual and for the Plural. The first of these may be called the *Inclusive*, and the second, the *Exclusive* form.

The *Inclusive Dual* comprises the speaker and the person spoken to. Hence it should be rendered into English by—*thou and I.*

The *Inclusive Plural* comprises the speaker and two or more persons spoken to; hence it means *you and I.*

The *Exclusive Dual* excludes the person spoken to : it comprises the speaker and some person distinct from the one who is addressed. Hence it means, *He and I* or *she and I.*

The *Exclusive Plural* excludes the person or persons addressed ; it comprises the speaker and two or more persons distinct from those who are spoken to. Hence it means *They and I.*

I consider the following as the original Personal Pronouns, and therefore as complete roots and not as mere truncations of the Emphatic Personal Pronouns—

	Singular	*Dual.*	*Plural.*
Ist Pers.,	*ing*, I.	Inclus., *lang*, thou and I.	*bu*, you and I.
2nd Pers.,	*me*, thou.	Exclus,, *ling*, he and I, she and I.	*le*, they and I.
3rd Pers.,	*i*, he or she.	*ben,* you two.	*pe*, you.
Impers. or Neut.,	*á*, it (i.o).	*king*, both, the two.	*ko*, they.
		á, both (i.o).	*á*, they (i. o).

These forms never occupy an independent position in the Proposition : they are essentially *suffixes* or *infixes*.

The following rules must be observed regarding their position :—

1st.—When they stand as Subject of a Proposition, they must be suffixed either to the Copula or to the word which immediately precedes the Predicate—

Pred.	Cop.	Subj.		Adv.	Subj.	Pred.	Cop.
Hiju'len -	a -	*ko*,—they came.		Hola -	*ko*	hijúlen -	a,—They came yesterday.

N. B.—These Pronominal Subjects when suffixed to Mundari Transitive or Intransitive Predicates give the latter a semblance of a conjugation. Hence beginners are inclined to always suffix them to the Copula. The Mundas by preference suffix them to the word immediately preceding the Predicate. It may even be stated as a general rule that they *must* be suffixed to Adverbs which may happen to immediately precede the Predicate. The same rule holds good of the Negative Particle *ka*, not, which in Negative Propositions always stands immediately before the Predicate, except in sentences where a Vocative of Address is used. In that case the Vocative frequently stands immediately after the Particle *ka* : thus—*ka gomke-ling sena!* —Sir, he and I will not go.

Remark.—To every Mundari Tense there corresponds an *Imperfect* which is obtained by adding *taeken* to the original Tense. When any of these Imperfects occur, the Mundas generally suffix the Simple Pronominal Subjects to the original Tense-form, so as to stand between it and the Suffix *taeken*. Here, then, it is *infixed* into the Predicate—

Def. Pros. Subj.	Imp, T. S. Co.	
leltan - *ing*	taeken - a,	I was seeing it then.
leltan - *em*	taeken - a,	thou wast seeing it then.
leltan - *e*	taeken - a,	he was seeing it then.

Remark.—When Nouns are used intransitively to denote either motion or rest, they take the Postpositions *te*, to, *tále*, towards, or *re*, in, *táre*, about ; then they infix the Pronominal Subject between these Postpositions and the Copula *a*. Thus—

Pred. Subj. Cop.

Oṛáte - ko - a; *literally*, to the house they it is, they to-the-house it, *i.e.*, they go home.

Oṛáre - ko - a; „ , in the house they it is, they in-the-house it, *i.e.*, they are in the house.

Pronominal Subjects occupy the same position when they stand as Subject either to the Predicate *mená*,—to exist, to be present ; *banó*, -not to exist, to be absent ; or to Adverbs of Place. Thus *mená-ko-a*, *they are present*; *bang-ko-a*, *they are absent*. *Nere* means *here* ; *nete* moans *this* way, *okore*? means *where* ? Hence *nere-ko-a*: they are here ; *nete-ko-a* —they come this way ; *okore-ko-a* ?— where are they ?

In the existing Present and Past tenses of this kind, the Pronominal Subject stands before the Tense-sign. Thus—

Hente-ko-jan-a,—they went that way.

However, the Perfect of *mená*, viz., *menáakan* never infixes Pronominal Subjects but follows the general rule of ordinary Predicates. Thus, *menáakange-a-ko*,—they continue there or here.

2nd.—When they stand as Direct Object to a Transitive Predicate in the Definite Present or the Definite Imperfect, they are *infixed* between the root of the Predicate and the Tense-sign. In all other Tenses they are suffixed to the Tense-sign, so as to stand between it and the Copula—

Root of Pred.	Dir. O.	Tense-sign.	Cop.	Subj.
D. Pr. Lel	- *ko*	- tan	- a	- le—Pronounce lel*ko*tanale,— we are seeing them.
*D.Imp.*Lel	- *ko*	- tantaeken	- a	- le " lel*ko*tantaekenale,— we were seeing them at that very moment.

R. of Pr. T. S. D. O. C. S.

Past. Lei - ked' - *ko* - a - le—Pronounce lelked'*ko*ale.—we saw them.

Perf. Lei - akad' - *ko* - a - le „ lelakad'*ko*ale,—we have seen them.

3rd.—When they stand as Indirect Object to a Predicate, they are preceded by a, meaning *to, for, against*, and, together with this Prefix, inserted according to the rule just given under 2—

	Dir. O.	Subj.	R. O.	Pr.	Ind. Obj.		Tense	S. Cop.
Def. Press.	Baba	-ing	om	-	*ako*	-	tan	- a,— I am giving them unhusked rice.
	Bulung-ing		om	-	*ako*	-	tantaeken-a,	—I was then giving them salt rice.

Remark—In some Past Tenses Indirect Objects are not preceded by *a*, whereas in others elisions take place, which will be explained in the Chapter on the Past Tenses.

The Pronouns *ing, me*, and *í* undergo some phonetic changes in certain positions—

Ist—Ing used as *Subject* suffixed to a word ending in *e* forms with this vowel a kind of diphthong in which the *e*-sound predominates strongly, whereas the *i* is hardly heard. At times the *i* appears to be entirely dropped.

Ranchire*ĭng* lelked'koa,—I saw them in Ranchi. Piṭĭte*ng* kultad'koa,—I sent them to the market.

Ing standing as infixed Subject (see above, Rem. 3) changes the *ng* into *ñ* before *a*. In this case the *i* of *ing* takes the jerk denoted by ('), and the preceding *e* of *re* or *te* is no longer heard.

Oṛátí*ñ*a,—I am going home. Ranchirí*ñ*a,—I stay or I am in Ranchi.

The same change of *ng* into *ñ* takes place whenever *ing* stands as infixed Direct or Indirect Object before *a*—

Ráí*ñ*ako,—they will call me. Oteko oma*iñ*a,—they will give me land.

2nd.—Me standing as *Subject* of a proposition always drops the vowel *e* except in the three cases given below :—

Pred.	Cop.	S.
Hasutan	-a-	*m*,—thou art sick.

When the Pronominal Subject *m* is suffixed to a word ending in a consonant, a short euphonic *e* is inserted between that consonant and the suffix *m*—

Ne loiong-*ĕ*-m kiringa chi ?—Wilt thou buy this rice-field ?

Me standing as Subject keeps the vowel *e*—

(1) When it is suffixed to the Copula *tan* in substantive propositions—

Munda tan-*me,*—thou art the village-chief.

(2) When it is suffixed to the words *mená*; to exist, to be present, and *banó,* to be absent, not to exist—

Mená*me*achi ?—Art thou present?

N.B.—The form mená*m*a is, however, also used.

(3) In the Second Person Singular of the Imperative Mood—

Hijú*me*! Come thou ! Senó*me* ! Go away !

N.B.—In two cases, however, the Imperative drops the *e* rather more frequently than not, viz.—

(*a*) When *ko*, they, stands as Direct or Indirect Object between the Predicate and the Pronoun—Rá-*ko-m*,—call them. Om-*ako-m*,—give it to them.

(*b*) When the Particles *kó* and *le* are inserted to form what may be called the Polite Imperative—Hijú*kó*m ! Do come, please ! sen*le*m ! go, please.

Here, however, *me* is oftener kept after *kó*. Thus hijúkóme occurs more frequently than hijúkóm.

Me very seldom drops the vowel *e* when it stands as infixed Direct Object. As Indirect Object it appears more frequently without the final *e*, especially in the Definite Present—

Om-*am*-tanae instead of om*ame*tanae,—he gives it to thee.

Kisi-*am*-tanae instead of kisi*ame*tanae,—he is angry with thee.

3rd.—The Pronoun *i*, *he* or *she*, preserves its original form only when it is suffixed as Subject to the Copula *tan*—

Urao*n* tan*i'*,—he is an Uraon.

When it stands as infixed *Direct Object*, it drops the peculiar jerk denoted by the mark (')—

Rá-i-me,—Call him.

When it stands as *Indirect Object*, it likewise drops the jerk, but it still preserves the *i* sound rather strongly, so that it cannot be said to form a diphthong with the preceding *a*—

Om-ai-me,—give it to him.

The same remark holds good with regard to í suffixed as *Subject* to the words *mená* and *banó*. Thus—

Mená*i*a,—he is here. Bangá*i*a,—he is not here.

In all other cases the Pronoun í is softened down into *e*: hence—

(1) Suffixed as Subject to words ending in *e*, it is hardly perceived except for the fact that it lengthens the preceding *e* slightly.

N.B.—In these cases the spelling *ee* is adopted instead of *e*. Thus: Ọrát*ee* nirjana—Pronounce ọráte,—he ran home.

(2) Suffixed to words ending in *a*, it forms with this vowel a diphthong, pronounced like *ai* in the English word *aisle*—

Senójan*ae*,—he went away. *Kae* hijúlena,—he did not come.

(3) Suffixed to words ending in *i*, *o* or a consonant, it is pronounced as a short ऍ —

Guṛũgadiriẽ lelnamtada, Enad'doẽ ȟalangkeda.—he saw on the ground a curry-stone. Then he picked it up.

Sadom-ẽ lelkia,—he saw the horse.

2.—Emphatic Personal Pronouns

Singular.	Dual.	Plural.
Ist Pers., *aing*, I.	Inclus. *alang*, thou and I.	*abu*, you and I.
	Exclus. *aling*, he and I or she and I.	*ale*, they and I.
2nd Pers., *am*, thou.	*aben*, you two.	*ape*, you.
3rd Pers., *aé*, he or she.	*aking*, both, the two.	*ako*, they.

In some tracts the simple form *ing* is used also emphatically instead of *aing*.

These compounds always occupy an independent place in the proposition: they are never suffixed to another word.

They are used—

Ist.—As Subject of a proposition whenever it is desired to lay a certain stress on the Pronominal Subject. These emphatic Pronominal Subjects stand before the Predicate though not always immediately.

To the question Senam-chi?—Wilt thou go?, the Munda answers Sena-*ing*,—I'll go.

To the question Okoi senae ?—Who will go?, the answer will be *Aing* sena,—I will go.

Dolabu Ranchite ! Come let's go to Ranchi! *Ape* seno-pe *aing* taina nerege,—Go *you* to Ranchi: *as for me I* shall remain here.

2nd.—Whenever it is required to specify or modify Personal Pronouns by means of a Suffix, as, *v. gr.*, in the phrases: of me or my, *aiñ-á*; towards me, *aing-tá*; for me, *aing-mente* ; on thee, *am-re*, with them, *ako-ló*, etc.

Remark—The enclytics *de, do, dang* or *derang* are very often suffixed to these emphatic subjects for the sake of stronger emphasis.

1. *Ge* is used to emphatically distinguish the subject from some other person. Hence *aingge, amge. aége*, etc., are best rendered into English by *I myself, thou thyself, he himself* etc. It may therefore be called a corrective enclytic.

N.B.—It would be a mistake to consider the forms *aingge*, *amge*, etc., as Reflexive Pronouns. There are no such Pronouns in Mundari. That deficiency is amply compensated by the *Reflexive Voice* of Transitive Predicates—

Aége bagraulá—*He himself* (*and nobody else*) has spoiled it.

2. Do suffixed to Pronominal Subjects is likewise a corrective enclytic, but it affects the whole proposition.

It may be asked—Are not the Emphatic or independent forms *aing*, *am*, etc., the original Personal Pronouns ? If so, the Suffix and Infix forms, which on page ?.

I call Simple Personal Pronouns, should have to be considered as results of phonetic decay. Moreover, *me* and *í* should, in the scheme given above, be replaced by *m* and *e*. This view has in fact been adopted by the existing Mundari grammars as well as by Skrefsrud in his Santhal Grammar. He gives the Singular forms thus: *n'* (ng), Í ; *m*, thou ; *e*, he or she, and says:—"When the words to which these suffixes are annexed terminate in a consonant, the full form is used in the first person singular and an *e* is either prefixed or affixed to the second person singular."

The following reasons show, I think, conclusively that *ing, me, í,* etc., are the original and complete Personal Pronouns, whereas the forms *aing, am, áe,* etc., are compound words:—

Ist.—A suffix *ng* for *ing* or *aing* cannot be said to exist in Mundari, for even after words ending in a vowel the *í* is always heard except in the one case mentioned on page ?. Thus Ka-ing sena,—I will not go; entedo*ing* sena,-then I shall go; gungu-*ing*, kiringa,—I shall buy a leaf-umbrella.

2nd.—The so-called suffix *m* occurs only as *Subjective* suffix after words ending in a vowel, *v. gr.,* leltana-*m*,—thou seest it. The statement that after words ending in a consonant an *e* is placed *either* before *or* after the *m* is, to say the least, misleading. The insertion of an *e* before the *m* is regulated by a definite law : it is only when *m* stands as suffixed *Subject* that an *e* is inserted *before* the *m*,—*never after* it. Thus Sar-*e*-m kiringa chi?—Wilt thou buy an arrow ?, *never* Sar-m*e* kiringa? Nor can it be said that this is owing to the fact that the Subjective Suffix is the last syllable of a compound word and therefore prefers the sound *em* to the sound *me* ; for in the Imperfect Tenses the Pronominal Subject is generally infixed into the Predicate. In this position too the *e* must precede the *m*. Thus Leltan-*e*-m-taikena,—thou wast looking on ; *never* leltan-*me*-taikena. Hence this *e* is evidently merely euphonic.

Whenever this Pronoun is infixed as Direct Object into the Predicate, the form *me* must be used after consonants, and is generally used even after vowels: thus Ter-*me*-aing,—I shall throw a stone at thee ; tam-*me*-aing,—I will strike thee ; rá-*me*-aing,—I shall call thee.

Again, *me* and not *em* is used whenever this Pronoun stands as *Possessive* Suffix to Nouns ending in a consonant—Hon-*me*-koṛa,—thy son. Now, if the *e* of *me* in these cases were merely euphonic, we should rather expect to see it before the *m* ; for *ter-em-aing, tam em-aing, hon-me-koṛa* would be more easily pronounced than *ter-me-aing, tam-me-aing, honmekoṛa*. Hence it may be admitted that this *e* is not euphonic, but belongs to the root of the Pronoun.

3rd.—If the original Pronoun of the third person singular were really áe, the would-be truncated or suffix-form would indeed be *e*. But in that case how explain the rise of *e* to *i* in, *v. gr.*, tan-*í*, he is; mená-*i*-a, he exists ; bangá-*i*-a,—he is not here ; Ranchir-*i*-a,—he is in Ranchi ; Ranchit-*i*-a,—he will go to Ṛanchi, as well as in all cases where the Third Person Singular is inserted into the Predicate as Direct or Indirect Object, *v. gr.*, lel-*i*-am,—thou wilt see him; om-a*i*-amg,—I will give it to him. The slight traces of the law of harmony of vowels, still existing in Mundari, can, in none of these cases, be said to require this rise of *e* to *i*. The ordinary laws of euphony would, in most of these cases, rather make us expect a lowering from *i* to *e*. Original strong vowels readily sink down to weaker ones, but original weak vowels never rise to stronger ones, except in obedience to the law of harmony of vowels in most Agglutinative languages. But that law cannot be invoked in the present case. Hence *í* must be considered as the original Pronoun of the Third Person Singular. The *e* of *áe* may be considered as a weakening of this original *í*.

4th.—The practice of inserting Personal Pronouns as Direct or Indirect Objects into predicates naturally necessitates a great and constant care to protect these inserted Pronouns against any phonetic decay ; for if they are to perform that function in such a position, they must be readily recognized by the mind as really complete Pronouns. But if they be not protected against phonetic decay by a continuous and, so to say, conscious effort, they would, in a very short time, be ground down by the preceding and following syllables of that word which they, as it were, cut into two pieces, in a manner which to any but Khol minds appears as very arbitrary and harsh. Since then the Khols have so pertinaciously clung to the practice of having Pronominal Objects infixed into their Transitive and Intransitive Predicates, it is natural that they should have preserved the pure original form of their Pronouns in that particular position more carefully than in any other. Hence it is in these infixed Pronominal Objects that we may expect to find the original forms. But, as already stated, the forms *ing, me*, and *í* are always used as infixed Direct or Indirect Objects, and they are so used even in cases where both the ordinary euphonic laws as well as the law of harmony of vowels would otherwise require either an elision or a weakening of *i* into *e*.

The Emphatic Pronouns *aing, am, áe*, etc., are, I think, compounds of the Impersonal Pronoun á and the Personal Pronouns *ing, me, í*, etc. It will be shown lower down that the Impersonal Pronoun á may, like any Mundari word, be verbalized, *i.e.*, used as an Intransitive Predicate, and that with this function it is equivalent to the English verb *to be* (the Latin *esse*) in its copulative meaning. In the compounds *a-ing a-m á-e* it is used with this function, and means *it is*. Hence these compounds are carious counterparts of the English, French, and German emphatic phrases : *It is me, c'est moi, Ich bin es.*

The explanation and analysis of Personal and Impersonal Pronouns is, as a rule, not more easy in the Agglutinative than in the Flexional languages. The reason of this difficulty seems to lie in the fact that even the nomadic tribes, though ever ready to throw out old words and replace them by new ones, stick to the more common and original words, such as Pronouns and Numerals, almost as much as the Aryan races. Hence we may expect to find in these forms strong elisions and signs of phonetic decay, and sometimes we may be obliged to look for the explanation of some forms in other Agglutinative languages which have apparently no connection whatever with the one we may be studying at the time. If a Pronoun of an Indian aboriginal language finds no counterpart except in Chinese, Japanese, or even in some Siberian languages, this ought to be pointed out; for in the present imperfect knowledge of Agglutinative languages, it is impossible to decide whether such a counterpart be a proof that the two tribes have both kept the same root as an inheritance from a formerly common stock, or whether one tribe borrowed it from the other at a remote date when they may have been, encamped for a time side by side, or whether it be a mere coincidence, if mere coincidences be at all admissible in languages.

Impersonal and Personal Pronouns of the Third Person Singular

If we may suppose that language in its genesis follows consciousness itself, then it should be admitted that the Impersonal and Personal Pronouns of the Third Person are perhaps the most original and therefore the simplest forms. For self-consciousness implies the consciousness of something distinct from self as a necessary and prior element: the Ego or self is primarily perceived as opposed to the Non-Ego, *i.e.,* something out of and distinct from self. The first aspect tinder which the Non-Ego presents itself to consciousness is that of *some-thingness* or *bare being* in its vaguest sense. But this, in language, is denoted by the Impersonal Pronoun. As thus conceived, this Non-Ego implies neither number nor life. The Non-Ego, as perceived in a living entity, is already much more precise. It implies number, inasmuch as the mind naturally conceives a living Non-Ego as an *individuality*, a concept it transfers from the Ego to the *living Non-Ego.*

In Mundari we find the vowels *a* and *i* used to denote these two most elementary concepts. The vowel, with the highest pitch, *viz.*, *i*, is used to designate in general the *living* Non-Ego, which must needs strike the mind more forcibly.

The sharp sound marked by (′) in *á* and *í* may possibly point to an original repetition of the simple sounds *a* and *i* for the purpose of emphatically pointing out the objects.

It is certainly a very peculiar fact that the Impersonal Pronoun á has no corresponding Dual and Plural forms. The direct consequence of this is the fact that even Nouns and other Pronouns denoting inanimate objects have no Dual and Plural.

All additional reason for considering the Persoŋal Pronoun *í* as a very original form seems to lie in the fact that this Pronoun does not connote Gender. No more do its corresponding Dual and Plural forms. In those languages in which the Impersonal and Personal Pronouns of the Third Person imply both Number and Gender, these pronominal forms can hardly be considered as simple and original forms; for the idea of Gender especially could scarcely have been superadded to the original vague concept without the addition of a second Demonstrative to the original root, unless we suppose that one of originally synonymous roots was gradually set apart for this distinct function.

As a signifying agent the Impersonal Pronoun is the vaguest of words. The *Personal Pronoun* of the 3rd Person Singular is a great deal more precise, inasmuch as it always points out one particular Non-Ego and represents it as *a living individual.*

N.B.—In Yakuti *a* occurs as Pronominal Suffix to Verbs. Boehtlingk in the Yakuti Grammar gives *a* as the Predicative affix to the 3rd Person Singular. But he says that this is referable to *ta* which is the Suffix of the 3rd Person Singular after simple vowels and heavy diphthongs.

The same author gives *a* as a lifeless Suffix (*erstarrtes affix*) in certain words, v .gr. *igiss,* to press against each other (intransitive) ikiss-*a*, that which is close by. *Cfr.* the Mundari na*n*ṛe near na*n*ṛe-á, that which is near.

Castren gives *a* as the real Dative Suffix in Burjätio. In Mundari *a* is a real Dative Prefix. It can, I think, be conclusively shown that this Mundari Prefix is nothing but the Impersonal Pronoun with a transferred function.

In Otaïti *a* and *e* denote existence. In Malay the same idea is rendered by *ada*.

The Personal Pronoun of the Third Person Plural

Compared with the Singular *í* the Plural form *ko*, *they*, is comparatively vague; for it simply designates a collection of living beings without specifying either the number of the collection or particularly pointing to one of the individuals of the collection. It directly means no more than the expressions—*More than one, a certain number, some*, It is therefore, functionally speaking, simply an *Indefinite Demonstrative.* Now in Mundari one of the ordinary Indefinite Demonstratives is *oko.* This denotes both one or more beings, whether living or inanimate. The initial *o* of *oko* is always very short—a mere set on as it were to the root *ko*. The Plural Pronoun *ko*, corresponding to the Singular *í* seems to be but this Indefinite Demonstrative root *ko*. If go, the Plural of Nouns, *v. gr.*, Hoṛo-*ko*, kula-*ko* would literally mean *man several, tiger-several*, *i.e.*, some men, some tigers.

N.B.—*Ko* is one of the Plural suffixes in Chinese.

The Pronoun of the First Person Singular

Since self-consciousness arises originally out of an antithesis of the Non-Ego to Self, and therefore implies the Non-Ego as a prior element, we may naturally expect the Pronoun of the 1st Person Singular to be a compound word containing in some way the Personal Pronoun of the 3rd Person Singular as one of its constituent elements. For if in its genesis language tends to follow consciousness, it would appear natural that the mind in framing a word to denote *Self* should have recourse to a method where the Non-Ego is already expressed, and thus signify Self by means of a word containing that very antithesis of the Non-Ego to the Ego which is contained in the original concept of Self. To obtain such an antithesis in words, the creation of a word exclusively denotative of Self is not necessary. In fact, the formation of such a root seems as impossible as the formation of an original concept exclusively representative of *Self.* All that is required is that in the compound to be formed, the Ego be signified in some way by *implication.* May it not be conjectured that the Mundari Pronoun *ing*, *I*, has been obtained in this manner ? Let us suppose this form to be a compound of *i*, *he* or *she* plus *ne*, *this* or *here,* and *ge*, another original Demonstrative emphatically pointing to something near. In that case the *i* would point out Self as a *living being*, and the use of two Demonstratives, both serving to specify as precisely as possible that particular living being, would sufficiently *imply* the speaker or the Ego himself. Thus the compound *i-ne-ge* would contain the required antithesis. That this should rapidly be contracted into *ing* is obvious in the case of a compound so constantly required. It is to be remarked that *ing* in its sharp pronunciation preserves as much as possible the sound denoted by ('). So far as functional precision is concerned, the Pronoun of the 1st Person is of all Demonstratives the most precise. Now the accumulation of Demonstratives indicated above, where each successive root specifies and narrows down the preceding one would appear eminently calculated to fit the compound *ing* for the very precise function it has to perform.

Personal Pronouns of the First Person Plural (exclusive form)

The existence of distinct Exclusive and Inclusive Dual and Plural forms of the 1st Person is met with in a certain number of languages such as Manchu, Yakuti, certain Polynesian and American languages.

With regard to precision, the Inclusive form *le* is more precise than the Plural of the 3rd Person ko ; for it does not simply denote a collection, but it specifies that collection, inasmuch as it indicates one individual of it, *viz*., the speaker, and it does in a way point out the other individuals as then and there standing in a particularrelation to the speaker. It means, in fact, *I and those with me.* Now in Mundari the Postposition *ló* means *with, together with, along with.* Hence the root of which *ló* is either the ground form or more likely a modification, is a Demonstrative which in Mundari has *de facto* been used for the particular purpose of denoting *a connection* between or an *association* of individuals as well as *contemporaneousness* of events.

May not the Plural *le* (*ice*, i.e., *they and I*) be considered as a particular form or even the original form of the root to which *ló* is to be referred. If so, it would answer the special meaning inherent in the Exclusive Plural form by designating a collection of individuals *as connected with the speaker*. The connection would be sufficiently designated *as referring to the speaker* by the fact of his using the form ; and this would dispense with the use of the Singular *ing*, *i.e.*, render superfluous the formation of a compound word in which the 1st Person Singular enters as an element.

Inclusive Plural form of the First Person

None of the Mundari Demonstratives seems to throw any light on the Inclusive form *bu,—you and I.*

Boehtlingk gives *bu* as a Yakuti Demonstrative, denoting *immediate* vicinity. It occurs only, he says, in the Casus Indefinitus. In other Cases as well as in derivations the ground-forms are *ba* and *man*. In Manchu the Inclusive Plural form is *be, you and I*. In Sonthali it is either *bo* or *bon* (compare this with *man*). This is evidently but a weakening of *ba* which Boehtlingk identifies with *bu*. That a Demonstrative denoting immediate vicinity should be used by the speaker to designate both himself and those whom he addresses (*i.e.*, those around him), and should thus come to mean *you and I* appears natural enough.

Pronouns of the Second Person

The same Demonstrative occurs as Personal Pronoun of the Second Person Singular in Mundari (*me*), in Cambodian *mè*, in Anamese *may*, and in Mon *m'neh*. Originally this, like the current Mundari Demonstrative *ne*, must have merely signified proximity. *Cfr.*, man = ba, which are given by Boehtlingk as ground-forms of *bu*, still denoting immediate proximity in Yakuti.

The dual *ben*, *you two,* may perhaps be accounted for as follows :

The consonants *m* and *b* are interchangeable, *m* being a weakening of *b* : hence *me, thou*, may be considered as a weak form of *be* or *me* = *be*. If the Demonstrative *n* (*en*, that) be added to *be*, we would obtain *ben,* literally meaning thou, that (one), *i.e.*, you two. Yakuti, Turkie, and even Sanscrit Plural forms of Pronouns seem to have been obtained by similar additions of Demonstratives which are synonymous or almost identical in meaning.

In *Mon*, which has several striking verbal resemblances with Mundari, the Plural of the Second Person is *pay*. This is evidently the same root as the Mundari Pronoun *pe, you*. *Pi*, which is mentioned by Edkins as an old Chinese Demonstrative meaning *this* and *he*, may perhaps be referred to the same root as the Mundari *pe* and the Mon *pay*.

If *me*, thou, *ben*, you two, and *pe*, you, be really only different modulations of one and the same root, then this would be an instance of a change of *meaning* attaching to a *consonantal* change in an Agglutinative language.

Inclusive and Exclusive Dual forms of the First Person

The forms *lang,—thou and I*, and *ling,—he* or *she and I*, have arisen after the Plural forms, and from their very nature must be compound words.

The Mundas have a very peculiar idiom which may perhaps throw some light on the composition of *lang* and *ling*. At the same time it appears to confirm the conjecture given above concerning the real nature of the Plural *le,—they and I.*

The expression *Paku and I* has no literal equivalent in Mundari. The Mundas do not say Paku *oró* aing, but they say either *Aling Pakuló* or *Pakuló aling*.

Pakutaking means *Paku and his companion*. Now the expression *Paku, his companion, and I* stands in Mundari thus: *Ale Pakutakingló* or *Pakutakingló ale*.

At first sight a foreigner would think that in the experssion *Aling Pakuló* or *Pakuló aling*, there is question of *three* individuals ; for it literally means *we two together with Paku*. And in the expression *Ale Pakutakingló* or *Pakutakingló ale* there seems to be question of at least *five* individuals ; for it literally means we (*i.e.*, they and I) together with Paku and his companion. However, in the Munda's mind each of these phrases is a double or compound phrase: the first part *enunciates* the *total*, whereas the second part *enumerates the individuals* which make up that total. It is as though it were written and translated thus:—

Aling, Pakuló,—*We two viz.* (*I*) *with Paku.*

Ale, Pakutakingló,—*We, viz.* (*I*) *with Paku and his companion.*

Remark that in the second part the Pronoun *I* (*ing*) is not expressed, although one of the individuals enumerated in that part be the First Person. Besides the Postposition *ló*, *together with*, requires the mention, either explicitly or implicitly, of the First Person as *the* one who is *together with* Paku. The reason of this omission of an explicit Pronoun of the First Person can only be this—that the Munda considers the First Person as already named in the *idioma* either explicitly or by implication. Now it would appear that in the phrase *Aling Pakuló* the first person is named *explicitly*, whereas in *Ale* Pakutakingló it is mentioned only *implicitly*. That *ale* in this phrase connotes the first person is evident from the meaning of the phrase. That the connotation is made exclusively by *implication* is clear from the fact that no trace of the Pronoun *ing* is to be met with in *ale*. Nor is there any reason to think that *le* is the result of much phonetic decay. So far, then, this *idioma* confirms the conjecture that *le* denotes a collection of individuals in which the First Person is *connoted* by the fact of its being used by the speaker.

That the First Person is signified explicitly in *Aling Pakuló* seems evident from the actual meaning of the Exclusive Dual, which is—*He* and *I* as well as from the very form *aling*, in which *ng* corresponds to the consonants *ng* in *ing*.

Presupposing the Plurals *le* and *alè* as having existed before the Duals, let us see how the Mundas would have applied the above *idioma* to the expression "he and I," corresponding to " Paku and I." They would naturally place the Plural *ale* first to denote the total, and then enumerate the individuals, viz.,*í* and *ing*, and thus obtain *ale-í-ing*, which would at once contract into *aling*, *i.e.*, *we*, viz., *he and I*.

In this hypothesis *ló* does not enter as a factor into the Dual *aling*. We may suppose too that by means of *ló* the form *aling* was obtained— thus, Aè-ló-ing; literally, *with him I*. In this hypothesis the form *ling* would really be a truncated form of *aling*.

The same *idioma* applied to the expression *thou* and *I* would stand thus: *Ale, am, ing*, we, viz., thou and I. The elision of *e* before *a*, the throwing out of the consonant *m*, and the elision of *i* would yield *alang*, meaning literally *We*, viz., *thou and I*. It is difficult to suppose that *alang* should have been obtained from *amlóing*, *thou with me*. Hence, by analogy, it is more probable too that *aling* is really obtained by the juxtaposition *ale í ing* than from *aé-ló-ing*.

Whatever may have been the actual process, the forms *aling* and *ling* contain parts of the Pronouns *ale* or *le*, *í*, and *ing*, and the forms *alang* and *lang* contain parts of *ale* or *le*, *am*, and *ing*.

III. DEFINITE, INDEFINITE AND INTERROGATIVE PRONOUNS

I.—Definite Demonstrative Pronouns

The Definite Demonstrative Pronouns are formed by suffixing the Simple Personal Pronoun of the Third Person *í*, *king, ko* to the Definite Demonstrative Adjectives *ne, en* (*hen*), and *han*, when the Demonstrative Pronouns denote living beings. The Impersonal Pronoun *á* is suffixed when the Demonstrative Pronouns denote inanimate objects.

Remark.—In the formation of these Pronouns some slight phonetic changes take place :

1. In *ne-í* this one (literally, this he or this she) the *e* elides with *í*; hence the form *ní*.
2. In all the compounds, in which the vowels *e* and *i* are not in immediate contact, the vowel *i*, influencing the weaker vowel *e*, raises it into *i*; hence the forms *inking* instead of *neking* these two (literally, this the two) ; *iní* instead of en-í that one (literally, that he or that she); *inking* instead of *en-king*, those two (literally, that the two).
3. The vowel *i* thus produced in the Singular *iní* and in the Duals *niking* and *inking* is, by a false analogy, very frequently kept in the Plural. But then it reacts on the *o* of the Plural Suffix *ko* and transforms it

into *u* to harmonize it with *i*. Hence the forms *inku* instead of *en-ko*, which would be the regular Plural, those ones ; *niku* instead of *ne-ko*, those ones.

However, the regular form *enko* occurs also.

The *í* of *ní* is always kept in the Plural. But it does not always influence the final *e* because it is itself already weakened by its position after the consonant *n*. Hence the form *niko* is heard, though it be not as frequent as *niku*.

	Singular.	Dual.		Plural.
L. bgs.	*ní*, this one.	*niking*,	these two.	*niko* and *niku*, these ones.
I. o.	*neá*, this one.	*neá*,	these two.	*neá*, these ones.
L. bgs.	*iní*, that one.	*inking*,	those two.	*inku* or *enko*, those.
I. o.	*ená*, that one.	*ená*,	those two.	*ená*, those.
L. bgs.	*haní*, yonder one.	*hanking*,	yonder two.	*hanko*, yonder ones.
I.o.	*haná*, yonder one.	*haná*,	yonder two.	*haná*, yonder ones.

N.B.—The strong form *hení* instead of *iní* never undergoes any change. Hence the Dual *henking* and the Plural *henko*.

Remark.—The i. o. forms *nea*, *ena* (*hena*) and *hana* are, in some parts, frequently used as Adjectives instead of *ne*, *en* (*hen*), *han*. Thus *Nea* daru instead of *ne* daru, this tree. *Hana* buru instead of *han* buru, yonder mountain.

The word *leka*, like, with the Personal Pronominal Suffixes *í*, *king*, *ko*, or with the Demonstrative Suffixes *ní*, *niking, niko*, may be suffixed either to the Singular or the Dual or the Plural of the Definite Demonstrative Pronouns to form Qualificative Demonstrative Pronouns: hence three double seta of such Pronouns are obtained, viz., one where the forms *lekai* (*lekaní*), *lekaking* (*lekanking*), *lekako* (*lekanko*) are suffixed to the Singulars *ní*, *iní*, *haní*; another where those forms are suffixed to the Duals *niking*, *inking*, *hankina*; and a third where the same form are suffixed to the plurals *niko*, *inku*, *hanko*.

Remark.—In the Dual and Plural Suffixes *lekaniking* and *lekaniko* the *i* of *ní* is dropped. Hence the forms *nilekanking*, *nilekanko*, etc., etc. The Impersonal *nea-leka-ena*, likewise drops the *e* after *a*. Hence the forms : *nealekaná*, *enalekaná*, etc.—

	Singular.		Dual.		Plural.	
L. b.	*nílekáe* or *nílekaní*	one like this one.	*nílekaking* or *nilekanking*	two like this one.	*nílekako* or *nílekanko*	some, several like this one.

I. o.	*nealekaá* or *nealekaná*	one like this one.	*nealekaá* or *nealekaná*	two like this one.	*nealekaá* or *nealekaná*	some several like this one.
L. b.	*inílekáe* or *inílekaní*	one like that one.	*inílekaking* or *inílekanking*	two like that one.	*inílekaá* or *inílekanko*	some, several like that one.
I. o.	*enalekaá* or *enalekaná*	one like that one.	*enalekaá* or *enalekaná*	two like that one.	*enalekaá* or *enalekaná*	some, several like that one.
L. b.	*hanílekáe* or *hanilekaní*	one like yonder one.	*hanílekanking* or *hanílekanking*	two like yonder one.	*hanílekako* or *hanilekanko*	some, several like yonder one.
I. o.	*hanalekaá* or *hanalekaná*	one like yonder one	*hanalekaá* or *hanalekaná*	two like yonder one.	*hanalekaá* or *hanalekaná*	some, several like yonder one

The second double set is obtained by adding the Compound Suffixes to Duals—*niking, inking, hanking*. Here the Impersonal forms do not exist—

Nikinglekáe or *Nikinglekaní*	one like these two.	*Nikinglekaking* or *Nikinglekanking*	two like these two.	*Nikinglekako* or *Nikinglekanko*	some like these two.

Etc.

The third double set is obtained by adding the same suffixes to the Plurals—*niku* (*niko*), *inku, hanko*—

Nikulekáe or *Nikulekaní*	one like these ones	*Nikulekanking* or *Nikulekanking*	two like these ones	*Nikulekanko* or *Nikulekanko*	some,several like these ones

The Compounds *lekáe* (*lekani*) *lekaá* (*lekaná*) may in the same manner be suffixed to any Pronoun, Noun or Adjective, and thus produce as many double sets of Qualifying Demonstrative Pronouns as there are Nouns, Adjectives, and Pronouns in the language, thus:—*Amlekáe* (*amlekaní*), one like thee; *Amlekako* (*amlekanko*), men of thy stamp.

Remark.—Circumstances or the context must show how the Compounds thus obtained should be rendered into English. Sometimes the English equivalent will closely resemble the Mundari word in its structure, *v. gr.*, *Ako lekaní* one like them. Sometimes it will be an Adjective, *v. gr, Jontulekaní*, a beastly man. At other times a whole English proposition will be required to give an intelligible rendering. The Tense of the Predicate, then, is decided be the context or the circumstances, *v, gr.*, *Okoilekanko* taikona ? Literally, which one like ones there? *i.e.*, which one (of us or of you or of them) did those who were there resemble ? If the Adjective to which the Compounds are suffixed are Participial ones, the Tense of the corresponding English Relative Clause is *ipso facto* indicated, *v. gr*. Anterior Past: *Hasúlen-lekanko*—Men who look as though they had been sick, or as though they had just passed through a sickness.

N.B.—These Compounds might of course be considered a Nouns. They are here classified as Pronouns because they are real Demonstratives, and in their formation follow the ordinary Demonstrative Pronouns.

2.—Indefinite Pronouns

These are formed by suffixing either the Personal Pronoun *í* or the Demonstrative Pronoun *ní* to the Indefinite Adjectives *oko, ja, jeta, jan, jetan, etá.*

The Impersonal or Neuter forms are obtained by suffixing *á*.

The Personal Pronoun is suffixed to *oko, ja, jan, jeta, jetan.*

The Demonstrative Pronoun is suffixed to *oko* and *eṭá.*

Remark.

1. *Eṭá* takes the Simple Suffixes *king* and *ko* for the Dual and Plural : hence the forms *eṭáking* and *eṭáko*.
2. *Ja* with a Pronominal Suffix always takes the Enclytic *ge* in the Singular.
3. The Suffix *í* is softened into *e* where it is preceded by a vowel. Hence the forms *okoe*, *jaege*, *jetae*,
4. In some districts the Impersonal *á* hardly keeps anything of the jerk denoted by (′).
5. *á* is never suffixed to *ja*,
6. The Impersonal form of eṭá inserts a euphonic *g* between the two *ás*; the jerk denoted by (′) falls away altogether from the *á* of *eṭá*. Hence the form *eṭagá*,— something else, another one.

Singular	Dual.	Plural.
L.b. *okoe*,—some one.	*okoking*,—some two.	*okoko*,—some.
I.o. *okoá*,—something.		
L.b. *okoní*—some ... some.		
L.b. *jaege*,—any one at all.	*jaking*,—any two at all.	*jako*,—any ones at all.
L.b. *janí*,—any one.	*janking*,—any two.	*janko*,—any ones.
I.o. *janá*,—anything.		
L.b. *jitae*,—some one.	*jetaking*,—some two.	*jetako*,—some ones.
I.o. *jetaá*,—something.		
L.b. *jetaní*,—some (any) one.	*jetanking*,—some two.	*jetanko*,—some ones.
I.o. *jetaná*,—some (any) thing.		
L.b. *etání*,—another one.	*eṭálking*,—two other ones.	*eṭáko*,—other ones.
I.o. *etagá*,—another thing.		

Sometimes two different forms are used together.

Of the Dual and Plural forms given above, *eṭáking* and *eṭáko* are the only one that are used regularly. The others are but seldom heard.

Instead of *okoko* the Reduplication *okoekoe* is generally used thus : Chiko hijúlena? Have they come? *Okoeokoeko* hijújana,—Some have come.

N.B.—Ko in okoeokoeko is not the Plural Suffix, but the Pronominal Subject to hijújana.

The Singular form *okoe* may perform a Plural function in Negative propositions. Then it generally takes the suffix, *o*, even, *v.gr.*, *Okoeo* bangkoa,—There is nobody here.

Okoní is chiefly used in disjunctive propositions. It may have a Plural meaning; the Predicate even in that case may stand in the Singular. *V. gr.*, some people can afford it, whereas others cannot afford it,—*Okoni daṛiae, okonido kae daṛia.*

The forms *jaege*, *jetae*, *janí*, *jetaní* are generaly used with a plural function. In Negative propositions they generally take the Suffix *o* even—

Jaege *ráaukom*!—Call anybody at all. Jetaeo *bankoá*,- There is nobody at home.

Remark.—Negative forms, such as, *v. gr.,* the Latin *nemo* do not exit in Mundari. The deficiency is supplied by *banó*,—not to be present, not to exit; or by the Negative Particle *ka*.

The Predicate *banó* may precede or follow the Indefinite Pronominal subject. Thus J*etaeo bangkoá* or *Bangkoá jetaeo*,—There is nobody here.

When these Pronouns stand as Subject to some other Predicate, the Negative Particle may be placed either after the Pronoun, followed by the Predicate or the Pronoun may follow the Predicate. In this case *ka*, of course, stands before the Predicate—

Jetaeo kako hijújana or *Kako hijújana jetaeo*,—Nobody at all has come.

Jetaná ka uiújana or *Ka uiújana jetaná*,—Nothing at all has fallen.

Similarly, these Pronouns may precede or follow the Predicate when they stand as Direct or Indirect Objects. In this case care must be taken to insert *Plural Pronouns* into the Predicate as Repeated Direct or Indirect Objects corresponding to the *l. b.* forms *jaege, jetae*, etc.—

*Kaing lelked'*koa *jetaeo* or *jetaeo kaing lelke'*koa,—I saw nobody: *jaegeo kae boro*akoa or *kae boro*akoa *jaegeo*,—he is afraid of nobody in the world; *jetanáo kaing lellá* or *kaing lellá jetanáo*,—I saw nothing.

A certain number of Indefinite Adjectives perform the function of Indefinite Pronouns without taking any Pronomial Suffix. All of them may stand indiscriminately both for Nouns denoting living beings or for such as denote inanimate objects. With the exception of *miad'*, one, any, they all have a Plural meaning. But *miad* too is construed as though it were a Plural—

Miad' one; *tara* several; *taratara,* or *tatara*, or *taramara* pretty many, pretty much; *purá*, many, much; *isupurá*, very many, very much; *huṛing* or *huṛingleka*, a few, a little; *huṛing huṛing* or *huḍuṛing*, very few, a very little; *huṛing huṛingleka* or *huḍuṛingleka*, very few or a very little; *kented'*, a great many, large numbers; plenty, heaps of; *mer mer*, immense numbers, no end of.

Remark.—*Miad'*, always takes the Suffix *o*, and is used only in Negative Propositions. The others generally take the Enclytic *ge*.

Miad'o bangko'a,—There is not even a single one here. *Miad'o kaing lelked'koa* or *Kaing lelked'koa miad'o*,—I have not seen a single one. *Puráge menákoa*,—There are many present. *Huṛing huṛingge namtad' koaing*,—I got a very few only. *Mer mergeko hunḍiakana*,—Large crowds are gathered.

Note.—One of the chief functions of *leka* is the formation of Adverbs of Manner : hence *Huringleka*, etc., may be looked upon as Advērbs of Manner. All the other Adjectives enumerated above, excepting *miad'*, may, without taking any Adverbial Suffix, be used also as Adverbs of Manner.

3.—Definite Interrogative Pronouns

The Definite Interrogative Pronouns are formed either by suffixing *the Definite Demonstrative Pronoun* to the Indefinite Adjective *oko* or by suffixing the *Personal* and *Impersonal Pronouns* to the Definite Adjectives, *chikan, chilekan*.

Remark.—The Definite Demonstrative Suffix *ní* drops the *í* in the Dual and Plural. Hence the forms *okonking ?* and *okonko ?*

L. b. *Okoní* ? Which one ? *Okonking* ? Which two ? *Okonko* ? Which ones ?

I. o. *Okonea* ? Which one ?

L. b. *Chikaní* ? What kind one ? *Chikanking* ? Two of what kind ? *Chikanko*? What kind ones ?

I. o. *Chikana* ? What kind one ?

L. b. *Chilekaní* ? Which line one ? *Literally,* one like which one ? *Chilekanking* ? Which like two ? Literally, two like which one ? *Chilekanko* ? Which like ones ? Literally, some like which one ?

I. o. *Chilakana* ? What like one ?

Okonking menákinga ? Which two are there? Soma Pakutaking, Soma and Paku. *Chikanko* hijúlenako—Uraon̲ chi Hoṛoko? What kind of people came—Uraon̲s or Mundas ? *Chilekanking* hende chi eselgeaking ? What were the two like—black or fair?

The Compound Definite Demonstratives described on pages ? and ? may all be used as Definite Interrogative Pronouns.

4.—Indefinite Interrogative Pronouns

The Indefinite Pronouns given in the preceding chapter may be used as Indefinite Interrogative Pronouns. What has been said there concerning the Dual and Plural forms as well as the Plural function of the Singular forms holds good also when those forms are used as Interrogative Pronouns.

Okoe? Who? frequently forms its Dual and Plural by inserting *te* or *ta* between the Singular form *okoe* ? Who ? and the Suffixes *king* and *ko*. Thus *okoeteking* ? or *okoetaking* ? Who (two) ? *Okoeteko* or *okoetako*? Who?

N.B.—*Te* and *ta* are similarly inserted into the Dual and Plural of Proper Nouns. They thus denote either *relationship* or *intimacy* or mere *companionship*. Hence *Somataking* may mean *Soma and* either *his wife, brother, sister*, or *any other relation junior to him* ; or it may mean *Soma and his friend* ; or *Soma and his companion,. i.e.*, the one who happens to be with him just now.

This idiom implies at the same time that the person whose name is expressed is the superior or senior or in some respect the most conspicuous of the collection signified.

From what has just been said, it may be inferred how the forms *okoetaking*, *okoetako* differ also in meaning from the reduplications *okoe okoe* ? or the rarely used simple Dual and Plural *okoking* ? *Okoko* ? Thus *okoetaking* ? might freely be translated : Who with his relation, friend or companion ? *Okoetako* ? Who with his family or who with his friends, etc. What gang ? or the like.

There are neither Relative nor Reflexive Pronouns in Mundari.

The deficiency of Relative Pronouns is compensated—

(1) by Transitive and Intransitive Predicates being used as Participal Adjectives, *v.gr.,* Hola *hijúlen* horo; *literally*, the yesterday having come man, *i.e.*, the man *who* came yesterday;

(2) by Nouns of Agency, obtained by suffixing the Personal Pronouns *í, king, ko* or the Demonstrative Pronoun *ni* to Participal Adjectives, *v. gr.*, Hola *hijúlení*,—The one *who* came yesterday;

(3) by the use of Co-ordinate propositions where we would use a Relative Clause as subordinate to some Principal Clause, or by means of an appropriate question and answer, *v. gr,*, Hola mid' hoṛo Ranchiete hijúlenae ; iníge ju ráauime: *literally*, a certain man came yesterday from Ranchi; go and call that one here; for, go and call the man *who* came yesterday from Ranchi. Or Hola mid' hoṛo Ranchiete bijúlenae chi ka? Ini'age mar ju ráauime? *Literally*, Didn't a certain man come yesterday from Ranchi? Well, go and call that one here.

The Definite Demonstrative *okoní* and the Indefinite *okoe* are *sometimes* used as Correlative Pronouns to the Demonstratives *ní* or *iní*. In this construction *okoni* or *okoe* always stands First. *Okoe* kae boroa *inígee* senóka,—Send some one (*literally*, let that one go) who is not afraid.

The deficiency of Reflexive Pronouns is compensated by the Reflexive Voice of Transitive Predicates, *v. gr. Dal*, to strike; *dalen*, to strike one's self.

No distinct roots exist for *Possessive Adjectives* or *Possessive Pronouns*.

The various ways in which this deficiency is compensated will be explained in the Chapter on the Equivalents of Declensions.

VI.—POSTPOSITIONS

These words correspond to our Prepositions; but since they are always suffixed to some other word, they are called Postpositions. Most, if not all of them, originally denote relations of space. The original meanings have been transferred to time as well as to other relations, which might be called moral relations, viz., such as are implied, *v. gr.*, in the propositions—He died *for* his country. He trusts *in* Providence.

There are very few original roots of this kind; but these, concurring with each other, yield a number of Compound Postpositions quite sufficient for the requirements of the language.

The functions of the Postpositions may be classed under four heads—

(1) They perform all the functions of our Prepositions.

(2) They replace the declensional and conjugational inflexions of Organic languages.

(3) They are used to form Adverbs of manner, time, place, and number.

(4) They take the place of the various Conjunctions, which, in Organic languages, introduce subordinate Final, Causal, Conditional, Temporal or other Circumstantial Clauses.

This function is one of the chief characteristics of the language. By its means our Subordinate Clauses are reduced to mere Qualifying Appositions to some part of the principal proposition. Thus our most complicated sentences can be rendered into Mundari by simple propositions, having but one Subject and one Predicate.

Detailed explanations of the second, third, and fourth set of functions performed by the Postpositions will be given in subsequent chapters.

The present chapter only sets down the various meanings of each Postposition, and points out the elements of Compound Postpositions—

Re (1) When used of space, generally denotes rest: hence, when it is suffixed to Nouns or Pronouns to denote mere spatial relations, it must be rendered by ... . *in, on, at.*

Hatu-re, in the village; *sakam-re*, on the leaf; *Ranchi-re*, at Ranchi; *sadom- re*, on the horse; *oṛá-re*, in the house, at home.

Remark 1.—The beginner must guard against restricting the use of *re* to phrases where in English the Preposition *in* occurs. For the Compound Postpositions *chetanre*, etc., *sirmare*, etc., are equivalent only to the English—*on the top of*, *on the summit of*, *on high*, *above*, Hence the English *on* is much more frequently to be rendered by *re* than by *chetanre*, etc.

Remark 2.—*Re* is rather frequently used where we would expects a Postposition denoting motion towards or from (see remarks 1 and 2 under *Te* and remark 1 under *Ete*).

(2) Transferred to time, *re* denotes both the past and the future. Hence, suffixed to Nouns to denote the future, it means ... ... *after*.
Suffixed to Nouns to denote the past, it means *before, ago,*

Chimtangem ruaṛa ? Api *má-re*,—When wilt thou return ?—*After* three days.

Chimtangem akiringkeda ? Isu *sirma-re*,—When didst thou sell it ?—Many years ago.

(3) It is suffixed to Nouns denoting the price for which something is bought or sold, and means ... ... *for*.

Ne lijá chimin *taka-re-m*, kiringtada ?—Bar *taka-re*,—*For* how many rupees did you buy this cloth ?—*For* two rupees.

Tá.—The root *ta* denotes *permanence*, *continuation* both in space and time. Thi appears evident from the functions it performs (1) in the Copula *tan*, (2) in the Static Tenses in *ta* and *tad*, (3) in the Imperfect Tenses, and (4) in the Compound Postpositions.

If this *ta* be used in transitively, it will mean *to continue*, *to last*, *to remain*. If thus used, it will take the Copula *á*, *is* or *it is*. Hence *taá* means *it remains*, *it continues*.

The Postposition *tá* seems to be nothing else than this *taá* contracted.

Hence *tá* is already a Compound Postposition ; in form and meaning a complete proposition, meaning *it continues, it remains*.

Now in Mundari there are no special forms or Suffixes to denote *correlation*. Hence the absolute or simple forms are used also with a correlative meaning. In propositions where words are used with a correlative meaning, there occur two Subjects, the second or correlative Predicate being under-stood. Thus, *iminung* means *that much*. The correlative sentence *I can lift up as much as thou canst* is literally rendered thus into Mundari: Thou that much I can lift,—*Am iminung-ing rimdaria*.

Thus, then, *iminung* means both *that much* and *as much as*. Similarly, *tá* means *it is* (*permanently* here or there) and *there where it is permanently*.

It is especially in its correlative meaning that *tá* concurs with *re*, *te*, *ete* (*ate*) to form the Compound Postpositions enumerated below. Thus, *daru táre* literally means, in there where the tree remains, *i.e.*, *at the tree*, *Daru táte*, literally, to there where the tree remains, *i.e.*, *to* or *towards the tree*.

1st. As a separate Postposition, *tá* is chiefly used to point out the spot where an action is going on. It is suffixed to Transitive or Intransitive Participles, and means ... ... *there ... where*.

Daru *má-tá* menáia,—He is there where (they) cut the tree. Chenṛeko *menáko-tá-e* kamitana,—He works there where the birds are (kept).

2nd. Suffixed to Nouns it denotes a more or less vague proximity, and means ... ... *about, in the surroundings of around.*

Ranchi-tá, about Ranchi around Ranchi

Sá is an equivalent of *tá* and occurs about as frequently as *tá.*

Pá is another equivalent of *tá.* In the Larksa district it is used as Postposition instead of *tá.* In the Upper Chota Nagpur parts it occurs only in a few Compounds.

Te—lst—Suffixed to Nouns denoting *places*, such as *countries, towns, mountains, etc., etc.,* signifies *motion towards*, and meanus .. ... *to, unto.*

Calcutta-te-king senójana,—Both are gone *to Calcutta. Bir-te*-ko nirlena, —They ran to the forest.

Remark 1.—*Te* suffixed to those Nouns denotes the exact terminus of the *motion towards*. It is therefore not an equivalent of the English *into. Into*, though denoting motion, must be rendered by *re* : hence when the above Nouns stand as Indirect Objects to the Intransitive Predicates *bolo*, to enter ; *dé*, to climb; *uiugó*, to fally, or their synonyms they take the Suffix *re*—

Gaṛa-te argunjanae,—He went down *to* the river. But

Gaṛa-re argunjanae,—He went down *into* the river.

Oṛá-te senjanae,—He is gone *to* the house or home. But

Oṛá-re bolojanae,—He entered *into* the house,

Daru-re déjanae,—He climbed up *in among the branches of* the tree.

Sadom-re déjanae,—He mounted a horse.

N.B.—He climbed or ascended the mountain may be rendered both by *buru-te* déjanae and buru-re déjana.

Remark 2.— Similarly, Nouns denoting objects there and then considered as a *place* or *receptacle* take *re* and not *te* when they stand as Indirect Object to the Transitive Predicates *do*, to place ; *uiú*, to drop ; *au* (*agu*) to bring, and their synonyms. Here, again, a real motion towards is rendered by *re.*—

Mej-re dotam! Put it *on* the table. *Kuan-re* uiúkom,—Drop or let them fall *into* the well. *Pindigi-re* aume,—Bring it *into* the verandah.

2nd.—Suffixed to Nouns not primarily signifying places, it denotes—

(*a*) *Instrumentality* in the strict sense, and means

--------- -- - - - - - - - - - - - - - - - *-by, with, through, by means of, on, in.*

Ari-te-ko hadiá,—They cut it *with* a saw. Sadom-*te* ling hijúlena,—We came *on* horseback. Kata-*te* senóme,—Go *on* foot. Reil-*te*-bu sena,—We shall go *by* rail; we shall take the train.

Te—(*concld.*)

(*b*) It denotes *the material* out of which something is made,and means ... . *of, out of, from, with,*

Duar *daru-te*-ko baiea,—They make doors *out of* timber.

Ne orạ́, *inta-te* baiakana,—This house is built *with* bricks.

(*c*) It denotes *the price* for which something is bought, sold or hired, and means ... .. *for.*

Moṇṛe *sai* taka-*te*-ng kiringked' kinga,—I bought both of them *for* five hundred rupees.

3rd.—Suffixed to Nouns denoting feelings, passions or any subjective dispositions, it denotes—

(*a*) *Cause*, and means ... ... *with, through, for, on account of.*

Kis-te rátanae,—He *cries through* rage. *Rasika-te* kaklatanae,—He shouts *for* joy. *Hasu-te* eklatanae,— He trembles *on account of* the pain.

(*b*) *Manner*. The compounds thus obtained are generally to be rendered into English by .... *some Adverb of Manner,*

or by ... ... *Adverbial phrases.*

Rasika-te kamitanae,—He works *cheerfully*, *with* pleasure.

4th.—In some expressions the Mundas use *te* where we would use *in*, because the idea of instrumentality, in the wide sense of the word, really exists in those phrases—

Nutum-te, in the name of . . . *Umbul-te*: literally, with the shadow of, i.e., in the name or with the authority of; as agent or attorney or plenipotentiary of ... *Rup-te*, in or under the (assumed) appearance of.

Note.—*Te* appears to be but a weak form of *ta*. The change of form causing a change of meaning is not of uncommon occurrence. *Ta* denotes permanence, *te* motion. Similarly, *kan*, as a Tense-sign, denotes the present whereas the weak form *ken* denotes the past.

Ló— Abstracts from the ideas of rest and motion.

It is used both of space and time—

1st.— In space it denotes accompaniment, connection, association : hence suffixed to Nouns or Pronouns depending on Predicates expressive of either *rest* or *motion*, it means ... *together with, with, along with.*

Aling-ló tainme,—Remain *with him and me. Nilu-ló* hijúlenae,—He came *with these ones.*

2nd.— Transferred to time *ló* denotes simultaneity. Thus it is suffixed to Participial forms, and yields equivalents of temporal clauses to be explained in a subsequent chapter.

Note.—*Le* is used as an Anterior Present and Future and Past Tense Suffix. This *le*, again, appears to be but a weak form of *ló* If so, it is another instance of a change of meaning being brought about by a change of form. Here the strong form denotes simultaneity, whereas the weak form denotes priority.

A.— Inserted Indirect Pronominal Objects are preceded by a simple *a* in the Indeterminate Tense, the Future, the Definite Present, the Simple Past, all the corresponding Imperfect Tenses and in the Imperative Mood—

Pred. I. O. Cop. Subj.

Om - *a* - ko - a - ing,—I will give (it) *to* them

Si - *a* - ko - a - ing,—Iwill plough *for* them.

Lel - *a* - bo - a - ing,—I will look *at* them ; I'll keep an eye on them.

Bai - *a* - ko - a - ing,—I will arrange the matter *on behalf* of them.

Kisi - *a* - ko - a - ing,—I will get angry *with* them or *against* them.

Suku - *a* - ko - a - ing,—I will be pleased *with* them.

Boro - *a* - ko - a - ing,—I shall be afraid *of* them.

These examples show the various words by which the relations, implied in the above Indirect Objects are rendered into English.

The greater number of such Indirect Objects depend on Predicate which denote a real transfer of something from one to another, such as *to give, to carry, to take to, to bring, to lend, to sell*, etc., etc., and their - synonyms. In these the relation primarily implied is one of *motion* in *space*, i.e., *motion* from an agent to a recipient. But to this primary relation a new moral relation is superadded in most cases, i.e., generally the transfer of a *right* or the relation of *ownership* as transferred from one to another.

The relations implied in the above examples by *for*, *at, on behalf with, against* and *of* can either be traced back to the one denoted by *to* or are so closely connected with it as to be easily derived from it. All of them are in fact real equivalents of the so-called Latin *Datirės of advantage or disavantage.* In *siakoaing* and *baiakoaing* it is the bestowing of a certain emolument or benefit on somebody i.e., a real transfer, just as in *omakoaing*. In *kisiakoaing and sukuakoaing* subective feelings are considered as directed to some one else. *Boroakoaing* is a peculiar idiom indeed, inasmuch as it exhibits the filling of fear as directed towards some one else. In all of them therefore, the relation implied is a double one, containing two distinct elements, viz., (1) a primary relation of space, a motion from one to another, (2) an additional relation, which abstracts from space, inasmuch as, over and above the material transfer it implies somethings, purely mental, i.e., a *right* or a *disposition* as transferred from one to another . It is this second element which constitutes the prominent feature of that double relation. In most cases the element of space is much effaced; it remains as it were a mere, hardly perceptible substratum of what might be called a moral relation. But it is and remains a real substratum, and the moral or intellectual side of the expression is gained, *not by a new word ad hoc,* but by *the simple transfer of one and the same word from the materials to the immaterial sphere, i.e., from space to mind.*

Now, is the relation which is, in the above examples, expressed by the English *to, for, at* , etc., signified explicitly by *a* in the Mundari construction, or is that relation merely implied, but not expressed in Mundari ? In other words, should it be said that in the above examples *ako* must grammatically be cut up into two parts, viz., (1) the Preposition *a* meaning *to, for, at,* etc., and (2) the Simple Pronoun *ko, they?* or may it be admitted that *ako* is simply one word, viz., the long or Emphatic Personal Pronoun ? In the latter supposition the rule concerning the Inserted Direct and Indirect Objects would run as follows :-

(I) In the case of *Direct Pronominal* Objects, the *Simple Personal Pronouns* are inserted into the Predicates. In the case of *Indirect Pronominal Objects* the long or *Emphatic Personal Pronouns* are inserted into the Predicate in the following Tenses : In the Indeterminate Tense, in the Definite Present, etc., etc. In the first supposition the rule would stand thus :

(II) In the case of Direct Pronominal Objects *the Simple Pronouns* are inserted into the Predicate in all Tenses.

In the case of Indirect Pronominal Objects, the Simple Pronouns, inserted into the Predicate, are introduced by the Preposition *a* in the following Tenses : the Indeterminate Tense, etc., etc.

Now, the rule marked (I) appears to be a gratuitous assertion. For—

(1) It leaves the Indirect Object forms without any intrinsic explanation.

(2) No extrinsic or mere phonetic reason can be adduced either for the use of the Emphatic instead of the Simple Pronouns. Since the Simple Pronouns are inserted as Direct Objects, it is plain that their use offers no phonetic difficulty.

(3) It seems altogether irreconcilable with the manner in which Indirect Objects are inserted into the Simple Past.

In this Tense the *a* occurs, but it is separated from the Pronoun by the Tense-sign *ked.* Such a separation is intelligible if that *a* be a separate word with a function of its own; but it becomes inexplicable if that *a* be really but the first syllable of the Emphatic Pronoun. In the Simple Past Direct Pronominal Objects stand between the Tense Suffix and the Copula *a.* Thus—

R. of Pr. Tens. S. D. O. Cop. Subj.
Lel - ked' - *ko* - a - ing,—I saw *them.*

In the case of Indirect Objects the *Simple* Pronoun occupies the same position, but the *a* which in other Tenses stands immediately before the Pronoun, and thus gives it the appearance of an Emphatic Pronoun, stands here before the Tense Suffix *ked.* Thus

R. of Pr. T. S. I. O. C. S.
Om - a - ked - *ko* - a - ing,—I gave (it) *to them.*

On the other hand, if the rule marked (II) be admitted as correct then these Indirect Object forms receive a rational explanation. For, since the relation described above attaches necessarily to Indirect Objects and to them only, it is natural that that relation should be expressed by a separate word, even as it is expressed in English by the words *to, at*, etc., etc. But the *a*, which occurs either mediately or immediately before the Simple Pronouns is the only word to which that function could be attributed in these constructions.

Two objections may be urged against the view taken here about the nature and function of the *a* under consideration, viz.—

(*a*) Demonstrative roots denoting relations of space, time, etc., are in Mundari either Suffixes (Postpositions) or Infixes. Why should *a* if it mean *to, for, at,* etc., be a Prefix or a Preposition ?

(*b*) If in the Tenses enumerated above, the relation attaching to Indirect Objects be expressed by the Preposition *a*, why is it not so expressed in a number of other Tenses, viz., in the Indefinite Present, the Indeterminate and Past Static Tenses, in the Anterior Future, the Perfect, the Pluperfect, and in all the corresponding Imperfects ? In these, Indirect Pronominal Objects are the Simple Pronouns, *v. gr.*, Omjad-*ko*-aing may mean I give them (the living beings) and, I give *to* them. Here circumstances and the context must decide whether the Inserted Pronoun be a Direct or an Indirect Object. Since the relation attaching to Indirect Objects is not expressed in these Tenses, why should it be expressed in the others ?

It may be replied: If these objections be real difficulties against the view defended here, they are at any rate not only no support to the opposite one, but go against it as much and even more ; for, to begin with the second objection, it may be said with the same pertinence : If the *Emphatic Personal Pronouns* are inserted as *Indirect Objects* in a certain number of Tenses, why are they not inserted in all Tenses ? Why do some Tenses insert the Simple Pronouns as Indirect Objects and others the Emphatic Pronouns ? If it be answered that in some Tenses the *a* of the Emphatic Pronouns is dropped for some phonetic reason, then that same phonetic reason holds good also for dropping the same *a* as Preposition. This objection therefore does not touch the question at all, but especially it leaves to the difficulty of the Past Tense its whole force against the supposition of the rule (I).

To the first of the above two objections it may be replied, first, in general, that the particular position of words in connection with each other is not so essential as to allow, from it alone, conclusions concerning the function of words, if those conclusions be not supported by any other intrinsic reason. Second, in particular, if it be true that, generally speaking, Demonstrative Mundari roots are Suffixes and in some cases Infixes, it is also true that two or more such Demonstrative roots concur with each other to express certain ideas. In these cases, then, one of those Demonstrative roots must stand first. Now Pronouns are Demonstrative roots primarily denoting relations of space, just as well as the so-called Postpositions. And it is particularly true that in all propositions the Simple Mundari Pronouns never take any Suffix. So much so that, when it is necessary to specify them by some Postposition, the Simple forms are no longer used, but the Emphatic ones take their place, even there where no kind of emphasis is required. Thus *with them* must be rendered by ako-ló and not by the Simple *ko*-1ó. The Simple Pronouns are always Suffixes or Infixes in Mundari, whereas the Emphatic ones are always independent words. Consequently it may be said that from the very fact that Indirect Objects are Infixes, it follows that those forms are not Emphatic but Simple Pronouns ; and since Simple Pronouns never take any specifying Suffixes, it follows that, if a Demonstrative root be required at all to specify them, that root will *precede* the Pronoun. This conclusion derives additional strength from the fact that in the Simple Past the *a* which is here described as a distinct Demonstrative precedes the Pronoun not immediately, but mediately.

A'.—The followmg constructions, identical in Mundari, but widely differing from each other in English, deserve particular attention :—

1st.—When Nouns or Pronouns *denoting living beings* depend on Compound Postpositions, whether of rest or motion, they take the Suffix *á*. But Nouns and Pronouns *denoting inanimate objects*, depending on the same Postpositions, take no Suffix.

It is to this difference of construction between words denoting *living beings* and words denoting *inanimate objects* that attention is drawn—

Aiarre denotes rest, and means *before, ahead, in front.*

Aiarte denotes motion, and means *ahead, beyond, in front, before*

Remain before me,—Aiñ-á *aiarre* tainme. Remain before the tree,—Daru *aiarre* tainme.

Go before, i.e., beyond me,—Aiñ-*á aiarte* senóme. Go before the tree,—
Daru *aiarte* senóme

2nd.—To have and *not to have* are rendered by *mená*, to exist, and *banó*, not to exist, respectively. In the phrases where this meaning is attached to *mená* and *banó,* the word denoting the object or being possessed, stands as Subject to the Predicates *mená* and *banó*, whereas the word denoting the owner takes the Suffix *á*—

I have land, *Aiñ-á* ote *mená*. He has no money,—Ae-á taka *banoá.*

3rd.—Possessive Genitives, depending on words denoting *inanimate objects*, are formed by suffixing *á* to the word denoting the *owner*—

The country of the Mundas,—Horoko-á disum.

4th.—Nouns or Pronouns take the Suffix á when they stand as Indirect Objects to the following Predicates:—

(*a*) those that denote a real or moral transfer ;

(*b*) those that denote the commission of a wrong to others;

(*c*) those that denote subjective states of mind or feelings towards others.

In 2nd, 3rd, and 4th we have again words denoting living beings which take the Suffix á ; for the construction under 2nd as well as the Possessive Genitive in á are strictly reserved for denoting *ownership* in the real sense of that term. Our more loosely used Possessive Genitives are in Mundari all Locatives, rendered by Postpositions exclusively denoting rest in space.

The following considerations will show—first, that this á is a complete root in itself, the same in all four constructions ; secondly, that it is identical with the *a* described above, which precedes Indirect Inserted Pronominal Objects.

The relation denoted by á in 1st is, of course, merely a spatial one. But the a does not in any way indicate the exact position in space. This is done by the particular Compound Postpositions occurring in this construction, such as *aiarre, aiarte, taiomre*, etc., etc.

What, then, does á express? Evidently nothing beyond the very *elementary relation of externality* to the speaker in the sentence aiñá aiarre: in other sentences, such as, *v, gr*, *Dasiá* aiarre in front of the servant it denotes the *mere relation of externality to a subject or livinq being.*

In this construction, then, the intellect has not superadded anything as yet to the simple element of space primarily denoted by *a*. Here *á* may be translated very approximately into English by— *With regard to*. Thus, *Aiñá* aiarre tainme may be literally rendered by— Remain in front *with regard to me.*

In the construction under 2nd the intellect superadds something to this elementary relation of space, viz., the relation of ownership. That the relation of space is the real substratum of the relation of ownership in this *á* is evident from the fact that in Mundari the *á* may in this construction be replaced by táre, meaning near or *about me*. Thus, I have land may be rendered by—Aiñ-*á* ote mená or Aing *táre* ote mená. This shows at the same time how the mind may transfer meanings from the material to the mental or moral sphere by simply superadding mental or moral to the material elements, bearing some analogy to the latter, and that without making use of special words or roots for the purpose.

Here, then, as in the *a* of the Indirect Pronominal Objects, *á* contains a double element, viz., first a relation of space as a substratum, and, secondly, a moral relation, ownership, implying an advantage to a living being or subject. Here, too, the element of space is nearly effaced, whereas the moral side is chiefly insisted on. The only difference lies in this that here the ownership (advantage) is considered as remaining with the subject, whilst in the Indirect Object forms it is considered as being transferred from one individual to another. But this difference is mainly due to the different meanings of the Predicates.

The relation expressed by *á* in the third construction, viz. , the Possessive Genitives in *á* is quite identical with the one that has just been described. This *a*, then, cannot be looked upon as a mere declensional desinence, the resultant of phonetic decay, which has no longer any meaning if taken by itself alone, but it is really a complete Postposition of space with a transferred meaning. This is further shown by the fact that other Possessive Genitives, viz., those depending on Nouns denoting living beings, are formed by means of the Postpositions *re* + the Demonstrative *n*, i.e., *ren* or by *tare* + *n*, i.e. *táren*. And those Genitive Suffixes may be replaced by *á* ; though for reasons given in the Chapter on Equivalents of Declensions, the forms *ren* and táren be preferred. Thus, the servant of Paku may be rendered either by *Pakutáren* dasi; literally, the servant, the one near or about Paku, or by Paku*á* dasi; literally, the servant *to* Paku.

If this *á* be, according to the genius of the language, used intransitively, it must be considered as a Participle, and becomes equivalent to a Relative clause. Hence we get literally, Horokoá disum the country *which is* to the Mundas.

The relation denoted by *á* in 4th is the very same as that denoted by *a* in most of the Indirect Pronominal Objects. It is a real *Dativus incommodi,* just like the Latin in *Tibi* peccavi.

Now, if the meaning and function here attributed to *á* be admitted, the four constructions under consideration receive a rational explanation; and it is readily perceived why the *á* should be used in all of them. Furthermore, it becomes evident that this *á* is in reality the same as the *a* which introduces Indirect Pronominal Objects, the loss of the sound denoted by (′) in the latter being due merely to the position *á* occupies when it introduces those Indirect Objects.

If the above considerations have any real value, the following would be a correct description of *á*:

A′ is a complete, original, Demonstrative root, primarily denoting one of the most simple relations of space, *viz., that of mere externality to a subject or living being,* or that which is implied when a subject considers some entity as out of and distinct from its own self.

This relation is generally transferred to the moral region. The analogy on which the mind bases this transfer seems to be the fact that in the spatial relation just described a certain proximity to the subject is implied, since the subject and the object are, as it were, placed over against each other on account of the complete abstraction made of everything else in the concept thus formed: hence the transfer to anything which is considered as closely related to the subject by affecting him directly either agreeably or disagreeably. That connection exists unmistakeably (*a*) in pleasurable or painful subjective affections; (*b*) in the relation contained in the notion of ownership; (*c*) in that which is implied in the transfer of ownership.

A′ (1st) Is used to form the Possessive case of Nouns denoting living beings. In this function it is suffixed —

(*a*) To Nouns denoting an owner when ever those Nouns depend on a word denoting inanimate objects, and sometimes when they depend on words denoting living beings. Hence it means ... ... *of*

Paku-á ora,—The house of Paku. Dasi-á talab.— The wages of the servant.

When thus suffixed to Pronouns it yields ... *Possessive Adjectives*

Aiñ-á ote, my land. *Am-á sadom, thy* horse. *Ae-á lijá, his cloth. Apeá* disum, *your* country.

(*b*)To Nouns and Pronouns denoting an owner, when they depend on the Predicates *mená* or *banó*. Thus it literally means ... *to*

Ako-á ote purá *mená*,—There is much land *to* them.

A'—(*concluded*).

But together with *mená* and *baná* it must be rendered into English by ... ... *to have or not to have.*

(*2nd*) It is suffixed to words denoting living beings when these depend on Compound Postpositions of rest or motion in space or of priority and posteriority in time. Thus it might strictly be rendered by ... *with regard to.*

But it has generally ... ... *no English equivalent.*

Aiñ-a aiarre senóme,—Walk in front of me. *Ako-á taiomre* hijúme,—Come after them (i.e., later than they).

(*3rd*) It is suffixed to Nouns and Pronouns standing as Indirect Objects to words meaning to offend against, to commit or cause a personal injury to, and means ... ... *against,*

Abu sobenko *Pormesor-á*-bu papkeda,—We all have sinned against God. *Ini-á* gunakedae,—He has committed an injury or injustice against him, also; he has violated her.

(*4th*) It is used as a Preposition to introduce Inserted Indirect Pronominal Objects in the following Tenses: the Indeterminate, the Future, the Definite Present, the Simple Past, the corresponding Imperfects and in the Imperative, and means ... ... *to, for, at, against, with, on behalf of,*

In this position it loses the sound denoted by (').

Om-a-meae,—He will give it *to* thee. Kami-*a*-koae,—He will work *for* them. Suku-*a*-bentanako,—They are satisfied *with* both of you.

Note.—The Postposition *á* is identical in form with the Neuter or Impersonal Pronoun. It may now be asked—Is this identity of form a merely casual resemblance or are the Postposition and the Pronoun but two different functions of one and the same primary root ?

If the views expressed here concerning the nature of the Postposition, and those given in the preceding chapter concerning the Impersonal Pronoun be correct, it follows that the Postposition and the Pronoun are in reality nothing else than *differently developed functions of one and the same root.* A short summing up will bear out this statement—

1st.—Pronouns are Demonstrative roots, primarily destined to point out relations of space. Those relations of space have, in the Pronouns, all reference to the Ego or Self, i.e., they show how Self is related to other entities.

2nd.—Postpositions are Demonstrative roots which are also primarily destined to denote relations of space. But in the case of Postpositions those relations do not necessarily refer to the Ego or Self. The relations denoted by these may exist either between the Ego and the Non-Ego, or they may exist between two or more beings out of the Ego. Hence the original function of Pronouns and Postpositions is *generally* the same, i.e., that of denoting relations of space. To this *generically identical function* the mind adds *specifically divergent functions* or *specifications* in either case.

3rd.—The Impersonal Pronoun in particular has for its own specific function to denote inanimate objects as out of and distinct from the Ego or Self : hence the relation denoted by it is that of *externality* with regard to Self, i.e., to ONE PARTICULAR *living being.*

4th.—The Postposition á has for its *specific* function to denote the same relation of externality, not exclusively to a particular living being, i.e.. Self, but to LIVING BEINGS IN GENERAL.

The relation, then, denoted by both the Pronoun and the Postposition is in this case *specifically* the same, though somewhat more extensive in the case of the Postposition than in that of the Pronoun.

The fact that the Postposition *á* is, in all the functions it performs as such, invariably referred TO LIVING ENTITY gives an additional significance to the *specific identity* of function attaching to the Pronoun and the Postposition, and goes far to prove that the Postposition and the Pronoun are one and the same root. The Pronoun is of course prior to the Postposition. Now the PRONOUN *essentially* refers to living entity. Hence, if this particular Pronoun be used with the function of a Postposition, it is natural that it should be reserved for relations referring to *living* beings. Furthermore, *á* is *the only* Postposition thus limited to relations referring to living brings. This limitation finds a rational explanation, if the Postposition be considered as a particular function of the Pronominal root ; otherwise it remains unexplained.

Ate or **Ete**—Primarily denotes motion *from* a place, and means ... ...*from, out of,*

The purely spatial meaning of *te* is very restricted. The original or spatial meaning of *ate* or *ete* is also restricted, though not with the same rigour as the primary meaning of *te*. The spatial function of *ate*or *ete* is by means co-extensive with the spatial function of the English Preposition *from*; for when- ever some living being or inanimate object is considered *in its totality* as the *terminus* from the immediate vicinity of which the motion takes place, *ate* or *ete* may no longer be used to render the English Preposition f rom (see *táate*, táete p. 101)

(I) In its primary meaning *ate* or *ete* is restrict

(1) To words primarily and directly signifying *space* or *places*, Such as Common and Proper Nouns of countries, islands, towns, etc., etc.

Bilait-*ate*-ko aulá,—They brought it *from* Europe. Ranchi-*ete* ling hijúlena,—He and I came *from* Ranchi. Bir-*ete*-e nirurungjana,—He ran *out of* or *from* the forest. Buru-*ete* argunjanae,—He came down *from* the mountain. Ora-*ete* nirjanae,—He ran away *from* home (from the house).

Sadom-*ete* argunme,—Come down from the horse. Daru-*ete*-e uiújana,—He fell *from* the tree. Chauli en tunki-*ete* dulurungme,—Pour the rice *out of* that basket. Lija-*ete* mod' takae urungiá,—He took a rupee *out of* his cloth.

(2) To Nouns and Pronouns denoting living beings or inanimate objects there and then considered as containers or receptacles.

REMARK.—In some cases really or apparently falling under the restrictions laid down above, the Mundas use *re* where we would expect *ate* or *ete*. This is the case (*a*) where the idea of motion is not attended to, because it is quite secondary; (*b*) where in reality there is no motion at all, though in English the Preposition *from* be used.

(*a*) Puru-*re* jomme,—Eat *out* of or *from* a leaf-plate. iala-*re* nújadae,—He drinks *out of* the cup.

(*b*) Ale hatu han burn-*re* lelóa,—Our village can be seen *from* yonder mountain. Ne kitab-*re* moiod' baria pirist parauaingme,—Read a couple of pages to me *from* this book.

(II) Suffixed to Nouns and Pronouns *denoting living beings* not considered there and then as containers or receptacles, *ate* or *ete* implies a *parting with, a separation from*, some object possessed, *a privation, a moral separation*, and means .. ... *from*.

Hence, the Compounds thus obtained are equivalent to such English Ablatives as depend on the Verb *to get, to receive, to accept, to take, to steal, etc., and their synonyms*—

Inku-*ete*-ng namtada,—I got it *from* them. Munda-*ete*-m kiringlä chi P?—Didst thou buy it *from* the **Ate or ete**—(*concld.*)

village chief ? Gomke-*ete*-king kumbrulá,—The two have stolen it *from* the master.

REMARK.—The Predicates *kumburu*, to steal; *ré*, to rob ; *hole*, to strip, to take off, and synonyms are generally construed with a double Accusative. Thus, they stole him his land. They robbed them their money.

The Noun denoting the living being from whom something is stolen, etc., must consequently be repeated in the shape of an Inserted Direct Pronominal Object.

Samu oteko kumburuk-í-a,—They stole Samu's land. *Senhoratanko*: takako réked'-ko-a,—They robbed the travellers of their money. *Chaprassi* sonoking holek-í-a,—They (the two) stripped the chaprassi of his coat.

(III) Transferred to time, *ate* or *ete* denotes the beginning of a period intervening between two events or between two points in time. Hence (1) to denote the time intervening between some past moment and the present, it is suffixed to Nouns or Adverbs denoting the past, and means ... ...*Since, ever since, from, for,*

Hola-*ete* baṇgáia,—He is absent *since* yesterday. Maha-*ete* misao kaing lelkía,—I did not see him once ever since last year, or for the whole of last year. En hulang-*ete* kaking eperangjana,—*From* that day they did no more quarrel with each other.

(2) When it is necessary to specify both the first and the last moment of a period, whether past or future, *ate* or *ete* is suffixed to the word which denotes the beginning of the period, whereas the word denoting the end of the period takes one of the Suffixes *joked' hami* or *táte, to.* Here, then, *ate* or *ete* becomes a correlative to *jaked', hami* or *táte*, and together with one of these it means ... *from* ...*to.*

REMAK—The strong form *ate* is generally used when there is question of a great distance or of a very remote time.

Munu-*ate* bongakole aewakoa, enamente náo kale bagedari-koa,—*Ever since* the very beginning we (Mundas) are worshipping the spirits, Therefore we cannot give them up now.

In ordinary cases *ete* is much more frequently used than *ate*. It may be said that *ate* occurs only for the sake of euphony.

N.B.—The initial *e* of *ete* is very short and weak, especially when preceded by a vowel. Thus, for instance, a foreigner unaccustomed as yet to the language will find it difficult to distinguish between *daru-te, with* the tree, and *daru-éte, from* the tree ; *orá-te, to* the house, and *orá-ete*, from the house.

Tare—Denotes rest within a certain area—

1st.—Suffixed to Proper or *Common Nouns* signifying space or places, it means ... *about, somewhere near, in the vicinity of the surroundings of.*

In connection with these Nouns it yields what might be called an *Indefinite Locative of rest.*

The *Definite Locative* of rest of the same Nouns is formed by means of the Suffix *re, v.gr.*, Ranchi-*re*, in Ranchi. Buru*re*,—On the mountain.

Ranchi-*táre*-ko taintana,—They dwell somewhere near Ranchi.

2nd.— Suffixed to other Nouns or Pronouns it means ... ... *with, near.*

In connection with these therefore it yields the *Definite Locative of rest*—

Han daru-*táre-e* namóa,—You will find him *near* yonder tree. Ale-*táre* kako taina,—They will not remain *with* or *near* us.

3rd.—In its transferred meaning *táre* denotes possession both in the strict and wider sense of the term. This meaning, however, requires to be completed by means of the Predicates *mená*, to be, and *baná*, not be.

Hence together with *mená* and *banó*, *táre* means

... ..*to have* or *not to have*

In this construction the name of the beings and objects possessed, or of the persons over whom a certain right is exercised, stands as Subject of the proposition; *mená* or *banó* stands as Predicate, and the Noun or Pronoun denoting the owner stands as Indirect Object with the Suffix *táre.*

Gomkee-táre taka mená,-The master *has* money. (*Literally*, With the master there is money.) Ale-*táre* dasiko bankoá,-We *have no* servants. (*Literally*, With us there are no servants.)

4th.—The Predicates *urú*, to long for, to yearn after, and *asrai*, to hope, to look to some one for something, to expect something from some one, always require *táre* as Suffix to their Indirect Object, *i.e.*, to the Noun or Pronoun denoting the object or being for which one longs, or the person from whom one expects something or to whom one looks for something. Hence here *táre* means .... *for, after, in, to, from.*

Engate-*táre-e urútana*,- He yearns *after* his mother. (*Literally*, he thinks towards his mother.) *Orá-táre-ko urútana,*—They are homesick. (*Literally*, they think towards their house or home.) Am-*táre*-le *asraitana*,-We hope *in* thee, or we look to *thee* (for help, counsel, etc.).

5th.—The Predicates *suku*, to be pleased with, to be satisfied with, to agree with; *ka... suku*, to be displeased with, to be dissatisfied with, to disagree with, and *kisió*, to be angry with, are sometimes construed in a similar manner.

Hence in connection with Indirect Objects to these, *táre* means ... ... *with, towards, against*

Mundako-*táre* khube *sukutana*, He is very well disposed *towards* the village-chiefs. Am-*táre* kae *sukutana*, He does not agree with thee. A-king-*táre* kented'ko kisiakana,-They are very angry *against* both of them.

Táte— Denotes motion towards.

1st.—Suffixed to Nouns denoting space or places, it yields an *Indefinite Locative of motion. The Definite Locative of motion* of these Nouns is formed by means of *te*; for in connection with these Nouns, *te* points out the exact terminus of the motion, whereas *táte* points out the direction of the motion only in a rather vague manner.

Hence it means ... ... *towards, in the direction of.*

Hatu-*táte*-ko senójana,-They went away *towards* the village. *Orá-táte-e* nirjana,- He ran *towards* the house. Sirma-*táte-e* sangilrakablá,—He looked up *towards* heaven.

2nd.—Suffixed to other Nouns and Pronouns, it assumes the same definite meaning which *te* has when suffixed to Nouns denoting space or places.

Hence it yields a *Definite Locative* of motion, and means... ... .. *to, up to.*

Han daru-*tate* senóme,-Go *up to* yonder tree. Ale-*táte*-king niraulá,-Both came running *up to* us.

Táate or Denotes motion from-— *Táete.*

1st —Suffixed to Nouns denoting space or places it yields an *Indefinite Locative of motion from*, and means ... ... *from the surroundings* or *the side of, from somewhere near,*

Ranchi-*táete*-ko *hijúlena*,-They have come *from somewhere near* Ranchi.

2nd.- Suffixed to other Nouns and Pronouns, it yields a *Definite Locative* of motion from, and means .... *from,*

Sadom-*táete* nirme,-Run away *from* the horse. Sengel-*táete* iditam,-Take it away *from* (near) the fire. But Sengel-*ete* urungtam,- Take it *out of* the fire.

3rd.-It is suffixed to Nouns and Pronouns denoting living beings, when they stand as Indirect Objects to the Passive Predicates—*kuló*, to be sent; *chutió*, to be dismissed, although the idea of motion be no longer either the only nor even the primary one implied. In this connection therefore it yields an equivalent to some of the Organic Ablatives, and must be rendered by ... *from, by.*

Raja-táete-ko Kuljana,-They were sent *by* the king. *Ale-táete*-king chutijana,- Both of them were dismissed by us.

Nouns denoting inanimate objects take *ete* when standing as Indirect Objects to those Passives, *v.gr.*, Jehel-*ete*-king chutijana,- Both were dismissed from prison.

Remark.—In *táate* and *táete* the *á* is checked very slightly, and the second *a* of *táete* as well as the *e* of *táete* are very short. Hence *táate* sounds almost like *táete*, and *táete* may easily be mistaken for *táte*.

Sáre, sáte sáate and sáete } Are equivalents of *táre táte, táate* or *táete*, and are used about as frequently as *táre*, etc, etc.

Nouns and Pronouns denoting living beings take the Suffix *á* when they depend on any of the compounds to be enumerated below. *V.gr.*, *Iniá* aiarre tainme,—Remain in front of him.

For the explanation of this construction see above (pages 91).

Aiar is both a Transitive and an Intransitive Predicate, meaning *to precede, to be,* or *go ahead, to continue.* V. gr., *Aiarkom*! Precede them. *Alom aiara*!

Don't go further ! don't go ahead ! *Aiarme* mar ! Continue your narration ! Go on with what you have to say.

N.B.—The form *aiûr*, a variation produced by the *i*, is rather rarely used.

Taiom is a Transitive and Intransitive Predicate, meaning to *be behind, to come* or *to go behind, to lag behind, to come later, to put something* or *some one behind*, v. gr., *Taiomime* ! Go behind him or put him behind ! Put him at the end!

In the sense of *to lag behind, to come behind* or *to come later* it is generally used in the Passive form, v.gr., *Taiomótanae*,- He is lagging behind. *Taiomjanako*,- They remained behind; they could not keep up with the others.

Doia or *dea* is primarily a Noun, meaning *the back*.

Sida is an Ordinal Numeral Adverb, meaning *first*.

Chetan is a Transitive and Intransitive Predicate, meaning *to be above, to put* or *place above, to be on the top of, to put* or *place on the top of.*

Suba is the contrary of *chetan*, and means *to be underneath, to be beneath, to put* or *place beneath.*

Sirma denotes the *cover, the roof*; also *the heavens*. It is also used as a Transitive or Intransitive Predicate, meaning *to raise on high, to lift on high, to be on high* (Passive).

Latar is a Transitive and Intransitive Predicate, meaning *to lower, to put lower, to be below (*Passive*).*

Tola is used both as a Noun and as a Transitive and Intransitive Predicate, meaning (1) *the middle*, (2) *to divide in the middle, to halve, to trace the middle.*

Racha denotes an open place outside in front of the house, *a kind of small yard,*

Kundam corresponds to *racha*, and denotes a place outside *at the back of the house.*

Biter is the Mundaricised Hindi word *bhitar*, inside. In its original form, i.e., without Suffix, it is a Predicate, meaning *to be inside (*Passive*), to put* or *place something inside.*

Danang is a Transitive and Intransitive Predicate, meaning to *screen, to hide behind something, to be screened* or *hidden* (Passive).

Japa is a Transitive and Intransitive Predicate, meaning *to be close* (Passive), *to put close by, to place against.*

Gena denotes *the edge* or *border, v.gr.*, of rivers, seas, lands. It may be used too as Predicate, meaning *to go along.*

Atom denotes the *edge* or *side of something*. Used as Predicate, *it means to put something aside, to remove something away from.*

The words enumerated above take the Suffixes *tá, te, táre, táte, táate or táete*, and thus yield the following set of Compound Postpositions. The Postpositions thus obtained are not Suffixes, but they occupy an independent position. They always stand immediately after the Nouns or Pronouns they govern, *v.gr.*, Gara *genatee* senjana,-He went *to* the riverside.

Aiartá is used of space. Its meaning is very vague (*cfr. tá*). It denotes both *motion* and *rest* within an ill-defined area, and means ... ... *somewhere ahead.*

Aiarre (*1st*) *used of space* denotes rest, and means ... ... *before, ahead of, in front of.*

Sadomá *aiarre* alom tinguna !-Don't stand *in front of the horse.* Mej *aiarre* dubme—Sit before the table.

(2nd) used of time, it means ... *ago.*

Moṇ̈re sirma *aiarre* neree taekena—He was hero five years *ago.*

Aiartáre denotes rest, but it is less precise than *aiarre*, and means ... *somewhere ahead;* ... *somewhere in front,*

Aiarte denotes motion and indicates the direction in a precise manner, and means ... ... *ahead, in front,*

Aiñá *aiarte* senóme—Go *straight in front* of me.

Aiartúte denotes motion, but indicates the direction more vaguely than *aiarte*, and means ... *somewhere in fronts.*

Aiarete denotes *motion from*, in a definite direction, and means ... *from in front of.*

Aiartáate or *aiarfáete* denotes motion from, in a vaguer way, and means ... ... *from somewhere in front of,*

Taiomre denotes rest in a definite place, and means ... ... *behind.*

Iniá *taiomre* tainme,—Remain behind him.

Taiomtáre denotes rest within a less well-defined area, and means ... *somewhere behind.*

Taiomte (*1st*) *used of space*, it denotes *motion towards*, and means ... *after.*

(2nd) used of time, it means ... *after.*

Aleá *taiomteko* hijúlena,—They came after us, *i.e.*, they came later than we. Api ma *taiomte* hijúruareme,—Come back after three days.

Taiomate or *taiomete* denotes *motion from*, in a definite way, *i.e.*, indi-cates the exact terminus from, and means } ... ... *from behind something* ; *from behind someone.*

Taimtáate or *taiomtáete* denotes likewise *motion from*, but does not precise the terminus from, in the same manner as *táiomete*. It means ....*from somewhere behind.*

Docare dare is used only as Definite Locative of rest of the Noun *dea*, back, and means *on the back.*

Doeate or *deate* is the corresponding *Definite Locative of motion* of the same Noun.

The Suffixes *táre, táte, táate (táete)* in connection with *doea* (*dea*) yield Compounds equivalent in meaning to *taiomáre* or *taiomre, taim*ete or taiomte, taiomtáte, taiomete or tiomtáete. But these Compounts with *dea* are, of course, restricted to cases where the Noun or Pronoun governed denotes human beings.

Sidàre is used of time. It is added to a word or phrase denoting a period of time, and denotes that a certain event preceded that period. The precedence thus signified is not an immediate one, but a more or less vague one. Hence *sidare* may be translated by ... . *more than* .... *ago.*

Mod'hisi sirma *sidareng* lelked' koa, —I saw them (once) more than 20 ,years ago.

Sidate (1st) is used of time, and, like *sidare*, suffixed to Nouns or -phrases signifying a period of time. It denotes that a certain action took place previous to that period. The precedence thus signified seems to be more definite *i.e.*, immediately preceding the period indicated. Hence it means .... *ago.*

Moṇṛe sirma *sidare* nereng *lelked'*koa, -I saw them here five years ago.

(2nd) Suffixed, to Nouns or Pronouns denoting living beings, it points out priority of one action or state over another, whether in the past or in the future, and means ... ... *before.*

Aiñá *sidateko* senkena,— They went before me, *i.e.*, before I went. Amá *sidate-e* senóka,—Let him go *before* thee, i.e., *before* thou wilt start.

Sidaate, sidaete points out a period lasting from some more or less well-defined moment of the past up to the present time, and means, } *ever since; ever since....ago.*

Mimid' sirma *sidaate* Horoko Chutia Nagporre menákoa,— The Mundas are (settled) in Chota Nagpore ever since year upon year, *i e.*, from time immemorial. Moṇṛe sirma *sidaete* nereng kamitangea,—I am working here ever since five years ago.

Chetanre denotes rest, and means ... *on the top or summit of,*

Buru *chetanre,*—On the summit of the mountain.

Chetante denotes motion to, and means ... ... *to the top* or *summit of'.*

Chetanate, chetanete denotes motion from, and means ... ...*from the top* or *summit of,*

To the above correspond the more indefinite Compounds :

Chetantáre ... ... *somewhere on the top of.*
Chetantáte ... ... *somewhere to the top of.*
Chetantáete ... ... *somewhere from the top of.*

Subare denotes rest, and means ... *near, underneath of, under.*

Mej *subare,*—Under the table, *i.e.*, near the legs of the table.

Subate denotes motion to, and means *under, underneath.*

Daru *subats* nirme,—Run *under* the tree, *i.e.*, close to the trunk of the tree.

Subaete denotes motion from, and means ... ... *from underneath.*

To these correspond the more indefinite compounds: *subátáre*, *subatáte, subatáae* or *sub'táete.*

Sirmare denotes rest, and must sometimes be rendered by

... *under, from, to.*

Oṛá *sirmare* hakakana,— It is hanging *under the house-roof.* Nájomko daru *sirmare* ko hakakoa,—They would hang sorcerers *to* the branches of a tree.

More frequently it must be rendered by ... ... *on, upon.*

Ora *sirmaree* tinguakana,—He is standing *on* the top or roof of the house.

Sirmate denotes motion to, and means

... ... *up to, to, to the top* or *roof.*

Sirmaete denotes motion from, and means

... ... *from, from the top* or *roof of* .

REMARK.—These three compounds are limited in their function as Postpositions to such words as denote houses, rooms, etc., *i.e.,* to covered or ceiled places.

Latarre denotes rest, and means ... *under, underneath.*
Latarte denotes motion to, and means ... *under, underneath.*
Latarete (*latarate*) denotes motion from, and means ...*from underneath.*

To these correspond the more indefinite compounds: *latartáre latartáte, latartáete* or *latartáate.*

REMARK —*Latarre latarte*, etc., is used only to denote the underneath of a covered place or a space, big or small, under some object, which allows of putting or shoving something under that object, Thus *mej latarre*, underneath the table; Topi *latarre*, under the hat.

Subare, subate, etc., is used to denote the *lower end* of something. *v. gr.*. There where a tree-trunk or a wall rises out of the ground. Daru *subaree* dubakana,—He is sitting under the tree, i.e., on the ground near the trunk. Daru *lataree* dubakana,—He is sitting under the kind of roof made by the projecting branches.

However, with regard to trees, *suba* is almost exclusively used even when the immediate proximity to the trunk is not strictly implied.

Amá kata *subareng* uiúntana,— I throw myself *at* thy feet. Ama kata *latarre*. mená—It is *underneath* thy foot, i.e., thou art treading or standing upon it.

Hence the compounds with *suba* are the contraries of those with *chetan*, whereas the compounds with *latar* are the contraries of those with *sirma*.

Tala denotes rest—

1st.—Suffixed to Nouns denoting space or places, it means ... *in the middle* or *the centre of.*

2nd—Suffixed to other Nouns, it means ... *amongst, among.*

Talate denotes motion to, and means { (1) *to the middle* or *centre of.* (2) *amongst, to the midst of*

Talaete denotes motion from, and means { (1) *from the middle of.* (2) *from amongst.*

To these correspond the indefinite compounds: *talatáre, talatáte, talatáate* or *talatáete.*

Biterre denotes rest, and means .... *inside, in the interior of.*

Biterte denotes motion to, and means .... *into the interior of, inside.*

Biterete denotes motion from, and means ... ... *from inside of, from the interior of.*

Add to these the indefinite compounds: *bitertáre, bitertáte, bitertáate* or *bitertáete.*

Rachare, rachate, etc., as well as *kundamre, kundamte* etc., etc., being entirely restricted to designate a small place out in front or at the back of the house are Adverbs of Place rather than Postpositions.

Danangre denotes rest, and means ... *behind, under cover of.*

Danangte denotes motion to, and means ... *behind.*

Danangete denotes motion from, and means ... *from behind.*

Add to these the indefinite compounds: *danagtáre, danangtáte, danangtáete.*

REMARK.—The Compounds with *danang* are used only when it is *actually* desired to imply that a living being or an object is actually hidden from sight by that behind which it is said to be. Hence Iniá *danangre* tinguakana,—He is standing behind him so as to be hidden from view. But Iniá taiomree tinguakana,—He stands behind him and can be seen.

Genare denotes rest, and means ... ... *on the border* or *the side of, near, along.*

Genate denotes motion to, and means ... *to the side of,* etc.

Genaete denotes motion from, and means ... *from the side of, etc.*

Add *genatáre, genatáte, genatáete or genatáate.*

Atomre denotes rest, and means ...

... *at the side, on the side on the edge, on the extremity of.*

Atomte denotes motion to, and means ... *to the side, etc.,* etc.

Atomete denotes motion from, and means ... *from the side, etc.*

Add *Atomtáre, atomtáte, atomtáate or atomtáete.*

REMARK.—*Atomre,* etc., etc., are used of the outer edge or side of any object, whereas *genare,* etc., are used only of rivers, seas, tracts of land, villages, etc.

Both sets of compounds are frequently reduplicated. In this case only the repeated form takes the Suffixes *re*, *te*, etc, etc., v. gr., Gaṛa *gena genare* tainme,—Remain close along the riverside.

These reduplications are sometimes used without the Suffixes *re, te, etc. V.gr.,* Gaṛa *gena gena* senme,—Go close along the riverside.

Japare denotes rest, in the immediate proximity to something or someone, and means ... ... *close to, quite near to, against.*

Japate denotes motion to, and means ... ... *against, up to.*

Japaete denotes motion from, and means ... *from against, from close to.*

Japare, etc.— Differ from *atomre, etc*., in this that the first indicate a point or place in immediate vicinity to or even contact with an object or living being, but still outside of it; whereas *atomre, etc*., denote the outer surface or limit of an object; thus *Mej atomre* dotam,—Put it on the edge of the table. But *Mej japare* dotam,—Place it near the table or against the table.

Hamí, habí, habid' or *hamé* —Indicate the distance between two points or the duration of a motion to, and point out the exact terminus of that distance or the motion ... *to, up to, until.*

They may be used alone or with the Suffixs *te*—

Ne daruete han daru *ham* or han daru *hamíte*—From this tree up to yonder tree.

The word indicating the terminus sometimes takes the Suffix *tá*— Han daru*tá* hamí senóme,—Go (from here) up to yonder tree.

Mente is the Instrumental Case of *men*, to say. It performs a variety of functions in connection with subordinate clauses. It has been transferred also to the function of a Postposition governing Nouns and Pronouns. In this function it is synonymous with *nagente, etc*., and means ... *for, on behalf of.*

Nouns and Pronouns depending on *mente* never take the Suffix *á*—

Am *menten*g auakada,—I brought this for theė. Honme *mentee* kiringiá,—He bought it for thy son.

Sam—Of Hindi origin, is used in some expressions as a synonym to *ló*, with, and means ... ... *with, together with,*

But it is never used of time. It is generally preceding the Noun it governs. However, it is also used as a mere Suffix—

Ne daru red'-*sam* tud'urungpe,—Pull out this tree *together with* its roots. *Sam*-kagaj ne tunkio hudumaratam,—Pitch away this basket together with the paper that's in it. *Sam-losod'*, besmeared with mud. *Sam-maiom*, besmeared with blood. *Sam*-maiomem tusingakana,—Thou art dressed (in cloths) *besmeared with blood.*

Begar, likewise of Hindi origin, is used, and means ... ... *without.*

This too precedes the Noun it governs, and that Noun frequently takes the Instrumental Suffix *te*—

Begar hake
or
begar hake*te* } ka mágóa,—There's no cutting without an axe.

Begar uríko
or
begar uriko*te* } ka siúa,—There's no ploughing without bullocks.

Note—The genuine Mundari construction consists of a Disjunctive proposition of which the first member is generally elliptic. If the first member be complete, the second member is elliptic—

Hakete karedo ka mágóa; *literally*. With an axe or else there is no cutting (it can not be cut).

Uṛíkote karedo ka siúa,—With bullocks or else there is no ploughing.

Hakete magóa, karedo ka,—With an axe one can cut, otherwise not.

Uṛíkote siúa, karedo ka,—With bullocks one can plough, otherwise not.

The fact that the Mundas often suffix *te* to the Noun governed by *begar* shows that they cannot quite resign themselves to the Hindi construction.

But this is shown still more forcibly by the combination of the Hindi and the Mundarí construction into a jumble which, if literally translated, would mean the opposite of what they intend to say—

Begar sadom karedo kaing sena
„ sadomte „ „ „ } I won't go without horse ; *literally*, Without horse or else I won't go.

Hamiate—Indicates the direction and duration of a motion by pointing out the exact terminus from which it starts, and may be rendered by ...

... *all along from, all the while from,*

Han orá *Hamite*ng niraujada, —I come running all the way from (as far as) yonder house.

Joked'—Is used both of space and time. It indicates the terminus of a motion or a duration.

1st.—When *Jaked'* is used of space the Postposition *tá* is frequently suffixed to the word denoting the terminus, and *jaked* is placed after *tá*. In this construction *joked'* is synonymous with *hamí*, etc., and may be rendered by

... *up to, as far as.*

Han darutá *jaked'* góiditam,—Carry it up to yonder tree.

2nd.—Used of time, *jaked'* may be rendered by ... ... *for.*

E chandu *jaked* tainóme,—Remain *for* seven months; stay *for the next* seven months.

Paromre—Denotes rest, and means ... *across, on the other side of.*

Gara *paromre* tangikom,—Wait for them on the other side of the river.

Paromte— Denotes motion to and means *across, to the other side,*

Paromete—Denotes motion from, and means ...

.... *from across, from the other side.*

Add *paromtáre, paromtáte, paromtáate* or *paromtáete.*

Horate—Is the Instrumental Case of *hora,*way, road. It is always used to signify the instrumentality of persons, and means ... ... *through by.*

The Noun or Pronoun denoting the person through whom something is done or accomplished takes the Suffix *á*—

Amá, horate le banchaujana,—We were saved, *by* thee. *Dasiá horate* ne chiti kultaime,—Send this letter to him *through* the servant.

Nagen or *nagente*—Has the same function as the Latin *pro*, and means ... *for, on behalf of.*

Nouns and Pronouns depending on this need not take the Suffix *á*—

Horoko *nagente*, for the Mundas. Ale, or *aleá nagente*, for us, on behalf of us.

V.—NUMERALS

I.—Cardinal Numerals

Distinct forms exist for the numbers from *one* to *ten* inclusively, and for the number *twenty.*

The numbers between *ten* and *twenty* are formed by adding the nine first numbers respectively to the word *gel*, 10.

No special Mundari word exists for any number higher than twenty, *hisi.* The higher numbers are divided into stages of twenties: thus 40 is called *bar hisi, i.e.*, two twenties; 60 is *api hisi, i.e.*, three twenties; 80 is *upun hisi, i.e.*, four twenties; 100 is, *monre hisi, i.e.*, five twenties ; 120 is *turui hisi, i.e.*, six twenties, etc.

The numbers from 20 to 40 are formed by adding the nineteen first numbers respectively to *hisi*, or *mid' hisi:* thus, 30 is *mid' hisi gelea, i.e.*, one twenty ten ; 31 is *mid' hisi gel miad', i.e.*, one twenty ten one.

The numbers from 40 to 60 from 60 to 80, etc., are formed in the same way. Thus, 50 is *bar hisi gelea, i.e.*, two twenties ten; 51 is *bar hisi gel miad',* etc.

The Mundari Numerals are being displaced more and more by the Hindi in districts where Hindi or Sadani is understood by the Mundas, and even in others where these languages are hardly understood at all.

The Hindi words *sau* or *sai*, a hundred, and *hazar* or *hajar,* a thousand, are now in common use almost everywhere.

However, *gel sai, i.e.*, ten hundred, occurs still frequently instead of *hajar*, a thousand—

mid' miad', moiad', or *mod'*	1	*maid' hisi gelea* —	30
baria — — —	2	*mid' hisi gel maid'* —	31
apia — — —	3	*mid' hisi gel baria* —	32
upunia — — —	4	*bar hisi* —	40
monrea — — —	5	*bar hisi gelea* —	50
turüia — — —	6	*api hisi* —	60
ēa — — —	7	*api hisi gelea* —	70
irilia — — —	8	*upun hisi* —	80
ārea — — —	9	*upun hisi gelea* —	90
gelea — — —	10	*monre hisi,* or *sau, sai, mid sai,*	
gel miad' — — —	11	*mod sai* —	100
gel baria — — —	12	*mod' sai miad'* —	101
gel apia — — —	13	*mod' sai baria* —	102
gel upunia — — —	14	*mod' sai gelea* —	110
gel monrea — — —	15	*mod' sai' mod' hisi,* or *turui hisi*	120
gel turuia — — —	16	*bar sai* —	200
gel ea — — —	17	*api sai* —	300
gel irilia — — —	18	*upun sai* —	400
gel area — —	19	*gel sai,* or *hazar, mod' hajar*	1000
hisi, isi, mid' hisi, or mod' hisi	20	*mod' hajar mod' sai gel baria*	1112
mid' hisi miad' — —	21	*mod' hajar iril sai upun hisi*	
mid' hisi baria — —	22	*gel upunia* —	1894

The last vowel of *apia*, *monrea*; *turuia*, *ea*, and *area* is always dropped when they are placed before the higher numbers—*hisi*, *sai*, *hajar'*. *Baria*, *upunia*, *irilia*, *gelea* drop the two last vowels before those higher numbers.

The same rule is followed whenever any of the ten first Numerals is placed before (*a*) words denoting measures of any kind, (*b*) the words *horo* (man), *orá* (house), *bó* (head), used as appositions in enumerations.

In enumerating the families of a village the word *orá* (house) is used as apposition in the same manner.

The word *bó* (head) is similarly used in enumerations of cattle.

N.B.—The words *horo*, *orá*, *bó*, when thus used as appositions, do not take the Dual or Plural Suffixes,

Bar gaudi, two leagues ; *api* tewa, three tewas (a grain measure); *gel* muka, ten yards; *upun* ghanta, four hours; *e* taka, seven rupees; ama chimmin honko menakoa? Kora-honko *api horo*, kuri honko *bar horo*,—How many children have you ? Three sons and two daughters. Ne hature *gel api ora* Mundako, oro *are orá* Uraonko menákoa, or No hature Mundako *gel api orá*, *oro* Uranko *are orá* menakoa,—In this village there are 13 Munda families and 9 Uraon families. Kerako *tunui bo* uriko *upun bó* menákoa,—There are six buffaloes and four bullocks.

II.—DISTRIBUTIVE NUMERALS

.Distributive Numerals are formed by the reduplication of the Simple Cardinal Numerals.

In the Compound Numbers this reduplication takes place only in the first Numeral of the Compound.

Sometimes even Compound Cardinal Numerals are used as Distributives without any change whatsoever—

mi-mid', or *mi-miad'*,	one each	*ge-gel miad*	eleven each
ba-baria,	two "	*ge-gel baria*,	twelve "
ap-apia,	three "	*ge-gel apia*	thirteen "
up-upunia	four "	*ge-gel monrea*	fifteen "
mon-monrea	five "	*hi-hisi or mo-mod' hisi*,	twenty "
tu-turutx	six "	*hi-hisi miad'*,	twenty-one "
e-ea	seven "	*ba-bar hisi*,	forty "
ir-irilia	eight "	*mon-monre hisi, or*	
ar-are a,	nine "	*sa-sai*,	a hundred "
ge-gelea,	ten "	*ba-bar sai*,	two hundred "
		ha-hajar	a thousand "

The forms given above are used adjectively.

When it is required to use Distributive Numerals adverbially, the Postposition *te*, as significative of manner, is suffixed to them—

mimid'te mimiad'te	one by one	*tuturiate*	six by six
babariate, babarte,	two by two	*eeate*,	seven by seven
apapiate,	three by three	*iririliate*,	eight by eight
upupuniate,	four by four	*arareate*,	nine by nine
monmonreate,	five by five	*gegeleate*,	ten by ten

Mimiad babar paisa omakom,— Give them two pice each. Daruko *apapiate* roakana, —The trees are planted three by three, three in a row. Paltanko *tuturiate* ko sesena,— The soldiers march six by six, six abreast.

REMARK—When there is question of human beings, the apposition *horo* often occurs where we would expect a Distributive Adverb only. In this case several different constructions may be used—

1. *Horo* is repeated and preceded each time by the *Cardinal Numeral* ; the second time *horo* takes the suffix *te*, v.gr.—

Bar horo bar horote senope, walk two by two.

2. *Horo* preceded by a Iristribative Numeral takes the suffix *te*, *v.gr.*,— *Monmonre* horote senope, walk five by five

3 In either of the two constructions given above *horo* generally drops the suffix *te* when the Predicate is by itself alone expressive of manner or arrangement, *v.gr.*, *panti*, abreast—

Upun horo upun, horo pantinpe, arrange yourselves into ranks of four and four—or *Upupun horo* pantinps.

The same rule is observed when such words as *nanti* are used, not transitively, but adverbially to specify some other Predicate. Then those words take the suffix *te*—

Monro horo monre horo *pantiteko* aiarka, let them advance a five by five.

III.—ORDINAL NUMERALS

There are only two forms in common use, viz., *sida*, the first, and *etá*, the second.

The Cardinal Numerals from three upwards are used with the function of Ordinals. This deficiency of Ordinal forms ought to give rise to many an ambiguous proposition when there is question of inanimate objects, because Nouns denoting inanimate objects generally take no Plural Suffix. Thus *api daru* may mean three trees and it may mean the third tree. This inconvenience, however, has never troubled the Mundas so far as to urge them to coin a compound that would do away with the ambiguity. They prefer to make themselves understood either by pointing out the object in question, or by having recourse to some circumlocution.

Thus to say, *cut the fourth tree,* they will say *api daru aiar-reá máeme; literally*, cut that one (which is) before the three trees.

Call the sixth boy,—*Monre korakoá aiar-reni ráime*, i.e., call that one who is before the five boys.

Or they will say *apia daru bageked'ie miad máeme,* i.e., leaving or having left three trees cut one.

To say, cut down *the four first trees,* they will point at the tree first and say: *En apia ló upunia* daru máeme ; literally, together with those three, cut four trees.

When the objects in question cannot thus be pointed out materially, then they point them out either by means of a statement, or more generally by means of a plain question ; thus :

Han hora genare gelbaria uli daru roakana, chi ka ? He mar ! apia bageked'te miad' máepe,—Along yonder road there are planted 12 mango trees, is it not so ? Very well, leaving three (i.e., the three first ones) cut down one (*i.e.*, the fourth one).

Han 'hora genare gelbaria daru roakana chi ka ? *He mar* ! *apialo upinia máepe,*— Are there along yonder road twelve trees or not ? All right! together with three (*i.e.*, the three first) cut four trees, *i.e.*, cut the four first ones.

IV.—PROPORTIONAL NUMERALS

Proportional Numerals are formed by suffixing *sá*, and in some districts *duang* or *duan* to the Cardinal Numerals.

The numbers from 2 to 10 inclusively drop the last or the two last vowels as indicated above under I (page 110)—

mid'sá, misá mosá	or	*mid'duang*	—	once.
barsá	"	*barduang*	—	twice
apisá	"	*apiduang*	—	thrice, three times.
upunsá	"	*upunduang*	—	four times.
moṇṛesá	"	*moṇṛeduang*	—	five times.
turuisá	"	it*ouruiduang*	—	six times.
êsá	"	*êduang*	—	seven times.
irilsá	"	*irilduang*	—	eight times.
aresá	"	*areduang*	—	nine times.
gelsá	"	*gelduang*	—	ten times.
gelmidsá	"	*gelmidduang*	—	eleven times.
mid hisisá	"	*mid hisiduang*	—	twenty times.
modsaisá	"	*mod saiduang*	—	a hundred times.

Approximations are expressed by juxtaposing two numbers without any conjunction, whenever the approximation is close to the exact number.

In Proportional Numerals the second only takes the suffix- *sá Moṇṛe turui hoṛo,* 5 or 6 men; *Api upunsá,* 3 or 4 times.

Doubtful numbers are expressed by suffixing leka to either the Cardinal or the Proportional Numerals.

Sometimes two numbers are uxtaposed and the second one takes the suffix *leka.*

Mod'hisi leka, about twenty. *Gelsáleka,* about ten times.

When these doubtful Numerals stand before a Noun the suffix *leka* is sometimes added to the Noun. But this position of *leka* seems to be anomalous—

Gelbaria *daruleka* or *gelbarialeka* daru máeme—Cut down *about twelve* trees.

When, in approximations, two or three multiples of 20, 100 or 1,000 are juxtaposed, the numbers *hisi, sai, hajar*, are used only once, *i.e.*, after the second or third multiplicant—

Bar api hisi leka, about 40 or 60. *Api upun saisa leká*, about about 3 or 4 hundred times.

In the shape of *Fractional Numerals* there exists only the word *tala* or *taṛa* meaning (1) the middle, the centre; (2) to halve to divide into two equal parts ; (3) half.

The requirements of their limited commercial transactions are sufficiently served by some special words denoting various fractions of the rupee or of some measures in ordinary use : *adeli*, an eight-anna piece; *ganda*, one anna, *sala*, 40 seers (of grain); *kandi*, 20 seers (of grain), etc.

If it be absolutely required to designate a fraction explicitly, the Mundas have recourse to some circumlocution, *v.gr*.

Cut off two-thirds,—*Apia hatingete baria hating* máeme (of three parts, out off two).

The first four Mundari Numerals occur in Mon, Cambodian Anamese and at least three other languages. Two, three, and four are monosyllables, viz., *baria*, two, is *bā̃* in Mon and *bar* in the others. *Apia*, three, appears as *pe* in three of these, in the others as *peh, pey* for *peng*.

Mon has *m'son* for *moṇ̈re*. In the other languages the Numeral *five* has no apparent resemblance to *moṇ̈rea*,

Turuia, six, occurs as *t'rou* in Mon and as *treon* and totron in two others. All the remaining Numerals are apparently quite different from the Mundari forms.

Sá ant *tá* are interchangeable in Mundari. Is it a mere accidental coincidence that Buṛjatic forms Iterative Numerals by suffixing *tá* to the Cardinal Numerals even as Mundari suffixes *sá* for the same purpose ?

In the same language Distributive Numerals are formed by adding the Instrumental Suffix to the repeated Cardinal Number just as in Mundari.

In Cambojan and Malay *isi* means *all*, and is used as one of the Plural Suffixes. If the Mundari *hisi* or *isi*, twenty, can be referred to this root, it would confirm the conjecture that this Numeral, which is the only distinct form the Mundas possess beyond *ten* was really intended to convey the idea of the great total of what probably formed their basis of counting, viz., the fingers *plus* the toes. The root *man*, *mun* or *bin*, meaning 100 in Wigur, 1,000 in Osmanli, 10,000 in Chinese, is similarly used to denote multitude, and hence means also *all*.

II. WORDS USED

I.—Adverbs

1. Most Adverbs of Place are formed by suffixing the Postpositions Interrogative Demonstrative. *Sá* is used as frequently as *tá* in these

nere — here | *enre* —

netáre	— }	here about, or	*entáre*	— }
nesáre	— }	somewhere here	*ensáre*	— }
nete	—	hither	*ente*	—
netáte	— }	this way, this direction	*entáte*	— }
nesáte	— }		*ensáte*	— }
neate	—	hence	*enate*	— }
			enete	— }
netáate	— }	from this side, from this	*entáate*	— }
netáete	— }	direction.	*entáete*	— }
nesaate	— }		*ensáate*	— }
nesaete	—		*ensáete*	— }
netá	— }	used in vague indications, denoting both rest and	*entá*	— }
nesá	—	motion	*ensá*	— }
okore ?	—	where?	*jetare*	—
okotáre	— }	where abouts ?	*jetatáre*	— }
okosáre	— }		*jetásare*	— }
okote	—	whither ?	*jetate*	—
okotáte	—	what way?	*jetátate*	— }
okosáte	—	what direction	*jetásate*	— }
okoate	—	whence ?	*jetáete*	—
okotáate	— {	from what side	*jetáate*	}
etc.	{	or direction ?	*etc.*	— }
sobentáre	— }	everywhere	*sobentáte*	— }
sobensáre	— }		*sobensáte*	— }

REMARK —The forms *nare*, here; *nate*, hither, occur occasionally instead of *nere* and *nete*. the Pronominal forms—nea-re, in this one; rea-te, to this one.

2. A certain number of Compound Postpositions are used as are cut away from all connection with Nouns or Pronouns, and are used

chetanre	—	above	*talare*	—
sirmare	—	above	*japare*	—
rachare	—	outside	*bitarre*	—
paromre	—	across	*doiare*	—
aiarre	—	ahead	*taiomre*	—

To these may be added—

ADVERBIALLY

OF PLACE

re, táre, re, táte, atc, ete, táate, táete to the Definite, Indefinite, and compounds—

there.	*hanre*	—	yonder.

somewhere, about there.	*hantáre* — *hansáre* —	somewhere yonder
thither.	*hante* —	yonder.
that way, or that direction.	*hantáte* — *hansáte* —	that way yonder to that side yonder.
thence.	*hanate* — *hanete* —	from yonder side.
from somewhere there from that side.	*hantáate* — *hantáete* — *hansáate* — *hansáete* —	from somewhere yonder.
used like *netá*.	*hantá* — *hansá* —	used like *neta'*.
somewhere.	*jare* —	anywhere at all.
somewhere about.	*jatáre* — *jasáre* —	anywhere about.
some way.	*jate* —	any way.
in some direction or another.	*jatáte* — *jasáte* —	in any direction at all.
from somewhere.	*jaete* —	from anywhere.
from some direction or another	*jatáate,* — etc.	from any side at all. from whatever side.
In every direction	*sobentáete*— *sobensáete*—	from everywhere.

These seem to be the stronger equivalents of the forms *nere* and *nete*, and not ccontractions of

Adverbs of place without undergoing any change whatever, *i.e.*, they simply to modify Transitive or Intransitive Predicates—-

in the middle	*subare* —	below, underneath
close by, near	*latarre* —	below, underneath
inside	*danangre* —	behind (hidden)
behind	*kundamre* —	behind (the house)
behind.		

Nanre, near; *sanginre*, far.

All the above take the Suffixes *te* or *ate*, *ete* when the Predicate to be

chetante — upwards *talate* —

chetanate etc.	—	from above	*talaete* etc.	—
sanginte	—	from far away	*sanginate*	—

The same words take the Suffixes *táre (sáre)*, *táte* (*sáte*), *táate* or denote either *rest within* a vaguely defined area, or *motion to* or *from*.

Hence another triple

chetantáre	—	somewhere above	*talatáre*	—
chetantáte	—	somewhere upwards	*talatáte*	—
chetantáete	—	from somewhere above	*talatáete*	—
etc.			*etc.*	

3. All the compounds under No. 2 may be rendered more precise

nechetanre	—	above here	*enchetanre*	—
nechetantáre	—	above here somewhere.	*enchetantare*	—
nechetante	—	up here	*enchetantae*	—
nechetantáte	—	up here somewhere	*enchetantáte*	—
etc.			etc.	

4. *Kŏre* and *kŏte* are added (1) to *ne, en, han*; (2) to *neta* (*nesa*) the Postpositions *chetan*, etc. enumerated above under No. 2, and to designate a place or to indicate a limit.

The compounds thus obtained with *kore* specify Predicates denoting indicate the place of rest or the limit or terminus of a motion vaguely

(1) *nekŏre*	—	somewhere here	(3&4) jetakore	—
(2) *netákŏre*	—	somewhere about here.	jetakote	—
nekŏte	—	about up to this point	jetakote	—
netákŏte	—	more or less up to this place.	chetanlore	
etc.			etc.	

Note.—The syllable *kŏ* in *kŏre*, *kŏte* sams to be but the Indefinite Demonstrative *oko* modified by them denotes *motion* to or *from* a place. Hence—

to the middle	*subate*	—	downwards.
from the middle	*subaete*, etc.	—	from below.
from afar	*nanrete*	—	near to (a place), close by.

táete (*sáate* or *sáete*) when the Predicates to be modified by them some less well-determined point of space, a vaguely indicated direction, set of Adverbs of Place

somewhere in the middle	*subatáre*	—	somewhere below
somewhere to the middle	*subatáte*	—	somewhere down ward.
somewhere from the middle	subatáte	—	from somewhere below.
	etc.		

by placing the Definite Demonstratives *ne*, *en*, *han* before them—

above there	*hanchetanre*	—	above yonder
above here somewhere	*hanchetantáre*	—	above yonder somewhere
up there	*hanchetante*	—	up yonder.
up there somewhere.	*hanchetantáte*	—	up yonder somewhere.
	etc.		

entá (*ensá*), *hantá* (*hansá*); (3) to *jetá, jatá, sobentá* (*sobensá*); (4) to compounds of the same with *tá* (*sá*); (5) to Nouns there and then used *rest;* those with kŏte modify Predicates denoting *motion* to. They or approximately, not very exactly—

somewhere about	(5) *Ranchikore*	somewhere in Ranchi.
to some point or place	*Ranchitakore*	somewhere about Ranchi.
to any place at all	*mukuribokote*	about knee-deep; *literally* about up to the head of the knee.
somewhere above etc.		

It may be remarked here that the Adverbs of place seem to clearly bear out the statement made in the Introduction that distinct parts of speech as such, *i.e.*, with permanent characteristics and with limited functions of their own, have not as yet been evolved in Mundari—

1st. We here meet with a set of words which, without undergoing any change, are used indifferently both as Postpositions and as Adverbs of Place. Such are the compounds *chetanre, etc.*, enumerated under No. 2.

2nd.— These same compounds may, again without undergoing any change of form, be used as Transitive or Intrasitive Predicates. For this it suffices to suffix to them a Pronominal Subject and a Copula, and, if need be, an appropriate Tense-suffix.

Pred. Subj. Cop. Pred. Subj. Cop.

Chetanre-ko-a —they are above *Chetante-ko- a*, They go above.

Pred Subj. Tense Cop.

Aiarte—ko—jan— a,—They went ahead.

The compounds under No. 1 are similarly used as Intransitive Predicates, *v. gr.*—

Okore-ko-a?—Where are they? *Okate-ko-jan-a* ?—Where did they go?

Okote-m-tan-a ? —Whither dost thou go now ? —*Hante-le-a*, we shall go to that place younder.

3rd —It has been stated in the chapter on Postpositions that *re*, *te*, *etc*, etc., are suffixed to Nouns and Pronouns to perform the functions which our Prepositions perform in connection with Nouns and Pronouns.

But here we see those same Postpositions suffixed to the unaltered

Demonstrative roots—*ne, en, han*. Now, in the preceding chapters we have met these Demonstratives with an Adjective function only. In this Adjective function they always precede the Noun or Pronoun they qualify, as in *ne hoṛo*,— this man; *en hoṛo*— that man; *handaru*.—yonder tree : or *in han*—í—yonder one; *han--king*,— those two yonder; *han-ko*.— those yonder. Here those same roots no longer qualify any Noun or Pronoun : they stand quite independently, and they take the suffixes *re, te, ete*, etc., in the manner and meaning in which these suffixes are attached to Nouns and Pronouns.

We may therefore say that the Demonstratives *ne, en, han* perform the functions of Nouns in the Adverbial compounds; that they are used Substantively, not Adjectively; they are by themselves alone equivalent to the English *Noun + Demonstrative*— this thing, this place *ne-re*, in *the* (this place). The same remark applies to the words *chetan, aiar*, etc. (see No. 2): hence the compounds *chetan-re, aiar-re*, etc., literally mean—in *the* above, in *the* ahead, etc. To sum up—

(1) We have first met the Demonstratives *ne, en, han* with a distinctively *Adjective function.*
(2) Here we find the same unaltered forms with a *Substantive function* for the purpose of forming *Adverbial compounds.*
(3) The compounds thus obtained are not restricted to their *Adverbial functions* ; they may without undergoing any change of form assume an *Intransitive function.*

Again—

(1) We have met the words *chetan, aiar*, etc., with a *Transitive* or an *Intransitive function* ; some such as *sirma tala*, with both a *Substantive* and *a Transitive* or *Intransitive function.*
(2} Here we find the same words assuming a Substanitive function for the purpose of forming Adverbial compounds or Postpositions.
(3) The compounds thus obtained are not restricted to their *Adverbial function* ; they may be useḍ with a *Transitive* or *Intransitive* function.
(4) These same compounds assume a *Substantive Function* in the complex Adverbs—*ne chietanre, en chetanre, etc*., because in these forms *chetanre* etc., are preceded by the Demonstratives *ne, en, han* used Adjectively, *i.e.*, as qualificative to a Noun

II.—ADVERBS OF QUANTITY

1. A certain number of Indefinite Demonstratives are used adverbially without undergoing any change in form—

isu, much.
isupurá, very much
purá, much

erage, very much
mermer, very much
timba, very much

betekan, very much
huṛing, little
huṛing huṛing, very little.

Ge is very frequently suffixed to the above as emphatic enelytic. *Era* seems never to be used without the suffix *ge.*

2. The *Definite* and *Interrogative Demonstratives* in which the quantitative *min* occurs are never used Adverbially without the suffix *áng* or *ung*. The change of *a* into *u* seems to be caused by the vowel *í.* The forms in *ung* are less frequent than those in *ang*—

chiminang, chiminung	how much?	niminang, niminung,	this much
iminang iminung	that much	haminang, haminung,	as much as that yonder.

REMARK.—The compounds *iminang, niminang, and haminang* are also used as Correlative Adverbs.

Paulus *iminang*ko oldaṛia,—They can write *as much* or *as well as* Paul. Ako *iminangdo* kaing sendaria—I cannot walk *as well* or *as far as* they can.

3. The suffixes *sá* or *duang* are added to the Adverbs under No. 2 and to *isu, purá, isupura, huṛing, and huṛing huṛing* to form comparative Adverbs of Quantity.

Isusá,—many times. *Chiminangsá*—how many times? *iminangsá*,—as often as that. The forms *iminangsá*, *niminangsá*, and *haminangsá* are also used as Correlatives.

4. *Leka*, suffixed to the compounds under No. 1 and to *isu, purá, huṛing, huṛing huring, isupurá* transforms them into approximate Adverbs of Quantity—

chiminangleka, about how much ?	*miminangleka*, about this much.
imianangleka, about this much.	*haminangleka,* about as much as that yonder.
isuleka, pretty much.	*puráleka*, pretty much
isupuraleka, very much	*huṛingleka*, a little, rather little.
huring huṛingleka, very very little	

REMARK.—*Iminangleka, niminangleka, haminangleka* are used also as Correlative Adverbs.

Paulus *iminanglekaing* hudumadaria,— I can throw *about as far as* Paul.

III.—ADVERBS OF MANNER

1. The following are used adverbially without taking any suffix :-

isu (asu), very	*mer mer*, very intensely.
erage, very.	*kented*, intensely, violently.
bodege, quickly, at once!	*betekan*, very much.
sekerage, quickly.	*birang, birage,* only, alone
rokage, suddenly	*eskar,* eskarge, only.
kaiom, unexpectedly.	
upaige, in vain, without rhyme or	

reason, unprofitably.
samage, in vain, without rhyme or reason for nothing, without profit, without clothes, with an empty stomach, without having eaten.

2. The Postposition *te* is sometimes used to denote manner. With this function it is suffixed to some of the words under No. 1 as well as to some others especially Intransitive Predicates, to form Adverbs of Manner.

maṇṛite, slowly, softly (of sound and motion).
maṇṛi maṇṛite, very slowly, very softly.
mid'te (*misate*), together.
hambalte, difficulty.
berelte, raw (not boiled).
landate, laughingly.
kakláte, quite loud (shoutingly).
eklatante, tremblingly (being trembling)
sukute, gladly, with joy.
borote, timidly, with fear.
sojete, straight, in a straight line.
sekerate, quickly.
bodete, quickly
andagate, suddenly.
rabalte, easily.
petote, raw (green, unripe).
ratante, cryingly, with tears.
landiate, lazily (*lit*., *lit*idlingly).
rasikate, gladly, joyfully).
ka-borote, fearlessly.
gandite, / *gaṇdete,* } crookedly.

REMARK:—Here, again, we have Numerals like *mid', misa,* Intransitive and Transitive Predicates like *bode, sekera kakla, boro, etc*., and even Definite Present Tenses like rátan, *eklatan*, and Qualitatives like *hambal*, *rabal, rabal, peto, berel,* assuming a substantive function and taking the suffix *te*.

If it be admitted that *thses* words have a Substantive function in the compounds enumerated here, then it is readily understood how the suffix *te* has come to denote manner, just as, *v.gr.*, the English termination ly, which later has no longer any meaning if taken by itself alone; for then these compounds must be considered as a kind of Instrumental Case. Thus *mid'te* means, literally with unity. *Misate*, with *ensemble*--

bodete, with celerity.
sekerate ,, ,,
eklatante, with actual tembling.
kaklate, with shouting.
landiate, with laziness.
rátante, with actual weeping.

3. A very ordinary mode of forming Adverbs and Adverbial phrases of Manner, consists in suffixing *leka* or *lekate* : (1) to the Definite, Indefinite and Interrogative Demonstratives ; (2) to Nouns and Pronouns ; (3) to Adverbs of Time ; (4) to Active and Passive Predicates with or without their Subjects or Objects —

(1) *chileka (chilekate),*	how? in what way?	*okoleka (enlekate),*	like what ?
neleka (*nelekate*), *neka (nekate),*	in this way.	*enleka (enlekate), enka (enkate),*	in that manner.
hanleka (hanlekate), *hanka (hankate),*	in the same manner as that younder.	*jeleka (jalekate),*	in any manner, any way at all.
		jetaleka (jatalekate,)	in some manner

The contracted forms *enka, neka, hanka, enkate, nekate, hankate* are used as frequently as the full forms—*enlekate,* etc.—

(2) *rajaleka, rajalekate,*	like a king, royally.	*dasileka, dasilekate,*	like a servant, in a menial way. etc.	*jontu'eka, jontulekate,*	like a beast, beastly.
aingleka, ainglekate.	like me.	*amleka, amlekate,* *etc.*	like thee.	*aéleka, aélekate,*	like him.
(3) *naleká, nálekate,*	like just now.	*enangleka, enanglekate,*	like a moment ago	*honderleka, honderlekate,*	like some days ago

etc. (See IV.—Adverbs of Time)

REMARK— The Adverbs thus obtained are used as correlatives, *v. gr.*—*Enanglekabu inunga,*—Let us play *as we did a while ago,* or let us play *the same game which we played a while ago.*

(4) *aiumóleka*	(*te*),	audibly—	(*literally* like being heard).
bujhauóleka	(*te*),	intelligibly	(,, like being understood).
atkaróleka	(*te*),	perceptibly	(,, like being perceived).
lelóleka	(*te*),	visibly	(,, like being seen).
neluṛumóleka	(*te*),	recognisibly	(,, like being recognised).
daṛióleka	(*te*),	possible (*v. gr.*, it looks possible)—	*literally,* like being feasible.

Etc.

REMARK.—Of all these the corresponding negatives are formed by prefixing *ka-Ka-aiu-móleka (te), inaudibly ; ka-bujauóleka (te),* unintelligibly.

Other compounds obtained by suffixing *leka to* Predicates must generally be rendered into English by some dependent clause—

Med' banólekatem senbaratana,—Thou walkest about as if thou hadst no eyes Ape kape *aiumjalekape* taintana hanre,—You fellows remain over there just as if you did not hear [as though you had not heard me (or some one else) calling you]. *Hasutanlekam* lelótana,—Thou lookest as if thou wert sick. Jultanleka lelótana,—It looks as if it were burning *i.e.,* it looks shining bright, it looks like fire.

5. *No*, *noge* are suffixed to Adjective Predicates with an Adverbial function. They must generally be rendered into English by the Adverb *pretty*—

sibil, tasty ; *sibilnoge,* pretty tasty.	*rabal,* light; *rabalnoge,* pretty light.
sibilnoge-a, it is pretty tasty.	*rabalnoge-a*, it is pretty light.

6. The following are suffixed to Transitive or Intransitive Predicates with an Adverbial function. These suffixes form a single Compound Predicate with the words to which they are suffixed : hence the Voice, Mood, and Tense-signs are placed behind these Adverbial suffixes.

Tab, dahb, or *ba,* quickly, fast ; *chaba*, completely ; *Ruaṛ, or ruṛa,* again. *Senotab*, to go fast. *Olruaṛ*, to rewrite, to write over again. *Bairuaṛ,* or *bairuṛa,* to repair. *Olchaba,* to write out completely, to finish off a writing. *Jomchaba,* to eat up completely, to finish off the whole food set before one.

Of the above, *chaba, ruaṛ or ruṛa* are also used as independent Predicates; *chaba* meaning to complete some work, *ruaṛ* or *ruṛa* meaning to return, to come back.

OBSERVATION.— The use of Adverbs is more restricted in Mundari than in our languages, because where we use a Verb with an Adverb, they often use of the word corresponding to our Adverb with a transitive or intransitive function.

Beginners, however, must beware of an indiscriminate use of this method ; for in a certain number of cases the use of a Predicate with an Adverb is the more ordinary construction, whereas in other cases Adverbs alone are used transitively or intransitively in their original meaning. Thus, *v. gr., liud* means crooked. *Enale liud'a* means that we *call* crooked. *Liud'me,* make it crooked. Practice is the only safe guide in this matter.

IV.—ADVERBS OF TIME

chimtang ? — *chimta* ? —	When ? At what time?
chiula ? —	When ? What day ?
ná —	Now.
imtang —	Then.
ne imtang — *nimtang* —	Just a moment ago.
enimtang —	Just a moment before that.
hahimtang —	Just a moment before that (*i.e.* an event

munure —	In the beginning, at first.
tundure —	In the end, at the end.
misá misá — *mosá mosá*—	Sometime, now and again.
isusá, purasá	Often, frequently.
isupurasá —	Very often.
isuduang, pura—*duang.*	Often.
isupuraduang	Very often.
tising, ising —	To-day.
hola —	Yesterday.

long since past).

ietaimtang —	At some time.
jaimtang —	At any time, at any moment.
jetaimtangka—	At no time, never.
jaimtangoka —	Never, at no time whatever.
jaula —	Any day.
chiulaoka —	Never.
janao —	Always.
jonom jonom—	Always.
janaoka —	Never.
neskan —	This time.
naike —, *nege* —, *garikad're* —, *lika* —	After a while, shortly ! Just a moment !
enang —	A while ago;
sida, sidare —, *sidate* —	Before, sooner, first, at first.
aiar, aiur, aiarre	Before, sooner.
taiom, taiomre —, *taiomte, taiomkote* on.	Afterwards, later, later *mutid.*
portonre —	In the very beginning.

gapa —	To-morrow.
holatare —	The day before yesterday.
gapadanang—, *meang* —	The day after to-morrow.
tisingapa —, *nimir* —	Now-a-days
honder —	Some days ago.
honder honder	Long ago.
han honder —	That time, long ago
musing, musing hulang.	Once upon a time, some day.
enbeter, enbetera, *enbeterang* —	At that time
singsatub' —	The whole day long.
ma, maha —	Last year.
kalom, kalomre, *kalomkore* —	After one year, next year.
dinaki —, *dinaki dinaki*—	Daily.
angoma, ango—	Every day, daily.
sirma sirma —	Every year, yearly.
mosat sirma —, *misat sirma* —	Two years ago.

Auri after a while, not yet, before. (For construction see Future, page 174).

To these may be added a list of words and phrases used by the Mundas to designate the different parts or hours of the day. Besides the natural divisions, such as the different positions of the sun, the Mundas have adopted some others taken from their daily work—

Simko auri ráre, long before daybreak ; *literally,* before the cocks crow.

Sida simko ráre, a little before daybreak ; *literally*, when to cocks crow first.

Angóre, angódipli, at dawn.

Singi turo, singi turóre ; Singiturtanre, at sunrise.

Aparana dipli, about 8 A. M.; *literally,* at yoking time, when oxen are yoked to the plough.

Landia tikin, about 10 A.M.; *literally,* lazy noon. *i.e.,* when lazy people leave their work.

Tikin, } at 12 o'clock ; *literally* { Noon.
Muli tikin } { Straight noon, exact noon.

Hare singi, about 2 P.M.; *literally,* at the crooked sun, when the sun is oblique.

Tara singi, about 4 P. M.; *literally,* when the sun stands midway between noon and sunset.

Etá sanj, afternoon, *i.e.,* the other half-day.

Basang dá dipli, between 4 and 5 P. M.; literally, at water-fetching time, *i.e.,* when women go to get water for the evening meal.

Urí ader dipli, between 5 and 6 P.M.; *literally,* when it is time to drive the cattle home.

Singi hasur, }
Singi dubui, } at sunset.

Mandi jom dipli, supper time, *i.e.,* after sunset.

Aiub', aiub're, evening, in the evening.

Tala nida, }
Tala nidare, } at midnight.

Enangsá, in to-day's forenoon.

Nasá, this afternoon.

Giti dipli, bedtime, time to lie down.

Nida, nidare, night, at night.

Mid'sanj, }
Mod'sanj. } half a working day, half of the full number of working hours.

VII.—CONJUNCTIONS

1st.—The various forms of the Indefinite Demonstrative *oro* are used as Conjunctions without taking any suffix.

They stand chiefly as a link between words in enumerations. They are less frequently used by the Mundas to connect propositions with each other—

Ad', adó, oró, ondó, ondo = and.

Munda *oró* pahanking hijúlena,—The village-chief and the sacrificer have comje ; *literally,* the village-chief + the sacrificer have come.

2nd.—The ordinary Co-ordinative Conjunctions connecting propositions with each other are formed by suffixing *te* to the Definite Demonstrative *en* or to the Pronoun *ena.*

It will be seen further or (page 230) that *te* is often suffixed to the Past Tense to denote a simple priority of one action over another. Here in the Compounds *ente, enate, te* has evidently the same function. Hence these Compounds may very accurately be rendered into English by—*that being so,* or *that being done,* or *that being said,* i.e., *thereupon, and then.*

Ente (entedo) ; enate (enatedo) ; enad (enad'do) ; ente enad',—and then, thereupon.

N.B.—The form *enad'* is most likely a contraction of *enate*do. If to this, again, *do* be added by a false analogy, the form *enad'do* is obtained.

3rd.—The Causal Conjunctions are obtained by suffixing *mente* to the Demonstrative Pronouns *nea* or *ena*—

Neamente for this ; *enamente,* for that, therefore.

N.B.—*Men* means to say ; *mente* literally means by saying, saying. (For the various transferred significations of this form, page 61)

Remark.—*Do* is generally suffixed to *neamente, enamente* when these Conjunctions are followed by the Negative Particle *ka,* as *neamentedo ka,* not indeed for this reason *; enamentedo ka,* not indeed for that reason.

4th.—Conditional Conjunctions are formed by suffixing *re* either to *en, ena* or to the Quantitative *imin ((*that much*).*

It has been stated that *re* is suffixed to Transitive and Intransitive Predicates to form Compounds equivalent to our Conditional clauses and Temporal clauses.

In the Compounds *enre, enare, iminre*, it occurs in the same function : hence these Compounds are correctly rendered into English, thus : *enre, during that, in the meanwhile ;* also, *if that be so; enare, if,* or *in case that be so.*

The Adverb *o*, too, also, even, is always suffixed to *iminre* and often to *enre*—

Enre { in the meanwhile.
notwithstanding.

Enreo, even if, even then.
Iminreo, even then notwithstanding; *literally;* even if it be so much.

Barsáaing rákía *iminreo* kae hijútana,—I called him twice, notwithstanding that he does not come.

REMARK.—In Negative Conditional Propositions no Conjunction is used, but *re* is suffixed to the Predicate.

If you do *not* come,—kam hijú-*re*. *If* he had *not* been sick,— kae hasulen-*re. Literally,* In thy not coming. In his not having been sick.

5th.—*Disjunctive Conjunctions* are formed by suffixing *re* to *ka* (not) or to *ban (banó,* not to be)—

Kare (karedo), or else, or if not ; (either)......or.
Banre (banredo), ,, ,, ,, ... ,,

Merom tolime *karedoe* nira,—Tie the goat or else it will run away.

Karedo, banredo may also stand after the Predicate—

Chatu nere alom dota, *rapudóa karedo,* —Don't place the waterpot here or else it will be smashed.

Only one Conjunction is used in Disjunctive sentences : there is no special word corresponding to *either* in the English Compound Disjunctive *either* .... *or.*

Nere *orá* saurite *karedo* kechoteko dabea,—Here they cover the houses *either* with straw *or* with tiles.

OBSERVATIONS.—Mundas pretty often merely juxtapose words and even propositions where we would use conjunctions.

In narratives, especially in rehearsing their scanty stock or popular stories, the Conjunctions *ente, enate, entedo, enatedo, enad, enad'do* are repeated with a most tedious profusion.

Honang is used in connection with Indicative Mood-forms to express that something would be done, would have been, etc., if a certain condition were fulfilled. (*See* pages 228 and 229)

AFFIRMATIVE, NEGATIVE, AND DUBITATIVE PARTICLES

He, hege, ea,	yes.	*kagedo, kaoró,*	certainly not, by no means·
he oró,		*idu,*	perhaps.
he derang, hegedang,	of course, to be sure.	*iduró,*	pherhaps, it may be.
		iduró,	who knows?
he honang,	truly, surely, it would be so if.	*idutam,*	I don't know.
		idu hale,	who can tell !
kachi,	isn't it ! indeed ?		
kaoró,	isn't it ! to be sure.		
ka, kage, banó, banóge, nala, nalage,	no.		

alo is a prohibitive or precative negative. particle, which takes the Personal Pronouns as suffixes. (For construction, see Part III, Page 117)

INTERJECTIONS

Mar ! all right ! go on ! go ahead ! (denotes approval).

martobe ! ditto (exhortative).

he mar ! all right *! (*answers to a statement or request).

dola ! come along (a familiar exhortative. It generally takes the Pronominal Suffixes *lang* and *bu).*

dollang ! come along thou ! let's go both of us !

dolabu ! come along you ! let's go all of us !

ju ! away *!* get away ! (This is a polite expression in connection with *senóme* only).

ju senóme ! mar senóme ! senóme mar !	good- buy ! good-bye then !
mar heu !	all right then ! come on then ! (a very familiar address
ela ! hela !	hallo ! (surprise, regret).

heina !
ajăga ! } alas ! (pain, sorrow, grief).
aianga!

ke ! indeed ! how wonderful ! Do you really mean to say so ?

Tirbole ! denotes intense joy and applause, at some one having, for instance, hit a mark or target with an arrow; or at some similar feat.

A ! is used only in familiar address, chiefly to children. It never stands alone ; it may be suffixed to any of the above Interjections, to Nouns, Pronouns, Predicates, or to any word representing a proposition, as, *v. gr.*, elliptical questions or replies.

In some districts children at play or in conversation with each other use this Interjection very freely.

Mar-a! all right. Hijúme-*a !* come thou ! am-*a !* thou there ! Tobepe-*a !* go ahead then you ! (here *tobe,* and then, is used intransitively in the Imperative Mood, with the Interjectional Suffix *a*). Okoi-*a*? Who (struck, understood) Patras-*a*. Peter (strcuk. understood). Peter protests saying, Kae-*a !* No ! (Here the *e* is merely euphonic.)

Eho ! hey ! (is familiar to grown-up men. *Ho* seems to be a contraction of *horo,* man. *Ho* is the ordinary form of *horo* among the Larka Khols).

Ga ! This is used familiarly to such women only as are related to the speaker. It is suffixed to *he* or *e,* yes, as, *ega !* to *ka (*no), *kaga ! to am* and *ape*, *amga* ! *apega !* and to Imperatives, *v. gr.*, *hijúmega !* come here *!*

Na ! is similarly suffixed in addresses to girls.

EMPHATIC, DUBITATIVE AND CORRECTIVE SUFFIXES

Ge is an Emphatic Suffix which may generally be translated by *indeed, certainly, of course.*

It may be suffixed to any word at all. If, however, it be used to emphasize a Transitive, Intransitive or Adjective Predicate, it becomes an *Infix*, since in that case it stands between the complete Predicate form and the Copula, *v. gr.*, He will come, *hijúae,* He will surely come, *hijú-ge-ae.*

Ja and *tera* are Dubitative Suffixes equivalent to *perhaps, perchance, may be.* If suffixed to Predicates, they stand after the Copula, *v. gr.*, May be he will come,—*Hijúae-ja* or *hijuae-tera.*

Do is Corrective Suffix.

1st.—It may very often be translated by b*ut, however*. In this function it is generally suffixed to the first word of the sentence, which in English would be introduced by *but*—

Iní-*do* kaeajana,—but that one did not agree. Gapa-*doe* hijúa,—but he will come to-morrow.

2nd.—It is used in really corrective replies, whether affirmative or negative, where in English no equivalent word would be used—

Is this the village-chief? Ní Munda taníchi ? No, this is not the Munda,— Ni Munda-*do ka.* Is that one the chief ? Ini Munda chi? No, this is the Munda,- Ká, ní-*do* Munda,or Munda-*do nige.*

3rd.—It is very frequently suffixed to the Conditional Mood-form in *re*—

If he be not at home, bring this letter back, but if he be, give it to him,— Bangáire ne chitti auruarme, menáire-*do* omaime.

4th.— It is used with a limitative function, and thus may often be rendered by the phrases *as far as that is concerned, so far as that goes.*

In this function it is suffixed to Predicates only. The Predicate must be repeated, viz., first stands the original form with *do* as suffix, and then the full Predicate with Copula, Voice, Mood, and Tense-Suffixes—

He can pay, he is the village-chief,—*Hal dariae, Munda taní.* He is the chief *so far as the name goes,* but he has no money,—Munda-*do* munda akanae takado banoátae.

I can reach it, but I cannot lay hold of it (i.e., as far as reaching it is concerned it can be reached), Teba-*do* tebagóa, mendo sab kaing daria.

Derang and *chimad'* are emphatic Particles which are not merely affixed to other words, but they occupy an independent position in the sentence. They are equivalent to the English *certainly, surely, to be sure, forsooth.*

Hijúae chimad', —He will surely come.

Derang is chiefly used in certain Conditional sentences (see page 228).

For the meaning and use of *honang* see pages 228 and 229.

EQUIVALENTS OF DECLENSIONS

1. The so-called *Cases* of Nouns and Pronouns, if considered as attributes of words, are indicative of the various relations in which Nouns and Pronouns stand to the Predicate of a proposition, or to each other as parts of a proposition.

2. As stated in the Introduction, three of those relations are never denoted in Mundari Nouns or Pronouns by any Suffix, viz. (1) that of the Subjects or *Nominative* Case ; (2) that of the Direct Object or Accusative to a Transitive Predicate ; (3) that of the Indirect Object or *Dative* to Transitive or Intransitive Predicates : hence we may say Mundari equivalents of Organic *Nominatives, Accusatives* and *Datives* of Nouns and Pronouns do not differ from each other in form. They are either the bare root, or the root *plus* the Dual Suffix, or the root plus the Plural Suffix.

The context of the proposition and to some extent the position occupied by a Noun or Pronoun in a sentence must show whether that Noun or Pronoun is the *Subject* or a *Direct* or an *Indirect Object.*

Regarding the position of these three Cases, it may be given as a more or less general rule that the Subject or Nominative stands first, the Dative second, and the Accusative third—

N. A.

Ex.— Gomke dasie rákía,—The master called the servant.

N. D. A.

Gomke dasi talabe omáía,—The master gave the servant his wages.

3. All the other relations denoted by declensional Cases with or without Prepositions in Aryan languages are in Mundari expressed by suffixing to Nouns or Pronouns some one or other of the Postpositions enumerated in the Chapter on Postpositions.

What has been there said concerning the various meaning of each Postposition suffices to show how our purely Locative Accusatives and Ablatives as well as all other Ablatives and Datives are to be rendered.

4. There remains, however, one difficulty, viz., the correct rendering or our *Genitive Cases.* As many as five different Suffixes are used to express the various relations connoted by the single Genitive Case-form. The reason of this is that the Mundas treat all these relations as merely local ones ; in other words, the Organic Genitive is by the Mundas split up into several *Locative Cases* or *relations.*

A few considerations to show how they view those relations is. These considerations will at the same time point out the reason for the use of each Suffix, and thus assist the memory and facilitate the) practical acquisition of these equivalents—

1st.—In a certain number of our Possessive and Partitive Genitives the spatial nature of the relation is easily discerned, *v. gr.*, the men *of the village,* the trees *of the forest.* What is directly indicated by these Genitives is a mere relation of space, viz., either the existence of inanimate objects in a certain place or the habitual dwelling of living beings within a certain area. These Genitives may even in English be rendered by a Preposition of Space: the trees *in* the forest, the men *in* the village.

This is mainly the mode of rendering them adopted by the Mundas:

(*a*) they suffix *re* (in) to the Noun or Pronoun denoting a place; then if the Genitive in question depend on a word denoting a living being, the Demonstrative *en* (that) is added to *re.* This yields the dompound Suffix *ren.*

Hatu-ren-en horo becomes *haturen* horo ; *literally,* that man in the village, *i.e.*, the man of the village.

The last part of the Compound Suffix *ren* is in reality a Demonstrative Adjective qualifying the Noun which governs the Genitive, *i.e.*, in the present instance the word *horo.*

Since no Adjectives take the Dual or Plural Suffixes, it is plain that the Suffix *ren* remains unchanged even if the governing Noun be in the Dual or Plural—

Hatu-ren hoṛoking,— Those two men in the village, *i.e.*, the two men *of* the village.

Hatu-ren hoṛoko,—Those men in tho village, *i.e.*, the men *of* the village.

(*b*) If the Genitive in question depend on a word denoting inanimate objects, the Impersonal Pronoun *á*(it) is added to *re*. I his yields the Compound Suffix *reá*. Hence—

The door of the house,—*Oṛá-reá duar,* means literally the door it in the house.

The trees of the forest,—*Bir-rea daru,* means literally the trees they in the forest.

2nd.—Such Genitives as *peace* OF MIND, *the meaning* OF THE WORD can, even in English, be intelligibly rendered by the Preposition *in,* although the relation here signified is no longer a *purely* spatial one: hence—

Mon-*reá* suku ; *literally*, peace it in the mind : peace *of* mind.

Kaji-*reá* mundi, *literally,* the meaning it in the word : the meaning *of* the word.

3rd.—Genitives denoting the *dimensions* of something, the material of which something is made, the *price* of something, and the *age* of some being are all rendered in the same way, viz.—

By the Suffix *ren* if they depend on words denoting living beings.

By the Suffix *reá* if they depend on words denoting inanimate objects.

Ex.—

A ring of gold,—*Samrom-reá* mudam ; *lit.*, the ring it *in* gold.

A bamboo of 3 yards,—*Api muka-reá mad' ; lit.*, the bamboo *it in 3* yards.

A cloth of 2 rupees, -*Bar taka-reá lijá* ; *lit.*, the cloth it *in* 2 rupees.

4th.—The family is conceived as a moral unit or totum. On this assumption the relation between its members becomes one of mutual *partnership* and not of *real ownership.* Consequently the Suffix used to denote it is the same as that which is used for Partitive Genitives. Of course the Demonstrative *en* is substituted for the Impersonal *á* because there is question of living beings : hence *re-en* = *ren* instead of *reá.* This is strictly observed to denote the relation between husband and wife—

Ex.—

The wife of the village-chief,—*Munda-ren kuṛi.*

Paku's wife,—*Paku-ren kuṛi.*

Sumi's husband,—*Sumi-ren koṛa.*

The relation between parents and children is frequently expressed in the same way. However, in this case, the idea of partnership is no longer so rigorously insisted on, and the ordinary Possessive Suffix *á* is used perhaps more frequently than the Partitive Suffix *ren* thus showing that the relation between parent and child partakes already of the nature of real ownership—

Ex.—Paku's son.—*Paku-ren hon* or *Paku-'a hon.*

5th.—The relation between a master and his servants is not conceived as one of real ownership, nor yet as that of real partnership, but merely as one of constant attendance : hence it is expressed by means of the Compound Locative Suffix *táre, about, near, around,* plus the Demonstrative *en,* i.e., *taren*—

Ex.—The servant of the village-chief,—*Mundá-taren dasi ; lit.,* the servant the one about the village-chief.

The relation between a master and his domestic animals is often expressed in the same way—

Ex.—Paku's cattle,—*Paku-táren uríko ; lit.,* the cattle those about Paku.

It is even used sometimes of children—

Ex.—Paku's children,—*Paku-táren honko* ; *lit.*, the children those about Paku.

REMARK.—The use of the purely Possessive Suffix *á*is apparently getting more common for the cases enumerated above. This must, I thing, be attributed to two causes—

(1) The ever-extending use of Hindi or Sadani.

(2) The very unidiomatic Mundari spoken by missionaries and imitated by their catechists and other servants.

6th.—All other *Possessive* and *Partitive Genitives* of Nouns and Pronouns denoting *living beings* are rendered by means of the Suffix *á (*to*)*—

Ex.—The house of Paku,— *Paku-á ora ;* literally, the house *to* Paku.

Thy cloth,— *Am-á lijá ; lit.*, the cloth *to thee.*

REMARK.—Partitive Genitives, such as the horse's head, the branches of the tree, may also be rendered by mere *juxtaposition, v. gr.*—

Sadom-bó, instead of Sadom-á bó, a horse head.

Daru-koto, instead of daru-*rá* koto, tree branches.

What has so fare been said may be summed up into the following rules :—

I.—Nouns and Pronouns standing as Subjects, Direct or Indirect Objects take no Suffix indicative of case relations.

II.—Possessive Genitives of Nouns and Pronouns depending on the word *servant* or *its synonyms* are *generally* rendered by means of the Suffix *taren, sometimes* by the Suffix *á*—

Jila gomke *táren* chaprassi chiṭṭi auakadae,—The chaprassi *of* the Deputy Commissioner has brought a letter. Samu *táren* dasie nirjana,—The servant *of* Samu has run away.

III.—Possessive Genitives of Nouns and Pronouns depending on the words *child, son, daughter, father, mother, brother, sister* are often rendered by means of the Suffix *ren,* sometimes by *táren*, more frequently by á—

Pahaṇṛ-*táren*
Pahaṇṛ-*ren*
Pahaṇṛ-*á* } kuṛi-hon Assamte arkid'idikiádo,—They (viz., the coolie-catchers) have taken the daughter *of* the sacrificer to Assam.

IV.—Possessive Genitives of Common or Proper Nouns and Pronouns *denoting persons* are rendered by means of the Suffix *ren* when they depend on the words *husband* or *wife*—

Munda-ren kuṛi hola ruatee goéjana,—The Munda's wife died of fever yesterday. Buduni-*ren* koṛa erágee hasuakana,—The husband *of* Buduni is very sick.

V.—All the other Possessive and Partitive Genitives of Nouns or Pronouns *denoting living beings* not enumerated in the preceding rules must be rendered by means of the Suffix *á*—

Am-tárem dasi-*á* lija lojaná,—The cloth *of* thy servant burnt. Sigin-*á* orá handirijana,—The house *of* Sigin has collapsed.

VI.—Genitives of Proper or Common Nouns or Pronouns denoting *seas, rivers, countries, towns, space or places,* or single objects there and then considered as a place or a container of something must be rendered by the Suffix *ren* when they depend on words denoting *living beings.* The same Genitives are rendered by *reá* when they depend on words denoting *inanimate objects*—

Ranchi-*ren* Uraoṇko Hoṛoteko jagara,—The Uraons *of* Ranchi speak Mundari, Ranchi-*reá* talaore marang haiko menákoa,—There are big fishes in the tank *of*

Ranchi. Bir-*ren* maráko erágeko chirgala,—The peacocks *of* the forest *(i.e.,* wild peacocks) are exceedingly shy. Bir-*reá* dá tut'kungea,—The water *of* the forest is cool.

VII.—Genitives denoting *age, price, dimension,* or *the material* of which something is made must be rendered by *ren* when they depend on words denoting *living beings.* When they depend on words denoting *inanimate objects,* they are rendered by *reá* or by *rá.*—

Turui sirma-*ren* hon,—A child *of* six years. Monre taka-*ren* merom,—A goat *of* five rupees, *i.e.,* a goat worth five rupees. Monre taka-*rea lijá,*—A cloth *of* five rupees. Mod'hisi muka-*reá* orá,—A house *of* 20 cubits, *i.e.,* a house measuring 20 cubits. Bar muka-*ren bing,*—A snake *of* two cubits, *i.e.,* measuring two cubits in length. Pital-*reá.* chipi,—A dish made *of* brass.

VIII.—Partitive Genitives of words denoting inanimate objects (*i.e.,* Genitives denoting a part of some inanimate object or whole) are generally rendered by means of the contracted suffix *rá,* rarely by *reá*—

En ote-*rá* hatingem namtadachi? Hast thou got a share *of* that land?

IX.—The Definite Locative of rest of Nouns or Pronouns is formed by the Suffix *re*—

Ne hatu-*re* Dikuko bangkuá,—There are no Hindus *in* this village.

The *Indefinite Locative of rest* is formed by *táre*—

Khunti-*táre* Teliko isu oteko eserakada,—About or around or near Khunti the Telis have got hold of much land.

X.—The *Definite Locative of motion to* of Nouns or Pronouns denoting *space* or *places* is formed by the Suffix *te*—

Ranchi-*te* senóme,—Go *to* Ranchi. Bir-*te* nirjanako,—They have run away *to* the forest. Ne lija gara-*te* idime,—Take this cloth to the river.

The *Indefinite Locative of motion to* of the same Nouns or Pronouns is formed by *táte*—

The *Locative of motion to* of *all other Nouns and Pronouns* is formed by táte.

Aing-*táte* niraujanae,—He came running *to me.* En haturen Munda-*táte* alom sena,—Do not go to the Munda of that village. Ne chitti gomke-*táte* iditab'me,—Take this letter quickly *to* the master.

XI.—The *Definite Locative of motion from* of Nouns and Pronouns denoting *space* or *places* is formed by the Suffix *ate* or *ete*—

Náuterge kula ne lata-*etee urunglena,*—A tiger came out just now *from* this den. Hatu-*ete* nirjanae,—He has run away *from* the village. Sirma-*ete uiújanae,*—He has fallen *from* the roof.

The *Indefinite Locative of motion from* of the same Nouns and Pronouns is formed by the Suffix *táate or táete*—

Han hatu-*táeteko* niraujana,— They came running *from* yonder village, *i.e.,* from somewhere near yonder village.

The *Locative of motion from* of all other Nouns and Pronouns is formed by the Suffix *táate or táete*—

Pahanr-*táetem* hijútana chi? Ka, Munda-*táete,*—Art thou coming *from* the pahan? No, *from* the Munda.

XIII.—The Instrumental Case of Nouns and Pronouns denoting *inanimate objects* or *irrational animals* is formed by the Suffix *te*—

Ne orá kecho-*te* dabakana,—This house is covered *with* tiles. Chipi diri-*te* karedo pital-*te* ko baiea,—They make dishes with (or out of) stone or with brass. Ne disumre uríko-*te*ko siea, sadomko-*te* do ka,—In this country they plough *with* bullocks, but never *with* horses. Banduk-*te* goéked'koae,—He killed them *with* a gun.

XIII.—The *Instrumental Case* of Nouns and Pronouns denoting human *beings* is formed by suffixing *á* to these Nouns and Pronouns and then adding *horate.* This *horate* is by itself the Instrumental Case of the word *hora (*way). It corresponds exactly to the Latin *viá*, and may therefore be rendered into English by *through*

Amá *horate* le banchaujana,—We were saved *by* thee.

XIV.—Ablative Cases of Nouns and Pronouns *denoting living beings* and depending on such words as *to receive, to buy, to steal, and their synonyms* are rendered by means of the Suffix *ete (*See *ete* in the Chapter on Postpositions)—

Ne sadom Samu-*ete*ng kiringkía,—I bought this horse *from* Samu.

REMARK.—The words *to steal, to rob,* and their synonyms generally take a double accusative—

Paku *Samu otee* rekíá, rather than Paku *Samu-ete* otee rékeda,—Paku has robbed Samu of his land. Hola dakuko *api horo senhoratanko lijako, tariko* ad' *takado* reked'koako,—Yesterday dacoits robbed three travellers of their cloths, their brass plates, and their money.

XV.—The Vocative may be preceded by the Interjection *e! he !* Very often the tone of the Voice alone distinguishes it from the Nominative form.

In familiar addresses it may take one or other of the Interjectional Suffixes given above (pages 127and 128).

The following schemes may serve as a synoptical recapitulation of these rules. The first scheme represents words denoting space or places. The second represents words denoting such inanimate objects as may at times be considered as places or receptacles. The third represents words denoting irrational animals. The fourth represents words denoting human beings :—

Singular, Dual, and Plural.

Subject, Direct and Indirect Object—		*Bir,*	the forest, a forest, forest or forests.
Locative Genitive.	dependent on words denoting living beings	*Bir-ren,*	(living beings) of the forest, &c.
	dependent on words denoting inanimate objects.	*Bir-reá*	(inanimate objects) of the forest, &c.

Definite Locative of rest—	*Bir-re,*	in the forest, &c.
Indefinite Locative of rest—	*Bir-táre,*	about, or somewhere in the forest, &c.
Definite Locative of motion to—	*Bir-táte,*	towards the forests, &c.
Indefinite Locative of motion to—	*Bir-táte,*	towards the forest, &c.
Definite Locative of motion from—	*Bir-ete,*	from the forest, &c.
Indefinite Locative of motion from—	*Bir-táate* or *táete.*	from the direction of the forests, &c.

Singular.

Nominative, Dative, Accusative—	*Sadom,*	the horse, a horse, horse.
Possessive and Partitive Genitive—	*Sadom-á*	of the horse, the horse's.
Definite Locative of rest—	*Sadom-re,*	on the horse, in the horse.
Indefinite Locative of rest—	*Sadom-táre,*	near or about the horse.
Definite and Indefinite motion to—	*Sadom-táte,*	to or towards the horse.
Definite Locative of motion from—	*Sadom-ete,*	from the horse.
Indefinite Locative of motion from—	*Sadom-táete,*	from near the horse.
Instrumental—	Sadom-te,	with or by means of the horse, on horse-back.
Ablative—	*Sadom-ete,*	from the horse.
Vocative—	*He sadom!*	horse!

The Dual *sadomking,* two horses, and the Plural *sadomko,* horses take the same Suffixes as the Singular—

Ex.—

Sadomkingá, of the two horses; *sadomkingre,* in or on the two horses.
Sadomkotáre, near the horses ; *sadomkoete,* from the horses.

Singular.

Nominative, Dative, and Accusative	*Munda,*	the village-chief.
Possessive Genitive dependent on the word wife	*Mundá-ren*	(the wife) of the village-chief.
Possessive Genitive dependent on the word servant	*Mundá-taren* or *á*	(the servant) of the village-chief.
Other Possessive Genitives—	*Munda-á,*	of the village-chief.
Definite Locative of rest—	*Munda-re*	in or on the village-chief.
Indefinite Locative of rest—	*Munda-táre,*	near or about the village-chief.
Definite and Indefinite Locative of motion to	*Munda-táte,*	to the village-chief.
Definite and Indefinite Locative of		

motion from	*Munda-táate,*	from the village-chief.
Instrumental—	*Munda-á horate,*	through the village-chief.
Ablative—	*Munda-ete,*	from the village-chief.
Vocative—	*He Munda !*	O village-chief !

The Dual *Mundaking* and the Plural *Mundako* take the same Suffixes as the Singular.

Pronouns take the Case-Suffixes which would be taken by the Nouns

Singular.

Masc. & Fem.

Nominative, Dative, Accusative	*Aing,*	I.
Genitives—	*aing-ren,* *aing-táren,* *ain-á,*	my.
Definite Locative of rest—	*aing-re,*	in or on me.
Indefinite Locative of rest,	*aing-táre,*	about me.
Definite and Indefinite Locative of motion to—	*aing-tate,*	to me.
Definite and Indefinite Locative of motion from—	*aing-táete,*	from me.
Ablative—	*aing-ete*	from me.
Instrumental—	*ainá horate,*	through me.

REMARK.—Nouns ending in *s* sometimes insert a euphonic *e* or *o* between this consonant.

Patronymics as well as other Proper and Common Nouns are obtain *ren* or *táren.* These Nouns take all the Dual, Plural, and Case-

The Singular forms thus derived from Proper names of men or whereas the Singular forms thus derived from Proper names of women

The Plural forms thus derived from Proper names of either men or *the family of, i.e.,* all the inmates of the house, grand-parents, husband

Pakurenko, Paku's family.

N.B.—If, however, such a Dual or Plural form be derived from the name of a man known

REMARK.—The expressions *the family of, the inmates of the house of* are more frequently family of Paku.

for which they there and then stand:—

Singular.		**Singular.**	
Masc.& Fem.		**Masc. & Fem.**	
Iní,	that one.	*Hana,*	that one yonder.
Iní-ren *Iní-táren,* *Iní-á,*	of that one.	*Hana-ren,* *Hana-reá,* *Hana-rá,*	of that one younder.

Iní-re,	in or on that one.	*Hana-re,*	in or on that one yonder.
Iní-táre,	about or near that one.	Hana-táre,	about or near that one yonder.
		Hana-te,	to and towards that
Iní-táte,	to that one.	*Hana-táte,*	one yonder.
		Hana-ete,	from,and from the direction of that one yonder.
Iní-táete,	from that one.	*Hana-táete,*	
Iní-ete,	from that one.	*Hana-ete,*	from ,,
Iní-á horate,	through that one.		
Iní-te,	(of irrational animals)	*Hana-te,*	by, with or out of that one yonder.

and the Possessive Suffix *á.* Hence the forms Paulus-o-á, Paulus-e-á, or Paulus-á, of Paul.

ed by suffixing the Personal Pronouns *í, king, ko* to the Genitive in suffixes of ordinary Nouns.

from Pronouns standing for such names always mean *the wife of;* or from Pronouns standing for such names mean *the husband of.*

women or from Pronouns standing for such names generally mean or wife, children, grand-children, *v. gr., Samu-rení,* Samu's wife.

as a polygamist, it may mean *the two wives of,* or *the wives of.*

rendered by suffixing *te,* followed by the Plural *ko* to the Proper name, *v. gr., Paku-te-ko,* the

Belait,	Europe.	*Belaitren,*	of Europe.
Ranchi,	Ranchi.	*Rachiren,*	of Ranchi.
Hatu,	village.	*Haturen,*	of the village.
Nagar,	town.	*Nagarren,*	of the town.
Iskul,	school.	*Iskulren,*	of the school.
Bir,	forest.	*Birren,*	of the forest.
Lau,	a boat.	*Lauren,*	of the boat.
Jehel,	jail.	*Jehelren,*	of the jail.
Raja,	king.	*Rajataren,*	of the king.
Soma	(man's name).	*Somaren,*	of Soma.
Sumi	(woman's name).	*Sumiren,*	of Sumi.
	the wife of Soma.		
Somarenking,	the two wives of Soma.		
Sumirenko,	the family of Sumi.		

Remark.—The Compounds derived from *Proper Names of Countries, towns and villages* immediately to the Nouns—

Ex.—Ranchirení, a Ranchiite ; *Ranchiking,* two Ranchiites ; *Ranchiko,* Ranchiites.

	SINGULAR.	DUAL.	PLURAL.
Belaitren-í	European.	*Belaitren-king.*	*Belaitren-ko.*
Ranchirení,	Ranchiite.	*Ranchirenking.*	*Ranchirenko.*
Haturení,	villager.	*Haturenking.*	*Haturenko.*
Nagarrení,	townsman.	*Nagarrenking.*	*Nagarrenko.*
Iskulrení,	school-child, a student.	*Iskulrenking.*	*Iskulrenko.*
Birrení	a wild beast. a savage. a stupid fellow.	*Birrenking.*	*Birrenko.*
Laurení,	sailor. passenger.	*Laurenking.*	*Laurenko.*
Jehlerení,	prisoner.	*Jehelrenking.*	*Jehelrenko.*
Rajatarení,	king's servant.	*Rajatárenking.*	*Rajatárenko.*
Somarení,	Soma's wife.		
Sumirení	Sumi's husband.		
Somarenko,	the wives of Soma, or the faily of Sona.		

frequenltly drop the Suffix *ren* in the Dual and Plural, the Pronouns *king* and *ko* being suffixed.

POSSESSIVE ADJECTIVES AND POSSESSIVE ADJECTIVE SUFFIXES

1st—The Possessive Genitives of Personal, Demonstrative, Indefinite, and Interrogative Pronouns are used as Possessive Adjectives.

As such, they stand before the Noun they qualify and remain always unchanged, *i.e.*, they take no Suffixes indicative of either Gender, number, or Case.

Example.—Aiñá sadom, my horse ; *amá* uríko, thy bullocks ; akoá loeong, their rice-fields ; *iniá* lijá, that one's cloth ; *okoiá* orá, whose house? *amtáren* dasi, thy servant. *Nitáren* honko, this one's children.

REMARK.—The Possessive Adjectives *aleá* and *akoá* often drop the Suffix *á* before the words *oṛá* (house) and *hatu* (village).

Example.—Our house,—aleá oṛá or *ale oṛá* ; our village,—aleá hatu or *ale hatu.*

Their house,—akoá oṛá, or *ako oṛá ;* their village,—akoá hatu, or *ako hatu.*

2nd.—The Possessive Adjectives *my, thy, his,* etc., are very frequently rendered by suffixing to the Noun denoting the beings or objects possessed the Compound Suffixes *taing, tam, tae, talang, taling, tabu, tale, tape, tako*—

Sadomtaing, my horse.
Oṛátam, thy house.
Lijátae, his cloth.
Hatutalang, our (my and thy) village.
Meromkotaling, mine and his goat.
Uríkingtaben, the two bullocks belonging to you two.
Simkotaking, the fowls belonging to the two.
Disumtabu, our (my and your) country.
Setakotale, our (my and their) dogs.
Haketape, your axe, or your axes.
Bakṛitako, their garden.

3rd.—When the Possessives *my* and *thy* qualify Nouns denoting family relations, they are generally rendered by suffixing simply *ing* and *me* or *m* to those Nouns. *Me* is suffixed to Nouns ending in a consonant, *v. gr- hon-me,* thy child ; *m* is suffixed to Nouns ending in a vowel, *v. gr. nga-m,* thy mother.

The corresponding Dual and Plural Possessives of the Is and 2nd Persons are rendered by means of the Suffixes *talang, taling, tabu, tale tuben, tape.*

The Possessive *his* or *her* is rendered by suffixing *te* to he same Nouns.

The *Inclusive Duals and Plurals* are formed by suffixing *talang* and *tabu* respectively to the Noun, *v.gr,, aputalang*, thy and my father; *aputabu,* your and my father.

But the *Exclusive Duals and Plurals* insert *ing* before *taling* and *tale.*

Example.—Apuingtaling, literally, my father, his and my.
Apuingtale, literally, my father, theirs and my.

Similarly, the 2nd Person Dual and Plural inserts *m* or *me* before *taben* and *tape*.

Example.—Bokomtaben, literally, thy junior brother, his and thy.
Bokomtape, literally, thy junior brother, their and thy.

The corresponding Dual and Plural Possessives *of the two* and *theirs* are rendered by suffixing *te,* plus *taking* and *tako,* respectively, to the Nouns in question—

Apuing,	my father	*Aputalang,*	my and thy father.	*Aputabu,*	my and your father.
		Apuingtaling,	my and his or her father	*Apuingtale,*	my and their father
Apum,	thy father.	*Apumtaben,*	the father of you two.	*Apumtape,*	your father.
Apute,	his or her father	*Aputaking,* / *Aputetaking,*	the father of the two.	*Aputako,* / *Aputetako,*	their father

The Compounds thus obtained with the Suffixes *ing, me* or *m* and *te* are very freely used with the declensional Suffixes. Thus—

Apuina orá, my father's house ; *apumá,* of thy father ; *aputeá, of his father.*

Apuingtáren dasi, my father's servant; *aqumtáren,* of thy father ; *aputetáren,* of his father.

Apuingtáte senome, go to my father ; *apumtáte,* to thy father ;

aputetare { at his father's. / with his father. }

REMARK.—The Dual and Plural, etc., forms, *aputalang,* etc., may likewise add the declenional Suffixes to the Possessive Suffixes *talang,* etc. But this is not often done. When the expressions *our father,* etc., *your father,* etc., stand in a Case different from the Nominative, Dative or Accusative, then they are generally rendered by the construction given under No. 1, viz., the Genitive of the Personal or other Pronoun is placed before the Noun, and then the Case-suffixes are added immediately to the Noun itself—

Example—

My and thy father's, *Aputalang-á;* more frequently *Alanged apua*

Our brother's servant, *Bautabutáren dasi,* more frequently *Abuá bautaren dasi.*

The same rule holds good, with a slight modification, for the formation of the Dual and Plural of the following Compounds:—

Nouns denoting family relations always take the Dual and Plural Suffixes after the Possessive Suffixes *ing, me* or *m* and *te,* but not immediately, for *te* is inserted between the Possessive Suffixes and the Suffixes *king* and *ko,*—

Example—

My two senior paternal uncles	...	*Gungu-ing-te-king.*
Thy two junior paternal uncles	...	*Kaka-m-te-king.*
His two sisters	...	*Misi-te-te-king.*
My senior brothers	...	*Bau-ing-te-ko.*
Thy junior brothers	...	*Boko-m-te-ko.*
His sisters	...	*Misi-te-te ko.*

The Dual and Plural Suffixes may, in the same manner, be taken after the Possessive Suffixes *talang, taling,* etc., etc., but in this case the construction given under No. 1 is more frequent—

Example—

My two senior brothers,—*Bau-ing-tale-ta-king* ; oftener *aleá bau-te-king.*

Your two junior brothers,—*Boko-m-tape-ta-king ;* oftener *apeáboko-te-king.*

Their sisters, { *misi-te-ko-ta-ko ;* oftener *akoa misi-teko* / *misi-te-teko;* or *akoa misi-te-te-ko.* }

N.B.-(1) In the Compounds *bau-ing-tale-ta-ko,* etc,. the inserted *te* is very often changed into *ta,* as in the examples given above.

(2) Nouns denoting family relations always insert *te* before the Dual and Plural Suffixes. Thus fathers, *apu-te-ko ;* mothers, *enga-te-ko ;* sisters, *misi-t-ko.*

The above Dual and Plural compounds, in which the Singular Possessive Suffixes *ing, me (m)* and *te* occur, always take the Case-suffixes ; whereas those in which the Dual and Plural Possessive Suffixes occur do so less frequently—

Example—

Gunguingteking-á orá	...	The house of my two senior uncles.
Kakamteking-táren dasiko	...	The servants of thy two junior uncles.
Misiteteko-ren korako	...	The husbands of his sisters.
Misiteteko-renko	...	

The Compounds *taing, tam, tae, talang, taling,* etc., may also be prefixed to the Noun denoting the object possessed.

Nea *tam* lijá ? Is this *thy* cloth? Ad'janae *taing* urí,—I lost *my* bullock. Idiked'koaks *taben* meromko,—They took away the goats *belonging to you two.*

This very remarkable transposition is not used as frequently as the forms where the Possessives *taing, tam,* etc., stands as Suffixes.

The *ta* of these Possessive Suffixes or Prefixes is no doubt the same as the *tá* in the Compound Possessive Suffixes *táren* and the Postposition *tá,* which, as shown above, is probably a compound of *ta* plus *á.* Hence *taing* wound literally mean *to me,* or *that which is to me, that which belongs to me.*

To judge from analogy, the Possessive Suffix *te, his* or *hers,* must originally have been a Pronominal Demonstrative equivalent to the 1. b. form í, *he* or *she,* or perhaps it was a Pronoun used both impersonally and personally. If it be admissible, as conjectured above, that the Impersonal Pronoun *á, it,* has been transferred to the function of a Locative denoting *to,* it may be supposed on the same grounds that the original Pronoun *te (he, she* and *it)* has been transferred to the same function, and that consequently the Locative Postposition *te, to,* is identically the same root as the Possessive Suffix *te.* The existence of the Impersonal and Personal forms *á* and *í* would naturally lead to the exclusive use of *te* in its *locative* function except in such original forms as the Possessives enumerated above.

In Yakuti *ta, tä* occurs as *Possessive* Suffix of the 3rd Person Singular, but not as *Subjective* Affix.

Possessive

1. Possessive Pronominal Compounds are obtained from Personal,
Demonstrative *ní, nea* for the Singular, and

Ist Person **SINGU**

LIVING BEINGS—	*Aiñá-ní*	mine	...	...
INANIM. OBJECTS—	*Aiñá-nea,* mine	...	...	

2nd Person

LIVING BEINGS—	*Amá-ní*	thine	...	...
INANIM. OBJECTS—	*Amá-nea,*			

3rd Persons

LIVING BEINGS—	*Aeá-ní,*	his or hers -- --
INANIM. OBJECTS—	*Aeá-ní*	

Demonstrativ

LIVING BEINGS—	*Niá-ní*	the one belonging to this one.
INANIM. OBJECTS—	*Niá-nea,*	
LIVING BEINGS—	*Iniáni,*	the one belonging to that one.
INANIM. OBJECTS—	*Inianea,*	
LIVING BEINGS—	*Haniá-ní*	the one belonging to that one yonder.
INANIM. OBJECTS—	*Haniá-nea,*	

Interrogative and

LIVING BEINGS—	*Okoiá-ní ?*	whose one
INANIM. OBJECTS—	*Okoiá-nea ?*	

LIVING BEINGS—	*Chilekaniá-ní ?*	...
INANIM. OBJECTS—	*Chilekaniá-nea ?*	...
LIVING BEINGS—	*Chikaniá-ní ?*	...
INANIM. OBJECTS—	*Chikania-nea ?*	...
LIVING BEINGS—	*Jetaiá-ní*	...
INANIM. OBJECTS—	*Jetaiá-nea*	...

Du

Aiñá-king, my two ones.	*Alangáking*	...
	Alingáking	...
Amá-king, thy two.	*Abená-king*	...
Aeá-king, his or her two.	*Akingá-king*	...
Niá-king, the two of this one	*Nikingá-king*	...
Iniá-king, the two of that one.	*Inkingá-king*	...
Hania-king, the two of that one yonder.	*Hankingá-king*	...
Okoiá-king ? whose two ?	*Okokingá-king*	...
Jetaiá-king, or	*Janjetaiá-king*	...

PLU

Aiñá-ko, mine	*Alangá-ko*	...
	Alingá-ko	...
&c. &c.,		
	Chilekaniáko ?	...
	Chilekankingáko ?	...
	Chilekankoáko ?	...
	Chikaniáko ?	...
	Jetaiá-ko ?	

Pronouns.

Demonstrative, and Interrogative Pronouns by suffixing to them the *king* and *ko* for the Dual and Plural—

LAR.

Alangá-ní	mine and thine	*Abuá-ní*	mine and yours
Alingá-ní	mine and his or hers.	*Aleá-ní*	mine and theirs.
Alangá-nea.	mine and thine.	*Abuá-nea,*	mine and yours.
Alingá-nea,	mine and his or hers.	*Aleá-nea,*	mine and theirs.
Abená-ní, / *Abená-nea,*	the one which belongs to you two.	*Apeá-ní,* / *Apeá-nea,*	yours.
Akingá-ní / *Akingá-nea,*	the one which belongs to the two	*Akoá-ní,* / *Akoá-nea,*	theirs.

Compounds.

Nikingá-ní / *Nikingá-nea,*	the one belonging to these two.	*Nikuá-ní* / *Nikuá-nea,*	the one belonging to these ones.
Indingá ní, / *Inkingá-nea,*	the one belonging to those two.	*Induá-ní* / *Inkuá-nea,*	the one belonging to those.
Hankingá-ní / *Hankingá-nea,*	the one belonging to those two yonder.	*Hankoá-ní,* / *Hankoá-nea,*	the one belonging to those yonder.

Indefinite Compounds.

Okokingá-ní? / *Okokingá-nea ?*	the one of which two?	*Okokoá-ní* or *okoiokoiá-ni ?* / *Okokoá-nea* or *okoiokoiá-nea*?	the one of which one's?

the one belonging to what sort of a (man or animal) ?

the one belonging to what sort of a (thing) ?

the one belonging to what kind or class (of living beings) ?

the one belonging to what kind or class (of thing) ?

any one's at all (living beings).

any one's at all (inanim. objects).

AL.

the two belonging to thee and me.	*Abuáking,* the two belonging to you and me
the two belonging to him and me.	*Abeáking,* the two belonging to them and me.
the two belonging to you and two.	*Apeá-king,* the two belonging to you.
the two belonging to the two.	*Akoá-king,* the two belonging to them.
the two belonging to these two.	*Nikuá-king,* the two belonging to these.
the two belonging to those two.	*Inkuá-king* the two belonging to those.
the two belonging to yonder two.	*Honkoá-king,* the two belonging to yonder ones.

the two belonging to which two ? | *Okoiokoiá-king,* whose two ?
the two belonging to any one at all

RAL.

those belonging to thee and me. | *Abua-ko,* those belonging to me and you.
those belonging to him and me (her). | *Alea-ko,* those belonging to me and them.
&c.

what is the one like, whose ones you ask ?

what are the two like, which you ask ?

what are those like, whose ones you ask ?

to what class belongs the one, whose ones you ask ? etc.

those of any one at all.

2nd.—Qualitative Possessive Pronouns are derived from the above by for the Dual, and *lekako* or ekanko for the Plural, Whenever these Pro

SING

Ist Person	LIVING BEINGS ...	*Aiñánilekaí* *Aiñániklekauí,* *Aiñálekaí,* *Aiñá-lekani*	one like the one which belongs to me ; one like mine.
	INANIM. OBJECTS	*Aiñá-nealeka,* *Aiñá-leka,*	one like mine ...

DU

Ist Person	LIVING BEINGS ...	*Aiñáni-lekaking,* *Aiñáni-lekanking,*	two like mine
	LIVING BEINGS ...	*Aiñá-lekaking.* *Aiñá-lekanking,*	two like mine.
	INANIM. OBJECTS...	*Aiñánealeka* *Aiñá-leka,*	two like the one belonging to me

PLU

Ist Person	LIVING BEINGS	*Aiñánilekako,* *Aiñánilekanko,* *Aiñá-lekako,* *Aiñá-lekanko,*	(some) like my one.
	INANIM. OBJECTS	*Aiñánealeka,* *Aiñá-leka,*	those or some like my one.

suffixing to them *lekaí* or *lekaní* for the Singular, *lekaking* or *lekanking* nouns denote living beings—

ULAR.

Alangá-ní-lekaí, *Alangá-ní-lekaní,* *Alangá-lekaí,* *Alangá-lekaní,*	one like the one belonging to me and thee.	*Abuá-nilekaí,* *Abuá-nilekaní,* *Abuá-lekaí,* *Abuá-lekaní,*	one like the one belonging to me and you.
Alingá-nilekaí *Alingá-nilekaní* *Alingá-lekaí,* *Alingá-lekaní,*	one like the one belonging to me and him (her).	*Aleá-ni-lekaí* *Aleá-ni-lekaní,* *Alcá lokai,* *Aleá-lekaní,*	one like the one belonging to me and them.
Alangá-nea-leka; *Alangá-leka,*	one like the one belonging to me and thee.	*Abuá-nea-leka,* *Abuá-leka,*	one like the one belonging to me and you.
Alingá-nea-leka, *Alingá-leka,*	one like the one belonging to me and him.	*Aleá-nea-leka,* *Aleá-leka,*	one like the one belonging to me and them.

AL.

Alangánílekaking, *Alangánílekanking,* *Alangá-lekaking,* *Alangá-lekanking,*	two like the one belonging to me and thee.	*Abuání-lekaking,* *Abuání lekanking,* *Abuá-lekaking,* *Abuá-lekanking,*	two like the one belonging to me and you.
Alingánílekaking, *Alingánílekanking,* *Alingá-lekaking,* *Alingá-lekanking,*	two like the one belonging to me and him or her.	*Aleánílekaking,* *Aleánílekanking,* *Aleá-lekaking.* *Aleá-lekanking.*	two like the one belonging to me and them.
Alangánealeka, *Alangá-leka,*	two like the one belonging to me and thee.	*Abuánealeka.* *Abuá-leka,*	two like the one belonging to me and you.
Alingánealeka, *Alingá-leka,,*	two like the one belonging to me and him (her)	*Aleánealeka,* *Aleá-leka,*	two like the one belonging to me and them.

RAL.

Alangánilekako *Alangánilekanko,* *Alangá-lekako,* *Alangá-lekanko,*	those or some like the one belonging to me and thee.	*Abuánilekako,* *Abuánilekanko,* *Abuá-lekako,* *Abuá-lekanko,*	those or some like the one belonging to me and you.
Alingánilekako, *Alingánilekanko,* *Alingá-lekako,* *Alingá-lekanko,*	those or some like the one belonging to me and him or her.	*Aleánilekako,* *Aleánilekanko,* *Aleá-lekako,* *Aleá-lekanko,*	those or some like the one belonging to me and them.
Alangánealeka, *Alangá-leka,*	those or some like the one belonging to me and thee	*Abuánealeka,* *Abuá-leka,*	those or some like the one belonging to me and you.
Alinganealeka, *Alinga-leka,*	those or some like the one belonging to me and him.	*Aleánealeka,* *Aleá-leka,*	those or some like the one belonging to me and them.

Similar Compounds are obtained from the Personal Pronouns of the Second and Third Persons, as well as from Definite and Indefinite Demonstrative Pronouns and from Interrogative Pronouns—

Amánilekaí, amálekai, etc., one like thine ; *abenánilekai,* etc., one like the one belonging to you two; *akoánilekaí,* one like the one belonging toe them; *nkingánealeka,* one (inan. obj.) like the one belonging to those two ; *haniáleka king,* two like the one belonging to yonder one; *okoiálekanko namtanam ?* Like whose ones do you want ? or to the one of which one must those resemble whom you want ? *Chilekankoálekaním idia ?* What are those ones like to whom belongs the one (living being) that resembles the one you intend taking away ?

The Compounds thus obtained may be further multiplied by substituting either the Dual *king* or the Plural *ko* to the Demonstrative *ní* in the first part of the Compounds—

Example—

Aiñá-king*lekai,* one like my two ; alangá*king*lekaking, two like the two which belong to me and thee; aleá*king*lekanko, those like the two which belong to me and them. Niku*áko* lekani,—One like the ones belonging to these ones.

Nouns are very often substituted for the Demonstrative *ní* or the Personal Pronouns *king* and *ko.* The Suffixes *lekaí* or *lekaní, lekaking,* or *lekanking, lekako* or *lenkanko* remain of course.

Ex.—

Chilekan sadomem mantana ? What kind of horse dost thou want?

Amá *sadom*-lekaníing namtana,—I want one like thy horse. Instead of—

Amá-*ni*-lekaníing namtana.

Okolekan setako sukukoam? What kind of dogs are to your taste ?

Amá *setaking*-lekanko,—Those that are like your two dogs. Instead of—
amá-*king*-lekanko.

The Possessive-Adjective Suffixes are added to Transitive and Intransitive Predicates with the function of Possessive Pronouns, thus:

If the Pronominal Subject precedes the Predicate, then the Possessive Suffixes are added to the Copula.

If the Pronominal Subject be suffixed to the Copula, then the Possessive Suffixes are added to the suffixed Subject—

S. Pr. C.

Meang ko idi-a-*taing* ...
Meang ko idi-a-*tam* ...
Meang ko idi-a-*tae* ...
} After tomorrow they will take my one, thy one, his one.

S. Pr. C.

Am iditan-a-*taking* ...
Am iditan-a-*tabu* ...
Am iditan-a-*tale*
} Now thou takest the one belonging to them, to me and you, etc.

S. Pr. C.

Hola - ko idiked a- *taing* ...
Hola- ko idiked a- *tam* ...
Hola- ko idiked a- *tae* ...
} Yesterday they took mine, thine, his or hers.

Pr. D.O.C. S.

Idi- ko- a- e- *talang* ...
Idi- ko- a- e- *taling* ...
Idi- ko- a- e- *taben* ...
} He (she) will take those belonging to me and thee, to me and him or her, to you two.

Pr. D. O. Tense. C. S.

Idi- ko- tan - a- m- *tape* ...
Idi- ko- tan - a- m- *tako* ...
Idi- ko- tan - a- m- *taing* ...
} Now thou takest those belonging to you, to them, to me.

Pr. D.O. C. S.

Idiked'- ko - a- ben- *talang* ...
Idiked'-ko - a- ben- *taling* ...
Idiked'-ko - a- ben- *taking* ...
} You two took those belonging to me and thee, to me and him, to the two.

Instead of the Adjective Suffixes *taing, tam, tae,* etc., the Genitive form, *i.e.,* the corresponding Pronominal Suffixes *taiñá, tamá, taeá, talangá, talingá,* etc., may also be added to Transitive and Intransitive Predicates in the manner indicated above—

Adjana-taiñá,—My one (inanimate object) got lost. *Nirjanae-tamá,*—Thine (living being) ran away. *Idi-ko-tantaekenape-talangá,*—You were taking away those belonging to me and thee. *Hijúakanako-taleá,*—Ours have come.

ADJECTIVES

Words restricted to the function of merely qualifying Nouns can hardly be said to exist in Mundari; for most of the words which denote qualities may, without undergoing a change of form, be used as Substantives, as Adjectives, or as Verbs, *v. gr., Hence* means blackness, black and to blacken. However, the differentiation of these Qualitatives into real Nouns, Adjectives, and Verbs has begun, as the following facts will show—

1st.—Abstract Nouns may, with a certain amount of liberty, be formed by inserting the Demonstrative *n* after the first *vowel* of the Qualitative and then repeating that vowel, *v. gr., marang,* great; *ma-n-arang,* greatness.

This mode of obtaining Abstract Nouns presents no phonetic difficulties in any word, and it is certainly very simple. It is therefore both curious and characteristic that it is not used as freely by the Mundas as we might expect. Some words are thus transformed into Abstract Nouns rather freely, whereas others are never so used. Again, some individuals will occasionally have recourse to this formation in the case of certain words which other individuals will leave in their bare original form. I have several times remarked that a man very much concerned about a particular matter will use this abstract formation when speaking earnestly or anxiously about it, whereas in ordinary circumstances he himself as well as others neglects it altogether. So far, then, this formation resembles a real commodity for which there exists as yet no extensive demand.

It will be easily seen how widely this mode of evolving a vague root into a distinct Abstract Noun differs from the Aryan method.

2nd.—Bugi means to be in good health, to be well, to make well, to cure, to be good. *Et'ka* means, to spoil, to be bad, to treat badly, to ill use. These two words can no longer be used as Adjectives to qualify Nouns. To use them with that function, the Demonstrative *n (this)* must be suffixed : thus a good horse, *bugi*-n *sadom ; literally,* good-*this* horse. A bad man, *et'ka*-n *horo ; literally,* bad-*this* man.

REMARK.—When the adjectives *bugin and et'kan* stand as Predicates, the Suffix *n* is dropped before the enclytic ge, *v. gr.,* —This horse is good, *Ne sedom bugin-áe,* or *ne sadom bugigeae.* This man is bad,—*Ne horo et'kanae* or *ne horo et'kageáe.*

The only other formations bearing any analogy to the above are the *exceptional* Demonstrative Adjectives quoted above (page 64) where the Personal and Impersonal Suffixes *i* and *a* are added to the ordinary Demonstrative Adjectives *ne, en, han : ní horo,* this man ; *literally,* this-*he* man instead of *ne horo. Hana buru,* yonder mountain ; *literally,* yonder-*it* mountain instead of *han buru.*

This manner of evolving a distinct Adjective out of the vague original forms *bugi, et'ka, ne,en han* is analogous to the Aryan method of forming Adjectives.

The two methods just described yields, for the generic ideas of goodness and badness, the following real Parts of Speech :—

Verb ...	*Bugi* ...	to be well, to be good, to make well.
Adjective ...	*Bugin* ...	well (in good health), good.
Noun ...	*Bun-ugi* ...	goodness.
Verb ...	*Et'ka* ...	to be bad, to spoil, to treat badly.
Adjective ...	*Et'kan* ...	bad.
Noun ...	*enet'ka* ...	would be the form for *badness*, but I never heard it used by any Munda.

3rd.—A somewhat more extensive mode of forming real Adjectives consists in adding the Possessive Suffix *an* to words denoting animate or inanimate beings as well as qualities. These compounds are entirely restricted to the Adjective function. They denote possession—

Senran wisdom, discretion, to have attained the use of reason, to be wise, to have recourse to such or such an expedient, to excogitate something—*senran-an* wise. *Taka,* a rupee, money ; *taka-an horo,* a monied man. *Merom,* a goat ; *merom-an horo,* a man possessed of goats, a man who possesses many goats.,

4th.—The very same ideas may be expressed adjectively by means of circumlocution containing the words *mená,* to have, and *banó,* not to have.

5th.—Many equivalents of our Adjectives are Perfect Participial forms, viz., the bare root-form *plus* the Perfect Tense-suffix *akan.* They are therefore analogous to such English Adjectives as *pointed, wounded,* etc.

Goja, a point, to point ; *goja-akan* sota, a pointed stick; *gau,* wound, to wound; *gau-akan* silib, a wounded deer ; *ol,* a scratch, a crack, a mark, to scratch, to crack, to mark, to write; *ol-akan chatu,* a cracked waterpot.

A certain number of words denoting qualities are used adjectively with as well as without the Perfect Participial Suffix—

Leser, to sharpen ; *leser katu* or *leserakean katu,* a sharp knife.

The Perfect Tense-suffix, however, may not be added indiscriminately to any word denoting quality. It is restricted to those cases in which the quality is known as the result of some work performed. It can therefore not be used to denote those natural qualities which are in no way the result of human skill or labour : thus *hende seta* means a black dog; *hendeakan seta* would imply that a dog of some other colour had been blackened artificially.

The Instrumental Suffix *te,* added to the Indeterminate Tense-forms *mená* and *banó* yields *menáte, banóte.* These forms are then transformed into real Adjectives by means of the Demonstrative Suffix *n, menáten* and *bonóten,* v. gr., *Taka menaten horo,*— A man who has money,or a monied man. *Peoe banoten sadom,*—A horse which has no defect, or a perfectly sound horse. Strictly speaking, Mundari did not stand in need of this formation ; for the bare Indeterminate Tense-forms used participally express the idea perfectly: *Taka mená horo,*—The man who has money. *Poé banó sadom,*—A horse which has no defect. The Simple Participles are used as frequently at least as the Compounds *menáten* and *banóten.* The latter are therefore chiefly interesting as indicating a tendency towards the evolution of Parts of Speech. In meaning *menáten* and *banóten* resemble the phrases *provided with, versehen mit, pourvu de* and their contraries ; but etymologically they differ widely from them.

DEGREES OF COMPARISON

The formation of the *Comparative Degree* differs from that which obtains in European languages. It is analogous to the corresponding Hindustani formation. The *Adjective* or *Qualitative* denoting the excess takes no Suffix. The Noun or Pronoun denoting the term of comparison takes the Ablativer Suffix, *ete.* Hence the sentence, *the elephant is bigger than the horse,* is rendered literally thus—From the horse the elephant is greater,—*Sadmoete hati marangae*. I saw a beast bigger than a leopard,—*Sonchitáete marang jontuing lelnamlia.*

The Superlative Degree has a double formation—

1st.—When it is desired to state the absolute excess of one or more particular beings over all the beings of the same species or genus, the Adjective *soben,* all, is placed before the term of comparison which stands in the *Ablative Case.* The Adjective remains unchanged, *v. gr.*, the elephant is the biggest animal,—*Soben jontukoete hati maranggeáe; literally,* from all animals the elephant is big or, among all animals, etc.

2nd.—Such Superlatives as are in English expressed by *very, exceedingly* are in Mundari rendered in two ways, viz.—

(*a*) by affixing *uter, utterly, exceedingly* to the Qualificative, *v. gr.*, *marang,* great; *maranguter,* very great;

(*b*) by placing before the Qualitative one of the words : *isu, purá, isupurá, kented', mermer, betekan.*

Isu may be used with any kind of Qualitatives, just like the English *very*—*Isu bugin horo,* a very good man ; *isu marang daru,* a very big tree. *Purá* is by preferences used with *Quantitatives. Kented'* is used with Qualitatives denoting energy, power or violence. *Mer mer* is used with Qualitatives denoting qualities disagreeable to taste and smell, *v. gr.*, mer mer haradá. It is exceedingly bitter. *Betekan,* although evidently the Hindi word *betekan,* is in Mundari pronounced *betekan,* and is synonymous with *isu, purá,* and *isupurá. Isupurá* is but an intensive form for *purá* and for *isu.* The Superlatives in *uter* seem to have been borrowed from the Sanskrit.

3rd.—Qualitatives denoting *dimensions* form their Superlatives by infixing the Consonant *p* after the first vowel and then repeating that vowel, *v. gr., narang,* great ; *ma-p-arang,* very great ; *jiling,* long ; *ji*-p-*iling,* very long; *moto,* thick ; *mo-p-oto,* very thick.

This distinctly un-Aryan formation may be supposed to have applied formerly to all Qualitatives. Here, as on several other points, the Burjatic dialects offer a striking analogy with Mundari ; for in them too the Superlative is formed by the insertion of *p* between the first vowel and its reduplication. The only difference being that they repeat the whole first syllable, *v. gr., Sagan, sa-p-sagan ;* whereas the Mundas repeat only the first vowel after the *p.*

EQUIVALENTS OF CONJUGATIONAL FORMS

As stated in the Introduction, every Mundari word, no matter what its primary meaning or function may be, can be used to denote a state or action as referred to a Subject and thus become a functional equivalent of an Organic Verb.

The Organic *Infinitive Mood* has either a characteristic desinence or auxiliary Preposition of its own, *v. gr.*, ambula-*re,* all-*er,* geh-*en,* to go.

The Mundari Infinitive is never characterized by any Suffix or Prefix ; it is always the bare root or the bare word-form—

Buru, a mountain : hence also ... (1) to heap up ; (2) to keep up certain feasts or to hold a fair (because they take place on mountains) ; (3) to call something a mountain.

Soje, straight : hence also ... (1) to straighten something ; (2) to go on straight ; (3) to call something straight.

Gapa, to-morrow ... (1) to put off to the next day, procrastinate; to express by means of the word *gapa.*

He *!* Yes ! hence also ... (1) to answer in the affirmative ; (2) to agree to something; (3) to grant some- thing to some one.

Hokaeabu ! Let us cease : hence also to express by means of the word *hokaeabu.*

Sim, a fowl : hence also ... (1) to acquire a fowl ; (2) to kill a fowl for one's meal ; (3) to call something or some one a fowl.

The Mundari Transitive or Intransitive Predicate differs very widely from the Organic Verb both in its material structure as well as in its functional capacity.

STRUCTURAL AND PHONETIC DIFFERENCES

In the Organic Verb as well as in its Mundari equivalent we distinguish between the *primary* and the *formative* elements.

The primary element is that part which directly denotes the state or action.

It is generally called the *predicative* or the *attributive root.* This may in itself be simple or compound, *v. gr.,* in *go* and *forego.* If compound, it may consist either of two originally predicative roots or of a predicative and a demonstrative root, or even of two originally demonstrative roots which by their conjunction acquired a predicative or attributive meaning.

The formative elements comprise (1) all those roots or remnants of roots which have been added (prefixed, infixed or suffixed) to the primary element for the purpose of connoting Voice, Mood, and Tense ; (2) the Personal Pronominal Subjects. These formative elements are generally *demonstrative roots.*

I.—Difference between the Primary elements

Reduplication of the first syllable is used in Mundari as well as in Organic languages, chiefly to form Frequentatives or Intensives—

1st.—In Organic Verbs reduplication is frequently accompanied with phonetic changes, *v. gr., fengw pefnga ; do, dedi.* These changes may become very considerable, *cfr.,* the German languages where reduplication has caused the so-called apophony (Umlaut), *v. gr., halten, to hold ; hielt, held,* from a former reduplicated form, *hialt.*

In Mundari reduplication never causes any phonetic change in the syllable reduplicated, *v. gr., dal,* to strike ; *dadal,* to strike repeatedly.

2nd.—In Organic Verbs the reduplicated syllable has assumed the function of a purely formative element. It is used extensively to denote the *Perfect Tense,* as in the above Greek and Lativc examples, or the *Past,* as in German and English.

In Mundari reduplication is strictly reserved to modify the meaning of the primary or attribute element. It can never serve to connote either Voice, Mood or Tense.

3rd.—In Organic Verbs the primary element is liable to phonetic changes even when there is no reduplication. To quote but two examples—(1) Strengthened and nasalized roots are weakened down to their originalform when the Augment attracts the tonic accent, *v. gr., fengw, efngon; lambánw elabon* (2) strong vowels descend the tonic scale before heavy accentuated syllables, *v. gr., émi,* I go ; *imás,* thou goest.

In Mundari the primary root remains perfectly unaltered through all the Voices, Moods, and Tenses, *v. gr.,* dal-*eaing,* I will strike ; dal-*tanaing,* I am striking now ; dal-*kedaing,* I struck; dal-*entanaing,* I strike myself; *dal-óaing*, I will be struck.

II.—Differences between those formative elements which connote Voice, Mood, and Tense.

1st.—In Organic Verbs the formative elements are of three specifically distinct kinds, viz. (1) reduplication of the predicative or primary root; (2) auxiliary words which are traced back (*a*) to an original Substantive Verb, meaning *to be ; (b)* to original Verb, probably meaning *to will*, *to desire*; (3) purely demonstrative roots. These may be (*a*) *Prefixes* as some Augments ; (*b*) *Suffixes, i.e.,* those which may be traced back to original Pronouns.

In Mundari all the formative elements connoting Voice, Mood, and Tense are *Suffixes,* and all of them are purely demonstrative roots, with the exception of the generic Imperfect Tense-suffix *taeken,* which is added to the ordinary Tense-suffixes.

2nd.—In Organic Verbs these formative elements hāve, so to say, no porotection against phonetic decay : hence the need felt in modern languages to replace them by independent Auxiliaries, *v. gr.*, in English , *to have, to be, to will* and *may.*

In Mundari these elements are comparatively safe : hence independent Auxiliary Verbs do not exist. The whole work of denoting Voice, Mood, and Tense is done by means of demonstrative Suffixes to the primary root.

III.—Differences regarding the Pronominal Subjects

1st.—In Organic languages the Pronominal Subjects have a fixed place : they are always Suffixes and have grown into the Verb-form to such an extent that they have dwindled down to mere desinences, having no longer a trace of meaning if considered by themselves along. So severely have they been multilated that even a desinence denoting the same Number and Person is not always identical in form through several Tenses, *cfr.*, audio, audiebam, audivi. Nevertheless, philology traces all of them back to a few original Pronouns : the Nominative theme—*aḥa;* the Oblique Case-theme *ma;* the themes *twa* and *ta,* and the Reflexives *sma* and *swa,* variously combined, with occasional strengthenings. and vowel insertions or Demonstratives. Hence the need felt in Organic languages of having recourse to a separate set of current Personal Pronouns for use independently of Verbs. As this decay was carried on further and further, the modern Aryan languages had to use these current forms even in connection with Verbs, although traces of the Subjective Affixes be still existing here and there.

In Mundari the Pronominal Subjects to Transitive and Intransitive Predicates are still the current Pronouns of the language. In no sense can they be said to have grown into the Predicates. They are not even restricted to one particular position; with regad to these Predicates as shown in the Chapter on Personal Pronouns (pages 66 and 67).

2nd.—In those Aryan languages which have resumed the current Personal Pronouns in connection with Verbs, these Pronouns may be replaced by Nouns or other Pronouns, *v. gr., He* came. *The king* came.

In Mundari the Pronominal Subjects must always remain in immediate contact with Transitive and Intransitive Predicates, even though the Subject be denoted already by a Noun or by another Pronoun—*Hijúlena-e, he comes. Raja-e hijúlena* or *raja hijúlena-e.* The omission of the Pronominal Subjects in these cases would be, so to say, a barbarism in Mundari.

Raja hijútana is quite as faulty in Mundari as the sentence *the king come* is in English. (The reason of this has been explained in the Introduction, from page 38 to 39)

IV.—Differences regarding the number of formative elements

1st.—The Mundari Transitive and Intransitive Predicates are always connected with the Subjects by means of the Copula *á* (*a*). This *a* has *a* fixed place in thePredicate : it is suffixed to the Root *plus* Voice, Mood, and Tense-suffixes. It occupies in fact that place which the Pronominal Subjective desinences occupy in Organic Verbs : hence we must consider it as one of the formative elements.

Organic Verbs have no Copula. They add the Personal Pronominal desinences directly to the complete Predicate, *i.e.,* the Root *plus* Voice, Mood, and Tense-desinences.

2nd.—In Mundari Direct and Indirect Pronominal Objects are an essentially formative element of Transitive and Intransitive Predicates. When the Objects denote living beings, Personal Pronouns *must* be inserted into the Predicates. Whenever no Pronoun is inserted it is understood that the Predicate either connotes an Inanimate Objects or that it denotes a realized possibility. Thus *Lel-ko-tanaing,* I see them ; *Leltanaing,* either I see *it* or *them* (them objects) or, I *can* see.

In Organic languages Direct and Indirect Objects are quite distinct from the Verbs. They are in no sense formative elements.

3rd.—Every Mundari Transitive or *Intransitive Predicate* is referred to its Subjects by means of a link-word, viz., the Copula *á* (*a*). This Copula remains absolutely unchanged through all Voices, Moods, Tenses, Numbers, and Persons.

Organic Verbs always add the Pronominal Subjects directly to the Tense-form without a link-word. It is only in the more modern Aryan languages that link-words are used in certain Tenses, *v. gr.,* he *is* coming. But, then, that link-word is itself treated as a Verb and it adds the Pronominal Suffixes to the roots, *cfr., am, art, is, are.*

From what has been said so far, we see that every Tense of a Mundari Transitive or Intransitive Predicate constitutes a ground-form or scheme, in which not only the primary or predicative root, but also all the formative elements connoting Voice, Mood, and Tense remain unchanged through all Numbers and Persons. The Pronominal Subjects and Objects alone change.

Again, the formative elements of Voice, Mood, and Tense, so far as these are denoted by a special Suffix, have their places perfectly fixed in the compound. The Voice-sign stands first, the Mood-sign second, and the Tense-sign third, the Copula fourth : hence if we denote the Root or primary element by *R,* the Voice by *V,* the Mood by *M,* the Tense by *T,* and the Copula by *C,* we obtain for all actual Predicates the following general formula $R + V + M + T + C$.

Of the formative functions, there are only four which are never denoted by a special Suffix, viz., (*1st*) the Active Voice (*2nd*) the Indicative Mood, (*3rd)* the Imperative Mood, (*4th)* the Future and the Indeterminate Tenses (these two being identical in form).

If, therefore, the student has learnt by heart all the existing Voice, Mood, and Tense-suffixes and remembers where to affix or to insert the required Pronominal Subjects and Objects, his memory lesson is finished for these Pronominal Subjects and Objects remain the same through all Voices, Moods, and Tenses for the same Person; thus, ko is both Subject and Direct Object in all Tenses.

By way of illustration I shall give here *in extenso* two Tenses— the Definite Present of the Active Voice and the Definite Present of the Passive Voice. In the Passive of course Direct and Indirect Objectds are not inserted. To avoid the insertion of an explicit Object in the Active forms, I shall give that Tense as implying an inanimate Direct Object. Since the Active Voice and the Indicative Mood have no special Suffixes of their own, the columns under *V* and *M* remain blank in the first scheme and the column under *M* remains blank in the second—

R.	*V.*	*M.*	*T.*	*C.*	*S.*		
dal-	...	...	*tan-*	*a-*	*ing,*	I beat it now.	
dal-	...	...	*tan-*	*a-*	*m,*	thou beats it now.	
dal-	...	...	*tan-*	*a-*	*e,*	he (she) beats it now.	
dal-	...	...	*tan-*	*a-*	...	it beats it now	
dal-	...	...	*tan-*	*a-*	*lang,*	thou and I	beat it now.
dal-	...	...	*tan-*	*a-*	*ling,*	he (she) and I	
dal-	...	...	*tan-*	*a-*	*ben,*	you two	
dal-	...	...	*tan-*	*a-*	*king,*	both of them	
dal-	...	...	*tan-*	*a-*	*bu,*	you and I	
dal-	...	...	*tan-*	*a-*	*le,*	they and I	
dal-	...	...	*tan-*	*a-*	*pe,*	you	
dal-	...	...	*tan-*	*a-*	*ko,*	they	

R.	*V.*	*M.*	*T.*	*C.*	*S.*		
dal-	*ó-*	...	*tan-*	*a-*	*ing,*	I am being beaten now.	
dal-	*ó-*	...	*tan-*	*a-*	*m,*	thou art being beaten now.	
dal-	*ó-*	...	*tan-*	*a-*	*e,*	he (she) is being beaten now.	
dal-	*ó-*	...	*tan-*	*a-*	...	it is being beaten now.	
dal-	*ó-*	...	*tan-*	*a-*	*lang,*	thou and I	are being beaten now.
dal-	*ó-*	...	*tan-*	*a-*	*ling,*	he (she) and I	
dal-	*ó-*	...	*tan-*	*a-*	*ben*	you two	
dal-	*ó-*	...	*tan-*	*a-*	*king,*	both of them	
dal-	*ó-*	...	*tan-*	*a-*	*bu,*	you and I	
dal-	*ó-*	...	*tan-*	*a-*	*lo,*	they and I	
dal-	*ó-*	...	*tan-*	*a-*	*pe,*	you	
dal-	*ó-*	...	*tan-*	*a-*	*ko,*	they	

Such a scheme is not hard to get by heart, but to correctly place the Pronominal Subjects and Objects as rapidly as conversation requires is immensely difficult for a foreigner. The difficulty is increased by the fact that the Pronominal Objects have two different position in different Tenses, and the Pronominal Subjects may have three different positions as shown in the Chapter on Personal Pronouns.

In the Definite Present and the Definite Imperfect the Objects stand immediately *before the Tense-suffix.* In all other Tenses they stand *immediately after the Tense-suffix.* In the Imperfect Tenses they stand between the particular Tense-suffix and the Auxiliary Imperfect word *taeken.*

The Subjects too stand between the particular Tense-suffixes and the Auxiliary *taeken* in the Imperfect Tenses ; but they are placed after the Objects. Thus, I was seeing them,—*Lel-jád*-ko *(O.) ing (S.) taekena.*

In all the other Tenses the Subjects are affixed to the word which immediately precedes the Predicate. If no word precedes, then they are suffixed to the Copula: hence, if we represent the Objects by *O*, the Subjects by S, and the Imperfect Tense-signs by T_1 and T_2 (the Auxiliary taeken*)*, we obtain the following schemes :—

Definite Present ... { R + V + M + O + T + C + S or
—S R + V + M + O + T + C.

Other Tenses ... { R + V + M + T + O + C + S
—S R+ V + M + T + O + C.

The insertion of the Subjects between the principal Tense-suffix and the Auxiliary *taeken,* although so frequent as almost to constitute a general rule, is nevertheless not a necessity. They may be suffixed also to the word preceding the Predicate or to the Copula : hene each Imperfect is represented by a triple scheme—

Definite Imperfect { R+ V + M + O_1 + T_1 + S + T_2 + C or
R + V + M + O + T_1 + T_2 + C + S or
— S R+ V + M + O + T_1 + T_2 + C

Other Imperfects { R + V + M + T_1 + O + S + T_2 + C or
R + V + M + T_1 + O + T_2 + C + S or
—S R + V + M + T_1 + O + T_2 + C.

In Organic Conjugation we have a real combination or blending of primary and formative elements into a new word.

In Mundari, as the above schemes show, there is a mere agglutination of the primary and formative element into a *loose compound.* The main tie keeping these elements together is their *pronunciation* as one word.

This structural difference between Organic Verbs and Mundari Transitive or Intransitive Predicates produces another, viz., *a functional* difference between them.This functioanl difference must appear even more striking to an Aryan mind, because it leads to methods of thought-rendering that have no analogy in Aryan words or propositions.

Functional differences between Organic and Mundari Tense-forms.

The term *bare Tense-form* is here used to denote that part of any Transitive or Intransitibe Predicate which denotes an action or state together with the circumstances of Voice, Mood, and Tense; hence it contains the primary root *plus* all those secondary elements which connote Voice, Mood, and Tense. Now, if this be applied to *Organic Verbs*, we find that they have only two parts, viz., (*1st*) the bare Tenseform, *(2nd)* the Pronominal Subjects ; for here, with the exception of the Pronominal Subjects, every change in, or addition to, the primary root has been made to serve the purpose of connoting either Voice, or Mood, or Tense. But in the Mundari equivalents we find *three parts,* viz. (1st) the bare Tense-form ; (2nd) the invariable *á* or á, which never connotes Voice, Mood, or Tense ; (3rd) the Pronominal Subject.

By way of illustration compare the following Tenses of the Verb *to give* in Greek, English, and Mundari :—

1. b. T. fr.	*2, Pr, S.*	*1. Pr. S.*	*2. b. T. fr.*	*1. b. T. fr.*	*2.*	*3. Pr. S.*
d*í*dwm	-μ*i*	I	give.	*omjad*	*-a-*	*ing.*
		I	am giving.	*omtan*	*-a-*	*ing.*
dws	-w	I	shall give.	*om*	*-a-*	*ing.*
edídw	-*v*	I	gave.	*omjad'taeken*	*-a-*	*ing.*
				omtantaeken	*-a-*	*ing.*
dedwk	*-a-*	I	have given	*omajad*	*-a-*	*ing.*

I. The bare Organic Tense-forms cease to have any current meaning as soon as they are severed from the Personal Pronominal Subjects. Thus the sounds d*í*dw, dws, ed*í*dw, and dedwk convey no meaning to the ordinary mind, no more do the English forms, *will give, gave,* etc. a defaced coin may still have the required weight, and will be accepted by a goldsmith and paid for according to the amount of precious metal it contains; but it is powerless as a buying agent in the general market : it is out of currency. Similarly, a bare Organic Tense-form will be recognized by the philologist as pregnant with meaning; but that meaning is, to the ordinary eye, quite latent. The form has no currency as a medium of exchange in the market of ideas.

In Mundari, on the contrary, the bare Tense-form is not something incomplete, requiring the addition; of a new element to give it currency. Thus the forms *omtan, omjad, om, omakad* are all, by themselves alone, so many complete and perfectly intelligible Mundari words—

(1) Any such bare Tense-form is primarily *an Abstract Noun* denoting the action together with all the circumstances of Voice Mood, and Tense.

When they perform the function of Nouns, these Tense-forms may of course take all those Postpositions of Case, Time, and Space which any ordinary Noun may take—

Olked denotes *a past act of writing : rá* is a Genitive Suffix denoting price.

Olked-rá gonong,—The price paid for a piece of writing done in the past.

Ol, besides denoting the act of writing in general, is also a Future, and thus signifies a piece of writing to be done in the future : hence—

Ol-rá gonong,—The price paid for a promised or future act of writing.

Ola' is the Indeterminate and Future Passive : hence it denotes the act of being written, *i.e.,* of having one's name written down or registered.

Oló-rá hukum,—The order of having one's name registered.

(2) The bare Mundari Tense-forms are Adjectives. As such, of course, they must be followed by a Noun; but, like the ordinary Adjectives, they never take suffixes indicative of Gender or Number, *v. gr.*—

Olked' hoṛo,—The man who wrote something.

Ol hoṛo,—A man whose ordinary occupation is writing, or a man who is about to write something.

These forms remain adjectives still, even when Direct or Indirect Pronominal Objects are inserted into them—

Olked'-ko hoṛo,—The man who wrote *them* down, *i.e.,* who registered their names.

Ol-aing dasi,—The servant who is generally writing for me, or theservant who is about to write *to me.*

(3) Instead of qualifying a Noun, these bare Tense-forms may qualify a Pronoun of *the Third Person ;* but such Pronouns are always suffixed to the Tense-form; hence a Compound Noun is obtained. These Nouns are Nouns of Agency in the wider sense. They denote an Agent or a Sufferer according to the Voice of the form. Direct and Indirect Objects may be inserted into these Nouns just as into the Adjectives described under (2)—

Olked-i,—The one who wrote ; *olked'king,*—The two who wrote ; *olked'-ko,*—Those who wrote.

Olked'ko-ni,—The one who wrote them; *olked'ko-king,*—The two who wrote them ; *olked'koko,*—Those who wrote them.

(4) The bare Tense-forms considered as Nouns may take the Instrumental Suffix *teá,* and thus they yield Nouns of Instrumentality. These Nouns express *nuances* that cannot be expressed in English, except by rather long circumlocutions—

Ol-teá, writing materials, *i.e.,* pencils, pens, ink, and paper or slate.

Olken is the Simple Past of the Passive or the Intransitive Active Voice.

Ne chiti olken-tea,—The particular pen (and ink) with which this letter was written.

(5) The bare Tense-forms may take the Impersonal Pronoun *á*as Suffix. A euphonic *e* often precedes this *á.* This yields Concrete Nouns of two kinds, viz.—

(*a*) Nouns denoting the result of an action :—

Olked'á,—That *which some one has* written.

Olo-á,—That which is about to be written.

(*b*) Nouns denoting the material on which a certain action is to fall :—

Jom, to eat; *jom e-á,* that which is eaten, eatables, food; *her,* to sow ; *here-á,* that which is sown, viz., the grain, but in the Passive *hero-á,* that which is sown with the grain, viz., land, fields.

Thus a man may say : *Hero-á do mena mendo hereá banoa,*—I have fields, but no seeds.

II. The moment a bare Organic Tense-form is brought into contact with a Personal Pronominal desinence, or (in the case of modern languages) with a current Personal Pronoun, its latent meaning is brought out clearly ; it becomes a perfectly intelligible word. But this word performs one function only—it is *a Verb.*

It cannot denote a state or action abstractly, but it must denote it as actually referred to this or that particular Subject or Agent.

Here attention is drawn to the fact that *reference* of the action to the agent is not *expressed.* There is nowhere a distinct word denotative of reference, nor is there even a remnant or trace of such a word. A real link-word or Copula, then, does not exist between the Transitive Predicate and its Subjects. Language uses mere juxtaposition of the word denoting a state or action (the bare Tense-form) and the word denoting the agent (the Personal Pronoun either in; full or as a desinence) and leaves to the mind the task of referring the one to the other.

Thus, then, what the coinage does for the precious metals, the Personal Pronouns do for the bare Organic Tense-forms, inasmuch as they give currency to word-forms which would be meaningless without them. In this sense the Personal Pronouns, whether in their full or multilated forms, enter as essentially constituent elements into the formation of Organic Transitive or Intransitive Predicates.

With the bare Mundari Tense-form the case is very different. Being by itself alone a current word with both Substantive and Adjective functions, it may take certain Suffixes to vary and multiply those functions, but it refuses direct contact with the Personal Pronominal Subjects. Were such a Pronominal Subject brought into direct contact with a bare Tense-form, that form would immediately lose all its current functions, and yet would not become a Transitive or Intransitive Predicate. It would simply be destroyed as a current word. The forms *omtan-ing, omjad-line, om-le* are not propositions like the corresponding *, *: they are simply meaningless. Hence the bare Mundari Tense-form is not like the bare Organic Tense-form, a readymade Transitive or Intransitive Predicate, requiring only contact with a Personal Pronominal Subject to give it actuality and currency as such. In other words, it is not a *functional equivalent* of the bare Organic Tense-form.

What, then, is required to turn a bare Mundari Tense-form into a Transitive or an Intransitive Predicate ?—The mere addition of the vowel *a.* The moment this *a* is suffixed, the bare Mundari Tense-form loses all its Substantive and Adjective functions and becomes a perfect functional equivalent of the bare Organic Tense-form. Thus, functionally—

omtan-a = *δίδωμι,* give ; *om-a* = *δωσ,* will give.

omakad-a = *δεδωκ,.* have given.

Like *dídwm*, *dws*, and *dedwk*, the forms *omtana, oma,* and *omakada* have no current meaning by themselves alone. Though they now have all that which on their part is required to be Transitive or Intransitive Predicates, they have not yet currency as such. Like their Organic equivalents, *dídwm*, *dws*, and *dedwk*, they now require a complement ; and this complement is the Personal Pronoun, and that Pronoun only.

Here, too, therefore the Personal Pronoun is that which gives the final touch to the Transitive or Intransitive Predicate : it is, so to say, the coinage which gives it currency—

Omtana-ing = *δίδω-μi,*—I give.
Omtana-m = *δiδω,–σ*,—thou give-st.
Omtana c – *δiδω–σ,*—he give-s.
Omtana-bu } = *δiδo–μεv,*— { You and I give.
Omtana-le } { they and I give.
Omtana-pe = *δiδo–τe,*—you give.
Omtana-ko = *δiδo–aσι,*—they give.

Whereas in Greek and other ancient Aryan languages the very place of the Pronominal Subjects is unalterably fixed, the Mundari Subjects are bound only by the law of *immediate proximity* to the Transitive and Intransitive Predicates: hence the Mundari Pronominal Subjects may, as already stated, be suffixed either to the Predicate or to the word immediately preceding the Predicate : it may even, in the case of Imperfect Tenses, be infixed into the Predicate.

The *Simple* Personal Pronouns may also be replaced by the corresponding Emphatic compounds. These compounds must precede the Predicate—

Aing omtana, I give ; *am omtana,* thou givest ; *ae omtana,* he or she gives, etc.

The reason of this greater liberty of the Mundari Pronominal Subjects seems to lie solely in the fact that these Subjects are at the same time still the current Personal Pronouns of the language.

In English, where the Pronominal desinences have been lost except in the Second andThird Persons Singular, the current Personal Pronouns have been resumed for conjugational purposes.

Though they must, as a rule, precede the Predicate, they enjoy a privilege which even the Mundari Pronominal Subjects never have; for (a) they may in certain cases be separated from the Predicate by intervening words, *v. gr., I* always give ; (b) they may be left out altogether in the Third Person Singular and Plural, provided the proposition have a Noun or some Demonstrative Pronoun as Subject, v. *gr.*—

This one gives, these ones give ; the king gives, the kings give.

The reasons of this lies in the fact that the English mind still feels the effects of the formerly existing desinences, all the more because two of these survive in the Singular, just as the Roman mind fancied a Personal desinence somehow in the final *o* of the Present Indicative Active, *v. gr., lego,* though that desinence had long ceased to exist. But Mundari Predicates never have had any Personal desinences *grown* into them : hence the Mundari mind cannot conceive them as complete Predicates without connecting with them what he possesses in the line of Personal Pronouns, *i.e.,* the current forms. He therefore cannot possibly replace the Pronominal Subjects by a Substantive or a Demonstrative Pronoun. The proposition *Rajako omtana* will appear as barbarous to the Munda as, for instance, *Reges da* would have appeared to a Roman or as the proposition *the king give* would appear to an Englishman.

The Munda must always use a Personal Pronominal Subject together with a substantive or a Demonstrative Pronominal Subject—

Ní omtana-e or *Ni-e omtana, literally,* this one give-*s* or this one *he* give.

Níku omtana-ko or *Niku*-ko *omtana, literally,* these ones give-*they* or these ones-*they* give.

Raja omtana-e or *Raja-e omtana, literally,* the king give or the kings-*he* give.

Rajako omtana-ko or *Rajako-ko omtana, literally,* the kings give-*they* or the kings-*they* give.

The above brings out clearly the fact that in Mundari, as much as in the Aryan languages, the Personal Pronominal Subjects are an essential complement of every Transitive and Intransitive Predicate. But if the Personal Pronoun is the necessary and final complement of the Mundari as well as of the Organic Transitive or Intransitive Predicate, then what is the *a* which must be added to the bare Mundari Tense-form to render it capable of coming into direct contact with the Personal Pronoun, and which has no apparent equivalent in the Organic Conjugations?

Without this *a* words denoting states or forms of activity are either mere Abstract Nouns or Adjectives : with the *a* they are perfect functional equivalents of our Verbs. This *a* has not only the power of changing into Transitive or Intransitive Predicates Nouns which denote already states or actions, but it transforms into a Verb *any* and *every* Munadi word it happens to touch. Concrete Nouns denotative of living beings or inanimate objects, Pronouns, Numerals, Postpositions, Adverbs, Interjections,—all are changed into words denoting states or actions as referable and actually referred to some subject or agent the moment this *a* is suffixed to them. Even complete propositions are by it retransformed into compound words capable of standing as Transitive or Intransitive Predicates in a new proposition, *v. gr., Hokalá-e,* he stopped ; *Neado-le hokaláe*-á. We express this by the word *hokaláe* or we express this by saying *hokalae.* We might therefore call this *a* the verbalizing agent of the Mundari language. But then this name does not explain anything. The question immediately arises *Why* is it the verbalizing agent? Whence does it drive this power of verbalizing every word or proposition; it touches ? What does it mean, and what is its origin?

In the Introduction (page 51) I stated that this áwas in reality nothing else than the Impersonal Pronoun used with an Intransitive function. That statement can, I think, be proved by the following arguments :—

1st.—The genius of the language leaves to Mundari words the largest possible functional elasticity, and thus allows every word to perform the function of an Intransitive or a Transitive Predicate, according to the nature of the concept originally denoted by the words : hence the Impersonal Pronoun ámay likewise assume an Intransitive function. Since á means *it* or *something,* it denotes being in general. If this concept be used intransitively, it can mean only two things, viz., either (1) *to be something* or (2) *to become something.*

2nd.—Mere Qualitatives or Adjectives are transformed into Nouns by means of the Suffix *á*, *v. gr., Pundi,* white ; *pundiá,* something white or *a white one* (inanimate object). There is no doubt that in this case the Suffix á is the Impersonal Pronoun *it.* The compound literally means *a white something ;* but the same form is used as a proposition and means also *it is* white, *v. gr., Ne kagaj pundia,*—This paper is white (*literally,* this paper a white-something). The word *a* is evidently the same in both expressions : only the *function* is different.

3rd.—Bare Tense-forms, *i.e.,* R+ V + M + T are in Mundari mere Qualitatives or Adjectives. Now the addition of *á*to these Tense forms transforms them into Nouns, just as Adjectives are transformed into Nouns, *v. gr., lelakan* is the bare Perfect Tense-form, meaning *having been seen :* hence *lelakan-a* means *that which has been seen (literally,* a having been seen something or *visum quid).*

Here, again, the áis evidently the Impersonal Pronoun. But the same form may stand as Transitive Predicate to a Subject : *lelakana, it has been seen (literally,* a having been seen something (is) it). Here, again, the á appears obviously as the same identical Suffix, but the function it performs is different

4th.—That the á here under consideration cannot be considered as a mere phonetic *débris* of a former more complete root, but is in reality the Impersonal Pronoun used intransitively seems proved beyond a doubt by the following fact. Mundari is much more particular in specifying the time to which an action; belongs than any Organic language : hence the number of its Tense-forms—*3 Present Tenses, 3 Past Tenses, a Perfect Tense, 2 Future Tenses* and *a General or Indeterminate Tense.* To each of these corresponds an *Imperfect Tense :* hence 9 *Imperfects.* Besides this, it has its *Static, Inchoative,* and *Completive* forms. In all these Tenses, with the exception of two, viz., *the Simple Future* and the *Indeterminate Tense,* the particular time signified by the Tense-form is denoted by a special and very distinct *Tense-suffix.*

The absence of a special Tense-suffix in the Indeterminate Tense would be conceivable. That a form which is used only in cases where the mind deliberately abstracts from any particular *time* should be devoid of a special *time* or *Tense-suffix* would have nothing surprising. But that alanguage which uses as many as *three* distinct suffixes to denote the *Present* should have no suffix at all for the

Future appears certainly very extraordinary at first sight. It is in fact *impossible* for the Munda mind in its present stage to denote an action; as future without his being implicitly conscious that the idea of futurity is in some way expressed by one of the formative elements in the Predicate. Yet the Simple Mundari Future is invariably Root + Copula + Pronominal Subject in the active Voice—I will or shall go,—*sen—a—ing.* They will come *hiju-á-ko.* In the other Voices the Future is R + V + C + S—I shall be seen,—*lel-ó-a-ing* (the *ó* is the Passive-Voice Suffix).

Now it cannot be maintained with a shadow of reason that *futurity* is in any way implied by the *root* of a Predicate, much less by the Pronominal Subject. Therefore, we msut admit that the Munda mind sees or is implicitly conscious of futurity being implied by the Copula á, which is the only remaining element of the Predicate. Now, if we admit that the Copula á is really the Impersonal Pronoun á used ntransitively, we shall find that this á really may imply futurity. Indeed, if the Impersonal Pronoun *it,* which directly denotes *being* in its vaguest sense as well as applied to a particular object, conceived merely in its most general or vaguest outlines, be used with an Intransitive function, it must mean either *to be* something or *to become* something. In other words, if the idea denoted by the Impersonal Pronoun be verbalized in Organic languages, it will yields the Verbs *to be* and *to become—sein* and *werden*, *être* and *devenir, esse* and *fieri.* But the Verbs *to become, fieri,* etc., necessarily imply a future time as opposed to present or realized entity. If this view be admitted, the Mundari Future Tense finds a rational explanation. In that case we may say—in the Future Tense the Munda uses the Impersonal Pronoun intransitively in the sense of *becoming.* Since this necessarily implies futurity, and implies it in a manner of which the Munda mind is instinctively conscious, he does not feel the need of a separate Tense-suffix for the Future. Here, then, the Impersonal Pronoun serves at the same time as Copula and as Tense-sign : hence the proposition *sen*-a-*ing* can literally be translated into English by going-*become*-I ; and *hiju*-a-*ko* means literally coming-*become*-they.

In all the other Tenses the Copula á is the Impersonal Pronoun used in its first meaning, viz., *to be.* Now, even as the Pronoun *it* makes abstraction of all particular specifications in the objects it may denote, so does the so-called Substantive Verb *to be* make abstraction of all particular times. In itself it only denotes being in its widest sense, whether real or purely ideal, past, present, or future. The bare rootform of any Verb does not imply any particular time: by itself alone it is indifferent to time. That Organic languages as well as a number of others use it without a spcial time affix to denote the present is indeed quite intelligible on the ground that when no particular time is mentioned, the speaker may naturally imply the present ; but that implication does not lie in the root-form as such. This prescinds from all time. The Mundas use the Intransitive

Pronoun *á* as meaning *to be,* precisely in this most abstract sense : hence this Copula is, in this meaning, perfectly compatible with Present and Past Tense-suffixes. Considered in this light, all Mundari Tense-forms can be literally rendered into English as follows, where the Noun *being* is substituted for its synonym *it*—

Definite Present—*Hijú-tan-a-ing,*—(*A*) coming-now-being-I.
Simple Past—*Sen-ken-a-ing,*—(*A*) going-then-being-I.

According to our organic habit of thinking, we feel the need of transforming the Pronoun *it* or *being* nto a Verb and say—

Sentan-a-*ing,*—Going-now *am* I.
Senken-a-*ing,*—Going-then am I.

Here we further feel the need of tearing the Past Tense Suffix from the Predicate and throwing it into our link-word. Thus, we get, going *was* I, or I *was* going.

The Munda of course does not feel the need of any change in the form of his Copula. The element of time is attached to the root by means of a Tense-suffix, and the consciousness that the Personal Pronoun acts as Subjects is sufficiently evoked by the immediate contact of the Personal Pronoun with the compounds *sentan, senken,* etc. In reality we do radically the very same thing as the Mundas; for we too suffix our Pronouns to roots modified by whole or partial time-suffixes or modificatory elements. It is only the loss of the explicit consciousness of their original meaning which makes us attach something like a mysterious or living meaning to our Verb-forms. In fact, the Organic Conjugation is in its origin even more rudimentary than the Mundari equivalent; for whereas the Munda uses a link-word, we use none : *eo, is, it,* etc., is literally only the juxtaposition of root the Pronominal subject thus, *go I, go thou, go he.* But the Munda says: *go being I, go being thou, go being he.* The work of referring the attributive root to the Pronoun as to its Subject is entirely left to the mind. All that language does is juxtaposition, and thus it leads the mind of the listener to refer the juxtaposed elements to each other as *Predicate* and *Subject.*

From the above we see that the Kholarian translates the mind's working more closely than we do ; for every concepts standing as Predicate is really made up of a fasciculus of notes or features. Among these there is one which is necessarily common to all possible concepts, viz. that of *being,* whether *real* or *ideal ;* this is, so to say, the foundation on which all our concepts are built up. The building up is done by superadding to this most vague and universal notion of entity other particular characteristics or features for the purpose of raising the vague idea of being to that degree of precision which the mind aims at in a particular concept.

But this is precisely what the Munda does in his spoken Predicates. He explicitly calls every Predicate *it* or *a something; a being.* And this *something* he specifies by adding to it roots denoting such characteristics as are there *and* then required. The order which he follows in adding these specifications is the same which he uses when specifying a Noun by means of Qualitatives, viz., the specifications precede the word specified. Just as he expresses the phrase—

A good and wise *man,—Bugin ad' seranan horo,*

so does he express the phrase—

Coming now,—

Hiju-tan a literally, *a* coming-now *being.* Hence, strictly speaking, this *á*is not precisely a *link-word* between the Subject and the Predicate. It is rather the common basis of all Accidental Predicates or the universal Predicate of Accidental propositions. And that compound which we call exclusively the Predicate, consists in reality only of those specifications which are added to the common or universal Predicate as so many qualitative appositions or limitations.

The Aryan does not in his Predicate express the common element of all concepts. Taking it for granted that the listener's mind will supply that element, he translates into language only the particular features of his Predicative concept. This greater liberty with which he translates thought into language renders his Predicates, if less regular, a great deal lighter, and thus more handy for practical purposes.

Besides those structural differences between Organic Verbs and Mundari Transitive and Intransitive Predicates, which have been pointed out above, there exists still another which it seems preferable to explain immediately before entering on a detailed description of the Tense, Voice, and Mood-forms. *The flexional process* is not uniformly the same in even one and the same Organic languages. It is subdivided into several classes or Conjugations, the number of which varies from language to language. Thus all the Latin Verbs fall under four different Conjugations.

The division is based directly on the exigencies of those phonetic laws which regulate the blending of the primary and secondary elements of a verb into one word.

In Mundari the process by which the primary and the secodary or formative elements are agglutinated into one word remains uniformly the same. For (1) the formative elements are always the same ; (2) the extent to which they submit to phonetic changes consequent on their subordination to the primary root never varies; hence if, for the sake of a name, we call the Mundari process conjugation, we should say that in Mundari there exists but one *Conjugation.* However, this Mundari Conjugation is subdivided into two constructions— *the Personal* and the *Impersonal construction.*—

I.—The Personal Construction is that in which the Subject is a *Personal* Pronoun. This Pronoun may occupy three different positions as explained above (pages 66 and 67).

II.—The Impersonal Construction is that which has the *Neuter* Pronoun *a* as Subject.

We too have Impersonal Verbs. but they do but partially coincide with the Mundari Impersonal Predicates. Thus, whereas we conceive the Subject of natural phenomena as *impersonal*, the Munda conceives it as *personal*. We say *it* rains, *it* hails, etc. The Munda says *he* rains, *gamajada*-e ; *he* hails, *ariljada-e*, etc.

In Mundari the Impersonal Construction is limited to two kinds of words—

1st. Words denoting purely subjective states or affections, such as joy, grief, etc. (*confer* the Latin *poenitet me, taedet me* etc.)

2nd. The so-called Substantive Verb *to be, i.e., to exist* or *to be present, mena,* and its contradictory *banó, not to exist* or *to be absent.*

In these two kinds of words the subject or being affected by joy, grief, etc., or the being of whom existence or non-existence is predicated is treated as an *inserted Pronominal Object*—

Hasu, sickness, pain : hence also, to pain. It will pain thee,—*hasu-ame-a;* it does pain thee,—*hasu-jad'-me-a ;* it did pain thee,—*hasu-ked'-me-a.*

In the case of the first kind of words the Impersonal Construction is subject to certain limitations. In the case of *mená* and *banó* it is confined to the Present Tense. Full explanations on this point will be given further on.

The terms *Voice, Mood,* and *Tense* may be kept in the etymological description of Mundari Transitive and Intransitive Predicates, because they do not directly imply the *flexional* process of Conjugation.

The particular names of the various Voices, Moods, and Tenses may, with a few obvious modifications and additions, be kept also.

VOICE

If we take the term Voice as denotative of a pure grammatical function, we may define it as the particular relation of *activity* or *receptivity* in which the Subjects of a judgment stands to a Transitive or Intransitive Predicate.

The Subject may stand to such Predicates—

(1) In the relation of an agent, *v. gr., I see.* This relation is called the *Active Voice.*

(2) It may stand to the Predicate in the relation of a *recipient.* In this case the Subject is in reality the terminus of an action performed by some one else, *v. gr., I am seen.* This relation is called *the Passive Voice.*

(3) The Subject may, in certain judgements, be conceived as both the agent and the recipient of an action, *v. gr., I see myself.* This relation may be called *the Reflexive Voice,* the term implying that the action is conceived as turning or falling back on the agent himself. It corresponds therefore to the Greek *Medium Voice.*

(4) A Subject may denote two or more agents. These may, in certain judgements, be represented as reacting on each other, *i.e.,* as being at the same time with regard to each other agents and recipients of specifically the same action, *v. gr., They see each other.* This relation may be called *the Reciprocal Voice.*

If now we consider the term *Voice* as directly applied to particular *word-forms* and only indirectly to the above functions or relations, we may define it as that form of a Transitive or an Intransitive Predicate which shows whether the Subject stands to the Predicate in the relation of activity, passivity, or of both activity and passivity.

Organic languages do not attach the relation of reciprocity to the Predicate form. That relation is expressed by the Reciprocal Pronouns standing outside the Predicate, *v. gr.*, by *each other* in the proposition,—*They see each other.* The relation of reflexivity too is in most of them detached from the Predicate and denoted by separate Reflexive Pronouns. Hence in most Organic languages Verbs have only two Voices—*the Active* and *the Passive.* In some we meet with three Voices—*the Active, the Passive,* and *the Reflexive* or *Medium.*

Mundari attaches all four of the relations described above to the Predicate. It has neither Reflexive nor Reciprocal Pronominal forms, and does not stand in need of them : hence here we have *four Voices—the Active, the Passive, the Reflexive,* and *the Reciprocal.*

MOODS

Considered as a grammatical function, the term *Mood* may be defined as the connotation of the manner in which the mind conceives a judgement. Considered as a word-form, we may define it as that form of a Transitive or Intransitive Predicate which connotes the manner in which a proposition is uttered. A proposition may be uttered *assertively, imperatively, conditionally,* or *dubitatively.*

Mood-forms have been very unevenly developed even in languages of the same group. In Mundari we meet with five Moods—the *Indicative,* the *Imperative,* the ordinary *Precative* or *Concessive,* the *Polite Precative* or *Optative,* and the *Conditional.* The *Infinitive* cannot be called a Mundari Mood in the sense of the above definition. The *Conditional* differs so radically from the other Mundari Moods that it can hardly be called a Mood at all; for in the clause which contains the condition, the Predicate is no longer connected with Subject by means of the Copula, and thus it loses its character as a real Transitive or Intransitive Predicate.

Details concerning the Voices and Moods presuppose a full explanation of the Tense-forms, whose function consists in pointing out the time to which an action belongs.

The connotative functions of the Aryan Verb are limited to Voice, Mood, and Tense. To these functions the corresponding Mundari Predicates add, as stated in page 70 and 71, *Case* or the signification of Direct and Indirect Objects. Besides this, the Mundari Predicates possess another very characteristic feature, which is altogether wanting in our Verbs.

There exists, in the Active Voice of Transitive Predicates, a form which is neither a *Mood* nor a *Tense.* It cannot be called a Mood because the Suffix by which it is obtained does not imply the manner in which the proposition is uttered.

It is not a Tense-form because the Suffix does not in any way connote time. It is obtained by suffixing *ta* to the root. It has a double connotation—

(1) It may signify *the intention of the agent* or *the instigator* of an action with regard to *the effects* of that action.

(2) It may signify *a particular state of mind* in which the agent performed the action, viz., it implied that the act is or was done *in spite of* a custom or an order—

Duar-ing niea means I shall open the door.

Duar-ing ni-ta means either (1) I shall open the door and *want it to remain open,* or (2) I *will* open the door, *happen what may, i.e., contrary to anybody's order or desire.*

This form occurs only in *the Indeterminate Tense,* as in the above example, in the *Simple Past* and in *the Imperative Mood.*

In the Simple Past the Tense-suffix *ked* drops the letters *k* and *e,* so that a Compound Suffix *tad* results which stand for *ta-ked*—

Duar-ing ni-keda,—I opened the door.

Duar-ing ni-tada,—either (1) I opened the door and *left it ajar,* or (2) I *did* open the door, *notwithstanding any orders to the contrary* or *notwithstanding any apprehended consequences.*

Direct Pronominal Objects are inserted according to the general rules, thus—

Uríko-ing ader-ta-ko-a,—(1) I shall drive the cattle in and *shut them up ;* or (2) I will drive the cattle in now, *though it be not yet time to do so,* or *though I have been told not to.*

Uríko-ing ader-tad'-ko-a,—I drove the cattle in and *shut them up (*so that they are even now inside), or I *did* drive the cattle in, *notwithstanding any custom* or *order to the contrary.*

This form would, from its nature, appear to be limited to Transitive Predicates, *i.e.,* such as do necesssarily presuppose a Direct Object or a real direct terminus distinct from the agent. Howevcer, the second meaning which it conveys, viz., that of a determination to act notwithstanding any moral or physical obstacles allows its transfer to purely Intransitive Predicates, such as *sen,* to go; *nir,* to run, etc. Thus, for instance, the sentence—I kept on walking fast (notwithstanding my fatigue or the heat, etc.) may very adequately be rendered by *khub-ing sen-tada.*

This very peculiar form has been called *the Reservative* and *the Static*. Though neither of the terms be an exact designation of the function performed, the term Static will be kept in the subsequent pages.

Instead of placing it under a separate heading as distinct from *Voice, Mood,* and *Tenses,* it will be classed with the Tenses, where it will figure as *Static Future* and *Static Past* respectively. The Imperative form will be classed as *Static Imperative.*

NOTE.—This is a very remarkable instance of the transfer of a meaning from the spheres of *time* and *space* to the purely *mental* and *moral* spheres. In the chapter on Postpositions it has been stated that *ta* denotes primarily *fixity* in space and *permanence* or *continuity* in time. Here we see the very same suffix used to denote (1) permanence or continuity of the effects of an action as *intended* by the agent (mental sphere); (2) fixity or firmness of *purpose* or *resolve* on the part of the agent to perform a certain action, notwithstanding any difficulties to the contrary (moral sphere).

TENSES

The Active Voice and the Indicative Mood are not connoted by special Suffixes: hence Predicates consisting only of the root *plus* the Copula, *plus* the Subjects, or of the root *plus* the Tense-suffix, *plus* the Copula, *plus* the Pronominal Subject, belong to the Indicative Mood of the Active Voice.

I. The Indeterminate Tense

We are in the habit of using a *Present* Tense-form to express certain actions or states which are not limited to the present time.

To this class belong (1) propositions stating general principles or universals truths; (2) propositions stating customs and habit not yet extinct, as well as regularly recurring actions and events.

To express these, the Mundas use no Suffix denotative of time, but subjoin the Copula *a* immediately to the Voice and Mood-form whenever no Pronominal Object is to be inserted. The first vowel of the root is lengthened.

If some Direct or Indirect Pronominal Object occur, then that is inserted between the Copula and the Voice and Mood-form.

This mode of expressing such statements is, in a way, more accurate than the use of a Present Tense-form, because the absence of any Suffix denotative of time is well calculated to imply that the statement makes abstraction of every particular time; that it holds good of the past, the present, and the future—

Hormo gojó-a, tama kae gojo-a,—The body dies, the spirit does not die. *Pormesor nel-bu-ae,*—God sees us (always). *Mundaka heró dipli-ko bonga-e-a,*—The Mundas offer a sacrifice at sowing time (a customes universally observed). *Orá chilekate-ko bai-e-a?* How are they in the habit of making (their) houses? *Garako urea enrege dáko dul-e-a enateko chapadea; chapad' kedchi en losod' pachri tapáteko idia,* etc.,—They first dig (a hole in the ground), into that they pour water and then knead (prepare the mud); having kneaded, they take that mud to build up the wall.

Bokomdo chikanmente kae taekena hature ? Why was not your brother in the village ? *Gupitee* sen-a *gomke.* He (always or usually) takes the cattle to graze, sir, *i.e.,* that is his regular daily work.

Nea chikana-ko kajia *?* What do they call this? *Chandaea-ko,* —They call it *chandae* (the caves of a roof) *Nea chikana-ko chika ?* What are (people) using this for ? What are they (generally) doing with this ?

Words ending in a checked vowel insert a euphonic *e* before the Copula in the Indeterminate and the Future Tense. In this case the checked vowel is broken up into two distinct vowels, of which the first keeps a slight check, thus—

Tí, hand ; *tíi,* to take the hand, to handle something, to lead or to take with one's own hand ; *chó,* a kiss; *chóo,* to kiss; *kú,* cough; *kúu* to cough ; *tíi-e-a-ing, chóo-e-aing, kúu-e-aing.*

Intransitive Predicates ending in a consonant never insert this *e*—

Debel, to swim; *debel-a-ing, sen,* to go, *sen-a-ko.*

Transitive Predicates, no matter what their ending be, insert an *e* before the Copula whenever their *Direct Object* is an inanimate being.

Lel-e-aing,—I shall see *it* ; *harub'-e-a ko,*—They will cover it up.

Any word used with the meaning *to call by such or such a word, to mean, to signify, to denote by such or such a word,* refuses the insertion of *e* before the Copula, even if it end in a checked vowel—

Chikana-ko tíia ? What do they mean by the word tíi ? *Ena-ko kú-ua*—that they express by the word kúu (to cough). *Nea-le-sirma-á*—We call this sirma (a roof). But *nea-le sirma-e-a,*—We shall make a roof of this (*i.e.,* of these materials).

II.—The Simple Future

This Tense is, in its form, absolutely similar to the Indeterminate Tense. The difference of function assumed by the same word-form is explicable only on the supposition that here the Copula á means *to become.* and thus implies futurity; whereas in the Indeterminate Tense the Copula means *to be* in its widest and vaguest sense, and therefore applies to all times, the past, the present, and the future. Needless to say that the identity in form of two quite distinct tenses presents great difficulties to a foreigner. The fact that the Indeterminate Tense has no counterpart at all in Organic languages will naturally mislead him into using a Mundari Present Tense where he ought to use the Indeterminate form. The same fact will lead him to mistake for Future the Indeterminate forms used by the Mundas until he has accustomed himself thoroughly to attribute to the context and the circumstances that amount of attention which in this as in many other constructions helps to fix the actual meaning of a proposition. Thus the sentence *En kora nete hijúae* may mean either that man *is in the habit of coming* here, or that man *will come* here. The lengthening of the first syllable in the Indeterminate Tense is generally not sufficiently pronounced to strike the foreigner easily.

For those who wish to acquire a practical knowledge of the language, it is absolutely necessary that they should, for some time, practise the insertion of all the Personal Direct and Indirect Objects into each of the three Persons in the Singular, Dual, and Plural. To give a complete scheme of all the possible insertions, even for a single Tense, is quite out of the question. For (1) the third Persons of the Singular, Dual, and Plural may take each eleven insertions: hence thirty-three different forms for the Indicative of these three Persons only. Each of the eight remaining Persons take ten distinct insertions : hence eighty more forms.

The following schemes may serve as models to practise both the correct use of the Pronominal Subjects and the insertion of the Pronominal Objects. The learner may, *mutatis mutandis,* transfer them to all the other Tenses.

Scheme for practising the correct use of the Subjects together with the 3rd Person Plural inserted as Direct Object.

Rá-ko-a-ing,	I shall call them.	*Gapa-ing*	*rá-ko-a,*
Rá-ko-a-m	thou wilt call them.	*Gapa-m*	*rá-ko-a,*
Rá-ko-a-e,	he or she will call them.	*Gapa-e*	*rá-ko-a,*
(Rá-ko-a	it will call them.)		
Rá-ko-a-lang,	thou and I will call them.	*Gapa-lang*	*rá-ko-a,*
Rá-ko-a-ling,	he or she and I ,, ,,	*Gapa-ling*	*rá-ko-a,*
Rá-ko-a-ben,	you two ,, ,,	*Gapa-ben*	*rá-ko-a,*
Rá-ko-a-king,	both or the two ,, ,,	*Gapa-king*	*rá-ko-a,*
Rá-ko-a-bu,	you and I ,, ,,	*Gapa-bu*	*rá-ko-a,*
Rá-ko-a-le,	they and I ,, ,,	*Gapa-le*	*rá-ko-a,*
Rá-ko-a-pe,	you ,, ,,	*Gapa-pe*	*rá-ko-a,*
Ra-ko-a-ko	*they* ,, ,,	*Gapa-ko*	*rá-ko-a,*

I, thou, he, etc., etc., will call them to-morrow.

Scheme for practising the rapid insertion of all the Direct Objects into the 3rd Person Singular.

Rá-iñ-a-e, he or she will call	*me.*	*Gapa-e*	*rá-iñ-a,*
Rá-me-a-e, ,, ,, ,,	*thee.*	*Gapa-e*	*rá-me-a,*
Rá-i-a-e, ,, ,, ,,	*him* or *her.*	*Gapa-e*	*rá-i-a,*
Rá-lang-a-e, ,, ,, ,,	*thee and me.*	*Gapa-e*	*rá-lang a,*
Rá-ling-a-e, ,, ,, ,,	*him or her and me.*	*Gapa-e*	*rá-ling-a,*
Rá-ben-a-e, ,, ,, ,,	*you two.*	*Gapa-e*	*rá-ben-a,*
Rá-king-a-e, ,, ,, ,,	*both of them.*	*Gapa-e*	*rá-king-a,*
Rá-bu-a-e, ,, ,, ,,	*you and me.*	*Gapa-e*	*rá-bu-a,*
Rá-le-a-e, ,, ,, ,,	*them and me.*	*Gapa-e*	*rá-le-a,*
Rá-pe-a-e, ,, ,, ,,	*you.*	*Gapa-e*	*rá-pe-a,*
Rá-ko-a-e, ,, ,, ,,	*them.*	*Gapa-e*	*rá-ko-a,*

To-morrow he or she will call *me, thee,* etc.,

In the first of the above schemes the Direct Object *ko* should be successively replaced by all the other Pronouns, whereas in the second scheme the Subject *e* should be replaced successively by the other Pronominal Subjects. In replacing the Subject *e* by other Pronouns, attention must be paid to the fact that where the Subject and Direct Object are one and the same person, the Active forms with Inserted Objects cannot be used. It must be replaced by the Reflexive forms.This coincidence of Subject and Direct Objects happens always in the Ist and 2nd Persons, Singular, Dual and Plural. I strike myself cannot be translated by *dal-in-a-ing.* It must be rendered by the Reflexive form *dal-en-a-ing.*

Similarly, thou strikest thyself is *dal-en-a-m,* not *dal-me-a-m.* He strikes himself is *dal-en-a-e,* not *dal-i-a-e.*

The form *dal-i-a-e* signifies that one third person strikes another third person.

In those Tenses in which the Indirect Pronominal Objects are preceded by *a,* the insertion; of these Objects must be practised separately—

Kul-iñ ae, kul-me-ae kul-i-ae, etc., means he will send *me, thee, him,* etc., *kul-aiñ-ae, kul-ame-ae, kul ai-ae,* etc., means he will send (some one or something) *to* me, *to* thee, *to* him, etc.

Auri followed by a *Future Tense* is equivalent to the English phrases *not yet* or *not as yet* followed by a *Perfect* or *a Pluperfect.*

He has not yet returned,—*Aurie ruara.* At that time they had not yet surveyed the fields in these parts,—En dipli nere ote *auriko mukaea.*

III.—Static Future

The formation and meaning of this compound has been explained above (pages 169 and 170).

Indirect Pronominal Objects are never inserted into the Static Future. *Direct* Objects stand between the Suffix *ta* and the Copula, *v. gr.,* I will sell off these horses,—*Ne sadomkoing akiring-ta-ko-a.*

When the Direct Object is an inanimate being (in which case no insertion is made), euphonic vowels are not interposed between the *a* of the Suffix and the Copula : hence these two *a's* are in immediate contact. This contact produces a single long *á* with the check. Thus *ni-tá-ing, ni-tá-m, ni-tá-e, ni-tá-lang,* etc.,— I, thou, he or she, thou and I, etc., will set the door ajar.

Ta is rarely suffixed to Intransitive Predicates. If affixed, it changes them into Transitives. *v. gr., Tising Ranchi jaked'ing sen-ta* means I will do the road from here to Ranchi to-day ; I will traverse to-day the distance from here to Ranchi.

IV.—The Anterior Future

It is formed by suffixing *le* to the root, and denotes the priority of one future action over another future action.

Transitive Predicates insert both Direct and Indirect Objects between *le* and the Copula. The Indirect Objects are, however, not preceded by *a,* so that the context or the circumstances must decide whether in certain cases the Simple Pronouns stand as *Direct* or as *Indirect* Objects. Thus, for instance, *Om-le-ko-aing,* may mean either I shall first give them (*v. gr.,* the horses) away to some one; or I shall first give it to them.

When the Pronouns *ing* or *í* stand inserted as Objects, the *e* of *le* elides with the *i* of *ing* and with *í.* The result is a long *í.* In this elision the Pronoun *í,* he or she, loses its check. Thus *Om-liñ-ae,*—He will first give to me; *rá-lí-aing,*—I shall first call him or her.

N.B.—Great attention must be paid to the correct pronunciation of these two forms, because they differ from the Anterior Past only by the absence of the check on the i : *Rálíñae* means he first *called* me ; *rálíñae* means he *will first call* me. *Rêlíae,*—He first *called* him or her ; *rálíae,*—He *will first call* him or her.

Le is not affixed as a mere Anterior Future Suffix to Intransitive Predicates, such as *sen, nir, hijú,* etc., in the Indicative Mood.

Intransitives form their Anterior Future in three different ways—

1st.—They may take the Suffix *kó* after the root. This Suffix generally performs the function of a Polite Precative or Optative, *v. gr.,Dub-kó-aing ?* May I sit down, please ? However, with Intransitive Predicates this function frequently disappears, and it is simply equivalent to the Future in *le* used in Transitive Predicates, *v. gr., Oráteng sen-kó-a,*— I shall first go home ; *Pittelang sen-kó-a,*—Let us (thee and me) go first to the market.

2nd.—The Simple Future Tense may be preceded by the Adverbs *sida* or *sidate,* first, *v. gr., sida* or *sidate pittelang sena,*—Thou and I will first go to the market.

3rd.—The Adverb *sida* may be suffixed to the root just as *le* is suffixed in Transitive and *ko* in Intransitive Predicates, thus *Nirsidaeaing,*—I will first run; *Nir-sidaeam,*—Thou wilt first run.

This construction has, however, generally a different meaning : *Nirsidaeam,*— Thou wilt be the first to run away. Here no precedence of one action over another is implied. In this sense, therefore, the form is a Simple and not an Anterior Future.

In the case of Transitive Predicates too the above constructions with *sida, sidate* are freely used instead of the Anterior Future form in *le. Meromko har-sida-ko-aing,*—I shall first drive the goats away.

If *sida* be suffixed to the root, inserted Indirect Objects are not preceded by *a :*

Talab om-sida-ko-aing,—I shall first give the wages to them.

The form *sen-le-aing* is the only case in which I have ever heard the Suffix *le* used with an Intransitive Predicate in the Indicative Mood. On enquiring into the correctness and the meaning of *senleaing,* I was told by some of the more intelligent among correct speakers that the form is used, but that it does not mean *I shall first go,* but I shall *try* to go, I shall *attempt the distance.* In this phrase *sen* participates of the nature of a Transitive Predicate. In have further been assured that *le* cannot, even in this sense, be used with other Intransitives, such as *hijú, nir,* etc.

Le is used to denote the idea of attempting or trying; but then it is followed by *k,* v. gr., *kuril-lek-aing,*—I shall try to jump (that height or length).

V.—The Definite Present

This Tense is formed by suffixing *tan* to the root of both Transitive and Intransitive Predicates. Direct and Indirect Pronominal Objects are inserted between the root of the Predicate and the Suffix *tan*—

Rá-ing-tan-ae,—he is calling me. *Om-ako-tan-aing,*—I give to them.

When the Second Person Singular *me* is inserted into the Definite Present as *Indirect Object,* it frequently drops the final *e*—

Om-ame-tan-aing or om-*am*-tan-aing,—I am giving it to thee.

Similarly, the *e* of *me* may be dropped when *me* is inserted as Direct Object into words ending in *a*. *Rá-me-tanae* or *rá-m-tanae,*— he calls thee.

VI.—The Indefinite Present

It is formed by suffixing *jad* to the root of the Predicate.

Direct and Indirect Object are inserted between the Tense-suffix and the Copula.

Indirect Objects are never preceded by *a,* so that the context and the circumstances must decide whether an inserted Pronoun stands then and there as *Direct* or as *Indirect* Object.

The *d of jad* is checked whenever the inserted Pronoun begins with a Consonant—*Lel-jad'-meaing, lel-jad'-lingae.*

Before the Pronouns *ing* and *í* the *a* is dropped altogether, and the *a* of *jad* is checked—*Lel-já-iñae, lel-já-i-aing.*

Concerning the use of Indirect Objects with this Tense, the following rules should be observed :—

Words denoting *to give, to lend,* and their synonyms generally insert their Indirect Objects, *v. gr., Takaing paincha-jad'-ko-a,*—I am lending money to them; *kami-e om-jad'-le-a,*—He is giving work to us.

Words denoting *to bring, to take, to carry,* and their synonyms generally do not insert Indirect Objects. The Object stands outside the Predicate with the Suffixes *táte* or *táre* according to the nature of the case. Hence *(a)* when the Indirect Object is a living being, denoted by a Noun, no Pronominal Object is used at all, *v.gr.*, I take this to thy brother,—*Nea bokom-táteng idijada* : never *Nea bokom-táteng idijaia ; (b)* when the Indirect Object is a Personal Pronoun, then the emphatic form with the required Suffix stands out of the Predicate—I take this to them,—*Nea ako-tateng idijada.*

3. Indirect Objects to most other words stand out of the Predicate with the Postposition *nagente* and synonyms (see pages 107 and 109)— *Ne loeong ae menteng sí-jada,*—I plough this field *for* him.

Distinction between the Definite and the Indefinite Present

The grammatical Present may be conceived in two ways: (1) an action may be conceived as actually going on at the present *moment, i.e.,* as belonging to the present in the strict and narrow sense of the word. (2) It may be conceived as going on or continuing, with such interruptions as circumstances may require, through that vaguely defined portion of time which we call the present in the wider sense of the word. The terms *Definite Present* and *Indefinite Present* would accurately designate these two modes of conceiving present actions. In Mundari grammer these terms, however, cannot be limited to this meaning.

The correct use of these two Tenses is difficult for a foreigner. Even an accurate description of their respective functions is not easy. For the functions are based on two distinct principles, viz, first and mainly on the manner in which the action itself is conceived, independently of the element of time, and only secondarily and exceptionally on the manner in which the present time is conceived.

If an action is conceived exclusively as a modification of the agent, it is, grammatically speaking, intransitive. This mode of conceiving may be extended even to those forms of activity which in reality must have an effect or terminus distinct from and out of the agent.

If, on the contrary, the mind considers an action both as a modification of the agent and as having an effect or terminus out of the agent, it is called transitive. It is these two modes of conception, the Munda mind adheres to throughout, and he expresses them in language by distinct Suffixes.

All Tense-suffixes ending in *n* are primarily *Intransitive Suffixes ;* those ending in *d* are primarily *Transitive Suffixes.*

As a general rule, the Munda does not distinguish between the *present moment* in the narrow or strict sense and the *present time* in the loose or wide sense. A thorough-going distinction therefore between a *Definite* and an *Indefinite Present* as defined above does not exist in Mundari grammar.

So far as the element of time is concerned, there is, generally speaking, but one *Present* Tense in Mundari. This Tense abstracts from the stricter and the wider present : it embraces both of these without particularly insisting on either. Hence the following rules :—

1st.—The Suffix *tan* serves to form the *Present Tense* of *Intransitive Predicates.*

. *2nd.*—The Suffix *jad serves* to form the *Present Tense of Transitive Predicates.*

Kamitanae may mean, He is working just now, or he has work these days.

3rd.—When it is desired tonecessary to point out that a *Transitive action* which is then and there conceived transitively is actually going on at the present moment, the Suffix *tan* must be used. In this case Direct and Indirect Objects denoting living beings must be inserted into the Predicate. The following example was given by a servant as an illustration of this rule : I and another servant stand near a table on which money is lying, and you, sir, are sitting at a distance. The other servant whispers to me : "Take one of those rupees." But you happen to be just then looking at me. So I whisper back : "I can't : the master is seeing me,"—

Kaing daria : gomkee lel-ing-tana.

Do you see those two birds ? No, I don't. I suppose they have now disappeared behind the leaves. Not a bit ! there they are ; I see them still,—*En chenreking leljad'kingam chi ? Kaing leljad'kinga ; sakamkóre danangjanakingja.Kage ! menakogea : naoing lel-king-tana.* Here the Predicate *leljad'kinga* is in both instances a *Definite Present.* But since no stress is so far laid on the exact moment, the ordinary Transitive Present forms are used ; but in the last sentence the Suffix *tan* must be used because the speaker desires to point out the exact or strict present moment.

This is the only case in which *tan* is used instead of *jad* for the particular purpose of obtaining a real *Definite Present* form.

In those parts where the Hindus and Uraons have not yet settled, and where the Mundas know and speak only Mundari, *jad* is hardly ever suffixed to Intransitive Predicates. It is in fact so rare that it may safely be considered as a mistake. I have been told by several of the best speakers that such forms as *senjadaing, nirjadaing* are used only by foreigners who do not know Mundari properly and by the Mundas who live among Hindus and Uraons.

Frequently the context will show whether this Tense-form is there and then performing the function of a strict Definite or a strict Indefinite Present in the case of Intransitive Predicates—

v. grt., My elder brother is not at home now; he works at the road,—*Bauing bangáia, horare kamitanae (Def. Pres.).*

What are you doing these days?—I am working at the road,—*Chikanam chikatana tising gapa ? Horarèng kamitana. (*Here *chikatanam* and *kamitanaing* are both *Indefinite Presents.)*

A man looking on at a carpenter engaged on some particular work, but not understanding what sort of implement or furniture he is making will ask : *Chikanam baijada ?*—What are you making ? The carpenter answers : *Kirking baijada,*—I am making a window. Here *Baijada* is twice used as a *Definite Transitive Present.*

So far all is easy and simple enough. The difficulty lies in the following rules :—

4th.—The Suffix *tan* must be used with *Transitive Predicates* whenever the speaker makes abstraction of the outward effect or terminus of the action in question, and considers it only in so far as it affects the agent. In that case Pronominal Direct and Indirect Objects (denotative of living beings) *are not inserted* into the Tense-form if these Objects occur as Nouns or Independent Pronouns in the sentence :

What art thou doing in this place ? (What is your occupation or work here these days?),—I am teaching the children of the village,—*Nere chikanam chikatana tising gape ? Haturen honkoing itutana. (*Here both Predicates are Indefinite Presents, and the Transitive word *itu,* to teach, does not take a Pronominal Object.)

Why is your brother not at home? Where is he just now? He is grazing the cattle,—*Baum chikanamente bangaia? okoría nado ? Uríkoe gupitana.* Here *gupitana* is a *Definite Present.*

VII.—The Continuative Present

It is formed by suffixing the transitive Perfect Tenses suffix *akad* to both Transitive and Intransitive Predicates.

The intransitive Suffix *akan* is used only with those Intransitives which denote rest or stillness, such as *tingun,* to stand ; *dub,* to sit ; *giti,* to lie down; *hapen,* to keep silence, and their synonyms. Direct and Indirect Pronominal Objects stand between the Suffix *akad* and the Copula. Indirect Objects are not preceded by *a.*.

The phonetic changes are the same as those indicated in the Transitive Present, in *jad,* p.p. 176 and 177.

It frequently takes the emphatic *ge,* which stands immediately before the Copula: *Sen-akad'-ge-ae,*—he keeps on walking or going ; *Lel-a-kad'-ko-ge-ae,* he keeps looking at them ; *Tingu-akan-ge-ae,*—he continues standing all the while ; *hape-akan-ge-ae,*—he persistently keeps silent.

The Continuative Present implies that an action already begun will or must be continued *uninterruptedly* through the Present into the Future until certain circumstances or explicit orders cause it to cease. It is of course chiefly used in teh Imperative Mood.

N.B.—The uninterrupted continuity here spoken of may apply either to numerically the same act or to numerically distinct acts of a homogeneous series. In the first case the continuative Present denotes a physical continuity of one and the same act, *v.gr.*—goakad'geaing, I keep carrying it, *i.e.,* I have never put it down for an instant. In the second case it denotes a morally uninterrupted continuity, and implies that each time an occasion presents itself for performing an act belonging to the series, that occasion will or may not be missed , v. gr., They still continue killing everyone who enters their country : *Náo akoá disumre bolotanko goeákad'kegeako.*

VIII.—The Simple Past

It is formed by suffixing *ken* to Intransitive and *ked* to Transitive Predicates, *Sen-ken-aing,* I went ; *lel-ked-aing,* I saw it.

Direct Pronominal Objects are inserted between the Suffix *ked* and the Copula.

When the Pronouns *ing* or *í* stand as Direct Objects, the consonant *d* of *ked* is dropped and the *e* elides with *i* of *ing* or with *i.* This elision causes the *i* of *ing* to be checked; hence the forms—

Lel-kiñ-ako, they saw me, instead of *lel-ked-íñ-ako.*

Lel-ki-ako, they saw him, instead of *lel-ked-í-ako.*

These strong elisions are limited to the Mankipati districts. In other places the complete forms are current.

When Indirect Objects are inserted, the Simple Past is so different in appearance that it would seem quite unconnected with the form in *ked*—

Om-áiñ-ae or *Om-ad'-iñ-ae,*	He gave it to me.	*Om-ad'-ling-ae,*	He give it to him and me.
		Om-ad'-ben-ae,	He gave it to you two.
Om-ad'-me-ae,	He gave it to thee.	*Om-ad'-king-ae,*	He gave it to both of them.
Om-ái-ae *Om-ad-í-ae,*	He gave it to him or to her.	*Om-ad'-bu-ae,*	He gave it to you and me.
		Om-ad'-le-ae,	He gave it to them and me.
Om-ad'-lang-ae,	He gave it thee and me.	*Om-ad'-pe ae,*	He gave it to you.
		Om-ad'-ko-ae,	He gave it to them.

A plausible reason why a distinct Tense-suffix should have been adopted in the case of Indirect Pronominal Objects cannot be assigned. The explanation given in the Introduction [page 63] shows, I think, conclusively that *ked* is the basis of the above forms. I there assume that that *a* which introduces Indirect Pronominal Objects, has, in this Tense, been placed beofore the Suffix *ked,* whereas the Pronoun follows the Suffix : thus *om-á-ked-iñ-ae.* The instinctive hurry to hasten from the *a* to its natural complement, the Pronoun, caused the two first letters of *ked* to be dropped, thus producing the forms *om-a-d-iñ-ae, om-a-d'-me-ae, om-a-d-i-ae,* etc. In the Mankipati district the forms *om-ad-iñ-ae* and *om-ad-í-ae* were then further contracted into *om-á-iñ-ae* and *om-á-i-ae.* In these two contractions the disappearance of the consonant *d* caused the *a* to be checked. This check reacting on the Pronoun *í* reduces it to an unchecked vowel *i.*

This Tense is called here the *Simple Past.,* because it simply represents the action as a past one without any further implication or connotation.

IX.—The Incomplete Past

This Tense signifies that an action has been interrupted or broken off before it was completed. It generally implies an intention of resuming and completing the action. By its very nature it is mainly limited to *Transitive Predicates.*

It is formed by suffixing *ken* to the root. Pronominal Objects are not inserted. The reason is because in this form the subjective element of the action is insisted on : in other words, the action is considered primarily as a past modification of the agent : hence it becomes virtually Intransitive. The form is often correctly rendered by the English phrase, *to have been busy doing this or that —Enangsanj mad'ing ma-kena,*—This morning I have been busy cutting bamboos (but I have not cut as many as I intend to cut). *En loeongem siakada?* Hast thou ploughed that rice-field ? *Sidoing si-kena, auring chabaea,*—I have been busy ploughing, but I have not finished it yet.

X.—The Anterior Past—A

This Tense denotes the priority of one past action over another. It is formed by suffixing *len* to Intransitive and *led* to Transitive Predicates.

Pronominal Objects are inserted between the suffix *led* and the Copula. Indirect

Objects are not preceded by *a.*

When *ing* or *i* are inserted as Objects, the same elisions take place which have been described in the Simple Past Tense. Hence the forms *Lel-linae* for *lel-led-in-ae,*—He first saw me, and *Lel-lí-ae* for *lel-led-i-ae,*—He first saw him.

A very strong contraction takes place when the Direct Object is inanimate, in which case Personal Pronouns are not inserted. The complete form is *lel-led-aing,*—I first saw it or them (inanimate objects). In the Mankipati district the *ed* of *led* is dropped, the Copula is checked and immediately suffixed to the *l:* hence the forms—

Lel-lá-ing, I saw it (them i.o.) first.	*Lel-lálang,* Thou and I saw it first.
Lel-lám, Thou sawest, etc.	*Lel-láling,* He or she and I, etc.
Lel-láe, He or she saw, etc.	*Lel-lá-ben,* You two, etc., etc.

REMARK— When there is question of one agent having performed a certain action before another agent performed the same action, the Anterior Past is not used, because this form denotes the priority of one past action over some other past action. In that case *aiar* or *sida* are suffixed to the root and followed by the Simple Past Suffixes *ken* or *ked* or some other Past Suffix. He was the first to run away,—*A'ege niraiarjanae.* I was the first to see these birds.—*Aing ne chenrekoin lelsidaked'koaing.*

The words hiju, to come, and *jonomó,* to be born, always form their *Simple Past* in *len.* The forms *hijú-kenaing hijú-kenam,* etc., are never heard from the Mundas themselves.

One frequently hears the Anterior Past used in cases where the real function of this tense would not justify its use. The following may be accepted as a correct general rule or description of the Mundas'; practice:—

Whenever there is really question to the priority of one past action over another, the Mundas invariably use the Anterior Past Tense form. In other cases they use it rather frequently instead of the *Simple Past.*

XI.—The Static Past

It is limited to Transitive Predicates, and is formed by suffixing *tad* to the root.

Pronominal Objects stand between the Suffix and the Copula. Indirect Objects are not preceded by *a.* The elisions described in the Simple Past take place here too when the Pronouns *ing* or *í* are inserted as Objects : hence the forms *tol-tá-iñ-ae* for *tol-tad-iñ-ae,* and *tol-tá-i-ae* for *tol-tad-i-ae.*

What has been said above concerning the double function or meaning of the Static Future applies also to the Static Past—

Dura nitada means { either, He has opened the door and left it open; or, He opened the door, although he ought not to have done so.

Uríko-ing adertad'-koa means { either, I drove the cattle in and they are still in the stable ; or, I drove the cattle in before the proper time or against orders.

XII.—The Perfect Tense

It is formed by suffixing *akan* to Intransitive and *akad* to Transitive Predicates.

Pronominal Objects stand between the Suffix *akad* and the Copula. Indirect Objects are not preceded by *a.* The elisions described in the Simple Past take place here too when *ing* and *i* stand as Objects : hence the forms *Lel-aká-iñ-ae,*— He has seen me, and *Lel-aká-i-ae,*—He has seen him or her.

The Perfect Tense directly signifies that an action is completed, and it implies that the effects or the state brought about by that action are continuing still. In other words, the Perfect Tense points out the present effects of a past and completed action.

The Mundas adhere strictly to the function of the Perfect as here defined. This gives rise to cetain idiomatic expressions in which particular Perfect forms are used where we would expect the Indeterminate Tense of *ituanaing,* I know ; *ituanam,* thou knowest, etc—

En horo lel-akáiaing,—I know that man ; *Kaing lel-akad'-koa,*—I do not know them ; *En hora kaing senakana,*—I do not know that road ; *Ama bharom kaing did daria go kaing heua-akana,*—I cannot take your luggage (load), I am not accustomed to carrying, *i. e.,* my shoulders are not hardened by having carried loads; *En jó chiulao kaing jomakada,* — I do not know how that fruit tastes (because I have never eaten any of it).

In the above and similar sentences Mundas use the Perfect Tense of certain Predicates in order to directly denote the effects or the state brought about by the actions signified.

The difference between the Perfect Tense and the Static Past may be defined as follows:—

The Perfect Tense is the simple statement of an accomplished fact with the accompanying connotation that the effects of the action are lasting as a matter of fact. It connotes nothing respecting the *intention* or *the state of mind of the agent.*

The Static Past, on the contrary, connotes or rather primarily denotes the *intention* or the *state of mind of the agent.*

The Perfect is a Tense-form in the strict sense of the term. The Static Past, on the contrary, is, so far as *ta* is concerned, rather a modification of the Predicate's meaning.

XIII.—The Indefinite Past

The Suffix *jan* is used with some *Intransitive Predicates* to form a Past Tense which may in a certain sense be called *Indefinite Past.* However, the name is not very accurate, and is used here chiefly for want of a better one. In the Active Voice the Past in *jan* is limited to *sen,* to go; *nir,* to run away ; *apir*, to fly away ; *hoka,* to cease, to stop. It implies that the being denoted by the Subject to these Predicates went, ran or flew away and is not yet returned, or that an action has been stopped for the moment and has not yet been resumed, though the intention of resuming it exist.

Example.— Hokajanale dá go,—We have, for the present, stopped carrying water. It differs from the Perfect, inasmuch as that Tense primarily denotes the definite or permanent absence brought about by the past acts of going, running or flying away, whereas the Indefinite Past does not imply a permanent absence. It simply connotes that so far the being signified by the Subject has not yet returned.

Okoria Soma? Nirjanae,—Where is Soma? He has run away (*v. gr.,* for fear of being scolded by you he ran away, just to avoid meeting you).

Nirakanae,—He is no longer here, *i.e.,* he has run away from this place definitively and does not seem to intend returning.

In narrations too this Indefinite Tense is generally used, *v. gr.*—

Enatedo tuiu ruṛajanae aeá oṛáte oṛo inioe senójana,—Then the fox returned home to his own house and he too (the stork) went home.

The Simple Past in *ken* is used only in enquiries or statements concerning a matter of fact, *v. gr.,* I told Soma to go to Ranchi. Did he (really) go ? Yes, sir, he did go. *Ranchite senme mente Somaing kajilia. Chia senkenae ? He, gomke, senkenae.* If this question be answered by *senjanae,* it would imply that he did go, and is not yet back.

Second function.- Jan is suffixed to both Transitive and Intransitive Predicates to signify that the Subject or Agent *went* to do a certain work or *began* some action, and that he has not yet completed or discontinued it: hence in English this very peculiar Tense-form must generally be rendered either by the Past of the Verb *to begin* or *to go*, followed by an Infinitive or a Participal Clause.

Transitive Predicates never insert Pronominal Objects in this form —

Durang-jan-ae, he *began* to sing *; Rd-jan-ae* he *began* to cry. *Inung-jan-ae,* he *is gone* to play*; susun-jan-ae,* he has gone to dance ; *senderu-jan-ae,* he is *gone* hunting ; *siú-jan-ae,* he is gone to plough. *Madle md-jan-a,* he is *gone* to cut bambos; *Urike-e gupi-jan-a,* he is *gone* to graze the cattle ;*Haike-e sab-jan-a,* he is *gone* to catch fish.

When *jan* is suffixed to *hoka,* to cease, to stop, it implies that a certain action is discontinued for the moment, though it be not definitively broken off or given up altogether.

Daru pataule hokajana,— We have (for the moment) stopped watering the trees.

The Perfect Tense, on the contrary, implies the complete giving up of the action. *Ne daru patau nadole hoke-akada,-* We have now stopped watering this tree (because it does no more require it, it has taken root.)

THE IMPERFECT TENSES

To nearly each of the Tences described so far there corresponds an Imperfect Tense. All these Imperfects are formed by adding *taeken* (seldom *taeken)* to the original complete Tense-form, so that the generic Imperfect Tense-suffix always stands immediately before the Copula, *v. gr., sentan-taeken-a-ing,-* I was going then. *Inungledtaeken-a-ko,-* They had been playing.

The Imperfect Tense-suffix never affects the position of the inserted Pronominal Objects. These remain in the position pointed out above; nor does it interface with any of the elisions described in the Indefinite Present, the Simple Past, etc, But this Suffix or rather Auxiliary does affect the position of the Pronominal Subjects. As a general rule the Mundas place the Pronominal Subjects immediately before *taeken*—

Senioan-ing-taekena, seldom: *santan-taeken-a-ing.*

*Inungled'-ko-taekena,*seldom : *inungled'-taeken-a-ko.*

Hence in those Tenses which insert the Pronominal Objects after the Tense-suffix, we have in the corresponding Imperfects two Pronouns standing side by side before the Auxuliary *taeken ;* the first of these being a Direct or Indirect Object and the Pronominal Subject—

Leljad'- ko-ing -taeken-a, I was seeing them at the time ; *Haiko sabled' ko-le-taeken-a,-* We had just been catching fish.

With regard to function, it may be said in general that the Auxiliary *taeken* does not change anything either in the denotation or connotation of the original Tense-forms. All it does with regard to them is this : it transfers them into the past time, and there assigns to them in relation to some past fact that particular position in time which the original Tense-form implies.

XIV.—The Indeteminate Imperfect

One of the functions of the Indeterminate Tense is to state universal truths, first principles or axioms. This particular funtion has of course no Imperfect.

Another function of the original Tense is to state customs not yet extinct or habits not given up, etc. This function has an Imperfect Tense.

Taeken added to the Indeteminate Tense represents as having exited formerly customs now extinct, habits now given up, occupations performed regularly at one time, but abandoned now.

Before the English arrived in our country the Mundas were in the habit of burning wizards and witches alive : *Aleá disumre Angrajiko auriko hijúre Mundako nojomko jid' jid' ge-ko (*Subj.*) atar-ko-taekena. Hen diplio sí-ko-taekena-* At that (remote) time too they were ploughing, *i.e.,* they performed the work of cultivators.

In the Active Voice there is no Imperfect corresponding to any of the three Future Tenses. The Imperfect form of the Transitive or Definite Present is commonly used to express the idea that some past action was on the point of being performed when the main event narrated took place.

However, when it is desired to insist on the idea of a futurity of a past action relatively to another, the following circumlocution is used which renders the difference berween the Simple, the Anterior, and the Static Future to a nicety. In this circumlocution the original Tense-forms occur in Direct-speech form, whereas the Auxiliary *taeken* is added to words meaning *to intend, to say:-*

Ex.— He was on the point of going to Ranchi when his wife fell sick, becomes *I shall go* to Ranchi, saying he *had intended,* but then his wife fell sick : *Ranchiteng sena mente moneakade taekena, entedo kuritae hasujanae.* Here *mone* is in the Pluperfect, because it means, he *had made up* his mind.

He was going to first sow that field and then start for Ranchi when he got sick, becomes, I shall first sow that field and then go to Ranchi saying he had made up his mind, when he got sick : *En loeonging herlea ente Ranchiteng sene mente moneakade taekena, mendo hasujanae,-* He was forbidden by the owner to cut that tree. Notwithstanding he was about to cut it, when a tiger came and carried him off, becomes......... nevertheless. I will cut it, saying he had determined ; but then a tiger, etc.- *En daru alom maea mente kisanre manalía. Enreo mataeaing mente moneakade taekena. Entedo kula birete unungjanchie idikia.*

XV.—The Intrasitive or Definite Present Imperfect

This performs two distinct functions :-

(1) It imlies that the action in question was going on in the past simultaneously with another past action spoken of or implied in the same sentence—

Ako dapalken imta enta're sitaning taekena,—I was ploughing there just at the same time they were fighting.

(2) It is also used as Imperfect to the Future instead of the above circumlocution—

Senótaning taekena,- I was (at that time) on the point of going, or I was about to go.

XVI.—The Transitive or Indefinite Present Imperfect

This is limited to Transitive Predicates. It performs the function described under (1) of the Intransitive Present Imperfect. It is also used as Future Imperfect. *Rajad'-ko-ing-taekena* may mean I was just then calling them, or I was just on the point of calling them.

XVII.—Imperfect of the Continuative Present

Whereas the Imperfects described under XV and XVI exhibits the action in question as merely simultaneous with some other past action, this Imperfect denotes that the action having begun before some other past act or event, continued uninterruptedly whilst that other act or event took place : *Hoiote aiñá bened' otangjanchi garare uiujana ; aingdo sadoming sadakái-taekena mente kaing sabdairijana,*- My pugri being blown away by the wind fell into the river; I could not catch it because at that moment I was (busy) holding the horse.

XVIII.—Imperfect of the Simple Past

The Intransitive form is hardly used except with *sen. Senken-ing-taekena,*-I had been going. The Transitive form is gererally replaced by the Anterior Past Tense-form with *taeken.*

XIX.—Imperfect of the Incomplete Past.

This is used with Transitive Predicates to show that a past action had been left in a state of incompleteness before some other past act or event.

I asked him whethe he had finished cutting those bamboos. He *had been busy cutting,* but he had not finished. Nevertheless, he told me he had finished,- *En mad'em machabakeda menteng kulikia. Mado ma-ken-e-taekena mendo kae chabaakad taekena. Enreo machabaakadaing mentee kajiruraíña.*

XX.—Imperferct of the Anterior Past

This Tense is generally used with both Transitive and Intransitive Predicates, both with its own particular function as well as in cases where we would rather expect the Imperfect of the Simple Past—

Inku auri tebare haiko sab'led'-ko-le-taekena,- We had been catching fish before they arrived.

XXI.—The Imperfect of the Static Past

This is used with both the meanings explained under III with that modification of time which the Auxiliary *taekena* denotes.

Aputee ruarimta uriko adertad'-ko-e taekena,— He had just driven in the cattle for the night (*i.e.,* permanently) when his father arrived, or he had just driven in the cattle (against orders or before the proper time) when his father arrived.

XXII.—Pluperfect or Imperfect corresponding to the Perfect Tense

This is used both with its own function as well as a substitute for an Imperfect corresponding to the Past Tense in *jan.*

Susunjanae,—He went to dance and is not yet back. The Imperfect is, *susunte senakane-taekena-a,* never *susun-jan-e-taekena.*

PASSIVE VOICE

This voice has a double formation. In *the Indeterminate Tense, the Future* and *the Definite Present* it is formed by affixing *ó* to the bare root-form. *The Imperative Mood* forms its Passive in the same manner, because this Mood-form is only the bare root *plus* a Personal Pronominal Affix, *v. gr., lel- me !* look thou! *lel -pe !* look you! *lel ben. !* look you two ! The Passive Affix *ó* therefore stands between the root and the Pronominal Affix : thus *dal,* to beat; *dal-ó-me!* be beaten ; *dal-ó-ben !* be beaten both of you !

In all the other Tenses the Passive is formed by affixing the *Intransitive Tense-suffixes* to Transitive Predicates.

Thus whilst *lel-led-aing* means I first *saw* it ; *len-len-aing* means I *was first seen.*

REMARK 1.—In the third Person Singular of the Indeterminate and the Future Tense the check (') is generally transferred from the Passive Affix *ó* to the Copula *a*, v. gr., *aium,* to hear ; *iumó,* to be heard, Nere hann gara *aiumoá,*— Yonder river is always heard from here. *Sajai,* to punish ; *sajaió,* to be punished; *sajaioáe,*— he will be punished.

The same rule is followed of course whenever the Pronominal Subjects are suffixed to a word preceding the Predicate, *v. gr., Gapa-ing sajaioá,*—I shall be punished to-morrow; *gapa-m sajaioá,*—thou wilt be punished to-morrow.

REMARK 2.—Monosyllables ending with *checked vowels* always insert a *g* before the Affix ó, v. gr., *dá,* water ; *da-g-ó,* to become liquid or to turn into water ; *ré,* to rob ; *re-g-ó,* to be robbed. Dissyllabic words containing no consonants and ending with a checked vowel also insert a *g* before the Passive Affix, *v. gr., uiú,* to drop, to let fall ; *uiú-g-ó,* to fall.

Dissyllabic words containing a consonant and ending with a checked vowel sometimes insert this *g* and sometimes they do not, *v. gr., toroé,* ashes ; *toroeó* or *toroe-g-ó,* to be reduced to ashes ; *lebé,* soft ; *lebeó* or *lebe-g-ó,* to become soft ; *peré,* to fill; *pereo* or *pere-g-ó,* to be filled up, to become full.

The checks of all final vowels disappear before the Passive ó even in those cases in which the check of ó is transferred to the Copula .

REMARK 3.—Te Affix ó changes very frequently, not to say generally, into *ú* when preceded by *i.* This is according to the law of harmony of vowels—

Kaji, to say ; Kaji-u-á, it is said (generally) or it will be said.

The Future Tense, which has no corresponding Imperfect in the Active Voice, has an Imperfect in the Passive Voice—

Daló taeken-ae,—He was on the point of being beaten when such or such an event occurred.

This Imperfect is even substituted for the Definite Present Imperfect.

The Static Future and the Static Past are wanting in the Passive.

The Anterior Future too is wanting. It may be replaced by the construction with *sidate* given under IV (pages ? and ?).

The Incomplete Past in *ken* being essentially an Active form is wanting.

The Suffix *jan* is used in the Passive to form the Simple Past Tense as well as an Indefinite Past.

The Passive of *the Indeterminate Tense* is frequently used to denote *feasibility* or *possibility.* For the purpose of this function Intransitive Predicates too take the affix ó in the Indeterminate Tense, *v. gr., Ne jó jom-ó-a,*—This fruit *can be eaten* or *is eatable ; Nere ka nir-ó-a,*—It is not *possible to run* here; *En kotore, sen-o-a,*—It is *possible to walk* on that branch; *Totraute ka durum-o-a,*—It is *impossible to sleep* on account of the uproar.

I do not believe the Passive Affix ó to be a *débris* of a formerly complete root. If, however, it be such a *débris,* it will hardly be possible to form even a reasonable conjecture concerning the original form and meaning of that root until the Kholarian dialects of India can be traced to a wider group with which they have some more striking remblances than those which have so far been discovered.

If, on the other hand, ó be a complete root, then the only explanation presenting itself to me is the following:

As has already been shown, *á* means both *to be* and *to become.* But the idea *of becoming,* besides implying *futurity,* does also imply the idea *of being acted upon, i.e.,* the idea of *passivity;* for the mind, as a matter of fact, *does not conceive* incipiency or effect without, at least implicitly, referring the effect or that which begins to *a cause* distinct from *the effect* : hence this *á (to become)* may, with as much reason, be used to signify the idea *of being acted upon* or the notion of *passivity* as it is to signify *futurity.* Suppose, now, that *á* be actually used for the purpose of denoting that particular *nuance* implied in the idea of *becoming,* we would, in the Indeterminate Tense, get this *á* twice immediately after the bare root thus *dal-á-á-ing ; literally,* Strike become being I, or more freely a *becoming* struck being I, *i.e., Becoming* or *getting* struck am I. Now in such a case it would appear natural that a vowel change should have been adopted to signify the implied *nuance* of passivity, and that the *á*-form should have been kept for the purpose of signifying futurity and that of link-word.

If this supposition be correct, it allows of the following statement : The Passive Affix ó is but an alternative form of á, *to become,* which has assumed as its primary meaning that particular *nuance* of the original concept which implies the correlation between cause and effect. Its precise function, therefore, consists in exhibiting the Subject of the proposition as being acted upon by a cause distinct from itself.

Mundari is not the only language which uses the idea of *becoming* as a functional exponent of both futurity and passivity : thus, *v. gr.,* German, when forced to replace worn-out formative elements by complete auxiliaries, instinctively turned to the Verb *werden, to become,* for the same purposes. Ich *werde schlagen*—

I will or shall strike ; literally means I *become* to strike. *Ich werde geschlagen.* I am being beaten ; literally means I *become* struck. In the Future of the Passive the same auxiliary occurs in both functions : *Ich werde geschlagen werden,* I shall be beaten; *literally,* I become becoming beaten. English auxiliaries too present a striking instance of that instinctive tendency which uses *nuances* or, if I may say so, *side-ideas* implied in a concept, for special functional or formative purposes. To quote but one: *To will* denotes self-determination ; but this implies the *origin* or the beginning of a new self-modification. It is therefore generically the same idea as that implied by *to become.* As such, it necessarily implies futurity. It is no doubt on acount of this *implied* futurity that the Verb *to will* has been chosen as an Auxiliary for the *Future Tense.*

REFLEXIVE VOICE

By *Reflexive Voice* we understand that form of a Transitive Predicate which implies that the action denoted by the Predicate falls back on the agent himself, or that the Subject of the proposition represents both the *agent* and the *terminus* of the action.

It is formed by affixing *n* to be the root or predicative element. Roots ending with a consonant insert a euphonic *e, o, i* or *u* before the *n.* The choice of the vowel is determined by the law of harmony. *Ex.—Dal,* to strike ; *dal-e-n,* to strike oneself ; *Ur,* to skin ; *ur-i-n,* to shed one's skin ; *Bingko urina,* snakes throw their skin.

The Reflexive *n* is affixed to the root only in *the Indeterminate Tense, the Simple Future, the Definite Present,* and *the Indefinite Past* in *jan* and in the corresponding Imperfects. In all the other Tenses the Intransitive Tense-suffixes in *n* are used for the Reflexive as well as for the Passive Voice.

The Mundari Reflexive Voice is not limited to the cases in which we would use a Transitive Predicate with a Reflexive Pronoun as Direct Object. This is mainly due to the fact that Mundas may use any and every root with a Transitive function. This obliges them in certain cases to have recourse to the Reflexive Voice where we use ready-made Intransitive Verbs. V. gr.—*Dasi,* a servant; *dasin,* to serve (*literally,* to make a servant of oneself). In other cases too, where we have Intransitive Verbs, they have recourse to the Reflexive Voice, *v. gr., to feign, to pretend,* is in Mundari rendered by the Reflexive form of *bai,* to make. He pretends to be ill,—*Hasu baintanae.* As will be seen from the two examples just quoted, the Reflexive *form* is not always purely Reflexive in *meaning* according to our ideas. We would expect *dasin* to mean *to serve one's self, to act as one's own servant in certain cases.* Again, a beginner is liable to translate *hasubain* by *to make one's self really sick.* In other cases the Reflexive form is used where the agent is, according to our way of thinking, the Indirect Object, *v. gr., dul,* to pour; *dulen,* to pour *on* or *over* one's self; *uiú,* to throw ; *uiun,* to throw (a cloth) *over* one's self, *i. e.,* to cover one's whole body with a big cloth which is thrown over the shoulders. A correct and idiomatic use of the Reflexive form can be learnt only through intercourse with the people.

I am inclined to think that the Reflexive Affix *n* is simply the Demonstrative *ne, this* (see page 65, *Note* (1) for the following reason :.—

According to the rules regulating the insertion into the Predicate of Direct Objects denoting living nbeings, we should expect the following forms, *v. gr.*-Pr. root. D. O. Pr. Tense. C. S.

Dal-ing -tan - a - ing	I strike me (myself).	*Dal-king-tan-a-king.*
Dal- *me - tan - a - m*	Thou strikest thee (thyself).	*Dal-bu -tan- a- bu.*
Dal - i - tan- a - e,	He (she) strikes himself.	*Dal-le -tan-a-le.*
Dal-lang- tan - a -lang,	Thou and I strike thee and me.	*Dal-pe -tan-a-pe.*
Dal-ling - tan - a- ling.	He and I strike him and me.	*Dal-ko -tan-a-ko.*
Dal-ben - tan - a - ben,	You two strike yourselves.	

Now it will be remarked that the form *dal-i-tan-a-e,*—he strikes him is ambiguous, because it does not appear from the form alone whether the Pronoun *i,* which stands here as Inserted Direct Object, denotes the same individual which is denoted by the Subject *e (*the weak form of *i)* or whether it denotes some third person different from the Subject.

The same ambiguity exists in the forms *dal-king-tan-a-king, dalko-tan-a-ko.* Again, in the Inclusive Dual *dal-lang-tan-a-lang,*—thou and I strike thee and me, it does not appear from the form whether I strike myself and the included second person strikes himself, or whether we strike each other mutually. A similar ambiguity exists for the Exclusive Dual as well as for the Inclusive and Exclusive Plural of the first Person.

But if, instead of the Direct Objects *i, king, ko, lang, ling,* etc., the Definite Demonstrative *ne,* this be inserted as Direct Object, then this Demonstrative could readily be understood as referring to or pointing out the Pronominal Subjects *i, king, ko, lang, le,* etc., for the purpose of thus identifying the Direct Object with the Subject.

The meaning of the Demonstrative *n* could then be translated into *that same he, those same two, those same ones,* etc.—

Dal-en-tan-a-e,—He strikes that same he, *i.e.,* himself.

The Inserted Demonstrative thus interpreted would remove all ambiguity and at the same time set the forms *dal-i-tanae, dal-king-tanaking, dal-ko-tanako,* etc., free to signify Subjects and Direct Objects distinct from each other. And in fact these forms are in constant use, but the Direct Objects *i, king, ko* are understood to denote third persons different from those denoted by the Subjects i, *king, ko* in the same compounds.

Dal-i-tan-ae means he or she strikes some other third person.

If the explanation here given as to the manner in which the ambiguity mentioned has been removed be admissible, it is easily understood how, for the sake of uniformity, the Demonstrative *n* should have come to be inserted as Direct Object also in the few cases in which there would be no ambiguity if the Personal Pronoun were inserted as Direct Object. This, then, would allow the following statement. The Definite Demonstrative *n* is inserted as Direct Object into Transitive Predicates whenever it is required to point out that the agent and the sufferer of an action are identical. *This insertion yields the Reflexive Voice.*

RECIPROCAL VOICE

By *the Reciprocal Voice* we understand that form of a Transitive Predicate which implies that the action denoted by that Predicate is reciprocal between two individuals or two sets of individuals. In other words, the Reciprocal Voice implies that the individuals denoted by the Subject of the Proposition reciprocate the same action on each other.

The Reciprocal Voice is formed by inserting the consonant *p* after the first vowel of a Transitive root, then repeating that vowel and adding to it the remaining part of the root—

om, to give ; *o-p-om,* to give to each other ; *nel,* to see; *ne-p-el* to see each other.
dal, to strike ; *da-p-al,* to strike each other ; *ré,* to rob ; *re-p-é* to rob each other.
kaji, to say ; *ka-p-aji,* to converse with each other. *erang,* to scold ; *e-p-erang,* to quarell.
má, to cut ; *ma p-á,* to fight with axes, swords or knives.

The Reciprocal Voice has of course only the Dual and the Plural Numbers.

NOTE.—The Pronoun *pe* or *ape* if used transitively means *to call some people you* or *to 'you"* some one's, *i.e.,* to put some people into the relation of *second persons* with regard to the speaker.

PJP May it not be that *pe* you, is, with a transitive function inserted into the root of Predicates for the purpose of signifying that the agents (*i.e.,* the Dual or Plural Subjects to such Predicates) put themselves with regard to each other into the relation of Second Persons, not indeed as speakers and parties addressed, but as agents and reagents, as reciprocating on each other the action denoted by he Predicates into which *pe* is inserted in the shape of the consonant *n.*

The idiomatic use of the Reciprocal Voice presents even greater difficulties than that of the Reflxive Voice.

Functionally it may be divided into the Direct Reciprocal, and the Indirect Reciprocal.

The Direct Reciprocal implies that the agents and reagents denoted by the Subject are at the same time the *Direct* Objects of the action signified by the Predicate, *v. g.,* thexse two always greet each other,—Niking jo-*p*-oaraking.

The Indirect Reciprocal implies that the *Direct* Object of the Predicate is some living being or inanimate objects *distinct* from the persons or animals denoted by the Subject, *i.e.,* generally something owned by them. The persons or animals denoted by the Subjects are *Indirect* Objects of the action signified by the Predicate, *v. gr.,* They show their bows and arrows to each other. In the war dance they strike (at) each other's swords. Hence sentences in which the Predicate is an *Indirect Reciprocal* contain a Noun or Pronoun denoting the Direct Object, whereas those in which the Predicate is a *Direct Reciprocal* do not contain such a Noun or Pronoun, *v. gr., Direct* Reciprocal—*Ta-p-amtanaking,*—the two hit each other. *Indirect Reciprocal—Tarauri-king ta-p-amtana*—They stirike (at) each other's swords.

Inasmuch as neither of the agents and reagents is the terminus or sufferer of the action, the *Indirect Reciprocal* participates of the nature of the *Active Voice*:- hence it is quite natural that in the Past Tenses the Transitive Tense-affixes ending in *d* must be used and not the Intransitive or Passive Affixes ending, in *n,* viz., *ked* for the Simple Past, *led* for the Anterior Past,k *tad* for the Static Past, and *akad* for the Perfect and the Continuative Present.

From the Active nature of the Indirect Reciprocal it also follows that Pronominal Objects should be inserted into this Reciprocal form whenever the Direct Object denotes living beings, *v. gr.*—

They show their hawks to each other,—*Lampiking u-p-udub-jad' king-a-king.*

In a word, the Indirect Reciprocal is in every respect treated like a Simple Transitive Predicate of the *Active Voice* regarding Mood and Tense-suffixes.

The Direct Reciprocal, on the contrary, is treated as a Transitive Predicate of the *Passive Voice,* because in this form the Subjects of the proposition are at the same time the sufferers or termini of the action denoted by the Predicate. However, the Passive Affix *ó* is not used because the Infix *p* is supposed to perform at the same time the function of that Passive Affix. Hence—

(1) In the Anterior Future the Tense-suffix *kó* must be used instead of *le, h. gr.,. tipi-kó-alang,*—Let us first shake hands ; never *tipi-le-alang.*

(2) The Indefinite Present in *jad* is always replaced by the Definite Present in *tan : eperang-tan-akó,*—They scold each other ; never eperang-*jad*-ako.

(3) The Past Tenses take the Tenses-suffixes ending in *n,* viz., *ken, len, jan,* and *akan.*

The very same word may be used as Direct and as Indirect Reciprocal—

Ti, hand; *tipí,* to take each other's hand, *i.e.,* to shake hands ; and *tipí,* to take up or to handle other's property, *v. gr.,* a bow.

Nel, to see; *nepel,* to see each other, to look at each other ; and *nepel,* to look at each other's property, or to show (*i.e.,* let see) each other's property to one another.

Udub', to show and to denounce; *upudub',* to denounce each other; and *upudub,* to show each other's property one to another.

The words *to steal, to rob, to give, to help,* and *their synonyms* are treated as Direct Reciprocals, even when in English a distinct Direct or Indirect Object is expressed in the sentence, *v. gr.*, They robbed each other of their rice.— *Babako repé-ken-a.* They helped each other with money,—*Takako depenga-ken-a,*—They gave presents to each other,—*Enemko opom-ken-a.*

The following table shows the Tense-suffixes of the Direct and the Indirect Reciprocals respectively : —

Direct Reciprocal	*Indirect Reciprocal.*
Indeter. T. —*Nepel-ako,*—They habitually see each other.	*Ásar-ko-nepel-e-a,*—They are in the habit of showing their bows and arrows to each other.
Simple Fut.—*Nepel-ako,*—They will see each other.	*Ásar-ko nepel-e-a,*—They will show their bows and arrows to each other.
Anter. Fut.—*Nepel-kó-ako,*—They will first see each other.	*Ásar-ko nepel-le-a,*—They will first show their bows and arrows to each other.
Defin. Pres.—*Nepel-tan-ako.*—They are seeing each other.	*Ásarko nepel-tan-a,*—They are now looking at each other's bows and arrows.
Indef. Pres.—Not used.	*Ásarko nepel-jad-a,*—They look at each other's bows and arrows.
Contin. Present.—*Nepel-akan-a-ko,*— They keep looking at each other.	*Ásarko nepel-akad-a,*—They keep looking at each other's bows and arrows.
Simple Past.—*Nepel-ken-ako,*—They saw each other.	*Ásarko nepel-ked-a,*—They looked at each other's bows and arrows.
Anter. Past.—*Nepel-len-ako,*—They first saw each other.	*Ásarko nepel-led-a,* —They first saw each other's bows and arrows.
Perfect.—*Nepel-akan-ako,*—They have seen each other.	*Ásarko-ne-el-akad-a,*—They have looked at each other's bows and arrows.
Indef. *Past.*—Not used.	*Ásarko nepel-jan-a,*—They have seen other's bows and arrows.
Intent. Past.—*Nepel-jan-ako,*—They are gone to see each other.	Ásarko nepel-jan-a,—They are gone to look at each other's bows and arrows.

When two words concur to form a Compound Predicate, the Reciprocal *p* is generally infixed in both words.

Ir, to reap ; *ré,* to rob : hence *ir-ré* means to rob some one by cutting his harvest : hence *i-p-ir-re-p-étanaking,*—The two are robbing each other by cutting each other's harvest.

Nir, to run, *darom,* against or towards : hence *nir-darom,* to run against or to run towards : hence *ni-p-ir-da-p-aromkenaking,*—They ran or rushed against each other.

Har, to drive, to run after ; *nir,* to run ; hence *Ha-p-arni-p-ir,* to play a game in which one must try to catch or overtake another who runs.

The insertion of the *p* may, however, be confined to the principal word, *v. gr., nirda-p-arom.*

ORIGIN AND MEANING OF THE TENSE-SUFFIXES

Tan seems to be a compound of the Static Suffix *ta* and the Demonstrative *ne.* The Static *ta* is identical with the root of the Postposition *tá* (see pages 87 and 88). This *ta* presupposes concrete existence which in Mundari is signified by *mená.* To judge from its meaning as a Postposition and as Static Suffix, *ta* would seems to primarily and directly denote *continuance, duration, permanency,* just as *eté,* signifies *beginning* and *chaba, completion.* According to the *genius* of the language it may be used with a Transitive or Intransitive function, and then mean either *to last, to continue (*Intransitive) or *to render permanent (*Transitive) just as *eté* may mean *to commence, to begin,* and as *chaba* may mean to *finish* or *to complete (*Transitive and Intransitive).

This, like other roots, may be added to a primary root for the purpose of modifying its original meaning, thus—

Ete, to begin; *tol-ete,* to begin to tie; *chaba,* to finish; *tol-chaba,* to complete the act of lying ; *ta,* to render permanent ; *tol-ta,* to render permanent the state brought about by the act of tying (first of the meanings explained above on page169) or to persist in the intention of tying (second meaning). The duration or continuance denoted by *ta* is in no way specified. It is an indefinite one: hence the peculiar meaning of the Static forms. If now it be desired to specify this duration; so as to refer or limit it to the present time only, the Demonstrative *ne* would naturally be used for that purpose ; for specification and limitation is the primary function of this Demonstrative : hence the Compound Suffix *ta-n* would directly denote a duration limited to the present time. It would in fact mean *to be busy with something now,*so that *tol-tan-aing* would literally denote a present tying and mean I am busy tying now. This is precisely the meaning of the Definite Present.

The fact that *ta* in the Static forms points *not to the action itself* as lasting, but to its effects, whereas *tan* directly denotes the present duration *of the action itself,* presents no difficulty. For indefinite duration, such as is signified by *ta,* cannot as a rule be predicated of actions themselves. These can last indefinitely only in their effects.

If *ta* really men *to continue, to last,* as is here supposed, then its Reflexive form would be *ta-en* and mean to make or cause oneself to continue indefinitely, *i.e., to remain;* but it so happens that the Mundari equivalent of the Verb *to remain* is precisely the word *laen* or *tain.* This no doubt supports the views just exposed concerning the meaning of the Static *ta* and the composition of *tan.* The generic Imperfect Suffix *taeken* is but a contraction of the Simple Past of *taen,* viz., *taenken.* This form is sometimes used instead of the contracted form.

viz., *taenken.* This form is sometimes used instead of the contracted form.

Ta and *ka* seem to be but two different forms of the same original root. At any rate they are perfect equivalents of each others as appears from the folowing facts. The Mundari and Sonthali dialects differ but slightly from each other. Now (1) the Sonthals use *ka* where the Mundas use *ta* to denote permanency of the effects of an action. (2) The Sonthals use *kan,* as Copula in Substantive propositions and as Definite or Intransitive Present Tense-suffix where the Mundas use *tan.*(3) In both dialects *akan (akad)* are used as Perfect and as Continuative Present Suffixes : hence whereas the Sonthals use *ka, kan, akan* for both the Present and the Perfect, the Mundas have reserved *ta* and *tan* for the Present.

Ken is plainly but a weak form of *kan.* In both dialects *ken* is used as a Simple Past Suffix. This is another striking instance of vowel-change being used for obtaining a change of meaning.

Akan.—The explanation of this as a Continuative Present and Perfect Tense-suffix presents some difficulty. I am inclined to think that the initial *a* of *akan* is not really a part of the Tense-suffix as such ; in other words, that this á does not directly belong as a specification to the Suffix *kan,* but rather to the root of the Predicate. If so, *kan* alone would be the Tense-suffix, and this Suffix is added, not to the bare root, but to the root *plus a.*

Strictly speaking, the *Perfect Tense* falls under the category of Present Tenses, inasmuch as it directly denotes a *present state* brought about by a completed or accomplished action. So far, then, the Present Tense-suffix *kan* remains within its proper function in the Perfect Tense ; but by itself alone it does in no way express that other connotation of this Tense, which consists in representing the action as an accomplished fact. This, I believe, is done by *a* being suffixed as a specification to the root. A root or word conceived then and there as an Adjective is transformed into a Noun by the Affix á, *v. gr., pundi,* white ; *pundiá,* something white. Similarly, *a* transforms into Nouns certain roots conceived then and there transitively or *intransitively : Jom,* to cat ; *jomeá,* that which can be eaten or that which is ready to be eaten, *i.e.,* eatables.

Now, may it not be supposed that *a* is similarily suffixed to roots conceived first transitively or intransitively for the purpose of changing them into Nouns denoting the action in question substantively so as to represent them as complete? Thus *hijú,* to come ; *hijúa,* the coming or *the arrival* ; *sen* to go; *sena,* the going or the having gone, *i.e., the absence.* The compound thus obtained can be made to resume its Transitive or Intransitive function by being referred to a Subject by means of the Copula *a.*

If to this new Predicate the Present Tense-suffix *kan* be suffixed, the Copula *a* refers the completed action to a subject as a *present* state—*Hijú-tan-ae* literally means coming-now-is-he ; *Hijua-kan-a-e* means Having-come-now-is-he.

If this be so, we should say that in the Mundari Perfect the action itself is denoted by the bare root of the Predicate, *v. gr., hijú;* the state brought about by the action is denoted by *a,* inasmuch as it transforms the root into a Noun denoting a state *hijú-a ;* the present duration of that state is denoted by the Suffix *kan.*

Ked and *a-kad.*—Just as the consonant *n* in *ken* represents a distinct Demonstrative root, so does the *d* of *ked* and *a-kad* represent a distinct original root. But here the question arises—Is this root the same as the one represented by *n,* or is it both with regard to its *original meaning and form* a different root? That Mundari should have two differently ending Suffixes for Transitive and Intransitive Predicates is in itself every remarkable.Transitiveness and Intransitiveness are not so much objective qualities of actions as subjective modes of conceiving actions. Even such actions as pre-suppose a terminus distinct from the agent may be conceived *exclusively in their relation to the agent, i.e.,* as Intransitive. Now these subjective modes of conceiving actions are not in other languages expressed by special distinct formative elements *ad hoc.* It would therefore be very extraordinary if the Mundas had recourse to a special root for the purpose or directly denoting transitiveness, if, in a wofd, the consonant *d* represented an original root which would both in *form* and *meaning* differ from *n.* The consonant *d* must, I think, be considered as a mere alternative for the consonant *n,* and the substitution of *d* for *n* has been caused solely by phonetic exigencies. If the Mundas did not insert Pronominal Objects after these Suffixes, *ken* and *a-kan* would no doubt be used with Transitive as well as with Intransitive Predicates. The forms *lel-ken-iñ-ae, lel-ken-me-ae, lel-ken-i-ae, lel-ken-lang-ae* are rather heavy. Hence the substitution of the dental *d* for the dental *n* has been made for the purpose of obtaining the lighter forms *lel-ked-in-ae, lel-ked'-me-ae,* etc. The check on *d,* which is used before consonants, renders this consonant still more similar to the *n* it replaces.

Len, led, and *tad* are evidently only contractions of *le-ken, le-ked,* and *ta-ked.*

Ló, as stated in the Chapter on Postpositions, denotes *simultaneity* in time and *concomitancy* in space.

Le, as appears from the function it performs in the Anterior Future and the Anterior Past, denotes *priority, i.e.,* a comparative or relative past. Both *ló* and *le* therefore denote relations of time. May not, then, *ló* and *le* be but different modulations of one and the same root, the difference of meaning being brought about by the change in the root-vowel, just as an analogous change of meaning has been caused by the vowel change in *kan* and *ken?*

Lá denotes excess in *extent,* in *duration*, and in *intensity.* It is used as a Pronoun, as an Adverb, and as a Transitive and Intransitive predicate. *Enate láge, more* than that, *further* than that ; *gel sirmaete láge, longer* than ten years ago, or *longer* than for ten years to come; *la-kedae,* he *exceeded* the distance, he *exceeded* the time. If *la, ló* and *le* be in reality but different modulations of the same root, they constitute an interesting example of changes in meaning being caused by mere vowel changes.

Yan is the Transitive equivalent of the Suffix *jan.*

The variations *yan, yad,* and *nad,* are used in certain districts instead of *jan* and *jad.*

I am unable to offer even a plausible conjecture concerning the real nature and original meaning of this Suffix.

Le and *ta,* as stated above, cannot be called *Tense-suffixes* in the strict sense of the word. We may therefore say that, with the exception of *jan* and *jad,* all the Mundari Tense-suffixes are but variations of the roots *ta* and *ne.*

Imperative Mood

This Mood, like the Indicative, has no special Affix.

The Personal Pronouns of the Second Person Singular, Dual or Plural are added to the root or to the root modified by a Tense-suffix or by a Voice-suffix—

Sen-me! go (thou) ; *nir-ben,* run (you two); *hijú-pe !* come (you).

It occurs in all the four Voices—*Abung-en-me !* Wash thyself ! *Dal-ó-pe !* Be beaten (you)! *Du-p-ular-pe !* Love each other !

Direct and Indirect Pronominal Objects are inserted immediately before the Pronominal Suffix.—*Lel-ing-me !* Look at me ! *Rá-i-ben !* You two call him! *Om-ako-pe,* Give it to them !

It is used in the following Tenses :—

1st.—The Indeterminate and *the Simple Future*—Whenever the Direct Object of a Transitive Predicate is an inanimate being, the vowel *e* is inserted before the Pronominal Suffix—

Lel-e-me! Look at it. *Do-e-ben!* Put it down (you two) ! *Hur-ang-e-pe!* Throw it away (you) !

2nd.—The Static Future—Tol-ta-i-me! Tie him down ! *Do-ta-ben!* Put it down and leave it there (you two), or Put it down all the same *or* nevertheless !

The vowel *e* of *me* is generally dropped when this Suffix is immediately preceded by the Static Affix *ta* or by the Pronominal Objects *ko* or *ako. Do-ta-m ! ra-ko-m !* Call them ! *Ader-ta-ko-m !* Drive them in and shut them up ! or, drive them in notwithstanding !

3rd.—The Intransitive Anterior Future in kó and *the Anterior Future in le.* Remark that *me does not drop its* é after *kó and le—Hiju-kó-me* ! *Rá-le-ko-m !* First call them (thou) !

N. B.—Whenever *kó* is suffixed to words which form their Anterior Future in *le,* the Suffix *kó* assumes the meaning of a polite invitation. *Sen-kó-me !* Go, please ! *Ol-kó-me!* Do write, please ! *Dub'-kó-pe !* Do sit down, please !

Even with those words which form their Anterior Future exclusively in *kó,* that Suffix frequently implies a polite invitation : hence circumstance must decide whether, for instance, *Hijú-kó-me !* means *first come here !* or *do come, please !*

The Suffix *len* is sometimes used in the Imperative and the Precative Mood for the purpose of expressing *defiance.* This form is restricted to Intransitive Predicates. *Hijú-len-me !* Come *if thou dare !* Come and thou wilt see something! *Sen-len-me !* Go *if thou dare !*

Mar enka *kahani-len-kae* ale menálere ! —All right let him dare to lie like that in our presence (when we are present).

4th.—The Continuative Present.—In the Active forms the *d* of *akad* is always dropped-–*Goaka-m !* Keep carrying it ; *Sabaka-ko-m!* Continue holding them ! *Otongaká-i-ben !* Keep following him (you two) ; *Senaka-m!* Keep on walking ! never stop walking !

The Affix *akan* is used with two distinct functions in the Imperative :—

1st.—To distinguish the strictly *Intransitive* from the *Transitive* functions in those words which have both functions:—

Birid', to raise—Imperative, *birid-aka-m! biriden,* to rise—Imperative, *birid-akan-me!*

Tingu, to put on end—Imperative, *tingu-aka-m ! tingun,* to stand'—Imperative, *tingu-akan-me !*

Hape, to silence—Imperative, *hape-aka-m ! v. gr.,* keep that drum silent, let that drum no longer he heard ! en dumang *hape-aka-m ; hapen,* to be silent—Imperative *hape-akan-me!*

2nd.—With *purely Intransitive* Predicates, such as *sen, hijú, nir,* etc., *akan* sometimes implies a threat and sometimes it conveys the idea of keeping out of reach so as to avoid a threat.

Sen-aka-m! Keep on walking ! but *Sen-akan-me !* Continue walking or going to such and such a place *if thou dare !* or Go *and remain away* (because it is no longer safe here for thee)! *Hiju-aka-me* ! Keep or continue coming !, but *Hiju-akan-me* ! Continue coming *if thou dare* ! or Come away *and remain away* (because it is no longer safe for thee over there) !

The very peculiar meaning of these forms is of a *Reflexive nature* for it is equivalent to the phrases *to expose one's self to a danger* by going, coming, etc., or *to save one's self from a danger* by going, coming etc.

The Imperative in *akan,* which have been mentioned under *(1st),* are all corresponding to Reflexive forms : hence I incline to think that the Continuative Present Imperative in *akan* is in all cases a Reflexive-Voice form, and that the final *n* is not belonging to the Tense-suffix, but that it is the formative element of the Reflexive Voice.

If this be so, it justifies the following statement : —

All Continuative Presents are formed by the Suffix *akad.* In the Imperative the final *d* is always dropped. In the Reflexive Voice the Voice-affix *n* stands between the Tense-suffix *aka* and the final Pronoun : hence the Imperative quoted above must be alanlysed as follows : —

Root. Tense. Voice. Pron.	Root. Tense. Voice. Pron.	Root. Tense. Voice. Pron.
birid - aka - n - me !	*tingu - aka - n - me !*	*hape - aka - n - me !*
sen - aka - n - me !	*hijü - aka - n - me !*	*nir - aka - n - me!*

The same explanation applies to the form *Hijulenme !* Come if thou dare ! *i. e.,* expose thyself to danger by coming ! hence the analysis *hiju-le-n-me.*

Prohibitions are expressed by placing the prohibitive and deprecative particle *alo!* don't before the bare root *plus* the Copula. In this construction the Personal Pronouns are suffixed to *alo! alo-m hiju-a !* Don not come (thou) ! *Alo -ben hiju-a!* Don't come (you to) ! *Alo-pe ra-ko-a!* Do not you call them ! *Alo-m dal-iñ-a !* Don't strike me ! *Alo-ben om-ai-a!* Don't (you two) give it to him !

PRECATIVE, CONCESSIVE OR OPTATIVE MOOD

This Mood-form implies that the speaker expresses a *desire* or that he asks or grants a *permission, a concession* or a *favour.*

It occurs through the four Voices in the Indeterminate Tense—the Simple, the Anterior, and the Static Fututre and in the Continuative Present.

The formative element of this Mood is the consonant *k.*

In the Indeterminate Tense and the Simple Future *k* stands immediately before the Copula *a*—

Sen-k-a-ing,—May I go, or let me go; *Chuti-ó-k-aing,*—Let me be released, or let me be dismissed. *Dasi-n-k-a-ing ?* May I engage myself as a servant ? *Depenga-k-a-lang !* Let us help each other (thou and I) !

Direct and Indirect Objects precede the Mood-suffix *k—Lel-ko-k-a-ing !* Let me see them ! *Om-aing-k-a-e!* Let him give it to me !

The vowel *e* is inserted whenever the Direct Object is an inanimate being.

Rim-e-k-a-e ! Let him lift *it* up. *Aium-e-k-a-e !* He may hear *it.* But *aium-k-a-e !* means let him listen ! *i.e.,* let him *pay attention !*

In the other Tenses the Tense-suffixes are affixed immediately to the root. Direct and Indirect Objects denoting living beings stand between the Tense-suffix and the Mood-suffix *k.*

Objects denoting inanimate beings are not inserted—

Lel-le-k-a-ing ? May I first see it ? *Tol-ta-ko-k-a-ing !* let me tie them (and leave them tied), or let me tie them notwithstanding.

The Static Future calls for no further explanations.

In the Anterior Future attention must be paid to the following points : —

1st.— *Kó* is used both as Anterior Tense-suffix and as a polite form with most Intransitive Predicates : hence *Sen-kó-k-a-ing* may mean *(a)* Let me *first* go, or *(b)* May I first go, *please ?*

2nd.— In the case of Transitive Predicates *le* is exclusively used as Tense-suffix. In this Mood as well as in the Indicative the *e* of *le* is dropped whenever *ing* or *i* is inserted as Direct or Indirect Objects. *Om-l-ing-k-a-e !* for *om-le-ing k-a-e !* Let him first give it to me ! *Rá-l-i-k-a-ing* for *rá-le-i-k-aing !* Let me first call him !

The remarks made in the Chapter on the Imperative apply throughout to the Precative or Concessive. Hence (*a*) in the case of purely Intransitive words, the following difference in meaning exists : —

Sen-aka-k-a-e ! Let him continue walking without interruption !

Sen-aka-n-k-a-e ! Let him continue going to such a place *if he dare,* or, Let him go to such a place and *remain there to save himself !*

(*b*) In words capable of both functions, *aka* stands for the Transitive and *aka-n* for the Intransitive, *i.e.,* the Reflexive function—

Dumange hape-aka-k-a-e ! Let him silence that drum for good and all !

Rutanko hape-aka-ko-k-ae,—Let him keep the drummers silent.

Hape-aka-n-k-a-e ! Let him remain silent !

The Suffix *len* is added to Intransitive Predicates for the purpose of implying a threat—

Hijú-le-n-ka-e ! Let him come if he dare !

The Suffix *kó* in connection with Transitive Predicates is used exclusively to express a desire or an invitation in a polite manner.

Refusals, prohibitions and requests for exemption are expressed in two ways, in each of which the Negative Particle *ka* is replaced by the Prohibitive *alo*—

1st.— *Alo* with the Pronominal Subject precedes the Simple Future of the Concessive Mood—

Alo-ing kami-k-a,—Let me not be obliged to work. *Alo-e sajai-ó-k-a,*—Let him not be punished.

However, this construction is rather exceptional.

2nd.— Generally the Mood-suffix *k* is detached from the Predicate and suffixed to *alo.* In the Second Person Singular as well as throughout the Dual and Plural a euphonic vowel is necessary to prevent the immediate contact of *k* and the consonants *m, l, b, p* and *k :* hence in this construction the Emphatic Pronouns *aing, am, ae, alang,* etc., replace the Simple Pronouns—

Alo-k-aing sena,—Let me not be obliged to go.

Alo-k-am sena ! Do not go ! or Let thee not be obliged to go.

Alo-k-ae-sena ! Let him not go ! or Let him not be obliged to go!

Alo-k-alang sena ! Let thee and me not be obliged to go ! or Let us not go!

Alo-k-aling sajai-ó-a,—Let him and me not be punished.

Alo-k-aking ra-iñ-a,—Let them (the two) not call me.

Alo-k-abu ep-er-anga,—Let you and me not quarrel.

Alo-k-ale dasi-n-a,—Let me and them not be obliged to engage as servants.

Alo-k-ape nira mente,—Lest you run way, in order that you may not run away.

Alo-k-ako hijúa,—Let them not come.

Of the above forms, the Third Person Singular, Dual and Plural are generally used as Imperatives, *i.e.,* for the purpose of conveying prohibitions or refusals.

The First and Second Persons Singular, Dual and Plural occur chiefly in negative Final clauses. In this function they are followed by *mente. Alo-k-ae sena mente nere kami rikajad' mea,*—He makes thee work here lest thou shouldst go, or, to prevent thee from going there, etc. *Ote-ng hating-ape-a alo-k-ape eperanga mente,*—I shall divide the land between you lest you quarrel, or to prevent you from quarrelling.

Attention must be paid to the requisite change of Person in translating these Final clauses from English into Mundari. In English the Subjunctive of the Final clause is in reality equivalent to the indirect speech-form (*oratio obliqua).* In Mundari this is replaced by the direct form : hence the Verb which in English stands in the First Person must in Mundari stand in the Third Person and *vice versa*—

He gave me money in order that *I* should not sue *him* stands thus in Mundari: In order that *he* should not sue *me* saying (to himself) he gave me money,—*Alo-k-ae nalis-iñ-a mente takae oma-ina.*

Whenever circumstances allow, the Predicate which we would expect to follow the forms *alo-k-aing,* etc., is left aside, and these forms are made into complete propositions by adding *a*—

> *Alo-k-aiñ-a !* Let me not be obliged to it !
>
> *Alo-k-ae-a !* Let him not do so ! or Let him not say so !
>
> *Alo-k-alang-a !* Let us not do it, let us not say it, let us not go, etc., etc.
>
> *Alo-k-aling-a !* Let him and me not be obliged to it !
>
> *Alo-k-aking-a !* Let them (the two) not do it, say it, etc.

The Second Persons Singular, Dual and Plural are replaced by the Imperative *alom, alo-ben, alo-pe* followed by *a,* v. gr., *alo-m-a !* Don't ! *Alo-ben-a !* Don't (you two)! *Alo-pe-a !* Don't you !

The Mood-suffix *k* must, I think, be referred to that root which we met in the Indefinite and Interrogative Demonstratives and Pronouns, *oko* and *okoe.* In these words the initial *o* is so short that it may be looked upon as a mere onset. The very function of the words *oko* and *okoe* shows that the root is expressive of doubt and uncertainty. Now if *k* represent that root, then the Mood-suffix would have to be looked upon as fulfilling the function of a *dubitative* or *interrogative* Adverb, similar in meaning to the English *perhaps.* Hence *kami-k-a-ing,— Perhaps* I shall work or, *may be* I shall work, *i.e.,* if thou desire or allow it. The Precative as such does indeed directly connote uncertainty, and it connotes this uncertainty as dependent on the good pleasure of some one distinct from the speaker.

The polite Suffix *kó* has plainly the meaning attributed above to the ordinary Suffix *k,* the only difference being the *kó* directly connotes the good pleasure of the person addressed, whereas *k* insists more directly on the uncertainty or doubt. *Dab-kó-me,*—be pleased to sit down. *Dub-kó-a-ing,*—may I sit down please ? is equivalent to *I* shall sit down if I *thou* be pleased. The Concessive or Precative *k* and the polite *kó* seem to be but different forms of one and the same Indefinite or Interrogative root, which occurs as *oko* in the Indefinite and Interrogative Adjectives, as *ko* in the Third Person Plural of the Pronoun, as *k* in the Dual *king,* and again as *ko* in the Plural of Nouns denoting living beings. Indefiniteness and consequently a certain vagueness or uncertainty is the common feature of all these words. It is therefore probable that the *k* which runs through all of them belongs to one and the same original root.

The explanation of the Conditional forms belongs to the Chapter on Subordinate Clauses. (See p. 227)

MENA' AND BANÓ

Concrete existence and presence in a given place are denoted by *mená.* Non-existence and absence from a given place are denoted by *banó.* In the Present Tense these two words insert the Personal Pronouns between the root and the Impersonal *á.*

The *n* of *banó* is nasalized throughout except in the Impersonal form. Hence *bang* instead of *banó*—

Mená-iñ-a,	I exist or I am present.	*Bang-iñ a,*	I do not exist or I am absent.
Mená-me-a,	thou existest.	*Bang-me-a,*	thou doest not exist
Mená-i-a,	he or she exists.	*Band-áia,*	he or she does not exist.
Mend,	*it or they (inan.obj.) exist.*	*Bano-á*	it or they (inan. obj) does not exist
Mená-lang-a,	thou and I exist.	*Bang-lang-a,*	thou and I do not exist.
Mená-ling-a,	he or she and I exist.	*Bang-ling-a,*	he or she and I do not exist.
Mená-ben-a,	you two exist.	*Bang-ben-a,*	you two do not exist.
Mená-king-a,	the two exist.	*Bang-king-a,*	neither of them exist.
Mená-bu-a,	you and I exist.	*Bang-bu-a,*	you and I do not exist.
Mená-le-a,	*they and I exist*	*Bang-le-a,*	*they and I do not exist.*
Mená-pe-a,	you exist.	*Bang-pepa,*	you do not exist.
Mená-ko-a,	they exist.	*Bang-ko-a,*	they do not exist.

In the Second Person Singular the form *menám-a* may be used instead of *mená-me-a.*

Bang-á-iña occurs frequently instead of *bang-iñ-a ; bang-ku-a* may be substituted for *bang-ko-a,* and in some places they say *bang-ú-i-a,* or *bang-uj-a* instead of *bang-á-ia.*

The phrases *to be here, to be there, not to be here, not to be there* are generally rendered by *mená* and *banó* without the Adverbs of Place. These Adverbs are used only when it is desired or necessary to emphasize the exact position. In this case the Adverbs generally take the emphatic Affix *ge* or the Corrective *do* according to the requirements of the proposition—

Nere-ge mená-ko-a, *hanre-do* bang-ku-a,—It is *here* they are, over there they are certainly not.

The phrases *to be still alive* and *to be dead* are very often rendered simply by *mená* and *benó*—

Mená-i-a,—he is still alive. Soma isu din táete *bang-á-ia*--Soma is dead since many years.

Similarly, the phrases, *to be at home* and *not to be at home* are rendered simply by *mená* and *banó,* respectively.

Particularly the Second Person Plural and the Third Person Plural are used to ask or answer the questions. *Are all of you at home ?* or *Are all the people of this house at home now?*

This *Mená-pe-achi ? Bau-ingtaking mená-king-a, apuingdo bang-ái-a.* Are all of you at home ? My two (senior) brother are at home, but my father is not, or my father is out. Hence context and circumstances must generally decide whether *mena* means *to exist* or *to be present* or *to be here or there,* or *to be at home,* or *to be still alive.* Similarly, the meaning of *banó* depends generally on the context or the circumstances.

Compound Postpositions and Adverbs of Place denoting either *rest in* or *motion* to a place are construed like *mená* when they are used intransitively. Even Nouns denoting places follow the same rule when they have the Suffixes *re* or *te.* In this construction the *e* of *re* or *te* elides with the *i* of *ing and* with the *í* of the 3rd Person Singular.

Ne-r-íñ-a,	I am here.	*Taiom-re-lang-a,*	Thou and I, he	*Oráre-bu-a.*	You and I.
Ne-re-ma,	Thou art here.	*Taiom-re-ling-a,*	and I, etc.,	*Orá-re-le-a,*	they and I.
Ne-r-ía,	He (she) is here	*Taiom-re-ben-a,*	are behind.	*Orá-re-pe-a,*	etc., are in
Ne-re-a,	It is here.	*Taiom-re-kin-ga,*		*Orá-re-ko-a,*	the house.
Hant-iñ-a,	I, thou , he,	*Aiar-te-lang-a,*	Thou and I, he	*Bir-te-bu-a,*	you and I
Han-te-m-a,	etc., shall	*Aiar-te-ling-a,*	and I etc.,	*Bir-te-le-a,*	they and I,
Han-t-í-a,	or will go	*Air-te-ben-a,*	will go on a	*Bir-te pe-a,*	etc., will or
	yonder.	*Aiar-te-king-a,*	a head.	*Bir-te-ko-a,*	shall go to
					the forest

Mená has a Continuative Present. *Mená-akange-a-ing, mená-akange-am, mená-akange-ae, menáakange-á, etc.* I am still here, or— I am still alive, or I am still at home, etc.

Banó forms a Past Tense with the Suffix *jan.* In this construction the Personal Pronouns remain suffixed to the root *bang* or *banó* just as in the Present Tense. The very meaning of the form limits it to the Third Person Singular, Dual and Plural : *Banga-i-jana-e,* he died or he has gone away from here and never returned since. *Banó-jan-a,* that thing or those things were lost or destroyed. *Bang-king-jan-a,* both died or went away and never returned. *Bang-ko-jan-a,* they died or they went away and never returned.

Adverbs and Nouns denoting place form a similar Past in *jan* when they take the suffix *te* indicative of *motion.* This Past Tense occurs in the three Persons and Numbers—

Bir-t-ing-jan-a,—I went to the forest.	*Aiar-te-lang-jan-a,*—Thou and I went ahead.
Bir-te-m-jan-a,—thou wentst to the forest.	*Aiar-te-ling-jan-a,*—he and I went ahead.
Bir-t-í-jan-a,—he went to the forest.	*Aiar-te-ben-jan-a,*—you two went ahead.

etc.

Taeken-a is used as Past Tense of *mena.*

Taeken-a-ing,—I existed; I was there ; I was at home.

Taeken-a-m,—thou existed ; thou wast there ; thou wast at home.

Taeken-a-e,—he existed ; he was there ; he was at home ; he was alive.

Taeken-a,—it existed ; it was there.

The corresponding Past Tense of *banó* is formed by placing the Negative Particle *ka* with the Pronominal Suffixes before *taeken*—

Ka-ing taekena, ka-m taekena, ka-e taekena, etc.

The Past of the Adverbial Compounds is formed by placing them with the Pronominal Suffixes before *taeken*—

Nere-ng taekena,—I was here : *Orá-re ka-m taekena,*—Thou wast not at home, etc.

Various words are used to perform the function of Future to *mená* and *banó*—

(1) In their strict meaning—*to exist* or *not to exist,* they take the word *taen* as Futrue whenever there is question of inanimate objects—

Ne orá api sirma taiomte ka taena,—This house will no longer exist after three years. When there is question of living beings, *jidó,* to be alive, is often used. But *taen* may be used too—

Ne haram api sirma taiomte kae jidóa or *kae taena,*—This old man will not be alive after there years.

(2) When they mean *to be present* or *to be absent,* they borrow their Future either from *taen* or from *namó* to be found—

Gapa nere kae taena or *nere kae namóa* { he will not be here to-morrow. / ,, ,, ,, present ,,

Mená and *banó* are also the Mundari equivalents of the Verbs *to have, to possess* and *not to have, not to possess.*

The construction to be used when they have this meaning has been explained in the Introduction (page 41-42).

Men means *to say.* Although this word may take all the Tense-suffixes, it is frequently used with a Present Tense meaning without Tense-suffix and without Copula for the purpose of quoting replies made by some third person, or in order to emphasize one's own words to some body—

Rear dá menáchi banoá mente kulikom. Kuliked' koaing, banoá-ko men,— Ask them whether there is fresh water or not. I did ask them *they say that there is none. Kako hijúakana-e men,*—He says that they have not come. *Kaing sena-ing men,*—I tell thee that I won't go. *C hikanam kajila ?* Kaing bujaubeskeda? — What didst thou say there ? I did not understand will. *Mar-ing sena-ing men,*—I said (just now) all right I shall go, or I said that I would go.

Ka as Transitive or Intransitive Predicate.

When the Negative Particle *ka* is used either transitively or intransitively it is construed like *mená.* It has the Indeterminate Tense, the Future, the Definite and Indefinite Present, the Definite Present Imperfect and the Indefinite Past with the Suffix *Jan.* It may mean *not to be willing, not to agree to something, to refuse*—

INDETERMINATE AND FUTURE: *Ka-iñ-á, ka-m-á, ka-e-á, ka-lang-á,* etc.

DEFINITE OR INTRANSITIVE PRESENT : *Ka-iñ-á-tan-a, ka-m-á-tan-a,* etc., I am unwilling.

TRANSITIVE PRESENT : *Ka-iñ-á-jad-a, ka-m-á-jad-a,*—I refuse it ; I don't agree to this or that.

IMPERFECT : *Ka-iñ-a-tan taekena, ka-m-á-tan taekena, ka-e-á-tan-taeken-a.*

PAST : *Ka-iñ-á-jan-a, ka-m-á-jan-a, ka-e-á-ja-a, ka-lang-á-jan-a,* etc.

The Neuter form of the third Person Singular is often used to denote that some inanimate object resists all efforts at producing a certain effect on it. Thus, *v. gr.,* after fruitless attempts at breaking a rock or moving some heavy object, the Munda will say *Ka-e-á !*— It won't break, it won't move ! In this form the *e* is purely euphonic.

When it is necessary to specify the refusal denoted by those forms in which the Personal Pronouns are inserted, the bare root of the specifying word is

Suku,	to be pleased, glad, or satisfied.
Rasika,	to be joyful.
Huringji,	to feel downcast.
Mukunin,	to feel peevish, homesick or lonely.

Chenta,	to be jealous.
Khis,	to feel angry.
Kurkur,	to feel angry.
Kadrau,	to feel impatient or annoyed.
Mamarang,	to feel proud.
Giu,	to feel ashamed.
Sanang,	to desire.
Haia, *Angau,*	to feel a strong longing or to be hankering after.
Akabakau,	to feel confused or confounded.
Akadanda,	to feel astonished.
Asadi,	to be tired of, to be disgusted with.
Hilang.	to feel a hatred, a horror, a dislike for.
Monduku,	to feel sorrow, regret for, to repent of.
Renge,	to feel hungry.
Tetang,	to feel thirsty.
Rabang,	to feel cold.
Tutkun,	to feel cool.
Lolo,	to feel hot.
Urgum ,	to feel cosily warm.
Jete,	to feel the rays of the sun.

placed before the forms, *v. gr., Sen ka-e-á,*—He will refuse to go *Kami ka-king-á,* —Both of them refuse to work. *Hijú ka-ko-a-tan-a,*—They now refuse to come. *Nir ka-iñ-a-jan-a,*—I refused to run away.

N.B.—The Indeterminate forms *ka-iñ-á, ka-m-á,* etc., are generally used with a present meaning. Hence, *v. gr., durang ka-e-u* may mean—

(1) He always refuses to sing (he never sings) ; (2) He will refuse to sing, or (3) He refuses to sing.

Words denoting purely subjective affections, such as *bodily feelings, passions* or *states of mind,* are construed *impersonally.* The Pronoun denoting the person who experiences these affections is inserted according to the rules given for *Indirect Pronominal* Objects.

The following list, which contains the greater number of those words, gives, besides the bare root, the first Person Singular of the Future, the Present, and the Simple Past Tenses. The remaining Tenses are also in use :—

suku-aiñ-a.	*suku-já-iñ-a.*	*saku-k-íñ a.*
rasika-aiñ-a.	*rasika-já-iñ a.*	*rasika k-íñ-a.*

hurinaji-aiñ-a.	*huringji-já-iñ-a.*	*huringji-k-íñ-a.*
nukunin-aiñ-a.	*nukunin-já-iñ-a.*	*mukunin-k-íñ-a.*
chenta-aiñ-pa.	*chenta-já-iñ-a.*	*chenta-k-íñ-a.*
khisi aiñ-a.	*khisi-já-iñ-a.*	*khisi-k-íñ-a.*
kurkur-aiñ-a.	*kurkur-já-iñ-a.*	*kurkur-k-íñ-a.*
kudrau-aiñ-a.	*kadrau-já-iñ-a.*	*kadrau-k-íñ-a.*
mamarang-aiñ-a.	*mamarang-já-iñ-a.*	*mamarang-k-íñ-a.*
giu-aiñ-a.	*giu-já-iñ-a.*	*giu-k-in-a.*
sanang-aiñ-a	*sanang-já-iñ-a.*	*sanang-k-íñ-a.*
haia-aiñ-a.	*haia-já-iñ-a.*	*haia-k-íñ-a.*
angau-aiñ-a.	*angau-já-iñ-a.*	*angau-k-íñ-a.*
akabakau-aiñ-a.	*akabakau-já-iñ-a.*	*akabakau-k-íñ-a.*
akadanda-aiñ-a.	*akadanda-já-iñ-a.*	*akadanda-k-íñ-a.*
asadi-aiñ-a.	*asadi-já-iñ-a.*	*asadi-k-íñ-a.*
hilang-aiñ-a.	*hilang-já-iñ-a.*	*hilang-k-íñ-a.*
monduku-aiñ-a.	*monduku-já-iñ-a.*	*monduku-k-íñ-a.*
renge-aiñ-a.	*renge-já-iñ-a.*	*renge-k-íñ-a.*
tetang-aiñ-a.	*tetang-já-iñ-a.*	*tetang-k-íñ-a.*
rabang-aiñ-a.	*rabang-já-iñ-a.*	*rabang-k-íñ-a.*
tutukun-aiñ-a.	*tutkun-já-iñ-a.*	*lolo-k-íñ-a.*
lolo-aiñ-a.	*lolo-já-iñ-a.*	*lolo-k-íñ-a.*
urgun-aiñ-a.	*urgun-já-iñ-a.*	*urgum-k-íñ-a.*
jete-aiñ-a.	*jete-já-iñ-a.*	*jete-k-íñ-a.*

Elang, to strongly feel the heat emanating from a flame or burning coals.

Balbal, to perspire.

Turtung, to feel the glare.

Sukul, to feel the smoke in one's eyes and throat.

Dulumulu,
Rusurusu,
Rusumusu, } to experience those sensations of shivering and which characterise an approaching fever.

Ruarabang, to have ague (feel hot and cold successively).

Kudbaur,
Uladeo, } to feel sick on the stomach ; to fell on the point of bringing up.

Osobondo, to feel that peculiar heaviness of limbs and fatigue which precedes an attack of fever.

Tatai, to feel *stiff* on account of having continued too long in the same position.

Ruiam,	to experience that peculiar *itching* in a limb arising from continuing too long in the same position.
Gamang,	to experience a ticklish sensation.
Laga,	to feel tired.
Hambal,	to find that something is heavy.
Rabal,	to find that something is light.
Babata,	to itch.
Gutu,	to feel a pricking sensation.
Usur,	to feel a smarting or burning sensation.
Bóbiur,	to feel giddy ; *literally*, to fel one's head turning.
Luturhunghun,	to have one's ears buzzing.
Ṭoṭoṛau,	to feel deafened with a noise.
Gungurud', *Datagamang,*	to feel one's teeth on edge.
Mer,	to find something bitter.
Harad',	to find something hot (like pepper).
Jojo,	to find something sour.
Heben,	to find something astringent.
Siṛiṇ,	to find something tasting stale.
Soan,	to experience a bad smell.

To these must be added to generic word *at'kar,* to feel, to experience, to be under the impression, to fancy.

The sentence or phrase denoting the subjective affections experienced takes the Suffix *leka,* like, as though, as if, just like, just as if, just as though. This Suffix replaces the Copula *a* of the Predicates, and thus transforms the whole sentence or phrase into a mere Adverbial phrase.

Ruatan-a-ing,—I have fever : hence *Ruatan-leka at'kar-já-iñ-a,*—I feel as if I had fever. *Chiulao kaing lelkía,*—I never saw him : hence

elang-aiñ-a,	*elang-já-iñ-a*	*elang-k-íñ-a.*
balbal-aiñ-a.	*balbal-já-iñ-a.*	*balbal-k-íñ-a.*
turtung-aiñ-a.	*turtungjá-iñ-a.*	*turtung-k-íñ-a.*
sukul-aiñ-a.	*sukul-já-iñ-a.*	*sukul-k-íñ-a.*
dulumulu-aiñ-a	*dulumulu-já-iñ-a.*	*dulumulu-k-íñ-a.*
rusurusu-aiñ-a.	*rusurusu-já-iñ-a.*	*rusurusu-k-íñ-a.*
rusumusu-aiñ-a.	*rusumusu-já-iñ-a.*	*rusumusu-k-íñ-a.*
ruarabang-aiñ-a.	*ruarabang-já-iñ-a.*	*ruarabang-k-íñ-a.*
kud'baur-aiñ-a.	*kud'baur-já-iñ-a.*	*kud'baur-k-íñ-a.*
uladeo-aiñ-a.	*uladeo-já-iñ-a.*	*uladeo-k-íñ-a.*

osobondo-aiñ-a.	*osobondo-já-iñ-a.*	*osobondo-k-íñ-a.*
tatai-aiñ-a.	*tatai-já-iñ-a.*	*tatai-k-íñ-a.*
ruiam-aiñ-a.	*ruiam-já-iñ-a.*	*ruiam-k-íñ-a.*
gamang-aiñ-a.	*gamang-já-iñ-a.*	*gamang-k-íñ-a.*
laga-aiñ-a.	*laga-já-iñ-a.*	*laga-k-íñ-a.*
kambal-aiñ-a.	*hambal-já-iñ-a.*	*hambal-k-íñ-a.*
rabal-aiñ-a.	*rabal-já-iñ-a.*	*rabal-k-íñ-a.*
babata-aiñ-a.	*babata-já-iñ-a.*	*babata-k-íñ-a.*
gutu-aiñ-a.	*gutu-já-iñ-a.*	*gutu-k-íñ-a.*
usur-aiñ-a.	*usur-já-iñ-a.*	*usur-k-íñ-a.*
bóbiu-aiñ-a.	*bobiur-já-iñ-a.*	*bobiur-k-íñ-a.*
luturhunghun-aiñ-a.	*l.hunghun-já-iñ-a.*	*l'hunghun-k-íñ-a.*
ṭoṭoṛau-a-iñ-a.	*ṭoṭoṛau-já-iñ-a.*	*ṭoṭoṛau-k-íñ-a.*
gungurud'-aiñ-a.	*gungurud'-já-iñ-a.*	*gungurud-k-íñ-a.*
d.gamang-aiñ-a.	*d.gamang-já-iñ-a.*	*d.gamang-k-íñ-a.*
mer-aiñ-a.	*mer-já-iñ-a.*	*mer-k-íñ-a.*
harad'aiñ-a.	*harad'-já-iñ-a.*	*harad'-k-íñ-a.*
jojo-aiñ-a.	*jojo-já-iñ-a.*	*jojo-k-íñ-a.*
heben-aiñ-a.	*heben-já-iñ-a.*	*heben-k-íñ-a.*
siṛiṇ-aiñ-a.	*siṛiṇ-já-iñ-a.*	*siṛiṇ-k-íñ-a.*
soan-aiñ-a.	*soan-já-iñ-a.*	*soan-k-íñ-a.*

Clriulao kaing lelkileka atkar-ja-iñ-a,—I am under the impression that I never saw him.

Gel gauḍi-ng senakada,—I have done ten leagues, or I have continued marching ten leagues : hence, *Gel gaudi senakad'-leka at'kar-k-iñ-a,*—I felt as though I had been marching ten leagues.

All the above words must be construed *personally* when they take the causative *rika* or *iṛi,* v. gr., *huṛingji-rika,* to cause some one to feel discouraged; *khis-iṛi* to cause some one to get angry. Pronouns are inserted as *Direct Objects, v. gr., giu-rika-ked'-ko-a-e,* he made them ashamed, he shamed them.

The following when construed personally either insert Indirect Pronominal Objects, or they take Objects introduced by *tá* and *táte* outside the Predicate :—

Suku, to like some one : *suku-ai-tan-a-ko* or *aétáte-ko suku-tana,* they like him.
Chenta, to envy; *chenta-ako-a-e,* he will envy them.
Khisió, to be angry with : *khisi-ale-a-ko* or *ale-tá-ko khisi-ó-a,* they will be angry with us.
Kurkur, to be angry with ; *kurkur-ad'-ko-a-e,* he got angry with them.

Boro, to be afraid of; *boro-am-tan-a-le,* we are afraid of thee.

The following are used as Transitive Predicates :—

Lolo, to heat ; *tutukun,* to cool; *urgum,* to warm ; *rabang,* to make cold.

Mer, to give a bitter taste to something by means of a particular ingredient.

Harad', to give a hot taste to something by means of a hot ingredient.

Jojo, to give an acid taste to something by means of tamarind.

Hasu, to be sick, *and rua* to have fever, are construed personally.

Hasutan-a-ing, I am *sick,* but *hasu-já-iñ-a,* it *hurts* or *pains* me.

Renge when construed personally means *to be poor; Renge-tan-a-ko,* they are poor; *renge-len-a-ko,* they had been poor; *renge-jan-a-ko,* they have become poor.

Suku construed personally means to be satisfied, to be happy, to be pleased; *Suku-tan-a-le,* we are satisfied; *Suku-jan-a-ko,* they were satisfied and are so still; *Suku-len-a-ko,* they were satisfied then.

Since the correct rendering of the English Verb *to be* presents considerable difficulties to the foreign students, it seems advisable to resume into a few rules all that has been said here and there in the preceding pages about the manner in which Mundari Predicates are connected with their Subjects—

1st—Whenever the Verb *to be* is synonymous with *to exist, to be still above, to be present, to be at home* it is rendered by *mená.* In the corresponding negative proposition it is rendered by *banó*—

Three *is* a God,—*Pormesor menáia,* Three *are* no witches,—*Nájomko bangkua Is* thy father *still alive ? Apun menaia chi ?* The village-chief and the sacrificer *are not present,—Munda pahaṇṛking bangkinga.*—My brother *is not at home,— Bauing bangáia.*

Mená is frequently replaced by the construction explained on page 154 when there is question of *presence* in a particular place which is designated either by a Noun or an Adverb of Place.

Banó can never be replaced by this construction—

They *are* here,—*Nere menákoa* or *Nerekoa.* Negat. *Nere bangkua.* He *is* in the house,—*Oṛáre menáia* or *Oṛária.* Negat. *Oṛáre bangáia.*

Where *is* the axe *? Hake okore mená* or *Hake okorea.*

2nd—Whenever the Verb *to be* is a mere *link-word* it is rendered either by *tan* or by *a* according to the following rules:—

1. When the Verb *to be* stands as Copula in a sentence where the *Predicate* is a *Noun* or *Pronoun* primarily and diectly denoting an *individual* or a *species* or a *genus* it must be rendered by *tan.*

Who *is* this? *Ní okoi tani ?* This *is* Pasana of Sarwada,—*Ní Sarwadaren Pasana toní. Are* these Mundas or Uraons? *Niku Hoṛoko tan-ko chi Uṛaonko ?* It *is a* sal tree,—*Sarjom taná.* it *is* himself, *Iníge taní.*

2. When the Verb *to be* stands as Copula in a sentence where the Predicate is

an Adjective or a Participle, it must be rendered by á. This *á* is always suffixed to the Predicate. Adjective Predicates very frequently take the emphatic *ge* as Suffix.

It *is* black, *Hendea* or *hendegea.* This mean *is* tall,—Ne *hoṛo salangigeáe.* Some *are* good, others *are* bad,—*Tara ko bugigeako taṛako et'kageako.*

Here it must be remembered that many Mundari equivalents of English Adverbs are treated as Intransitive Predicates. Of these, most stand in the Perfect or Continuative Present Tense—

He *is* rich, *Pungiakanae;* literally, he is enriched. This knife is sharp,—*Ne katu leserakana;* literally, is sharpened or has been sharpened. Some stand in the Intransitive Present—

He *is* poor, *Rengetanae;* literally, He hungers or he wants. They *are* sick, *Hasutanako.*

3. When the Verb *to be* stands as a Copula in a sentence where the Predicate is a *Noun* primarily denoting an individual, but *directly* connoting a *dignity,* an *office* or a *state of dependence,* it must be rendered by á. In this case the Mundari equivalent of the English Noun is treated as an Intransitive Predicate and stands in the Perfect Tense—

Who *is* chief in this village ? *Ne hature okoi mundaakanae ?* These two *are* the servants of the sacrificer,—*Niking pahaṉṟtáreking dasiakana.* He *is* the king of this country,—*Ini ne disumree rajaakana.*

REMARK.—It often happens that the *dignity* or *office* connoted by these Nouns is entirely neglected, and that the designation of the individuality is solely intended by the speaker. In this case the Mundari equivalent of the English Noun retains the function of a Noun and is connected with its Subjects by means of the Copula *tan.*

Who *is* this man? *Ne hoṛo okoi tani?* He is the chief of Sarwada,—*Sarwadaren Munda taní.* Who are these two young men ? *Ne dangra king okoi-king?* They are my servants,—*Aiñá dasiking tanking.*

FUNCTION OF REDUPLICATION

Reduplication consists in the repetition of the first syllable of a Transitive or Intransitive Predicate, *v. gr.. dal, da-dal; sen, se-sen*—

Words beginning with a simple or an aspirated vowel reduplicate, not by a distinct repetition of that vowel, but by lengthening it *v. gr., hijú, hijú, aium, áium.*.

This simple lengthening of the vowel in the first syllable is very freely used even in words beginning with a consonant, *v. gr., dál* for *dadal ; sén* for *sesen. Certaiṉ* words beginning with a consonant do not admit of real reduplication. Lengthening of the first vowel is all they allow, *v. gr., jágar, jagar,* never *jajagar. Si,* to plough, is rarely reduplicated, *sisi* being hardly ever heard. If its first syllable is lengthened it is followed by *u.* Hence *siu* is equivalent to *sisi.*

Reduplication is used—

Ist.—To denote *natural dispositions* or *habits, customs,* and *natural phenomena.* With this function; it naturally occurs chiefly in the Indeterminate Tense. It may in fact be stated as almost a general rule that the Indeterminate Tense-form reduplicates or lengthens its first syllable. It is by this that it is chiefly distinguishable from the Simple Future—

Ne hoṛo dadalae, or *dalae,*—This man *is in the habit of beating* or this man is quick to beat. *En jo kako jojoma,* or *joma,*—They do not eat that fruit, *i.e.,* that fruit *is never eaten* or it *is not eatable. Asarre gamaeae,* in Asar (middle of June to middle of July) it *(always)* rains.

2nd.—It is used to denote *an àttempt* at something or *a purpose* to begin something. In this case the reduplicated Predicate either takes the Locative Suffix *te,* to, and is followed by *sen,* to go, or it takes the construction explained on pages 203 and 204 without *sen.*

Nenelteng sena or *neneltiña,* }
Nelteng sena or *neltiña,* } I shall go to see.

Aiumte-bu sena or *áiumte-bu-a,*—You and I will go to listen.

In the Imperative the Exhortative Particle *dola* generally takes the Personal Pronominal Suffix : *Dola-bu nenelte,*—Let us (you and I) go to see. However, the other constructions are also used. Thus *Dola ! siu-te-bu-a* ! or *Dola ! siu-te-bu sena !* Come ! let us (you and I) go to plough.

3rd.—It is used to denote *successful beginnings : Ne hone sesena* or *sena,*—This child *begins to walk.*

This particular phrase is used in the Perfect Tense with a slightly different meaning. *Ne hon sesenakanae,*—This child *has learnt to walk* or, *can walk. Ne koṛa nodoe ola,*—Now this boy *begins to write.*

FORMATION OF COMPOUND PRIMARY (PREDICATIVE) ELEMENTS

In the preceding chapters we have seen how the secondary or formative elements agglutinate with the primary or predicative elements for the purpose of forming integral and intelligible parts of a sentence.

The present chapter shows how new *primary elements* are obtained either by the concurrence of several predicative roots or by the concurrence of a predicative with a demonstrative (formàtive) root.

In Mundari these *Compound Primary elements* are obtained by mere juxtaposition of two complete roots or words, *v. gr., sadom-bó,* horse-head ; *sen-aiar,* precede.

In Organic Compounds of this kind there *always* exists a *functional interdependence* between the component parts. Thus in the compound *horse-head* the first Noun acts as a *Qualificative* of the second. In *fore-see fore* acts as a *Modification* of the Verb. Hence we may say that in these Compound words one of the components does in a way assume the function of a formative element, although it be a predicative root and although the result of the composition be itself a primary element which in its totality is as susceptible of the ordinary secondary or formative elements as any simple root or word.

Mundari forms similar compounds, and it does so even more extensively than Organic languages. But besides these, it forms a set of Compound words in which the component elements are not only materially juxtaposed, but also functionally *co-ordinate, i.e.,* neither of the juxtaposed words acts as specification or modification to the other. These co-ordinate Compound words are of two kinds—

1st—Natural or conventional groups of men or animals or collections of objects, such as, *v. gr.,* sets of implements, are denoted by juxtaposing the names of two individuals of the group or the names of two objects of the collection.

In analogous expressions of Organic languages the Conjunctive Particle must be used, *v. gr.,* kith *and* kin ; goods *and* chattels.

2nd—Many of these co-ordinate Compounds are used to directly denote quite a *distinct idea* which we generally express by means of an *Abstract Noun.* The idea thus denoted arises by implication from the collection originally signified.

I here subjoin a list of such Compounds which give a fair idea of the Munda's degree of civilization and of his ambitions, fears, and pleasures : —

Enga-apu (mother and father), *parents.*

Haram-buria (the old man and the old woman), *the heads of the family.*

Hon-hopon (child and grandchild), *the children of the house.*

This includes daughters-in-law as well as any adopted children.

Boko-boea (brother and sister), applied to all the children of the same parents without distinction of sex or seniority. It is equivalent to the German word *Geschwister.*

Misia-barea (sister and brother). Like *bokoboea, the children of the same parents.*

Hon-buri (child and old woman), *wife and children.*

Hon-mis (child and sister), *female relations.*

Dasi-guti (servant and slave), *dependants, c.fr.,* the Latin *familia.*

Munda-pahanr (chief and sacrificer), *the authorities of the village.*

Raja-takur (rajah and takur), *the authorities of the land* (includes all official persons).

Raja-parja (the king and peasant), *the whole population.*

Rayat-parja (tenants with and tenants without occupancy right) *the subjects.*

Bing-kiding (snake and scorpion), *venomous reptiles* (includes centipedes and bad spiders).

Jiu-jantu (life and beast).—*1st, every living thing* (except man) ; *2nd, everything* *living that cannot fly (*except man).

Chenre-chipurud' (bird and ?), *the birds of the air,* v. gr., *Nida dipli jiu-jantuko senbara chenre-chipurudko duruma.*

Ote-sahan (land and firewood), *wealth in immoveable property.*

Daru-sing (tree and tree), *orchard (*includes all fruit trees).

Dhan-kurji (a bag in which goods are packed and loaded on packbullocks and goods). *wealth* in moveable property.*

Taka-paisa (rupees and pice), *cash, ready money, riches.*

Uri-merom (ox and goat), *cattle.*

Sim-sukuri (fowl and hog). This is a complement to *urí-merom,* and implies that a man's *farmyard and poultry* is all that can be desired.

Urí-aranran (bullock and yoke), *wealth in cattle* (it implies that a man is *rich* in cattle, and that he can turn out several yokes of oxen).

Sadom-chatom (horse and umbrella) *greatness, highest wealth.*

Sadomchatom menáteni, a great man, an aristocrat (literally, one possessing a pony and an umbrella).

Kutum-kupul (relations and friends), *Haga-boea* (relations and brothers) } *Good and extensive family connexions, good social position*

Kutum kupulko menakoátaiá,—He is a man of good connexions, *i.e.,* he is received as a guest (with rice beer) in many families.

Taṛi loṭa (a brass-plate and a brass vessel) is the Mundari equivalent of *crockery and plate* of a wealthy European family. It implies a house where the meals are served in the best style.

Sakam-karkad' (leaf and tooth-cleaner, *i.e.,* a thin stick of green salwood is turned into a tooth-brush by chewing one end of it for a while. Some leaves are stitched together with wooden needles so as to form a kind of dish. In this dish the food is placed). This Compound might be said to denote the ordinary man's *table-service* if the Mundas possessed any tables. As it is the Mundas squat on the ground to eat. The fingers of the right hand serve as spoon and fork.

Chaṭu-lundi (earthen pot and ladel), *cooking utensils.*

Haṭá-tunki (winnowing-shovel and basket), *the housewife's working utensils.*

Naiul-araṇraṇ (plough and yoke), the cultivators' gear.

Nangili-pal (a leather strap wherewith plough is attached to yoke and a plough share), *the cultivators' gear.*

---

* This expression is purely Hindi. The Mundas never use bullocks for the purpose of carrying anything.

Gaiṇti kud'lam (pickaxe and hoe), *the earth-worker's implements.*

Á-sar (bow and arrow), *a bow.*

Kapi-taṛauri (axe and sword),
A-sar-kapi (bow, arrow and axe), } *Weapons, armaments.*

Lija-sini (cloth and ?), *a good wardrobe* (implies wealth).

Sered'-lijá (a rag and a cloth), *the necessary clothing.*

Mandi-utu (cooked rice and stew), *abundant food. Mandiutu menáteni,*—One who has a good fare.

Ili-saba (rice beer and dregs), *a grand dinner.*

Aṛá-sakam (herbs and leaves, *i.e.,* the leaves of some trees which are eaten), *vegetables.*

Tasad'-busu (grass and straw), *abundant fodder for cattle.*

Sunum-bulung (oil and salt), *the bare necessaries of life. Sunum bulung kam purauiare chikanamentem dokiá !* is a frequent reproach of the mother-in-law : Why didst thou marry my daughter if thou canst wilt not give her even *the bare necessaries of life !*

Bulung-tamaku (salt and tobacco), *the weekly market purchases, the weekly bazar.*

Orá-duar (house and door), *one's circumstances* (of poverty, ease or wealth, especially used in the expression: *Oráduar nenel,* to go and enquire into some one's circumstances before arranging a marriage. With *mená* without any qualification it means *to be established in life, to have a house and home of one's own.*

Susun-karam (dance and karam, i.e., a certain religious ceremony used in many parts), *a feast.*

Dumang dangiṛi (drum and girl), *a dance.*

Gaṛa-dora (river and ravine), *broken ground.*

Buru-bera (mountain and plain), *everywhere, all over.*

Dub-tingun (to sit and to stand), *to be on speaking terms, to be friendly with,* v. gr., *Nidó alelo dubtinguno kaeá,*—This man is on bad terms with us, *i.e.,* he does not even sit or stand with us.

Nala-tumbal (to work for wages and to glean), *to live fròm hand to mouth,* v. gr., *nado nalatumbaltcle asulótana,*—We are now living from hand to mouth.

Gerang-ruiud' (to moan and to pine), *to be in great pain, severe illness. En oráre gerang-ruiud'-tangeako,*—There is severe illness in that house.

Ol-parau (to write and read), *learning, education,* v. gr.' *Ol-parauakanae,* he has a good education ; he is a *learned man.* (Note the Passive form ; *literally,* he is a *written* and *read man.)*

Adjectives are similarly co-ordinated without any Conjunctive Particle. *Hendeará,* black *and* white ; *pundiara,* white *and* red.

ORDINARY COMPOUND WORDS

I.—Compound Nouns

In these Nouns the specifying word stands first just as in English, *v.gr., oráduar,* house-door ; *sadombó,* horse-head. This kind of composition is used more extensively in Mundari than in English. Hence the specifying Noun has sometimes to be translated into English by an Adjective, sometimes even by a Relative Clause : *Birsim, a wild* fowl ; *birsukuri, a wild boar ; birhoro,* a caste of men *who live exclusively in the forests.* Hatusim, a *tame* fowl.

Sometimes it must be translated by a Noun depending on a Preposition, or even by an Adverbial phrase—

Chatomorá (chatom, an umbrella), a house with a roof like an umbrella, *i.e., with a roof sloping down on all four sides.*

The formation of Compound Nouns by means of the Pronominal Affixes *i (ni), king* and *ko* to the Possessive forms in *ren* or *ten* has been explained in the chapter on Equivalents of Declensions (pages 136 and 138) and on Possessive Adjectives.

Instrumental Nouns are formed by suffixing the Impersonal Pronoun *á, it, something* to the Instrumental Case of Participles. These Participles may stand in the Indeterminate, the Present or the Past Tenses. *Ka* may be prefixed like the a privativum. *Lumó,* to get wet. *Ka-lumóteá* a water-proof, *i.e.,* something by means of which one won't get wet.

Uiugo, to fall : *Ka-uiugoteá,* a parapet, *i.e.,* something by means of which one won't fall.

Ol, to write. *Oltea,* writing materials (paper, pen, and ink). *Ne pata olkenteá,*— The *pen with which* this deed *was written., Botoé,* a waist-cloth for men to cover one's self decently. Hence *botoén (*Reflexive Voice) to tie a cloth round one's own waist. Hence *botoéntéa,* a cloth wherewith to cover one's self decently. *Suru,* to shelter. *Surun* to shelter one's self. *Surunteá,* a shelter against rain or sun, *an umbrella* or anything of that kind.

Nouns denoting materials are obtained by adding the Impersonal Pronoun *á* to the bare root or to the Passive in *ó.* An *e* is generally inserted between the bare root and *á.*

Jom, to eat, *jomeá,* eatables. *Her,* to sow ; *hereá,* seed grains; *heró,* to be sown ; *heroá,* land to be sown.

II.—Compound Predicates

In most cases the modifying word, whether predicative or demonstrative, stands second.

(1) *Compounds consisting of a Predicative root and a Postposition.*—In

Mundari the Compound Postpositions denoting *rest* or *motion* to or *from* are freely used by themselves alone as Transitive or Intransitive Predicates. In these cases Predicative roots denoting *motion,* such as *sen, nir,* etc., and equivalents or synonyms of the Verb to *put,* such as *do*, etc., are generally to be understood from the context or the circumstances, *v. gr., aiar, to put something or some one before some one else (anteponere)—Aiaró,* to *be ahead, to go ahead. Taiom, to place behind (postponere), to put off. Taiomo, to lag* behind, to *be* left behind *Chetan,* to *put* or *place above* or *to raise up. Chetano, to be raised, to be above.*

On account of this use of the Postpositions, Compound Predicates, consisting of a Predicative root and a Postposition, are comparatively rare in Mundari ; *Aiar, sida* and *parom* are almost the only Postpositions used freely in Compounds: *lelaiar,* to look ahead, to foresee ; *aiumsida,* to first hear and to be the first to hear ; *nirparom,* to run across.

Such words as the Latin *retrospicere, superponere* must be rendered by using the Postpositions adverbially, *v. gr., taiomsáte lel,* to look *backwards ; chetanre do,* to put *above* or *upon* or *on top of.*

Transfer of Postpositions to the moral or ideal sphere having hardly begun in Mundari, such Compounds as *to suppose, to respect, to imply, to condescend,* etc., etc., do not exist.

Some of these words can hardly be rendered at all in Mundari ; others must be rendered by circumlocutions, and some of the ideas denoted are expressed by distinct words, chiefly of foreign, origin *v. gr., chema,* to *con*done, to *par*don; *manating,* to *respect* ; *puja, to* adore, to worship ; *marang,* to *ex*alt, to praise.

A very common way of forming Compounds consists in juxtaposing two and sometimes three Transitive or Intransitive Predicates. The Voice, Mood, and Tense-suffixes are added to the last of the juxtaposed words. In these Compounds the first word generally performs the function of a modifying *Participial Clause of Cause or Manner.* Hence it can frequently be rendered into English by means of the word *by introducing* a Participle. However, other modes of rendering the modifying or first part of these Compounds must occasionally be used as the following examples will show : —

Buló, to be drunk. *durum,* to sleep. Hence *buldurumó,* to fall asleep on account of being drunk, to fall asleep in a fit of drunkenness. *Jetana kae mundia, buldurumakanae,*—He won't understand anything : he is asleep in a fit of drunkenness.

Hered', to weed; *nala,* to gain a daily wage. Hence *hered'nala,*— to earn one's (daily) sustenace by weeding (other people's rice-fields).

Tiga, to tread, to trample ; *nam,* to find, to discover. Hence *tiganam,* to find or discover something by treading on it. *Hola aiub ne chakuing tiganamlá,*— Yesterday evening I found this penknife by treading on it. *Bagrau,* to spoil. Hence *tigabagrau,*—to spoil something by tampling on it. *Birsukuriko babataeko tigabagraukeda,*—The wild boars have destroyed his paddy by trampling on it.

Rebed', to force or squeeze in between ; *goé,* to kill ; *gojó* (for *goeó*), to die. Hence *rebed-goé,*— to kill by squeezing between two objects, and *rebed'gojó,* to be killed by being squeezed. *En kera huangre uiujanchie rebed' goéjana,*—That buffalo falling into a precipice was killed by being jammed (between two rocks).

N.B.—Although the word *rebed'* in this example be itself in the Passive Voice, it does not take a separate Passive Affix—

Har, to drive ; *urung,* to take, or carry out, to cause to go out.

Hence *harurung, to drive out, to expel.*

Ader, to take, bring or carry inside, to cause to go inside. Hence *harader, to drive in.*

Tuing, to shoot an arrow ; *goé,* to kill. Hence *tuinggoé,* to kill with an arrow.

Toṭe, to shoot with a gun. Hence *taṭegoé,* to kill with a gunshot.

Tam, to strike with a club or stick. Hence *tamgoe,* to kill with clubs or sticks.

Gaṛa, to dig. Hence *garaurung,* to dig out, to unearth.

Topa, to bury. Hence *topagoe,* to bury alive, *i.e.,* to kill by burying.

Kaji, to say, to speak; *denga,* to help. Hence *kajidenga,* to help by speaking (for some one), to plead, to intercede for. This is always Transitive in Mundari : *Jetaeo kako kajidengajáia,*—There is nobody to intercede or plead for him.

Si, to plough. Hence *sidenga,* to help somebody to plough.

The examples given above suffice to familiarize the student with this kind of formation to which there is, so to say, no limit in Mundari. However, certain compounds belonging to this class present greater difficulties to the foreigner, not only because they cannot be translated *literally* into any Aryan language, but also because it is impossible to lay down any uniform or general rule for their translation.

Lá denotes *excess* in general. It may be used as a Quantitative Adjective. In this case the *terminus* which is exceeded takes the Suffix *ete.*v. gr., *Sai takaete láge,—More* than one hundred rupees *Iniete láe kuril daṛia,*—He can jump *further* (or *higher)* than that one.

La is frequently used as an independent Predicate. If so, the particular act in which the excess takes place is gathered from the context or the circumstances. *Lákedako* (treansitive) may denote an excess of any kind, *v. gr.,* they *dug* further or deeper, they *rose* higher, they *went* or *ran* further, etc., etc.

When it is desirable or necessary to *specify, i.e.,* to explicitly state the nature of the act in which an excess takes place, then a compound is formed by placing the word denoting that act before *lá.* But the terminus which is exceeded is generally not expressed in Mundari, and since in these compounds *lá* does not denote an *absolute* but a relative excess, the terminus must generally be rendered into English by some circumlocution.

Jom-lákedako,—literally, they exceeded in eating. But this does not imply an absolute excess. Hence it does not mean *they ate too much,* but it means *they ate more than their usual amount.*

Om-láad'koae,—literally, he exceeded in giving to them. This means either: he gave *more than he owed them,* or: *more than he usually does.*

When *lá* concurs in this way with an *intransitive* Predicate, the resulting compound becomes *Transitive.* Hence the Transitive Tense-suffixes must be used in the Past Tenses, *v. gr., Sen-lákedae,*—He went beyond this or that terminus.

When the terminus which is exceeded is expressed, it takes the Suffix *ete, v. gr., Holaetee jomlákeda,*—He ate more than he did yesterday.

Bage means to *abandon, to relinquish.* In compounds it assumes two different meanings :—

(1) It may retain the original meaning just quoted. In this case the compound may be rendered into English either (*a*) by a co-ordi nate compound sentence in which the equivalents of the words constituting the Mundari Predicate are connected by means of the Conjunction *and*—*Ne lijáe huduma-bagekeda,*—He *threw* this cloth *away and left it there; Gopoé etéjanchi Soma sangikotae nirbageked'koae,*—As soon as the fight began Soma *ran away and abandoned* his companions. (*b*) Either word of the Mundari compound may be rendered by a Participial clause: *Sangikotae nirbageked'koae,*—He ran away, *abandoning* his companions, or, he abandoned his companions *by running away.*

N.B.—A very remarkable feature of these compounds consists in the fact that, although the compound, as a grammatical unit, be Transitive, the Intransitive part may still have its own Locative Case. *Et'kan kurie taikena, honko Assamtee nir-bagetad'koa,*—She was a bad creature : she *abandoned* her children *and ran away to Assam.*

(2) *Bage* may mean to leave *undone.* These compounds, like those described under (1), cannot be translated literally by a corresponding English Compound Predicate. They may be rendered either *(a)* by a Negative proposition in which the equivalent of the first word in the Mundari compound stands as Predicate, whereas *bage* is simply translated by the Negative Particle *not* or by the phrase *not to do. Daru japare si-bagekedako,*—They *did not plough* (the spot) close to the tree. *Ne upun kaji ol-bageakadae,*—He *has not written* these four words.

In Imperative propositions *bage* is generally equivalent to the Prohibitive Particle *alo! Daru japare si-bagetam ! Don't plough* close to the tree ! *Jilu jombagetam, kam sukuredo !* If thou do not like it (meat), then *don't eat* the meat. This implies that meat is *mixed* up with the food served, and has consequently to be left aside by the peculiar process of *eating* what is with it.

(*b*) The Compounds may be translated by rendering *bage* by means of *to leave, to omit.* In this case the first part of the Compound must be rendered either by a Passive Participle with the Prefix *un* or by an Infinitive Clause—

Darujapare si-bagekedako,—They *left* (the spot) near the tree *unploughed.*

Ne upunia kajie ol-bagekeda,—He *omitted to write* these four words, or, he *omitted* these four words *when writing.*

Saré means *to leave over ; sareó,—to remain over, to be over.* In Compounds it is, like *bage,* used with two distinct meanings—

(1) It may keep its original meaning. In that case the first part of the Mundari Compound is reduplicated, *v. gr., ool-saré, joom-saré, lala-saré, siu-saré.* In rendering these Compounds the equivalent of *saré* stands as Predicate, whereas the reduplicated first part is translated by an Active or a Passive Infinitive Clause.

Aiub'mente huringlekaing joom-sareakada,—I have kept or *left* a little *over to eat* in the evening. *Etá sanjamente bar priste ool-saré akada,*—He *has left* two pages *over to be written* this afternoon (he has left *for* this afternoon two pages to be written).

(2) *Saré* is sometimes used as a synonym of *bage* in the Compounds described on page 112 under (2). In this case the first part of the Compound is not reduplicated—

Daru japare si-saretam, or *si-bagetam,—Don't plough* close to the tree. *Jilu jom-sarekadae,* or *jom-bagekedae,—He did not eat* the meat (which was mixed with his food).

Urum is not used independently. Added to words denoting sense perceptions, it means *to recognize :* thus *lel-urum,*—to recognize by sight ; *aium-urum,*— to recognize by hearing ; *soan-urum* or *ji-urum,*—to recognize by smelling ; *jom-urum,* —to recognize by the taste ; *chapu-urum,*—to recognize by the touch ; *chapad-urum,*—to recognize by the feeling an object causes on the sole of the foot when it is trodden on.

Since there is no general term equivalent to the English Verb *to recognise,* the foreign student must be careful to prefix the right word to *urum* in every particular case. A few examples by way of illustration—

Will you recognize those men if you see them? *En horokom lelurumkoachi?* (Here the clause *if you see them* is sufficiently rendered by the word *lel).* I did not see him, but I *recognized his voice,—Leldo kaing lelkia mendo aiumurumkíaing. Sonchita ne lataria, soanurumjáiaing,*—The leopard is in this den : I reconize him by the smell.

The following deserve special notice on account of the change of meaning which, from our point of view, they undergo when added to other Predicates :-

Au (agu) means *to bring, to fetch.* In Compounds it is used with two distinct meanings—

(1) It primarily denotes a motion from a distance to the speaker or to a fixed point. Thus it is synonymous with *ete., from.* Hence when suffixed to a Predicate, it implies that the action or effect denoted by that Predicate is conceived as approaching the speaker, *v. gr., Soanjáiná,*—I perceive a smell. *Soan-aujáiña,*—I perceive a smell coming from a distance in this direction. *Lel, to see.* Hence *lel-aujad'koaing,*—I see them *coming this way ; lel-auiaing,*—I shall wait here to see *him come in.* These examples suffice to show how much the hearer has to gather

from context and circumstances for a correct understanding of these Compounds as well as for a correct rendering into English. Like *ete, from,* the above primary meaning of *au* in Compounds may be transferred to time. If so, *au* implies that the action denoted by the first part of the Compound has been going on from a more or less remote past up to the present time with a physical or moral continuity—

Ne haturenko modhisi sirmatáete malko omaujada aingtá,—The people of this village have *always* paid their rent to me for the last twenty years. *Neado nangrenkotaete aium-aujana.*—This is a tradition since time immemorial; *literally,* this has *always* been heard from those of former or olden times.

(2) *Au,* inasmuch as it is equivalent to the English *to fetch,* i.e., *to go and bring,* implies a *going from one place* for the purpose of performing the action denoted by the first part of the Compound, and then and *immediate return* to the place one had left. These Compounds can neither be rendered literally into English, nor yet always by the same kind of circumlocution.

Auri heu ! dáing nu-au-k-a ! Wait a moment hey ! till I have been for a drink! *Literally,* Not yet hey ! (*i.e.,* don't start as yet). Let me go to drink and return (to you).

Ju lel-aume ! Go and *bring news,* i. e., *Go, see* what is going on and *return* to inform me or us.

Aege aium-auláe,—He *has been to bring news, i.e.,* he has been to *hear* by himself (what was being said or done) and has come back to report it. *Lijakole nur-aukoa !* May we *go,* please, *to wash* our clothes !

N.B.—From the Munda's point of view *au* does not undergo any change of meaning. He seems to conceive the first part of the Compound substantively—*Nu,* a drink ; *lel,* a look ; *aium, a hearing ; nur,* a wash. Hence to him *nu-au, lel-au, aium-au, nur-au* means, literally, *to bring or to fetch a drink to bring or to fetch a look (at something), to bring or fetch a hearing, to bring a wash.*

Idi means *to take something* or *some one some place or person.* In Compounds it denotes a *continuation* or a *constant repetition* of the action denoted by the first word of the Compound—

Parau-idime ! Continue reading ; literally, take the reading *further* on. *Setako han daru hubí solka-idikiako,*—The dogs continued or kept biting (the bullock) up to yonder tree.

N.B.—*Niridi* simply denotes a running *from,* just as *nirau* denotes a running to the speaker. *Niridiláe,*—He ran to such or such place or person.

Peré means *to fill.* It is added to other Predicates with its original meaning, but in a manner in which we would hardly expect it. In translation *peré* must be rendered separately either by the Verb *to fill* or by the Adjective *full* or sometimes by the Adverb *entirely* or the phrase *in full,* v. gr., *Dub'-perélako,*—The whole place was *full* of people *sitting down ; [literally ;*—They sat (the place) full]. *Turu-perékiako,*—They *stung* him *all over. Hal-peréad'koae,*—He paid them *in full, i.e.*, as much as he owed them.

Giṛi means *to throw away.* Added to other Predicates, it denotes *a Superlative degree, an excess* or a *climax.* It is generally synonymous with the Superlative Affix *uter,* but it is used only to denote *mental* or *physical states. Balu-giṛljanako balu-uterjanako,*—They got *utterly* dumbfounded. *Abuá kajite miad' kitab pere-girikedabutaiá,*—We have *filled entirely* one of his books with our words. *Ne daru cham-giriakana,*—This tree is *entirely seasoned.*

En inung mukuṇiṇ-giṛijanaing,—I am *perfectly disgusted* with that game.

Pharchi means *to cleanse, to clean away.* In Compounds it becomes synonymous with the Superlative Affix *uter.*

Whereas *giṛi* in Compounds always denotes a *state* as the result of some action, *pharchi* exhibits the action itself as carried right through to its natural terminus or completion.

Misa gitite ang-pharchiaing,—(If I) once get to lie down *I down it entirely. Ang* means *down ;* used intransitively it means to continue till daybreak. In the above sentence the Predicate *ang* derives its particular meaning form its proximity to *gitite,* which means *to go to sleep (literally,* to go to lie down). Hence here *ang* means to continue *to sleep* till daybreak. *Pharchi* added to *ang* implies that the sleeping is not interrupted even for a single moment. Hence the sentence may be rendered thus : Once I go to sleep, *I never wake till daybreak.*

Riṛing-pharchikedaing,—I have entirely forgotten it, I can't remember *anything* of it, however much I may try to.

Bai means *to make,* to arrange, to prepare, *v. gr., Oṛále baitana,*—We are busy making (building) a house.

In Compounds it keeps this signification whenever it stands first. *Nekate bai-biurkako,*—Let them arrange it right around in this way. *Pachrie bai-rakab'-keda,*—He has raised the walls (*literally,* he made thae walls up to the top).

When *bai* stands second in Compounds, it becomes equivalent to the English Adverbs : *carefully, properly, well, one by one.*

Biur-baikako,—Let them turn it round *carefully. Entedoko rakab'-baikeda,*—Then they raised it *carefully. Kaing aium-baikeda,*—I did not hear it *properly. Ne Jo halang-baipe,*—Gather up these fruits *one by one.*

Hindi means *to gather, to collect.* It keeps this meaning in Compounds when it stands first. But when it stands second it becomes equivalent to the English *many, plenty. Duarbu ni-hundita !* Let us open *plenty of* outlets or doors.

The English Verbs to see, to hear, to feel, and their synonyms have often an Infinitive or a Participial Clause as Direct Object, *v. gr.*, I saw *him come in ;* I heard *him singing.* The corresponding Mundari words *lel, aium,* and *at'kar* differ from each other in their construction.

Lel admits of four different constructions :—

1st.—It may take a *Participle* as modifying a Pronominal Direct Object. The

Object itself is of course inserted into *lel:* I saw him Ploughing that field,—*En piri sitan-ing lelk-í-a.*

2nd.—The same construction may be used with this difference that the bare Participle takes the Postposition *re,* and is consequently transformed into an Adverbial Clause of Time : *En piri sitanre-ng lelk-í-a,*—I saw him *when he was ploughing* that field.

Both these constructions are, however, ambiguous because the Participle may refer to the Subjects as well as the Object, so that *sitaning lelkiá* or *sitanreng lelkia* may mean also, I saw him when *I was ploughing.* Hence when either of these constructions is used, the context and the circumstances must be attended to.

If instead of *re* the Postposition *ló* be suffixed to the Participle, it is understood that the Participle is an Adverbial Clause modifying the Subjects and not the Object. *Sitanlóing lelk...a,*—I saw *him* whilst *I was ploughing.*

3rd.—Instead of the constructions described under 1st and 2nd, the Mundas very frequently form a Compound Predicate in which *lel* stands first, and the word denoting the action which is seen stands second. *Lel-siked'-koaing,*—I saw them ploughing. *Lel-nirjad'koaing,*—I see them running away. *Lel-olked'meaning,*—I saw thee writing.

In these Compounds the ambiguity mentioned in 1st and 2nd does not exist. But whenever the second part of the Compound is a Transitive word, there arises an ambiguity of a different kind. The Transitive word may have a Passive meaning, but it can never take a Passive Affix, because the Voice of the Compound as such is detemined by *lel* which is necessarily Active in the Compound. Thus *lel-tam-ked'koaing* may mean either I saw them *whilst they were beating* one or more others, or I saw them *being beaten.* Here, again context and circumstances must decide.

Aium.—*1st.*—It may take a bare Participle preceding the Pronominal Subject, *v. gr., Jagartan-ing aiumkia,*—I heard him speaking.

2nd.—Instead of a Participle it may take the Infinitive or bare root, *v. gr., Jagar-ing aiumkia,*—I heard him speaking ; *Durang-bu aiumkoa !* Let us hear them singing.

3rd.—Sometimes it forms a Compound with another Predicate. If so, it stands second. This construction seems to differ from the above only by the transposition of the Pronominal Subject—

Jagaraiukiaing,—I heard him speak ; *Durangaiumkiaing,*—I heard him seing.

At'kar, which is generally constructed impersonally, does not concur with other Predicates to form Compounds. The Participle depending on it takes the affix *leka, like, as though, as if.* I Ifelt a snake pass over me,—*Bing leng paromjaingleka at'karkina, : literally, I felt as though a snake were creeping across me.*

Permissives and *Causatives* are formed by adding any of the three follwing to Transitive or Intransitive Predicates : *rika, iri* or is'i.

The context and the circumstance must decide whether these Compounds do in a given case denote *real causation* or a mere *permission,* or a favour—

Hiju-rikaked'koae ...	may mean	either He *caused* them to come.
Hiju-iriked'koae ...		he *made* them come, or
Hiju-ichiked'koae ...		he *allowed* them to come.

Iri and *ichi* are used only as Causative or Permissive affixes.

Rika is used also as an independent Predicate, meaning *to do. Chilekateko rikakeda ?* is equivalent to *chilekakedako ?* How have they *done* it?

Idiomatically *rika* is also used to denote a *sound thrashing. Khub'ko rikakia,—* They gave him a *sound thrashing.*

Ruar or *rura* menas to return. Added to other Predictes, it performs the function of the Latin and English Prefix *re.*

Ol, to wirte ; hence *ol-ruar, to rewrite.* Om-ruar, reddere, to retunr, to give back. *Bai-ruar,* reficere, to repair.

Ete means *to begin.* Added to other Predicates, it yields *Inceptives.*

Ol-ete, to commence writing. *Inung-ete,* to begin to play.

Hoka means *to cease, to stop.* Added to other Predicates, it implies that the action denoted by them ceases.

Ol-hoko, to cease writing. *Inung-hoka,* to stop playing.

Chaba means *to complete, to finish.* Added to other Predicates it yields *Completive Compounds.* These differ from the Compounds with *hoka,* inasmuch as they imply the *real completion* of a work or action, whereas those with *hoka* denote a *mere cessation* of a work or action which does not necessarily imply completion.

*Ol-chabakedae,—*He finished the whole piece of writing which he had undertaken. *Jomchabakedae* may mean he has finished his meal, *i.e.,* he has eaten as much as he wanted, or, he has eten everything that was set before him.

The following occur only as Affixes in compound words : *bara, tab* or *ba.* They perform the function of Adverbs, but they are no longer used as independent Adverbs. *Bara* means *about, here and there, now and then.*

Sen-bara, to walk or go *about. Bu-bara,* t pierce or make holes *here and there* in something. *Chuk-bara, I to make a mistake now and then.*

Tab Ior ba means *quickly, fast. Hijutab,* to come quick. *Nir-tab,* to run fast. *Ol-tab,* to write fast.

Tuka is used only as an afix, and has the same meaning as the Hindi *rakhna* in the expression *bolrakho.*

It implies that an action already begun is to be interrupted for the prupose of doing that which is denoted by teh word to which *tuka* is prefixed. It may also imply the momentary leaving of a place for the purpose of doing the act denoted by the word ot which *tuku* is suffixed.

*Kaji-tukaime ! Tell him (*this or that) first (*and then continue your present work,* or, *and then return). Ne horoko lel-tukakom ! See these mean safely out* (or in) (*and then continue your present work or and then return).*

Adverbs are by preference suffixed to their Predicates so as to form a Compound. In these Compounds the Adverbial Affixes Ite, leka or *lekate* are never used with the Adverbs.

Bes, well. Hence *Kaing lel-besked'koa,*—I did not see them well. *Marang,* long ago, in the beginning. Aege *eser-maranglae,*—He was the first to take possession. *Bai-poktaakadae,*—He has made it solidly.

When Adverbs are separated from their Predicates they generally take the Affixes *te, leka* or *lekate re, ete* or *ate. Beslekate kaing jelked'koa. Marangree eserla. Poktatee baiakada.*

SUBORDINATE CLAUSES

Since In Mundari the Syntax or description of the Proposition as such coincides with the Etymology of the language, a special syntactical part would amount only to a repetition of what has already been explained in the Introduction and through the various chapters on Etymology.

Nevertheless, because the rendering of English subordinate clauses presents such considerable difficulties, I here subjoin a summary recapitulation on this subject with a number of examples which I give word for word as I noted them occasionally from the lips of Mundas who are ignorant of Hindi. To these I add a number of similary collected examples in which words are transferred from their primary functions, to the function of Trnansitive or Intransitive Predicates. These examples must not be looked upon as exceptional and rare idiomaticisms which the average Munda would but seldom use. On the contrary, the less a Munda knows of Hindi, the more he is given to this characteristic transfer of function.

I.—Relative Clauses

The Substantive and Adjective functions of Tense-forms have been fully explained in preceding pages. (See Introduction; from pages 27 to 32 and 53 and 54 and Grammer, pages 120 and 121)

Marheu ! sidalenko hijúpe ! He ! those who came in first, come here ! *Samrom namken gomkeko ne bangaloreko taikena,—The Eurpeans who were looking for gold* lived in this bungalow.

Ne Nanedo med banólekai senbaratanae.—That Nane walks about *like one who has no eyes.*

Ale paraukentea kitabing namtana,—I want the book *in which we were reading,* i.e., *which served as our reader.* (Note how in this the Participle *parauken* is turned into an Instrumental Noun, although it qualifies the word *kitab.)*

Ka dulakana duleban,—Water those (plants) *which have not been watered.* (Note how the word *dul,* which means to *pour anything,* is used here in the sense of *to water* owing to the context. The sentence was used by a gardener directing two boys whilst watering the garden.) *Patraakana enaka gutuea,*—They use the word *gutu* to designate *a place which is covered with shrubs.*

Netáre miad ka-urungjan diyaselaing namla,—Here I found a *match which has not yet been fired. (Urungó, to come out,* is used of matches like the English *to go off* is used of explosives.)

Ranchitenko auriko ruara,—Those who go to Ranchi (i.e., those who are in charge of this law-suit, and who consequently have to go to Ranchi for each hearing of the case) are not yet back.

Hen merom kule mukíu goéai honder horo kaetaikena mentel, We did not cut (*i.e.,* kill) that goat the other day because *the man for whom we were to kill it* was not there (at our place), *i.e.,* because the *guest,* in whose honour we were going to kill it, did not turn up. (Here we have the Future Tense with an Indirect Pronominal Objects : *goé-ai.)*

En oṛá ondorled'leka nádo leloá,—Now that house looks *as if some one had recently burnt it down (put fire to it).*

Kula huakaiá maiomre tupuakad lijá kako tusinga, mendo pagrireko tolmodea karedo maiangkoreko doea dhotiló oṛó dhoti banónído botoére,—They (the Mundas) do not wear around their neck a cloth *which they have dipped into the blood of a man whom a tiger has killed (*literally, bitten), but they tie it up together with their turban or they put it somewhere about their waist in their *dhoti,* and *he who has no dhoti* (puts it) into his *botoé* (a very narrow waist cloth). This sentence was given in an explanation of the various charms Mundas wear against tigers, snakes, and sickness.

The two preceding examples illustrate the Munda's preference for the use of *Active Past Participles* in cases where we would rather use *Participles of the Passive Voice.*

Participial Nouns may without any other affix perform the function of a Circumstantial Clause of Manner—

Saurwadare Sant Petrus chabi sabakadi menáia neredo judalekae chapaakana,—In Sarwada Saint Peter is represented with the keys in his hands, but here he is pictured differently ; *literally,* In Sarwada there is St. Peter, *one who keeps in his hands* (Continuative Present) the keys.

Indefinite Pronouns are sometimes used in correlation with Definite Demonstratives, and thus perform the function of Relative Pronouns (page 64). In reality, however, the sentence thus obtained consists of two *Co-ordinate Propositions.* The construction is comparatively rare in districts where Hindi is unknown.

Oko kaji kaji sanajáia ena kae puchid'besdaṛia,—Some words which he desires to say he cannot pronounce well. (He desires to pronounce some words, those he cannot, etc.)

Okoe chetanre med'ea iní pojo med'le kajia, okoe bitterre medéa iní undumed',—Some one is in the habit of opening his eyes wide (of eyeing above) him we nickname *pojo med'* ; some one is in the habit of keeping his eyes half-closed (eyeing inside) he is (*nicknamed)* an *undu med',* i.e., *those who* make big eyes are nicknamed, etc.

Okoe balbajadi racharee gitian, okoe rabangjadi biterre gitiae,—Those who perspire sleep outside in front of the house, and those who feel cold sleep inside. *Literally,* some one there is who perspires (or a perspirer) he sleeps outside, some one there is who feels cold, he sleeps inside. *Babbaljadia,*—he feels perspiring. Hence *balbaljadí,*—one who, etc. *Rabangjadia,*—he feels cold. Hence *rabangjadí,*—one who feels cold.

Lekani lekanking, lekanko suffixed to Nouns must sometimes be translated by an English Relative Clause, the Predicate of which has to be gathered from the circumstances of the case.

Pakulekanko auriko sabchabavá,—Those who are of the size of Paku are not yet all caught. *Deosailekanko haltabeako,*—Those *who are as rich as Deosai* will pay quickly.

English sentences containing a Relative Clause are often cut up into a question and an answer, thus yielding two Simple Principal Propositions.

Hensáre api horo dasiko kamitanako chika ? Mid' horo ráauime !— Go and call one of the three servants who work over there. (Are there three servants working over there or not ? Go and call one of them hither.)

II.—Conditional Sentences

A conditional sentence is one which states a contingency or fact as depending on a given condition. In Organic languages it is always a compound sentence. The principal proposition is that which states the fact. The dependent proposition is that which states the condition. It is called the Conditional Clause, *v. gr., If he come* (Conditional Clause) *I will leave* (Principal proposition). The condition may be expressed either as *realizable* or as *unrealizable.* A realizable condition, again, may be expressed as *probable* or as *improbable.* In Organic languages these differences attaching to the manner in which the condition is expressed cause changes in the Tense and Mood of the Verbs of both the Conditional and the principal proposition.

In the sentence *If he come I will leave,* the condition appears as both *realizable* and *probable* or at least as *apprehended.*

A change of Tense in the Conditional and of Mood in the Principal Proposition will make a realizable condition appear as improbable or not apprehended, *v. gr., If he came I would go.*

Unrealizable conditions always demand a similar change of Tense and Mood.

In Mundari the Conditional Sentence is really a simple proposition, inasmuch as it contains but one Subject and one Predicate. The whole Mundari Conditional clause is reduced to an Adverbial Compound.

A further difference between Organic and Mundari conditional sentences lies in the fact neither the nautre of the condition nor the manner in which it is expressed ever cause any change of Tense or Mood.

Condition is expressed by the Postposition *re, in.*

The following may be accepted as a safe, though purely mechanical, method to form Conditional Clauses. The substitution of *re* for the Copula *a* transforms any Mundari Tense-form into a correct Conditional Clause.

Sen-a-ing,—I will go. *Sen-re-ng,* if I go. *Kaing sen-a,*—I won't go. *Kaing sen-re,*—If I do not go. *Raleko-a-ing,*—I shall first call them. *Ráleko-re-ng,* If I were first to call them. *Ráked'ko-a-m,*—Thou didst call them. *Ráked'ko-re-m,*—If thou hadst called them.

Daló-a-ko,—They will be beaten. *Daló-re-ko,* If they be beaten. *Dapaljan-a-king,* They had a fight (were beating each other). *Dapaljan-re-king,*—If they had been beating each other. *Dasin-a-ko,*—They will engage themselves as servants. *Dasin-re-ko,*—If they engage as servants.

In these Conditional forms the Pronominal Affixes *ing (ng), m, e, lang, ling,* etc., etc., must, I think, be considered as *Possessive Affixes,* just as in the expressions *apu-ing, enga-m.*

The Tense-form together with its Pronominal Objects becomes a Noun by the fact of its being no longer referred to a Subject by means of the Copula *a* see Introduction, 53-55). *Sen,*—the act or the case of going. *Ráleko,*—the act or the case of first calling them, *Ráked'ko,*—the act or the case of having called them. In the Locativ Case in *re* these compounds may be rendered thus : *Sen-re,*—*in* the case of... going. *Raleko-re,*—in the case of ...calling them first. If to this the Possessive Affixes *ing, m, e,* etc., be added, we get : *Senre-ng,*—in my going, or, in the case of my going. Ralekore-m,—In thy calling them, or, in the case of thy calling them.

The Conditional Clause may follow the Principal Proposition ; but as a general rule it precedes it.

The Principal Proposition stands in that Tense of the Indicative Mood which it would stand in if it were absolute, *i.e.,* independent of any condition.

Ranchite senreng naua lijáing auamea,—If I go to Ranchi, I will bring a new cloth for thee.

The word *honang* or *honanga* placed after the Conditional form implies that the condition is either unrealizable or at least that it is considered as one which will certainly or probably not be realized, though it might possibly be fulfilled.

Ranchite senreng honang lijáing auamea,—If I were to go to Ranchi (which, under the circumstances, I cannot or will not do), I would bring a cloth for thee.

Honang may also be placed after the Principal proposition—

Ranchite senreng lijáing auamea honanga.

Rálekorem honang kachiko hijua ? If thou wert first to call them would'nt they come? or *Ralckorem kachiko hijúa honang. Gara paromdarijanre Ranchiteng senkena honang,*—I would have gone to Ranchi if it had been possible to cross the river.

If it be desired to imply that the event spoken of in the Principal proposition would *certainly* take place if the condition; were fulfilled, then *honang* must be placed after the Conditional Clause and *derang* or *chimad'* are placed after the Principal Clause. *Derang* and *chimad'* are not used after Predicates in the Past Tense. *Ranchite senreng honang lijáing auamea derang,*—I would certainly bring a cloth for thee if I went (could go) to Ranchi.

Rálekorem honanga hijúako derang,—If you were to call them, they would certainly come.

Conditional Clauses which in English are introduced by *but* or *even suffix* do or *o* respectively to *re,* v. gr.—

But If you had called them, they would have come,—*Raked'kore-do-m hijúlenako honang.*

If in Past Tense propositions it be desired to state that the event would *certainly* have taken place had the condition been fulfilled, then the Adverb *sartige* or *sartige dang* is used instead of *derang.* This Adverb precedes the Predicate, whereas *honang* follows it. *Ráked'kore-do-m sartigedangko hijúlena honang,*—But if thou hadst called them, they would most certainly have come.

Ráked'kore-o-m kako hijúlena honang,—Even it thou hadst called them, they would not have come.

The ordinary construction of the Principal proposition may be replaced by the following idiomatic construction :

The Instrumental Suffix *teá* is substituted for the Copula after the Predicate of the Principal Clause, and the Pronominal Subject is affixed to the word immediately preceding the Predicate—

Raked'korem sartigeko hijújan-teá honang, for *hijújana honang.*

Taka taekenre honang en hatuing auked'teá for aukenda,—If I had had money (*literally,* If there had been money), I would have taken (*i.e.,* bought) that village. *Sadom kae taekenre kae sendariteá honang,*—If he had had no horse, he would probably be unable to go. *Sadom bangáire honang kae sendaritea derang* or *chimad',*—If he had no horse, he would certainly be unable to go.

The only explanation I can offer of the construction in *teá* is this : It may be considered as an elliptical impersonal proposition, in which the Predicates *there is, there would be, there would have been a means* are understood.

Thus *Taka taekenre on hatuing auked'tea ... honang,*—Had I had money, *there would have been* wherewithal to buy that village or wherewith I might have bought that village, = *Taka taekenre en hatuing aukenteá taekena honang.*

Sadom bangâire kae sendariteá honang = ae sendariteá ka taekana honang,—If he had no horse, there would be *no means* of his going or *no means* whereby he could go.

In all the above constructions the use of the Simple or the Emphatic Personal Pronominal Subjects follows the rules given above (pages 50 and 51).

When the Subject of the Conditional Clause is the same as that of the Principal proposition, it need not be expressed twice—

If *I* go, *I* will give it to you,—*Senre-ng omamea.* In this case the Affix *ng* after *senre* must of course be considered as Subject to *omamea* and no longer as Possessive Affix to *senré.*

Isolated Conditional Clauses are fequently used in conversation to replace a negative reply. These replies are generally followed by *chi* or *oró or chi oró.* They contain the reason of the expected negative reply. The same construction is often used sarcastically.

Didst thou bring a cloth for me ? *Lijam auáiñachi ?* Instead of simply replying *no, I didn't,* the Munda will very feequently assign the condition on which the bringing of a new cloth depends, *v. gr.,* If I had money ! *Paise menáre chi !* or *paisa menárechi oro !* or If I had gone to the market,—*Pitteng senkenrechi !*

Have you sown that field ? *En pirim herakada ?* Not yet ? *Silerechi !* Here even the Pronominal Affix is wanting, If I had first ploughed it (then I might have sown it). A free but correct translation of the idea implied is this : Sowed that field ! Why that presupposed ploughing, a thing I have yet to do. The Principal Clause is often added to these replies.

Lijám auáiñcahi ? Paisa menáreching auamea honang ! If I had money, I might bring a cloth for thee. *En pirim herakedachi ? Silerechi heroa honanga!* If I first plough it, then there will be means of sowing.

The Conditional Clause form is also used to make a polite suggestion, *v. gr., Inta pantisoje dolekórebu honang,*—Suppose we were to arrange the bricks side by side in a straight line.

III.—Circumstantial Clauses of Time

1. *Re* is used to express in a more or less loose manner the concomitance of a secondary event with that which is spoken of in the principal proposition. Hence in this function *re* is translated by *when, at the time of.* Circumstantial Clauses of Time are therefore obtained by detaching the Copula *a* from any Mundari Transitive or Intransitive Predicate and affixing *re* instead of the Copula.

Upudub'tan-re enlekadole kajia,—We say so (we use the word chundul) *when* we are actually pointing out one another.

Hasu-reko patia, They will believe this (a warning to abstain from bad meat) *when they shall get sick;*

Aing itukire khube monelá ; nádoe landiajana,—He applied himself seriously (to study) *at the time when I was teaching him ;* but now he has become lazy ;

Uiúilen-reng gaulena,—I got wounded *when I had fallen down* or rather *when I had first fallen.* (Note the Anterior Past form which is used to show that the act of falling immediately preceded the wound, and is therefore considered as the cause.) *Uríko bankuátako-re uríko menáko-táreko siea,—When they (*the Mundas) *have no oxen* (of their own) then they plough with those who have cattle.

To a question concerning the meaning of the word *ta goe* the following reply was given : *Mochate jomjan-re enako tagoea,—When (*something*) has been eaten by or with the mouth* that they call *tagoe,* i.e., *to masticate.*

Hansárem taeken-redoing kajijad taekena,—But I was relating it whilst you were over there.

2. *Ló* and *imta* or *imtang* are used instead of *re* to denote *concomitance* or simultaneity in the strict sense of the term. They must therefore be rendered by *at the moment, at the very time, just as, etc. Gomke hijú-lóge ghanta saripe !* Ring the bell *as soon as the master comes.*

Am kam tebaled-imtange nirjana,— He ran away *just a little before you arrived.*

Te suffixed to any Predicate implies that the act or state signified by it precedes the fact or state spoken of in the principal proposition.

Misa gíti-te angpharchiaing,—When or *after* (I) *lie down,* I sleep in one stretch till day-break. *(N.B.*—Here *giti* is in the Indeterminate Tense because it denotes a habit or natural disposition.)

Mara ! dá han darure dulepe abungkó-te,—He you ! pour water on (*i.e.,* around) yonder tree, *after you have first washed yourself.* (*Abungkó* is the Anterior Future Tense-form.)

To a complaint about thc difficulties of the Mundari language the following reply was give : *Api-chanḍúko-tedo huṛing huṛingem bujauea,*—But *after three months will first have passed* thou wilt understand a little. (Here the phrase *api chanḍú, three months,* is used as an Intransitive Predicate and stands in the Anterior Future Tense.)

Chi is suffixed *to Past Tense-forms* to denote priority.

Enad'do apuing miad sadom *idikí-chi* oráte aururalíña,—Then my father having taken a pony to that place brought me back home. *Jomked'chiko joarkía ad'*

ko senójana,—Having eaten they greeted him and went away.

Ate suffixed to a Tense-form implies that the state spoken of in the principal clause has continued *uninterruptedly* ever since the event signified by the Tense-form took place. These Temporal clauses are often preceded by *mod'* or *mid'* used adverbially and meaning *in one stretch*—

Mod' hijúlen-ate misao kae nirlena,—From the moment he came up to the present, he did not run away. *Ne orạ́ mid' baiakan-ate jetatáre ka bagrauakana,*— This house has never got spoiled anywhere *ever since it has been built (made) Am hijúakan-ate kako siea etwar hulang,*—

Ever since you have come here they do no more plough on Sundays.

Reá or *rá* may be suffixed to a Tense-form to denote a loose simultaneity. Temporal Clauses of this kind are so characteristically idiomatic that they defy any literal translation.

Neado apuing menái-rá kajige,—This happened *at the time when my father was still alive.* (*Kaji, a word,* is often used as an equivalent of the English *an occurrence, an affair.* Here the Principal Clause is elliptical : *Neado kajige* for *neado kaji taná,*—This is an occurrence. The Genitive of Time *apuing menáirá* depends on *kaji* We might say an occurrence *of my father's time.* But we could never use a Present Tense-form even in the circumlocution : This is an occurrence! of the time when my father *was* still alive). *Neado sidareá, baiar sid'jan-rá,*— This happened before that, *namely, on the occasion when the rope snapped.*

IV.—Causal Clauses

Te may be suffixed to Tense-forms to denote *cause* and thus transform them into Causal Clauses.

(*Buṛi) hola boloken-te chi oṛó ná kae taina !* Won't (the bear) be there now (in the den) *since he entered yesterday ! i.e.,* the bear is sure to remain in the den still now *because* he entered it yesterday.

Inungo ka rasika taṛako kakoatan-te,—There is no pleasure in playing *since* or *because some (boys) refuse (to play).*

Pusio bangáire pusi ! pusi ! chikanamentem koklatana ? Miṇauṇ miṇauṇ ae menea-te,—What art thou shouting for a cat ! a cat ! when there is no cat (about this house) at all ? *Because he (*the cat) *says miau miau !*

Sonsorod'ko baba jomchabajadakotaiñá auri auri auritege,—The grasshoppers are eating up my whole crop of paddy because of my long delay to reap it. *(Auri* means *not yet.* Here it is used intransitively, and therefore means *to delay, i.e.,* to be always saying not yet ! not yet not yet ! That the delay refers to the reaping must be gathered from the context.)

Riringkedale isudinjan-te,—We forgot it *because it happened long ago (*because many days have passed). (Here *isudin,* many days, is used intransitively.)

Sentences containing Causal Clauses are often cut up into two co-ordinate Propositions.

Ísu dinjana ; énatele riṛingkeda,—Many days have passed since : on account of that we forgot it.

Tarako kakoaana ; ena-te inungo ka rasika,—A certain number of boys refuse (to play) : on account of that there is no pleasure even in playing.

Mente. This is the causative form of *men, to say* (see pp. 101 and 215). This *men* is not confined to the denotation of audible speech. It is often used to signify an interior speaking to one's self, and thus it becomes equivalent to the English *to believe, to think, to suppose, to be under the impression.* Hence when it is suffixed to Tense-forms for the purpose of denoting *cause,* it does by its very nature denote a *subjective cause, a reason,* the perception of which impels a living agent. Accordingly the Clause preceding *mente* is treated as a Direct-speech form, *v. gr.,* He punished *me* because *I* came late, becomes in Mundari, Saying "*thou* camest late, " he punished me,—*Bilamjanam mentee sajaikíña.*

However, *mente* as Causal Affix is no longer restricted to this its original meaning. It is now often treated as a mere Causal Affix in which the signification of *men, to say,* is obliterated. Hence *mente* may, like *te,* be used to denote *cause in general* and be construed also in the same way—

Bilamjana-ing mentee sajaikíña,—He punished me *because* I came late. *Ote keteakana mente chalu ka itua,*—It is impossible to hoe *because* the ground is hard.

Causal Clauses are also formed by means of the Affix *rá.* These, like the Temporal Clauses in *reá* or *rá,* are characteristically idiomatic—

Ne upun paisa, botol ka perejan-rá, Here are four pice over *because the bottle has not been filled.* (Literally, Here the four pice of the not having been filled up bottle, *i.e.,* the four pice due back to you for that amount (of oil) which is wanting towards the filling of the bottle.)

To signify that a certain effect is not obtained notwithstanding the existence of a cause which was thought sufficient to produce that effect, the Affix *o, even,* is added to a Causal Clauses in *te.*

Hela ! am upuniamedakan-te-o kam leljáiam,—Hallo ! thou doest not see him (the bird), although thou beest four-eyed. (This was said to me by an old Munda who had tried in vain to point out a bird to me in the foliage of a tree. *Upunia med'* four eyes, is used here in the Perfect of the Passive Voice, and is intended to denote spectacles which, added to the natural eyes, make up the four eyes spoken of by the old man.)

Gonoé kabu nirdaṛia rajaakan-te-o-ka,—None of us can escape death, not even *though we be kings.*

Rokage niridiled'te-o kae tebakia,—He did not reach him (find him alive any more), although he ran thither at once.

When the principal proposition is affirmative this construction implies that a certain effect is produced notwithstanding the existence of a cause which was thought sufficient to prevent that effect—

Jetana ka gunaked'te-o-le sajaijana,—We were punished, *although* we had committed no fault whatever.

The Affix *o* is sometimes omitted, especially in sarcastic apostrophies—

He ! am ! seṛaṇakan-te-m kam daṛia ! What ! thou ! being such a smart chap, thou canst not do it !

V—Final Clauses

1st—They may be obtained by suffixing *mente* to the Optative Mood-forms. Here it is necessary to keep in mind what has been said concerning the rendering of the English Indirect-speech forms into Mundari (see Introduction, pages 54-55).

With these Clauses *mente* really denotes a desire. Taken in connection with the Optative form, it literally means, *because I say (to myself), because thou sayest (to thyself),* etc., *let this or that be done.* But this implies a desire.

Nirkae mente janaue erangjaíña,—He is always scolding me in order that *I* should run away ; *literally,* Because he says (to himself) : "Let *him* run away!" he is always scolding me.

Horare alokako boroa mente banduke omad'lea ; literally, Because he says (to himself) : "Let *them* not fear on the way " he gave us a gun. Hence freely : He gave us a gun in order that *we* might not fear on the way.

Mundaókaing mente khube rikantana ; literally, Because he says (to himself) : " Let me become village-chief ! " he bestirs himself a great deal. Hence, freely, He bestirs himself a great deal *in order to become village-chief (in order that he should become village-chief).*

2nd—The optative without *mente* may be used to denote purpose. The result is a Compound Sentence in which two propositions are co-ordinated without any link-word *ad hoc*—

Auláing nellekae—I brought *in order that he might see it ; literally,* I brought, let him see it.

3rd—The Instrumental Suffix *te* added to Tense-forms yields sometimes Compounds which are best rendered into English by a Final clause.

A boy asking another, who was digging a trench, what he was up to received the following reply : *Am topa-te gara,*—(I am digging) a grave *to bury thee.*

4th.—The Substantive Instrumental Affix *teá* is used similarly : *Miad' jo idikóaing Thomastá rasikanteá gomke omláe mente ?* May I take one fruit to Thomas *wherewith or whereat he may rejoice himself* because the master has given it, literally, May I take one fruit to Thomas, a *wherewithal to rejoice himself,* because he will say the master gave it. *Chikanaben namtana ?* What do you two want? *Tin-hon dáling dul-teá,*—A small tin in order that we (he and I) may pour water (on the flower pots) ; *literally, a wherewith to pour water we two.*

5th.—*Leka,* like, yields strongly idiomatic Final clauses—

Guri suid'besepe hasaló midó-leka,—Knead the cow manure properly *in order that it may mix perfectly with the earth ;* literally, *to become like one thing with the earth ;* or knead the cowdung *like becoming one thing with the earth.*

Ne ari ghari hardarió-leka chakareabu—Let us broaden this dam, *so that a cart may be driven over it ;* literally, let us broaden this dam *like a cart being able to be driven.*

VI.—Subordinate Clauses of Manner introduced by "as though," "as if"

They are rendered into Mundari by affixing *leka* to any Tense form. These clauses are sometimes strongly elliptic, much having to gathered from the context and the circumstances for their complete understanding.

Sojege oltana roltad'-leka,—He writes quite straight *as though he had ruled* (his paper). *Rol* is the Mundarized English Verb *to rule.* Hence *roltadae,* he has ruled (his paper).

En piala sab'teá banólekam sabakada,—Thou art holding that cup *as if it had no handle.*

Iskulhonko nindirko jomkí-lekako latabia,—The schoolboys will cut his hair (so as to make him look) *as though the white-ants had eaten him* (his hair).

Julab botolre *nutabó-leka leloa mendo itilitila,*—Caster oil when in a bottle looks *as though it could be drunk fast (i.e.,* it looks as flued as water),but it is very fatty.

When Clauses with the Affix *leka* modify the words *tor, at'kar, biswas, boro* they express *a belief, an impression* or *an apprehension,* and therefore are equivalent to English clauses introduced by *that, lest,* or Clauses standing as Direct Objects without any introductory word—

En kaji olakan-lekaing torkeda,—I am under the impression *that that word has been written down.*

Batire sered' banó-lekaing torkeda,—I believe *there is no wick* in the lamp.

Chaprasi padaing-lekaing borojada,—I fear *the chaprassi is goint to kick me;* literally, I apprehend the chaprassi *as being about to kick me.*

VII.—Restrictive Clauses

Restrictive or limitative clauses which in English are introduced by *as for . . . . , as far as . . . . is concerned, with regard to,* etc., are in Mundari rendered in two ways:

1st.—The bare root-form of the Predicate generally with, sometimes without the Affix *do* is placed either before or after the complete —Predicate, *i.e.,* the Predicate with its formative affixes—

Kako tigakeda tigado, as for trampling on it, that they have not done.

Aledo kale bongatana bonga, as far as devil-worship is concerned, we do not worship devils.

Nírdo kale nira, as for running away, that we won't do.

2nd.—The repeated Predicate root is made to depend on the word *kaji* and therefore takes the Suffix *rá.* In these expression; *kaji* means *a matter, an affair,* and it generally takes the Affix *do. Tebaeako tising teba-rá kajido,*—They will reach to-day so far as the mere matter of reaching is concerned.

VIII.—Correlative Clauses of Manner

Since there are no distinct Correlative forms in Mundari, our Correlative

Clauses of Manner are rendered by simply suffixing *leka* or *lekate* to Tense-forms. The correlation must be guessed from the context. These clauses are sometimes strongly elliptic.

Merom ating-lekae olre sekeraea,—He writes *as fast as a goat grazes ; literally,* When writing he hastens as much as (the mouth of) a grazing goat.

Gerkí-lekae latab'jana,—He is shorn as unevenly as if rats had nibbled off his hair ; *literally,* He is shorn as if rats had nibbled or gnawed him.

Ka sunumakan-lekae lelóa,—He looks as untidy *as one who has no rubbed oil on his hair and body. (Sunumen,* to oil one's self).

Nea ale honder lumamko aukenteá-lekana (koto),l—This is a branch of the same kind *as the one on which we brought the silk-worms the other day.*

IX.—Correlative Clauses of Place

Soma daru má-tá menáia,—Soma is *there where* they cut the tree. *Tuinglí-tá sakidakan maiom menáakanagea,*—There is still now coagulated blood *there where they shot him with an arrow.*

Enad'do bintiked' chi sobenko mod' rele jojoma, oṛó ka-bijanído aeá titege oṛó jomae, ad' bijankodo apan jomkented chipi gasarkeate apan jomken taead'rege dubhapeakanko taena eṭáko auri jomchabajaked,—Then after saying the prayers we would all eat together, and if any one had not enough *(literally,* and the not satiated one), he would of his own accord take and eat more, and those who had their fill, having cleaned the vessel from which they had eaten, would sit still *in the place in which they had eaten* until the others would finish eating.

Examples Showing The Transfer of Words From Their Original Functions To That Of Transitive Or Intransitive Predicates

Duṛa, dust. Duṛaótanaing,—I am getting covered with dust.

Sirma, roof ; chandae, eaves of a roof. Enado kale sírmaá chandaeale,—We don't call that roof ; we call it eaves.

Ang, name of a Hindi letter. Ne aksar okoate Angótana ? By what (additional sign) does this letter (the Hindi *a)* become *Ang ?*

Hasa, earth. Enare oṛóle hasaea ? Shall we throw more earth into that ?

Bir, forest. En hora bejai birakana,—That road leads through dense forest. (Note that *biró* does not here mean *to be covered with forest,* as it would, *v. gr.,* in the sentence *En disum birakana.)* The present meaning, *to lead through a forest,* must be gathered from the nature of the Subject, *hora, a road,* which of course cannot be *covered* with forest.

Lacho, lip. Atiri-kandomlekam lachoakana ! Thou hast got lips like the rim of a chatu-cover.

Dar, the edge of a knife or *sword. Mid'sa darakana chi baransá ?* Is it single-edged or double-edged ?

Badnam, bad reputation. Aiñáe badnamtana ! He gives me a bad reputation.

(Note the Affix *á* to *aing, cfr.* Postpos. pages 82 and 85)

Nilidá, honey (literally, bee-water). *Niliko kako dákeda,*—The bees have not made honey. (Note how the word *nilada* is truncated because the first part of the compound occurs as Subject of the sentence—

Gitiorá,—The village dormitory for young people. In most villages all the boys and unmarried young men sleep, not in their respective houses, but altogether in a separate house, or if there be that commodity, in the dancing-house, called *akra.* The girls sleep in another house under the guardianship of some old woman, generally a widow. These dormitories are called *gitiorá. Gitiorádo kale gitioratána,*—As for the public dormitories, we do not sleep there.

Bó, head. Nesám bóea chi hansá ? Shall I put your pillow this side or that side ? *Literally,* Will thou put thy head this side or that side ?—*Setahonking misáreking bóakana niralge !* The two pups are so nicely sleeping head against head !

Dá, water. Dáakana neredo,—Here (it is watered) there is too much water. (This was used by one of the collies who was beating concrete in the foundations, and it was intended to convey the idea that there was too much water in a particular part of the lime and stone mixture.)

Turam, bifurcation, v. gr., the point at which a branch starts from the trunk. *Nesáte miad horaakana hansáteo miad' horaakana enaoko turama,*—When one road leads this way and another road leads that way, that too they call *turam,* bifurcation, *i.e.,* They also use the word *turam* (bifurcation) to denote the branching off of a road in two different directions. (Note the use of the absolute or categorical forms *horakana* instead of the conditional forms, *Nesáte miad' horaakanre,* etc.)

Orá, house (in the Reflexive Voice). *Aeá kurio oránjanae,*—His wife too left him, *i.e.,* has gone back to her parents' house.

Konea, bride. Entedo en kuri oroe koneanjanae,—Then that woman (a widow) married again, *i.e.,* again made a bride of herself.

Kanada or *kandae, a compartment, a room, a separate place in a house, etc. Jimbiri kandaegea* or *kandaakana,*—The *jimbiri, i.e.,* a peculiarly constructed fish-trap, has several compartments.

Kuri, wife. Bariae huriked'kinga,—He took two wives.

Jomti, right hand (literally, the eating heand). *Buruma hatulang parcmeachi? Ka gomke jomtialang,*—Shall we (thou and I) pass through the village of Buruma? No, Sir, we shall leave it to our right-hand side, *i.e.,* we shall pass on the left of Buruma.

Daru, tree, Neredang darulena,—It is in this place that the tree stood. (Note the Anterior Past, *darulena,*—There was a tree here formerly.)

Nida, night, Mandiale nádo gomke, nidaólea karedo holaleka,—We will cook now, Sir, otherwise the night will again overtake us like yesterday. *[Literally,* It will become night (for) us.] Here the Noun *nida* is first used in the Passive Voice; then this Passive form is retransferred to the Active function, and thus it takes the Inserted Pronominal Direct Object *le.*

The more ordinary construction with such words as *nida, aiub',* etc., consists in using them simply as Passive forms with the Personal Pronouns as Subjects. *Nidaóale;* literally, we shall be nighted, *i.e.,* we shall be overtaken by the night. *Entedoko aiub'jana,*—And then *they were delayed till evening.*

Dokan, a shop. Nado chikanae kamitana ? Chungi gomkee dokanakada,—What is he doing now ? He is selling cigars ; *literally,* he has made a cigar shop.

Taka, rupee, Baba akiringóre takaoá,—If one can afford to sell paddy, then one can make money. *(Literally,* If paddy be sold, repees wil become.)

Urí, bullock . Mahae uríked'koa,—He acquired bullocks last year.

Miad'em meromked'kore Dikue kumtruia, miad'em simked'kore inío eidia,—The zamindar robs us of every goat or fowl we rear. *(Literally,* If thou near a goat, the zamindar steals it : if thou rear a fiow that too he takes. (For explanation of the Plural forms *ko* as Direct Objects after *miad'* see pages 71-72)

Dá, water. Nea chikana ? Dá chimad'. He mar nume daredo. What is this? Water to be sure ! All right, drink it then *if it be water.*

Daru, wood. Ne huka chikana ? *Daruge. Hela ! darure chiamente ka loa ?* What is this pipe (what's it made of) ? It is wood. How that ! *If it be wood,* why does it not burn?

Diku : Hindu. Oróe dikuiña,—Then he would again address me in Hindi (Here the Indeterminate is used because the sentence occurred in a vivid narration). Proper Nouns when thus used to denote a particular language are more frequently construed *intransitively.*

Am Horore horoaingme tobe ! chikanam dikuaingtana ! If thou be a Munda, well, then, speak Mundari to me ! What art thou addressing me in Hindi for ?

Gomkedang Dikukíña oró ! But it was the master who nicknamed me *Diku. Chikanamentee enkaked'ma ? Misa misaing dikubaraea mente,*—Why did he call thee thus ? Because sometimes I speak a bit of Hindi.

The way in which Patronymics are used transitively or intransitively is especially puzzling—

Tenja-ing or *tenja-ng,*—My junior brother-in-law.

Tenjangaiaing,—He is my junior brother-in-law, *i.e.,* I say to him : *my brother-in-law.*

Tenjan-gaiam ? Is he thy junior brother-in-law, *i.e.,* Doest thou say to him: *my brother-in-law ?*

Tenjangaiae,—He is his junior brother-in-law, *i.e.,* He says to him : *my brother-in-law.*

Tenjangameae ? Art thou his junior brother-in-law, *i.e.,* Does he say to thee : my junior brother-in-law.

The Possessive Affix may be omitted. In that case the Transitive construction is preferred—

Mamu, maternal uncle. *Mamu-iñ-ae,*—I am his maternal uncle, *i.e.,* literally, he *maternal-uncles* me or, he calls me maternal uncle.

Mamu-i-aing,—He is my maternal uncle, *i.e.,* I call him maternal uncle.

Horo, man. Mimid' hororе babar horoked'kingae mentee darijana, karedo honang kage,—He would most likely not have got the victory in that fight had he not put two men against each one of their men ; *literally,* Because *against* or *for each one man* (of theirs) he (put) *two men,* he succeeded, if not probably not.

Bhanda, an earthen waterpot half the usual size, which is used only by little girls of from 8 to 10 years old to fetch water in.

Ne hon bhandadáakanae,—This girl is about 8 or 9 years old. This stands for *Ne hon bhandare dá audariae,*—This child can bring water in a *bhanda.* Instead of that *bhandare dá* is turned into a compound : *Bhandadá,* bhanda-water, *i.e., half a chatu of water.* This, again, used Intransitively denotes *ability to carry* half *a chatu* of water. That ability is given as an approximative index of the age.

Satom (Adverb of Time), *after two years.* To a question about the meaning of the word *satom* I received the following reply : *Bar sirma taiom enale satoma,*— After two years that we call *satom,* i.e., *Satom* means after two years.

Honder, before yesterday. *Honder honder* may mean *some weeks ago* and also *some months ago. Bar apidchandú sidare enado chilekateko kajia ? Enagekoo honder honderá,*—What do they say for : two months ago ? That too they express by the word *honder honder.*

Martobe ! all right then ! Come on then ! martobepea ! *Do say martobe ! i.e.,* begin the work !

Enka, like that. Enkaeako,—They *say, do, think, run, stand, work,* etc., etc., like that.

Taiom, after, at the end. *Darom taiomeme !* Place the word *darom* after or behind (such another word).

Sonje, straight. Ente gomke hantátele sojea,—Then, Sir, we shall go straight that way.

Tala, the middle, half. Miad' garado talaeabu nere ! Ka baiúa en pabita daru talatana,—Let us dig one trench here in the middle (between two trenches which were already dug.). It won't do that papaya tree *stands in the middle.* [Note how in these two sentences the word *tala* is first used Transitively : let us middle the trench, *i.e.,* dig a trench in the middle. Then it is used Intransitively; *daru talatana,* the tree middles it (between the two trenches), *i.e.,* stands in the middle. *Gande, crooked ; Enatedo hora gandeótana,* and then the road turns, *(i.e.,* becomes crooked).

Ek ! do ! tin ! One ! Two ! Three ! used as signal to begin a race.

Ek do tineabu ! Let us agree to start at the signal *ek ! do ! tin !*

Ekdoakana ! Take care you will be too late ! *i.e.,* One ! two ! has already been shouted: hence in a moment the race begins.

Mid', one ; mid'jangeale ! We are one, *i.e.,* we are equal (in a game).

Aiar, ahead ! Enlekako aiartana ne durangre,—Like that this song continues; *literally,* like that they go ahead in this song.

Okoe ? who ? Neado okoeáakana ? And this whose share has it become ? To whom has this been given or adjudicated ?

Oṛo oṛó, more and more. Hence *Oṛó oṛoá,*—Other and still other things. (These things may denote circumstances, sentences, words, etc., etc.) *Latarte ko kajiachi ? Kajiako oṛó oṛoákóre,*—Do they say *latarte ?* They do when the occasion presents itself, *i.e.,* when they happen to use other and other sentences.

Saṛaoṛo'pe,—Pour more manure.

Auri,—not yet, wait a moment. Chimtangking arandia ? Aurikinga,— They will wait still ; they won't marry just now.

(Note here the Impersonal Construction used with an Adverb of Time, see pages 212-215)

Jomtisáte,—to the right-hand side. Ama heu ! jomtísatem ! Thou there ! Go to the right !

Ghakarno, pretty broad. Ne aribu chakarnoea,—Let us make this ridge pretty broad.

Haní, yonder one. Haní haníejada,—(The one you look for) is yonder. (Literally, yonder one he yonders.)

Pechang, a chip of wood. Pechangoá chika ? Won't the chips fly about?

Rotod', topknot of hair (a Hindu fashion of wearing hair). *Nídoe rotod' akana,*—This one wears a topknot ; *literally,* is topknotted.

Basidá, water in which is poured on boiled rice and which is left standing for a day so as to turn acid. This is the ordinary drink of Mundas. They very seldom will drink plain water—*bereldá,* raw water, as they call it. *Niral, nice. Basidá niralakana,*—The rice-water is just at the right stage of acidity, *i.e.,* is nicely ready.

Upun diring, foru horns. *Upuniako diringakana,*—(That kind of deer) are four horned, *i.e.,* each horn has two branches.

Upuniae kataakana,—(That animal) is four legged.

(Note how the Numerals qualifying Nouns are here separated from the Nouns by means of the Pronominal Subjects *ko* and *e.* It is on account of this separation that the Numerals resume the final *a* which they drop whenever they are in immediate contact with the Noun)—

Kented', many. Kented'jaíñako, kaing dariaokoa. They are too many for me, I can't get over them. (They out-number me.)

Enka, like that. Pakudange enkaled'mea,—Sure it's Paku who first called thee thus (who first gave thee that nickname).

Janao, always. Hewaoá janaoredo,—One gets accustomed to it when one *does it always.*

Hemar ! all right. Hemarláe mendo taiomtee nirjana,—He agreed (to come with me) at first, but afterwards he ran away.

Hemartobe ! all right then ! Hemartobeáiña,—He told me all right then ! He agreed to it.

Hereo kareo baiúgea,—It will do anyhow whether they agree (to the proposal) or whether they do not, *i.e.,* Their or his saying yes or no does not matter one way or the other.

Maparangmed', very big eyes. *Maparanggee med'baṛajada,*—He opens big eyes at it, *i.e.,* he is very much surprised.

Nida-med', literally, *night eye,* is the name given to a peculiar weakness of the eyes on account of which people thus affected can see nothing at all any more after sunset. *Nidamedotanaing,*—I can no longer see anything after sunset, *i.e.,* I am affected by that eye disease.

Apan (Hindi Possessive), *his own. Goako kaing namkoa; gota haturenkoe apanked'koa,*—I shall not get any witnesses : he has got the (people of the) whole village over to his side (*Literally,* he made them his own).

Barsá, twice. Barsákenaing, misao kaing tólá,—I aimed (threw, hit or shot at it) twice, but did not hit it even once.

Naua, new, Hankue nauaakad'koa,—He has engaged or appointed yonder ones *as new hands;* he has appointed new men, viz. yonder ones.

Rabang, cold. Hoṛoko aingsáko rabangjana,—The men turned me the cold shoulder *(literally,* became cold towards me).

Ale, we (exclusive). *Ale aleredo jeman chile rojotoa,*—When we are amongst ourselves (*i.e.,* when no foreigners are with us) don't we bring out a lot of this stuff. (After having for a couple of hours listened to and noted down the meanings Mundas attach to their dreams and to certain omens, I asked the company whether there was anything more to be added on that subject. Then a young man gave the above reply to show there was more, but that, to find it all, they must be *en famille,* so that one may bring out what another happens to forget, *Rojoto* is used to denote a *consultation.)*

Mipiad', one by one ; also *one here, one there, a few here and there.* A boy who got over the worst of an attack of chicken-pox was consoled by a visitor with the sentence : *Nádo am mipiad' akanam,*— Now thou hast (only) a few here and there (*literally,* now *thou art one-here-one-there-ed).*

Chi ? Interrogative Interjectional Affix. A young man who had a somewhat peculiar style of speaking being asked why he did not speak like others answered : *Chiaing oró ? mochataing enka senoá,*—What am I to do ? My mouth goes that way. (Other people would rather say *chikaeaing ?)*

In the follwing complete propositions are treated as Transitive or Intransitive Predicates :—

Baiuá,—It will do. Kaling baiúáa,—He and I won't agree to that ; *literally,* we two will not (say) it will do.

Prachare ituana,—The catechist knows it. Pracharituanaaking,—Both of them say or maintain that the prachar knows about it (both of them say pracharituana). Note that the Pronominal Subject *e* is dropped after the word *prachar* to avoid having two Pronominal Subjects.

Banoá,—There is none. Banoáako,—They say that there is none. *Hokaalang! Let us stop (thou and I). Aledo hokaalanga,*—But we (Mundas) would express that by saying *hokaalang.*

Sartiakana,—It is true. Sartiakanaako,—They will believe it (They will say, it is true.)

Appendix

I.—THE ASUR LEGEND

Sirmare inígebu Singbonga-tana.

That one (who is) in heaven we (call) Singbonga.

Aking kulbuṛiaking kapa-jitana.

Both husband and wife are conversing with each other.

Sida biam sida sangain ...

The first marriage, the first love (theirs was).

Sona satarangge Singbonga dubakanae, sona taiṇṛi-danda.

On a golden throne Singbonga is seated: a golden sceptre-staff (he holds).

Imtangking kapajitana ...

At that time both were conversing with each other.

Pati peté petétekoa, mimiad' miu miutekoa.

They have plenty of rice ; they have plenty of cattle.

Ranki gundi piuri gaiking arjitana Singbongatá : Upal-bá pukuri, tarai-bá bandela dundátana. Chara kaling namjada, singsandom, tasad'-rurá soben rongotana. Chimti-pipiri, charai-chunguni dá kako namjada, chara kako namjada.

The heifer with turned-up horns, the cow with turned-down horns both complain to Singbonga : the tank (with its) floating flowers, the band (*a kind of tank) (*with its) marsh-flowers is drying up. We two find no food: tree and shrub, grass and stalk all is withering. The creeping insects and the flying birds do no longer find water ; they do no more find food.

Sirmare singbongae elangtanae aiurtana.

In heaven Singbonga is scorched by the heat ; he is reached by the heat (emanating from the Asurs' furnaces).

Sona satarangire dubakanatee aiumtana ; kisjanae.

Seated on the golden throne, he (Singbonga) hears (these plaints) ; he got angry.

Kacha kanḍajanae, ṭuṇṭa pirinjanae : Hasur-honko magirikoaing.

He armed himself with a single-edged sword and shielded himself with a plain shield : "I will cut the Asurs to pieces."

Ente kuṛie kajiaitana: Aloma! eskarge kaṃ dariakoa, sangiako haga, sangiako boea. Inku nidaoko sipud'tana singioko sipud'tana. Amdom eskargeam; mapa tupuingte kam dariakoa. Bara bidu, tero chaiakoe metáia. Hemarkedae.

Then his wife said to him : Don't ! alone thou wilt not get over them. There are multitudes of them (Literally : they are many a relation, they are many a brother.) They work (their) furnace-fellows by night too and they work (their) furnace-bellows by day too. But thou art alone; in a mutual fight with the sword and with the bow and arrows thou canst not overcome them. Wisdom and craft ! she said to him. He agreed to that (he said: all right !)

Enate dingchua maru ente kerkeṭa jagu kuldutam ked'-kingae Hasurhonkotá.

Then he sent the energetic kingcrow and the watchful kerketa (*a bird who cries repeatedly during night)* as messengers to the Asurs

Inking kajijada : Kajichaling autada, baḳạnrachaling setertada. Nidape sipuḍ'redo singi alopea ! singidope sipud'redo nida alopea! Upal-bá pukŭri taṛai-ba bandela anjed'tana ḍunḍátana. Ranki gunḍi piuri gai dá kaking namjada, chara kaking namjada menteking kajitana. Chimṭi-pipiri, charai-chunguni dá kako namjada, chara kako namjada. Otere tasad'-ruṛá, sing-sandom soben rongotana. Sirmare Singbongae elangtanae aiurtana menteking kajitana.

Those two said : We two have brought a message; we two have reached here with a request. If you work the furnace-bellows by night, then don't (work them) by day. But if you work them by day, then don't (work them) by night ! The tank with its floating flowers, the band with its marsh-flowers are drying up, are getting dry. The heifer with turned-up horns, the cow with turned-down with horns both do no more find water, both do no longer find food, saying the two (birds) say. The creeping insects and the flying birds do no more find water; they do no more find food. On the earth grass and blade, tree and shrub are withering. In heaven Singbonga is scorched by the heat; he is reached by the heat, saying the two (birds) say.

En Hasurhonko kajikeda : Ale Singbongatelea, ale maṛang deotatelea, jetaeá kaji kale manatinga.

Those Asurs said : We are greater than Singbonga; we are above the great deities; we won't obey the orders of anybody.

Alege ang maṛangakana, alege tur maṛangakana. Aleáte jetae maṛang bangáia. Nidaole sípud'a, singiole sípud'a mente-ko kajirurakingtana. Kadalkandile kandiakana, jumbulijurile juria-kana. Dunda pahalle kidub'tana, dunda, pahalle angaratana, ale jetaeá kaji kale manatinga menteko kajikeda.

We are prior to the dawn; we are prior to the sunrise. There is nobody prior to us. We will work (our) furnace-bellows by night too; we will work (our) furnace-bellows by day too, saying they replied. We are clustered together like plantains in a bunch; we are close together like clusters of fruit (*we are very numerous).* We gain; to-day's food by making short ploughshares; we secure to-morrow's food by preparing short ploughshares. We will not obey the orders of anybody, saying they said.

Dingchua kuila durateko herkía, kerkeṭa bicha duṛateko herkía.

"Ju senóben ! okoetáreben udub'ea !"

Inking senójanaking, Singbonga-táreking udub'jada : "Hela gomke ! alingdo jatiate bejaitijana !"

Senóben abená jatitáte ; sobenko mid'gepe lelóae kajijad'kinga.

Enteking senójana ad'king lelked'koa, mid'geako.

Ente sonadidi rupadidi kulked'kingae. Inking Hasurhon-koking kajiakotana : Kajichaling autada, bakaṇṛa chaling seṭertada: etc.

Ente kotaiteko maraked'-kinga, ente sandasomteko maraked'kinga.

Ju senben ! okoetare ben udub'ea nádo menteko kajiad'-kinga.

Ente lipi susari, kaua bandari inkinge kulked'kinga Hasur-honkotá. Ente inking hijulena oṛóking kajiakotana: kajichaling, etc.

Ente kaua kuila-durateko herkía, lipi bicha duṛateko herkía, etc.

Ente lang-cheṇre Lakan, bochochenre kajure kuldutam-ked'kinga, etc.

Bocho cheṇre sasang-dáteko hichirkía, lang cheṇre chad'lomko tauijilingkía, etc.

They strew coal-dust on the kingcrow; they strew iron-ore dust on the kerketa.

"Off ! begone ! to whom will you complain !"

Both of them went away. They complain to Singbonga : "Alas, Master! we two (he and I) have become outcasted from our caste.

Go (back) you two each to his own caste; you will all look alike (*i.e., all kingcrows will henceforth look black and all kerketas will henceforth look grey)* he says to them.

Then both went away, and they saw them (those of their own kind), they are all one (*they all look alike*).

Then he sent the golden vulture and the silvery vulture. Those two tell the Asurs: We two have brought a message; we two have reached here with a request, *etc., as above. (The reply of the Asurs too is the same as above.)*

Then they struck both of them with a hammer; then they struck both of them with the large iron pincer.

Off ! Begone ! to whom will you complain now saying they said to both of them. *(Thier complaint to Singbonga and the latter's reply is the same as above.)*

Then he sent the worshipping lark and the leading (the forward) crow to the Assurs. Then both of them came and they said to them : We two have, etc. (same as above. The asures' reply too is the same.

Then they threw coal-dust on the crow and iron-ore dust on the lark, *etc. (as above.)*

Then he sent Lakan the lang (a small bird with two long feathers in tail) and Kajur, the bocho, *etc.*

They threw saffron-water on the bocho and they lengthened the lang's tail by pulling at it, *etc.*

Ente Singbonga baro bidu tero chayaked'kinga.

Then Singbonga had recourse to wisdom and craft *(Literally :* he twelve-knowledged and thirteen-appearanced it.)

Ekasi piri tirasi badi dasiko ṛa mátan chalutanae. Ente enre Singbonga kasra herkeda iniá hormore. Ente ní gaujanae. Gaujanchi, sona richi soridikíae iníta.

A servant is clearing (cutting) and hoeing the eighty-one high grounds, the eighty-three high rice-fields. Then there Singabonga sowed itch on that one's body. Then that one got wounds. When he had got the wounds, he (Singbonga) flew a golden hawk towards him (went out hunting with a folden hawk whom he made fly towards that servant).

Enteee metaitana; Chi de ! aing chalulea misa. Ente en kasraakaní kajiruṛaitana: Aingdo kasragaute soben kud'lam harangite topechabaakana, amdo nelekan pharchi horo kaing omamea mentee kajiáia.

Then he said to him. Come now ! let me try once to hoe. Then that itch-covered one replied to him : On account of itchwounds my whore hoe is entirely besmeared with the liquid oozing out of the wounds. I will not give it to thee who art such a fair man, saying he told him.

Ente Singabonga inígе chutaub're sab'kía ad'e sokoekía. Hotorjanae. En urte Singbonga sonójanae. Enatee senójana Hasurhonkotáte. Huṛi patṛate jirentana rokoko hartanteá. Pati rokoko harjáia, pati tijuko uiuiditana.

Then Singbonga took hold of him by the top-knot of hair and shook him. He got out of his skin (like a snake). With that skin Singbonga clothed himself. Then he went away to the Asurs. He twirls a leafed branch of a huribush round about himself to drive away the flies. As many flies as would fill a pati (*grain-measure containing two pounds)* are driving him ; he goes along dropping a pati full of maggots.

Ente Hasurhonkoa hatue tebakeda.

Then he reached the Asurs' village.

"Chi hale ! dasipe dodoa chi ? Simkoing harnala."

Chi hale ! will any of you engage a servant ? I will gain my wage by driving off the fowl (from the grain).

Ente Hasurko kajitana : Juna kuriko Q lelipe. Enteko lelkia. Enateko lelkichiko chichijadako, durdurjadako, bejadako. "Kalea, kale dodoa ganrakotale chalauoa." Ente aiar hatutee senojana.

Then the Asurs said : He ! you women ! have a look at him. Then they looked at him. And then having seen him, they (say) chichi! they (say); away ! away ! they spit. We won't ! we don't engage a servant. Out children will be infected ; our offspring will be infected. Then he went to the next village.

"Chi hale ! dasipe dodoa chi ! etc. . . ganrakotale chalauoa. Ju seno me ! hansa tolate seno me, Mundaking menakinga Lut'kum haram Lut'kum, buria. Inking asid', honko bangkua, dindageaking. Aledo kalea."

Ente inkingtáe senójana.

"Chi hale ! jiangking tantangking, menábenachitabu.

Inking dasiking dokia. Ente simkoe harnalatana.

Ente musing hulang dine kajiakingtana : Simjarom namatukaingpe, gaute haiajaina. Enteking namatukaia. Ente Hasurhonkotae senojana. Inkulo inung nagene senotana. Akoa meed guli, kasra kora a simjarom guli Hasur honko kapajitana : simjaromtae rapid'eabu, led'eabu, Mara oraumeko metaitana. Oraukedae. Ente inia guli kako tókead. Ente iniá guli kako tókeda. Ente, mar ape oraupee menjada. Ente iní gulikedae. Ente simjarom gulite mered' gulikoe tokorapudkeda. Ente inku ringinijanako. Aurile udub' mea Lut' kumharamta kingt'are ! Babado patireking tasitukaad' meaking; simko jomchabakedako menjada.

Enate haram buriakingtáre enkateko udub'keda. Buria Kistótanae : "Chinalang joma ! soben simko jomchabakeda. Ne kasra kora dasi kalang dodoiaing metad'mea; doigealangem menkeda."

Chi hale ! will any of you, etc. (*as above*) . . . . . our offspring will be infected. Get away ! go to the hamlet yonder ; there there are two Mundas : Lutkum the old man (and) Lutkum's old wife. They perchance (will engage thee), there are no children; they are chldless. As for us, we won't (engage thee). Then he went to those two.

Chi hale ! you two my grandmother and my grandfather, are you two at home, ar we you and I ?

Those two engaged him as a servant. Then he gains his wage by driving off the fowl (from the spread-out grain).

Then some day he says to both of them : Do get some eggs for me. On account of my wounds I experience a strong craving for them. Then they got them for him. Then he went to the Asurs. He goes to play with them. They (had) iron marbles ; the itch-covered by had eggs for marbles. The Asurs said to each other : we shall break his eggs; we shall fry them, they say. All right, do thou first place thy marbles. He first placed his marbles, Then they did not his his marbles. Then, all right now you place your marbles. Then he rolled his marbles. Then with his egg-marbles he hit and broke the iron marbles. Then they took it ill. Just thou wait a while, we shall denounce thee to old Lutkum and his wife. Sure they had spread paddy on a mat for thee (to watch it) ; the fowl have eaten it all up, they say.

Then they reported like that to the old couple (the old man, the old woman—both). The old woman gets angry : What are we going to eat ! the fowl have eaten up every grain of it. Let us not engage this itch-covered boy as a servant, I told thee ; we (thou and I) will certainly engage him thou saidst.

Miad' babajang en kasra-koṛa halangrurakedae. Patiree dokeda, pati perẽjana ; oratee idikeda. Sehelree, dokeda, sehel peréjana. Tunkiree dokeda, ṭunki peréjana. Haṭáree dokeda, hatá peréjana.

The itch-covered-boy picked up again one grain of paddy. He placed it on the mat -- the mat got filled. He took it (the grain) to the house. He put it into the husking pit - the husking pit got filled. He put it into the basket - the basket got filled. He put it on the winnowing shovel—the winnowing shovel got filled.

Ente haṛamburiaking lelkedaking.

Then the old couple saw this.

Okoeá am kumbuṛukedam menteking kajiaitana ?

Whose (paddy) didst thou steal, saying, both said to him?

"Jetaeá jiangking tatangking kaing kubuṛutada. Abuáge saratingtana-baratingtana. Singbongae omabutana."

I have stolen nobody's (paddy). my grandmother (both), my grandfaterh (both). Yours and mine (paddy) is increasing (getting plentiful). Singbonga gives it to us.

Ente oṛó eṭá hulangrá din : aben hale ! Jiangking tatangking lupólad' baiatukaingben, gaute haiajáiña mentee kajiakingtana. Ente inking lúpulad'king baiaia. Ente lupúlad' sab'ked'tee senójano Hasurhonkotá ínungte.

Then again on some day : Halé you two! my grandmother, my grandfater, prepare some husk-bread for me. On account of (my) wounds I feel a strong craving for it. Then taking up those husk-cakes he went away to the Asurs to play.

Ente inku : Mara lupúlad' katitam, oṛaumeko metaitana. Ente inku katikeda, kako tókeda. Mar nado ape oṛauepee metad'koa. Ente katikedae Katikotako rapudótana, mered' katiko lupúlad'katite. Ente inku ringinijanako, etc.

Then they : Go on use the husk-cakes as kati, place (thy) kati first, they tell him. Then they threw their katis, they did not hit. Go on now you place your katis, he told them. Then he threw his kati. Their katis break, iron katis with a kati made of husk-cake. Then they did not take it well, *etc. (as above, viz., the accusation and the multiplication of grain).*

Ente Hasurhonko mered'e ghatuked'koa. Ente : dea ! chaulijang lelalem ! kasrakorako metaitana.

Then he caused the Asurs to run short of their supply of iron. Then, Come now ! do please examine the rice-grains for us (*i.e., act as soothsayer for us that we may know what sacrifice is needed in our present distress)* they said to the itch-covered boy.

Dub'o kaing daṛia, gau hasujáiña, chilekateng lelapea mentee kajiṛuraad'koa. Ente inkusenoṛuratanko taikena.

I cannot even sit down : (my) wounds are paining me so ; how can I examine (the rice-grains) for you, saying he replied to them. Then they were going to go away.

Daea ! omaingpe chaulijang, gitilellekaing mentee kajiru-raad'koa. Ente seta hijupeng udubapea.

Come, then ! give me the rice-grains. I shall examine them lying down as I am, saying he replied to them. Then you come (in the) morning, I shall show you (what's required).

Ente inku setáko senruṛajana. Chia ? chilekatem namkedako kulijáia ?

Then (next) morning they went back (to him) : Well ? how hast thou found matters to stand, they ask him?

Singbongare punḍi sim bongaipe, imtangtape meṛedóa.

In (honour of) Singbonga you sacrifice a white fowl; then you will find iron (then to you iron will become).

Ente inku punḍi simko bongakia; ente huringlekatako mered'jana. Enteko rasikajana.

Then they sacrificed a white fowl, whereupon they found a little iron. Then they rejoiced.

Ente oró eṭá hulangtako ghaṭaujana. Ente oṛó chaulijangko idiruráia. Daea lelalem chaulijang, meṛed'tale ghaṭaujana. Held gaute kaing dub'daṛiae metakotana. Ente Hasurhonko hijuruṛatanko taikena Ente : da ! omaingpe, gitilelle kaing, setá ruṛapee kajiruraad'-koa. Setá angjanchi en Hasur honko sennamkíako. Chiam lelad'leam menteko kulijáia ? Punḍi bakra bongaipe, huṛinglekatape meṛedoá. Ente bakrako bongakíetako mered'jana. Ente inku rasikajana.

Then again some other day their (iron) ran short. Then once more they took the rice-grains to him. Come now do please examine the rice-grains for us: our iron has run short. Alas, I am unable to sit up on account of my wounds, he says to them. Then the Asurs were on the point of coming away again. Then, come then ! give them (rice-grains) to me. I shall try to examine them whilst lying down ; come back in the morning, he replied to them. In the morning, as the day broke, the Asurs went to (find) him. Well, hast thou examined them for us they ask him? Sacrifice a white he-goat, you will (then) find a little iron. Then having sacrificed the he-goat they found iron. And then they rejoiced.

Ente oró etá hulang, etc. ... Singbongare bale mindi bongaipe. Inku bale mindi bongakíte mered' huringlekatako mered'jana. Ente inku, ḅesudubad'buae menteko rasikajana.

Then, again, *etc. (as above)* ... Sacrifice a young sheep in honour of Singbonga. Having sacrificed a young sheep they found a little iron. Then they rejoiced, because he had shown them the right sacrifice (then he has shown us aright, saying they rejoiced).

Ente etá hulang oṛótako ghaṭaujana, *etc.* . . . . Chiam namad'lea menteko kulijáia. He aing named'pea mentee kajiakotana : Horo-danṛejanatapeae

Then agains some other day again their (iron) ran short, *etc. (as above.)* Well, hast thou found it (the kind of sacrifice) for us, they ask him. Yes, I have found it out for you, he says to them : A human sacrifice

metad'koa. Enate inku haikatejanako. Hela kasrakoṛa, okorele namiako kajiruṛaitana. Ju ! senópe Doisa parganate, Kulkura parganate ; enre Mundako menákoa. Kulikope ! chi akiringkoape mente kulikope. Hela chikanatekọ omalea, chinatele kiringiako metaitana. Ente : ne kakaurking samroming omapetana: senópe ju! Kiringtee metad'koa.	has become (necessary) for you, he told them. Then they became dumbfounded. Alas, itch-covered boy, where will we find one (a man) they reply to him. Go to the Doisa district, to the Kukura district ; there there are Mundas. Ask them ! he ! do you sell them (men) ask them. Alas, for what (as price) will they give to us (a man), with what shall we buy him, they say to him. Then I give you these two pumpkins, (they are) gold ; all right ! go now to buy, he said to them.
Ente inku Doisa parganateko senójana : Chi hale ! hoṛokope akiringkoape chi menteko kulijad'koa ; bongaialae !	Then they went to the Doisa paragnah : Chi hale ! do you sell men, saying, they asked them ; we are going to sacrifice one !
Okoea namtana engateá roga! dalipe ! Mod'baleatebu asultaia! Bongainí okoe namtana dalipe !	Who then is asking a mother's darling (child) ! hit him ! From the tenderest childhood we have reared him ! The one who wants to sacrifice him strike him !
Ente inku nirjanako. Enate kasrakorako metaitana : Hela kale namkía hoṛo !	Then they ran away, and then they tell the itch-covered boy : Alas, we have not got a man !
Chilekape kajikeda ?	How did you say (ask) ?
Chigheu ! honkope akiring koape chi ? bongaiale mentele kajiakotana.	Chigheu ! do you sell children ? we are going to sacrifice one, saying we told them.
Enaddoe ? metakotana.	And then (what happened?) he says to them.
Nirjanaleko metaitana.	We ran away they tell him.
Ainggea tobe ! bongakingpee metakotana. Gaute erágeng dukutana, nida singi harangige lingitana mente kajiakotanae.	Here am I myself then ! do sacrifice me, he says to them. I am suffering much pain on account of my wounds; matter is flowing out day and night he says to them.
Ente Lutkum haṛam Lutkum buria kaling omma menteking kajiruṛaitana;okoe oṛá horoalinga?	Then the old man Lutkum and Lutkum;s old wife : We won't give thee (up), saying both of them said, who will watch our house for us ?
Inkinge metakingtana : Bongakingkako jiangking tatangking !	To those two he says : Do let them sacrifice me my grandmoter dear, my grandfather dear !
Ka amo ! okoe alingdo asul-	No thou too ! (*i.e.,* what doest thou think

linga ?

Aben aloben uṛúa ! asulógeaben. Aben táreng kajitukatana. Chi nea kaji udubabentanaing metadkinga. Ape Mundahonkotáre ne kaji tainka mente kajitukaad'kinga. Hatu talare pahaṇṛá hon sing subareng dubatukaiaing. Ini aben mainbena, bare misa, bataulire misa, magere misa.

Inking : he martob ! ne kaji kaling riringea mentekíng kajiruṛaitana.

Ente Hasurhonko idikia bongai nagen.

Ente inku auri bongai sidaree kajiad'koa : Pundi merom bakra potaipe ur, naua ghandiking baipe, naua binghal baipe, baba-holong rurungepe, kodeholong rurunggundaepe ; dinḍa kuṛiking rurungeka mentee kajiad'koa, katabakanate.

Mar nádo iladepe !

Ente en kutite bolotanimtang kajiatukaakotana : Dinḍa kuṛiking sipudeka, api ma kata-bakanate. Nida singiking sipudeka. Sutambinda naua chatute dáking auka, uli daurate-king hirchienṛeka ! Mar ! nádoing bolojana, iladkesedingpe !

Enatedoking sipud'keda nida singi. Enatedo api ma hobajanchi

of) who then will support me and her?

As for you two, don't worry yourselves! You will surely be supported. I leave my word for it to you two. Now this promise I reveal to you two, he says to both of them. Let this word of mine remain (be ever remembered) amongst you Mundas, he impressed it on them (he impressively said to them) : I will seat the pahan's son (the sacrificer) under a tree in the middle of the village. He will sacrifice to you, (*i.e.,* he will offer to you two the essences or souls of the fruits, flowers, and animals he sacrifices) once on the flower feast, once on the batauli feast, and once on the mag feast.

Then both of them : All right then ! he and I (we two) won't forget this word, saying they reply to him.

Then the Asurs led him away in order to sacrifice him.

Then before they sacrificed him he said to them : take the skin of a white he-goat (*to make bellows with)* make new bellow-sticks, prepare a new bellow-nozzle, husk rice into flour, husk marrua *(a small grain)* into flour ; let two virgins do the husking after having fasted, saying he said to them.

All right now plaster up (the furnace).

Then at the moment he was entering into that furnace he impressed it upon them (as follows): Let two virgins who have fasted since three days work the bellows. Let them work the bellows by night and by day. Let them on a head cushion made of cotton thread bring water in a new earthen pot and let them extinguish the fire by sprinkling (water on) it with a twig of a mango-tree. All right ! now I have entered ; plaster me up !

Then the two (virgins) worked the bellows day and night. Then when three days sutambinda naua chatute dáking agulá, uli daurateking hirchienṛekedaking. Enate kutiking rurungutunṛkeda.

Enate angtanleka turtanlekae urunglena. Sona rupatege somparauakanae ; lota taṛigee sabana.

Khubchi menáko kulijáia ?

Haṇ ! haṇ ! khub mená mentee kajiakotana. Hagape sangia, apedo purápe aguea. Enate kutiundute bolopee metaad'koa, koṛa hon bhari ! Koṛahonko aguchabakope ; taimotepe repéa karedo. Ente, sirmare sonadidi rupadidiking jalatingtana. Mar suba seromilte lelnamkoben, chuti kangsulilte lelnamkoben, merako ukuna, mentee kajiakotana.

Hasurhonkodo : chabajanale menteko kajiaitana. Koṛahon-ko-bhari sobenkole auchabaked' koa.

Ente inku sobenko bolocha-bajanchi : marna kuṛiko ! ilad'-kesed'epe bichadurate kuiladu rate ! Ilad'kesed'kedako. Marna kuṛiko ! sengel salgau ad' sipudepe! Sipud'jadako ; ena tedo kutichetanre kuilako dul jada ad' khub'ko sipud'jada. Chaïṇ chuïṇtanko ragoentana.

Helaea ! am bedaked'leako metaitana.

Marna kuriko sipudepe ! repétanako, kako dongótana ! sekerage sipudepe !

had passed, they brought water in new earthen pots on head cushions made of cotton-thread ; they extinguish the fire by sprinkling (water on) it with twigs of a mango-tree. Then they broke the furnace down with husking poles.

Then he came out like the dawn, like the rising sun. He is covered with golden and with silver ornaments ; he holds a drinking vessel and a plate.

Is there plenty more of it (treasure), they ask him?

Yes ! yes ! there is plenty more of it, saying he tells them. You are many brethren, you'll be able to bring out a lot of it. And then : enter through the hole of the furnace, he said to them ; Men only (will do) ! Bring together all the men, or else later on you will rob from each other. And then : under the roof (of the furnace) a golden and a silver vulture both are soaring. Examine them underneath at the feathers under the wings and at the feathers which are at the end of the wings, perchance they may hide (their treasure) saying he tells them.

But the Asurs : we are all here, saying they tell him. So far as the men are concerned, we have brought all of them together here.

Then when all of them had entered : all right ! now you women, plaster up (the furnace) with iron-ore dust and with coal-dust. They plastered it up. All right ! now you women, light the fire and work the bellows ! They work the bellows. Then on the top of the furnace they pour coal and they work the bellows with energy. (Those inside) are crying desperately *chaïṇ chuïṇ*.

Alas, thou has cheated us they (the women) say to him.

'Tis all right now you, women ! work the bellows ! They are robbing each other ; they do not all get enough ; work the bellows fast!

Entedo lada ladatan urungótana maiom gera horate nari horate.

Heleam ! bedaked'lea, chi maiom naeadoko metaitana.

Kana ! kuriko, pan kasailiko jomtana, enako béurungjada, Marna kuriko ! khub sipud'ta- bepe, sekerage !

Ente, rongojan torked'kochi rurungutunrepe mentee kajiad'koa.

Enteko rurungutunrekeda. Jang eskargeko namkeda, rankaroretanko namkeda.

Helaeam bedaked'lea ! nakamente kale torked'mea ! Korakotale sipud'goerikaked'-leam menteko kajiaitana.

Hela na ! kerketa jagu, dingchua maru kuldutamled'-kingaing. Inkingá kaji kape manatingjana mentee kajiakotana. Ente : aiñá hal hukumpe manatinga chi na mentee kajiakotana.

Hanle manatingako men. Kale manatingkóre *chilekatele asulóa oróko* metaitana.

He martobe ! asulótea horaing udubapea mentee kajirurakotana.

Patguru, Tura chelaking dotukakingtana. Hulabara chaulijang, sete bara kudijang dia sengel poro sengelteko *salanam pitinampeako.* Patguru Turachela inkingtáre alope ukuna menteng kajiapetana.

And then the blood flows out abundantly through the passage for molten refuse and through the air-passage of the bellows.

Alas thou hast deceived us : isn't this book they say to him.

No you women ! they are eating pan and kasail it is that they are spitting out. Go on now ! yo women, work the bellows fast with energy, quickly !

Then, when he knew that they were burnt, not break the furnace with your husking poles, he said to them.

Then they broke it with husking poles. They found only bones, rattling dry they dound them (the bones).

Alas ! thou has deceived us. We did not think that thou wouldst act like that ! Thou has made us burn our men to death.

Well now ? I sent the watchful kerketa and the energetic kingcrow as messengers (to you); You did not obey their orders, saying he told them. And then : will you then now obey my commands and orders, saying he says to them.

Yes, we will obey, they say. Unless we obey *how in the world* can we find a living! they say to him.

All right then ! I shall show you a means (way) whereby you will be supported, saying he answers.

I am going to establish the Patguru and his disciple Tura, both of them (the sooth sayers). These two will consult you (*approach you for adivice, approach you for direction)* by means of half-broken rice-grains, by means of half-husked kudi grains, by means of lamplight, by means of straw-torch light. I order you not to abscond (not to hide anything) from the Patguru and Turachela (*i.e., always reveal to them the causes of disease and the sacrifices required).*

Hatu talare Mundahon pahanṛe taina, sing suba, daru suba. Manatingpeae metad'koa.

Enate iní sirmatee rakabentana.

Entedo en Hasurkuṛiko iniá lijáreko sabentana. Ente chutaub're sub'ked'kochi huṛang'giriked'koae.

Bururе uiújaní burubongajanae, ikirre uiújaní ikirbongajanae, piri úiujaní oṛó lor tundukóre nagebongajanae ; ente maṛang bururе uiújana, maṛang burubongajanae, desaulire uiú- janí desaulibongajana, chondo- rikirre uiújaní chondorikirbongajanae, chandire uiújaní chandib ongajanae.

In the middle of the village a Munda shall dwell as sacrificer, under a tree, under a tree. He will worship you he said to them.

After that he rises to heaven.

And then those Asur women cling to his clothes. Then he, catching them by the top-knot of hair threw them down.

The one (who) fell on a hill became a buru- bonga, the one (who) fell into deep water become an ikirbonga, the one who fell on high fields or near the end of ravines became a nagebonga ; then the one who fell on a high mountain became a marang burubonga, he who fell on a wooded spot became a desaulibonga, he who fell on a wooded spot near a spring (low ground) became a chondorbonga, he who fell into a grove on the open field or a height became a chandibonga.

II

RICE-CULTIVATION AND AN ORDINARY DAY'S WORK IN A MUNDA VILLAGE

(Written by Johann Rongo, a Mundari school-boy)

Sidako síchataea, enateko ruṛaea. Apisáko síked'chiko taerikaea. Enate dá gamakeate kachaluakad aṛikoko chaluea. Tara sidare chaluakad aṛiko herejeṭea jeṭesingirege. Asar ad' Sawan chanḍú tebakochi sóbenko achraea oṛó taramarako roaea. Sobenko herchabakead' enate omonoá, omonjanate maparangoá. Enate soben loeongko durumleka leloá. Enate huṛingleka pandu pandu lelóimtangko karaea; karaekeateko hokaea. Enate baḅako dembooá, ente geleoá, enate toako pereoá, enate enage sakid'kóchi jaromoá.

First they open (the ground) by ploughing, then they replough. Having ploughed it three times, they let it lie. Then after it has rained (once) they hoe those fields which they had not hoed before. Some fields which they had hoed before they summer-sow in the hot season itself. When the month of Asar and Sarvan has arrived, all sow in the water (standing in the fields) and some people plant (*i.e.,* transplant the seedlings). When all have finished sowing then it springs up, having sprung up it grows big. After that all the rice-fields look one mass of green. After that, when it begins to look a little greyish they press it down (by dragging a long piece of wood over it); having pressed it down they stop (*i.e.,* there is nothing more to be done).

Then the paddy grows into incipient ears, then it forms ears, then (the grains) become filled with milk, then when that has solidified, it ripens.

Jaromjanatedoko sirea; datromteko irked'chi kolomteko godupilea oṛó tara marakodo sagariteko har-rakabea. Enate kolomreko paṛoea. Paṛoekeate oṛoko arguea ad'ko dauṇria (enea). Laud'janchiko kotaea, enateko aturea. Peté baḅakoko giṛia, jang babakodoko auea. Enateko potomea. Potomko sagariteko haridia; oṛáko tebaked'chi potomko aderea adingre, Tara potomko hitaea, tarako jomea.

After it has ripened they reap it; having cut it with the sickle they carry it on their shoulders (the men) and on thier heads (the women) to the threshing floor, and some do drive it up on sagars (bullockcarts). Then on the threshing floor they place the sheaves with the ears upwards (to dry entirely). After having thus dried them, they thresh it (by driving cattle over it round and round). When it has become soft, they shake (out the grain from the straw) then they winnow it. The empty husks they throw away, those with seeds in them they take (keep). Then they pack it into bales. The bales they carry (drive) away on sagars; having reached home they put the bales into the store-room. Some bales they reserve for seed, the others they eat.

Sidate miad' potomko bongoéea. Ena sidako hoṇdéea, enate jetereko tasia, enate roṛojanchi sehelre tukuteko rurungea, enate chauli urungoá. Soben auri chaulichabaóimtang setéakanako metá; mipiád mipiad' eskar babako taiúimatang talaakanako metá. Mirad'o baba banó ad'burud'leka chauli pharchi lelóimtang sóakanako metá. Enchauligeko mandia.

A first they make a hole into one bale. That (grain which they take out daily through this hole) they parboil, then they spread it out on a mat in the sun. Then when it has become dry, they husk it with husking poles in the husking pit, and then clean rice comes out. At the time when all is not yet become perfectly clean rice, they call it *seté* (they say : it is become seté , *i.e.,* husks begin to fall off). When only here and there a grain of unhusked rice remains, they call it *tala i.e.,* half clean. When not even one grain of unhusked rice is left and the rice looks shining white, they call it *só, i.e.,* clean rice. That rice they cook for food.

Mandi imtang sida dáko ladia, enate basangoá. Basangjanchi chauliko harub'ea, enate mandi isinoá.

When cooking they (the women) first put water (in a pot) on the fire, then that boils. When it has become boiling they pour in the rice and then it gets cooked into food.

Isinjanchi chipiko gasarea;

When it is cooked they clean (scrub) the

gasarked'chi mandiko hatingea; hatingkedchi koṛakoko kajiakoa : abungenpe ! Enateko abungena enate mandiko joma. Enate kuṛiko joma ad' soben kuṛihonko. Sobenko jomked'chi, hon hopon apan apan giti jomtekoa.

Setá angkóte soben apan apan kamitekoa : kuṛikodo setá gurí ko giṛia ad' koṛakodo uríko pasartekoa, ad' honkodo sengeltáre dubakanko (dubakanteko) jiruba ad' jeṭeketé ked'chi honko merom urí gupitekoa, oṛó koṛako siú kamia. Tikinjanteko raṛakoa ad' aṛanṛakoko gókead' karkadenteko senóa. Karkad'kóate oṛá tekoa ad' tikin mandiko joma.

brass vessels having cleansed them they deal out the cooked rice ; having dealt it out they say to the men : wash yourselves ! Then they take a wash and then they eat their food. And then the women and the girls eat their food. When all have eaten then every one (literally : child and grand child) betake themselves to their night's rest.

In the morning when the day has broken, all betake themselves to their work: the women they clean the stables (they throw out the cowdung), and the men they turn out the cattle to graze and the children, they being seated near the fire warm themselves, and when the sunshine has become strong the children go to graze the goats and cattle and the men go to the ploughing work. When it has become noon they unyoke them (the oxen) and, carrying the yokes on their own shoulders, they go to brush their teeth (at the nearest steam or pool); having brushed their teeth they go home and take their midday meal.

III
HARAM BURIAKINGA KAHANI

Baria haṛamburiaking horeking herlá. Enaddo janau saráko hoṛe jomko sentan tai kena. Enamente janao haṛamdo hoṛe horoe sentan taikena.

Enaddo musing hulang hasue baintan taikena oṛó buṛiae kajiáia : Ama, buriatalang aing hasuing baina oṛó amtalang ráema oṛó neka kajime : Okoe gore ! ne haṛamko iditukairedo goṭa gora hoṛeing omakoa.

Enaddo hasue bainjana oṛó buṛia rátane taikena : Okoe goṛe ! ne haṛam iditukairedo goṭa goṛa

Two married people (an old man, an old woman) had sown kurti (*a coarse pulse).* And then the baboons were always going to eat the kurti. Therefore the old man was always going to watch the kurti.

Then one day he was going to feign sickness (making himself sick), and he said to the old woman: Thou he ! my dear old wife (thou he ! old woman thou and I !) I will pretend to be sick and thou, my dear, cry and say like this : Alas ! if any one would carry this old man away, I would give them a whole field of kurti.

Then he pretended to be sick and the old woman was crying : Alas ! if any one would carry this old man away, I would give them horeing omakoae menjada.

Entedo banda sará rátane aiumlía. Enaddo sarákoe kajiakotana : oko buria ratanae metakotana ? Enad'doko kajiaitana : Okorea ! banda amge erá-gem aiumjad'koa metaitanako! Auritoa ! oró misabu aiumliae menjada. Enaddo oróe rájada : Okoe gore ! ne haramko iditu kairedo gota gora horeing omakoa ! Eatedoko aiumkía.

Enad'doko niraulá, enatedoko kulijáia : Chikanam menláko metaitana ? Enaddoe kajiad'koa : Kaea babu ! ne haram derang okoe iditukaia gota gora horeing omakoa.

Enatedoko kajiáia : Alo buriam ráea ! Mar iditukaialeko metaitana. Enad'doko sab'kía ad'ko idikía.

Enad'do oráko tebaked'chiko kajiaitaina : Chi buria ! netárele dotaiko metaitana ? Euad'doe kajiad'koa : Kaca ! hen gonrasáte idiipe metad'koa. Enatedoko idikía. Enaddo buria duare handed'tada oro korae metaitana lelkoma, talanga ! gota gora horeko jomchabajada koe metaitana.

Enad'do hakege sab'tab'kedae oroe mágoéked'koa.

a whole field of kurti.

Then a tailless baboon (one who had lost his tail) first heard her crying. Then he says to the baboons. Listen ! What old woman is crying, he says to them ? Then they say to him : Where at all ! thou tailless one, thou art hearing them very much indeed ! they say to him. Just wait awhile ! We shall first listen to her once more he says. And then she cries once more : Alas ! if any one were to carry this old man away, I would give to them a whole filed of kurti ! and then they heard her.

And then they came running up to her and then they ask her : What didst thou say, they say to her ? And then she said to them: What I mean to say is this, sir ! (No, indeed! sir) if any one will carry this old man away, I will give them a whole field of kurti.

And then they said to her : Don't cry, old woman ! (Don't old woman thou cry!) all right we shall carry him away, they say to her. Then they took hold of him and they carried him away.

And then having reached the house they say to her : What (do you say) old woman ! shall we put him down and leave him here, they say to her ? Then she said to them : No dear ! take him to that stable yonder, she said to them. And then they took him (thither) and then the old woman fastened the door down and said to (her) husband : Look to them, my dear ! they are eating up a whold field of kurti ! she says to him.

Then he (the husband) quickly laid hold of his axe and killed them by cutting them to pieces.

PART II

INTRODUCTION

To enable especially missionaries in the shortest possible time to understand the Mundas and converse with them is the chief aim of the following pages. This aim has dictated the plan or method adopted.

The book is divided into *Exercises*, the scope of each exercise being indicated in an introductory heading. In each Exercise only so much of grammatical explanations is given as is absolutely necessary to thoroughly understand the sentences with which the Exercise concludes. These explanations are mainly and often verbatim taken from my Mundari Grammar, but they purposely avoid all purely theoretical considerations.

I must, I suppose, submit to the apparently well-founded criticism that so far as method and order are concerned, these are chiefly conspicuous by their absence. Whilst admitting that other and better methods may be found, I take the liberty of reminding the critic acquainted only with Aryan languages, such as English, Hindi and the like, that any of the methods adopted in Grammars or Exercise-books of such languages, would prove an obstacle rather than a help to the study of Mundari, All plans of Aryan Grammars are mainly based on the division of the whole subject matter into Etymology and Syntax, and the Etymological part follows the division of words into Parts-of-Speech. But in Mundari Etymology is so mixed up with Syntax that they cannot be rigorously separated from each other. He who has understood the whole of Mundari Etymology, has got the Syntax into the bargain: he knows the whole language. Since Mundari ignores the separation or distinction of words into Parts-of-Speech, it will not submit to be explained by separate Chapters on Nouns, Pronouns, Verbs, Adjectives, etc. Hence the adoption of such a method would not only give no assistance towards explaining the *real* difficulties in a *rational manner*, but it would create *new* and *purely imaginary* difficulties even where no real ones exist.

The student then, whose first glance over the book is a search of Declensions and Conjugations in order to get these by-heart as a sort of key to the intricacies of Mundari, looks for things that do not exist. Regarding Declensions, separate *Nominative Case-ending* he will find nowhere. He must accept five distinct equivalents for his English *Genitive Case*, and these he is not at liberty to use indiscriminately; cfr. the following : The house *of* Pasana : Pasana-*a*' ora'. The cattle *of* Pasana : Pasana-t*aren* uriko. The wife *of* Pasana : Pasana-*ren* kuri. The birds *of* the forest: Bir-*ren* chenṛeko. The trees *of* the forest: Bir-*rea*' daru. A ring *of* gold: Samrom-*ra*' mudam. For the formation of a number of *Instrumental*, *Causative* and *Locative Cases* he has first to get by heart and understand will the meaning and nuances of a long list of simple and compound Locative vocables which are always affixed and are therefore called Postpositions. Finally he must resign himself to look for most *Accusatires* and *Datives* and even for some *Ablatives*, not at the end of Nouns or Pronouns, but somewhere in the center of the Transitive or Intransitive Predicates. If he insist on calling this sort of thing a *Declension*, he shall have the satisfaction of declining not only Nouns and Pronouns but Adverbs, Postpositions and Verbs too and even whole Propositions or Clauses.

Regarding Conjugations the student will probably be surprised that in the whole first part of the Exercises he nowhere finds the conjugation of the Mundari equivalent for the English to *be*, because this may seem to him an essential factor in the formation of even the simplest sentences. That is so indeed for English. In Mundari the Verb *to be* has not one, but six equivalents, i.e., six distinct forms and constructions which have no phonetic resemblance to one another. And the foreigner who confounds one of these with the others, will not only speak very un –idiomatic Mundari but he will say things which he never intended to say at all, and understand what was never said. By way of illustration compare the following sentences : He *is* a Munda : Horo *tani*. He *is* a village-chief: Munda-*akance*. He *is* good (buginge) : Buginge-*ae*. He is here (nere): *Ner-ia*. He *is not* here: *Bangia*. There is a God : Pormesor *menaia*.

By way of compensation for this complication the student will be spared the usual, tedious list of *Irregular Verbs*. For in Mundari all Verbs are regular and all words are Verbs or at any rate something equivalent of English Verbs so far as meaning and function is concerned. And all this endless array of so-called Verbs is subdivided into two very regular conjugations. Only these conjugations are nothing like what he is accustomed to and probably expects to find: They are two *moulds* into which the principal or predicative root is thrown together with a number of Affixes and Infixes denotative of a variety of functions such as *Voice, Mood, Tense, Intention, Purpose, Defiance* and *Case*. To these must be added Personal Pronouns, which, though always the same in form (barring two of the slightest phonetic changes) occupy varying positions in this Verb-like agglomeration, and they have the power of changing the meaning of the whole by simply interchanging their respective places. V.gr. Dal-led-*le-a-ko* means: They first struck us. Dal-led ko-a-le: we first struck them.

Besides the ordinary number of Moods, these would-be-Conjugations have four Voices instead of two, the *Reflexive* and the *Reciprocal* being added to the Active and the Passive Voices, and of Tenses there are only just over twenty.

When he has mastered all this, the student finds himself confronted with yet another difficulty, *viz.*, that of a correct handling of this formidable array of compounds, for the purpose of forming subordinate propositions, such as Relative, Conditional and various circumstantial Clauses. This handling is so different from anything he is accustomed to that at first it will appear to him illogical or paradoxical. And yet it is all of a perfect regularity and will appear so to him as soon as he has grasped the main principles on which this very original and very primitive agglutinative language rests.

Then again he must accustom himself to do without certain things which he may so far have considered as essontial factors of all languages as such, *viz.*, *Definite* and *Indefinite Articles, Ordinal Numerals, Relative* and *Reflexive Pronouns, Grammatical Genders* and to some extent even *Grammatical Numbers*. For the Mundas, instead of classifying all things as either *Masculine, Feminine* or *Neuter*, divide them into two very different categories: *Animate* and *Inanimate beings*. By Animate beings they understand all that is endowed with animal or with intellectual life. Hence plants are treated as inanimate. On the other hand celestial bodies as well as causes of natural phenomena such as rain, hail, etc., are considered as *animate*, or personal. Now all words denoting inanimate beings have no Grammatical Numbers. The same form is therefore used for one or several such things: *daru* means, *trees*, as well as a *tree*. But words denoting animate beings have invariably three Numbers: *the Singular*, the *Dual*, and the *Plural*. Personal Pronouns of the First Person may in a sense be said to have five Numbers: *The Singular*, the *Inclusive Dual, the Exclusive Dual, the Inclusive Plural* and *the Exclusive Plural*.

These remarks on some of the more striking characteristics and peculiarities of the language will suffice to show that the methods suitable to the explanation of Aryan languages cannot with any good results be applied to Mundari.

The plan adopted here as based on and guided by the fact that, in Kolarian languages, a thorough knowledge of the correct and idiomatic use of Transitive and Intransitive Predicates is practically equivalent to the knowledge of the whole language. Hence the gradual explanation of the Mundari Equivalents of Aryan Conjugations runs as a leading line through the whole book. Other matters are inserted gradually as subservient to this plan and as required by the widening scope of sentences in the successive exercises. The Exercises begin by explaining the use of Imperatives, not because this presents any particular difficulty but for the purpose of affording an opportunity for framing simple and useful sentences from the outset.

Like all other languages Mundari has its dialectical variations, all of which can of course not be adopted together if Mundari is ever to become a written language. The dialect spoken in the tract called Mankipattis is adopted in these Exercises because this has not been affected so much by alien influences as those of other tracts where Mundas live side by side with Hindus or hinduized

Aborigenes. In such tracts they have adopted not only a much greater number of foreign words but also certain alien constructions which no Munda not acquainted with *Sadani* or *Hindi* would ever think of using.

That the whole subject-matter is not published in a single issue is mainly due to want of leisure. A missionary has of course a great many things to do which are more important than publishing books, and these duties are but too often of a nature the very reverse of favoring serious study and careful writing. The severally issued fascicules do not constitute so many theoretically distinct and closed grammatical parts; they simply represent such parts of the whole subject matter as leisure and circumstances allowed to get ready for the press.

The longer dialogues and descriptions are no mere arbitrary compositions but are as much as possible taken from real incidents for the purpose of offering a realistic picture of Mundari life and strife at existing at the present time.

MUNDARI VOWELS AND CONSONANTS

The vowels *a*, *e*, *i*, *o*, *u* are pronounced as in Latin or German. Any two vowels may stand side by side: *ae*, *ai*, *ao*, *au*, *ea*, *ei*, *eo*, *eu*, etc. When thus occurring together each vowel retains its original sound. Fusions of two vowels into a new sound, such as occur, *v. gr.*, in the English word *broad*, do not exist, nor are two vowels together used to form a long one. Each vowel is either long, short, or neutral, *i.e.*, so short that is difficult to distinguish between an ᾰ and ĕ.

All the vowels may be nasalized. In that case I use the mark *n* after the vowels, *v. gr.*, *a n̲ ṛ i*, a fig-tree ; *che n̲ ṛ e*, a bird. They occur only before. *ḍ* and *ṛ*.

The semi-vowels *y* and *w* are rare. *y* is used only instead of *e* when this occurs between two vowels, *v. gr.*, *loyong* for *loeong*, a rice-field. *w* takes the place of o between two vowels, *v. gr.*, *heua* for *heoa* , accustom.

The consonants *f*, *x* and *z* do not exist.

g is always pronounced like the *g* in *good*, never like the *g* in *George*.

j is a purer sound than the English *j*. It may be said to stand between the German and the English *j*; but it has nothing of the French *j*. The same remark applies to *ch*.

d and *t* are pure dentals as in German, hence different from the English sounds.

r is always pronounced distinctly as in German, never like the affected French guttural.

s is a sharp palatal rather than a dental consonant.

n (1) in the beginning of a word is pronounced like the English *n* in never.

(2) In connection with a dental it becomes a pure dental.

(3) When it precedes the consonants *g* or *k* it is pronounced like the *n* in the English *ring* and the German *Enkel*.

In this conjunction of *n* and *g* is pronounced like in the English *ring* when it is the last letter of the word; but when it is followed by another letter, the *g* ispronounced somewhat harder like in the English *linger*, *v. gr.*, *dungui*, short. With regard, however, to this combination of *ng* and *nk*, attention must be paid to the following rules :-

(1) When the vowel following *g* is the first part of a distinct Suffix, *v. gr.*, the Perfect Tense Suffix *akan*, then the *g* is pronounced like the *g* in the word *English* or the German word *Engel v. gr.*, *dingakana*, -full of water.

(2) When the *n* preceding the consonants *g* or *k* belongs to the Demonstrative Prefix *en* that, then the *n* must be pronounced as a distinct dental, *v. gr.*, *enkate* = *en-kate*, that way or thus; *inku* = *in-ku*; *literally*, that they, *i.e.*, those.

In this we see the instinctive tendency of an Agglutinative language trying to preserve the primary root against even the slightest encroachments on the part of secondary roots.

I do not think it necessary to adopt a diacritic mark for the purpose of distinguishing between the cases where the *n* and *g* or *k* sounds are preserved quite pure, and those where they are, so to say, melting into each other, because a slight knowledge of the language will naturally lead a foreigner to observe the above rules.

Besides the *n* described above, there exists in Mundari the so-called *n mouille*. This I write *ñ*. It is used when the Pronoun *aing* or *ing* of the first Person Singular is followed by the Suffix *a*, *v. gr.*, the Possessive *aiña'*, to me or of me, my ; *kaiña'*, I won't.

To the above consonants must be added the cerebral *d*, *t* and *r*, which is readily interchanged with *d*.We might add *n*, which is used to transform ordinary vowels into nasals before *ḍ* and *ṛ*.

h occurs both in the beginning as well as in the body of words, *v. gr.*, *hoṛo*, man ; *mahara*, cowherd.

Moreover, all consonants may take the aspirate; hence *dh* and *ḍh*, *ṭh* and *th*, etc.

It is a curious fact that the Mundas of the Mankipati districts, who are generally not acquainted with Hindi or Sadhani, frequently drop the aspirate in adopted Hindi words.

• It is difficult for most Europeans to get into a correct pronunciation of the aspirate consonants, and especially of the cerebrals *ḍ, ṭ, ṛ*, and *n*. But it is, I believe, quite impossible for any foreigner to acquire a perfectly correct pronunciation of the peculiarly checked vowels which occur so frequently in Kholarian languages. All the vowels may be thus checked. This peculiar sounding of the vowels may be described as follows: The pronunciation of a vowel, commenced in the ordinary why, is suddenly checked by a rapid partial contraction of the muscles used in its formation, and then, by a relaxation of those muscles the breath or sound is allowed to flow out without receiving any further modulation. This process gives to the vowel the sound of two vowels, of which the first is very distinct, smart, and short; whereas the second sounds somewhat like a slight short echo of the first. I represent these sounds by a wedge-shaped apostrophe; *a' e' i' o' u'. a,* a bow sounds somewhat like a-a, de', to climb *de'-e*. The consonants b and d preceded by vowels are frequently treated in the same manner For *d* this is the case not only at the end of words, but also each time that this letter is followed by a *k* or a *t* in the middle of a word *v*. gr, *ub*', hair; *med*', eye; *had*', to cut. *Ked* is the Simple Past Tense Suffix. The *d* of this becomes *d*' in *v*. gr. leike*d*' koaing,—I saw them; lelke*d*' te,-having seen it. The consonant *b* thus checked sounds somewhat as though it were followed by a slight m; ub' = ub-m. The consonant d' sounds as if it were followed by a slight n, me*d*'-med-n. In reality, however, there is neither an m nor an n attached to these consonants. These *m*-and-*n*-like echoes arise naturally from the flow of the breath after the check whilst the lips and tongue are still in that position in which they were when the formation of the consonants *b* and *d* was commenced.

The consonant *t* in *et'kan*, bad, seems to undergo the same check . The checking of *d* in the Tense-suffixes before *k* and *t* seems to be used for the purpose of preserving this final letter of a tense-form which would otherwise naturally become *t* before and in contact with *k* and *t*.

These checks disappear and reappear in certain connections in a manner which seems to be almost arbitrary. Again, some Mundas will use them where other do not use them. As I have so far not been able to fully ascertain the laws which regulate them, it would hardly be of use to put down here such observations as I have been able to make.

In dissyllabic words the accent is generally on the first syllable even when the last syllable is checked, *v. gr., lijá*, a cloth ; *rebed*', squeeze. There are few exceptions to ths rule. They must be learned by practice. I have so far not ascertained the reason of the accentuation of the last syllabe in those words. In general it may be said that accentuation is by far not as pronounced as in German or English. Barring some very short vowels, the accentuated has hardly more stress than the non-accentuated syllable.

The law of harmony of vowels which plays such a prominent part in Ural-Altic languages has comparatively little influence in Mundari. Vowels of Tense-suffixes, for instance, never change for the purpose of harmonizing with the root-vowel, *do-akad, dé-akad, tí-akad, nu-akad.*

However, some vowel-changes are evidently traceable to this law. *V.gr*., the Plural kuri*ku* used as well as kuri*ko*. Again, inr-instead of *e*nr, etc.

I-EXERCISE

This Exercise draws the student's attention to some of the most striking peculiarities of the Mundari language, viz., 1° regarding Nouns, the absence of Articles and of Grammatical Genders; 2° regarding Mundari words in general, the capacity of every word to perform the function of a Verb, *i.e., to stand as*

Transitive or as Intransitive Predicate in a sentence.

For the purpose of offering a few simple sentences, the Exercise explains the formation and use of the Imperative Mood of Intransitive Predicates.

1. There is neither a *definite* nor an *Indefinite Article* in Mundari *Ora'* may mean: *a* house or *the* house ; *horo*: a man or *the* man ; *hoṛoking* : two men or the two men ; *sadomko*; horses or *the* horses.

2. The Mundas do not recognize any grammatical distinction between *Genders*. A very limited number of words only connote sex. Generally speaking, one and the same word denotes both male and female beings.

Sadom may mean: a *stallion*, or a *mare*; *sin*: *a hen*, or a *cock*.

When it is desired to explicitly designate the sex of animals the words *sandi*: *male* and *enga: mother*, are prefixed respectively to the Nouns in question.

Sandi-sim: a *cock*; *enga*-sim : a *hen*.

The only Mundari Nouns connoting sex are the Patronymtics, *i.e.*, words denoting family relations, *v gr*.

apu	: father, Vocative : *aba !*	*enga*	: mother, Vocative : *eanga !*
ko ṛa	: man, husband.	*ku ṛi*	: woman, wife.
herel	: husband.	*era*	: wife.
bau	: senior brother.	*misi*	: sister.

3. Every Mundari word may be used as a Verb, *i.e.*, as a *Transitive* or *Intransitive Predicate*.

In dissyllabic words the accent is generally on the first sylla when the last syllable is checked, *v. gr.*, *lijá*, a cloth; *rebed'*, There are few exceptions to this rule. They must be lea practice. I have so far not ascertained the reason of the accẹ of the last syllable in those words. In general it may be accentuation is by far not as pronounced as in German or Barring some very short vowels, the accentuated has hard stress than the non-accentuated syllable.

The law of harmony of vowels which plays such a prominen Ural-Altaic languages has comparatively little influence in Vowels of Tense-suffixes, for instance, never change for the pt harmonizing with the root-vowel, *do-akad, de'-akad, ti-akad*,

However, some vowel-changes are evidently traceable to *V. gr.*, the Plural *kuriku* used as well as *kuriko*. Again, *ini of eni, etc.*

4. *The Infinitive* Mood has no special Affix or Prefix ; it is the bare root or the bare word-form.

Buru means mountain ; hence it also means : 1° *to heap u hold a fair* (because fairs are usually held on mountains), *3° something a mountain.*

orá means : *house*. Hence it also means : *1° to make a house acquire a house, 3° to call something a house.*

urí means : *bullock*, hence it also means : *1° to acquire cattle. Call some one* a bullock.

soje means : *straight*. Hence it also means : *1° to straigthen*, 2° *something or some one straight, 3° to denote* or *express by me the word soje.*

he ! means *yes* ! Hence it also means : 1° *to answer in the tive, 2° to agree to something, 3° to grant something to some one.*

5. The *Imperative Mood* is formed by affixing the P **me** ; *thou*, **ben** ; *you two* or *Pe* ; *you* to the Infinitive.

v. gr., *Buru-me* ! heap up ! *soje-pe*! Straighten you it !

DEMONSTRATIVE ADJECTIVES

6. Ne this; **en** that ; **han** yonder.

DEMONSTRATIVE ADVERBS

Nere	here;	**enre**	there;	**hanre** in that place
nete	bither;	**ente**	thither;	**hante** to that place

Aragun-me !	Come down !	Nere kami-ben !	Work her
Jagar-pe !	Talk ! (don't keep Silent).	Susun-ben !	Dance yo
		Nete hiju-me !	Come her
Ente sono-ben !	Go thither both of You !	Hante nir-pe !	Run to place !
Nere tain-me !	Remain here !	Enre tingun-ben !	Stand th two !
Hanre dub-pe !	Sit down in yonder Place !	Ente de-me !	Climb up
Enre giti-me !	{ Lie down there ! Go to sleep there!	Nere tangi-me !	Wait her
		Hanre inung-pe !	Play in place !
Happen-me !	Be silent ! keep quiet!	Enre chalu-me !	Hoe ther

II—EXERCISE

This Exercise continues the explanation of the Imperative Mood :It shows the correct use of Transitive *Imperatives when their* Direct *Object is a word denoting* inanimate *beings.*

7. *Mundari Nouns* and *Pronouns* take no Case-Affixes in the *Nominative*. Nor do they take any case-Affixes in these *Dative* and *Accusative Cases* which depend on Transitive Predicates. Hence the bare root or the bare word-form constitutes *the nominative, the Dative* and *the Accusative*. Apu : *father* is therefore equivalent to the three Latin forms : *pater, patri, patrem.*

8. Whenever a Transitive Predicate has for its Direct Object a Noun or Pronoun denoting some *inanimate being,* then the vowel e must, in the *Imperative Mood*, be inserted between the Infinitive form and the Pronominal Affixes **me**, **ben**, **pe**.

Remark.—This inserted e is always very short : *her* : to sow, her-ĕ-me : sow it.

In words ending with i, u, or au a short ĭ generally takes the place of *e*. *Idi* : to take away , *idi-ĭ-me* ! take it away. *Au* to bring, *au-ĭ-me* bring it. *Ru* : to beat a drum, *ru-i-me* ! beat the drum ! This change of *e* into *i* is merely euphonic and the *i*-sound is so slight that it can hardly be distinguished from *e*.

Angelus ghanta	Angelus bell.
au	to bring.
ba	flower.
bai	to make; to prepare.
bati	a lamp ; a light.
binti-hisir	a rosary (prayer-beeds).
bura	to draw (water).
chandoa	a medal.
chitti	a letter.
da	water.
darn	tree.
diri	a stone.
dul	to pour.
gasar	to scrub clean.
ghanta	a beel ; an hour.
kobi	cabbage.
kot*e*	to break with a hammer or stone.
lagau	to arrange ; to put on.
lijá	a cloth ; cloths.
lu	to ladel out, to deal out food.
ma′	to cut.
manḍi	cooked rice ; food.
mej	a table.
nambṛa	to seek ; to look about for smoething.
naua	new.
oṛa'	a house.
pabita	a papaya.
gilas	a glass
giṛi	to throw down ; to throw away.
god	to pluck (only of flowers and fruits).
her	to sow.
idi	to take ; to take a way.
jang	a seed (grain or stones) ; a bone.
janum	a thorn.
jo	a fruit.
jo	to sweep.
jom	to eat.
kagaj	paper.
kiring	to buy.
parau	to read.
parkom	a bed.
patau	to water.
pilet	plate, dish.
piri	high-field.
ranu	medicine.
roa	to plant.
salgau	to light, to kindle.
saṛa	manure.
sari	to ring. / to sound.
satalu	a peach.
taiar	to prepare ; to make ready.
tamras	a goava.

9. ADVERBS OF TIME

na' nado	now.	naike	at once, immediately.	gaṛikad' gaṛikad're	after a while
sida	first.	ente entedo	and then.	taiomte	afterwards.
seta' seta're	in the morning.	tikin tiking dipli	at noon.	aiŭb aiŭbdipli	in the evening.
oro' ad' ondo	and.	tising	to-day.	gapa	to-morrow.

Setáre oṛa jo-ĕ-me ente parkom bai-i-me! Nado mandi taiar-ĕ-me taiomte mej lagaui-me! Gaṛikadŕe manḍi au-i-ben! Ne gilas oṛo' en pilet idi-i ben oro gasar-ĕ-ben! Sida ne diri koṭe-ĕ-pe, ente han tamras-daru paṭau-ĕ-pe! Airbdipli bati salgau-i-me, ente Angelus ghanta sari-i-me ! Da bura-e-pe oṛo ente dul-e-epe! Naike nere kobi-jang here-ĕ-ben oṛo naibdipli ne sataludaru hanre ora-e-ben ! Sida sara dul-ĕ-pa taiomte her-ĕ-pe oṛo patau-ĕ !Tising naua lija kiring–ĕ-me! Ne chitti parau-ĕ-ben ! Ne kagaj giṛi-ĭ-me! Chandoa nambara-ĕ-pe! En binti-hisir idi-ĭ- me! Ne daru me-ĕ-ben ente hante idi-ĭ-pe! Tikin dipli en ranu nu-ĭ-me oṛo gilas gasar–ĕ-me! Ne satalu jome-ĕ-me oṛo jang giṛi-ĭ-me. Nado mandi lu-ĕ-pe oṛo jom-ĕ-pe ente inung-pe, taimote en piri chalu-ĭ-pe ! Aiubdipli binti-me, ente nere gitĭ-me ! Gapa ranu kiting –ĕ-pe.

III—EXERCISE

This Exercise points out two other striking characteristics, viz., 1° the Grammatical Distinction *between* animate *and* inanimate *beings; 2° The formation of* Grammatical numbers *as based on that distinction.*

As a basis for practising the points explained,. -the formation of the Present *Tense of* Intransitive *Predicates is given in the 3 rd Person Singular, Dual and Plural.*

10. The distinction between *animate beings* and *inanimate objects* must he carefully and constantly attended to. The term *animate beings* is not commensurate with the term *living beings*; for it comprises only those beings which are endowed with *animal* or *intellectual life*.

11. Hence plants are treated as *inanimate objects*.

12. On the other hand the Mundas consider celestial bodies, such as the sun, the stars, the moon, as *animate beings*.

13. Natural phenomena too, such as rain, hail, are attributed to an *animate cause*.

From a grammatical point of view this distinction is of the highest importance; for it regulates 1° the Grammatical *Numbers* of Nouns and Pronouns; 2° the *Grammatical Numbers* and *Persons* of Transitive and Intransitive Predicates.

NUMBERS OF NOUNS

14. Nouns denoting *animate beings* have three numbers-*the Singular, the Dual* and *the Plural.*

15. *The Singular* is always the bare root or the bare world-form.

16. *The Dual* is formed by affixing to the Singular the Pronoun *king* which means : *the two or both, v. gr. hoṛo* : man, *hoṛo-king* (literally man-the two) ; two men; *sadom* : horse, *sadom-king* : two horses; *ipil* star, *ipil-king* : two stars.

17. The *Plural* is formed by affixing to the Singular the Pronoun *ko* which means *they.*

hoṛo : man, *hoṛo-ko* (literally *man-they*) : men; *sadom* : horse, *sadom-ko* : horse; *ipil* : star, *ipil-ko* : stars.

18. Nouns denoting *inamimate objects* generally do not take the Dual and Plural Affixes. Hence the bare root or word-form may denote one or more objects. The context must decide what number of objects is there and then denoted by a given word.

daru { a tree / trees   *diri* { a stone / stones   *bati* { a lamp / lamps.

19. *Exception.*—In *enumerations* of inanimate objects, every Noun of the series takes the Affix *ko.* v. gr. Buy salt, tobacco and rice : *Bulung-ko, tamaku-ko* ad' *chauli-ko kiringěme* !

20. The same rule is followed in enumerations of parts of the body. v. gr. Head, chest, stomach, (in a word) my whole body is ailing me : *Bo-ko, kuram-ko, lai'-ko,* goṭa *hoṛmo-ko* hasujaina.

Even when a single part or member is spoken of as ailing, the Affix *ko* is often used. *v. gr Kuram-ko* hasújáiña: My chest is paining.

21. In all other cases the Mundas affix *ko* only occasionally when they desire to lay great stress on the plurality of objects. I say, *occasionally,* because even this cannot be taken as a general rule.

22. The distinction between *animate and inanimate beings* shows itself equally in the form of Transitive and Intransitive predicates. Let us illustrate this by a few examples :—

23. In Mundari, Transitive and Intransitive Predicates are made up of several elements which remain unchanged throughout all the Ńumbers and Person of the same Tense. Two of these elements, viz., *the bare root* and the *Copula* or *Linkword a,* are common to absolutely all Tenses. A distinct. *Tense-Affix* is added to the root in all Tenses except two.

24. In the *Present of Intransitive Predicates* the Affix *tan* stands between the *root* and the *Copula a.*

Gojo' menas *to die*. Hence *gojo'-tan-a*, is the unchangeable ground form of *the Intransitive Present*.

25. When this ground-form stands as Predicate to a Noun denoting animate *beings*. It has three Numbers, the Singular, the. Dual and The Plural.

26. The *Singular* is formed by affixing to the ground-form the weakened Personal Pronoun *e* which mans *he* or *she*. (the original form is *i*). This horse is *dying* : Ne sadom *gojo'tana-e*.

The Dual is formed by adding the Pronoun *king* which means *the two* or *both*.

These two horses are dying: No sadomking *gojo'tana-king*. *The Plural* is formed by affixing the Pronoun ko : they.

These horses are dying : Ne sadomko *gojo'tana-ko*.

27. But when the same ground-form stands as Predicate to Nouns denoting inanimate objects, it takes *no* Affix indicative of any Number; Not even then when such Nouns do themselves take the Affix *ko* (see 19 and 20).

This tree is dying : Ne daru *gojo'tana*

These two trees are dying : Ne baria daur *gojo'tana*.

These trees are dying : Ne daur *gojo'tana*.

The rice, urid, mustard are dying this year : Ne sirma babako ramrako ad' maniko gojo'tana.

apir	to fly.
aṛăgun	to come or climb down.
aril	to hail.
ating	to graze.
baria	two.
binti	to pray.
chanḍu	moon.
dangṛa	a young man.
dangṛi	a marriage-able girl.
dasi	servant.
duṛa	dust.
durang	to sing.
eṇṛeo'	to get extin-guished.
gama	to rain.
gara	a river.
handiṛio'	to tumble down.
harao'	to grow.
hasuro	to set (of the Sun, etc).
hichir	to lighten, to flash.
isu	many, much.
itun'	to learn.
jaromo'	to ripen.
jete	to be hot (of sunshine).
jo	to bear fruit.
kami	to work.
kuṛil	to jump.
kulai	a hare.
lelo	to be visible ; to appear
lingi	to flow.
lo	to burn.
otango	to be carried away by the wind.
pereo'	to get full, to rise (of rivers).
ra'	to weep.
sari	to sound.
sengel	fire.
seta	a dog.
sim	a fowl.
sukul	to smoke.
turo'	to rise (of the Sun).
uri'	bullock, also cat-tle in general.

Ne jo jaromo'–tana. Dura otango'-tana. En honking ra-tana-*king*. Nere kobi khub harao'-tana. Hanre hoṛo-ko duramg-tana-*ko*. Ne hon binti-tana-*e*. Isu diri *uiugo-tana*. Uri-ko ating-tana-*ko*. En baria ora lo-tana. Nado hon-ko itun-tana-*ko*. Baria ghante sari-tana. Tising aiub dangṛi-*ko* susun-tana-*ko* oṛo dangṛa-ko durang-tana-*ko*. Ne oṛa handiṛio-tana. Hanre hon-ko inung-tana-*ko*. En baria bati enreo-tana. Nere da lingi-tana. Kulai-ko kuṛil-tana-ko . Ne sengel isu sukul-tana. Han sim-king apir-tana-*king*. Aril-tana-*e*. Singi turo-tama-e . Chandu' hasuro'-tana-*e*. Ipil-ko lelo'-tana-*ko*. Tising jete-tama-e . Gaṛa pereo'-tana. Nado han hoṛo-king aṛăgun-tana-*king*. En hon-*ko* jagar-tana-*ko*. Seta-king nir-tana *king* .Dasi-ko kami-tana-*ko*.

IV EXERCISE

The Exercises IV, V and VI attack the greatest practical difficulty of the language, viz., the insertion of Pronominal objects into *Transitive Predicates.*

By way of graduating the necessary explanations, the present Exercise limits itself to the insertion, into Transitive Imperatives, *of the Personal Pronouns of the3rd Person Singular, Dual and Plural, viz.* i *: he or she;* king *: the two, both of them and* ko *: they,*

28. The distinction between *animate* beings and *inanimate* objects affects Mundari Transitive Predicates still in another way and renders them so very different from the Verbs of most of the existing languages.

29. We have seen already **(8)** that Transitive Predicates insert a *short* e or, sometimes a *short i* in the Imperative, when they have as *Direct Object*, a Noun or Pronoun denoting inanimate objects. This *e* is probably but a weak form of the *Impersonal Pronoun* a: it. The short *i* used occasionally, is but a euphonic change of the *e*, determined by the preceding vowel.

30. Now whenever a Transitive Predicate has for its *Direct object* a Noun or Pronoun denoting *animate beings* then a *Personal Pronoun* corresponding in *Number* with the *Direct object* must be *inserted* into the Predicate.

31. *Ra'* means *to call*. Whenever this has for *Direct Object* one single animate being, then the *Original Personal Pronoun* 3rd Person, Singular, *viz.*, *i*: he or she is inserted. This I must be pronounced *distinctly*.

Do thou call *him* or *her*! Ra'-i-me You two ! call him or *her* ! Ra'-i-ben ! You ! call him or her ! Ra'-i-pe!.

32. When the *Direct Object* denotes *two* animate beings. Then the 3rd Person of the Dual of the Personal Pronoun, viz. king, both or the two be inserted.

Do thou call both of them! Ra-king-me !

You two ! Call both of them! Ra'-king –ben !

You ! call both of them! Ra'-king-pe !

33. When the Direct object denotes more than two animate beings, the 3rd person Plural ko : they, must be inserted.

Do thou call them ! Ra'-ko-me!

You two ! Call them! Ra'-ko-ben !

You ! call them! Ra'-ko-pe !

Remark.—After the inserted Pronominal Object *ko* the imperative Affix *me* generally drops the vowel *e.* Ra'-ko-*m*! is much more frequently used than ra'-ko-*me*!

34. These Pronominal Objects must be inserted even then, when the Direct Object is already expressed in the sentence by a *distinct Noun or Pronoun.*

Do call the servant !	*Dasi* ra'-*i*-me !
You two ! Call the servant !	*Dasi* ra'-*i*-ben !
You ! call the servant!	*Dasi*-ra'-*i*-pe !
Do thou call the two servants !	*Dasiking* ra'-*king*-me !
You two ! call the two servants !	*Dasiking* ra'-*king*-ben !
You ! call the two servants !	*Dasiking* ra'-*king*-pe !
Do thou call the servants !	*Dasiko* ra'-*ko*-m !
You two ! Call the servants !	*Dasiko* ra-*ko*-ben !
You ! call the servants !	*Dasko* ra'-*ko*-pe !

NUMERALS

35.

Mid', miad' / moiad', mod'	...	1	turuia	...	6
baria	...	2	eea / eia	...	7
apia	...	3	irilia	...	8
upunia	...	4	area	...	9
monrea	...	5	gelea	...	10

36. The last vowel of *apia, monrea, turuia, eea* and *area* is always dropped when they are placed before words denoting measures of any kind, v. gr. *Bar* gaudi, two leagues; *api* tewa, three tewas (a grain measure) ; *gel* muka, ten yards; *upun* ghanta, four hours ; *e* taka, seven rupees.

37. In *enumerations* of *men, families* and *cattle* the words *horo, bo* and *ora* are generally used as appositions and then take no dual and Plural Suffixes. When they are thus used, numerals standing before them follow the rule just given under *36.*

Three sons and two daughters	Api *horo koro* honko ad' bar *horo kuri* honkin Kora honko api *horo* ad kuri honking bar hor

Ten Munda families and eight Uraon families.	Gel *ọrá* Mundako *ọrá* iril *ọra* Uraonko. Mundako gel *ọrá* ọro Uronko iril *ọrá* .
Six buffaloes and four bullocks.	Kerko turui *bo ọrá* uriko upun *bo.* Turui bo' kerako *ọrá* upun bo uri'ko.

akiring to	sell.	kumburu	thief.	rarura to	call back
buri	a bear.	lel	to see.	sab	to cathch.
chimin ?	how many ?	meang	after to-morrow,	sabrura	to catch an bring agai
dudmul	a pigeon.	mente	for.	sekera	quick.
gupi	to graze cattle.	merom	goat.	senbaṛa	to go about
harurung	to drive away, to drive out.	munḍa	village-chief.	sobenta'	all over.
itu	to teach.	nam	to seek.	tol	to tie.
khasi	gelded goat.	ol	to write.	toṭe	to shoot with a gun.
katekisem	catechism.	parob	feast.		
kuli	a porter.	rahunḍi	to call together.		

Remark.—*Rika* is both *causative* and *permissive*. Hence, added to a Predicate it means either: to *cause, order* or *force* some one to do the action in question, or te *allow, to permit, to let*, v .gr. Sen-*rika-ko*-m ! *Make* them go ! *order* them to go Q or: *Let them go*! *Allow* them to go!

Sadom taiar-*i*-me Garikad're en bar horo honking au-*king* – ben ! Ed uriko lel-*ko*-m, harurung-*ko*-m! Gapa simko kiring-*ko-pe* ! Ne baria dud'muliking hante idi-king-me ! Meang iril hoṛo kuliko nam-*ko*-pe. Tising meromko gupi-*ko*-m, gapa en piri chalu-*e* me !Bar horo honking nirtanaking ; nirpe! Sabrura-*king*-pe. Han buṛi lel-*i* me, sekera! toṭe-i-me ! kumburuking sab –*king* -pe *ọrá* nete au-*king*-pe ! Gapa Munḍa mente keṛako upun bo' ad' uriko turui bo' kiring-*ko*-ben ! Ne sadomking akiring-*king*-me ! Dasiko ra'-hundi-*ko*m! Setaking nirtanaking rárụra-*king*-me. En upunia meromko sab-*ko*-pe oṛo nere tol-*ko*-pe. Nere chimin honko itun-tanako ? Gel horo. Nado be monṛea dangrako katekisĕm itu-*ko*-m, taiomte hanre chalu-*rika-ko*-m! Setare honko parau-*rika-ko*–m, aiub'dipli ol-*rika-ko* m !

V—EXERCISE.

This exercise explains the insertion of the same pronouns i, king *and* ko *into the Present Tense of Transitive Predicates in the* 3 rd person *Singular Dual and Plural of that Tense.*

38. The Present of Transitive Predicates is formed by affixing *jad* to the Infinitive. Hence the unchangeable ground-form of the Transitive Present is Root + jad + a.

Let means to *see*. The Present will be lel-jad-a.

39. If the Direct Object of this Predicate denotes one *single animate being* then the Personal Pronoun *i* must be inserted between *jad* and *a* ; v. gr. She sees him :

lel-jad-i-ae.

40. *Remark.*—In the Mankipati Districts the latter *d* is always elided before the inserted Direct Object *i* and the vowel *a* is checked. In other Districts the original form is generally kept.

He or she him or her :	Lel-*jad-i*-a-e,	or : lel-*ja-a-e*.
Both of them see him or her	Lel-*jad-i*-a-king,	or : *lel-ja-i-a-king,*
They see him or her:	Le-*jad-i*-a-ko,	or : lel-*ja-i-a-ko*.

41. When the Direct Object *two animate being*, then the Pronoun *king* : the two or both of them, must be inserted between the Affix i *jad* and the Copula *a*.

N. B.—The letter *d* is always checked before consonants.

He or she sees both of them :	Lel-jad'-*king*-a-e.
The two see both of them :	Lel-*jad'-king*-a-king.
They see both of them :	Lel-*jad'-king*-a-ko.

42. When the Direct Object denotes *more than two animate beings* then the Pronoun *ko* : they, is inserted between *jad* and *a*.

He or she sees them :	Lel-jad'-*ko*-a-e.
The two see them :	Lel-jad'-*ko*-a-king.
They see them :	Lel-jad'-*ko*-a-ko.

43. When, in a sentence, any word precedes the Predicate, then the Pronominal Subjects *i* : he or she, *king* : the two and *ko* : they, are generally suffixed to that word rather than to the Copula *a*.

v. gr. He sees him to-day :	Tising-*e* lelja'ia.
Both of them see him to day :	Tising-*king* lelja'ia.
They see him to-day :	Tising-*ko* lelja'ia.

alu	Potatoe.	gomke	master.	pahanr	sacrificer.
ara	vegetable.	gupini'	cowherd.	prachar	prachar, catechist
asi	to ask.	har	to drive, to drive away.	pusi	cat.
bagran	tro spoil.	hua	to bite.	racha	to pull, to draw v.g. water.
bairura	to repair.	iskulhon	school-boy.	sipai	soldier, policeman.
banria	a merchant.	kadal-daru	plantain tree.	tikinmandi	dinner.
chapi	to wipe, to clean.	mali	gardener.		
chini	sugar.	mandini'	cook.		
goe	to kill.				

Prachar baria dangr'aking-*e* itu-*jad*-king-a. Mandini' tikinmandi mente baria siming-e goe'-jad'-king-a. Dasi gilas-*e* chapi-*jad*-a. Iskulhonko da'-*ko* racha-*jada-a*. *oro* daru-*ko* patau-*jad*-a. Hanre pusi dud'mul-*e* jom-*ja'*-i-a. Upunia sipaiko en baria kumburu-king-*ko* sab-*jad'-king*-a. Mali kobi-*e* roa-*jad*-a. Na'do saiz sadom-*e* taiar-*jai'*-*i*-a. Ne kuli jo-*e* au-jad-a. En dangraking chitti-*king* ol-*jad*-a. Gupini kerako hante-*e* har-*jad'*-ko-a. Urriko en kadal-daru-*ko* bagrau-jad-a. Tising gomke baria sadomking-e kiring-*jad'-king*-a.

Hanre are horo kuliko horo-*ko* bairura-*jad*-a. Gomke dasiko-*e* rahundi-*jad-ko*-a. Ne honking chini-*king* asi-*jad*-a. Ne banria aluko, a rako oró joko-*e* akiring-*jad*-a. En setaking meromko-*king* hua-*jad'-ko*-a. Munda miad' khasi-*e* idi-*ja'-i*-a. Upunia honko meromko gupi-*jad'-ko-a-ko*. Ne dan-graking uriko hanre-*king* tol *jad'*-*ko*-a. Ne horoking baria honking idi-*jad'-king-a-king*. Tising pahanr baria dasiking enre-*e* chaluriaka-*jad'-king*-a.

VI--EXERCISE

This Exercise extends the preceding explanations to all the Persons of each Number, i. e., it shows the insertion as Direct Objects of all Personal Pronouns *into all the Numbers in certain Tenses of transitive Predicates in general. Hence*

1° It gives a complete list of all the Simple Personal Pronouns.

2° It explains the form *and the* position *of these Pronouns when they stand as* Subject *to any Predicate whatever.*

3°. It explains the position *occupied by the Pronouns* within the Predicate, *when they stand as* Direct Objects *(a) in the Present Tense, (b) in the Simple Past Tense, (c) in the Simple Future Tense.*

To this are added a few points necessary for the formation of appropriate sentences illustrating the rules laid down in the Exercise.

PERSONAL PRONOUNS

44. *There are two sets of Personal Pronouns : the Simple or Unemphatic, and the Compound* or *Emphatic.*

45. The Pronouns of the I st and 2 nd person, of course, always denote *animate beings*. In the 3 rd person there is one form to denote *animate beings, viz., i : he* or *she*, and another form for *inanimate objects, viz., a : it.*

46. Pronouns denoting animate beings have three Numbers : *Singular, dual* and *Plural*. The Impersonal or Neuter Pronoun *a'=it* has no distinct form for the Dual or Plural ; hence *a'* may mean : *it*, or ; *the two*, or : *they* i.e. many *inanimate objects*.

47. The Personal Pronoun of the 1st person *ing* : I, has two distinct forms for the Dual, *viz., lang* and *ling*, and two dintinct forms for the Plural, *viz, bu* and *le*. These may be called the *Inclusive* and the *Exclusive* forms respectively.

The *Inclusive Dual lang* denotes the speaker and the person addressed ; hence it must always be translated by : *thou and I.*

The *Exclusive Dual ling* excludes the person spoken to ; it denotes the speaker and some other third person ; hence it must be translated by : *he and I*, or *she and I.*

The *Inclusive* Plural *bu* denotes the speaker and the persons addressed ; hence it means ; *you and I.*

The Exclusive Plural *le* excludes the person spoken to ; it denotes the speaker and two or more third persons ; hence it means ; *they and I.*

N. B.-It is important for the beginner to constantly keep in mind these translations of *lang, ling, bu* and *le.* In translating his thoughts into Muṇḍari he must eliminate the English pronoun *we* altogether as having no equivalent in Muṇḍari. The precise phrases : *thou and I, he and I*, or *she and I, you and I, they and I* must be substituted for the vague pronoun *we.*

48.—

	Singular.	*Dual.*	*Plural.*
First pers.	*ing* : I.	Inclus: *lang* : thou and I. Exclus. *ling* : he and I, she and I.	*bu*: you and I *le* : they and I.
Second pers.	*me* : thou.	*ben* : you two	*pe* : you.
Third pers.	*i'* : he or she.	*king* : both, the two	*ko* : they.
Impers. or Neuter.	*a'* : it (i. o.)	*a'* : both (i. o.)	*a'* : they (i.o.)

49. REMARK 1—The ng in *ing* is a palatal nasal sound, pronounced like *ng* in the English word *king* or in the German word *ging.* When *ing* takes the suffixes *a* (Copula) or *a'* (Possessive Suffix), then *ng* is pronounced like *gn* in the French word *accompagna.* Hence in those two cases the spelling, *ñ* is substituted for *ng* v. gr. omaiñako : they will give it to me ; kaiña ! : I won't.

50. REMARK 2—When the pronoun *me* : thou, is suffixed as subject to any word (except tan and roots in the Imperative Mood), it drops the final *e* : sentana*me*' thou art going, never sentana*me.*

When the word, to which this Pronoun is suffixed, ends with a consonant, then a euphonic *e* is inserted between that consonant and the abridged pronoun *m.* v. gr. Meang-*e-m* sena ? Wilt thour go after-to-morrow ?

51. REMARK 3—Whenever the Pronoun *i' : he* or *she* is suffixed as Subject to any word whatever, it is softened down into a plain short *e* and loses the peculiar jerk denoted by the sign (') v. gr. Tisingĕ sena ; he will go to-day. Gapadoe hijua : but to-morrow he will come.

52. When the Simple Personal Pronouns stand as Subject, they are always suffixes.

53. In short Propositions, where the Predicate is not preceded any another word, these Pronominal subjects *must* be suffixed to the Copula.

54. Whenever some word precedes the Predicate in a proposition, the Mundas almost invariably suffix the Pronominal Subjects to that word. *Ka* means *not*.

sentana - *ing*	I am going, thou art going, etc.	ka - *ing*	sentana	I am not going now, etc.
sentana - *m*		ka - *m*	sentana	
sentana - *e*		ka - *e*	sentana	
sentana		ka	sentana	
sentana - *lang*		ka - *lang*	sentana	
sentana - *ling*		ka - *ling*	sentana	
sentana - *ben*		ka - *ben*	sentana	
sentana - *king*		ka - *king*	sentana	
sentana - *bu*		ka - *bu*	sentana	
sentana - *le*		ka - *le*	sentana	
sentana - *pe*		ka - *pe*	sentana	
sentana - *ko*		ka - *ko*	sentana	

55. When the Pronoun *ing* is thus suffixed to a word ending in *e*, then the *i* of *ing* is dropped, v. gr. I am staying here, nere-*ng* taintana.

56. In **39**, **40**, **41** and **42** we have seen that Personal Pronouns of the *Third Person* Singular, Dual and Plural are *inserted* into Transitive Predicates when they stand as *Direct. Objects*.

Pronouns of the Ist and 2 nd Person Singular, Dual and Plural are *similarly* inserted when they stand as Direct Objects.

57. When the Personal Pronoun ing stancs as inserted Object in the Present tense' then the consonant d is elided in the Mankipati Districts, and the *a* of *jad* is checked. Cfr. No. 40. Furthermore the consonant *g* of *ing* falls away before the Copula *a* and the consonant *n* is pronounced like *gn* in the French word *accompangner*. This sound is here represented by *ñ* (cfr. No. **49**) v. gr., He sees me : *Lel-ja-iñ-ae* instead of *lel-jad-iñ-ae*.

58. This insertion of Pronominal Objects is one of the chief difficulties of the language. It is absolutely necessary to practise it for some time with regard to *each particular Tense*. To give a complete scheme of all the possible insertions, even for a single Tense, is quite out of the question. For the Third Person of the Singular, Dual and Plural may take each eleven insertions ; hence thirty-three different forms for the Indicative of these three Persons only. Each of the eight remaining Persons take ten insertions : hence eighty more forms.

59. The following schemes may serve as models to practise both the correct use of the Prenominal Subjects and the insertion of the Pronominal Objects.

Scheme for practising the correct use of the Subjects together with the 3 rd Person Plural.

Ko inserted as Direct Object in the Present Tense.

Ra'-jad'- ko-a-*ing*,	I call them.	Ka-*ing* ra'-jad'-ko-a
ra'-jad'- ko-a-*m*,	thou callest them.	Ka-*m* ra'-jad'-ko-a
ra'-jad'- ko-a-*e*,	he or she calls them.	ka-*e* ra'-jad'-ko'a
(ra'-jad'- ko-a,	it calls them).	(ka- ra'-jad'-ko-a
ra'-jad'- ko-a-*lang*,	thou and I call them.	Ka-*lang* ra'-jad'-ko-a
ra'-jad'- ko-a-*ling*,	he or she and I call them.	Ka-*ing* ra'-jad'-ko-a
ra'-jad'- ko-a-*ben*,	you two ,, ,,	ka-*beu* ra'-jad'-ko-a
ra'-jad'- ko-a-*king*	both or the two ,, ,,	ka-*king* ra'-jad'-ko-a
ra'-jad'- ko-a-*bu*,	you and I ,, ,,	ka-*bu* ra'-jad'-ko-a
ra'-jad'- ko-a-*le*,	they and I ,, ,,	ka-*le* ra'-jad'-ko-a
ra'-jad'-ko-a-*pe*,	you ,, ,,	ka-*pe* ra'-jad'-ko-a
ra'-jad'-ko-a-*ko*,	they ,, ,,	ka-*ko* ra'-jad'-ko-a

60. In this scheme the Direct object *ko* should be successively replaced by all the other Pronouns. However, in doing so, attention must be had to the fact, that, Whenever the Subject and the Direct object are *one and the same person* the Active forms with inserted objects cannot be used. They must be replaced by the Reflexive Voiceforms.

This coincidence of Subject and direct Object happens always in the 1st and 2nd person Singular, Dual and Plural. Hence : *I strike myself* may not be rendered by : dal-jad-*iñ*-a-ing. Similarly : *thou strikest thyself, he strikes himself*, etc., cannot be rendered by : *dal-jad-me-a-m, dal-jad-i-a-e*, etc. The form : dal-jad-*i*-a-e or dal'-ja-i-a-e signifies that one-third person strikes another third person. The corresponding forms of the Reflexive Voice will be explained in a subsequent chapter. For the present ñ when practising the insertions, the Reflexive forms must simply be passed over.

1st Substitution : Ra'-jad-*iñ*-a-m or ra'-ja'-*iñ*-a-m ; ra'-jad-*iñ*-a-e or ra'-ja'-*iñ*-a-e : ra'-jad-*iñ*-a-lang or r-ja'-*iñ*-a-lang,etc.

2nd Substitution : ra-jad'-*me*-a-ing ; ra-jad'-*me*-a-e ; ra'-jad'-*me*-a-lang, etc.

3rd Substitution : ra'-jad-*i*-aing or ra'-ja'-*i*-a-ing ; ra'-jad-*i*-a-m or ra'-ja'-*i*-a-m; ra'-jad-*i*-a-e or ra'-ja'-*i*-a-e, etc.

61. Scheme for practising the rapid insertion of the Pronominal Objects into the 3rd Person Singular.

He or she calls me, thee, him or her, thee and me, etc.	He or she does not call me, thee, him or her, thee and me, him and me, etc.
ra'– jad' – *iñ* – a – e	ka – e ra' – jad – *iñ* a
ra'– ja' – *iñ* – a – e	ka – e ra' – ja' – *iñ* a
ra'– jad' – *me* – a – e	ka – e ra' – jad'– *me* a
ra' – jad'– *i* – a – e	ka – e ra' – jad'– *i* a
ra' – ja' – *i* – a – e	ka – e ra' – ja' – *i* a
ra'– jad' – *lang* – a – e	ka – e ra' – jad'– *lang* a
ra'– jad' – *ling* – a – e	ka – e ra' – jad'– *ling* a
ra'– jad' – *ben* – a – e	ka – e ra' – jad'– *ben* a
ra'– jad' – *king* – a – e	ka – e ra' – jad'– *king* a
ra'– jad' – *bu* – a – e	ka – e ra' – jad'– *bu* a
ra'– jad' – *le* – a – e	ka – e ra' – jad'– *le* a
ra'– jad' – *pe* – a – e	ka – e ra' – jad'– *pe* a
ra'– jad' – *ko* – a – e	ka – e ra'– jad' – *ko* a

62. Here the Subject *e*, he or she, should be successively replaced by all the other subjects. The Reflexive forms or those in which *the* Subject and the Object are one and the same person, must again be passed over. Hence we get-

Ist Substitution.	*2nd Substitution.*	*3rd Substitution.*
ra'-jad'-me – a-*ing.*	ra'-jad-*iñ* – a-m.	ra'-jad – *iñ* – a–*lang.*
ra'-jad-i – a-*ing.*	ra'-ja'-*iñ* – a-m.	ra'-ja' – *iñ* – a–*lang.*
ra'-ja'-i – a-*ing.*	ra'-jadi – a-m.	ra'-jad – me – a–*lang.*
ra'-jad'-lang – a-*ing.*	ra'-ja'-i – a-m.	ra'-jad – i – a–*lang.*
ra'-jad'-ling – a-*ing.*	ra'-jad'-lang – a-m.	ra'-ja' – i – a–*lang.*
etc.	etc.	etc.

63. SIMPLE PAST TENSE

The Simple past tense of *Transitive* predicates is formed by affixing *ked* to the root. V. gr. ra'-*ked*-a-ing; lel-*ked*-a-ing.

64. Pronominal Objects are inserted between *ked* and the Copula *a;* *v.*gr. ra'-ked-*ko*-a-ing : I called them.

65. When the Pronouns *ing* and i are inserted as objects, then the Consonant *d* is dropped in the Mankipati Districts. Since the vowels *e* and *i* would thus come into immediate contact, the *e* is elided. As a compensation for this, the vowel *i* is then checked v. gr. ra'-k-iñ-a-e instead of ra'-ked-iñ-a-e ; ra'-k-a-e instead if ra'-ked-i-a-e.

66. **Ist Scheme**

Ra' – ked'– ko – a – *ing*	I, thou, he or she, etc., called them.	Hola – *ing* ra' – ked' – ko - a	Yesterday I, thou, he or she, etc., called them.
ra' – ked' – ko – a – *m*		hola – *m* ra' – ked' – ko - a	
ra' – ked' – ko – a – *e*		hola – *e* ra' – ked' – ko - a	
ra' – ked' – ko – a – *lang*		hola – *lang* ra' – ked' – ko - a	
ra' – ked' – ko – a – *ling*		holo – *ling* ra' – ked' – ko - a	
ra' – ked' – ko – a – *ben*		holo – *ben* ra' – ked' – ko - a	
ra' – ked' – ko – a – *king*		holo – *king* ra' – ked' – ko - a	
ra' – ked' – ko – a – *bu*		holo – *bu* ra' – ked' – ko - a	
ra' – ked' – ko – a – *le*		hola – *le* ra' – ked' – ko - a	
ra' – ked' – ko – a – *pe*		hola – *pe* ra' – ked' – ko - a	
ra' – ked' – ko – a – *ko*		hloa – *ko* ra' – ked' – ko - a.	

1st Substitution.	*2nd Substitution.*	*3rd Substitution, etc.*
Ra' –ked – iñ-a-m.	Ra' – ked'-*me*-a-ing.	Ra'–ked –*i*-a-ing.
ra' –k – iñ-a-m.	ra' – ked'-*me*-a-e.	ra' – k –*i*-a-ing.
ra' –ked – iñ-a-e.	ra' – ked'-*me*-a-lang	ra' – ked –*i*-a-m..
ra' –k –iñ – a-e.	ra' – ked'-*me*-a-ling	ra' – k –*i*-a-m.
ra' –ked – iñ-a-lang.	ra' – ked'-*me*-a-ben.	ra' – ked –*i*-a-lang.
ra' –k –iñ- a-lang.	ra' – ked'-*me*-a-king.	ra' – k –*i*-a-lang.
etc.	etc.	etc.

67. **2nd Scheme.**

Ra'- ked' – *iñ* – a – e	He or she called me, thee, him or her, etc.	Hola – e ra' – ked – *iñ* – a	Yesterday he or she called me, thee, him or her, etc.
ra' – k – *iñ* – a – e		hola – e ra' – k – *iñ* – a	
ra' – ked' – *me* – a – e		hola – e ra' – ked' – *me* – a	
ra' – ked' – *i* – a – e		hola – e ra' – ked – *i* – a	
ra' – k – *i* – a – e		hola – e ra' – k – *i* – a	
ra' – ked'– *lang* – a – e		hola – e ra' – ked' – *lang* – a	
ra' – ked' – *ling*– a – e		hola – e ra' – ked' – *ling* – a	
ra' – ked' – *ben* – a – e		hola - o ra' – ked' – *ben* – a	
ra' – ked'– *king* – a – e		hola – o ra' – ked' – *king* – a	
ra' – ked' - *bu* – a – e		hola – e ra' – ked' – *bu* – a	
ra' – ked' – *le* – a – e		hola – e ra' – ked' – *le* – a	
ra' – ked' – *pe* – a – e		hola – e ra' – ked' – *pe* – a	
ra' – ked' – *ko* – a – e		hola – e ra' – ked' – *ko* – a	

1st Substitution.	*2nd Substitution.*	*3rd Substitution, etc.*
Ra'-ked –me – a-*ing*.	Ra'-ked' –*iñ* – a-*m*.	Ra'-ked–iñ – a-*lang*. }
ra'-ked –i – a-*ing*. }	ra' –k – iñ – a-*m*.	ra' –k –Iñ – a-*lang*. }
ra'-k –i – a-*ing*. }	ra' -ked – i – a-*m*.	ra' –ked–m – a-*lang*.
ra'- ked –lang – a-*ing*.	Ra'-k – i – a-*m*	ra' -ked –i – a-*lang*. }
ra' –ked–ling – a-*ing*.	Ra'-ked'-lang – a-*m*.	Ra'-ked–i – a-*lang*. }
etc.	etc.	etc.

68. THE SIMPLE FUTURE

The Future has no distinct Tense Affix. It consists of the *root* plus the Copula *a*. Hence *sen-a-ing* means I will or shall go.

Transitive predicates having as Direct Object a noun or Pronoun denoting one or more *inanimate objects*, insert the bowels *e* or *i* according to the rules given above under **8** for the Imperative ; v. gr. lel-ĕ-a-ing : I will see it, or I shall took to it.

Transitive Predicates having as Direct Object a Noun or Pronoun denoting *animate being*, insert the Personal Pronominal Subjects *between the root and the Copula* a, v. gr. Ra'-*me*-a-ing : I shall call thee; ra'-iñ-a-e ; he or she will call me.

69. 1 St Scheme.

Ra' – ko – a – *ing*	I shall call them, thou wilt call them, etc.	Gapa – *ing* ra' – ko – a	I shall call them to-morrow, thou wilt call them tomorrow, etc.
ra'– ko – a – *m*		gapa – *m* ra' – ko – a	
ra' – ko – a – *e*		gapa – *e* ra' – ko – a	
ra' – ko – a – *lang*		gapa – *lang* ra' – ko – a	
ra' – ko – a – *ling*		gapa – *ling* ra' – ko – a	
ra' – ko – a – *ben*		gapa – *ben* ra' – ko – a	
ra' – ko – a – *king*		gapa – *king* ra' – ko – a	
ra' – ko – a – *bu*		gapa – *bu* ra' – ko – a	
ra' – ko – a – *le*		gapa – *le* ra' – ko – a	
ra' – ko – a – *pe*		gapa – *pe* ra' – ko – a	
ra' – ko – a – *ko*		gapa – *ko* ra' – ko – a	

1st Substitution.	*2nd Substitution.*	*3rd Substitution, etc.*
ra' – *iñ* – a – m	ra' – *me* – a – ing.	ra' – *i* – a – *ing*
ra' – *iñ* – a – e.	ra' – *me* – a – e	ra' – *i* – a – *m*.
ra' – *iñ* – a – lang	ra' – *me* – a – lang.	ra' – *i* – a – *e*.
etc.	etc.	etc.

70. **2 nd Scheme.**

Ra'-*in*	– a – e	He or she will call me, thee, etc.	Gapa – e	ra – in	– a
ra '–*me*	– a – e		gapa – e	ra – me	– a
ra' – *i*	– a – e		gapa – e	ra – i	– a
ra' – *lang*	– a – e		gapa – e	ra – lang	– a
ra' – *ling*	– a – e		gapa – e	ra – ling	– a
ra' – *ben*	– a – e		gapa – e	ra – ben	– a
ra' – *king*	– a – e		gapa – e	ra – king	– a
ra' – *bu*	– a – e		rapa – e	ra – bu	– a
ra' – *le*	– a – e		gapa – e	ra – le	– a
ra' – *pe*	– a – e		gapa – e	ra – pe	– a
ra' – *ko*	– a – e		gapa – e	ra – ko	– a

To-morrow he or she will call me, thee, etc.

1st Substitution.	*2nd Substitution.*	*3rd Substitution, etc.*
Ra' – me – a – *ing.*	ra' – iñ – a – *m.*	ra' – iñ – a – *lang.*
ra' – i – a – *ing.*	ra' – i – a – *m.*	ra' – me – a – *lang.*
ra' – lang – a – *ing.*	ra' – lang – a – *m.*	ra' – i – a – *lang.*
etc.	etc.	etc.

ad'	and.	enka	in that way	maha	last year.
aium	to hear.	erang	to scold.	mastar	school master
barhi mistri	carpenter.	hasu	sickness ; to be sick.	misa	once.
				nea	this thing.
barsa'	twice.	hege !	yes, of course !	okore ?	where ?
bir	forest.	honder	before yesterday.	ol	to write.
birsukurei	wild boar.			oró	still.
bugin	good.	hukum	an order ; to order.	otong	to follow.
chia ?	Interrogative Particle.	iduoró !	I don't know.	padri	the priest.
chikana	what ? what is it?	iskul	school.	Pormesor	God.
		kented'	very much.		
chikanamente	why ? wherefore ?	kul	to send.	purage	very much.
		kula	tiger.	ráau	to call hither.
chimtang ?	when !	kuli	to ask.	rayat	a tenant.
chiulaoka	never.	lampi	a haswk.	renge	hunger ; poor.
dal	to beat.	lelau	to visit, to look up.	sendera	hunt ; to hunt.
daramkaji	religious instruction.			sobensá	everywhere.
		lelurum	to recognise.	talab	pay, wages.
denga	help ; to help.	loró	to lie in wait for.	tebá	to reach, to come up to.
diku	zamindar.				

REMARK 1.—Munḍari adjectives never take amy Affixes indicative of either Gender, Case or Number. *Bugin* hoṛo, a good man ; *bugin* horoko ; good men ; *bugin* ote, good land ; *bugin* horokoa, of good men.

REMARK 2.—*Te* suffixed to Proper or Common Names of places denotes motion towards and means to; v. gr. Ranchi*te'*, to Ranchi ; ora'te, to the house ; hatu*te*, to the village.

REMARK 3.—*Mente* suffixed to a Predicate means : *because*. Kajikiñako: they told me ; kajikiñako-*mente* : because they told me. Lelked'koale : we saw them ; lelked'koale-*mente* ; because we saw them.

Mente suffixed to Nouns or Pronouns means : *for, on behalf of*, etc., v. gr. Sadomking*mente* : for the two horses.

REMARK 4.—*Chi* is often suffixed to the last word of a sentence to show that the sentence is an interrogative one.

When *chi* is not suffixed, the tone of the voice must show that the sentence is interrogative; because the order of words in interrogative is the same as in affirmative or negative sentences.

REMARK 5.—Bara suffixed to Transitive or Intransitive Predicates means *about, here and there* ; v. gr. *sen* : to go, *senbaṛa* : to go about ;

nir: to run, *nirbaṛa* : to run about; gaṛa: to dig, *garabaṛa* : to dig here and there; bu : to bore , *bulbaṛa* to bore holes here and there.

Baṛa forms a Compound Predicate with the words to which it is suffixed. Hence Tense and Mood Suffixes stand after *bara*; v. gr. *senbaratanae*: he is going about. Nirbaṛame: run about.

Honder kula enrege bari'a urikinge goeked'-*king*-a. En kulam lelk *i'*-a ?	The other day a tiger killed two bullocks there. Didst thou see that tiger?
Hege, barsa'ing lelk-*i'*-a misa' ne uri'e loṛobarak-*i*-a, mendo kae sabk -i'-a.	Yes, I saw him twice; once he lay in wait for this bullock, but he did not catch him.
Ne chanḍu sadom kaing kiring-*i'*-a.	I won't buy a horse this month.
Honder lampi baria dud'mulkings sabked'-*king*-a.	Before yesterday a hawk caught two pigeons.
Pormesor singi, chandu oṛo' En ipilkoe baiked' –*ko*-a.	God has made the sun, the moon and the stars.
Chimtangben seno'a? Meangling seno'a.	When will you two leave? He (or she) and I shall leave after to-morrow.
Hola munda ne honko purag'ee erangked' –ko-a egerked ko-a-toscold.	Yesterday the village-chief scolded these children very much.
Ne sadomking okoreben kiring-	Where did you two buy these two

ked'-king-a ?

horses?

Han setaking ne meromking huak-v-a.

Those two dog bit this goat.

Gapa baria kasikingbu kiring *king*-a ?

To-morrow we (you and I) shall buy two gelded goats.

Tising uriko han birtee harked' - *ko*-a

To-day he has driven the cattle to yonder forest.

Ne dasikingem raked'-*king*-a ?

Hege, naike Ranchiteng kul-*king*-a

Didst thou call these two servants? Yes, I am going to send them to Ranchi just now.

Chikanamente soben honko nerem rahundi-ked'*ko*-a ?Gomke enkae hukumk-*iñ*-amente. Men do chikanamente enkae humumked'-m*e*-a ? Tising daramkajie itu-*ko*-amente.

Why hast thou gathered all the children here? Because the Mas ter (missionary) has so ordered me. But why has he ordered thee thus? Because to-day he will (teach) give them religious instruction.

Ne chiti chikanamente kam oljada?

Why doest thou not write this letter.

Tising oṛó kamime; aiub tala-bem name-*e*-a.

Work still to-day; this evening thou wilt get thy pay.

Sipaiko ne rayathko sobensa otonbaraked'-*ko*-a oṛo'keṇṭed'-'ko dalked'-ko-a. Chikanamenteko enkaked'-*ko*-a ? Dikue hukumke'-*ko*-amente.

The constables followed these tenants all about and thrashed them very severely. Why did they treat them thus? Because the zemindar ordered them to.

En honko kul-*ko*-ben ; nere bintiko ituna.

You two send those children, they will learn their prayers here.

Pahanr chikanamente monrea kasikoe kiringjad'-*ko*-a ? Iduoṛo'.

Why does the pahanr buy five gelded goats? I don't know.

Apia simkoing adked'-ko-a, nambaṛa-ko-m.

I lost three hens, look for them.

Honderle aiumked'-*king*-a.

We (they and I) heard both of them the other day.

Chia ? honking iskultem idi-ked'-king-a? Ka, Gomke, gapaing idi- *king*-a.

Did you take the two children to the school? No, sir, I shall take them to-morrow.

Maha nere birsukurikkobu senderaked'-*ko*-a.

Last year we (you and I) were hunting wild boars here.

Ne naua sadom chimtangem de-i'-a ?

When art thou going to mount that new horse?

	new horse?
Setaking okoreben lelked'- *king*-a.	Where did you two see the two dogs?
Ne daru gojo'tana, ma'-e-me.	This tree is dying, cut it down.
Chiulao kaing dalked'-*pe*-a.	I never beat you.
Chimtangko raked'-*me*-a ? Holako ra'k-*iñ*-a.	When did they call thee? They called me yesterday.
Chikanamente baṛhi mistri nere kae kamitana ? Tisinge hasuta-namente.	Why does the carpenter not work here? Because to-day he is sick.
Maha ne renge horolang dengak-i'-a.	Last year thou and I helped this poor man.
Padri Gomkeko pur'ageko itu-ked'-*bu*-a.	The Missionaries have taught us (you and me) very much.
Mastarking neaking kulik –iñ-a.	The two masters asked me this.
Chiulao kaben lelauk-*i*-a.	You two never went to see him.
Chikanape aujada? Baria bugin setakingle aujad'-*king*-a	What are you bringing? We (they and I) bring two good dogs.
Prachar kae lelurumked'-*lang*-a.	The prachar did not recognize thee and me.
Dasiking okorem tangiked'-*king*-a ?	Where didst thou wait for the two servants?
Hanreko tebaked'-*ling*-a.	They reached (overtook) us (him and me) in yonder place.

VII. EXERCISE.

By way of completing the theory of Personal Pronouns this Exercise explains the correct use of the Compound of Emphatic Pronouns. *But it chiefly aims at a practical recapitulation of al the preceding Exercise.*

COMPOUND OR EMPHATIC PERSONAL PRONOUNS.

71. The Emphatic Personal Pronouns are obtained by prefixin a to the simple Pronouns. In this composition the Pronoun *me* drop the final *e*, and the Pronoun *i'* is softend into *e'*.

Singular.		*Dual.*		*Plural.*
1 st Person-*aing* : I.	Inclus. *alang*	: thou and I.		*abu* : you and
	Exclus *aling*	: he and I, or she and I.		*ale* : they and
2 nd Person-*am* : thou.	*aben*	: you two.		*ape* : you.
3 rd Person-*ae* : he or she	*aking*	: both, the two.		*Ako*: they.

N. B.—In some districts the Simple Pronoun *ing* is used also emphatically.

72. These Pronouns are use whenever it is desired or necessary to lay some stress on the Pronouns.

They are treated as Nouns; They are never mere suffixes but always occupy an independent position in the sentence. Hence-

1° When they stand as Direct of Indirect Object to a Transitive or Intransitive Predicate, a corresponding Simple Pronoun *must be inserted* into the Predicate as Repeated Object.

Chia! *aingem* lelkiñam ? What! Was it me you saw?

2° When they stand as Subject a corresponding Simple Pronoun is *generally used* as Repeated Subject. However. However this Repetition is not strictly necessary.

Okoe senae? *Aing-ing sena*, or ; *aing* sena-*ing*, or: *aing* sena. Who will go? I for one, I will go.

73. a' is one of the suffixes used to form the Possessive Case in Mundari. Hence when this is suffixed to the Emphatic Personal Pronouns, *Possessive are* obtained.

aiña' : my.
ana' : thy.
aa : his, her.
Aaa to precede
asnan- a book containg the doctrine to be learned mefore receiving baptism.
harom a load, luggage.
to lodge, pass the night.
an insinuating Interjection.
antae. there, in that place.

{ *alanga* : thy and my. / *alinga* : his and my. }
abena : you two's
akinga : the two's
ghanta an hour.
gota' entire, whole.
haram an old man.
hasutan sick.
he oro ! that's plain.
hiraau to visit.
ju ! away, get away.
Kada plantain.
karedo or else
Khub very early.
idangre

{ *abua* : your and my. / *alea* : their and my. }
apea : your.
akoa : their.
kulibara to examine.
ma day.
martobe all right then.
meang – after to-mor row.
kote row.
kote row.
nagente for.
rara to untie.
pap udub confession.
ruar to return.
saiz servant in charge of horse

Remark-1. *Leka* means like whenever it is suffixed to Nouns or Pronouns; v. gr. *amleka*: like thee ; *honleka* : like a child.

Suffixed to Numerals it denotes approximation and means :*about*,

Thus them it yields approximate Numerals, v.gr. *barialeka*: about two some two; *gelealeka*; about ten, some ten.

2° *Chaba* denotes completion. It may be suffixed to any Prędcate to dentoe that the action signified by that Predicate will be, being or has been completed. It is generally to be rendered in English by some Adverb or Adverbial phrase: v.gr, jom: to ea *Jomchaba* : to eat up entirely, also : to complete one's meal. *Ol* : write olchaba : to complete or finish a certain writing.

DIALOGUE

Am ju! aiña saiz oṛo′ kuli raau-king-me,

Go thou and call both my sys and my carrier.

Chikanamentem raked-ling-a, Gomke?

Sir, why didst thou call hi and me ?

Naike Nauatolitebu sena. Am, Johan, aiña sadom taiar-*i*-me, oro am, Paulus, bharom Baime !

You and I will presently go Noatoli ; Hohan, get my hor ready, and thou, Paulus, Prepa the luggage.

Nauatolirebu deraea chi?

Shall we (you and I) stay over night in Noatoli.

Hege, tising entarebu ḍeraea; gapa Buruhaturen kristankoing hiraau-ko-a oṛo meangkotebu ruara.

Yes, to-day we shall stay (over night) there ; to-morrow I shall visit the Christians of Buruhat and after to-morrow we (you an I) will come back.

Entedo manḍiníoe sena ?

Then will the cook go too ?

He oṛo! Karedo chikanaing joma ? Simko upunialekae idi-ko-a, oṛo' ladko, aluko, koffiko, kadalko api ma nagente.

Yes, of course ! or else who shall I eat ? He shall take wit him some four fowls, nnd brea and potatoes and coffee and plantains for three days.

Entedo kasi kam kiring-*i*-a, Gomke?

Then, Sir, you won't buy khasi ?

Api mare goṭa kasi chilekateng jomchaba –i-a !

How can I eat up a who khasi in three days !

Ela, Gomke, ale huringlekale jomdenga-me-a.

Oh, Sir, I and they will hel you a little in the eating.

Martobe, miad'bu kiring-*i*-a. Nado prachar raau-i-ben !

All right then ! we (you and I) will buy one. Now call the prachar hither.

Prachar, tising Nauatolitebu sena. Am aiar-*le*-me, honko hunḍi-ko-m, oṛo itu-*ko*-m. Gapa asnan-puti aing kulibra-ko-a. Ente khub idangre Buruhatutem senoa oṛo baria hasutan haṛamking hiraau-*king*-me, oṛo pap

Prachar, to-day we (you and I) shall go to Noatoli. Do thou precede us (them and me), gather the children and teach them. Tomorrow I will ask hem all about in the asnan puti. Then thou goest very early in the morning

Mundari	English
udub mente taiar-king-me. Ente honko rahundi-ko-m oṛo binti itu-*ko*-m !	to Buruhatu and look up the two sick ole men and prepare them for confession. Then call the children together and teach them the prayers.
Saiz ! sadomem taiark-i-a?	Syce ! didst thou get the horse ready?
He, Gomke.	Yes Sir.
Bharomdo?	And the luggage !
* *Enao taiarakana.*	That too is ready.
Martobe nado abeno senóben !	All right then, now you two also go on !
Chia ? Kaling tangi-me-a?	What ! we (he and I) shall not wait for thee?
Kage !	No !
Mando, Gomke, sadom okoe raṛa-i-a?	But, Sir, who is going to untie the horse!
Ainging raṛa-i-a oṛo mod ghantareng teba-ben-a	I shall untie him myself and within an hour I will overtake you two.

* **N. B.**—*o* affixed to a word means *too*.

Taiarakana is the impersonal form of the Perfect Tense in the Passive Voice, meaning literally: *It has been prepared.*

VIII. EXERCISE

This Exercise extends the some subject (viz., the insertion of Pronominal Objects into Transitive Predicates) to a peculiar Mundari Tense, the Indeterminate Tense, *which has no counterpart in European language.*

Hence it gives the formation *and explains the specific used of this Tense form.*

For the practical acquisition of the points explained three se of sentences are givenunder A, B and C.

The sentences und C aim more especially at the practical did crimination between the Indeterminate *Tense and the* Simple Future.

THE INDETERMINATE TENSE

74. There exists in Mundari a Tense which has no equivalen separate Tense form in European languages. It may be called the Indeterminate Tense, because it makes abstraction of every particular time for the statements made in this Tense form are equally true in the past, the present and the future.

Its correct use presents great difficulties to the European student because all the statements which, in Mundari, stand in the *Indeterminate Tense*, are, in our languages, expressed by the *Present*.

75. The Indeterminate Tense is used:—

1°—To express necessary, universal truths and phenomena of inan mate as well as animate nature (hence also the needs, peculiarities an natural habits of animals and men) whenever they are spoken of general : God sees all ; Wood burns ; Man speaks.

2°—To express freely adopted habits of individuals or still existir customs of whole tribes and races. Hence in this case the Indetermnate Tense is very accurately rendered into English by the phrases be in the habit ..., to be *accustomed to* ... This man is in the habit of getting drunk ; Mundas bury the dead.

3°—To express trades, professions or the ordinary occupations individuals, casts or tribes. Telis prepare oil ; This man keeps the cattle, i.e., he is a cowherd.

76. All the statements falling under the above numbers 2°and 3° directly imply a repetition.

The statements under No. 1° imply at least the possibility of a constant repetition.

Hence the formation of this Indeterminate Tense must contain an element denoting repetition.

77. But in Mundari ordinary Frequentatives are formed by the reduplication of the Ist syllable of a word ; v, gr. da, dadal ; nel, nenel.

78. We should therefore expect redupliction in the Indeterminate Tense. However instead of explicitly reduplicating, the Mundas simply lengthen the first syllable of the Predicate in the Indeterminate Tense, whereas explicit Reduplication is used only to denote a merely accidental repetition of the same act ; v. gr. :—

dadal : to strike repeatedly ; dal : to be in the habit of striking.

nenel : to look repeatedly ; nel : to be in the habit of looking, or to have the office of looking ; to be an overseer. Since this Tense abstracts from all particular time, it takes no special Affix. We may therefore say :

79. The indeterminate Tense is formed by adding the Copula *a* to the root and lengthening the first vowel of the root.

80. From this it is evident that both in speaking and in listening the beginner must pay the greatest attention to this lengthening of the first vowel, or else he will constantly confound the Future and the Indeterminate and thus actually say what he did not intend to, or understand what was not said.

The rules given above under **No. 8**. for the insertion of *e* and *l* in the Imperative apply also to the Indeterminate Tense ; v. gr. Baraiko pahalko kote-e-a : Lohars forge ploughshares.

N. B.—Intransitive Predicates too insert an euphonic e in the Indeterminate Tense. Words ending in a *checked vowel* reduplicate that vowel and then insert the euphonic e v. gr. *Ku* to cough. *kuueako*.

Asur Asur (a caste).
akiring ruar / akiring rura } to re-sell.
badi a second class rice field.
Barai a blacksmith (Lohar).
bepari to trade.
Bhogata a Bhogata (a caste).
Birhor Birhor (a caste).
bonga a spirit, a deity requiring sacrifices.
buru a mountain
chaṭāka a grain basket made of bamboo mats about 3 or 4 feet high and about 2 feet diameter.
chaṭu an earthen waterpot.
chauli husked rice.
ḍaṭom a squaire hasket about 8 or 10 inches high.
Diku a Hindoo.
eṭa′ other.
go to carry on the shoulder
guiu a leaf covered or straw covered hut in the shape of a roof directly resting on ground.

hasa earth.
hatu a village
Hoṛa a Munda.
huring-leka a little.
iṇṭa a brick.
jan any.
jana anything.
jilu fleshmeat, flesh
jǒjom to be in the habit of eating something
kanchi a small round basket used by women to carry on their heads.
keti to till.
kiring hundi to buy together.
Korara a Korara (a caste).
koṭe { to break with a hammer, to forge iron.
kuila to burn charcoal.
Kumbar a Khumbar (a caste).
loeong a 1st class rice-field.
madṙea' paṭi a bamboo mat.
mahajon a money lender, merchant.
māl rent.
Mahali a Mahali Munḍa (a caste).
mered iron.
pāhal a ploughshar
Perain a Weaver caste).
piri a field on high ground.

purá much, many
rung to husk.
seru-rung to smelt (to) of)
si′ to plough.
sikuar bangirope.
suku to like.
sukuri-jilu pig's flesh.
sunum oil.
taben raw rice bantaen quite bro.
ṭaiad place.
tamakn tobacco.
tain to remain.
tasil to levy ren.
Teli a Teil (jom maker). caste).
teng to weave.
Tuṛuku a Mahomed
Turi a Turi (bal maker caste).
ur to dig.

Hoṛoko bir-ko maea, loeongko, badiko, piriko-ko baiea ; si'ea ko ad-ko senderaea. Eta kamido ka-ko sukua.

Mundas clear (cut) the forest make first and second class rice fields and tanrs ; they plough and they hunt. Other work they do not like.

Mundako mal-ko tãsilea.

Village-chiefs collect the rent.

Pahaṇṛko bõngaen-ko.

Sacrificers offer sacrifices.

Perainko lija-ko tẽngea.

Weavers weave cloth.

Baraiko pahal-ko koteea.

Lohars forge ploghshares.

Kumbarko chatu-ko baiea.

Khumbars make chatus.

Bhotatako taben-ko rurungea.

Bhogotas prepare (beat) flat rice.

Mahajonko lijako, bulungo, tamakuko-to akiringea.

Mahajans sell cloth, salt and tobacco.

Mahaliko ote-ko kamia, oroke bepaira.

Mahali Mundas till the ground (work land) and they trade.

Turukuko janage ko kamia.

Mahomedans will do any work.

Uronko si'ea-ko, hasa-ko ura, benta-ko baiea, bharom-ko go'ea pro' jan eta kami-to ituna.

Uraons plough, dig earth (do earth-work) make bricks, carry loads and learn (are ever ready to learn) any other work.

Dikuko urijila ka-ko jojoma.

Hindoos (never) eat cow's flesh.

Turukuko sukurijila ka-ko jojoma.

Mahomedans (never) eat pig's flesh.

Horoko and Uraonko janageko jojoma.

Mundas and Uraons are in the habit of eating anything.

Teliko sunum-ko lenea, chauliko kiringhundia oro'geko akiringruara (or: akiringruraea.)

Telis prepare oil, they buy up (husked) rice and then they resell it.

Turiko datomko, kanchiko, chatakako oro madrea patikoko baiea.

Turis make square and round baskets, rice-reserviors and bamboo mats.

Koroako kuilaea-ko, sendernea-ko oro burukore huringleka-ko ketia; loeongdo ka-ko baiea.

Karoas burn charcoal, they hunt and cultivate a little bit here and there on the hills; but they make no rice fields.

Birhor-ko ote ka-ko kamia, hatuo ka-ko baiea : birkore guir-ko baibaraea; sikuar-ko baiea oro'-ko akiringa. Jan taiadre pura chandu ka-ko taina.

The Birhors do not cultivate the ground, they also do not villages; they also do not make villages; they make leafhuts here and there in the forests ; they make bangiropes and sell them. They (never)

The Asurs smelt iron. | remain many months in any (the same) place. Asurko mered-ko serurungea.

B.

baturi a bull.
brin a snake.
bu' to bark.
ching { to neigh. (cry of kites.)
chui a calf.
chunin chunin (cry of a mouse).
chutu a mouse.
enga-sim. a hen.
gai a cow.
garjau to growl (of tigers).
gonen gonen to grunt.
gugun-chu to coo (of doves).
gundi a cow used for plonghing.

hara abullock (this is used only in in contradistinction of gundi).
huuker { to low (of cattle). to growl (of leopards).
kaka to caw (of crows).
katea a rat.
kau a crow.
kead kead (cry of parrots).
kenr kenr (cry of mainas).
keo keo to cacke
kiki { to neigh to laugh in a particular manner.

kokore-cho to crow cocks).
konr kinr (cry rats).
kurid a kite.
maina a maina.
meon meon (cry cats).
omba (cry of calve
putam a dove.
ra { to cry, to carki (cry of goa and jackals
sandi-sim a cock.
sipu to hiss.
sonchita a leopard.
sukuri a pig.
tuin a jackal

Kula-e gārjauea.	The Tiger growls.
Sonchita-e luukera.	The leopard growls.
Gaiko, uriko, baturiko oro gundiko huukera.	Cows, bullocks, bulls an ploughing cows low.
Sadomko chingeako.	Horses neigh.
Kurid-e chingea.	The kite screams.
Chuiko-ko o'mbaea	Calves low.
Sadom-e kikia.	The horse neighs.
Pusiko meonmeongeako.	Cata mew.
Setako buiako.	Dogs bark.
Sunkuriko gonengoneneako.	Pigs grunt.
Meromko ad tuiuko-ko raea.	Goats bleat ; and jackals yell.
Sandi-simko kokorechoeako.	Cocks crow.
Enga-simko keokeoeako.	Hens cackle.
Chutuko chuninchunineako.	Mice squeak.
Kateako-ko konrkonrea.	Rats squeak.
Putam-e gugumchuea.	The dove coos.
Kau-e kakaea.	The crow caws.

Bingko-ko sipuia.	Snakes hiss.
Mainako kenrkenreako.	Mainas chatter.
Keadko keadkeadeako.	Parrots chatter.

C

ki	liquor distilled from the mowa fruit.	galang	to plait.	kita pati	a palm loaf mat.
		gojo	to die.		
		hormo	body.	nam	to want.
ma	spirit, soul.	ili	rice beer.	nea	this.
halu	to hoe.	keleng beleng	to molest much.	nu	to drink.
bilekate ?	how ?			pudgi	sandfly.
nkana.	those things, such work, such things.	kented'	very, intensely.	sikinrin	mosquito.
		kita	a palm-tree.	Sukurbar hulang.	Friday.

REMARK 1.—*Dari* : to be able, to know how to do something, is placed after another Transitive or Intransitive Predicate so as to form a compound word with it ; v. gr. *baidariaing* : I can make, I know how to make.

2.—*Ituan* means : knowing, (one) who knows : *ituan horo* : a man who knows about it. If this Adjective be used as an Intransitive Predicate, the tonic accent falls on the *u*, and the long *a* of the Adjective becomes short ; v. gr. *ituanaing* : I know.

3.—*Ja* is always a suffix equivalent to *perhaps*, *may be*. It must be suffixed to the word on which the doubt or the probability falls ; v. gr. hiju'ako-*ja : may be* they come, *perhaps* they come. Tising-*jae* nijua ; *it is probably* to-day that he will come.

4. *o* is always a suffix. Munda-*o* : the village chief *too*. O o-ing ituana. I can wrie *also*.

Pud'giko oro sikinrinko horoko purageko kelengbelengkoa.	The sandflies and the mosquitoes molest people very much.
Horoko chikana-ko kamia ?	What (kinds of) work do the Mundas work ? (*i.e.*, which are the Mundas' ordinary occupations?)
Sieako, chalueako, bir-ko maea, loeongko, badiko, pirikoko baiea ad'-ko senderaea.	They plough, they dig (wi hoes), they clear the forest, they make 1 st and 2 nd class rice-field and high-fields and they hunting.

Tising-em chalu'ea ?
Wilt thou dig to-day ?

Kage ! tising han loeong-ing siea'.
No ! to-day I shall Ploug yonder rice-field.

Lija-m tẽng daria ?
Canst thou weave cloth ?

Tẽngeaing !
I do weave (*i. e.*, I am a weaver

Entedo ne honmente miad lija tengeme.
Well then weave a cloth this child.

He mar ! gapa-ing tengea.
All right ! I will weave it tomorrow.

En dangṛa tising pahale koṭedaṛia ?
Will that young man be able arrage (forge) this ploughshar to-day?

Ka-e ituana ; Hoṛoko pahal ka-ko kote'a ; Han baṛai- e Kote'a.
He does not know how to forget Mundas never forge ploughshar Yonder Lohar will arrange it.

Ne ḍaṭom-em akiringeam chi !
Wilt thou sell this square be ket?

Ka-ing akiringea ! ne kami mente-ng namtana.
I won't sell it. I want it now for this work.

Entedo naua ḍaṭom baime.
But then make a new basket

Mendo ka-ing ituana. Turiko enkana-ko babaia, Horokodo ka.
But I can't. Turis make *su* articles, but not the Mundas.

Chia Hoṛoko paṭio ka-ko galena?
Do the Muṇdas not make mats either ?

Mad'rea paṭi ka-ko bãia mendo kuriko kitapati-ko galangea.
They (never, make bamboo mats but the (Muṇḍari) women plait palm-leaf mats.

Neam-*nued* chi ?
Wilt thou drink this ?

Chikana' ?
What's it ?

Ilige !
Rice beer !

Ka-ing nuea.
I won't !

Chia ! ili ka-m (nunuea) ?
What ! doest thou (never) drink ili.

Nũdo-ing nuea, mendo tising kaing nuea ; huṛingleka-ing hasutana.
I do drink it, so far as that goes, but to-day I won't drink it : I am a little unwell just now.

Arki-m nũea ?
Art thou in the habit of drinking arki ?

Kaing nuea !
I never take it.

Jilu-em joma ?	Wilt thou eat meat ?
Ka-ing joma tisingdo.	I won't eat any to-day
Chikanmente ka ?	Why not ?
Ale Katholik Kristanko Sukurbar hulang jilu ka-le jõma.	We Catholic Christians (never) eat meat on Fridays.
Kula chilekate-e rãea !	How does a tiger shout ?
Garjaueae. Hola miad' kula en burure-e garjaukena ; aĩub oṛo-e garjauea ja.	He growls. Yesterday a tiger growled in that mountain probably he will growl again this evening.
Ne hoṛo kenṭ'ed-e hasutana ; iduoṛo-e gojoa ja.	This man is very sick. Who knows ! he may die.
Hoṛmo gõjoa atmado ka-e gõjoa.	The body dies, but the soul never dies.

IX. EXERCISE

This Exercise treats of the insertion into Predicates, of the ***Indirect Pronominal Objects****.*

By way of giving a larger scope to the formation of appropriate sentences, the manner in which invitations and prohibitions are expressed, is added.

INSERTION OF INDIRECT PRONOMINAL OBJECTS

81. When the *Indirect Object* to A transitive or an Intransitive Predicate is a Personal Pronoun, it must be inserted into the Predicate according to the rules given above for the Direct Pronominal Objects.

82. In the *Indeterminate Tense*, the *Future*, the *Definite Present* and in the *Simple Imperative* the inserted Pronouns are preceded by a meaning *to, for, on behalf, with, against*.

Indet. Tense.	God gives good things *to* us :	Pormesor bugina' om-*abu*-ae.
Future	He will plough *for* them :	Si-*ako*-ae.
Def. Present.	He is pleased *with* them :	Suku-*ako*-tanae.
	He is angry *against* them :	Kisi-*ako*-tanae.
Imper.	Give it to me :	Om-aing-me.

83. In the *Simple Past* the *a*, being placed before the Tense-Sign *ked* causes a strong contraction : the consonant *k* and the vowel *e* are thrown out. Thus instead of om-*a*-ked-*ko*-ae we get om-*ad'*-*ko*-ae : he gave it to them. In the first and third Person Singular the *d* is regularly thrown out and replaced by a jerk (') on the *a*, in some districts, whereas in others it is kept.

N. B.—This elision is the same as the one explained above under **40**.

om-*ad-iñ*-ae om-*a-iñ*-ae	he gave to me.	om-ad-*ben*-ae	he gave to you two.
		om-ad-*king*-ae.	he gave to both of them.
om-*ad-me*-ae	he gave to thee	om-*ad-bu*-ae	he gave to you and me.
om-*ad'i*-ae om-a'-i-ae	he gave to him or her.	om-*ad'-le*-ae	he gave to them and me.
		om-*ad'-pe*-ae	he gave to you.
om-*ad'-lang*-ae	he gave to thee and me.	om-*ad'-ko*-ae	he gave to them
om-*ad'-ling*-ae	he gave to him and me.		

84. REMARK.—In the 2nd Person Singular of the Definite Present the *e* of *me* is often dropped. Thus om-*am*-tanae instead of om-*ame*-tance ;

85. In all the other Tenses Indirect Pronominal Objects are not preceded by *a*. Hence the context must decide whether in those Tenses an inserted Personal Pronoun stand as *Direct* or *Indirect Object.*

Akiring-jad'-*ko*-ae may mean { he sells them (the living beings) *or* He sells to them.

86. These indirect Pronominal objects *must* be inserted even though the Object be already expressed in the sentence by a separate Noun or Pronoun.

87. REMARK 1.—Nouns or Compound Pronouns, standing as Indirect Objects, do not differ in form from the Nominative Case, i. e., they take no suffix indicative of Case. Hence the context must show whether or not a given Noun or Pronoun stands there and then as Indirect Object.

He gives the letter to the master: Chiṭṭi *gomkee* om-*ai*-tana.

The master gave the wages to the servants: Gomke *dasiko* talabe om-*ad'*-ko-a.

INVITATIONS AND PROHIBITIONS

88. Invitations to one or more persons in the *Inclusive forms* are expressed by the *Indeterminate Tense*-form with or without the exhortative particle *dola* ! come! come now ! come on !

Sena-lang ! let us go (thou and I) ! *sena-bu* ! let us go (you and I)!

When *dola* ! is used then the Pronouns *lang* and *bu* are generally affixed to *dola* ! Before *lang* the *a* of *dola* is dropped.

Dol-lang om-ako-a ! Come, let us (thou and I) give it to them ! *Dola-bu* nira ! Come, let us (you and I) run away !

REMARK 3. Prohibitions are expressed by means of the Prohibitive Particle *alo* and the *Future Tense-form*. The Pronouns *m* (for *me*) : thou, *ben* : you two, *pe* you, are affixed to the particle *alo*.

Alo-m sena ! sena don't go! *Alo-ben* sena ! don't go (you two) ! *Alo-pe* sena ! don't go (you) !

achu	to engage for work
aium	to hear
ata	to parch, to fry (used of grains only).
auri aurige	not yet
baiua !	it will do, it is alright.
bakshis	reward.
bujaubes	to understand properly.
bulu	1° thigh. 2° leg, v. gr. mindi bulu: a leg of mutton.
chandu	month.
chankau	to stew in oil or ghee with spices.
chuti	1° leave. 2° dismissal. 3° to give leave. 4° to dismiss.
dali	dal.
enka'	to do so, to say so
enkate	like that.
ente	and then.
gajara	carrot.
hai	fish.
hatu	village.
hulang	day.
holong	flour.
ini'	that one.
isin	1° to boil hard eatables till they acquire the desired softness, v. gr. rice. 2° to cook or bake soft eatables till they acquire the desired consistency, v. gr. sggs, dough, etc. 3° used sometimes of bricks and lime : to burn bricks, to burn lime. 4° to ferment : in the Passive isino' : to attain the desired degree of fermentation.
joar	to great, a greeting.
kora hon	boy.
kosoran	1° to parboil husked rice for rice beer. The rice thus boiled is kept in a chatu for fermentation. 2° a chatu of parboiled rice.
Kuri hon	girl.
la'	1° to exceed, 2° to give over and above.
lad'	1° cakes of anything, bread. 2° to bake anything (v. gr. dough, hashed meat, small fish) by packing it in leaves and placing the packet on burning coals or in hot ashes.
leka	(affix), as , by way of, in the shape of.
matar	pea.
med'bara	to turn the eyes all about, to look about.
mendo	but.
mundi	1° meaning,

	signification. 2° to explain, to make clear.
nakal	a copy of some document.
ni'	this one.
oiong	to boil in plain water without any condiment (used of roots and tubers).
olrura	to write back, to answer.
pit	market, week.
rabang	to be cold.
rapa'	1° to roast eatables directly on coals or ashes. 2° to burn bricks or lime.
rasika	to be happy.
re	(affix) after.
ro	to burn the hair of an animal by means of flame.
running	to husk the paddy.
sanga	sweet potato.
seer	a seer.
si	to plough.
tara	some.
tarako	some of them.
teo	to fry in a little oil or ghee.
tiki	1° to parboil eatables previous to stewing them. 2° to parboil unhusked rice previous to husking. 3° to boil cloths in water and ashes previous to washing.
tising gara	these days.
upades	instruction.
utu	1° stew. 2° to stew.

Ne dali ata-aing-me.	Fry this dal for me.
Ne gajara oro sanga oiong-*aling*-me.	Boil these carrots and sweet potatoes for him and me.
Haiko chilekateng taiar-*ape*-a? lod'ko-aing ching utukoa?	How shall I prepare the fish for you? Shall I bake them into cakes or stew them ?
Tarako lad'-*ale*-m, tarakodo utu-ale-me.	Make some of them in cakes for us (them and me) and stew us the others.
Korahonking lija tiki-*aking* me.	Boil their cloths for these two boys.
Ne matar isinme, ente jilulo' chankau-*alang*-me.	Parboil these peas and then stew them in spices with the meat for us (thee and me).
Ne kurishone rurungea; am tiki-*ai*-me. Ena kae ituana ; isinchabaeaeja.	This girl will husk the paddy; but do thou parboil it for her. She does not know that; she would probably boil it altogether.
Tisingdo kobi chilekatem taiar-*aling*-tana ?	How art thou preparing the cabbages for him and me to-day?
Teo-*ad'-ben*-aing tising, gapado jiluloing utu-*aben*-a.	To-day I fried them in a little oil for you two, but to-morrow I shall stew them for you with the meat.

Upun marebu parobea. Ne monre seer chauli dasiko kosoran-*ako*-m.

After four days we shall have a feast. Parboil these five seers of rice for the servants (to make rice-beer).

Tising gapa purage rabangtana, Gomke ; upun mare ka isinoa. (Simple Future Passive).

It is very cold these, sir ; in four days will not ferment.

Chika-*ako*-alang tobe?

What then shall we (thou and I) do for them ?

Hature miad' ililang kiring *ako*-a, ad parob' hulang holonging lad'-*ako*-a oro jiluing chankau-*ako*-a. Ente khub'ko rasikea.

Let us buy them a pot of rice beer in the village, and on the feast-day I will make some flour into cakes and fry some meat in ghee and spices for them. Then they will be quite happy.

He mar ! enkaealang !

Very well ! we shall do so !

Dasiko talabem om-*ad'-ko*-a ?

Hast thou given the wages to the servants ?

Aurige, Gapaing om-*ako*-a.

Not yet. I will give them tomorrow.

He mar ! Johando mod' taka bakishis-leka la-*ai*-me. Ne chandu' khube kamikena.

Alright ! Give one rupee extra to Johann by way of bakshis. He has worked very hard this month.

Paulus chitti ol-*ain*-a; hasutance. Oro mod pitmente chutie asijad- me-a.

Paulus wrote a letter to me ; he is seek. He asks thee leave for another week.

Olrur-*ai*-am?

Have you answered him ? (written back of him).

Aurige. Gapaing olrur-*ai* a.

Not yet. I will answer him tomorrow.

He mar ! en hature oro bar horoking hasutana. Gapa prachar ranu idi-*aking*-a. Inr ama chitti Pauluse om-ai-a.

Very well! There are two more men sick in that village. The prachar will take medicine to them to-morrow. He will give your letter to Paulus.

Tising Patras huringleka ili oro moiad' kasibulue au-*ad'-me*-a joarmente.

Patras brought some rice beer and a kasi leg for thee by way of a greeting.

Ama' hon gapaesi-*ain* a ?

Will thy son plough for me to-morrow ?

Ka, Gomkee daria. Gapamente Munda sobenkoe achuked'lea. Chalu-*ai*-ale. Mendo meang aina hon oro aingling si-*ame*-a.

He won't be able to, sir. The village-chief has engaged all of us for-to-morrow. We shall hoe for him. But after to-morrow my son and I will plough for thee.

Enao baiua !	That will do also.
Nido chikanae chikatana?	What is this one doing here?
Nakale parau-ale-tana.?	He is reading a copy of a judgment for us.
Chia ! en nakalem bujautana ?	Doest thou understand that copy ?
Paraudoing paraudaria, mendo kaing bujaubesea. Am Gomke mundi-ako-me.	I can just read it, but I do not understand it properly. Sir, do thou explain it to them.
He mar ! nakal udub'-aing-me !	Very well ! show me the copy !
Ne sadom akiring-aing-me !	Sell this horse to me !
Kaing akiringia, Gomke.	I won't sell it, sir.
Enkate alom med'baraea, mendo aingge lel-aing-me oro upades aiumbeseme !	Do not turn thy eyes all about like that, but look at me and listen attentively to the instructions (hear the instruction well).

X. EXERCISE

The Mundari equivalents of certain English Transitive Verbs *are* Intransitive *and vice versa. The Exercise points out these Mundari Predicates with their peculiar constructions. To this is added the formation and use of* Perfect Tense.

89. The following Predicates insert an *Indirect Object* in Mundari.

Boro : to fear some one, to be afraid of some one ; bor-*am*-tanae ; he (or she) fears thee.

Suku : to like some one, to be pleased or satisfied with some one ; suku-*am*-tanae : he (or she) likes thee.

Kisi or **khisi :** to be angry with some one ; kisi-*am*-tanae : he (or she) is angry with thee).

Kurkur : to be angry, to be very angry against some one.

Dari primarily means : *to be able, to manage* to ; dariaing (In-determinate Tense): I am able to do it, I can do it, I can manage it.

I. Dari is generally used in connexion with other Transitive or Intransitive Predicates ; viz :-

1 ° it may be suffixed immediately to the root of those Predicates and thus forms an ordinary compound Predicate with them. *Nirdariae*: he can run ; *nirdaritanae* ; he can run Now ; *kae nirdaria*: he is unable to run, etc.

2° The Pronominal Subject with or without the Negative Particle ka may stand between the root of the Predicate specified by *dari* and the suffix *dari*. *Nir-e-daria*: he can run ; *nir-e-daritana*, he can run now ; *nir kae daria* : he cannot run ; ect.

N. B.—The insertion of the bare Pronominal Subject between the specified root and dari is very rare. But the insertion of the Negative Particle+the Pronominal Subject is rather frequent, though not as common as the construction mentioned under 1°.

II. Whenever dari is suffixed to *Transitive Predicates*, the compounds obtained become *Intransitive* and therefore inset *Indirect* Pronominal Objects.

Lel-ko-tanaing: I see them now ; kaing *lel-dari-ako-aing*: I cannot see them now.

Sab-ko-aing: I will catch them ; sabdari-*ako-aing* : I can catch them.

Tolked'-ko-ae: he (or she) tied them ; *toldari-ad'ko-ae*: he managed to tie them

III. Used alone dari often means : 1° to *get the better of some opponent ; to overcome some one ; to manage some one. 2° to actually hit game, other animals or men one is aiming at with a bow or a gun*. In both meanings it insert Indirect Pronominal Objects. *Ne sadom kaing dari-ai-a*: I won't be able to *manage* this horse. *Dikuko kale dari-ako-a*: we cannot *get over* the Hindoos. *En kulai kaing daria-ia*: I did not *hit* that hare. Putamkoing *dari-adko-a*: I did *hit* the doves.

90. The following Predicates take a *Direct Object*:

Hewa: 1° to get accustomed to someone's ways or to someone's company.

2° to accustom animals to oneself so that they allow themselves to be touched, milked, led, yoked, etc.

Na'do iskulhonkoe hewaakad'-*ko*-a : now he *has go used to* the schoolboys' company, i. e. *he feels at home wih* the schoolboys.

Kerakole hewa-*akad'-ko-a*: the buffaloes *are used to us*, or the buffaloes *allow us to approach, to feed, to yoke them*, etc.

Hendo : to speak against some one ; criticise some one ; to find fault with some one's every word or action. Hedoja-*in* ako: they find fault with all I say or do.

Hisinga is the Hindi equivalent of *chenta*. It is rather frequently used by the Mandas and construed like chenta.

Chenta : to be jealous of some one ; to envy some one. Chen-taja'-*iñ*-ako : they are jealous of me.

Landa : to laugh at some one. Landaked'-ko-ako : they laughed at them.

Nogor primarily denotes the growling of a dog. It also means to grumble at or against some one.

Raji in the sense of: to settle a dispute between two persons or two parties, generally requires the static Future or Past Tense. *Raji-ta-ling*-me Gomke : Sir, do settle this dispute between him and me. Raji-*tad'-ko*-aing: I have settled their dispute, I have caused them to come to an agreement or an understanding. Raji-*ta-ko-aing*: I will settle their dispute, I will make both parties to come to an understanding.

Salha has the same meaning and is construced in the same manner as *raji.*

Tangi: to wait for some one. Mod' ghantalekaing tangik-*i*'-a : I waited about one hour for him.

Saating or *sahating*: to bear up with some one ; to have patience with some one ; to suffer some one. Oro do kaing saating-*ko*-a: I will bear no longer with them.

Uru : to think of some absent person *with regret* or *affection* ; to miss some one. Am senore isuing uru-mea : if thou go away I shall thing (much) often of thee, or I shall miss thee very much.

N. B.—This is however (often) construed with the Suffix *ta*' or *ta're* added to a separated Pronominal or Substantive Object. Am-*ta'le* uru'tana : we miss thee, we think of or long for thee, literally : *we think towards thee.*

Suku : to love some one, is, like *u ṛ u*, frequently construed with *ta*' or *ta're.* Ae'ta'e sukutana : he lover her. En dangrata're kae sukatana : she does not care for that young man.

Asra : to hope in some one, to expect help protection or support from some one, is generally construed with *ta*' or *tare.* Am*tale* asratana : we expect help from thee. Muuḍa-*tare* kale asraea : we don't expect any assistance from the village-chief.

It is sometimes construed with a Double Accusative, thus : tising *karacha*ling asra-jad'-*me*-a : we expect a day's food from thee-to-day.

The Predicates *akiring*: to sell some one, *au* or *agu* : to bring to some one, *idi*: to take to some one, *kul* : to sen to some one, *ol* : to write to some one, may , instead of an *Inserted* Indirect Pronominal Object take a *Separate* Object with the Suffixes *ta', tare* or *ta'te*, Ne ote am-tare-ng akiringa or: ne oteng akiring-*ame*-a: I will sell you this land.

THE PERFECT TENSE

91. The perfect Tense directly denotes that an action is completed, and it implies that the effects or the state brought about by that action are continuing still.

92. It is formed by suffixing *akan* to Intransitive and *akad* to Transitive Predicates.

Direct and Indirect Objects are inserted between the Tense-Suffix *akad* and the Copula. Indirect Objects are not preceded by *a*, so that the context and the circumstances must decide whether an inserted Pronoun stands as *Direct* or as *Indirect* Object.

93. The *d* of *akad* is checked whenever the inserted Pronoun begins with a consonant, *lelakad'-ko-aing* : I have seen them.

94. The elision described in the Indefinite Present (*No. 40*)

take place here too when *ing* and *i* stand as Objects ; hence the forms lel-aka'-iñ-ae : he or she has seen me, and lel-aká-i-ae : he or she has seen him or her.

FIRST SCHEME

hiju'-*akan*-a-ing	I have come.	Lel-*akad'-ko*-a-ing	I have seen them.
hiju'-*akan*-a-m	thou hast come	lel-*akad'-ko*-a-m	thou hast seen them
hiju'-*akan*-a-ẹ	he or she has come.	lel-*akad'-ko*-a-e	he or she has seen them.
Hiju'-*akan*-a-lang	thou and I have come.	lel-*akad'-ko*-a-lang	thou and I have seen them.
hiju'-*akan*-a-ling	he or she and I have come.	lel-*akad'-ko*-a-ling	he or she and I have seen them.
etc.		ect.	

SECOND SCHEME

lel-akad-iñ-a-e	he or she has	lel-*akad* –*i*	–a–e	he or she has seen
lel-akad-iñ-a-e	see me.	le-*aka* –*i*	–a–e	him or her.
lel-akad-me-a-e	he or she has seen them	lel-*akad'*-lang	–a–e	he or she has seen thee and me.

etc.

N. B.—The *Perfect* of *lel* is frequently used with a *Present* meaning, and then signifies : *to know, to recognize*. En horaing *lelakada ; I know* that road. En horoing *lelaka'ia* : I *know* or I *recognize* that man.

bai	to arrange a marriage.	jagar	to speak.
bẹtekan	very much.	jaked'	up to.
buṛia	old man, old woman.	janau janau	everlasting.
ḍarpokena	coward.	lelgod'	to see for an instant to catch a glimpse of.
ḍarpokenaja-nam	thou hast become a coward.	misa	once.
		misaoka	never once.
dutam	matchmarker.	oko?	What?
engam apum – taking	thy mother and father, thy parents.	ruru	to leave in peace.
		Somar	Monday.
ela !	ah ! hela ! hallo !	ta'	(postposition) to (motion).
enate	by that, thereupon.		
erang	abuse, quarrel.	tab	(affix) quickly.
hiju' darijana-	I could come.	tobe	well then.

Amge Sigin ! Ne api chandu nere misao kale lelgod'ked'mea !	Is it you Sigin ! For three months we have never once caught a glimpse of you here !
Ela, Gomke, kaing hiju' darijana.	Ah, sir, I could not come.
Chikana tobe na'do ?	Well then what is the matter now.

Am taing hijutana, Gomke.

Hege, enado lelo'tana ! Chikanamentem hiju'akana ?

Kajige, Gomke.

Kajige ! kajige ! haramkoleka jagarem etejade. Urungtabeme ama' kaji.

Kajido neage : Buruhature aing nagenteko baikeda.

Oko orareko baikeda.

Mundaa orare, Gomke.

Dangriem lelkr'a ?

Hege ! Dutam Buruhatutee idikíña. Mendo en dangri kaing sunkaitana. Ena udubing hijuakana.

Kam sunkaitana? Entedo ena engam apumtaking kajiaking me

Ela ! Gomke, misaing ajiad'kinga; entedo beteanking Dangkinger. Najakedoking kisiaingtana.

Entedoem hekeda?

Chiakeaing oro? No bar pit misao kaing ruruingtana. Enedo Somar hulang hekedaing.

Ela! Enatem bagraua kadam Amo nado dorpokenafanam

Darpoekna do; Gomke, ka ! Mendo en janau Janau erang okoe oro saa'ting? Aing eskarge en haram buriaking kaing dariakinga. Na'do amating asratana. Am, Gomke, jagarkingme: boroamtanaking.

I am coming to thee, sir.

Yes, that is plain (visible) ! Why hast thou come ?

On business (for a word), sir.

Business ! business! Thou beginnest to talk like the old men. Out quickly with that business.

The matter is this : they have arranged a marriage for me in Buruhatu.

In what house (family) have they arranged it ?

In the house of the village-chief, sir.

Didst thou see the girl.

Yes, the matchmaker took me to Buruhatu. But I do not like the girl. It is to tell this that I have come.

So, thou doest not care for her? Then to tell that to thy parents,

Hela ! sir, once I told them; and they scolded me fearfully. Up to now they are angry with me.

So then thou didst agree to the marriage? (thou saidest Yes?)

What else am I to do? For these two weeks they do not leave me in peace even once. So Monday I agreed to the arrangement.

Hela ! by that thou hast spoiled it (matters). So thou too hast new become a coward.

Not exactly a coward, sir. But who in the world can stand this everlasting abuse? I alone connot get over the load couple. So now I look for help from thee. Do thou, sir, speak to them, they are both afraid of thee.

Jagardoing jagarkinga. Iduording manatinga chiking ka! Amo en dangri kaing doia mente kajiakingme.	As far as that goes, I shall speak to them. But I don't know whether they will listen or not! Thou too must tell them that thou wilt not marry that girl.

XI. EXERCISE

This Exercise explains the use of those very idiomatic Mundari ***Possessive Affixes*** *which especially foreign influences tend to replace by the possessive Adjective given above (pp.29-73).*

To this is added an explanation of the formation and the various uses of the ***Indefinite Past Tense****. The student's attention is particularly drawn to these explanations because a correct use of this Tense-form presents very great difficulties.*

POSSESSIVE SUFFIXES

95. Instead of Possessive Abjective *aiña', ama', aea'*, etc., the Mundas do very frequently use another construction, quite different from anything to be met with in English :

To the Noun denoting the being or object or owned, or possessed they suffix the following compounds:-

Sing.	*Dual.*	*Plural.*
aing : my.	*talang* : thy and my.	*tabu* : your and my.
tam : thy.	*taling* : his (her) and my.	*tale* : their and my.
tae : his (her).	*taben* : of you two (your).	*tape* : your.
	taking : of both (their).	*tako* : their.

Sadom-*taing* : My horse	sadom-*talang* : thy and my horse. sadam-*taling* : his (her) and my horse.	sadom-*tabu* : your and my horse. sadom *tale* : their and my horse.
sadom-*tam* : thy horse.	sadom-*taben* : the horse of you two.	sadom-*tape* : your horse
sadom-*tae* : his (her) horse.	sadom-*taking* : the horse of the two.	sadom-*tako* : their horse

sadomking-*taing* : my two horses, etc; sadomko-*taing* : my horses, etc.
ora-*taing* : my house or my houses; ora-*tam* : thy house or houses, etc.

96. Whenever the Adjectives *my*, *thy*, and *his* or her refer to relatives close or distant, the suffixes *taing*, *tam*, *tae* are replaced by *ing*, *me* or *m* and *te*.

N. B.—*Me* is suffixed to Nouns ending in a consonant; *m* is suffixed to Nouns ending in a vowel, v. gr. Hon-*me* : thy son. Enga-*m* : thy mother.

The *Inclusive Duals* and *Plurals* are formed by suffixing *talang* and *tabu*, respectively, to the Noun. But the *Exclusive Duals* and *Plurals* insert *ing* before *taling and tale*.

Similarly, the 2nd Person Dual and Plural inserts *m* or *me* before *taben* and *tape*.

The corresponding Dual and Pluural Possessives : *of the two* and *their* are rendered by suffixing *te* plus *taking* and *tako*, respectively, to the Nouns in question.

		apu-*talang*	: thy and my father.	apu-*tabu*	: your and my father.
Apu-*ing*	: My father	apu-*ingtaling*	: his (her) my father.	apu-*ingtale*	: their and my father.
Apu-*m*	: thy father.	apu-,*mtaben*	: the father of you two.	apu-*mtape*	: Your father.
Apu-*te*	: his (her) father	apu-*tetaking*	: the father of the two.	apu-*tetako*	: their father.

97. The word *parents* is in Mundari rendered by the juxtaposition of the words *enga apu*. Whenever both parents are thus named, the Possessive Suffixes *ing*, *m* and *te* are suffixed to either word, and the Compound Daul Suffix teking or *taking* is added to the second word.

Engaing apuingtaking : my (father and mother) parents.
Engam apumtaking : thy (" " ") parents.
Engate aputetaking : his (her) (" " ") parents.

98. When the Plural and Dual Possessives refer to both parents individually the independent Possessive Adjectives must be used; thus

Our (my and thy) parents : *alanga'* enga apu.
our(his or her and my) parents : *alinga'* enga apu.
your (of you two) parents : *abena'* enga apu.
their (of both) parents : *akinga'* enga apu.
Our (your and my) parents : *abua'* enga apu.

Predicates referring to *enga apu* in these phrases must of course stand in the *Dual* v. gr. Alanga' enga apu hasutana-*king* : thy and my father and mother are both sick.

When there is question of the parents of two or more people who are not brother and sisters then the Possessive Adjectives *abena'*, *akinga'*, *apea'*, *akoa'* are used and Predicates referring to the words *enga apu* in such phrases stand in the Plural.

Abena' enga apu-*ko* hasutana-*ko* : The parents of you two are sick. Chia ! apea enga apu-*ko* hijuakana-*ko*? Have the parents of all of you arrived?

99. The possessive Affixes *ing, me, te* are not used in connexion with the word *kuri* when it signifies wife. A Munda speaking of his own wife generally uses the Plural form kuriko without any Possessive Adjective. The Possessive *aiñá* is however heard too. For *thy , his* etc. the forms ama', aea' etc. are used : kuriko or *aiñá* kuri : my wife, *Ama' kuri* : thy wife. Aea' kuri his wife.

THE INDEFINITE PAST

100. The Indefinite Past Tense is formed by affixing *jan* to the root of the Predicate.

This Tense has two distinct functions.

101. *The first function* is limited to the Intransitive Predicates *sen* : to go; *ruar* : to return; *nir* : to run away; *apir* : to fly away *hoka* : to cease, to stop, and to their synonymes.

With these the Indefinite Past implies that the being denoted by the subject *went, came back ran* or *flew away* and is not yet returned, or that an action *has been stopped for the moment* and *has not yet been resumed*, though the intention of resuming it exist.

Soma okoria ? *Nirjanae* : Where is Soma ? He has run away. *Daru pataule hokajana* : We have (for the moment) stopped watering the trees.

In narrations too the Indefinite Tense is generally used, v. gr. *Enatedo tuiu* rurajanae : Then the jackal returned home.

102. *Second function. Jan* is suffixed to both *Transitive* and *Intransitive Predicates* to signify that the Subject or agent *went* to do a certain work, or *began* some action, and that he has not *yet completed* or *discontinued* it; hence in English this very peculiar Tense form must generally be rendered either by the Past of the Verb *to begin* or *to go*, followed by an infinitive or a Participal Clause.

REMARK. Transitive Predicates never insert Pronominal Objects in this form.

Durang-jan-ae : he began to sing. *Sendera-jan-ae* : he is gone hunting. *Haikoe sab –jan-a* : he is gone to catch fish.

I. SCHEME

nir-jan-a-ing	I have run away.	nir-*jan*-a-king	both of them have run away.
nir-jan-a-m	thou hast run away.	nir-*jan*-a-bu	you and I have run away.
nir-jan-a-e	he or she has run away.	nir-*jan*-a-le.	they and I have run away.
nir-jan-a-lang	thou and I have run away.	nir-*jan*-a-pe	you have run away.
nir-jan-a-ling	he or she and I have run away.	nir-*jan*-a-ko	they have run away.
nir-jan-a-ben	you two have run away.		

II. SCHEME

durang- *jan*-a-aing.	I *began* to sing.
durang – *jan*- a -m.	thou *beganst* to sing.

durang – *jan* – a – e.	he or,she *began* to sing.
durang – *jan*- a – lang.	thou and I *began* to sing.
durang – *jan*- a- ling.	he or, she and I *began* to sing.
durang – *jan*- a – ben.	you two *began* to sing.

etc.

III. SCHEME

Uri'ko – ing	gupi – *an* a.	I *went* to graze the cattle.
uri'ko – m	gupi – *jan* – a.	thou *wentst* to graze the cattle.
uri'ko – e	gupi – *jan* – a.	he or, she *went* to graze the cattle.
uri'ko – lang	gupi – *jan* – a.	thou and I *went* to graze the cattle.
uri'ko – ling	gupi – *jan* – a.	he or, she and I *went* to graze the cattle.
uri'ko – ben	gupi – *jan* – a.	you two *went* to graze the cattle.

etc.

aminangge	so much.	kupulo'te seno	to go on a visit.
aṛakata	(arkata) roof beam	langṛa	to limp.
auri	not yet.	leser leser	very sharp.
denga	to help.	marang	big.
girja	church, chapel.	mid'rege	together.
hered'	to weed.	nindir	white ant.
joro	to leak.	rokage	suddenly.
jata	a small piece of wood.	tiga to	tread.

En marang loeong-*tabu* sidengamente Pasana koṛabu achuia !	Let us (you and I) engage Pasana to help us to plough that big rice-field of ours !
Inid'o kae hijudaṛia.	That one cannot come.
Chikanamente ka ?	Why not ?
Enga-*te* apu-*tetaking* kupulot'eking senojana, oṛo api ma mente kaking ruaṛa.	His parents are gone on a visit and they will not return for three days.
Seta-*taing* nirjanae ; chia apea' hature kape lelkra ?	My dog has run away. Did you not see him in your village ?
Ka Gomkele lel-*akaia*.	No, sir, we have not seen him.
Sadom-*taben* akiring mente tising boko-*m* apu-*inglo* piṭte senae chi ka ?	Will thy brother go to the market-to-day with my father in order to sell your (thy and his) horse ?
Tising book-*ing* kae sendaṛia ?	To-day my brother cannot go.
Chikanamente kae sendaṛia. ?	Why can he not go ?
Oṛa-*tale* jorotana : ninkirko	Our house is leaking because the

aṛākata-ko jomchaba-*akada*-ko mente. Entedo hola naua daruling ma'-*jana*. Entedo birre leser leser jatae tigakeda oṛo tisingo pura'gee langratana.	white ants have completely eaten the arkatas (roof beams). So we went yesterday to cut new trees. Then in the forest he trod (on) a very sharp piece of wood and even to-day he is limping very much.
Dola tobe am semme !	Come on then ! go thou thyself !
Chilekateng sena ! Boko-*ing* koṛae langṛatana oṛo enga-*ingo* hasutanae, Orare okoe kamiae oṛo !	How am I to go ! My brother is lame and my mother too is sick. Who then will work at home ! (who is to do the house work !)
Dolang girja-ora'te ! Padri Gomkee hijuakana. naikeẹ upadesbua.	Come along (thou and I) to the chapel ! The priest has come, after a while he will give us an instruction (instruct us).
Auri ! enga-*ing* book-*ing* kuṛilo' hered-*jan*-aking ; inking-ing ra'aukinga ente sobenko midregebu sena.	Wait a while ! My mother and my younger sister rare gone to weed (my mother with my younger sister are both gone to weed) I shall call them hither, then we shall all go together.
Boko-*m* piṭte senakanae chi !	Has thy junior brother gone to the market ?
Kage ! si-*jan*-ae.	No ! he is gone to plough.
Chikanamente aminanggee boroaingtana ? Honder huṛinglekaing erangkra entedo rokagee ra'-jan-a.	Why does he fear me so much ? The other day I scolded him a little and then he began at once to cry.
Sadom-*taing* taiarime. Ruitolateng sena.	Get my horse ready. I shall go to Ruitola.
Tising hoṛoko kam namkoa ; soben korako sendera-*jan*-ako.	To-day thou wilt not find the people ; all the men are gone to hunt.

XIII. EXERCISE

This Exercise explains the formation and use of the Anterior Past. *By way of giving still larger scope for the formation of appropriate sentences, it explains the formation of* Conditional Sentences.

THE ANTERIOR PAST

103. This Tense denotes the priority of one past action over another. It is found by adding *len* to Intransitive and *led* to Transitive Predicates. *Pronominal Objects* are inserted between the affix *led* and the Copula. *Indirect Objects* are not preceded by *a*.

When *ing* or *i* are inserted as Pron. Objects the same elisions take place which have been described in the Simple Past. (p. 22. 65.)

I. SCHEME

nir-*len*-a-ing	I first ran.	nir-*len*-a-lang	thou and I first ran.
nir-*len*-a-m	thou first ranst	nir-*len*-a-ling	he or she and I first ran.
nir-*len*-a-e	he or she first ran.	nir-*len*-a-ben	you two first ran.
nir-*len*-a	it first ran.	nir-*len*-a-king	both of them first ran.

II. SCHEME

Ra'– *led'* – ko – a– *ing* ra' – *led'* – ko – a – *m* ra' – *led'* – ko – a –*e* ra' – *led'* – ko – a – *lang* ra' – *led'* – ko – a – *ling* ra' – *led'* – ko – a *ben*	I, thou, etc. first called them.	ra' – *led'* – *ko* – a – king ra' – *led'* – *ko* – a – bu ra' – *led'* – *ko* – a – le ra' – *led'* – *ko* – a – pe ra' – *led'* – *ko* – a – pe	The two you and I, ect. First called them.

III. SCHEME.

Ra-*led-iñ* –a-ko ra –*l* – *iñ* –a-ko	They f. c. me	ra-*led'-ben* –a-ko	They f. c. you two.
ra-*led'-me*-a-ko	They f. c. thee.	ra-*led'-kin*-a-ko	They f. c. both of them.
ra –*led'-i* –a-ko ra-*l-i* - a-ko	They f. c. him or her.	ra-*led'-bu* –a-ko	They f. c. you and her
ra- *led'-lang* –a-ko	They f. c. thee and me.	ra-*led'-ee* -a-ko	They f. c. them and me.
ra-*led'-ling*-a-ko	They f. c. him and me.	ra-*led'-pe* –a-ko	They f.c. you.
		ra-*led'-ko* -a-ko	They f. c. them.

104. A very strong contraction takes place Transitive Predicates when the *Direct Object* is an inanimate being, in which case Pronominal Objects are not inserted. The complete form would be v. gr. lel-led-a-ing : I saw *it* or *them* (inanimate objects). Now, in the Mankipati districts the *ed* of *led* is dropped, the Copula *a* is checked and immediately suffixed to the *l*. Hence the forms :

Lel-*l'-a*-ing	I first saw it.	lel-*l'-a*-king	both first saw it.
lel-*l'-a*-m	thou f. sawst it.	lel-*l'-a*-bu	you and I f. s. it.
lel-*l'-a*-e	he or she f. s. it.	lel-*l'-a*-le	they and I f. s. it.
lel-*l'-a*-lang	thou and I f. s. it	lel-*l'-a*-pe	you first saw it.
lel-*l'-a*-ling	he or she and I f. s. it.	lel-*l'-a*-ko	you first saw it.
lel-*l'-a*-ben	You two f. s. it.		

105. One frequently hears the Anterior Past forms used in cases where the real function of this Tense would not justify its use. The following may be accepted as a general rule or description of the Mundas' practice :

Whenever there is really question of the priority of one past action over another past action by the same agent, the Mundas invariably use the Anterior Past Tense-form. In other cases they use it rather freely instead of the *Simple* Past Tense-form.

106. REMARK.—Whenever there is question of *one agent* having performed a certain action before *another agent* perfomed the same action, the *Anterior Past* is not used. In that case the words *aiar* : to precede or *sida* : first, are suffixed to the root of the Predicate and followed by the Simple Past Affix *ken* (intrnas.) or *ked* (Trans.) or by some other appropriate Past Tense suffixed.)

Some nir-*aiar-jan*-a-e : Some was *the first* to run away (understood : the others ran away after he had run.) Aege tam-*sida-k-i-ñ*-ae enamenteng rukía : He struct me *first*, that's why I thrashed him with (my) stick (He *began* the fight). Aing ne horoko knobijang om-*sida ad'-ko*-a-ing. I was the *first* to give cabbage seeds to these people. (*I introduced* the cultivation of cabbages among these people.)

107. REMARK.—The words *hijú*: to come ; *teba'* and *seter* to arrive; *jonoma*: to be born, always form their *Simple Past* in *len* and not in *ken*.

Hiju' –*len* – a – e instead of	huju' – *ken* –a – e he came.
teba' –*len* – a –e	teba' – *ken* – a – e he arrived.
seter – *len* – a – e	seter – *ken* – a – e he arrived.
jonom – *len* – a – e	jonom – *ken* – a – e he was born.

CONDITIONAL SENTENCES

108. A conditional sentence is one which states a contingency or a fact as depending on a given condition. In English it is always a compound sentence : The *principal proposition* is that which states the contingency or fact, the dependent *Conditional Clause* is that which states the condition. v. gr. *If he come* (Conditional Clause) *I will leave.* (Principal Proposition).

109. A condition may be expressed as either *realizable* or as *unrealizable.* Again a realizable condition may be expressed as either *probable* or *improbable.*

All these differences attaching to the *manner* in which the condition is enunciated, cause changes in the Tense and Mood of the Verbs of both the Principal and the Conditional Clause.

v. gr. In the sentence : *If he come, I will leave* the condition is implied not only as realizable but also as probable, or at least as actually apprehended.

A change of Tense in the Conditional Clause and of Mood in the Principal proposition implies that a realizable condition is considered as improbable. V. gr. *If he came, I would leave.* Unrealizable conditions require a similar change of Tense and Mood. V. gr. *If* men *could* fly, bicycles *would* hardly be used.

110.—In Mundari a Conditional Sentence is always a simple proposition inasmuch as it contains but one Subject and one Predicate. The *Conditional Clause* is reduced to a mere Adverbial Compound.

Condition is expressed by the Postposition *re* (in) if. The substitution of re for the Copula *a* transforms any Mundari Tense into a *Conditional Clause.* The Compounds thus obtained imply that the condition is both realizable and probable.

INTRANSITIVE PREDICATES

SIMPLE FUTURE TENSE

Categorical propositions.		*Conditional Clauses.*			
Sen –*a* – ing sen – *a* – m sen – *a* – e sen – *a* – lang sen – *a* – ling etc.	I, thou etc. will or shall go.	Sen – *re* – ng sen – *re* – m sen – *re* – e sen – *re* –lang sen – *re* – ling etc.	*If* I, thou etc. do go.	Ka – ing sen – *re* ka – m sen – *re* ka – e sen – *re* ka – lang sen – *re* ka – ling sen – *re* etc.	*If* I, thou etc. do not go

SIMPLE PAST TENSE

Senken-*a*-ing senken-*a*-m senken-*a*-e senekn-*a*-lang senken-*a*-ling etc.	I, thou etc. did go.	Senken-*re*-ng senken-*re*-m senken-*re*-e senken-*re*-lang senken-*re*-ling etc.	If I, thou etc. really did go.	Kaing senken-*re* kam senken-*re* kae senken-*re* kalang senken-*re* kaling senkin-*re* etc	If I, thou etc really did not go.

PERFECT TENSE

Senakan-*a*-ing senakan-*a*-m senakan-*a*-e senakan-*a*-lang senakan-*a*-ling etc.	If I, thou etc. have gone.	Senakan-*re*-ng senakan-*re*-m senakan-*re*-e senakan-*re*-lang senakan-*re*-ling etc.	I, thou etc. have gone	Kaing senakan-*re* kam senakan-*re* kae senakan-*re* kalang senakan-*re* kaling senakan-*re* etc.	If I thou etc. have not gone.

111. When the subject is a Noun or a Pronoun different from the Simple Personal Pronouns, the Personal pronominal affixes need not be used. To use them is however no mistake.

Ne horo sen-*re*	: If this man do go.	Ne horoking senken-re	: If these two men have gone really did go.
Ne horo senakan-*re*	: If this man really did go.	Ne horoko sen-re	: If these men do go.
Ne horo senaken-*re*	: If this man have gone.	Ne horoko senken-re	: If these men really did go.
Ne horoking sen-*re*	: If these two men do go.	Ne horoko senakan-re	: If these men have gone.
Ne horoking senken -*re*	: If these two men really did go.		

112. Transitive Conditional Clauses insert Pronominal Objects according to the rules given for Transitive Predicates of Categorical Sentences.

FUTURE

Lel-*ko-re*-ng lel-*ko-re*-m lel-*ko-re*-e lel-*ko-re*-lang lel-*ko-re*-ling etc.	If I, thou, etc., do see them.	Kaing lel-*ko-re* kam lel-*ko-re* kae lel-*ko-re* kalang lel-*ko-re* kaling lel-*ko-re* etc.	If I, thou, etc., do not see them.	En horo lel-*ing* -*re* en horo lel-*me* -*re* en horo lel-*i* -*re* en horo lel-*lang* -*re* en horo lel-*ling* -*re* etc.	It that man do see me, thee, etc.

PRESENT

Leljad'– *ko* – *re* – ng leljad' – *ko* – *re* – m leljad' – *ko* – *re* – e leljad' – *ko* – *re* – lang leljad' – *ko* – *re* – ling etc.	If I, thou, etc., see them now.	Kaing leljad' – *ko* - *re* kam leljad' – *ko* - *re* kae leljad' – *ko* - *re* alang leljad' – *ko* - *re* kaling leljad' – *ko* - *re* etc.	If I, thou, etc., do not see them now.

En horo	leja'	–	*ing*	- *re*	If that man see me, thee, etc., now.
en horo	leljad'	–	*me*	- *re*	
en horo	lelja'	–	*i*	- *re*	
en horo	leljad'	–	*lang*	- *re*	
en horo	leljad'	–	*ling*	- *re*	

SIMPLE PAST

Lelked'– *ko* – *re* – ng	If I, thou, etc., really did see them.	Kaing lelked' – *ko* - *re*	If I, them, etc., really did not see them.
lelked' – *ko* – *re* – m		kam lelked' – *ko* - *re*	
lelked' – *ko* – *re* – e		kae lelked' – *ko* - *re*	
lelked' – *ko* – *re* – lang		kalang lelked' – *ko* - *re*	
lelked' – *ko* – *re* – ling		kaling lelked' – *ko* - *re*	

Apum	lelk'	–	*ing*	- *re*	If thy father really did see me, thee, etc.
apum	lelked'	–	*me*	- *re*	
apum	lelk'	–	*i*	- *re*	
apum	lelked'	–	*lang*	- *re*	
apum	lelked'	–	*ling*	- *re*	

113. Conditional Clauses which in English are introduced by *but, on the other hand* and synonymous expressions, affix *do* to *re* in Mundari. If the Pronominal Affixes do not precede the clause, then they are affixed to *do*.

Sen-*re-do-ing* : But if I do go ; Kale sen-*re-do : But* if we do not go. Senken-*re-do-m : But* if thou really didst go . Kako senakan-*re-do* : But if they have not gone. Lel-ko-*re-do-e : But if he* do see them. Kaking raked'-pe-*re-do* : *But* if these two really did not call you. Dalled-me-*re-do-e : But* if *he* first struck thee. Bauing mo-akad'-ko-*re-do : But* if my brother have given it to them.

114. Conditional clauses which in English are introduced by *even* or synonymous expressions, affix *o* to the conditional form in *re*.

En Dikum nalisi-*re-o* kam dariaia : Thou wilt not get the better of that zemindar *even* if thou do sue him. En horo kulae leljai-*re-o* kae borotana : That man does not fear even when. He sees a tiger.

115. No changes of Mood and Tense ever take place in Mundari Conditional Sentences. The connotations implied by those changes in English Conditional Sentences are expressed by the word *honang* or *honanga*.

Honang (honanga.) denotes mere possibility, probability and *some-times desire*. It is used only in connexion with Transitive or Intransitive Predicates.

If added to Conditional forms in *re* it signifies that the condition is considered by the speaker as a contingency which is merely desired but either impossible or at least improbable.

Ranchiteng *sen-re honang*, lija'ing au-amea derang : If I were to go to Ranchi (a thing which I desire but under the circumstances cannot do) I would certainly bring a cloth for thee.

Bauming *leljái-re honang*, ama' chitting omaia : If I do chance to see thy senior brother to-day, I will give him thy letter.

Teba'ked*king-reng honanga* sajaiked'kinga chimad' : If I had over taken them (a thing I desired, but could not accomplish) I should certainly have punished both of them.

116. If *honang* be added to the predicate of the Predicate of the Principal Preposition it represents the event as depending only contingently, or probably on the realization of the condition.

Ranchiteng *sen-re* lijaing *auamea honang* ; I might probably bring a cloth for thee if I do got to Ranchi.

Tising bauming *namja'i-re, erangiaing honanga* : If I do meet thy brother to-day I shall probably (possibly) scold him (i.e) I have desire to do so but have not quite made up my mind for it.

Baganreng *tebaked'king-re sajaiked'kingaing honanga* : If I had overtaken the two in the garden I would probably have punished both of them.

Neutaki'-rem-o kae hiju'jana honanga : He would probably not have come even if thou hadst invited him.

117. *Honanga* ! added to conditional forms, yields complete phrases equivalent to English sentences expressive of desire whether realizable or unrealizable.

Seno-re-ko honanga ! O if only they were to go away ! Engaing oro' misaing *leli-re honanga* ! O if I could but once more see my mother again ! *Neuataki'-rem honanga* ! O if only thou hadst invited him ! I wish thou hadst invited him. En kulabu *goe'akái-re honanga* ! Would that we had killed that tiger.

ader	to enter, to drive in.
aege	he or she herself.
aiumkumburu	to listen stealthily, to ovehear, to spy out by overhearing.
aji	sister
amin	surveyor.
apakiring	to sell each other.
aṛakati	cooli-catcher.
arkid'	to carry off.
auri	not yet.
bagan	garden.
bahi	register.
baranking	both of them.
beda-urung	to cheat away.
bejaiti	to deprive one of his
dondo	stupid.
emanko	such ones.
ena (Pron.)	that (impers. Pron.)
enkage	like that.
enkan	such.
enreo	nevertheless.
enta'	there.
entarege	there, in that very place.
era'ge	much.
eskar eskarte	separately ; by one self alone.
eṭani	another one.
eṭasare	somewhere else.
eta'eta	various.
-ete (postposition – form, out of.)	
gara	river.

	caste, to spoil one's. caste
bes	well, to treat well.
bichar	to judge, to conclude.
biswas	to believe.
biuro	to be turned.
bolo	en enter.
bajau	to understand.
bul	to make drunk.
chalan	to take away, to take to jail, to march some one off to a dept.
chanḍu	every month.
daṛ̣ra	to seek.
dastur	custom.
din	day.
dinaki	every diay.
dipu	colli depot.
dip-babu	the babu in charge of a dept
dipu-gomke	the European in charge of a dept.
dismiss	to reject to dismiss a case.
do	to marry.
jana jetana	anything at all.
jati	a caste.
jawab	to say, to reply.
jetasa're	somewhere.
jima	to make over.
jira	to cross-examine.
kachcheri	court.
kahan'ni	a story, to tell a story, to yarn.
kupulko	relations.
lelnam	to see, to find
main ! (Voc. Of girl!	Child daughter !

gati	companion.
gerang	to weep.
girmiti	agreement.
gititora	sleeping house.
golmallena	there was trouble.
haji	to present.
hagako	relations.
hakim	judge.
hati kuti	in all kinds of way.
hatom	aunt.
herel	husband.
hiju-nam	to come for some one, to come in search of some one.
hobajana	it has become.
hosro	a lie, to lie.
idang idangre	very very early.
iminangge !	enough !
ja (Indef, Pron.)	some.
-ja (suffix)	perhaps.
jaege (Ind. Pron.)	any one.
jelekate	somehow.
phuslau-idi	to cajole away.
purasa'	very often.
pura'te	chiefly.
Rajput	Rajput.
rangakan	coloured.
regiseteri	registration ; to register.
-reni'	suffixed to a Proper name of a man means the wife of.
rinti	to deny stubbornly.
sabuti	proof.
sahi	to sign.
ama	useless.

	address).
men	1° to think.
	2° to say.
mi-mid'te	one by one.
mid're	together.
misa misa	sometimes.
motaite	by force, out of spite.
muka	to measure, to survey.
musing	once.
nails	to bring a case.
namo'	to be taken.
nekage	like this.
nutum	name.
nutumten	called, by name.
nutumtei'	the one called.
okil	pleader.
okoni'	some
panchal	cunning, crafty.
parom	to cross.
phalna	such.
phuli	strong arak.
sanjokte	by a chance.
sarasari	to exact an explanation.
sarkar	government.
sukute	freely.
sumdi	father of one's son-in-law.
tae'te	(post- since, from. Pos.)
taekenae	he or she was.
taka-lobte	with greed of money.
-tat'e (Postpos.)	to (motion).
-te (Postpos.)	by means of, under, by.
tor	to know.
ujur	to object.
udub'	to report,to reveal.
uku	to hide.
uru'	desire.
uter	very, utterly.

N.B.—*jeruṛakanre* : If need there be
Karedo : but if not, or else; *karedo ka* : or else not at all.

118. *REM. 1.*- Locative Genitives depending on Common or Proper Nouns denoting persons are formed by suffixing *ren* to the Nouns denoting place.

Ranchi-*ren* gomke : a gentleman of Ranchi. Ranchi-*ren* Uraonko : the Uraons of Ranchi. Burudi-*ren* Soma : Soma of Burudi.

119. Rem. 2.—Possessive Genitives depending on the word *ku ri*: wife, are generally formed by means of the same affix *ren* being added to the husband's name: v. gr. Pasana *–ren* kuri: The wife of Pasana.

Hence the Pronominal form of this affix, viz., *reni*, added to the Proper name of a man, always means: *The wife* of, v. gr. Pasana *–reni'*: The *wife* of Pasana.

A Munda when speaking of his own wife generally uses the Plural form *kuriko* without any Possessive Adjective or Affix. Hence *kuriko* often menas: my wife.

Am Samu! bar pittaete ama hature aminko mukajadako oro am eta'sarem taintana!	Why Samu ! the surveyors are measuring (surveying) in your village for the last two weeks and thou remainst somewhere else!

Hela gomke aiña orare erage golmallena : Barwada-*ren* arakati hon-*ing* kuri diputee idili'a; en honing nambarakia.

Chimtange idili'a!

Bar pit hobajana.

Sukurbar hulang hon-*ing*-kuri hatu-*ren* dangrikolo Soeko pittee senkena. En, hulang orate kae rurajana. Ente Sanichar hulang kuri-*ko* en dangriko kulibara- ked'koako. Inkudo: Palo Jiurite seno'janaeko metakotana. Jiuri - *ren* Moso pahanr boko-*ing* – kurie doakaia. Enamente, hatomtea oratee senakana oro' gapae ruaraing menjada.

Etwar hulango kae rurajana, enateng danrabarakia. Jiurire kaing namkichi, Otongorateng senkena, kupulko-*taing* – *tat'e*. Inkuo kale lelaka'ia menteko metaingtana. Enatedo Baridi-*ren* sumdi-*taing*-ing kulik*ía*. Inio, Kae hiju'lena mentee Kajiaingtana. Ente enatedo ja arakati arkid'kiae menteng bicharkeda.

Enreo oro api ma mente eta eta hatukoreng nambarakia. Orateng rurajanchi kuriko nea-geko udubkina: Tising seta Deosai-reni, abena hon Barwa-daren arakati Asamtee akiring-kiaking metalingtana. Chile-kate-ben torkeda-ling kuliked-king-chi-king neka-aling-tana : Tising gapa dangriko alinga orareko gitioratana, oro hola nida –ling aiumkumburuked'koa. Nekajada-ko I duoro en Barwada-ren Sau kora Paloe bedaakiringkia ja !

O sir, a great trouble arose in my house (family): A coolicatcher of Barwada took my daughter to a cooli-depot; I was in search of that daughter.

When did he take her away?

Two weeks ago. (It has become two weeks). On Friday my daughter went to the Soeko market together with the girls of the village. That day she did not return home. Then on Saturday *my wife* asked those girls here and there. But they: Palo went to Jiuri, they said to her. Moso pahanr of Jirui has merried *my junior* sister. Therefore I thought she had gone to her aunt's house and would return the next day.(Literally: therefore, she has gone to her aunt's house and she will return to-morrow, say I.) On Sunday too she did not return, therefore I went about seeking her. Not having found her in Jiuri I went to Otongora,to my relatives They too told me that they had not seen her.(They too, we have not seen her, saying, they said to me.) And after that I asked my *sumdi* (the father of my daughter's husband) of Baridi: he too said that she had not come. Then at last I concluded that some cooli-catcher had carried her off.

Nevertheless I Still looked for her, for three days in various villages. Having returned home, *my wife* told (reveald) me this: This morning *Deosai's wife* said to me: a cooli-cathcer of Barwada has sold your child to Asam. Having asked her, how she knew, she replied thus to me: (Literally: Having asked her: how do you know ?) These days the village girls use my house as dormitory (Literally: they sleeping-house it in my house) and

Tising ae eskarge hatutee rura-jana.

yesterday night I overheard them: They spoke like this: Who knows, that man Sau of Barwada has sold Palo by deceiving her. To-day her returned alone to (his) village.

Entedo *tising* idangre Chan-du-*ling* kuliki'a. Ini'do, Soeko pitre Barwada-*ren* Sau kara Palolo'king jagar-*jana* . Entedo, domeaing mentee metaia: Enatedo paloe meta'ingtana: Ne ko-ralo' Barwada'teng senoa' ad' ini'lo'ing taena. Hature rokage alope udubiña! Jiuritee senakanae *mente* enga-*ing* apu-*ing*-takingta'te kajipe. Otongora're aingmenteking baikeda. Mendoen Otongora'ren kora aing kaing sukuaitana. Ne Sau koralo'ing taina. Mod' pit taiomte uduba-kingpe. Entedo mid'teking se-no'jana. Mendo hola Etwari en Sau kora, Barwadaree lelnamki'a. Palo*do* Barwadare kae taekena. Entedo Etwari aji-*te*-e kuliki'a. Ini'do, hege! Sukurbar hulang aiubsa Sau kora miad dangrie aukia; mendo Sanichar hulang baranking. Seno'janaking. En kora isu horokoe akiringked'koa. Nado ne dangrio ja diputee chalankia chimad'.

Then early this morning I asked Chandu. She related to me this: In the Soeko market place Sau got into conversation with Palo. Then, I will marry (keep) thee, saying he said to her. And then Palo says to me: I will go to Barwada with this man, and with him I will remain. Do not report me at once in the village! Say to my father and mother: She is gone to Jiuri. They (my father and mother) arranged a marriage for me in Otongora. But I don't like that man of Otongora. I will remain with this man Sau. After one week tell it to them. And then both went away together. But yesterday Etwari saw that man Sau in Barwada. *As for* Palo she was not in Barwada. Then Etwari asked her sister. She (said), yes indeed! on Friday towards evening Sau brought a girl, but on Saturday both of them went away. That man has (already) sold many people; now forsooth he also marched that girl off to some cooli-dept.

Entedo am Barwadatem sen-kena chi?

Then didst thou go to Barwada?

Kaing senkena Gomke. China ohikateng sena oro!

I did not go, sir. What for should I go there! (To do what should I go!)

Chikana chikate oro ! En Sau kora sarasari mente!

To do what indeed! To exact an explanation from that man Sau!

Ela gomke ena samagea ! *hen** arakatijatiko sobena jan-augeko rintia.

Alas, sir, that is useless! *Those wretched* cooli-cathers always deny everything stubbornly.

Entedo jetana kam chika-keda ?

Then thou didst do nothing at all?

Ka gomke ! rokage Ranchi-teng senkena, oro enta mod pit dinaki kachcherireng loro'kena hon-*ing*

No, Sir! I at once went to Ranchi and there for a whole week I every day watched (sat watching) to see whether

* The demonstrative *ken* often denotes contemple or scorn.

mente.

Mendo jetasa're kaing lelgod-kia.

Iduoro am auri tebareko chalankia chimad'!

Ka gomke! Dipuree taekeña. Hanre ainggeko lelurumkina enamente en soben din kach-cherite kako idiki'a.

Na'dom kahanitana! Ranchire amge okoe lelurummea oro! Oro hon-*me* kuri dipuree taekena mente chilekatem ituana?

Kaing hosrotana. Sartige. dipuree taikena. Ranchi-*uter-ren ko* aingge kako lelurumiña honanga; mendo arakatiko Kachiko torakaina !

Mendo am Ranchite aurim seno're en Barwada-*ren* arakati hatutee ruralena. Chilekate tobedo Ranchiree udubmea honanga !

Ini'do gomke ka, mendo aea gatiko. Arakatiko eskar eskartedo kako kämia. *Misa misa api upun* horote mid' horogeko akiringia: Mid' horo dangri ora-etc karedo pittaete bēdaurungia, etani ja haturee ukuia, jerurakanre, ente dipute idiia oro' mid horo Ranchiree loro baraea, enga apuko hijunamiako chiko ka mente. Ini, en kuri apute kared'o aea' korae lelki're, ente dipu-babu, alope hajiria, mentee ūdubaia. Entedo apu-*te* chi herel' auri seno'jaked' geko ūkuia.

they would bring my daughter for registration (literally: will they bring or will they not (bring) my child for registration, saying).

But I could no where see her at all (catch a glimpse of her).

Who knows! Most probably they dispatched her (to Assam) before thou arrivedst.

No, Sir! She was in the depot.

Over there (in Ranchi) they recongnized me; that's why all those days they did not take her to the court.

Now thou art telling stories! Who would recognize thee in Ranchi! And how doest thou know that thy daughter was in the depot?

I am not lying. She was certainly in the depot. The people of Ranchi itself (*those living altogether in Ranchi*) would not recognize me: but the cooli-catchers don't they know me? (literally: have not they known me !)

But that cooli-catcher of Barwada returned to (his) village before thou wentst to Ranchi. How then should he reveal thee (point thee out) in Ranchi !

Not indeed that one, but his companions. For cooli- catchers are not in the habit of working separately (each by himself alone). It sometimes take three or four men to sell one man (cooli) (lierally: sometimes by three or four men they sell one). One man will cheat a girl out of her house or away from the market place, another one will hide her in some village, if need there by, then he will take her to the depot and one man will watch in Ranchi to see whether the parents are coming to get her back. That one, if he have seen the father or the husband of that

Mendo Sarkara hukumte jaege dipuree bolo daṛia aea hon karedo aea kuṛi nam mente!

Bolodoko bolo daṛia mendo nā̃m kako namkoa.

Ena alom kā̃jia ! Dipu gomkeko kako bē̃da.

Ka jako bē̃da, Mendo arakatiko oṛo dipuren dasiko akoa gomkeko bedakoako. Purasa horoko eṭa nutumteko aderkoa. Tobedo gomkem kajiaire : phalna nutumten hoṛo omru'raingme mente, aea' bahie lelea oṛo' : nete kae hijuakana mentee meta mea ?

Mendo am soben hoṛoko mimid'te leldaṛiakoam !

Enao hege! Mendo gomke kae sē̃nbaṛaea amlo; oṛo dipuoabuko oṛo aṛā̃katiko panchal-geako. Jalekateko ukukoa. Sanjokte mod hoṛo nā̃moae karedo ka. Enamente nado dipukore kale nā̃mbarakoa.

Entedo environmental soben aṛā̃katiko Munḍa-honko chi?

Kage ! Peṉaaiṉko. Baraiko, emankoo enageko kã̄mia, mendo purate ale Munḍ'a-honko tising-gapale apakiringtana (Reciprocal form). Dipugomkeke, kare-do akoa' dasiko taka-lobte enkatege koṛa kuṛi

woman, will tell the babu in charge of the depot: don't present her (for registration). Then they will hide that woman until her father or husband is gone.

But by the order of the government any one may enter a depot to get back his child or his wife.

So *far as entering is concerned*, they can enter, but as *for finding* (them) they will not find them (their own).

Don't say that. The Europeans in charge of depts do not cheat.

Perhaps they do not cheat. But the cooli catchers and the dept servants cheat their masters. Very often they enter coolies under another name, Then if you tell the gentleman: Give me back the person of such and such a name, he will look into his register and tell thee: he or she has not come to this place.

But thou canst (go) and see all the coolies one by one.

That too yes! (I will grant). But the gentleman does not go about with thee (the one who seeks) and the depot babus and the arkaties are cunning. They hide them (the coolies in question) somehow. By a chance one is discovered or else not (*i.e.* generally not). Therefore we do generally not look for them in the depots.

Then (are) all the cooli-catchers Mundas?

No ! weavers, blacksmiths and the like also do that work. But now-a-days it is chiefly we, Mundas, who sell each other. The depôt-owners or their servants are thus utterly corrupting us, men and women, with greed for money.

bagrauchabaked' leako.

Chia ! kuṛikoo hoṛoko ãkiringdengakoako !

Hela gomke ! ena kam ituana ! Akoge puṛate dangṛiko *beda*-üṛungkoak. Okonido misi-*te-a* karedo bau-*te-a'* hon kupulo'tee jdiia ente eta' arakatitatee jïmaia oṛo inigee chãlania. Ente enuter kuṛi environmental dangṛi engaapukinloe nãmbaṛaia oṛo khube gërangea. Okonido honte kuri nekage ãchuia; ju main am phalna dangṛi: dola ! Assamtelang sena mente phuslauidiime. *Honte-kuri* environmental dangṛi beda-daṛiaire ente baranking moiad arakatitateking sēna. Ente nido aṛaãkati-buṛia hon-*te*-kuri horaetee kūlruṛaia oṛate oṛo eṭani diputee chãlania.

Purat'edo piṭhu*langgeko* bēdakoa : rangakan lijako Üdubakoa, phuli-arkiteko būlkoa enteko ïdikoa ja htute Batai karedko Penrain karedo Rajputkoa orate.

Enkage bejaitijad'koako. Hoṛokoa dastur nekagea : Ja kuṛieṭa jatiren hoṛokoa oṛare musing mente jomked're karedo taejanre mod' nida, ente aea' hagako environmental kuṛi chïlaniako. Chikaeako tobe ! diputeko seno'gea, stkute karedo motaite.

Iduoṛo' ! enkan kajiko okoe bïswasea !

What ! do women too help to sell people?

Alas, Sir ! doest thou not know that ? They indeed (it is who) mostly cheat away young girls. Some (even) take a sister's or a senior brother's daughter to a visit and then make her over to another cooli-catcher and that one will send her off. Then that very woman will help the parents of that girl to seek her and she will weep and groan very much. Some will engage their own daughters like this (put up their own daughters to the following trick) : go child and keep cajoling such a girl : come on ! let us two go to Assam, saying. Then if their daughter succeeds in deceiving that girl, both will go together to some arkati-friend. Then that one will send the arkati-woman's daughter back home from the way and take the other one to the depot.

But chiefly they cheat them away on market days : they will show them some coloured cloth, make them drunk with strong mowa liquor and then they take them to some village to the house of some Blacksmith or Weaver or Rajput.

Like that they deprive them of their caste. The Mundas' custom is like this : Whenever any woman eats in the house of men of another caste or if she have remained there, one night, then her relations treat her as an out-cast. What are they to do then ! they are sure to go to the depot, freedly or else by force.

Strange ! who can believe such things !

Hela gomke ! am biswasreo kam biswasreo, enkagea. Am ïsu' din nerem taenre, entedo amo enam bujauia. Ne soben kajirea' sabuti nao aing omdaṛiamea. Leleme, honder Topadiren Guti-*ta'ren* kuṛi-hon As-samte senojanae. Hatomte...

Iminangge ! enarea sabuti kaïng namtana. Ama' huṛi-hon dipureko unkuki'amente ena chilekatem sabutiaña ?

Hon-*ing* hola oṛatee ruṛajana oṛo' aege udub'kiña. Somar Hulang idange idangre nirjanae dipuete. Environmental hulang neren naua padri-gomke Ranchiate ruralenae chi ka ?

Hege !

Oṛo' Sabunãrika gṛata ama dasi Sahadeo nutumteni, sandomloe tangikṛa chika, gaṛa parom mente ?

Ena Hege !

Enta'rege Sahadeoe lelurumki'a oro'e kajikia : Nege patri gomkee hijua. Ini' gaṛa parom-ked're ainglo Khuntite senome. Entare dipurenko kako nambaṛ-amea. Padri gomkeo lelkia oṛo Sahadeo : ne kuṛi tising idangre dipuete nirjanae mentee udu-baia. Gomke kachie udub'ad'-mea ?

Udub'ki'ñae mendo ni ama hon-*me* kuṛi taekenae mente kae torla. Amdo na'do chikanam chikaea ? Environmental Barwada-*ren* ho-ṛom nalisia chi ?

Chikanaing nalisia ! Ale don-ḍo Hoṛoko enkan kaji kachcherire kale sabuti daṛia. Okilko hati kutiko jïrabaralea, bo *biurd'eka,* ente borote

Alas Sir ! it is like that, whether, thou believest it or not. If thou remain long here then thou too wilt understand it. Of all this I can give thee proof even now. Look here, the other day the daughter of Guti of Topadi went to Assam. Her Aunt...

Enough ! I want no proof of that. But how doest thou prove that they hid thy own daughter in the depot ?

My child returned home yesterday and she herself has told it to me. On Monday very very early she ran away from the depot. On that same day the new Father of this place returned also from Ranchi, is it not.

Yes !

And did not thy servant, called (the one with the name) Sahadeo, waif for him with a pony near the Sabunrika river to cross the river ?

That too is true.

There Sahadeo recognized her and he told her : Just now the Father will come. When he has crossed the river, then go with me to Khunti, there the depot-men will not look for thee. The Father too saw her and Sahadeo told him: this woman ran away from the depot early to-day. Did not the Father tell it to thee?

He did tell me, but he did not know that that was thy daughter. But as for thee now, what art thou going to do ! wilt thout bring a case against that Barwada man ?

Why should I sue him ! We stupid Mundas can never prove such things in court. The pleaders cross-examine us in all kinds of ways *so as* jana jetanale jawabea oro' ente hakim alea' nalise dismisea. Hon-*ing*-kuring namruṛaaka'ia ! iminangee ! Oṛo' chikanaing namtana !

to make our heads turn, then out of fear we say anything at all and then the judge rejects our case. Now I have *got my daughter back ! That's enough*! What more do I want sill !

Mendo chikana mente Assamte sẽnpe borotana ? Enre oṛa', talab sobenape namea. Bagan-*ren* gomkeko besjad'peako oṛo mahata-ete Sarkarea hukumteo chandu chandu mod' taka talab'ko lajad'-pea.

But why do you fear to go to Assam ? There you get a house, pay and everything. The planters (the gentlemen of the gardens) treat you well, and since last year by the order of government they increase your pay one Rupee per month.

Hela gomke environmental mod' taka chikanale chika ! Talab huring-gea mentedo horoko kako ujurtana. Mendo akoa' uruleka kako hijuruar daria.

Alas Sir ! what are we to do with that one Rupee ! The people do not object saying : the pay is small. But they cannot come back as they lie (like their own desire). That's what we fear.

Enale borotana. Monre sirmarea' girmiti sahi-rĭkameako mendo gel sirmareo kam ruardaria ; okonido : he mar, monre sirmamenteng sena kajijada oro chiulao kae ruara. Sidaman chimin horoko, taekenako ne Munda disumre. N'ado huring-nogeako mente amom ituana gomke. Assamte idichabajad' leako' !

They make one (thee) sign an agreement for five years and one cannot even return after ten. Some people say : alright I will go for five years and they never return at all. How many people there were formerly in the Munda country ! And now, thou too knowest, Sir, that there are pretty few. They are taking us all to Assam.

Kako idichabapea ! Isugeko senakana, enado hege ! Nere sobenko asulotea nâm-dari-*janre* ka chimad'ko senkena honanga. Oro' isu Horoko akoa monsukute hanreko tâena. Hanre oṭe saham sobenako namakada mente.

The won't take all of you away! Many have gone, that's true ! If all had been able to find a living here they would most probably not have gone. And a great many Mundas remain over there out of their own free will, because there they have got land and wood and every-thing.

He gomke, tara mara monsukute hanreko taena mente, enadole ituana. Enreo, tara mara ruar sanajad'koa mendo kako daria. Oro' enale borotana. Alea' uru-leka hiju'-*senorikalere honanga* !

Yes Sir, we know that a certain number remain there of their own free will. Notwithstanding that, a certain number want to come back here but they cannot. And that is what we fear. If only they let us go and come according to our own free will !

XIV. EXERCISE

This Exercise explains the formation and uses of the Anterior Future, *the* Continuative Present *and the* Incomplete Past.

To this is added the whole theory of the Mundari Definite, Indefinite *and* Interrogative Demonstratives, *viz. 1° their form when they are used* adjectively *i. e. to specify a Noun ; 2° their formation when they are used as* Independent Pronouns.

THE ANTERIOR FUTURE

120. If is formed by suffixing *le* to the root, and denotes the priority of one future action over another future action.

121. Transitive Predicates insert both Direct and Indirect Objects between *le* and the Copula. The Indirect Objects are, however, not preceded by *a*. Thus: *om-le-ko-aing* may mean either : I shall first give *them* (v.gr. the horses) away to some one, or I shall first give it to *them*.

When the Pronouns ing or I' stand inserted as Objects, the *e* of *le* elides with the I of *ing* and with I'. The result is a long ï. In this elision the Pronoun I', *he* or *she*, loses its check. Thus : om-*liñ*-ae, he will first give to me ; ra-lï-aing, I shall first call him or her.

122. N. B.—Great attention must be paid to the correct pronunciation of these two forms, because they differ from the Anterior Pasy only by the absenceof the check on the I: *ra'-language-I'-ñae* means he first *called me*, *ra'-language-ï-ñ-ae* means he *will first call* me ; *ra'-language-I'-ae:* he first *called* him or her, *ra'-language-ï-ae* : he *will first call* him or her.

123. *Le* is not affixed as a mere Anterior Future Suffix to Intransitive Predicates, such as *sen, nir, hijw,* etc., in the Indicative Mood.

124. Intransitives form their Anterior Future in three different ways.

1st.—They may take the Suffix *ko*' after the root. This Suffix generally perfomrs the function of a Polite Precative or Optative, v. gr. *Dub'-ko'-aing* ? May I sit down, please? However, with Intransitive Predicates this function frequently disappears and it is simply equivalent to the Future in le used in Transitive Predicates; v. gr. *Orateng sen-ko'-a.* I shall first go home : *Pittelang sen-ko'-a*, Let us (thee and me) go *first* to the market.

2nd.—The Simple Future Tense may be preceded by the Adverbs *sida* or *sidate*, first; v. gr., *sida* or *sidate pittelang sena*, thou and I will first go to the market.

3nd.—The Adverb *sida* may be suffixed to the root just as *le* is suffixed in Transitive and *ko*' in Intransitive Predicates: thus: Nirsidaeaning, I will *first* run ; *nirsidaeam*, thou will *first* run.

This construction has, however, generally a different meaning; *Nirsidaeam*: Thou wilt be *the first* to run away. Here no precedence of one action over another is implied. In this sense, therefore, the form is a Simple and not an Anterior Future.

125. In the case of Transitive Predicates too the above constructions with *sida, sidate* are freely used instead of the Anterior Future in *le. Meromko har-sida-ko-aing* : I shall *first* drive the goats away.

If *sida* be suffixed to the root, inserted Indirect Objects are not preceded by *a. Talab om-sida-ko-aing*, I shall first give the wages to them.

THE CONTINUATIVE PRESENT

126. It is formed by suffixing the transitive Perfect Tense suffix *akad* to both Transitive and Intransitive Predicates.

127. The intransitive Suffix *akan* is used only with those Intransitives which denoe rest or stillness, such as *tingun* : to stand; *dub*' : to sit ; *giti* : to lie down ; *hapen* : to keep silence; and their synonyms.

Direct and Indirect Pronominal Objects stand between the Suffix *akad* and the Copula Indirect Objects are not preceded by *a*. The phonetic changes are the same as those indicated in the Perfect Tesne (cf. Part I No. 94)

128. The Continuative Present frequently takes the emphatic *ge*, which stands immediately before the Copula ; *sen-akad-ge-ae* : he keeps on walking or going ; *lel-akad'-ko-ge-ae* : he keeps looking at them ; *tingu-akan-ge-ae* : he continues standing all the while.

129. The Continuative Present implies that an action already begun will or must be continued *uninterruptedly* through the Present into the Future until certain circumstances or explicit orders cause it to cease. It is of course chiefly used in the Imperative Mood, as will be explained.

130. N. B.—The uninterrupted continuity here spoken of may apply either to *numerically the same act* or to *numerically distinct acts of a homogeneous series*. In the first case the Continuative Present denotes a physical continuity of one and the same act, *v. gr. go'akad'geaning* : I keep carrying it, i.e. I have never put it down for an instant. In the second case it denotes a morally uninterrupted continuity, and implies that each time an occasion presents itself for performing an act belonging to the series, that occasion will or may not be missed, *v. gr. Nao akoa disumre bolotanko goe'akadkogeako* : they still continue killing everyone who enters their country.

THE INCOMPLETE PAST.

131. – This Tense signifies that an action has been interrupted or broken off before it was completed. It generally implies an iutention of resuming and completing the action. By its very nature it is mainly limited to *Transitive Predicates.*

It is formed by suffixing *ken* to the root : ol-*ken-aing*, ol-*ken*-am, etc.

132. Pronominal Objects are not inserted. The reason is because in this form the subjective element of the action is insisted on ; in other words: the action is considered primarily as a past modification of the agent; hence it becomes virtually Intransitive. The form is often correctly rendered by the English phrase: *to have been busy doing this or that.* Enangsanj mad'ing *makena* : this morning I have been busy cutting bamboos (but I have not cut as many as I intend to cut).

DEFINITE DEMONSTRATIVE ADJECTIVES

133. *Ne*: this ; *environmental* : that; *han* : that, that ... yonder; *nimin* : this much of, this number of; *niminang* : just this much ; *imin* : that much, so much, *iminang* : just that much, just so many.

The forms *nimin* and *imin* qualify Nouns denoting animate beings, whereas *niminang* and *iminang* qualify Nouns denoting inanimate objects.

Ne sadom tasad' omaime : Give grass to *this* horse. *Environmental* koṛako ra'aukom Call *those* men hither. *Han* dangr'aking manḍi idiakingmc Take food to *yonder* two young men. *Nimin* hoṛoko lelkad'koaing : I saw so *many* men. *Niminang* taka gachauakoaing : I'll promise them *this much money*. *Imin* honko ituked'koae : He has taught *so many* children. *Iminang* oteng akiringamea : I'll sell *so much* land to thee.

N. B.—The strong form *hen* for *environmental* is sometimes used to express hatred or contempt, v. gr. *Hen* arakatiko : *Those scoundrels* of coolicatchers. *Hen* gaasiko ! *Those wretched* gaasis.

INDEFINITE DEMONSTRATIVE ADJECTIVES

134. *Jeta*: some, any ; *ja* : any at all. These two are used only with Nouns denoting animate beings.

Jetan : some, any ; *jan* : some, any. These are used only with Nouns denoting inan, objects.

The following are used indifferently with any kind of Nouns :

Oko : some.
mid' (*miad', moiod' or mod'*) : one, some one.
huṛing (huḍuring) : a few, a little
hupuṛing : very little, very few.
huṛingleka : some few, a little.
isw : many. Much,
Pura' : many, much.
isupura' : very many, very much,

tara tarara (tatara) : a certain number, a certain amount of.
tara mara : a certain number, a certain amount of.
nimpirung (nimpirang) : this little, this trifling amount of.
jaiminung (jaiminang) : any number of , any amount of.
oro' (odo') : more
eta' : other, another.

Ja hoṛo omaime : Give it to any man *whom so ever*. *Jeta* dasiking kulkingme: Send *any* two of the servants. *Jetan* daru ma'eme : Cut down *some* (one) tree. *Jan* loyong kiringaingme : Buy for me *any* rice-field *at all*. *Oko* honko ituntabeako, *oko* honkodo kako ituntabea: *Some* children learn quickly whereas others (literally: but *some* children) do not learn quickly. *Mid'* horo seno'kae ! Let *some one* man go ! *Huringleka* chauli omaime ! Give him a *little* rice. Hola horare *isupura'* horokoing lelked'koa : yesterday I saw a great *many* men on the road. *Nimpirung* diri upunialeka halangaingme : Pick up for me some four or five *little* stones *of this size* ! *Tara horokoe* halrurad'koa : He has repaid several men. *Jaiminung* Dikuko kale boroakoa : We are not afraid of *any number of* Hindus. Oro horoko achukom ! Engage *more* men !

135. REMARK.—The Enclitic *ge* is always suffixed to the above Demonstratives in short replies to questions, when the Noun qualified by the Interrogative in the question, is understood but not expressed in the answer.

Chimin horoko senako ? How many men will go ? *Purage* : Many. Oro manding omamea ? Shall I give you more cooked rice ? He mar oroge ! Alright (give) more !

INTERROGATIVE ADJECTIVES

136. *Oko* ? What ? *Chikan* ? *what* kind or what sort of ? *Chilekan* ? what quality or description ? *Chimin* ? how many ? (is used with Nouns denoting animate beings). *Chiminang* ? how much ? how many (used with Nouns denoting inanimate objects).

Oko darum akiringea ? *What* tree wilt thou sell ? Ne daruge. This tree. *Chikan* darum akiringea ? *What kind* of a tree wilt thou sell ? Uli daruge. A mangoe tree. *Chilekan* darum akiringea, huringa chi maparanga ? *What description of tree* wilt thou sell, a small one or a very big one ? Han salangi daruge. Yonder high tree. *Chimin* horoko hijulenako ? *How many* men came ? Huringlekage. A few. Chiminang baba potomakadae ? How much rice has he stored or packed ? Isupurage. A very great quantity. *Chiminang* takako halaiña ? *How many* rupees are they going to pay to me.

II

DEFINITE DEMONSTRATIVE PRONOUNS.

137. The Definite Demonstrative Pronouns are formed by suffixing the Simple Personal Pronouns of the Third Person *i'*, *king*, *ko* to the Definite Demonstrative Adjectives *ne, environmental* an *han*, when the Demonstrative Pronouns denote animate beings. The Impersonal Pronoun *a'* is suffixed when the Demonstrative Pronouns denote inanimate objects.

138. REMARK 1.— A few phonetic changes occur when the Pronouns are suffixed to *ne* and *environmental* : 1° the *e* of *ne* falls away ; hence the form ni'' instead of *nei.* 2° in the Dual the *e* is changed into a simple *I* for the sake of making it harmonize better with the i of king ; hence niking instead of *neking.* 3° This simple i of the Dual is generally kept in the Plural, though not always. If kept it influences the *0* of *ko* and raises it to an *u* ; hence niku instaed of *niko.* If the simpel i be not kept then the regular form *neko* is ued. 4° The initial *e* of environmental, being influenced by the suffixed I and king, becomes a simple i in the Singular and Dual; hence the forms ini' instead of eni, inking instead of enking. In the Plural the initial e is sometimes kept and then the regular form *enko* is used. But more frequently the i of the Singular and Dual is transferred also into the Plural. Then the form *inku* is used.

Singular.		*Dual.*		*Pural.*	
An. Bgs. *ni*	: this one.	*Niking*	: these two.	*Neko or niku*	: those ones.
In.objs. *nea'*	: this one.	*Nea'*	: these two.	*Nea'*	: these ones.
An. Bgs, *ini'*	: that one.	*Inking*	: those two.	*Niku or enko*	: those ones.
In. objs.*ena'*	: that one.	*Ena'*	: those two.	*Ena'*	: those ones.
An.bgs, *hani'*	: yonder one.	*Hanking*	: yonder two.	*Hanko*	: yonder ones.
In. objs, *hana'*	: yonder one.	*Hana'*	: yonder two.	*Hana'*	: yonder ones.

139. REMARK 2.—No Phonetic change takes place when the Personal Pronouns are suffixed to the strong form *hen* : that. Hence *heni'* : *henking* : those two ; *henko* : those ones.

140. REMARK 3.—In some parts the Pronominal forms *nea, ena, hana* are frequently used as Adjectives instead of the real Adjective forms *ne, environmental , han.* Thus : *nea* daru instead of *ne* daru : *ena* hatu instead of *environmental* hatu ; *hana* buru instead of *han* buru.

INDEFINITE DEMONSTRATIVE PRONOUNS

141. These are obtained by suffixing either the Personal Pronouns or the Definite Demonstrative Pronouns to the Indefinite Adjectives.

The Personal Pronouns are suffixed to : *oko, ja, jeta, jan, jetan*. The Definite Demonstrative Pronouns are suffixed to *oko* and *eta*'. The Impersonal or Neuter forms are obtained by suffixing the Neuter Pronoun *a'* to the Indefinite Adjectives.

142. Phonetic changes occurring in these compounds :

1° The Pronominal suffix *i*' is softened down into *e* whenever it is preceded by a vowel. Thus : *okoe* instead of *okoi*'.

2° The Singular *jae* : *any one at all*, always takes the Enclytic *ge*- The Adjective *ja* never takes the Impersonal suffix *a'*.

3° *Eta*' always takes the Simple Suffixes *king* and *ko* in the Dual and Plural.The Impersonal form of *eta'* always inserts an euphonic *q* befre the suffix *a'*. The jerk (') falls away from the *a'* of *eta'* Hence the form *etaga'* : another one.

4° In some districts the Impersonal *a'* hardly keeps anything of the jerk denoted by (') in any of the Inanimate Pronouns.

143. *Singular.* *Dual.* *Plural.*

Amin.	bgs. *oko-e*	: some one.	*oko-king*	some	*oko-ko*	: some
In.	objs. *oko-a'*	: something.		two.		one's.
Anim.	bgs. *oko-ni'* some	... *okoni'* : ... others.				
Anim.	bgs. *ja-ege*	: any one at all.	*ja-king*	: any two at all.	*ja-ko*	: any one's at all.
Anim	bgs, *ja-ni'*	: any one.	*jan-king*	: any two.	*jan-ko*	: any one's.
In.	objs. *jan-a'*	: anything.				
Anim.	bgs. *jeta-e*	some one.	*jeta-king*	: some	*jeta-ko*	: some
In	objs. *jeta-a'*	something.		two.		ones.
Anim.	bgs. *jeta-ni'*	any one, someone.	*jetan-king*	: some two.	*jetan-ko*	: some ones.
In.	obj. *jetan-a'*	anything. something.				
Anim.	bgs. *eṭa-ni*	another one.	*eṭa-king*	: two others	*eta'-ko*	: others, other ones.
In.	onj. *eṭa-ga'*	another thing.				

144. Of the Dual and Plural forms given above *eta'king* and *eta'ko* are the only ones that are used regularly,The others are seldom heard. Instead of *okoko* the reduplication *okoe okoe* or *okoeteko* is generally used. *Okoe okoe* ko hijujana: Some of them have come. *Okoeteko* seno'a ? Who are going ?

The Singular form *okoe* has often a Plural function in negative propositions. In that case it generally takes the suffix *0* : even. Thus : *Okeo* bangkoa :Literally: they are not here (not) even some one, i.e. There is nobody here.

145. Okoni' .... Okoni' is used in disjunctive propositions. Though it have a Plural meaning, its Predicate stands in the Singular. The repeated form generally takes the Suffix *do. Okoni'* dariae *okoni'do* kae daṛia : Some people can afford it whereas others cannot afford it.

146. The forms *ja-ege, jeta-e, ja-ni'* and *jeta-ni'* are chiefly used with a Plural function. In negative propositions *jetae, jani'* and *jetani'* generally take the Suffix *o* : even.

Hence when they stand as subject of a proposition, the corresponding Predicate takes the Plural form, v. gr. *Jetaeo bangkoa'* : There is nobody here.

When they stand as Direct or Indirect Object, the Pronoun *ko* must be inserted into the Predicate as Repeated Direct Object or *ako* as Repeated Indirect Object, v. gr. *Jaege* ra'*aukom* : Call hither any one at all. *Jani'* oma*kom* :Give it to any one.

147. REMARK. — Negative Pronouns such as v. gr. The Latin *nemo* : *Nobody*, do not exist in Mundari. The deficiency is supplied by *bano'* : not to exist, or : not to be present, or by the Particle *ka,* in conjunction with the positive forms.

The Predicate *bano'* may either precede or follow its Pronominal Subject, v. gr. Jetaeo *bangkoa*, or Bankoa jetaeo : There is nobody here.

The Negative Particle *ka* may either be placed after the Pronominal Subject then be followed by the Predicate v. gr. Jetaeo *kako* hiju'jana : Nobody has come. Or the Pronoun may be placed after the Predicate. In this case too *ka* precedes the Predicate v. gr. *Kako* hijujana jetaeo. The same order is followed when the Neuter forms are used : Jetana' *ka* uiu'jana or *Ka* uiu'jana jetana : Nothing has fallen.

148. A certain number of Indefinite Demonstrative Adjectives perform the function of Indefinite Demonstrative Pronouns without taking any Pronominal Suffix. All of them may stand indiscriminately for Nouns denoting animate beings or for such as denote inanimate objects. With the exception of *miad'*, they all have a Plural meaning. But *miad'* too is construed as though it were a Plural.

Miad,'	one.	*huṛing huring,*	very few, very little.
tara		*huḍuring,*	
taratra	pretty many	*huṛing* huṛingleka	very few, a very
taramara	Pretty much.	*huring huḍuringleka*	litle.
pura',	many, much.	*kented',*	a great many, large
insupura',	very much.		numbers ; plenty,
	very much.		heaps of.
huring, :	a few, a little	*mer mer,*	immense numbers,
huṛingleka,			no end of.

149. N. B.—*Miad'* always takes the suffix *o*, and is used only in Negative Propositions. The others generally take the Enclytic *ge*.

Miad'o bangkoa : there is not even a single one here. *Pura'ge* menakoa : there are many present. *Mer mergeko* hundiakana : large crowds are gathered.

DEFINITE INTERROGATIVE PRONOUNS

150. The Definite Interrogative Pronouns are formed either by suffixing the Definite Demonstrative Pronoun to the Indefinite Demonstrative Adjective *oko* or by suffixing the Personal and Impersonal Pronouns to the Definite Demonstrative Adjectives *chikan, chilekan.*

REMARK.— The Definite Demonstrative Pronoun ni' sometimes drops the *i'* in the Dual and Plural. Hence the forms *okonking* ? *and okonko* ?

An. b	*Oko-ni*?	Which one ?	*Okoniking ?*	Which	*Okoniku* ?	Which
In. o.	*Oko-nea'* ?	Which one ?		two ?		ones ?

An. b, *Chikan-i* ?	What kind one ?	*Chikan-king ?*	Two of what kind ?	*Chika-ko* ?	What kind ones ?
In. o. *Chikan-a'* ?	What kind one ?				
An. b. *Chilekan-i*?	Which like one ?	*Chilekan-king* ?	Which like two ?	Chilekan-ko?	Which like ones ?
In. o. *Chilekan-a*'?	What like one ?				

Okonking mena'kinga ? Which two are there ? Sōma Pakutaking : Soma and paku. *Chikanko* hijulenako, Uraon chi Horoko ? What kind of people came, Uraons or Mundas ? Chilekanking hende chi eselgeaking ? What were the two like, black or fair ?

INDEFINITE INTERROGATIVE PRONOUNS

151. The Indefinite Demonstrative Pronouns given n° 142 may be used as Indefinite Interrogative Pronouns. What has been said there concerning the Dual and Plural forms as well as the Plural function of the Singular forms holds good also when those forms are used as Interrogative Pronouns.

Okoe ? Who ? frequently forms its Dual Plural by inserting *Technology* or ta between the Singular form okoe and the Suffixes king and ko : Thus : okoeteking? or okoetaking ? : who to ? ; *okoeteko* ? or *okoetako* ? : who ?

N. B.— Lists of new words will no longer be prefixed to the subsequent exercis, Idiomatic expressions will be indicated by being underlined in the Mundari text as well as in the corresponding English translations.

Naian Haram—Tobedo Soma am na'do nere *mali*-em kamitana ?	So then Soma thou art now working here (as) *gardener* ?
Soma—Hege ! turui chanduta'ete.	Yes for six months.
N. H.—Gomke chiminang talabe omamtana ?	How much pay does the gentleman give thee ?
S—*Chandu-chandu* monre taka.	Five Rupees *monthly*.
N. H.—Ke ! Han Asam chanbaganreo mon-monre takako kamia chandur chandu. Amdoama ora-duar japare aminangem *halangjada*! ad' oro' kami rabalge lelo'tana, *Majjaem* namakada amdo !	Indeed ! In the far-away Assam gardens too they work (get) five Rupees a months. But thou art picking up that much before thy house door ! and then the work looks easy too. Thou hast got *high life* indeed ! (anything easy, pleasant, to one's entire liking is called majja).

Chikanamente ne began *aminanggem kanda-kandaakadam* ?

Why *hast thou divided* this garden into so many *little plots* (parterres) ?

S.—Gomke enkage hukumakaiña. Akoa dastur judagea. *Kisim-kisimrea'ko* rōaea : mod' kandare risa-said, mod' kandare poṭom-salad, ed' enkage *kanda kandare* haṭikutiko hērea ad'ko gāchia adko rōa-ruraea : seleriko, salgamko, gajarako, matarko, likpiajuko, potom-kobiko, ba-kobiko, parsiliko, kiresko ad' eta—eta' arako, abu Horoko chiulao ka *lelakad*lekana.

The master has ordered me like that. Their ways are different (from ours). They plant all kinds of things : in one parterre endives (curled salad), in another lettuce (bundled up-salad) and so on, in *different parterres* (each in its own parterre) they sow, repick and replant all sorts of things : celery, turnips, carrots, peas, leek, cabbage (bundled up cabbage), caull-flower (flower-cabbage) three four kinds of beans, parsley, cress and sundry other vegetables, *the like of which* we Mundas have never seen, [litrly (as) we Mundas have never seenlike ones].

N.H. —Kiresem *menla'*, ena chikana' ?

Thou *didst say cress(just now)*. What kind of thing is that !

S.— Ena'do miad' aṛage; *berelteko* jômea.

That's one (kind of) herb; they eat it *raw* (without boiling).

N. H —Chilekan aṛa ?

What's like (what like herb) ?

S.—Dunguigea, *ibil-ibilge* omonoa ad' *risa risage. Tagoelere* abua mani-aṛaleka at'karoa'. Chaoṇ-chaoṇtana

It is short and comes up densely and it is curly. *If (one) masticate* it, it tastes like our mustardleaf vegetable. It is pungent.

N. H. — Piajūkodoing jomakada. Mendo likpiaj ena' chilekana' ?

As for onions, those I have eaten. But what is leek like (what-like thing is it) ?

S.— Ena'do piajūleka tejge at'karoa mendo red' jaked sojege ad'etangnogc taena ; da bano'a.

That tastes smart like onions ; but it remains straight and pretty thin down to the root ; *there is no bulb*.

N.H. —Selerido chikana'geko sëleria ?

What kind of thing do they call celery ?

S.— Ena'do *Belaitiuter jati*. Ne disumre jango ka jangoa. Tejge ad' judauterge soana. Aingdo kaing sūkua. Khub' saralere hobaoa karedo ka, Baksareko hērea, ente gachiled'chi ikirno gaṛareko rōaea. Entedo haranojanchi environmental garageke pēre'-dīa.

That is *something altogether European*. It won't even grow into seeds in this country (seed even it won't become seed). It smells very strongly and *quite differently (from anything I know)*. I for one do not like it. If one manure (the ground) very much it succeeds (it becomes) otherwise not. They sow it in a box, then after having

N. H. — Moiod' ara mente aminanggechiko kamia !

S.—Akoa *jati* enkagea ; sobena *baibaite*ko rîkaea.

N. H.— Ene' gomkee hijutana ! erangiñae chi ?

S.—Kae erangmea ; chikanamentee erangmea ?

N. H. — Mar gomke joar !

Gomke. — Chi Naian Haṛam ! maliem dengaja'ia?

N. H. — Dengado gomke ka ! Ape gomkeko *chiļeka-chilekatepe* bãganea enaing leltana. Apea dastur judautergea ! miad'o ale Horokoleka kape rĩkaea. Chikanam herjada, chilekate omono'a mente ena sobena' ne Soma koraing kulija'ia.

G. — Entedoe udubad'mea ?

N. H. — Oko-okoado udubaiña, oko-okoado aurige. *Hatikutidangpe* hërea ape. Chikana' chilekana mente, iduoro mod' pitreo kaing ïtuchabeaea *ja*' !Okoape *kirësia*, okoapa *sëleria*, okoado *chikanape lütumbaraìa* ! rokage okoe ero' sobena' pähamdaria ?

Enkana ne distire lelo kale lelakada oro lutumo kale lutumakada.

G.——Apeodang *kisim-*

first repicked it, they plant it in a pretty deep trench. And then when it has grown pretty much they keep filling in that trench.

What ! They work that much for the sake of one vegetable !

Their *nature* is like that ; they set about (do) everything *with care and trouble.*

There the gentleman is coming! will he scold me ?

He won't scold thee ; why should he scold thee ?

Good day. Sir !

Well old man (Elder) Naian ! art thou helping the gardener ?

Not exactly helping, Sir ! I am just looking *how you* (gentlemen) *arrange a garden*. Your ways are altogether different. You do everthing differently from us Mundas. (Not even one thing do you do like we Mundas). I am asking this (man) Soma what he is sowing and *how it appears when sprouting.*

Then did he explain it to thee ?

Some things he explained (to me) and some not yet. *You people forsooth* you sow *no end of differnet things*. What kind of things ? and what like ? *Well I suppose* I could not learn it all in a whole week. What thing you call cress. What *you call celery* and what (other things) *you call by what names*! who *indeed* can remember all that *at* once ?

In this country we have neither seen *such things* nor have we a name for them. (As for seeing, we have not even seen them, and as for naming, we have also not named them).

But surely you too plant *various*

kisimrea-pe röaea.

N.H. —Ela gomke ! aledo jargidadipli mod' barialekale röaea ente orodo ka.

G—Chikanape roaea ?

N.H.—Kakaruko, taiarko, kaitako, jhingako, ad manalko ; okonido nea, okonido ena ora *kundamasarele* hërea, ente jajetalekan koto jakãmentele bidea ad entele *bageta*. Hobajanre hobaoa karedo ka.

G.—*Rabangdinkore* chika'-namente jetana kape rõaea ? Gajãrako, salgamko, kobiko, aluko *rabangsa'* khub hobaoa' honanga apea bakrire ; *sarate* hende'gea *dang*.

N. H.— Ena'do hege ! Mendo jang okorele nāmea ? *Bulungtamaku* kīringmente paisa kale pūrau daiṛa ; *nelekan* Belaiti hitako chinatele kiringea honanga' !

G.— Dola bangalote ! Kobi –jang ad' salgam-janging omamea !

N. H.— Ka Gomke ! Kaing herea. *Nekana* khub paṭaulere *hobaoa* karedo ka. Kuaṇdo chiulao kale gaṛaakada ad' ḍaritale sangingea. *Okoe oro* dinaki pataumente da' goau? pâṭaulermo samagea : simko, mẹromko, uriko jetana kako *banchauia; miado kako sareia ja.*

kinds of things.

Ela ! Sir ! we plant one or two things *in the rainy season* and then no more.

What kind of things do you plant ?

Pumpkins, cucumbers, kaiṭhas jhinga and beans ; one will sow this, another one the other *at the back of the house*, then we stick a branch of any shape by way of stalk and then we leave *things to their own fate*. If they succeed they succeed, but if not then not.

Why don't you plant anything *in the cold season* ? Carrots, turnips, cabbages and potatoes would succeed splendidly during the cold season in your gardens ; for they (the gardens) are black with manure.

That is true ! But where are we to get the seeds from ? We cannot (i.e., we often can hardly) get enough money *for our weekly market purchases* (literally : do buy tobacco and salt). With what would or could we pay European seeds *like this* !

Come on to the bungalow ! I will give thee cabbage seeds and turnip seeds.

No, Sir ! I won't sow (any). *Things like these* (vegetable) *succeed* if one water them very much, otherwise they don't But we never have dug any wells, and our *village-spring* is far away. *Who in the world* is going to fetch water every day to water ! And even if one were to water them it would be useless : the fowls, the goats and the bullocks won't *spare* anything, they *would* not *leave* even a *single* (plant).

G.—Bakṛibiurlerem tobe ?

N. H. —Enreo ka Gomke ! Simko meromko kam daiakoa, bakṛiteo ka. Alelo miad' oṛareko tâena ad' janam chikalereo musingeko paromea ad sobena'ko jom-chabaea. Leleme Gomke ! maha am Sarwadren Gaasi muṇda kobi gachin omlia' chi ka ! Entedo oṛa' kundamsa' roaked'chie bakṛibiurtada ad' *paṭauidijadae paṭauidijadae.* Na do taiarakanatae kobi ! Khube rasikalena. Meangkotelang jomea mente Sau koṛae neutakia. Entedo environmental hulang uterge aea merom *chilekatee paromjana chilekate ka*, mendo kobi *jomchabatanure* Gaasi environmental merome teba'kia ; kentedo khisjanchi enta'rege koṛam-goeuterta'ia. Entedo Sau koṛatate senojanchie metaitana : Meromdo kobitaing jomakadae ! Chikaealang oṛo' na'do ! Mar merombu jomia. Entedo goṭa haturen koṛakoe achuked'koa : mod' *sanjgeko* sia'ia oṛo aege meromjilue omad'koa.

But if thou wert to put a hedge round !

Not even then, Sir ! You *can't get over hens and goats*, not even by means of a hedge. They live in the same house with us and whatever you may do, some day they will get accross or thorugh (the hedge) and then they will eat up everything. Look here, Sir! last year you gave cabbage seedlings to Gaasi Munda of Sarwada, is it not? Then he, having planted them at the back of his house, put a hedge around and he *goes on watering and watering*! Now at last his cabbages are ready ! he got quite happy. Then he invited Sau saying : After to-morrow we shall eat (cabbage). And then that very day his own goat, *nobody knows how* got through (into the garden), but Gaasi came on that goat *just as it was finishing off his* cabbages. Getting mighty angry he clubbed her to death on the spot. Then he went to Sau and said : The goat has eaten my cabbages. What can you and I do now ! We shall eat the goat. And then he engaged the men of the whole village: They ploughed for him half a day and he gave them goat's flesh.

XV EXERCISE.

This Exercise shows how the want of Relative Pronouns *is compensated for in Mundari. It further explains the formation and use* of those very characteristic Predicates *which, for want of a better name, are called* Static forms.

152. There are no Relative Pronouns in Munḍari.

153. The deficiency of Relative Pronouns is compensated in various ways.

(1) The Bare *Tense-forms* of Transitive or Intransitive Predicates, being used as Participal Adjectives, yield Subordinate Relative Clauses.

The term Bare *Tense-form* is here used to denote that part of any Transitive or Intransitive Predicate which signifies an action or state, together with the circumstances of Voice, Mood and Tense ; hence it contains the primary root *plus* all those secondary elements which connote Voice, Mood and Tense. Thus the Bare Tense-form of the Predicate *sen* : to go is *sen* or *sesen* in the Interminate Tense ; in theSimple Future it is sen, in the Simple Present it is sentan; in the Simple Past it is *senken*, etc., etc.

154. All Bare Tense-forms may be used adjectively to qualify a Noun. If so used they precede the Noun, and together with it are equivalent to an English Relative Clause v. gr. *Senken dasi* : the servant *who went ; senken dasiking* : the two servants *who went senken dasiko* : the servants *who went.*

We may therefore, from the English point of view, lay down the following rule :

155. In order to transform *any Mundari proposition* into a *sub ordinate Relative Clause*, place the subject of that proposition immediately behind the Predicateand deprive the predicate of its Copula and its Pronominal Subject.

REMARK.— Demonstrative and Indefinite Pronouns qualifying the subject of the proposition do naturally no longer occur in the Relative Clause.

Ne dasi dakoṛa'te sesen-ae	: This servant always goes to the postoffice.
Dakoṛa'te sesen dasi	: *the servant, who always goes* to the post office.
Environmental hoṛoko gapa Ranchite-ko sen-a	: Those men will go to Ranchi to-morrow.
Gapa Ranchite *sen hoṛoko*	: The men, who will go to Ranchi to-morrow.
Hanre *sadomtam nirtance*	: Thy horse is running away over there.
Hanre *nirtaṇ sadomtam*	: Thy horse, *which is running away* over there.
Honder ne dasiking birte-king senkena	: Before yesterday these two servatns went to the forest.
Honder birete *senken dasiking*	: The two servants, *who went* to the forest before yesterday.
Honme kora mad'-e ma'jan-a	: Thy son is gone to cut bamboos.
Mad' majan honme kora	: Thy son, *who went to cut* bamboos.

156. Nouns qualified by these Bare Tense-forms may stand as Subject, as Predicate, as Direct or Indirect Object or perfomr any other function in a new proposition. And in this way Mundari renders any *Compound English sentences* Containing a principal clause *plus* a subordinate relative clause. By one *simple proposition* having but one subject and one Predicate.

Subj. *Pred.*

Dakorate seasen dasi hasutanae : The servant, *whose business it is to go to the postoffice*, is sick.

Subj *Predicate.*

Ne horo *gomkea dakorate seasen dasi tani* : This man is that servant of the gentleman *whose business it is to go to the post office.*

Direct Object. *Predice.* *Sub.*

Ranchite senken dasiking lelked'kinga –ing : I saw the two servants who *went to Ranchi.*

Indirect Object *Dir. Obj.* *Predic.* *Subj.*

Honorataete ruarakea honko mandi omakoa-ing : I shall give their meal to the boys *who have returned from the walk.*

Apposition to Subject. *Subj.* *Predicate.*

Mad' ma'jan dasia aputee hijuakana : The father of the servant, *who went to cut bamboos*, has arrived.

157. Instead of qualifying a Noun the Bare Tense-forms may qualify a Personal or a Definite Demonstrative Pronoun. The Pronouns thus qualified are suffixed to the Bare Tense-forms.

The Compounds thus obtained are real *Nouns of Agency* which must generally be rendered into English by *Relative Clauses* :

Intransitive Tense-forms ending in a vowel take the Demonstrative suffix *ni*, those ending in a consonant take the Personal Pronoun *i*.

These Compound Nouns form their Dual and Plural according to the ordinary rules.

INTRANSITIVES

Indet. *sesen-i'; sesen-king; sesen-ko* : the one who always goes; the two who…, those who…

S.Fut. *hiju-ni'; hiju'-king; hiju'-ko* : the one who will come the two who…, those who …

S. Pres. *hiju'tan-i; hiju'tan-king; hiju'tan-ko* : the one who comes; the two who…, those…

S. Past { *hiju'len-i ; hiju'len-king* ; hiju'len-ko : the one who came; the two who…, those…
senken-i; senken-king; senken-ko : the one who went; the two who …, those… etc.

TRANSITIVES

158. Transitive Compounds of this kind keep the inserted *Pronominal Direct* and Indirect Objects. In the Singular they always take *ni'* as suffix, even if the Compound ends in a consonant.

INDETERMINATE TENSE

itu-ing-ni'	*itu-ing-king*	*itu-ing-ko*
itu-me-ni'	*itu-me-king*	*itu-me-ko*
itu-i-ni'	*itu-i-king*	*itu-i-ko*
itu-lang-ni'	*itu-iang-king*	*itu-lang-ko*
Itu-ling-ni'	*itu-ling-king*	*itu-ling-ko*
Itu-ben-ni'	*itu-ben-king*	*itu-ben-ko*
Itu-king-ni'	*aking itu-king*	*itu-king-ko*
Itu-bu-ni'	*itu-bu-king*	*itu-bu-ko*
Itu-le-ni'	*itu-le-king*	*itu-le-ko*
Itu-pe-ni'	*itu-pe-king*	*itu-pe-ko*
Itu-ko-ni'	*itu-ko-king*	*ako itu-ko*
The two who teach me, thee, him or her etc. or my, thy, his or her etc. two teacher.	The one who teachers me, thee, him or her etc. or my, thy, his or her etc. teacher.	Those who teach me, thee, him or her etc. or my, thy, his or her etc. teacher.

REMARK 1.— Since the Indeterminate Tense denotes regularly returning and therefore also professional occupations, it is evident that transitive Compounds of this Tense may frequently be translated by English Nouns qualified by a Possessive Adjective, as shown in the above scheme.

REMARK 2.—In all Tense where the Pronominal Objects *king* and *ko* immediately precede the suffixes *king* and *ko*, the Objects are by preference placed before the Compound in their emphatic form. Hence: *aking-ituking* the two who teach these two or both teachers of these two instead of : *ituking-king*.

SIMPLE FUTURE

Gapa ra'-ing-ni', gapa, ra'-me-ni', gapa ra'-i-ni', etc. The one who will call me, thee, him or her to-morrow.

But: Gapa *aking ra-king* : the two who will call both of the to-morrow. Gapa *ako ra'-ko* : those who will call them to-morrow.

FUT. WITH INDIR. OBJECT : *Om-aing-ni', om-ame-ni', om-ai-ni', etc.*: the one who will give it to me, thee, him or her, etc.

Om-alang-king, om-aling-king, om-aben-king, akingta' om-king : the two who will give ti to thee and me, etc., etc.

PRESENT WITH DIRECT OBJECT : *Dengaja'-ing-ni', dengajad'-me-ni' dengaja-i-ni*, etc. : the one who is helping me, thee, etc.

Dengaga'-ing-ko, dengajad'-bu-ko, dengajad'-pe-ko, ako dengajad'-ko : those who help me, you and me, you , them.

DEF. PRESENT WITH INDIRECT OBJECT : *Om-aing-tan-i', om-ame-tan-i', om-ai-tan-i'* : the one who gives, it to me, thee etc.

Om-aling-tan-king, om-aben-tan-king, om-aking-tan-king : the two who give it to me and them, to you two, to both of them.

SIMPLE PAST WITH DIRECT OBJ. : *Ra'ki-ñ-ni'-ra'ked-me-ni', ra'ki-ni'*, etc. ; the one who called, me thee, him or her, etc.

Ra'ked'-lang-king, ra'ked'-ling-king, ra'ked'benking, but. : aking ra'-ked'king or aking ra'kenking (see below p. 94, No. 160).

SIMPLE PAST WITH INDIRECT OBJECT : *Oma'-ing-ko, omad'-me-ko, ema'-i-ko* : those who gave it to me, thee, him or her, etc.

But : *Akingta' omked' king* or *omkenking* and *akota' omked' ko* oro *emkenk* : the two who gave it to both and those who gave it to them.

ANT. PAST. : *Ra'li'-ko* : those who first called him.

PERFECT : *Haruṛungakai'-ko bu naliskoa* : Let us bring a case against those who have driven him out.

159. When Transitive Tense-forms qualify a Noun, the insertion of Pronominal Objects of the 1st and 2nd persons Singular, Dual and Plural is considered rather heavy and therefore often avoided, in some Tenses more, in others less.

When this is the case the Pronominal Objects stand before the Bare Tense in their emphatic form. Indirect Objects then take an appropriate Postposition.

Indeterm. Tense.

Aing barhi-kami *itu* Diku, rather than : barhi-kami *itu-ing* Diku : the Hindu *who teaches me carpentry.*

Am mente Mãnḍi buṛa, rather *Manḍi-ame buṛia,* : the old woman *who (always) cooks for thee.*

Simple Future

Aben sab sipaiking hiju'tanaking, rather than ; *sab-ben* sipaiking : The two constables *who will arrest you two*, are coming.

Abu nagente gowa hoṛoko karachabu omakoa, rather than : *gowa-abu* hoṛoko, Let us give food and travelling expenses to the men, *who will give evidence for us.*

160. When the Pronominal Objects are not inserted in the Bare Tense-forms, but placed before it, then the specifically Transitive Tense Suffixes *jad* (Present) and *ked* (Simple Past) are generally replaced by the corresponding Intransitive suffixes *tan* and *ken.*

But in the Anterior Past, the Perfect and the Static Past the Transitive Suffixes *led*, *akad*, and *tad* must be kept even if the Objects are not inserted.

Simple Past

Ale denga-ken Uraoṇko, rathern than : *dengaked'-le* Uraonko : the Uraons who helped us.

Apeta'tie chitti olken hagako rather than : chiṭṭi *ol' ked-pe hagako* : the brethren who wrote a letter to you.

Present Tense.

Alang loṛo-tan sipai, rather than : lorojad'*-lang sipai*; the constable *who is on the look out to catch thee and me.*

Aling talab omtan gomke, rather than : talab *omalingtan* or omjad'ling gomke : the gentleman, *who gives wages to him and me.*

Tamli'-ing, tamled'-me, tamled-lang, etc., koṛa : the man who struck me, thee, thee and me, etc., or : Aing, am, alang tam-*led* koṛa, *never tam-len koṛa.*

Ra'aka-ing dasi or Aing ra'-akad' dasi : the servant who has called me.

Omaka'-ing, omakad'-me gomke, or Aingta, amta' *om-akad'* gomke : the gentleman who gave it to me, to thee, etc.

Ale toltad' daroga, seldom *toltad'* le daroga : the darogah who has put these handcuffs on them and me (who has tied us and keeps us tied).

REMARK.— When it is not absolutely required to lay stress on the particular nuances or relations of time expressed by the Anterior Past, the Perfect and the Static Past, the Mundas very frequently substitute the Simple Past Suffix *ken* for *led*, *akad* and *tad* in Relative Clauses.

Thus : aing, am, alang, aling, aben, abu, ale, ape neuta-ken Soma stands often for aing, etc., *neutaled* or *neutaakad* or *neutad* Soma.

161. Whenever the Direct or Indirect Object of a Bare Tenseform used as Relative Clause is a Pronoun in the 3rd Pers. Singular, it must be inserted.

Soma tol-i darogah: The darogah who will handcuff Soma.

Dal-*ja'i* sipaikingbu harkinga : let us drive away the constables who beat him.

Denga-*ki*' dasi ra'auime : Call the servant who helped him.

Kula goea-*kai'* horoking gegel taka omakingme : give ten Rupees to each of the two men who have killed the tiger.

Pinḍigire merom tol-*ta'i* hon erangime : Scold the boy who against orders tied the goat in the verandah.

162. In all the cases explained so far the Bare Tense-forms used as Relative Clauses qualify either Nouns or Pronouns of the 3rd Person Singular, Dual or Plural. In other words : The Subject of the corresponding English Relative Clauses stand in the 3rd Person Sing., dual or Plural.

But the subject of a Relative Clause may also be a Personal Pronoun of the 1st or 2nd Person Sing. Dual or Plural.

To transform any Mundari proposition of this kind into a Relative Clause the following rule must be observed :

Place the Pronomunal subject in its emphatic form before the Transitive Predicate, deprive the latter of its Copula but let the Pronominal Objects tand as they were in the original proposition. Nouns standing as Direct Objects must be placed after the Bare Tense-forms.

Dasi-em ra'-i-a : thou wilt call the servant, becomes :
Am ra'-i dasi : the servant, whom thou wilt call.

Kulai-ing goë'ki'a : I killed a hare, becomes :
Aing goe'ki' kulai (omamtanaing) I give to thee the hare, *which i killed.*

Aingta' uri'm akiringa'kaiam : Thou hast sold a bullock to me .
Am aingta' akiringaka'i uri goe'janae : The bullock thou hast sold to me, died.

163. Remark. – When the Direct Object is a Noun in the Dual or Plural, the corresponding Pronominal Objects are generally. Not expressed in the Bare Tense-form :

Am mente dasiking achuakad'king-aing : I have engaged two servants for thee, becomes.
Aing am mente achuakad' dasiko (gapako hiju'a) : the servants whom I have engaged for thee will arrive to – morrow.

Honkom itujad'koa : thou art teaching the children.
Am itujad' honko alom tamkoa : Don't beat the children, whom thou art teaching.

164. When the Subject of the Relative Clause (*aing or am*) is at the same time Subject or Direct or Indirect Object of the Principal Clause, then the Demonstrative Pronoun *ni*' must be affised to the bare Tense-form.

Isu' sirma menteng ituked'pea : I taught you for many years : becomes:
Aing isu' sirmamente ituked'pe-ni', na'do neaing hukumjad'pea : I, who taught you for many years, now give you this command.

Pura'gem dengaakad' leam : thou hast helped us very much.
Am pura'ge dengaakad'leni' chiulao kale bagemea : We shall never abandon thee who hast helped us (so) very much.

165. (3) The Mundas frequantly use Co ordinate propositions where we would use a Relative Clause as subordinate to some Principal Clause. Often too they have recourse to an appropriate question and answer, v. gr.

Hola mid' horò Ranchiete hijulenae ; inige ju raauime, *literally* : a certain man came yesterday from Ranchi ; go and call that one here ; for : go and call the man *who* came yesterday from Ranchi. Hola mid horeo Ranchiete hijulenae chi ka ? Inigi mar ju raauime, *lit.* : Didn't a certain man come yesterday from Ranchi ? well, go and call that one here. you this command.

Puragem dengaakad leam : thou hast helped us very much.

Am purage dengaakad'leni' chiulao kale bagemea : We shall never abaudon thee who hast helped us (so) very much.

166. The Definite Demonstrative *okoni*' and the Indefinite *okoe* are *sometimes* used as Correlative Pronouns to the demonstrative *ni* or *ini*'. In this construction *okoni*' or *okoe* always stands First. *Okoe* kae boroa *ini'gee* seno'ka (Imperative 3rd Person) : Send some one (*lit*, let that one go) who is not afraid.

STATIC FORM

167. There exists, in the active Voice a form which is neither a *Mood* nor a Tense. It cannot be called a Mood because the suffix by which it is obtained does not imply the manner in which the proposition is uttered. It is not a Tense-form because the suffix does not in any way connote time.

168. It is obtained by suffixing *ta* to the root, and has double connotation.

(1) It may signify *the intention of the agent* or *the instigator* of an action with regard to *the effects* of that action.

(2) It may signify *a particular state of mind* in which the agent performed the action, viz., it implies that the act is or was done *in spite of a* custom or an order.

169. This very peculiar form has been called *the Reservative* and *the Static*. Though neither of the terms be an exact designation of the function performed, the term *Static* will be kept here.

It occurs only in the *Future Tense*, in *Simple Past*, and in *the Imperative Mood.*

THE STATIC FUTURE

170. It is formed by suffising *ta* to the root.

Indirect Pronominal Objects are never inserted into the Static Future. *Direct* Objects stand between the suffix *ta* and the Copula, *v. gr.* :

Ur'iko-ing *ader-ta-ko-a*, means {
either (1) I shall drive the cattle in and *shut them up*;
or (2) I will drive the cattle in *now, though it be not yet time to do so, or though I have been told not to.*
}

171. When the Direct Object is an inanimate being (in which case no insertion is made), euphonic vowels are not interposed between the *a* of suffix and the Copula ; hence these two *as* are in immediate cantact. This contact produces a single long a with the check. Thus *ni'-ta'-m, nï'-ta'-e, ni'-ta'-long*, etc.: I, thou, he or she, thou and I, etc., will set the door ajar.

Duar-ing *ni'-ta'* means either { (1) I shall open the door and *want it to remain open* ; or (2) I will open the door, *happen what may, i.e., contrary to-any body's order or desire.*

172. *Ta* is rarely suffised to Intransitive Predicates. If affixed, it changes them into Transitives, *v. gr.* Tising Ranchi jaked'ing *sen-ta'*, means : I will *do the road* from here to Ranchi to day ; I will *traverse* to-day the *distance* from here to Ranchi.

THE STATIC PAST

173. It is formed by suffixing *tad* to the root. (Probably a contraction of ta + ked)

Pronominal objects stand between the suffix and the Copula. Indirect Objects are not preceded by a. The elisions descrided in the Simple Past (cfr. No. 65) take place here too when the Pronouns *ing* or are inserted as Objects ; hence the forms *tol-ta'-ie for tol-tad-in-ae and tol-ta'-i-ae for tol-tad-i-ae.*

Duare *ni'ada* { He has opened the door and *left it open* ; or He opened the door, *although he ought not to have done so.*

Uri'ko-ing *adertad-koa* { I drove the cattle in and *they are still in the stable*; or I drove the cattle in before the proper time, or *against orders.*

174. *Tad* is rarely suffixed to Intransitive Predicates. If affixed, it changes them into Transitives, *v. gr*.: Khub'-ing *sentada* : I kept on walking fast, I kept up a brisk step.

Chaukidar.—Salaam hajur ! Khuntiren daroga ne chiṭṭi kulakadae.	Salaam Your Honour ! The subinspector of police of Khunti has sent this letter.
Gomke—Hela chaukikar ! ne kaji chikanamente hola kam udub'aiña ? Hola seta' ama' hatu japarega buṛiako (buṛiko) mid' horogeko goe'ki'a oro' *nega* ga pabu	There now ! chowkidar, why didst thou not inform me of this matter yesterday ? Yesterday morning bears killed a man near thy very village, and *here now* (just now, this instant) the

senderakoa mente daroga olaingtana ! Tisinggebu *denraked' kore* honangar !

Gapa jaked' ka ja'ko taena en birre.

Samu Haṛam—*Tiki kaji,* Gomke! Kako taena. Kasurkedabu mente eṭa'teko nira

G—Enamentedo ka, Haṛam ! Janageko kajidariṛe honanga, entedo beskedabu menteko kajiia derang, Birrenko kasurrea' kaji kadangko ituana.

S.—Ela Gomke, sartigeko ituana

G.—He mar, Haṛam, ama' uṛuleka. Na'do chaukikar nea' chilekajana sobena *baibaite* udubalem !

Ch.—Nelekajana Gomke : Buruhaturen ṭuṭi barai han Iṭiburu bir bitterre *hurṛinglekae ma phailtada* ad' ne kalom *enrege* hoṛee herla.

Entedo hola en hoṛe tudmente kuṛiloking sentan tae kena. Buru aṛaguntanre en koṛa rutue orongjana. Orangtanae—orongtanae, ente hoṛegoṛa japare apia buriko rokage birete niruṛungjanchiko *darom ked'kinga.* Kuṛi lelsidakedkochi dolang nira koṛae kaklaaitana, ad'e nirtabjana, Tuṭidoko tebakia. Kapi *kae sabakada* entedo chikakoae oṛo' ! Miadnido daṛioae (Pass.) honang mendo apia buriko

darogah writes to me that we all shall hunt them to-morro. *We should have had a beat for them* to day (O if only we had sought them out to day!)

Perhaps they will not remain in that forest till to morrow.

Very true, Sir ! (literally : a correct word) they will not remain. They will run *to some other place* because of their crime (we have committed a crime saying to each other, they will run elsewhere).

Not indeed on that account, old man ! If they could say anything at all, they would be sure to say : we have done well. But the wild beasts (those in the forests) have no notion of guilt (do not know the matter of guilt).

Sir, they certainly do know it ! (their guilt).

All right, old man, as you like it. Now, chowkidar, relate to us everything *in detail (carefully)* as to how this thing happened.

It happened this way, Sir : Tuti the blacksmith of Buruhatu *has cleared a little plot* (lit. : cut-clear) inside the forest of younder Iti mountain and this year he had sown kurti *in that clearing*).

Then yesterday he went with his wife to pluck that kurti. As they were descending the mountain—(side) that man *began to play on the flute*. He plays and plays, then near the kurtifield three bears having suddenly run out from the forest *made for both of them* (went againt both). The wife, having seen them first shouted out of her husband : come let us (thou and I) run away ! and she ran fast. But they (the *eskarte* okoe dariakoa! Batiliako, *tagombarakiako*, go honang mendo apia buṛiko eskarte okoe daṛiakoa ! Batilrako, tagombarakiako, *godarkiako* ad' oṛo' ente bojang *poakichi hatangko* godarurungkia. Kuṛido hatute nirauledcjhi : dola sekeṛa ! Koṛatainggeko goejaiae kaklatana. *Okoiteko* goejaiale kulijaia; entedo buriako *namtaia* han Iṭiburu goaṛaree menjada. Entedo *a'-sar-kapi* sabtabkedchi sobenkole niridila'. Namkiale, goe'akanae; lelurumo kale lelurumkia'. Buṛikodo okosateko nirjana ! Kale lelnamked'koa.

G.—Chia en Ṭuṭi haṛam hoṛoe taekena chi ?

Ch.—Ka, Gome ! dangṛa hoṛoge; ne sirma kuṛie aulia.

G.—Entedo chilekate kae nirjana ?

Ch.—Ela Gomke, ena okoe kajidaṛiae ! Roka borote, chinirtanre ja ḍuṭure chi dirire tod'janchie uiulena, chi chilekajana ! mendo khub peṛe'akan dangṛae taekena.

G.—Daroga *tadaruktee* senkena ?

Ch.—Auri, Gomke ! gapae sena.

Samu Haram—Ena do bugin kaji, Gomke, Gapa amom sena senderamente, entedo daroga *taka kae* tudkoa.

G.—Chikanamente ṭake aukoa ?

bears) overtook Tuti. *He had not even* a battleaxe *in his hand* : so what could he do against them ! One (bear) might possibly be overcome, but who can *single-handed* get the better of three ! *They threw him on the ground, they mauled him all over, they tore him with their claws*, and then *having broken open* his skull—bones they scratched out his *brains*. His wife meanwhile running into the village shouited : Come on quickly ! they are killing my husband ! *Who (what gang of men)* are killing your husband ? We ask ; then she says : the bears *have got hold of him* in yonder kurtifield on the Iti mountain. Then laying hold hurriendly of our weapons we rushed thither. We found him, he was dead; we could not so much as recognize him. As for the bears they had run who knows whither ! we did not see them.

Was that Tuti an old man ?

No, Sir ! he was a young man;l he married (brought a wife) this year.

Then how is it that he did not run away ?

Alas, Sir, who can say ! Was it on account of a sudden fright or that, having stumbled over a stump of a tree *or a stone, he fell or how did it happen* ! but he was a very strong young man.

Did the subinspector of police go *to hold an enquiry* !

Not yet, Sir, he will go tomorrow.

Old Samu—That's a hapy chance, Sir : thou too wilt go there tomorrow for the hunt, then the darogah *won't take money from them* (lit : pluck them (of) rupees).

Why should he take money from

S.H.—Buṛiko en hoṛoko goeki'a mente,

them ?

Because the bears have killed that man.

Ch.—Ela Gomke, kae aukoa ; ne haṛam *samagee* enkajada.

Hela, Sir, he won't take (money from) them; this old man says so *without rhyme or reason.*

S.H.—Ela Gomke, samage kaing kajitana : kula karedo buṛia karedo bing ja hoṛogeko huagoe'kiṛe janau ṭakako tud'ḳoa, renge hoṛota moṇre ṭakaleka, punji hoṛota'mod'hisi moṇre ṭaka *habe'geko* auia. Hoṛo dumbuigoe janreo ṭaka, daruete uiujanreo ṭaka, oṛalojanreo ṭaka. Enado ne chaukidaro kachie torakada.

Hela, Sir, I am not saying it without reason. Whenever a tiger or a bear or a snake has killed (bitten–dead) a man they take money, from a poor man five rupees, from a rich man up to twenty-five. When a man gets drowned then too (it is) money ! when (one) falls from *a* tree (and dies) then too (it is) money, when a house is burnt thn too (it is) money. Doesn't this chowkidar also know that !

Daroga aea' mochatedang kae asikoa hoṛoko oṛo aea' titeo kae telaea; mendo chaukidarko ad' sipaiko tasilrikakoa. He chika chaukikar ? Alom *rinṭia* na'do. Ne Gomke holado kae bololena nere.

The darogah himself to be sure, does not ask people for the money with his own mouth nor receive it into his own hands ; but he makes the chowkidars and constables collect (raise) the money. Is n't it so chowkidar ? Now don't *deny a known fact.* This gentleman has not entered here yesterday (is not a new arrival in this country).

Amin sirma ne disumre hobajante, aegeo poliskoa' dastur huṛingleka ituanae chimad' ! Kachi Gomke ?

Being so many years (lit. : having become so many years) in this country, he too forsooth knows a little about the habits of the policemen. Isn't it Sir ?

Ch.—He mar, ape Hoṛoko enkajadape; aing *bole* chainaing kajidaṛia !

All right, you Mundas say like that ; and *what in the world* am I to say now !

G.—Mendo, Samu Haṛam, ape Horoko taka chikanamentepe omjad'koa ? Ape hoṛoko ṭaka alope tud'koa mente sarkar polis-horoko hukumakad'koa. Enate lage : Ja daroga chi sipai chi chaukidar moṭaite chi ghuslake ṭaka asikedae mente sarkar

But, Samu, why do you Mundas give them money ? The government has ordered the policemen saying : don't you take any money from the people (has forbidden them to take money from the people). More than that ; If the government obtain sabuti namkedre kentede sajaikoa : dankekoa ade jehelkoa,

evidence that some darogah or constable or chowkidar has taken money either forcibly or as a bribe, then it will severely punish them : it will fine them and imprison them.

S.H.—En do sobena'ole ituana, Gomke; mendo polisko pan chalgeako; sabuti kale sabutidaṛiakoa.

That we all know, Sir, but the policeman are cunning ; we cannot convict them. (lit; : as for proofs we cannot prove them (*i.e.* guilty).

Ḍonḍogeale, enate kale dariakoa.

We are stupid, that's why we can't get over them.

G,—Ḍonḍora ranu serange, oro' en ranu ape *kapea*. Ale, honko iskulrikakopele metapere entedo, meromko okoe gupikoa oro'pe menea. Chimin din apea' honko kape ituṙikakoa imin dinjaked' jetaeo nekan landphandete kako banchaudariapea. Ne kaji nad'obu bageta ! senderarea'bu jagarea.

The medicine for stupidity is education (litrly : wisdom) and that medicine *you don't want*. Whenever we tell you to send your children to school then you reply : and who will look after the goats ? So long as you won't let your children get instructed, so long can nobody save you from trickeries. Now let us leave this matter alone ! we shall talk about the hunt.

Tobedo, chaukikar, en sendara mente chikanape *bandobasakada* ?

Well now, chowkidar, what *have you arranged* for that hunt ?

Ch.—Tising Gomke Bandgaoṇreko pitina. Energe tara chaukidarko gapa Iṭiburure senderao'a (Pass. Fut.) menteko hakauiako, tara ko do *singiturosarea* haturenko rahundikope mente darogae hukumakadkoa. Entake e-sai. horoko habegeko hijua chimad'.

Today Sir, there is market in Bandgaon (lit . :—they market) There some chowkidars will proclaim (shout out) that there will be a hunt (lit. :— it will be hunted) to-morrow on the Iti mountain ; the darogah has ordered other chowkidars to call together the villagers of the east. Like that up to seven hundred men will most probably come.

G.—Kepesed'do chiminta'pe baikeda.

In how may places (litrly. : how many where) have you arranged *stands* ? (litrly. mutual closings *i.e.* places where the hunter and the hunted must close with each other).

Ch. Monreta' machanle baiakada.

We have made machans in five places.

G.—Chiminangpe salangikeda ?

How high ? (litrly : how much have you heightened them).

Ch—Bar pursage. Enre daru

Twice as high as a man can

kotore montono *opad'ko gandetele* toltada dubmente ad' oro birrenko enre *dubakani* aloakako lelgodiamente pataratele kesedbiiurkeda.

reach. There in the branches of the trees we have tied pretty thick *youug trees horizontally* to sit down on and besides we have closed it (the seat) in with *young* leafed branches in order that the wild beasts may not catch a glimpse of *the one who is seated there.*

G.—Sobenape beskeda, miad eskargepe *chukno'kede.* Tising-do ka senderao'a, oro' gapajaked' en sakam kachi rorochabao'a ! Entedo enre dubakanr ja huringlekate eklabaranre (Refl. Fut.) sakam saria. En sari birenko *aiumegeako* ad' ente atatate kako niridia. Patarako deimtage lagau hobao'a, *berel* berelte, ente daru sakamleka lelo'a ad' sario ka saria. Gapa tobe naua patarabu lagauia.

You did everything well, only in one point you have made a bit of a mistake (litrly.: one (thing) only you have mistaken a bit) To-day of course the hunt will not take place and tomorrow those leaves will be entirely dry ! And then if the one seated there moves (shakes himself) ever so little, the leaves will rustle (sound). That rustling the wild beasts *are sure to hear* and then they will not run towards that *stand.* The leafed branches must always be tied at the moment of climbing (the machan), *quite fresh* then they look like the leaves of the tree and they will also not rustle at all. So then to-morrow we shall put new branches.

XVI. EXERCISE

This Exercise explains the formation and use of the Imperfect Tense.

This is preceded by a set of rules showing how the Cases of Nouns and Pronouns are to be rendered in Mundari.

EQUIVALENTS OF DECLENSIONS

175. Nouns and Pronouns standing as Subjects, Dirct or Indirect Objects take no suffix indicative of case relations. The reason of this is because the relations indicated by our Datives, Accusatives and certain Ablatives are plainly indicated in the form of Transitive Predicates by the insertion of Direct and Indirect Objects.

Gomke dasi talabe omara : the master gave the servant his wages.

176. *Possessive Genitives* of Nouns and Pronouns depending on the word *servant* or *its synonyms are generally* rendered by means of the *suffix taren*, (literally : the one about, the one near), *sometimes* by the suffix a (litrly.: to) Jila Gomke-*taren* chaprassi chittie auakada : the chaprassi of the Deputy Commissioner has brought a lettor.— Samu-*taren* dasie nirjana : the servant *of* Samu has run away.

177. *Possessive Genitives* of Nouns and Pronouns depending on the words *child, son, daughter. Father, mother, sister* are sometimes rendered by means of the suffix *taren*, often by *ren* more frequently by *a'*.

Pahaṇṛ-*taren*
Pahaṇṛ-*ren*
Pahaṇṛ-*a'*

} kuṛihon Assamte aṛki'd idikiako : they (viz. the coolie catchers) have taken the daughter *of* the Sacrificer to Assam.

178. *Possessive Genitives* of Common or Proper Nouns and Pronouns *denoting Persons* are rendered by means of the suffix *ren* when they depend on the words *husband* or *wife.*

Muṇḍa-*ren* kuṛi hola ruatee goe'jana : the Munda's wife died of fever yesterday.

179. REMARK.—Patronymics as well as other Proper and Common Nouns are obtained by suffixing the Personal Pronouns i', *king, ko* to the Genitive in *ren* or *taren.* These Nouns take all the Dual, Plural and Case-suffixes of ordinary Nouns.

The Singular forms thus derived from Proper names of men or from pronouns standing for such names always mean *the wife of*; whereas the Singular forms thus derived from Proper names of women or from Pronouns standing for such names mean *the husband of* v. gr. Samu-*reni'* : Samu's wife.

The Plural forms thus derived from Proper Names of either men or women or from Pronouns standing for such names generally mean the *family of*, i. e., all the inmates of the house : grand-parents, husband or wife, children, grand-children ; v. gr. Paku-*ren.ko* : Paku's family.

N. B.— The expressions *the family of*, the *inmates of the house of are* more frequently rendered by suffixing *te*, followed by the Plural *ko* to the Proper name : v. gr., Paku-*te-ko* : the family of Paku.

180. *All the other Possessive and Partitive Genitives* of Nouns of Pronouns *denoting animate beings* not enumerated in the preceding rules must be rendered by means of the Suffix *a.*'

Amta'ren dasi-*a'* lija lo'jana : The cloth *of* thy servant got burnt.—Sigin-*a'* oṛa handirijana : the house *of* Sigin has collapsed.

181. *Genitives* of Proper or Common Nouns or Pronouns denoting *seas, rivers, countries, towns, space, or places* or single objects there and then considered as a place or as a container of something must be rendered by the Suffix *ren* when they depend on words denoting *animate beings*.

The same Genitives are rendered by *rea'* when they depend on words denoting *inanimate objects*.

Ranchi-*ren* Uraonko Horoteko jagara : the Uraons *of* Ranchi speak Mundari. — Bir-*ren* mara'ko era'geko chirgala : the peacocks of the forest (i.e. wild peacocks are exceedingly shy.—Ranchi-*rea'* talaore marang haiko mena'koa : there are big fishes in the tank *of* Ranchi.—

Bir-*rea'* da' tutkungea: the water of the forest is cool.

182. *Genitives* denoting *age*, *price, dimension*, or the *material* of which something is made must be rendered by *ren* when they depend on words denoting *animate objects*.

When they depend on words denoting *inanimate objects*, they are rendered by *rea'* or *ra'*.

Turui sirma-*ren* hon : A child *of six* years.—Monre taka-*ren* merom : a goat of five rupees , i. e. a goat worth five rupees.—Bar muka-*ren* bing : a snake *of* two cubits, i.e. measuring two cubits in length.— Monre taka-*rea'* lija : a cloth of five rupees.—Mod' hisi muka-raw ora : a house of 20 cubits, i. e. a house measuring 20 cubits.—Pital-rea' chipi : a dish made *of* brass.

183. *Partitive Genitives* of words denoting *inanimate objects* (*i.e.* Genitives denoting a part of some inanimate objects or the whole) are generally rendered by means of the contracted suffix *ra*,' rarely by *rea'*.

En ote-*ra'* hatingem namtada chi ? : Hast thou got a share *of* that land ?

184. The *Definite Locative of rest* of Nouns or Pronouns is formed by the Suffix *re*.

Ne hatu-*re* Dikuko bangkoa' : there are no Hindus *in* this village.

The *Indefinite Locative of rest* is formed by *ta're*.

Khunti-*ta're* Teliko is oteko eserakada : *About* or *around* or *near* Khunti the Telis have got hold of much land.

185. The *Definite Locative of motion* to of Nouns or Pronouns denoting *space* or *places* is formed by the Suffix *te*.

Ranchi-*te* senome : Go to ranchi,— Bir-*te* nirjanako : they have run away *to* the forest.

The *Indefinite Locative of motion to* of the same Nouns or Pronouns is formed by *ta'te*.

The *Locative of motion to of all other Nouns and Pronouns* is formed by *ta'te*,

Aing-*ta*'te niraujanae : he came running to *me*.— Ne chitti gomke- *ta'te* iditabme : take this letter quickly *to* the master.

186. The *Definite Locative of motion from* of Nouns and Pronouns denoting *space* or *places* is formed by the Suffix ate or etc.

Nau'terge kula ne lata-*etee* urunglena : A tiger came out just now *from* this den. —Hatu-*ete* nirjanae : he has run away *from* the village.

The *Indefinite Locative of motion from* of the same Nouns and Pronouns is formed by the *suffix ta'ate* or *ta'ete*.

Han hatu-*taeteko* niraujana : they came running *form* yonder village, i.e. form somewhere near yonder village.

The *Locative of motion from* of all other Nouns and Pronouns is formed by the suffix *taate* or taete.

Pahaṇṛ-ta'eten hiju'tana chi ? Ka, Munḍa'-*ta'ete* : Art thou coming *from* the sacrificer ? No, *from* the village — chief.

187. The *Instrumental Case* of Nouns and Pronouns denoting *inanimate objects* or *irrational animals* is formed by the suffix *te.*

Ne oṛa' kecho-*te* dabakana : this house is covered *with* tiles.—

Chipi diri-*te* karedo pital-*te*-ko baiia : they make dishes with (or out of) stone or with brass.— Ne disumre uriko-*te*-ko siia, sadomko-*te* do ka : in this country they plough *with* bullocks, but never *with* horses.

188. The *Instrumental Case* of Nouns and Pronouns denoting *human beings* is formed by suffixing *a'* to these Nouns and Pronouns and then adding *horate.* This horate is by itself the Instrumental Case of the word *hara* (way). It corresponds exactly to the Latin viā and may therefore be rendered into English by *though.*

Am-*a' horate*-le banchaujana : we were saved *by* thee.

189. *Ablative Cases* of Nouns and Pronouns denoting *animate beings* and depending on such words as *to receive, to buy, to steal* and *their synonyms* are rendred by means of the suffix *ete.*

Ne sadom Samu-*ete*-ng kiringki'a : I bought this horse *from* Samu.

REMARK.— The words *to steal, to rob*, and *their synonyms* generally take a double Accusative.

Paku *Samu ote-e* reki'a, rather than Paku *Samu-ete* otee rekeda : Paku has robbed Samu of his land.

190. The *Vocative* is often preceded by the Interjection *e'* ! he ! or the familiar *ate.* Very often the tone of the Voice alone distinguishes it from the Nominative form.

THE IMPERFECT TENSES

191. To each of the Tenses described so far, excepting the three Futures, there corresponds an Imperfect Tense. All these Imperfects are formed by adding *taeken* (seldom *taenken*) to the original complete Tense-form, so that the generic Imperfect Tense suffix always stands immediately before the Copula, v. gr., sentan-*taeken*-a-ing : I was going then.—Inungled'-*taeken*-a-ko : they had been playing.

192. The Imperfect Tense-suffix never affects the position of the inserted. Pronominal Objects. These remain in the positions pointed out above ; nor does it interfere with any of the elisions described in the Indefinite Present, the Simple Past, etc. But this suffix or rather Auxiliary does affect the position of the Pronominal Subjects. As a general rule the Mundas place the Pronominal Subjects immediately before *taeken.*

Sentan-*ing*-taekena, seldom : sentan-taeken-a-*ing*.

Inungled'-*ko*-taekena, seldom : inungled'-taeken-a-*ko*.

Hence in these Tenses which insert the Pronominal Objects after the Tense-suffix, we have in the corresponding Imperfects two Pronouns standing side by side before the Auxiliary *taeken* ; the first of these being a Direct or Indirect Object, and the second the Pronominal Subject.

Leljad'-*ko-ing*-taeken-a : I was seeing them at the time. —Haiko sabled'-*ko-le* taeken-a : we had just been catching fish.

193. With regard to function, it may be said in general that the Auxiliary *taeken* does not change anything either in the denotion or connotation of the original Tense-forms. All it does with regard to them is this : it transfers them into the past time, and thus assigns to them in relation to some past fact that paticular-position in time which the original Tense-form implies.

THE INDETERMINATE IMPERFECT

194. One of the functions of the Indeterminate Tense is to state universal truths, first principles or axioms. This particular function has of course no Imperfect.

Another function of the original Tense is to state customs not yet extinct or habits not given up, etc. This function has an Imperfect Tense.

Taeken added to the Indeterminate Tense represents as having existed formerly customs now extinct, habits now given up, occupations performed regularly at one time, but abandoned now.

Alea'n disumre Angrajiko auriko hijure Munḍ'ako najomko jid'jid'ge-ko (Subj.) *atar-ko*-taekena. Hen diplio *si'-ko-taikena* : Before the English arrived in our country the Mundas were in the habit of burning wizards and witches alive. At that remote time too they were ploughing, i-e. they performed the work of cultivators.

THE INTRANSITIVE OR DEFINITE PRESENT IMPERFECT

195. This performs two distinct functions :

(1) It implies that the action in question was going on in the past simultaneously with another past action spoken of or implied in the same sentence :

Ako dapalken imta entare *sitan-ing-taekena* : I was ploughing there just at the time they were fighting.

(2) It is also used as Imperfect to the Future.

Seno'tan-ing taekena : I was (at that time) : on the point of going, or I was about to go.

THE TRANSITIVE OR INDEFINITE PRESENT IMPERFECT

196. This is limited to Transitive Predicates. It performs the function described under (1) of the Intransitive Present Imperfect. It is also used as Future Imperfect. *Ra'jad'-ko-ing-taekena* may mena : I was just then calling them ; or : I was on the point of calling them.

197. REMARK.— It has been stated already that, in the Active Voice, there is no Imperfect corresponding to any of the three Future Tenses. The Imperfect forms of the Transitive and of the Intransitive Presents are commonly used to express the idea that some past action was on the point of being performed when the main event narrated took place (cfr. Nos. **184, 185** p)

However, when it is desired to insist on the idea of the futurity of a past action relatively to another, the following circumlocution is used, which renders the difference between the Simple, the Anterior and the Static Future to a nicety. In this circumlocution the original Tense-forms occur in the Direct-speech form, whereas the Auxiliary *taeken* is added to words meaning to *intend, to say and synonymes.*

He was on the point of going to Ranchi when his wife fell sick, becomes: *I shall go* to Ranchi, *saying, he had intended,* but then his wife fell sick : Ranchit*eng sena mente, moneakade taekena*, entedo kuri-tae hasu'janae. (Here *mone* is in the Pluperfect because it means : *he had made up his mind*).

He was going to first sow that field and then start for Ranchi when he got sick, becomes : *I shall first sow* that field and then go to Ranchi, *saying, he had made up his mind,* when he got sick : En loeong*ing herlea* ente Ranchiteng sena mente, *moneakade taekena,* mendo hasujanae.

He was forbidden by the owner to cut that tree. Notwithstanding he was about to cut it, when a tiger came and carried him off, becomes : ... *nevertheless I will cut it, saying, he had determined*; but then a tiger etc. : En daru alom ma'ea mente kisaṇṛe manalia. Enreo *mataeing mente, monekade taekena.* Entedo kula birate uṛunjạnchie idikia.

THE IMPERFECT OF THE CONTINUATIVE PRESENT

198. Whereas the Imperfects described under **184** and **185** exhibit the action in question as merely simultaneous with some other past action, this Imperfect denotes that the action having begun before some other past act or event, continued uninterruptedly whilst that other act or even took place:

Hoiote aiña bened' otangjanchi ga'ṛare uiu'jana ; aingdo sadoming *sabaka-i-taekena* mente kaing sabdaṛijana : My pugri being blown away by the wind fell into the river; I could not catch it because at that moment I was (busy) holding the horse.

THE IMPERFECT OF THE SIMPLE PAST

199. The Intransitive form is hardly used except with *sen*. *Senken-ing-taekena* : I had been going.

The Transitive form is generally replaced by the Anterior Past Tense form with *taeken* (cfr. No. **192.**)

THE IMPERFECT OF THE IMCOMPLETE PAST

200. This is used with Transitive Predicates to show that a past action had been left in a state of incompleteness before some other past act or event.

En mad'em ma'chabakeda menteng kuliki'a. Ma'do *ma'-ken-e-taekena* mendo kae chabaakad taekena. Enreo ma'chabaakadaing mentee kajirurakiña : I asked him whether he had finished cutting those bamboos. *He had been busy cutting*, but he had not finished. Nevertheless, he told me he had finished.

THE IMPERFECT OF THE ANTERIOR PAST

201. This Tense is generally used with Transitive and Intransitive Predicates. Besides performing the function of an *Anterior Past*, it occurs also in cases where we *should rather* expect the Imperfect of the *Simple Past*.

Inku auri teba're haiko *sab'led'-ko-le-taekena* : We had been catching fish before they arrived.

THE IMPERFECT OF THE STATIC PAST

202. This is used with both the meanings explained under No. 157 with that modification of time which the Auxiliary *taekena* denotes.

Aputee ruarimta uri'ko *adertad'-ko-e-taekena* : He had just driven in the cattle (against orders, or : before the proper time) when his father arrived.

PLUPERFECT OR IMPERFECT CORRESPONDING TO THE PERFECT TENSE

203. This form, besides being used as an ordinary Pluperfect, is used also as Imperfect to the Incomplete or Inchoative Past in *jan*.

In cases in which the Past in *jan* means, *to begin to* ... the Imperfect is formed by adding the Pluperfect of *ete'* to the bare root form of the original Predicate.

Durang-janae :*he began to sing Durang ete'akad-e-taekena* : he had begun to sing.

When the Past in *jan* means : *to go to* ... then the Imperfect is formed by affixing *te* to the bare root form of the original Predicate and adding the Pluperfect of *sen*.

Susun-janako : they went to dance *Susan-te senakan-ko-taekena* : they had gone to dance.

Gomke—Gapa idangre tambu uiuipe oro' Jikilatate goidiipe.

Early to-morrow morning take down (litrly : throw down) the tent and take it to Jikilata.

Mandini'—Chotahazarido gomke okorem jomea ?

The Sir where will you take your chota hazari ?

G.—Hupuring mej ad en mora, enado mad'chauki nere bagepe ente ne daru umbulre chota hazaring jomea. Taeomte am oro saizmej oro' mora Jikilatate *idijaben* (**N.B**. *ja* added to *au* or *idi* means *with*)

Leave the very small table and that mora, that is the bamboo-chair here, then I shall take chota hazari in the shade of this tree. After wards thou and the groom will take the table and mora *with you* to Jikilata.

Hanre naua khuntako baire honang kako *bid'tabea*. Enamente sam tambulo' ne taiarakan khuntako idiipe mente *gogo'ko* hukumakom.

If they were to prepare new tentpegs over there they won't *erect* (the tent) *quickly*. Therefore order *the carries* to take these ready made pegs together with the tent.

M.—Aing na'doing seno'a chiamgeng tangimea ?

Shall I go ahead now or shall I wait for you ?

G.—Seno'me mar ; aingdo egara *bajeleka* hanreng tebaea.

All right—go; I shall arrive over there at *about* elevan o'clock.

G.—Chia ! moṉṟe ghanta sidarepe urunglena oṟo na'jaked tambu auripe bidea !

What ! you (carries) have left five hours in advance (of me) and up to this moment you have not yet put up the tent.

Gogoko.—Ela gopmke, okorebu bidea mentele ara'urutanle taekena. Ne apia khantaradaru subare umbuldo khub umbulakana (Perf. Pass). Mendo oṟa' japare ka' jaem sukua. Nidadipli misa misa buriako epeṟangako misa misa huṟing honko ra'eako. Kam *hewaakante* durum ka jaem daṟia ! En *tikurare* khube hoiojada, mendo umbal aminanang ka umbulakana.

Oh, sir, we *were doubting* as to where we should erect it (where shall we erect it saying, we were doubting). Under these three jackfruit-trees there is a very good shade indeed (as for shade it is beautifully shaded.) But thou wilt perhaps not like it so near the houses. At night sometimes the old women will be quarrelling, and sometimes the little children will be crying. Perhaps thou wilt not be able to sleep because thou art not accustomed (to this sort of thing). On yonder *height* there is a nice breeze (it breezes beautifully) but there is not much shade.

G.—He mar tikurate, idiĭpe ad'

All right take it to the height and

bid'tabepe en ulidaru subare ; jojodaru subare sadom mente baiipe.

Gogoko—Okosa'rele *duara* ?

G.—Dakinsa.

Gogoko.—Ale Horokodo *dakin* kale kajja, *borkandurile* meta.

G. Chikanamente ?

Gogoko—Enado gomke ale dangrako kale ituana. Haramko enkageko *kajiau'jada* Ene' ! Joto harame hijutana. Ini kajidariae chimad.

Joto Haram—Mar gomke joar! G. Johar haram ! *Taukautergem* hijuakana, aingge, moiad kaji itu mente.

J. H.—Ela gomke aing dondo haram chikanaging tiumea oro ! Ape gomkeko sobenadangpe ituana.

G.—Sobenado kale ituana : apea jagarko, dasturko ape kape udubalere chilekatele ituna oro' ?

Ne dangrako nado, *dakin* ena'do alele *bokanduriako* metaingtana. Chikanamentepe enkaeaing kulijadkoa, entedo kale, ituanako men. Apea dangrako enkana kako ituanre, ale Belaitrenko chilekatele tordaria !

J. H.— He Gomke ena'do ainging udub'amea mar ! En kaji nekagea : Haram horoko nakage-ko kajiaujada : Munure abu Horohonko Hansa' asu' sangin disumrebu taekena ; ente ensa'ete urungjanchi ne disumrebu aragujana." Enamente na'do goea'kan hagokole topakore, alea' *nangrea'* disum mulitele katakoa, hante senruralekage. Enatedo bo nekasao'a (Pass Indet.) chika ? Topa imta miad

erect it quickly under that mango tree. *Arrange (a place)* for the horse under the tamarind tree.

On what side shall *the entrance be* ? (On what side shall we door it ?)

On the south side.

We Mundas don't say *dakin* (south), we call it *head-rest.*

Why ?

That, Sir, we young men don't know. The old people speak in that way from time immemorial. There ! old Joto is just coming, he will most probably be able to tell thee.

Well Sir good day ! (a greeting) Good day old man ! Thou hast come *just in the nick of time* (altogether appropriately to teach me something.

Oh, Sir, what in the world could I a stupid old man teach thee ! Youi gentlemen of course know every thing.

But we do not know every thing : Your language and your customs, if you don't explain them to us, how are we to learn them.

Just now these young men say that you call the south *head rest.* I ask them why you do so and they tell me they don't know. If your own young men do not know such things then how can we Europeans know them !

Oh yes, sir, that I will explain to thee. That matter is like this : Our ancestors have handed down the following tradition (litrly., bring down this saying); In the beginning we Mundas (Sons of men) lived (were) in that direction in a country *far far away,* then having gone out from there we came down into this country." Therefore now whenever we bury some deceased brethren we put their feet in sered're chauli karedo kodele potomkedchi, bo' subarele dota kanduri-leka. Enamente *dakin bokan durile* meta. Ad' okoa' Dikuko utarea ena' ale Horoko *katajambarle* kajia, kata ensa *muliakana* (perf. Pass) mente.

J.—Erne' ! na'dom ituakaiña. Ja jetan kami mentem hiju'akana ja ?

J. H.—Ka Gomke, kami mentedo ka. Ne tambutam chilekateko bidea, ena neneling hijuakana.

G.—Chia ! tambu chiulao kam lellakada ?

J. H.—Leldoing lelakada gomke. *Is usirmare* han Chaibasata kamitaning taekena. Entedo musing enta'te miad' hakime hiju'lena; *haramnogee* taekena. Entedo aea' dasiko tambu bidmenteko hukumkedlea. Okonido khuntale *gojahunḍijada*, okoni'do' busule goaujada, okoni'do kud'lamte en taunrle *phaijada*. Rimbil saritana mente, mara ! mara ! sekeraepe mente chaprasiking kaklabarajadaking. Bidtabkedale. Nado gomke sadomtee *niraujada*. Ae'ge tambu bolo imta daloge marang hoio hiju'tanae Tambudo hente nete eklabarao'tana (Pass. Def. Pres.) Aledo *surun* (Reflex. Indet.) mente miad' daru subatele niridila'.

Ensa'ete en' tambu leljad'le

the direction of our ancient (first) countrty *as if going back* thither. And thereby does not the head come this way (litrly become this way) ? At the moment of burying, we pack some husked rice or kde in a rag and place it under the head like a cushin. It is for that we call the suoth *head rest*. And that which the Hindus call north we call *katajambir (the lay of the feet)* because the feet *are pointing* that way (are lining it *i.e.* are stretched out line—like in that direction).

There now ! thou hast been teaching me. Hast thou perhaps come here about some business ?

No Sir, noit about business. I have come to see how they put up this thy tent.

What ! hast thou never seen a tent ?

As for that Sir, I have seen one. *Many years ago* I was once working (in some place) yonder about Chaibasa. Then one day a judge (any court-officer) came to that place; he was an *elderly* man. Then his servants ordered us to put up his tent. Some of us are busy *preparing a number* of tent-pegs (pointing-gathering) some are bringing straw and some are *clearing* that spot with hoes (slicing away, the grass. As it is thundering the two chaprassies are shouting all round : get on ! get on ! make haste ! We erected it very quickly. Now the gentleman is running in on horse back. The moment he enters the tent a strong wind comes on with rain. The tent is shaking hither and thither. As for us we ran for *shelter* under a tree (litrly, to shelter ourselves.)

From there We were looking at

taekena, ad', nege uiugoa ! ne'ge uiugo'ale menjado. Sekeraepe ! sekeraepe ! kaklala'ko mente enhupuring khuntako kale kilaaderbesla, pagakoo aminang kale *chanrila* Nado *ganamate* ote *lebeotana*. Oro misa hoio khube *udurtana* : ensarea khun'tako tudo'tana ad' *patken* uiugotana tambu. Sam gomkelo api horo dasiko topalenako' (Pass. Anter. Past) Inku, *bapare baparejadako*, gomkedo chikanae *men*-jada kale mundi darijana; mendo *oretanle* landakeda. Entedo nado gomkea bo lelotana, oborurungentanae tambuate. Er-angleae mente *lutur medmunan-rale hakatabkeda*, mendo kae lelked'lea. Hatutate *niridilae* ad' sida ora'ree nirbolojana. O'role landakea. Entedo en dasiko entaneta bo urungked'chi oborurungenjanako. Landado ale kale *keseddarijana*. Hankudo kented'-geko erangked'lea. Alebole chikaeale oro' !

that tent and there it goes (falls) there it "goes" ! we were saying. Because they had been shouting Make haste ! Make haste ! we had not driven these small tent pegs in properly the ropes too we *had not been stretching* so tight (as they should have been.) Now with *the rain* the ground is *softening*. Once more the wind *pushes* strongly : all the pegs on that (the windside) side *are pulled up* and *with a thud* the tent falls down. Together with the gentleman three servants *were buried*. Those (servants) shout *bapare bapare* ; as for the gentleman we could not understand what he was saying; but we were laughing *to split our sides*. And now suddently the gentleman's head is visible ; he creeps out from under the tent cloth. Lest he scold us we *quickly put on long faces*. (He will scold us, saying, we quickly hung down our ears and faces.) But he did not see us. He *rushed towards* the village and ran into the first house. Then we laughed again, and those servants putting out their heads in this and that direction crept out. As for laughing, that *we could not suppress*. And now those fellows scold us fearfully. What in the world were we to do in the circumstances.

G.—Entedope bidruratada ?

Then did you erect it again ?

J.H. Kage, ganama hoka imta gomke sadomte Chaibasatee nirrurajana. Entedo en tambu enkatege potomruraked'chi Chaibasatele *tebatada*, en nidage.

No indeed ! the moment the rain stopped the gentleman rode off back to Chaibasa. And then we packed up that tent like that (wet as it was) and that very night took it to Chaibasa *and left it there*.

G.—Tisingo marang hoio ganama botongjadbuae. *Jetejadae kented'rea* oro' han singi aiubsa hende' rimbil rakabjada. Enateja, idu ne

To day also a heavy storm with rain is threatening us. *The sun* is frightfully hot and yonder in the west a black cloud is rising (it is getting gomkeo enkao'a mentem *bicharkeda,* ad' aingge landamentem hijuakana ! he chi ka ?

clouded blackly). Perhaps on that account *thou calculatest* that the same thing will happen to me (this gentleman too will fare like that, saying (thou judgest,) and thou hast come to have a laugh at me ! Isn't it so ?

J. H. Ka gomke ! amdo kam enkao'a. Ama tambu ku *batio'a* Lelked'koaing ; Soben khuntako khub'ko kilaadertada, pagakoo mimiad'geko chanṛiakada; *mutkul khuntaking* mod'chokoe'o ka eklaoa ad baran sirma lijaking dumang-leka chanṛiakana. Ja aminang hoioreo jetana ka chikao'a.

No, sir ! thou wilt not fare like that. Thy tent *won't be thrown over.* I looked at them (thy servants). They have driven in all the tent-pages very well, the ropes too they have stretched one by one; the two *tentpoles* don't shake even one bit, and the two roof-cloths they are stretched as tight as a drum. Let it blow ever so hard, *nothing will happen.*

XVII. - EXERCISE

In the preceding Exercises all the Tense-forms of the Active Voice have been explained. Before going over to the Passive, the Reflexive and the Reciprocal forms, it seems advisable to explain at some length the various Mundari words and constructions which are equivalent to the English Verbs to be, to exist, to have and their contraries.

205. The English word *to be* expresses several really distinct ideas. In the sentence : This fruit is tasty, *to be* is a mere linkword referring the Predicate *tasty* to the Subject *this fruit.* In the sentence : There certainly *is* a God, the word *to be* is no longer a mere linkword but a complete Predicate denoting real existence. It is equivalent to the Verb, *to exist.* The Munda renders these distinct ideas by different words. In the sentence : The servant *is* here, *to be* is not a linkword but an independent Predicate denoting *presence* in a given place. This idea is akin to that of real existence ; yet, it differs from it, inasmuch as it adds some specification to it. Although it may be rendered by the same word which denotes *real existence*, it is more generally rendered by quite a peculiar construction, *viz.*, by a kind of impersonal conjugation of Adverbs of place and Nouns denoting localities.

So far then, we have *three* different Mundari constructions to render the English Verb *to be* according to the three different meanings that Verb is capabel of. We must admit that this process of thus discriminating between distinct ideas is rather logical, and, were it to stop here, the practical diffculty would not be great. But the Munda mind goes a step further. When the Verb *to be* is a mere linkword, then he insists on distinguishing between the nature of the Predicates which are to be referred by that linkword, and, according to the nature of the different Predicates, he uses different modes of connecting them with their subjects.

of the Predicate.

In the sentence : This fruit *is* tasty, the Predicate is an Adjective denoting a quality, a something quite accidental. Here the Munda uses as linkword the Copula *a*, the same which he uses for all Transitive and Intransitive Predicates. This denotes *being* in its widest and vaguest sense. It is therefore equivalent to one of the significations of the English Verb *to be*. Ne jo sibil-*a*.

In the sentence : This man *is* an Uraon, the Predicate is a Noun or Substantive. It does not denote a merely accidental quality, but a feature inseparable from his personality.. Born of Uraon parentage, the man remains an Uraon, as long as he lives. Predicates of this kind are referred to their subject by means of the Copula *tan*. This word is composed of the root *ta, plus* the specifying Demonstrative *en* or *ne*. Ta denotes fixity and permanence in general; so that the compound is expressive of the idea implied by the remain, to continue, to be always. Hence, the Copula *tan* connotes, in a manner, the nature of the Predicate, so that *ne horo Uraon tani'* might be rendered by : this man remains an Uraon.

In the Sentence : This man *is* a servant, the Predicate is also a Noun. But, unlike the preceding one, it does not denote a permanent feature of the subject's personality. It signifies a state or condition which may change any day. The man may *be a master* to-morrow. The Munda treats Predicates of this kind in a manner which, at first sight, may appear extraordinary, but which, in reality, is very logical. He transforms them into Transitive Predicates, puts them into the Perfect Tense of the Passive Voice, by affixing the Tense-sign *akan*,and then refers this Predicate to its subject by means of the Copula a. Dasi : a servant; hence, dasi-o' : to become a servant, to be received into service; dasi-*akan* : to have become a servant, to have been received into service. Hence : Ne horoe *dasi-akan-a*, this man *is* a servnat. Similarly : This man *is* a king, ne horoe *raja-akan-a*, i.e., this man has become a king, or, this man has been *king-ed*, even as in English we say : this man has been *knighted*.

To sum up : When the Verb *to be* is a linkword or Copula, it has three distinct Mundari equivalents, determined by the nature of the Predicate to be linked or referred to the subject. When it is itself a complete Predicate, denoting either real existence or presence in a given place, it has two Mundari equivalents. Furthermore the negation of real existence is not formed by the ordinary negative Partical *ka*, but by a special word. Hence, altogether six different Mundari equivalents for the single word to *be* :

	Cop.	*Pred.*	*Pred.*	*Cop.*
That man	*is*	tall:	en horoe'	salangi- *a*.
That man	*is*	an Uraon :	en horo	Uraon *tan-i'*
That man	*is*	a servant :	en horoe'	*dasi-akan-a*.
That man	*is*	alive [exists]	en horo	*menai'a*.
That man	*is*	here :	en horo	*neria*.
That man	*is*	no more :	en horo	*bangai'a*.

This shows how very important it is that the student should thoroughly familiarize himself with the following rules which expose the whole matter in a more grammatical terminology and explain the details of the different constructions.

I. TO BE AS COPULA OR LINKWORD.

206. RULE 1. Whenever the Predicate of a Sentence is an *Adjective* or a *Participle*, it must be referred to the Subject by means of the Copula *a* being suffixed to the Adjective.

207 *ge* is very frequently, almost generally, affixed to the Adjective Predicate, so as to stand between it and the Copula a.

It is white : Pundi-*a*, or, pundi-*ge-a*. That fruit is sweet : En jo sibil-*a*-, or, sibil-*ge-a*.

208. When the *Subject* of the Sentence denotes an animate being, then a *Personal pronominal Affix*, corresponding with the Subject in *Number* and *Person* must be added to the Copula.

I am tall ;	salangige-*a-ing*.
Thou art tall ;	salangige-*a-m*.
He or she is tall :	salangige-*a-e'*.
It is tall :	salangige-*a*
Thou and I are tall :	salangige-*a-lang*.
He or she and I are tall :	salangige-*a-ling*.
You two are tall :	salangige-*a-ben*.
The two or both are tall :	salangige-*a-king*.
You and I are tall :	salangige-*a-bu*.
They and I are tall :	salangige-*a-le*.
You are tall :	salangige-*a-pe*.
They are tall :	salangige-*a-ko*

Thy two bullocks are lean : Ama' uri'king usu'ge-a-*king*.

His dogs are small : Setakotae huringge-*a-ko*.

209. Qualities which are the result of human skill or of some natural process such as, *v. gr.*, sickness, are rendered in Mundari by Perfect Participles of the Passive Voice (root + *akan*) of Transitive Predicates.

Leser, to sharpen, *leser-akan*, that which has been sharpened ; hence, sharp; *goja*, to point, *goja-akan*, that which has been pointed, pointed, *liṛu*, to bend, *liṛu-akan*, bent, crooked.

This class of Adjectives does not take the affix *ge* except in emphatic assertions.

Ama' katu ka leserakan-*a* : thy knife is not sharp. Leserakan-*ge-a* : it *certainly* is sharp.

210. The English, *poor*, is always rendered by the Indicative Present in *tan*: renge-*tan-aing*, renge-*tan-am*, renge *tanae'*; renge-*tanalang*, renge-*tanaling*, *etc.* : I am poor, thou art poor, *etc.* A few other Adjectives *denoting bodily* afflictions are sometimes rendred in the same way : langra-*tanaing*, langra-*tanam*, etc. : I am lame, thou art lame, *etc.* Hasu-*tanaing*, I am sick : kanra-*tanaing*, I am soreyed. However, these, as well as all other Adjectives denoting bodily afflictions, are generally rendered by means of the Participial form in *akan*. Langra-*akanae*', kaṇra-*akanae*'; : gau-*akanae*' : he is wounded ; mari-*akanae*' : he has got small-pox ; kasra-*akanae*': he has got itch.

211. Most of the English Adjectives endingin *ible* or *able*, such as *visible*, *audible*, *legible*, *edible*, *adorable*, *etc.*, are in Mundari rendered by affixing *leka* to the Indeterminate Passive form, *i.e.*, the root + *o*', Thus, *lel-o'-leka*, literally : like being seen, or, rather, like something that can be seen; aium-*o'-leka*, literally : like something that can be heard ; parau-*o'-leka* : legible ; jom-*o'-leka* : eatable ; sewa-*o'-leka* : adorable. Adjectives of this kind generally affix *ge* before the Copula a : lelo'leka'-*ge-a* : It is visible.

212. In short replies to questions, the Englishman often omits the Adjective Predicate and expresses only the linkword. The Munda does just the opposite. He omits the Copula *a*, and uses only the Adjective Predicate. In this case *ge* must always be affixed.

Am kiringakad daru jiling-*a* chi : Are the trees thou hast bought long ? Jiling-*ge* : They are.

213. RULE 2. — When the Predicate of a sentence is a Noun primarily and directly denoting *an individual, a species, a genus, a easte* or *a class*, it is referred to its Subject by means of the Copula *tan*.

214. A Pronominal Affix, agreeing with the Subject in *Number* and *Person*, must be suffixed to *tan*.

Here again, therefore, we meet with something akin to a conjugational scheme :

I am a Munda :	Horo	*tan-ing.*
Thou art a Munda :	Horo	*tan-me.*
He or she is a Munda :	Horo	*tan-i'*
Thou and I are Mundas :	Horoking	*tan-lang.*
He and I are Mundas :	Horoking	*tan-ling.*
You two are Mundas :	Horoking	*tan-ben.*
The two or both are Mundas:	Horoking	*tan-king.*
You and I are Mundas :	Horoko	*tan-bu.*
They and I are Mundas :	Horoko	*tan-le.*
You are Mundas :	Horoko	*tan-pe.*
They are Mundas ;	Horoko	*tan-ko.*

215. When the Subject is a Noun or Pronoun denoting one or more *inanimate* objects, the Impersonal Pronoun *a*' is is suffixed to *tan*.

Nen daru tan-a' : this is a tree. Ena diri tan-a' : those are stones.

216. REMARK 1.—In short questions and replies, the Copula *tan* is very frequently dropped, the Subject and Predicate being merely juxtaposed. In this elliptic construction the following three points must be carefully attended to :

(1) The Simple Personal Pronouns cannot stand as Subject ; in their stead the corresponding Compund Pronouns must be used.

(2) The Compound Pronouns generally stand first, the Substantive Predicates, second.

(3) The emphatic *ge* is almost invariably suffixed to the Substantive Predicates. Hence :

Aing	*Horo-ge*	=	Horo	*tan-ing.*
Am	*Horo-ge*	=	Horo	*tan-me.*
Ae'	*Horo-ge*	=	Horo	*tan-i'*
Alang	*Horoking-ge*	=	Horoking	*tan-lang.*
Aling	*Horoking-ge*	=	Horoking	*tan-ling.*
Aben	*Horoking-ge*	=	Horoking	*tan-ben.*
Aking	*Horoking-ge*	=	Horoking	*tan-king.*
Abu	*Horoko-ge*	=	Horoko	*tan-bu.*
Ale	*Horoko-ge*	=	Horoko	*tan-le.*
Ape	*Horoko-ge*	=	Horoko	*tan-pe.*
Ako	*Horoko-ge*	=	Horoko	*tan-ko.*

The elliptic construction is generally used when the Predicate is qualified by a Possessive Pronoun or Suffix. This man is my servant : Ne horo aingtaren dasige. That one is the father of the village chief : Ini' Mund'a apute. Is that thy house ? Chia ena oratam ?

217. REMARK 2.— Animate Predicates denoting individuals, species, etc., may drop the Dual and Plural Suffixes in this construction, so that Horo tan-lang, Horo tan-ling, Horo tan-bu, etc., are equivalent to Horo-king tan-lang, Horo-king tan-ling, Horo-ko tan-bu, etc

218. RULE 3.— Tan is never used as Copula in Negative Sentences. In these, mere juxtaposition of Subject and Predicate is the rule. Here, too, three points must be attended to :

(1) The Compund or Emphatic Personal Pronouns must be used, and they stand first.

(2) The Substantive Predicates stand second, and generally take the Suffix do.

(3) The Negative Particle ka follows the Substantive Predicate, and generally takes the Suffix ge.

Nala-ge is very often used instead of ka-ge.

Aing	Horo-do ka-ge	I am not a Munda.
Ame	Horo-do ka-ge	thou art not a Munda.
Ae'	Horo-do ka-ge	he or she is not a Munda.

Alang	Horoking-do ka-ge	thou and I are not Mundas.
Aling	Horoking-do ka-ge	he or she and I are not Mundas.
Aben	Horoking-do ka-ge	you two are not Mundas.
Aking	Horoking-do ka-ge	the two are not Mundas.
Abu	Horo-do ka-ge	you and I are not Mundas.
Ale	Horo-do ka-ge	they and I are not Mundas.
Ape	Horo-do ka-ge	you are not Mundas.
Ako	Horo-do ka-ge	they are not mundas.

COMPARISON OF ADJECTIVES

219. The formation of the *Comparative Degree* is analogous to the corresponding Hindustani : formation. The *Adjective* or *Qualitative* denoting the excess takes no Suffix. The Noun or Pronoun denoting the term of comparison takes the Ablative Suffix, *ete*. Hence, the sentence : The *elephant is bigger than the horse*, is rendered literally thus : From the horse the elephant is greater, *Sadomete hati marangae'*, I saw a beast bigger than a leopard, *Sonchitaete marang jontuing lelnamli'a.*

220. The *Superlative Degree* has a double formation—

1*st.*— When it is desired to state the absolute excess of one or more particular beings over all the beings of the same species or genus, the Adjective soben : all, is placed before the term of comparison, which stands in the *Ablative Case*. The Adjective remains unchanged, *v.gr.* The elephant is the biggest animal,—*Soben jontukoete hati maranggeae'* : literally, from all animals the elephanth is big, or, among all animals the elephant is big.

221. 2*nd*—Such Superlatives as are in English expressed by *very*, *exceedingly*, are in Mundari rendered in two ways, *viz.*—

(*a*) by affixing *uter* : exceedingly, utterly, to the Qualificative, *v.gr.*, *marang*:great; maranguter : very great ;

(*b*) by placing before the Qualificative one of the words : *isu, pura', isupura'*, *kented', mer-mer, betekan.*

222. *Isu* may be used with any kind of Qualificatives, just like eht English *very.* — *Isu bugin horo* : a very good man ; *isu marang daru* ; a very big tree. *Pura'* is by preference used with *Quantitatives. Kented'* is used with Qualificatives denoting energy, power or violence. *Mer-mer* is used with Qualificatives denoting qualities disagreeable to taste or smell, *v.gr., mer-mer harada.* It is exceedingly bitter. *Betekan*, although evidently the Hindi word betekan, is in Mundari pronounced *betekan*, and is synonymous with *isu, pura'*, and *isupura.' Isupura'* is but an intensive form for *pura'* and for *isu.*

223. 3*rd.*—Adjectives denoting dimensions form their Superlative by suffixing the Consonant *p* after the first vowel and then repeating that vowel, *v. gr., marang* : great, *ma-p-arang* : very great ; jiling : long, *ji-p-iling* : very long ;

moṭo : thick, *mo-po-oto* ; very thick : *huring*, small, *hu-p-uring* : very small.

Before proceeding with the study of the remaining rules let the student read the following English sentences and apply the three preceding rules without looking at the Mundari trnaslations. After that let him go through the Mundaṛi text and see which Copula might be used in sentences where the Subject and Predicate are merely juxtaposed.

Aing hola kiringakad lija' bar muka chakar-*a* oṛo' khub ibilge-*a*; mendo ka rang-akan-*a*.

The cloth I bought yesterday *is* two yards broad and very thick; but it *is* not coloured.

Okorem kiringla ?

Where didst thou buy it ?

Tapkara piṭre, gelbar ganḍate.

In the Tapkara market, for twelve annas.

Gelbar ganḍa ! Bedaked'mea-ko! Ama lija-ete aiñaga' jiling oṛo' chakar-a' ad, amaga' aminang ibil-ge-a', oṛo' rangakan-*a*; enreo gelbar ganda eskargeng halkeda. En ama' lija' iril gandarea' chij *tana'*.

Twelve annas ! They have cheated you ! My cloth *is* longer and broader than yours, and it *is* as thick as yours and, besides that, it *is* striped; and yet I *paid* only twelve annas. That cloth of yours *is* a thing of eight annas.

Ni okoe *tan-i'* ? Honme-koṛa chi ?

Who *is* this ? Your son ?

Honing-*do*, gomke, *kage*; kupul hoṛo-*ge*.

He *is* not my son, sir; he *is* a visitor.

Ama' honlekae' leloa.

He looks like your son.

Enado hege ! Bokoingta'ren hon *tani*. Mendo aina hon-*ete* salagino-akan-*ae'*.

That's true ! (*lit.* : so far that, yes.) He *is* the son of my junior brother. But he *is* a trifle taller than my son.

Dikulekae' eselge-*a*.

He *is* fair, (*i.e.*, light-brown) like a Hindu.

He gomke ! Tara mara Munḍahonko ẹselnoge-*ako*. Sobenko kale barabariakan-a. Okoni'do hendeno-ge-a; okoni'do hendeuter-ge, okon'ido esel-*ge*.

Yes, sir ! Some Mundas *are* pretty fair. We *are* not all alike. Some *are* pretty dark; others *are* entirely black, and some *are* fair.

En buṛia okoe ? Pura'ge *rengetanae* chimad'; usuge-ae' ad' lija'-tae' checha'akan-a.

Who *is* that old woman ? She *is* very poor, to be sure; she *is* lean and her cloth is torn.

Munda engate, gomkẹ.

She *is* the mother of the village chief, sir.

Munḍa engate ! Ini'do khube phunjiakan-*a*.

The mother of the village chief ? But, he *is* very rich !

Phuṇjidoe' pbunjiakan-*a*, mendo

Rich, indeed, he *is*; but he *is* very miserly. Because his mother can now isu kutuge-ae'. Engate na'do kae' kamidaria mentee harurung-ki'a oro' jetanao kae' omaitana.

Iduro' ? Ne kajido pura' et'kage-*a* ! Ka biswaso'lekage-a !

Sartige-*a* Kam biswasingredo ni'ku kulikom tobe.

Chia ! Apea' munda engate kae' asulja'ia ?

Kae' asuljiaa. Huringnia' oraree' taentana oro' in'roe' *rengetanna*.

Munda bokotekora rengetanae'!

He oro' ! Munda soben bugin loeong aege autada, bokote badiko barie sarea'ia. Bokote chikaeae' oro' ! Ale dondo horo'koge. Munda marang horo *tani* oro' sobenkole boroaitana.

Ena chikan daru ?

Kantaradaru *tana'*.

Kantarajo sibil-*a* chi ?

Era'ge sibilge-*a*, gomke. Jiluole jojoma, jangole jojoma; jiludo heremge-*a*.

Darudo isu niralge-*a*.

He gomke ! Ibilge sakamakan-*a* oro' jete singio kantaradaru umbulre khub tutkunge-*a*.

Ne dangra okoe ?

Aingta'ren dasi.

Horo tani' chi Uraon ?

Horoge gomke, Netaren Horoko Uraon dasiko kale achukoa.

Mendo Uraonko khub kamia horokoge.

Kamiageako, enado hege ! Mendo alea' jagar kaka mundia oro'

no longer work, he has driven her out of his house and he gives her nothing at all.

Is it possible ? This *is* too bad It *is* incredible !

It is true. If you don't believe me, ask these people then.

What ! Does your village chief not support his own mother ?

He does not support her. She stays in the house of the younger brother (of the Munda), and that one too *is* poor.

What ? The brother of the village chief *is* poor !

To be sure ! The village chief has taken all the good rice-fields himself; he left only some uplands to his younger brother. What is the junior brother to do ! We *are* stupid people. The Munda *is* a great man, and we are all afraid of him.

What kind of a tree *is* that ?

It *is* a jack-fruit tree.

Is the jack-fruit tasty ?

It is very tasty. We eat the pulp as well as the seds. The pulp is sweet.

The tree is very nice, indeed.

Yes, sir! it is shady (lit., it is leadfed thickly) and, even in summer, it is very cool in the shade of a jack-fruit tree.

Who is this young man ?

He is my servant.

Is he a Munda or an Uraon?

He is a Munda, sir. We, Mundas of these parts, don't engage uraon sevants.

But the Uraon are very hard-working men.

They are hardworking, that's tru; but they don't understand our language, and they are men of another caste.

eta jatiren hoṛoko *tanko.*

Nea chikan-*a'* ?

Nea a *tana'* ena sar-*ge.*

En chen̲ṛekodo *chikanko*, huaṛako chi kead'ko *tanko* ?

Huaṛakodo ka, gomke ! Kead'koge. Inku'-*ete* huaṛako marang-ge-*a*-ko. Tara mara kead'ko huara aminang marang-*a*-ko mendo inku judageko ranga-kan-*a*. Inkudo kead'ko kale nutumkoa.

What *is* this?

This *is* a bow, that'*s* an arrow.

And those birds yonder, what *are* they, reen pigeons or parrots ?

They *are* not green pigeons, sir ! They *are* not green pigeons, Sir ! They are parrots; green pigeons are bigger than those. Some parrots are as big as green pigeons, but they are of a different colour (*lit.*, We do not call those *keads.*

224. RULE 4.— When in an English sentence the Predicate is a Noun denoting an individual, but at the same time directly connoting an office or function, a dignity, prerogative or a state of dependence, the equivalent is generally not treated as a Noun, but as a Perfect Participle of the the Passive Voice in akan, and is therefore referred to its Subject by means of the Copula a, just like the Adjective Predicates in *akan.*

Munḍa : village-chief; hence, *munḍa-o'* (Passive) : to become a village-chief ; hence, *munda a-akan* : to have become, *i.e*, to be a village chief.

Raja : a king ; *raja-ö'* : to become aking ; *raja-akan* : to have become, *i.e.*, to be a king.

Dasi : a servant ; *dasi-o'* : to become a servant ; *dasi-akan* : to be a servant. *Gomke* : master, owner ; *gomke-akan* ; to be a master or owner. *Paltan* : soldier; *paltan-akan* : to be a soldier.

225. Predicates denoting religious persuasions are very frequently treated in the same way.

Sansar : a pagan ; sansar-o' to become a pagan; *sansar-akan* : to have become, *i.e.* to be a pagan. *Kristan* : a Christian ; *kristan-akan* : to be a Christian.

226. As a consequence of this change in the nature of the Predicate, *English Genitives* depending on the *English Substantive Predicates* do in *Mundari* become Locatives of rest. (See P. II. P. 107, **184**).

His father is *the village-chief of Sarwada*, becomes : Apute *Sarwada-re munda-akanae'*. My son is *the servant of the sacrificer*, becomes : Honingkora *pahaanr-ta're dasiakanae'*. Their senior brother is the *rajah of Tamar* : Bautetako *Tamar-re-e' raja-akana.*

It would be quite wrong use the Possessive affix *ren* in these constructions and say, *v.gr.*, Apute Sarwada-*ren* munda-akanae'.

N.B.—The discrimination between different Christian denominations is generally made by adding such Locatives to *kristan-akan* as Mundas think appropriate.

We are all *Catholics* : Ale sobenko *Raman-re* kristanakanale. All the people of that village are *Anglicans* : En haturenko sobenko *Angraji-reko* kristanakanā. These two are *Lutherans* : Niking *Germani-re*-king kristanaka.

227. Whenever the speaker desires to prominently insist on the *personality* of an individual and not on his *office, prerogative* or *status*, Predicates of this kind are treated as Nouns, just as in English. In that case they are either referred to their Subjects by means of *tan*, or they are merely juxtaposed with the Subject. (See **217**). In this construction the Possessive Affix *ren* must, of course, be used.

These men are the village-chiefs of that pati : Ne horoko en pati-*ren* Mundako *tanko*, or : Ne horoko en pati-*ren Mundako-ge*. Who is that ? The maharaja of Chota-Nagpore : Ini' okoe ? Chota-Nagpo*ren* maharaja *tani'*, or : Chota-Nagpor-*ren maharaja-ge*.

II. TO BE USED AS PREDICATE OR AS SO-CALLED SUBSTANTIVE VERB

228. RULE 5.— When the Verb *to be* is used to denote *real existence*, it must be rendred into Mundari by means of the word *mena'*: to exist. Besides denoting existence as such, *mena'* is also used as equivalent to the English phrases: *to be still alive, to be present, to be here or there, to be at home.*

230. *Bano'* is the negative of *mena'*. Hence, it means : *not to exist, to be dead,* or : *to be no more, to be absent, not to be here or there, not to be at home.*

231. *Mena'* and *bano'* insert the Pronominal Subjects between the root and the Copula *a*.' Hence the following schemes :

Pred. Subj.	*Cop.*			
Mena'-iñ	*-a*	I exist	or	: I am present, etc.
mena'-me	*-a*	thou existest,	"	: thou art present, etc.
mena'-i	*-a*	he or she exists,	"	: he or she is present, etc.
mena'		it or they exist,	"	: it or they are present, etc.
mena'-lang	*-a*	thou and I exist,	"	: thou and I are present, etc.
mena'-ling	*-a*	he or she and I exist,	"	: he or she and I are present, etc.
mena'-ben	*-a*	you two exist,	"	: you two are present, etc.
mena'-king	*-a*	both of them exist	"	:, both of them are present, etc.
mena'-bu	*-a*	you and I exist,	"	: you and I are present, etc.
mena'-le	*-a*	they and I exist,	"	: they and I are presne, etc.
mena'-pe	*-a*	you exist,	"	: you are present. Etc.
mena'-ko	*-a*	they exist,	"	: they are present, etc.

232. REMARK 1.—Instead of *mena'me'a*, the contracted form mena'ma may be used.

Bang – iñ	*- a*	I do not exist,	or	: I am absent.
bang – me	*- a*	thou dost not exist,	"	: thou art absent.
bang – a'i	*- a*	he or she does not exist,	"	: he or she is absent.

bang – a it or they not exist, " : it is or they are absent.
bang – lang- a thou and I do no exist, " : thou and I are absent.
bang – ling - a he or she and I do not exist, " : he or she and I are absent.
bang – ben - a you two do not exist, " : you two are absent.
bang – king- a both of them do not exist, " : both of them are absent.
bang – bu - a you and I do not exist, " : you and I are absent.
bang – le - a they and I do not exist, " : they and I are absent.
bang – pe - a you do not exist, " : you are absent.
bang – ko - a they do not exist, " : they are absent.

232. REMARK 2.— Instead of the form *bangiña*, the form *bangaiña* may be used. In some parts *bangu'ia* or *banguja* is used instead of bangaia. The form *bangkua* occurs frequently instead of *bangkoa*.

233. REMARK 3.— *Mena'* and *bano'* denoting presence in or absence from a given place are generally standing alone. Adverbs of place or the Locative Case of a Noun is added only when it is absolutely necessary, as, *v. gr.* in questions, or when it is desired to emphasize the exact whereabouts.

Ne bir-re kulako mena'koa chi ?	Are there tigers in this forest ?
Bankua.	There are none.
Khuntirenko mena'koa chi *bankua* ? *Mena'kua.*	*Are* the Khunti people *here* or *are* they not ? They *are here.*
Nere mena'koa, haṇredo bankua.	*It is here* that they are, and not over there.
Chimin Pormesorko *mena'koa*?	How many Gods *are* there ?
Miad' eskarge Pormesor *menaia.*	There *is* only one God.
Mimiad' hature mimiad' munda mena'ria,oṛo' mimiad patire mimiad manki menaia.	In each village *there* is one chief, and in every pati (district) *there* is one manki.
Mod' patiredo chiminang hatu *mena'* ?	And in one pati how many villages *are there* ?
Okooko patire mod'hisi karedo mod'hisi gelea habe' ; mendo pura'te mod' patire gelbarialeka *mena'*.	In some patis there are twenty or even up to thirty villages ; but generally *there are* about twelve villages in one pati.
Manki *mena'i* haturedo munḍa *banga'ia* ?	*Is there no* chief in the village in which the manki lives (or dwells) ?
Mena'ia ?	*There is one.*
Netarrea' birko're jiluko *mena'-koa* chi ?	*Is there* any game in the forests of these parts ?
Khub *mena'koa*, gomke ! Kulaiko *mena'koa*, silibko kisimrenk *mena'koa*,	*There is* plenty, sir ! *There are* hares, *there are* deer of several kind,

birsukuriko *mena'koa*, sonchitako ad' kulakoo *mena'koa*.	there are wild boars, *there are* leopards and tigers.
Hatikodo ?	*Are there* any elephants ?
Bankua, gomke !	*There are none*, sir !
Apeta'ren muṇḍa haṛam najaked' *menai'a* ?	*Is* your old village chief *still alive* (*lit*., up to the present moment).
Api chanḍu'taete banga'ia, bing huagoe'ki'a	He *died* three months ago (*lit*., since three months ago he is no more), a snake killed him (*lit*., bit him dead).
Apum oṛo' Soma haṛamdo ?	And your father and old Soma ?
Inkingo *ḅankinga*.	*Both of them are dead too*.
Ne goṛare pura' diri *mena'*.	*There are* plenty of stones in this high field.
Ne mulire diri *mena'*, hansa'do maido diri *bano'a*.	In this direction there *are* stones; but, over there, there is *not* a single one.
Tising sobenko *mena'pea* chi ?	*Are* you all *at home*-at-day ?
Mena'lea ; bauing *eskarge* banga'ia, siujanae.	*We are* ; only my senior brother *is not at home*, he is gone to plough.
En naua oṛa're okoe *mena'ia* ?	Who *is living* in that new house ?
Pahanṛge.	The sacrificer.
Mena'ia chi ?	*Is he at home ?*
Banga'ia, mad'e majana.	*He is not at home*, he is gone to cut bamboos.

235. Instead of using mena' to denote presence in a particular place, the Mundas use, by preference, another rather peculiar construction :

Re : in, on, at, is suffixed to Nouns ; thus : Ora're : in the house ; bakrire : in the garden ; burure : on the mountain ; Kalkattare : at Calcutta. Now, to say, for instance : They (Subject) are (Predicate) in the house (Adverbial phrase), the Mundas place the Adverbial phrase first : Ora're-to this they add the Pronominal Subject ko—and then suffix the Copula a.' The whole compound is pronounced like one word : Ora'rekoa' : they are in the house. Hence :

236. RULE 6.—To express *presence in a particular place*, Adverbial phrases in *re* are used as Intransitive Predicates, and the Pronominal Subjects are inserted between the Adverbial phrase and the Copula *a*.

237 . N. B.— In the first and third perosn Singular, the vowel i of *ing* and i elides with the *e* of *re* and yields a long *i*. The jerk denoted by (') remains on the Pronoun *i*.

Ọra' – r - iñ - a : I am in the house.
Ọra' – re - m - a : thou art in the house.
Ọra' – r - i' - a : he or she is in the house.
Ọra' – re - a : it is or they (inan. Objects) are in the house.
Ọra' – re - lang - a : thou and I are in the house.
Ọra' – re - ling - a : he or she and I are in the house.
Ọra' – re - ben - a : you two are in the house.
Ọra' – re - king - a : both of them are in the house.
Ọra' – re - bu - a : you and I are in the house.
Ọra' – re - le - a : they and I are in the house,
Ọra' – re - pe - a : you are in the house.
Ọra' – re - ko - a : they are in the house.

238. REMARK.— *Ọra'-r-iñ-a' etc*., are used, when it is desired to insist on the presence *inside the house*. They are hardly ever used to render the English phrase *to be at home*. This, as already stated, is generally rendered by *mena'*.

Ner-iña	: I am here.	*Nerebena*	: you two are here.
Nerema	: thou art here.	*Nerekinga*	: both are here.
Ner-i'a	: he (she) is here.	*Nerebua*	: you and I hare here.
Nere-a	: it is they (i.o,) are here.	*Nerelea*	: they and I are here.
Nerelanga	: thou and I are here.	*Nerepea*	: you are here.
Nerelinga	: he (she) and I are here.	*Nerekoa*	: they are here.

Okoriña ?	where am I ?	*Okorelanga* ?	where are thou and I ?	*Okorebua* ?	where are you and I?
Okorema ?	where art thou ?	*Okorelinga* ?	where are he (she) and I ?	*Okorelea* ?	where are they and I ?
Okori'a ?	where is he or she ?	*Okorebena* ?	where are you two ?	*Okorepea* ?	where are you ?
Okorea ?	where is it ? or where are they (*i.o.*) ?	*Okorekinga* ?	where are both of them ?	*Okorekoa* ?	Where are they ?

239. The construction just described is used also with Adverbs and Postpositions denoting motion to a place, and with Nouns standing in the Locative case with the Affix *ta'* or *ta'te*. The compounds thus obtained are equivalent to the English phrase *to go to* or, according to circumstances, *to go unto* orunto.

They are used with a Present as well as with a Future meaning.

The elision described in **237** takes place in these constructions also.

Ọra'-t – iñ -a I am going home, or : I shall go home.
Ọra'-te –m -a thou art going home, or : thou wilt go home.
Ọra'-t –i' -a he or she is going home, or : he or she will go home.

Oṛa'-te –lang-a	thou and I are going home,	or :	thou and I will go home.
Oṛa'-te –ling -a	he or she and I are going home,	or :	he or she and I will go home.
Oṛa'-te –ben -a	you two are going home,	or :	you two are going home.
Oṛa'-te –king -a	the two are going home,	or :	the two are going home.
Oṛa'-te –bu -a	you and I are going home,	or :	you and I are going home.
Oṛa'-te –le -a	they and I are going home,	or :	they and I are going home.
Oṛa'-te –pe -a	you are going home,	or :	you are going home.
Oṛa'-te –ko *-a*	they are going home,	or :	they are going home.

Oḳa'-t -iñ -a?	Where am I to go to ?	or : Whither shall I go ?
Oḳo -te-m-a?	where art thou goint to ?	or : where wilt thou go to ?
Oḳo -t -i' -a ?	where is he or she going to ?	or : where will he or she go to ?
	etc.	

Han-te-lang-a	thou and I	are going,	or : will go to yonder place.
Han-te ling-a	he or she and I	" "	or : " " "
Han-te-ben-a	you two	" "	or: " " "
Han-te-king-a	both of them	" "	or: " " "

All the difficulties concerning the correct translation of the Verb *to be* are restricted to the *Present Tense.*

240. The Past Tense of the Copulas *tan* and *a'* as well as the Past Tense of *mena'* in all its significations is *taeken.* This takes the Copula *a.* The Pronominal Subject in affixed either to *taekena* or to the word immediately preceding.

He was village-chief :	Mundae' taekena.
They were pagans :	Sansarko taekenako.
They and I were soldiers:	Paltanko taekenale.
He was very good :	Isu bugine taekena.
You were poor :	Rengegepe taekena.
You and I were far way:	Sangingebu taekena.
He was here:	Taekenae'.
He and I were at home:	Taekenaling.
Last year he was still alive :	Mahae' taekena.
You and I were in the garden :	Bakrirelang taekena.
Both of them were on horseback :	Sadomreking taekena.
Wert thou inside (the house) ?	Ora'regem taekena ?

241. In Negative Sentences the Particle *ka* precedes taekena.

He was not the village-chief: .	Ini Mundado kae' taekena.
They were not far away :	Sanginge kako taekena.
You werenot at home:	kape taekena.
You two were not here :	Kaben taekena.
Neither of them was inside (the house) :	Orare kaking taekena.

242. *Mena'* has a Continuative Present Tense in *akan*. This generally takes the emphatic *ge*.

Mena'-akan-ge-a-ing	: I am still	alive, or : here,	or : at home.	
Mena'-akan-ge-a-m	: thou art still	" or : "	or : "	
Mena'-akan-ge-a-e'	: he or she is still	" or : "	or : "	
Mena'-akan-ge-a	: it is still existing	or : "	or : there.	

etc.

243. *Bano'* forms a Past Tense in *jan*. In this Tense-form the Personal Pronominal Affixes remain attached to *bano'* as they stand in the construction given above. (See **232**).

This Tense-form is, owing to its meaning, naturally limited to the third Person Singular, Dual and Plural.

Bangai' -jan-a : he or she died, *also* : he or she disappeared form here.
Bano' -jan-a : (that thing) disappeared.
Bangking -jan-a : the two or both of them died or disappeared.
Bangko -jan-a : they died or disappeared.

244. Adverbs of place and Nouns signifying *localities* or *places* form a similar Past Tense, when they have the Suffixes *te* or *ta'te* denoting *motion* to, *towards, into or unto*.

This Past Tense has all the Persons of the three Numbers.

Oṛa'-t-ing -jan-a : I went home.
Oṛa'-t-m -jan-a : thou wentest home.
Oṛa'-t-i -jan-a : he or she went home.
Oṛa'-t-lang-jan-a : you and I went home.
Oṛa'-t-ling -jan-a : he or she and I went home.
Oṛa'-t-ben -jan-a : the two or both went home.
etc.

245. Various words are used to perform the function of the Future Tense to *mena'* and *bano'*.

1st : When there is question of inanimate beings, the word *taen* is used to denote *existence* or *non-existence* in the *Future*.

In negative sentences *oṛo'do* : no longer, often precedes the negative particle *ka*.

After three years this house will no longer exist: Api sirma taeomte ne *ora'* ka *taena*, or : oro'do ka *taena*.

2nd : When there is question of living beings, *jido'* : to be alive, is often used instead of taem.

Ne haram api sirma taeomte orodo kae' jido'a : this old man will not be alive after three years.

246. When *mena'* and *bano'* mean : to be present, to be absent, to be at home, to be away, or, not at home, they borrow their Future either from *taen* or form *namo'* : to be found.

Munda gapa *kae' taena*, or : *kae' namo'a* : to-morrow the village-chief won't be here ; or : won't be at home. Chia mean geking *taena*, or : *namo'a* ? will both be at home, or : present, after to-morrow ?

MENA' AND *BANO'*
DENOTING POSSESSION OR THE CONTRARY

247. The Mundas have no *Transitive* equivalent of the English Verbs : *to have, to possess, to own.* The Intransitive Predicates *mena'* and *bano'* are used to render those English Verbs. Instead of saying : *I have a house*, they use a construcution analogous to : *A house is to me. I have no house*, becomes : *A house is not to me.*

This is done by suffixing the Possessive Suffixes *taing, tam, tae, talang, taling, taben, taking, tabu, tale, tape, tako* to the word *mena'* in Affirmative Sentences and to *bano'* in Negative Sentences. The Possessive affix *a'* is frequently added to *taing, tam, tae, etc.*

Oṛa' mena'taing	or : *mena'taiña'*	I have	a house
Oṛa' mena'tam	or : *mena'tama'*	thou has	" "
Oṛa' mena'tae	or : *mena'taea'*	he (she) has	" "
Oṛa' mena'talang	or : *mena'talanga'*	thou and I have	" "
Oṛa' mena'taling	or : *mena'talinga'*	he (she) and I have	" "
Oṛa' mena'taben	or : *mena'tabena'*	you two have	" "
Oṛa' mena'taking	or : *mena'takinga'*	both of them have	" "
Oṛa' mena'tabu	or : *mena'tabua'*	you and I have	" "
Oṛa' mena'tale	or : *mena'talea'*	they and I have	" "
Oṛa'mena'tape	or : *mena'tapea'*	you have	" "
Oṛa'mena'tako	or : *mena'takoa'*	they have	" "

N. B.— The *e* of *tae* is very rarely heard with the jerk denoted by (').

248. In this construction again attention must be paid to the distinction between living beings and inanimate objects. When, as in the example given above, *that which is owned* is an inanimate object, the form *mena'* or *bano'a* must be used, even if more than one object be owned, *v.gr., baria* ora' menata'ing : I have two houses.

249. But, if that which is owned be a living being, the forms *mena'ia* and *banga'ia* must be used.

I have a horse : Sadom *mena'iataing.*

Thou hast no horse : Sadom *banga'iatam.*

250. If *two* living beings be owned (or the contrary), the forms *mena'kinga* or *bankinga* must be used.

Baria dasiking *mena'kingatae* : he has two servants.Baria dasiking *bangkingatale* : they and I have not got two servants.

251. If more than two living beings be owned (or the contrary), the forms *mena'koa* or *bangkoa* must be used.

You have no servants: Dasiko *bangkoatape.* They have servants : Dasiko *mena'koatako.*

252. Instead of using the Possessive Suffixes *taing (taiña, tam (tama') etc.*, the independent Possessive Adjectives may be used. If so, there Adjectives stand before the Noun denoting that which is owned.

Aiña oṛa' mena' :	I have a house.
ama'oṛa' banoa' :	thou hast no house.
aea'oṛa' mena' :	he (she) has a house.
alanga' ora' banoa' :	thou and I have no house.
alinga' sadom *mena'ia* :	he and I have no horse.
abena' sadom banga'ia :	you two have no horse.
akinga' baria sadom king mena'kinga :	these two have two horses.
abua' baria sadomking bangkua' :	you and I have not got two horses.
alea' dasiko mena'ko*a* :	they and I have servants.
apea' dasiko bangku*a* :	you have no servants.

253. REMARK.— Mundas, who do not know Hindi, prefer the use of the Suffixes *taing, tam, etc.* They use the independent Possessive Adjectives only when it is desired or necessary to lay stress on the person of thw owner, *v.gr.* : As for me, I have fields and cattle ; but thou hast nothing at all in this village : *Aiña*' oṛa'o mena' urikoo mena'-koa, *ama'do* jetanao banoa'ne hature.

254. If the owner be denoted by a Noun, then that Noun with the Suffix *a*' precedes the word which signifies that which is owned. The construction is the same as the one just given.

Pakua' loeong mena' :	Paku has rice fields.
Pakua' Paisa banoa' :	Paku has no money.
Pakua' dasi mena'ia :	Paku has a servant.
Pakua' uri'king bangkinga' :	Paku has not got two bullocks.
Pakua' Meromko mena'koa :	Paku has goats.
Pakua' honko bangkua :	Paku has no children.

255 . For the Past Tense taekena is substituted for *mena*' in Affirmative Sentences and *ka taekena* in Negative Sentences.

Oṛa'taekena-taing or : *taekena-taiñ-a*' : I had a house.

Ora'taekena-tam or : *taekena-tam-a'* : thou hadst a house.
Ora'taekena-tae or : *taekena-tae-a'* : he or she had a house.
etc.

Aiña' ora' Taekena : I had a house.
Ama' ora' Taekena : thou hadst a house.
Aea' ora' Taekena : he or she had a house.

256. When there is question of living beings being owned then Personal Pronominal Affixes of the required Number must of course be suffixed to taekena.

Miad'eskarge uri' taekena-e'-taea' : he had only one bullock. Baria sadomking taekena-king-taea : he had two horses. Uri meromko tae-kena-*ko-tako* : they had cattle.

257. In Negative Sentences these Pronominal Affixes must be added to the Particle *ka.* They may even then be repeated after the Possessive Affixes *taing, tam, tae, etc.*

Uri' ka-*e*' taekena-tae : he had no bullock. Baria sadomking ka-*king* taekena-taea' or : ka-*king* taekena-*king*-taea' : he had not got two horses. Honko ka-*ko* taekena-taking or : ka-*ko* taekena-*ko*-taking : The two had no children.

258. When the Subject of the Sentence is a Noun, a Demonstrative or Interrogative Pronoun, then that Noun or Pronoun takes the Possessive Affix *a'* and stands first.

Paku-*a'* taka ka taekena : Paku had no money.
Ini-*a'* uri' meromko taekena-ko : That one had cattle.
Okoe-*a'* sadom taekena-*e'*? Who had a horse ?

259. *The Future Tense* is taken from *nam* : to get.

Taka-doing *namegea* : I shall have money. Kalomkote uri'kom *namkoa* chi? Wilt thou have bullocks next year?

260. Sometimes the Passive form *hobao'* is used. This either takes the Possessive Affixes *taing, tam, tae,* etc., or else it is preceded by the Possessive Pronouns *Aiña', ama', aea'* or *aeaga'*, etc.

Kakatetaking goejanre en soben loeong akinga *hobaoa'* : These two will have or get all those rick-fields when their junior uncle dies. Oro' barpitileka gamaere honang baba khub' *hobaoa'tabu* : If it continue raining for two weeks more, all of us shall have plenty of paddy.

261. A person may own something, *i.e.* have the right of ownership over something, without having that thing with, on him or by him at a given moment. The constructions explaiend above, *viz., mena'*and *bano'* with the Possessive Affixes or prceded by Possessive Genitives in *a'* all denote simply the right of ownership, but they are not used to render the English *phrases to have on, with* or *by oneself, to have here at the present moment.* These phrases are rendered by means of *mena'* or *bano'* preceded, not by Possessive Genitives in a' but by the *Locative Case* in *tare.*

Has any one got a knife here ? Jetaeta're katu *mena'* ? Have you got money with you ? Apeta're ṭaka *mena'* ? I was quite close to a sleeping hare ; I would have shot him but I had not got a bow and arrows with me : Durumakan kulai khubing naṉṟelia, tuingkiaing honanga mendo *aing-ta'ṛe* a'-sar *ka taekena.*

In short replies to questions the Locative is of course frequently omitted. Ne lija'ing ki'ringea honanga' mendo *aing-ta're* paisa *bano'a, amta're mena'* chi ? Bano'a, I would buy this cloth, but I have no money with me ; hast thou any here ? I have none.

262. Instead of the above construction the Perfect Tense forms of *au* : to bring, or *nam* : to get, are often used.

Am-ta're katu *mena'* chi *bano'a* ? Kaing *auakada.* Hast thou got a knife here or not ? I have not brought one.

263. The technical expression : *to be in possession of* is rendered by the Hindi *dakal* in the Locative Case and *mena'*. The Locative *dakal-re* is preceded by a Possessive Genitive in *a'*.

Mutru is in possession of that piece of land, becomes : That piece of land is in Mutru's possession. En ote *Mutru-a' dakalre mena'*.

264. When the object of the actual occupation or possession is not mentioned in the sentence, then *dakal* stands in the Nominative.

Who is in possession ? becomes : whose possession is there ? *Okoea' dakal mena'* ? Mutru is not in possession : *Mutru-a' dakal banoa'*.

265. The Possessive Affixes *taing, tam, tae, etc.*, or *taiña', tama'*, taea', etc. are often detached from the beings or objects owned and suffixed to the Predicate of the Sentence. When this is done the Possessives *taiña*,'tama; *taea'* are used by preference.

Thus instead of : Uri'ko-*taing* goe'janako, we get : Uri'ko goe'janako-taiña' : My bullocks have died. Meromkoe' akiringked'koa-*taea'* for meromko-*tae* akiringked'koae' He sold his goats.

Ne loeong okoea' tana' ?	To whom, does this rice-field belong ?
Ṭiprua'ge gomke.	It belongs to Tipru.
Babado besno'gea mendo tasadte pere'akana. Chikanamente kae' heṛed'jada ?	The paddy looks well enough, but it is full of grass. Why does he not weed it ?
Kae' daṛia na'do. Honko bankua'taea'. Maha hontekuṛi Asamtee' nirjana, seno;jan chandu bar hoṛo honking hobahasuteking goe'jana musingre oṛo'. barsing taeomte kuṛio	He cannot do it now. He has no children. Last year, his daughter ran away to Assam ; last month, two of his children died of cholera in a single day ; and two days later, his wife also

goe'janataea'. Na'-do eskarakantee' chikaea ! Paisa mena're chi hered'nalakoe' achukoa honanga', mendo enao bona'.

what can he do ? If, at least, he had some money, he could hire weeders by the day, but that too (*viz.* money) he has not got.

Ote khub' chi mena'taea' ?

Has he got much land ?

Mena' gomke. Uri'koo mena'koatae. Mendo en soben otena'do kae' kamidaṛia. Kalomko'te Taradoe' siea taradoe' marchaea. Uri'ko maharaakad'koae'. Ae'ge da' aujada, ae'ge manḍitana. Eskarge chiminunge, kamia !

He has, Sir. He has bullocks too. But he cannot now cultivate all that land. Next year, he will plough part of it, and part of it he will let lie fallow. His bullocks he has confided to the care of the cow-herd. He himself is fetching water (for cooking); he himself is cooking. How much is he alone to work !

Nakan hoba sirma ale Hoṛokomente isu et'kagea. Neleme gomke, ne bar chanḍure ale hature modhisi gel-e horoko goe'janako.

Cholera years like this are very bad for us, Mundas. See, Sir, within these two months, thirty-seven people have died in our village.

Ape Horokoa' jetan hoba-ranu banoa' chi ?

Have you Mundas got no cholera-medicine ?

Enarea' ranu banoa'. Ena rogge. Hasu sab'koa kamita' karedo uri'gupita' karedo orare. Musing karedo mod sanjlekageko hasua, enteko gojo'a. Misa misa musingre mod' ora're bar api horoko banogoa'. Topamenteo hambala oṛo' gota hatu si'soegea.

There is no remedy against that That is an epidemic. The disease will catch them whilst they are at work, or grazing the cattle, or in the house. They will be sick for a day or about half a day; and then they die. Sometimes, two, three people will die in a single day in one hour. It is seven difficult to bury them, and the whole village is in a state of confusion.

Uri'ko mena'kuatama' chi bangkua'?

Hast thou got any bullocks, or hast thou got none ?

Upunia mena'koataing. Maha turui bo taekmenako. Miad'ni goejanae' entedo inia' juring akiringta'ia.

I have got four. Last year I had six head. One of them died, and then I sold the pair to it.

Samua'do menakoa chi ?

And Samu has he any ?

Miad'o bangkua'taea nimirge.

For the moment he has not got a single one.

Maha ale hature uṛi-rog uṛungjans, enate sobenko goe'janakotae. Mendo inia'taka paisa

Last year, cattle-disease broke out in our village, and all his cattle died of it. But, he has money; he will mena; nauakoe' kiringkoa.

Chimin meroko mena'ko-atama.

Upunia eskarge mena'koataing. Maha khub'geko taekena. Entedo musing taniko nereko teba'jana goṭa got, gelturuialeka. Han daruta' aina meromko namked'koako oṛo' mod' ghaṛikad're upuniageko jomked'koa. Huring din taeomte oṛo' tuiu moiode' goe'kia.

En taniko chilekanko ?

Ara'geako, setalekako leloa' mendo chad'lomtako tuiu-chad'-lomleka ibilgea. Gupitan honko miad'o kako boroakoa; meromko kako goe'sidakoako mendo jid' jid, geko jomkoa khub'sekerage. Monre turui marang horoko khub' kakla kaklateka niridire bagekoako karedo ka. Monre turui sirmare misalekako hijua.

Ape hature jetaea banduk mena' ?

Goṭa hature miad'o kam namea, jataea laisens banoa. Mimid' horoa' a-sar kapi mena' enate senderare kulaiko, silib'ko birsukurikole goe'koa.

Amta're katu mena'chi ?

Kaing auakada. Bokoingta're mena'. Omameaingchi ?

Ne loeong okea'? Kented' chakara oṛo' buginuterge leloa'.

Loeongdo Pakua'ge, mendo tising-gapa inia' dakal banoa'. Bar sirmata'ete Ṭeṭea dakalre mena'.

Pakua' mena'redo, dakal

buy others (*lit.* new ones).

How many goats hast thou goten ?

I have only four. Last year, I had a lot. Then, one day, the wild dogs, a whole herd of them, about sixteen, reached here. Near yonder tree they found my goats, and in an instant they devoured four of them. A few days later, again, a jackal killed one of them.

What are those wild dogs like ?

They are red, they look like dogs; but their tails are busky like a jackal's tail. They do not fear the goat-grazing children one bit; they do not kill the goats first, but they eat them alive very fast. If five or six grown-up men run towards them with loud shouts, they abandon them (the goats), otherwise not. They come once about every five or six years.

Has any one in your village a gun ?

You won't find a single one in the whole village ; no one has a license. Every man has a bow, arrows and a battle-axe; with those (weapons) we kill hares, deer and wild boar in the hunt.

Hast thou got a knife with thee ?

I have not got it with me (have not brought it). My younger brother has one here. Shall I give it to thee ?

Whose is this rice-field ? It is exceedingly broad and looks to be very good.

The field belongs to Paku;l but, for the moment, he is out of possession. Since two years, it is in the possession of Tete.

If it belong to Paku, then how has he lost possession ?

chilekate ad'kedae ?

Enado nakajana : Ṭeṭe Murumkelaren hoṛoge. Neren Joraṛa Tete misitee' doaka'ia. Entedo turui sirma sidare Jorora han marang piri ad' baria badi jorpeskite Ṭeṭee omaia. En dipli Ṭeṭea' nere oṛa duaro ka taekena. Entedo en ote bar sirma mente aea hatuate kamikedchi, Jorara kundamsae oratada. En uter sirma ale hature hoba-hasu urung-janchi pura horoko goe'jana. Joraraa' bar horo kora-honkingoking bankujana. Nado Joraraa' bar horo kuri-honking eskarge mena'kinga.

Enamente Joraṛa gojo're aea' soben ote bokote-kora Pakua'age hobaoa. Eta bokoboeako bankua'taea. Ale Hoṛokoa' dastur enkagea.

Isu dintaete Joraṛaa'ad Pakua' kuṛikinga' eperang taekena. Entedo Joraṛa hontekorataking goe'-janre, kurite mer mere' kisjana, oṛo' Pakureni' honing-korakinge' jomked'kinga mente sobensae' jagarbaṛakeda. Entedo haturenko sokata'te chaulijangko idila'. Ni'do Pakureni najome' udub'ki'a. En diplita'ete haturenko Pakuageko bairijana. Kristanakanae mente danre kako aukia (1) tamo kako tamkia mendo' hagareko bageta'ia, enado ini'lo dub-tingun (2) oṛo' jom-nu kakoa

That happened this way : Tete is a Murumura man. Jorara of this place married Tete's sister. Then, six years ago, Jorara gave yonder big tanr and two pieces of high-lying terraced rice-fields in mortgage to Tete. At that time, Tete had no house nor any thing in this place. Then, after having cultivated that land from his own village for two years, he made a house at the back of Jorara's house. Just that year, cholera broke out in our village and many people died. Two sons of Jorara also died. Now Jorara has only two daughters.

Therefore, when Jorara comes to die, all his hands, will go to his junior brother Paku. He has no other brothers. Such is the custom among us Mundas.

Since a long time ago, there has been a quarrel between the wives of Jorara and Paku. Then, when the two sons of Jorara died, his wife became very angry and she was saying all over that Paku's wife had eaten her two sons (*i.e.* produced their death by means of witchcraft). Then the people of the village carried rice-grains to the soothsayer (*i.e.* they went to consult the soothsayer). This one point out Paku's wife as a witch. Since that time, the villagers turned against Paku (became enemies to Paku). They did not take

(1) When the soothsayer has pointed out some one as a witch or wizard, he also indicates in detail the number and kind of animals which must be sacrificed in order to appease the particular *bonga* (spirit) who, on account of the witch's spell, has caused the disease or death. The sacrificial animals must be supplied by the family of the witch or wizard, and the expense in always a heavy one. This is called *danre au* : to take the sacrifices.

(2) *dub-tingun* (*lit.*, to sit and stand with some one) means to hold the usual friendly intercourse with some one.

oṛo' jan nalis uṛungo're ini'a kako gowana.

Entedo api sirma sidare Joṛara am en marang loeong i'reme mente Ṭeṭee uskurki'a, oṛo' Ṭeṭee' irkeda.

Chia ! Paku jalekateo kae' ujurkeda ?

Chikaeae' oṛo' ? Monṛe ora'ren horoko kora kuṛi sobenko Ṭete-geko irdengaki'a. Paku eskarakante dapal kae daṛijana.

Mendo tana nanregea oṛo' Ranchire hakimko dubakana !

Ela, gomke, nakan kajire tanarenko oṛo' kacherirenko kumbuṛuko daua ad' peṛe'geko omakoa.

Enado alom kajia ! Tanarea' kaing kajia, mendo kacheriren hakim gomkeko ghus kako auea oṛo' sojegeko bicharea; enado aing taukageng ituana.

Enado', gomke, aingoing ituana, aing eskarge ka mendo ale soben Horoko enale torakada. Angraji hakim ghus kae' auea oro' ae'ge lelja'lekage khub taukagee' bicharea. Mendo ale disumre na'jaked' jataea' ote ka mukaakana. Hakim horokoa' gowakajileka bichar hobaoa', oro' enate sobena ultapultaotana. Neleme gomke, en loeongrea' Paku Ranchire naliskedae'. Entedo kacherire mid' horo

the prescribed sacrifices from him, nor did they beat him for fear of the missionary, because he is a Christian. But they have abandoned him in the brotherhood, *i.e.*, they refuse to speak to him and to eat and drink with him and, if a law-suit come on, they won't give evidence for him.

Then, three years ago, Jorara instigated Tete to reap that big rice-field and Tete cut it.

Why ! did not Paku object in any way ?

What is he to do ! The inmates of five houses, men and women, all helped Tete to cut (the field). Paku being quite isolated was unable to fight.

But, the police station in quite near and there are judges sitting in Ranchi !

Alas, Sir ! In a matter like this the police and the courts (those in the thana and those in the courts) do only give formal right and power to the thieves.

Do not say such a thing ! I won't speak of the thana : but the judges in the law-courts take no bribes and they judge justly; that much I know for certain.

That, Sir, I also know. Not I only, but we Mundas all of us know that. An English judge will take no bribe and he will judge straight according to his own lights (*lit.*, as he sees things). But in our country nobody's fields are surveyed up to date. The judge must judge according to the evidence given by the people, and thereby every thing gets upside down. Look here, sir ! Paku brought a habe ini'mente kako gowajana. Ena eskargedo kage : Monre horoko, oṛo' inkure Jorara ae'tege Ṭeṭeta're gowako omla. Tetaa' dakare mena Ṭeṭe' sikedae' Ṭeṭe herkedae' mente Kiriako jomkeda. Entedo hakim chikaea ? Pakua'nalise' dismistada oro' dewanime mentee' hukumkeda. Chinate `dewania ? Dewanire pura taka seno'a, oṛo' na'do Pakua' taka paisa bono'a.

case in the Ranchi courts about that rice-field. Then, in court, not a single man gave evidence for him. Not only that; but, five men, and among them Jorara himself, gave evidence in favour of Tete. They swore j(they ate an oath) that it (the field) was in Tete's possession, that Tete ploughed it and that Tete had sown it. In such a case, what can a judge do ? He dismissed Paku's case and ordered him to go to the civil court. With what *is* he to bring a civil case ? In a civil case a lot of money is spent (goes), and now Paku has no money.

Mena'reo, jetana kae' daṛia. Dewanireo sobena hoṛokoa' gowa kajite bicharo'a, oro' Paku gowako kae' namkoa. Na'do jana chiko're Ṭeṭe en nalisrea' nakale' udubea.

But, even if he had, he could not do anything. In the civil case, too, all is being decided according to men's oral evidence, and Paku will get no witnesses. Now, if anything happen, Tete will show a copy of that case.

En uter nakalte aea' dakal sabutio'a oro' Pakua' asal daua rapud'chabao'tana. Enamenteng kajiamtana : Tanarenko ad' kacherirenko kamburuko daua oṛo' peṛe'geko omakotana.

By means of that copy his possession will be proved and Paku's genuine right will be broken utterly. Therefore I say to thee : the police and the courts give legal rights and support to the thieves.

Amdo chikanamente Pakua kam gowea ? Aea' daua menamental torakada.

Why doest not thou give evidence for Paku ? Thou art aware that the right is on his side (is his).

Enadoing ituana, mendo enreo kaing daria. Inia' aing goware honanga', aingoge Paku lekateko ritaiña.

That I know; but, notwithstanding that, I cannot do it. If I were to give evidence for Paku, they would treat me like Paku, (*i.e.* as they treat Paku).

Ale Horokore hangareke bagemre entedom ad'jana; jetaeo kako banchaudaṛiamea.

If amongst us Mundas they exclude you from the ordinary brotherly relations, then you are lost; nobody can save you.

Ne apea' najomkaji 'isu et'kagea oro' baluuterge. Amo, Pakua' kuṛi najom tani' mentem biswastana ?

This witchcraft business of yours is very bad and utterly stupid. Doest thou too believe that Paku's wife is a witch ?

Aingdo kaing biswastana, oro' tara mara Horoko tising gapa enkan kajire kala biswasea; mendo chikaeale! Purate Horoko sokaa' kajire khub ketete'ko patia. Inkua' borote ka-biswastanio hapeakangee' taena. Misa mid' horo najome' sabjanre ente jetaea' daia-maia bano'a ini'mente. Angrajiko auri hijure ale. Horokoa nelekan dastur taekena : Najomgeko sabia, darureko hakaia, bo' latarki'ate ; ente latarre sengelgeko tingea oro' on najom jid'-jid'geko rapaia. Enado tising-gapa sarkar borote kakoa. Mendo najom ora'renko hatuate harurungmente, inkulo' jomu-u, dub-tingun kakoa, arandio kako omakoa oro' jalekate bedakalkoa. Nao ukuta kented'geko tamkoa. Enamente tising-gapajaked' najom sabakanko misa-misa hatu ora'-duar, ote sobenageko nirbagea. Tarakodo kristanentanako. Ente padri oro' sarkar umbulte jalekateko taen daria hature.

As for myself if I don't believe and now-a-days there are a certain number of Mundas who do no more believe in such things. But what are we to do ! By far the greater number of Mundas believe most firmly in the soothsayer's words. For fear of those even the man who does not believe will keep quiet. If one's person be proved (by the Soka's word) to be a wizard or witch, then nobody has any pity or consideration for him. Before the English come, there existed among us, Mundas the following custom : They would lay hold of the wizard or witch, they would hang him on a tree, head downwards (*lit.,* having put him with his head downwards) ; then underneath they would kindle a fire and then roast the wizard or witch alive. Now-a-days, they won't do that for fear of the Government. But in order to drive all the inmates of a wizard or witch's house out of the village, they will neither eat nor drink nor converse with them; they will also not intermarry with them (*lit.,* give them marriage). Now, too, they do beat them frightfully on the sly. Therefore, even now-a-days, people convicted of witchcraft will occasionally leave their village, house, lands and everything by running away. Some of them because Christians. Then they can somehow or another stay in the village under the protection (the shadow) of the missionary and the Government.